THE WORLD'S CLASSICS

DOCTOR FAUSTUS AND OTHER PLAYS

CHRISTOPHER MARLOWE, the son of a Canterbury shoemaker, was born in early 1564. He won a scholarship to the King's School, Canterbury, before he was 15, and two years later matriculated at Corpus Christi College, Cambridge. He received his BA degree in 1584 and went on for the Master of Arts degree, though the university authorities would have withheld it because of his extensive absences had not the Privy Council intervened on Marlowe's behalf. They asserted that he had been engaged 'in matters touching the benefit of his country' for which he was 'defamed by those that are ignorant in the affairs he went about'. Marlowe was granted his MA in 1587, at about the same time (1587–8) that both parts of *Tamburlaine* were first performed in London. Marlowe then moved to the vicinity of the London playhouses, and at one point shared a writing chamber with his fellow playwright Thomas Kyd. Between 1588 and 1592 he wrote *Doctor Faustus*, *The Jew of Malta*, and *Edward II* for the Lord Admiral's men. In 1593, an atheistic lecture was found in Kyd's residence; under torture, Kyd claimed that the seditious papers were Marlowe's. A warrant for Marlowe's arrest was issued on 18 May, but before he could appear before the Privy Council, Marlowe was murdered, apparently in a brawl, on 30 May.

DAVID BEVINGTON is the Phyllis Fay Horton Professor in the Humanities at the University of Chicago, where he has taught since 1967. His studies include *From 'Mankind' to Marlowe* (1962), *Tudor Drama and Politics* (1968), and *Action Is Eloquence: Shakespeare's Language of Gesture* (1985). He is also the editor of The Bantam Shakespeare, in 29 paperback volumes (1988), and *The Complete Works of Shakespeare*, HarperCollins (1992), as well as the Oxford *1 Henry IV* (1987) and the Cambridge *Antony and Cleopatra* (1990).

ERIC RASMUSSEN is Assistant Professor of English at the University of Nevada, Reno. He is joint editor with David Bevington of *Doctor Faustus* in the Revels Plays series (1993). His publications include *A Textual Companion to 'Doctor Faustus'* (1993), and many articles on Shakespeare and Marlowe.

MICHAEL CORDNER is a Senior Lecturer in the Department of English and Related Literature at the University of York. He has edited editions of George Farquhar's *The Beaux' Stratagem*, the *Complete Plays* of Sir George Etherege, *Four Comedies* of Sir John Vanbrugh and, for the World's Classics series, *Four Restoration Marriage Comedies*. He has also co-edited *English Comedy* (Cambridge University Press, 1994) and is completing a book on *The Comedy of Marriage 1660–1737*.

PETER HOLLAND is Judith E. Wilson University Lecturer in Drama in the Faculty of English at the University of Cambridge.

MARTIN WIGGINS is a Fellow of the Shakespeare Institute and Lecturer in English at the University of Birmingham.

DRAMA IN WORLD'S CLASSICS

Christopher Marlowe
Doctor Faustus and Other Plays

Arthur Wing Pinero
Trelawny of the 'Wells' and Other Plays

Oscar Wilde
The Importance of Being Earnest and Other Plays

Chapman, Kyd, Middleton, Tourneur
Four Revenge Tragedies

THE WORLD'S CLASSICS

===

CHRISTOPHER MARLOWE

Tamburlaine, Parts I and II
Doctor Faustus, A- and B-Texts
The Jew of Malta
Edward II

===

Edited by
DAVID BEVINGTON and ERIC RASMUSSEN

General Editor
MICHAEL CORDNER

Associate General Editors
PETER HOLLAND   MARTIN WIGGINS

Oxford New York
OXFORD UNIVERSITY PRESS
1995

Oxford University Press, Walton Street, Oxford OX2 6DP

Oxford New York
Athens Auckland Bangkok Bombay
Calcutta Cape Town Dar es Salaam Delhi
Florence Hong Kong Istanbul Karachi
Kuala Lumpur Madras Madrid Melbourne
Mexico City Nairobi Paris Singapore
Taipei Tokyo Toronto
and associated companies
in Berlin Ibadan

Oxford is a trade mark of Oxford University Press

First published as a World's Classics paperback 1995

British Library Cataloguing in Publication Data

Data available

Library of Congress Cataloging in Publication Data
Marlowe, Christopher, 1564–1593
Doctor Faustus / Christopher Marlowe; edited by David Bevington and Eric Rasmussen.
p.   cm. — (World's classics) Includes bibliographical references.
1. Faust, d. ca. 1540 Drama. 2. Magicians—Germany—Drama.
I. Bevington, David M. II. Rasmussen, Eric, 1960–   . III. Title. IV. Series.
PR2664.A2B48 1995   832'.4—dc20   94–12318   CIP
ISBN 0–19–282737–5

3 5 7 9 10 8 6 4 2

Printed in Great Britain by
Biddles Ltd,
Guildford & King's Lynn

CONTENTS

ACKNOWLEDGEMENTS

THE editors of this volume wish to thank Kevin Ewert for checking our play texts against the original editions. We are also grateful to Michael Cordner for the extraordinary pains he took in reviewing every stage of our work, and to Elizabeth Stratford and Sue Whimster at the Oxford University Press for truly expert copy-editing. Susie Casement and Frances Whistler have been supportive in every way as editors at the Press for the World's Classics drama series. We are happy to have had a part in launching that enterprise, and wish it well.

We should like to dedicate this volume to Tristan Rasmussen, newly arrived into this world.

DAVID BEVINGTON AND ERIC RASMUSSEN

INTRODUCTION

CHRISTOPHER MARLOWE'S heroes 'make their fortunes by exercising virtues which conventional morality might well regard as vices', writes Harry Levin (in *The Overreacher* (1952)). From first to last in his brief and meteoric career, Marlowe appears to have been fascinated by challenge of the established order in its cosmic and human dimensions. We sense in this, as we read or experience his plays in the theatre, the projection of a self that was no less daring, yet at the same time caught up in guilt and remorse. Even though we cannot interpret the plays as straightforward autobiography, no body of dramatic literature in the Renaissance makes us more curious to know the dramatist himself, for the plays seem to us intensely personal.

Marlowe's biography is shrouded in the mystery and controversy of one who became notorious in his own day. He was born in 1564, the same year as Shakespeare, to the family of a shoemaker and professional bondsman in Canterbury. Educated at the King's School there, he went to Cambridge in 1580, was elected to a scholarship established by Matthew Parker, Archbishop of Canterbury, and took his BA in 1584. During prolonged absences from university in 1581–3 and after June of 1586, he may have been serving in confidential government service, for a Privy Council letter of June 1587 to the university orders that Marlowe's MA degree should be conferred as usual in view of his having been sent to Rheims 'in matters touching the benefit of his country'. Sir Francis Walsingham, in charge of gathering secret information about Catholic conspiracy on behalf of Mary Queen of Scots, had good reason to keep an eye on the English Catholic seminar at Rheims. A second cousin of this powerful minister, Thomas Walsingham, was engaged in secret government service in the 1580s and was also Marlowe's patron. By the late 1580s Marlowe was in London, enjoying sensational success as playwright and poet. He spent time in gaol for his involvement in a fatal duel. In May of 1593 he was arrested on order of the Privy Council in connection with an investigation into religious heterodoxy and disloyalty to the Crown, though we do not know the severity of the offences with which he may have been personally charged. Shortly thereafter he died violently in a private house (perhaps a tavern) in Deptford at the hands of one Ingram Frizer.

Although the underlying causes of Marlowe's last quarrel may have been political—one of his companions that day was Robert Poley, a government secret agent of questionable reputation—many commentators on the notorious event were not slow to see divine retribution. The Puritan Thomas Beard, in his *Theatre of God's Judgements* (1597), sees Marlowe's death as an exemplary punishment for 'atheism and impiety':

Marlin [i.e. Marlowe], by profession a scholar, brought up from his youth in the University of Cambridge but by practice a playmaker and a poet of scurrility who, by giving too large a swinge to his own wit and suffering his lust to have the full reins, fell, not without just desert, to that outrage and extremity that he denied God and his son Christ, and not only in word blasphemed the Trinity but also (as it is credibly reported) wrote books against it, affirming our Saviour to be but a deceiver, and Moses to be but a conjurer and seducer of the people, and the Holy Bible to be but vain and idle stories, and all religion but a device of policy. (pp. 147–8)

Beard sees divine justice in the fact that Marlowe's death was self-inflicted: having caught hold of his attacker's wrist, the dramatist managed to stab his own dagger (which Frizer had seized) into his own head. By such means did God compel the 'hand which had written those blasphemies to be the instrument to punish him, and that in his brain, which had devised the same'. Marlowe's death is for Beard as edifying as it was terrible: he 'cursed and blasphemed to his last gasp, and, together with his breath, an oath flew out of his mouth, that it was not only a manifest sign of God's judgement but also an horrible and fearful terror to all that beheld him'.

Beard is alluding to Marlowe's 'monstrous opinions' as set down in the unreliable testimony of a spy called Richard Baines (published 1594), in two letters of 1593 by Thomas Kyd (who was himself under investigation for free-thinking and libel against the State), and in still other documents. Baines accuses Marlowe, for example, of having said that Christ was a bastard and a homosexual who deserved crucifying. Kyd asserts that it was Marlowe's 'custom when I knew him first—and as I hear say he continued it in table talk or otherwise—to jest at the divine scriptures, gibe at prayer, and strive in argument to frustrate and confute what hath been spoken or writ by prophets and such holy men'. Robert Greene, a playwright and poet who was clearly envious of Marlowe, speaks in a preface to *Perimedes* (1588) of 'daring God out of heaven with that atheist Tamburlaine', and later repents the folly of having said in his heart, like a certain 'famous grocer of tragedians' (i.e. Marlowe), that 'There

is no God' (*A Groatsworth of Wit* (1592)). These and other testimon-
ials need to be discounted for their exaggeration and for their having
been produced under legal circumstances we would regard as a
witch-hunt. Still, there can be little doubt that Marlowe explored and
even revelled in the intellectual scepticism articulated by the mathe-
matician and astronomer Thomas Harriott, by Giordano Bruno (who
visited England in 1583–5), and by others whom the age generally
regarded as free-thinkers and 'atheists'. No one at any rate seems to
have doubted that Marlowe was what Kyd had called him, 'irreligious'
and 'intemperate, and of a cruel heart'. The reputation is a reality, even
if we cannot be certain of the exact degree of Marlowe's nonconformity.

Tamburlaine the Great, written and performed in two parts in
1587–8 by the Lord Admiral's men and published in 1590, proclaims
its impatience with tradition in many ways. The Prologue to Part I is
a manifesto, both literary and ideological, written by a self-assured
dramatist who proposes to rescue his spectators from 'jigging veins of
rhyming mother-wits' and other pathetic 'clownage' of a previous
theatrical generation, and who invites his audience instead to 'hear the
Scythian Tamburlaine | Threat'ning the world with high astounding
terms | And scourging kingdoms with his conquering sword'. The
lofty, even arrogant tone is in keeping with the vision of a 'tragic glass'
or spectacle of greatness; the daring of the speaker matches the
heroism of the conquerer whom the dramatist will immortalize.

Both the vastness of Tamburlaine's achievement and the bloodiness
of his acts are manifest in the description of him on the 1590 title
page: '*Tamburlaine the Great, who, from a Scythian shepherd, by his rare
and wonderful conquests became a most puissant and mighty monarch, and
for his tyranny and terror in war was termed the scourge of God.*' The
play's two parts are to be seen as '*tragical discourses*' with no place in
them for low comedy; as Richard Jones's preface explains, presumably
with Marlowe's concurrence, the text omits 'some fond and frivolous
gestures, digressing, and, in my poor opinion, far unmeet for the
matter, which I thought might seem more tedious unto the wise than
any way else to be regarded, though haply they have been of some
vain-conceited fondlings greatly gaped at, what times they were
showed upon the stage in their graced deformities'. Whether Marlowe
or (as seems more likely) someone else wrote the comic scenes thus
described, they were to have no part in the literary monument to
greatness being presented to sophisticated readers.

The two parts of *Tamburlaine* have been described as a ten-act
whole by Roy Battenhouse (*Marlowe's 'Tamburlaine'* (1941)) ending

in the death of a protagonist whose downfall has a providential meaning. Yet the theatrical reality in 1587–8 must have been otherwise. Marlowe wrote Part I as a single play, and thus was it performed with Edward Alleyn in the title role. To perceive these plays as Elizabethan audiences did, we must imagine a performance of Part I all by itself—a performance so successful as to require a sequel.

The subversive thrust of Part I of *Tamburlaine* begins with its portrayal of life at the top. None of the rulers whom Tamburlaine overthrows is worthy to occupy a throne. Mycetes of Persia, with whom we begin, is an effete ninny, unable to muster the 'great and thund'ring speech' his cause of complaint would seem to require. In his comic cowardice and ineffectuality he is no match for his conspiring brother, Cosroe, who proceeds with Tamburlaine's help to unseat him. Cosroe is no better. One who treacherously buys the loyalty of his own brother's courtiers deserves to be outdone at his own game, and that is what Tamburlaine accomplishes—not through treachery, but by open competition for Cosroe's followers. Tamburlaine moves on next to Bajazeth, Emperor of the Turks, whose tyrannies and blustering rage deny him anything more than fleeting sympathy when he is defeated in battle, forced to act as the footstool of the triumphant Tamburlaine, and driven at last to brain himself in despair against his cage. Tamburlaine's last opponent in Part I, the Sultan of Egypt, is allowed to live in defeat because he is the father of Tamburlaine's beloved Zenocrate, but even here we extend little sympathy to one who pleads in vain for the assistance of the Egyptian gods and who allows the virgins of Damascus to beg for a deliverance from attack which the Sultan is himself unable to provide. Authority, as practised in the Middle Eastern world by autocratic rulers, is corrupt and incapable of defending itself. Tamburlaine's opportunity for limitless self-advancement arises from the universal failures of the present power structure.

Tamburlaine is not slow to meet the challenge. He knows he is destined for great things, though of humble origin: 'I am a lord, for so my deeds shall prove, | And yet a shepherd by my parentage' (1.2.34–5). By simple assertion of his unbendable will he can apparently accomplish anything, especially since the lack of true authority at the top of the social order creates the kind of vacuum that Nature abhors. Tamburlaine invokes the concept of Nature, in fact, to bolster his contention that it is natural to aspire: 'Nature, that framed us of four elements | Warring within our breasts for regiment, | Doth teach us all to have aspiring minds' (2.7.18–20). To be human is to climb always 'after knowledge infinite', restlessly exerting ourselves 'Until we reach the ripest fruit of all, | That perfect bliss and sole felicity, | The sweet fruition of an earthly crown' (ll. 24–9). The examples of the 'restless spheres' in the heavens, and of 'mighty Jove' himself, afford us cosmic precedent for ceaseless activity and the assertion of the individual will. A great part of Tamburlaine's enormous appeal for an audience lies in his embodying the idea that we can make of ourselves what we will, and that a dying patrician social order will fall before us. The idea galvanizes us even as we see its revolutionary implications. Human aspiration is potentially both constructive and destructive; most of all, it is an irreducible fact.

Tamburlaine's appeal manifests itself in his mesmerizing ability to win followers, in his serene self-consistency in the art of war or wooing, in his utter loyalty to those who serve him, in his vision of greatness. His destructive side manifests itself in the succession of conquests and the denial of all restraint for which his enemies denounce him. His 'giantly presumption' leads him 'To cast up hills against the face of heaven | And dare the force of angry Jupiter' (2.6.2–4). He is a 'devilish thief' who must be opposed 'In love of honour and defence of right' (ll. 20–1). He is inhumanly cruel, and laughs at the suffering of his victims. His self-vaunting can easily turn to rant, as when he boasts: 'I hold the Fates bound fast in iron chains | And with my hand turn Fortune's wheel about' (1.2.174–5). He is both a darling of the gods and a terrible scourge; he both acts in the name of the powers above and seeks their overthrow. 'Some powers divine, or else infernal, mixed | Their angry seeds at his conception' (2.6.9–10). He is alternatively a 'god, or fiend, or spirit of the earth' (l. 15).

In Part II, the warring elements in Tamburlaine grow more at odds. He attempts to deny the death of Zenocrate by encasing her in a sheet of gold and keeping her always with him. She has been, indeed, a compensating and tempering influence in his life, offering beauty, softness, compassion, and the awareness of mortal limits that he so visibly lacks. Partly aware of his own mortality through her death, he turns his attention to making heroes out of his three sons, and slays the one who does not measure up to his fierce standard of self-assertion. Increasingly, his own deeds mock him; even his unbroken string of victories over the princes of Europe and the Middle East can do little more than remind him that, like Alexander, he will soon have no more kingdoms to conquer. Yet his belief in himself and his mission remains unbroken. Death finally achieves a victory over him, after he has once more defied Muhammad by his burning of the Koran. Yet even here, the force that prevails against him is more surely a process of nature than the anger of some god. Tamburlaine pronounces his own sentence, as though the author of his own fate at last: 'For Tamburlaine, the scourge of God, must die' (5.3.248). Both parts of *Tamburlaine* dramatize the limitless assertion of the individual will, even if they also perceive the ironies and paradoxes of human striving.

In *Doctor Faustus*, written perhaps in 1588–9, a quest for power in the form of infinite knowledge exacts an immeasurably great cost. Doctor Faustus is both scholar and black magician. 'Graced with doctor's name', he excels all in the study of theology and other liberal arts, but cannot rest content with what traditional learning brings him. A Tamburlaine-like striving becomes, in Faustus, the 'cunning of a self-conceit' that drives him (like Icarus) to mount on waxen wings 'above his reach' until the heavens conspire his 'overthrow'. Such is the view of the Prologue, which goes on to deplore in Christian terms the 'devilish exercise' that tempts Faustus to surfeit 'upon cursed necromancy'. The play's final Chorus similarly offers Faustus as a clear example of one whose 'hellish fall' and 'fiendful fortune may exhort the wise | Only to wonder at unlawful things'.

At the same time, the final Chorus laments the tragic waste of a 'branch that might have grown full straight', a 'laurel bough' dedicated to Apollo 'That sometime grew within this learnèd man'. More ominously, the Chorus sees the tragedy of Faustus as that of a man who, like other 'forward wits', allowed his 'deepness' to 'entice' him 'To practise more than heavenly power permits'. The idea of a heavenly limit on human longing to know the secrets of the heavens recalls the Prologue's observation that the heavens 'conspired' Faustus's overthrow. (In contrast, Tamburlaine boasts that 'The chiefest God, first mover of that sphere . . . Will sooner burn the glorious frame of heaven | Than it should so conspire my overthrow,' Part I, 4.2.8–11.) The language of *Doctor Faustus* establishes an adversarial relationship between humanity and the gods. Just as Icarus' story could be read two ways in the Renaissance, as an instance of foolish human aspiration and as proof that the gods will not tolerate Promethean challenge of their authority, *Doctor Faustus* can be seen both as an object lesson of hubris and as a dark speculation on what is intolerable and tragic about divine limits placed on human will.

Doctor Faustus may seem a Renaissance morality play, all the more so because its chief figures are derived from conventions of a dramatic genre that flourished until shortly before Marlowe arrived in London. The Good and Evil Angels are abstractions from the morality play, the one offering Faustus wise counsel and the other the temptation of despair. Other characters too are grouped in pairs around the central figure. The Old Man in Act 5 bids Faustus repent his 'vile and loathsome filthiness' (5.1.41), as a counter to Mephistopheles' instructions in how to 'abjure the Trinity | And pray devoutly to the prince of hell' (1.3.53–4). The Scholars urge Faustus to 'look up to heaven' in remembrance that 'God's mercies are infinite' (5.2.12–13), while Valdes and Cornelius, as fellow magicians, hold out to Faustus the promise that all nations will canonize him and offer rich rewards for the miracles of magic (1.1.121–50). Even the comic scenes are from the morality play; the alternation of serious action with scenes of buffoonish revelling in sin is a recognizable feature of morality plays from *Mankind* (c.1471) on down to *The Longer Thou Livest The More Fool Thou Art* (c.1567) and other early Elizabethan dramas. Most of all, Faustus himself as the protagonist is the central figure of a soul-struggle in which he veers back and forth between dissipation and a longing to be better. Faustus is the 'mankind' figure of his own morality play, and accordingly we are told his whole life's history from birth in Germany to death and damnation.

As morality play, *Doctor Faustus* lends itself to orthodox Christian interpretation. Heaven and hell are realities, attested to by Mephistopheles himself. When Faustus proposes that 'hell's a fable', the devil wryly bids him 'think so still, till experience change thy mind' (2.1.127–8). Mephistopheles has already assured Faustus that he serves Lucifer, prince of devils, who was once an angel beloved of God until, for his 'aspiring pride and insolence', God 'threw him from the face of heaven' (1.3.68–9). When Faustus observes that he and Mephistopheles are free to walk together and dispute (2.1.138–9), he suggests how little he sees to fear in the hell where Mephistopheles claims to be confined. Indeed, Mephistopheles' account of his own spiritual condition might seem to encourage a metaphorical notion of hell as a state of mind ('Why, this is hell, nor am I out of it', 1.3.77) rather than a place of physical torment. Nevertheless, Reformation theology affords a view of Faustus's shortsightedness in speaking as he does. Calvin concedes that metaphors of unquenchable fire and the gnawing of worms are ways of expressing the terrors of hell to our limited human understanding rather than literal truths, but does not allow that such a view in any way denies the reality of hell, which is eternal absence from God. Faustus is a fool to deny this reality when Mephistopheles stands before him as 'an instance to prove the contrary' (2.1.136).

Heaven is no less real, and in the same spiritual rather than narrowly physical sense. Mephistopheles is reluctant to tell Faustus 'who made the world' (2.3.65), but he knows well enough, for he has already confessed that he once 'saw the face of God | And tasted the eternal joys of heaven' (1.3.78–9). The Good Angel urges Faustus to 'think of heaven and heavenly things' (2.1.20); the Old Man bids him seek mercy 'of thy Saviour sweet, | Whose blood alone must wash away thy guilt' (5.1.45–6). For all his scepticism in earlier scenes, Faustus perceives in his last terrible moments that 'Christ's blood streams in the firmament' and that one drop would save his soul (5.2.70–1), even if he cannot reach out for that grace.

The orthodox Christian view of Faustus as a benighted sinner readily explains what is so increasingly deplorable in his behaviour. Even his longing to master all fields of learning, and then to go beyond what rhetoric, medicine, law, and theology have accomplished, soon dissolves into false pride, hair-splitting, and sophomoric misquotation of the Scriptures. His humanist dreams of public service are immediately swallowed up in a frenzy of self-indulgent pleasure; a voyage of discovery to the wonders of Rome turns out to be little more than the occasion for some infantile practical joking at the expense of the pope. The show of the Seven Deadly Sins is at once typical of the kind of distraction he needs to keep his mind off his spiritual state and a reminder that Faustus himself practises all the Deadly Sins. The broadly comic scenes show us how frivolously easy it is to conjure, since the devil will come to any who call him. Faustus's immense powers of magic enable him to do little more than bamboozle a horse-courser or horse-dealer into buying a horse that dissolves into a bundle of hay, or to impress the royalty of Europe by fetching grapes in winter-time.

Calvinist theology also attests to the justice of Faustus's terrible fate. At one point Faustus declares, 'If it [heaven] were made for man, 'twas made for me', and so he resolves to 'renounce this magic and repent'. Yet his resolution is short-lived: 'My heart's so hardened I cannot repent' (2.3.10–11, 18). In the Old Testament, it is God who hardens Pharaoh's heart, though somehow this fact does not relieve Pharaoh of responsibility for his stubborn persistence in evil. In Calvinist doctrine, a similar paradox holds: God has made the will free, and yet some persons are predestinately evil and will not avail themselves of mercy. Even though divine dispensation in these matters is inscrutable, we are not to question its justice.

The paradox of free will and predestination, so central to *Doctor Faustus*, is continually dramatized in that play by rival spokesmen for the opposing sides of good and evil. When the Good Angel assures Faustus that 'God will pity thee', the Evil Angel retorts, 'God cannot pity thee'. The difference of view is not about God's nature, but about contrasting expectations of Faustus's moral capacities. When Faustus pleads that 'God will pity me if I repent', since God can forgive the worst of sinners, the Evil Angel replies by denying not the first possibility of God's power to forgive, but the second: 'Ay, but Faustus never shall repent' (2.3.12–17). In that fact lies the presumed justice of Faustus's doom. His crime is that of despairing of God's mercy.

The orthodox reading tends to condemn Faustus, and thus weaken his tragic stature, by trivializing his learning and by seeing him as a fool. Yet many spectators and readers respond with enormous sympathy to a man who, however recklessly, dares to take on heaven itself and the divine 'conspiracy' hinted at repeatedly in the play. Faustus's sceptical refusal to believe that 'after this life there is any pain' (2.1.134) is a natural enough consequence of his intellectual investigations, even if he turns out to be wrong. So is his persistent curiosity about the nature and origin of the cosmos. Here, at the heart of the play, is the question that teased the minds of Renaissance intellectuals and indeed was in the process of leading to major breakthroughs in scientific thought.

Faustus may be an epicure and practical joker much of the time, but part of him longs to know if there are many spheres above the moon and if they all revolve around 'this centric earth' (2.3.37 ff.). When Mephistopheles blandly replies with the accepted Ptolemaic astronomy of the day, or at least a version of it, postulating that all the spheres move 'upon one axletree, | Whose terminine is termed the world's wide pole', Faustus is understandably impatient with 'slender questions Wagner can decide', these 'freshmen's suppositions'. He moves on to the hardest issue of all for astronomers in the late sixteenth century: how are we to account for the retrograde motions of the planets and the fact that we do not have 'conjunctions, oppositions, aspects, eclipses all at one time, but in some years we have more, in some less'? The retrograde motion of the inner planets such as Mars—that is to say, the occasional backtracking of Mars through the fixed stars—seemed hard to explain in terms of an earth-centred universe, and required mathematical convolutions in the form of epicycles on top of cyclical spheres. What is Mephistopheles' explanation of this momentous puzzle? '*Per inaequalem motum respectu totius*', 'on account of their unequal motion with respect to the whole' (2.3.64). Faustus's wry reply—'Well, I am answered'—bespeaks his acknowledgement that he has been put off by a masterful equivocation, one that obfuscates the whole problem. Is Faustus answered thus because there is no other possible answer, or because heavenly powers will not 'permit' him to know more?

A similar question insistently returns to Faustus when he asks the even harder question of why he is the iconoclast that life has somehow made him. If Calvinism has its own answer, that God has hardened Faustus's heart as a sign of and in preparation for his predestined damnation, we may also perceive Faustus as a Marlovian kind of seeker who aspires simply because he is human. His inquiring intellect cannot let go of a desire to know more, even if that knowledge may be illusory. Even when he perceives clearly that his essential nature is what damns him, he cannot be other than he is. In that perception lies the human tragedy of this great and foolish man.

Doctor Faustus exists in two early texts, both printed in this edition, one published in 1604 (the so-called 'A-text') and the other in 1616 (the 'B-text'). The above analysis has quoted solely from the A-text, since in the opinion of the present editors it more nearly represents the play that Marlowe wrote in about 1588—very probably with a collaborator for the scenes of comic horseplay. The A-text probably derives from the authorial papers of this collaboration. Because *Doctor Faustus* was enormously popular, however, and was revived in the theatre a number of times, the acting text may have been changed substantially. In 1602, Philip Henslowe, proprietor of the theatre in which the play was acted, paid two dramatists to write additions to *Doctor Faustus*. Edward Alleyn, the leading actor of the Admiral's men and one of the greatest performers of his time, undertook the title role in this revival as he had done in the original production and in other of Marlowe's plays (including Tamburlaine, and Barabas in *The Jew of Malta*). The B-text seemingly incorporates the additions of 1602.

With its expanded treatment of the comic business and its fascination with magical effects in the theatre, the B-text gives us a lively picture of how one of the great tragedies of the Elizabethan period evolved through theatrical experiment in the early decades of performance after Marlowe's death. The B-text also provides a new theological emphasis, paradoxically giving Faustus more volition in his choice of evil and Mephistopheles a more active and sinister role in his temptation of his victim; see A-text 2.3.78, 82 and note, and B-text 5.2.91–7. These are a few of the reasons why today's reader should be familiar with both the A- and the B-texts as separate entities, created under different circumstances. The two texts should not be conflated into one; each deserves to be read in its own right.

If *Doctor Faustus* reflects Marlowe's view of himself to any significant degree, it suggests a man whose heterodoxies have come home to haunt him. *The Jew of Malta*, originally produced in about 1589–91, focuses more sardonically on an alien figure whose revenges against an unfeeling society create in us a deeply divided response. Barabas, a rich merchant on the Christian island of Malta, is another towering Marlovian figure, like Tamburlaine and Faustus, always at the centre of the action. The role, indebted as it is to the Vice of the morality play, is intensely theatrical, and must have provided a fine vehicle for Edward Alleyn in its early performances. Barabas boasts to us in soliloquy of his wealth and is disarmingly frank about his motives. We cannot help being impressed by his skill as he manipulates his oppressors, resourcefully concocts new plots, and deceives even his fellow Jews when necessary. Watching him act, we are drawn into complicity with a stranger who shows us so unsparingly the hypocrisy of a nominally Christian world. At the same time, the monstrosity in Barabas himself complicates our feelings toward this unorthodox protagonist.

Machiavel speaks the prologue, and indeed hovers over the entire play as a cynical mentor in the art of expedient intrigue. Reflecting a stereotypical and even hysterical view of Niccolò Machiavelli, the hated author of *The Prince*, this Machiavel insists that political rule is a matter of simple might, that religion is 'but a childish toy', and that 'there is no sin but ignorance'. He is what many Englishmen professed to fear most in Machiavelli, an atheist who believes that conscience and morality are mythologies which the crafty prince uses to keep his subjects in awe. When Machiavel recommends Barabas to us as one whose money 'was not got without my means', we are led to expect a gloating villain.

Yet when Barabas is set before us, he is hardly that. He is immensely wealthy through commercial enterprise, proud of his success, shrewd, devoted to his only daughter Abigail, and ready to settle for peaceful rule under Christian governors so that he can continue to gather in the plenty that heaven provides. The approaching Turks are of no concern to him, even if war should result, 'So they spare me, my daughter, and my wealth' (1.1.151). He does mislead his fellow Jews into a false sense of security by not sharing with them his worries that the Turks may demand more tribute than Malta will be able to pay, but this is only to say that Barabas believes in every man for himself.

Moreover, when Ferneze meets the Turkish demand for tribute by levying the whole amount from Malta's Jewish minority population, and then refuses to give Barabas even a moment to reconsider his initial refusal to pay, the manifest injustice of the action gives Barabas an opportunity to speak feelingly on behalf of those who are persecuted. Even if Jews were to be generally condemned for their sinfulness in Christian eyes, he asks, 'Shall I be tried by transgression?' His words ring with the simple eloquence of one who has been wronged: 'The man that dealeth righteously shall live; | And which of you can charge me otherwise?' (1.2.116–18). His point is all the more telling because of Ferneze's sanctimoniousness in preaching Scripture to confirm what amounts to simple theft in the name of political expediency. Marlowe unconventionally invites sympathy for a Jewish alien who suffers at the hands of a hypocritical and nominally Christian society, as Shakespeare was later to do in *The Merchant of Venice*—a sympathy complicated in both cases by the villainous role that the Jew is then called upon to play.

Barabas's villainy soon reveals itself to be as colossal in scale as his gathering of wealth, going well beyond any kind of rationally motivated revenge for the way he has been treated. Machiavel has already led us to expect to find in him a man with no conscience. Barabas plays the suffering victim to his fellow Jews, but confides to us in soliloquy when they have left the stage that he has nothing but contempt for 'the simplicity of these base slaves' who think, because they 'have no wit themselves', that other sufferers are like them. 'Evils are apt to happen every day', he reflects matter-of-factly, taking the present crisis of financial ruin as just one more occasion for resourcefulness in the competition of daily life (1.2.215–24). He plans with Abigail a plot of 'policy' (l. 274) against the Christians, and accordingly bids her dissemble as a nun (since his seized house has been converted into a convent). Later, when she falls in love with a Christian (Don Mathias) and thus appears to be disloyal to her father, Barabas concocts a plot whereby Mathias and Lodowick, Ferneze's son, kill one another as rivals for the favour of Abigail. Brokenhearted, Abigail concludes sadly that 'there is no love on earth, | Pity in Jews, nor piety in Turks' (3.3.47–8), and retires from the world in earnest.

Like Zenocrate in *Tamburlaine*, Abigail is a true-hearted woman whose simple loyalties and belief in virtue offer a rare perspective on the fierce amoral competitiveness of the male world around her. Once she has disappeared, all constancy and goodness die with her.

Barabas's partner in villainy for much of the play is a slave he buys named Ithamore, and it is in their scenes together that we discover the enormity of their comic resourcefulness in crime. Barabas boasts to Ithamore, in their first encounter: 'As for myself, I walk abroad a-nights | And kill sick people groaning under walls; | Sometimes I go about and poison wells' (2.3.175 ff.). He reviews a career in which he has practised medicine only to kill as many patients as possible, served as an engineer in the wars in order that he might slay 'friend and enemy with my stratagems', and turned to usury so that he might fill the gaols with bankrupts through his 'extorting, cozening, forfeiting'. In this way, Marlowe creates for us a composite character, part victimized Jew but part generic villain. Ithamore too can boast a varied career, setting Christian villages on fire, chaining eunuchs, taking a position as hostler in an inn where he might steal travellers' purses and cut their throats, strewing poison on the steps of shrines at Jerusalem, and the like (ll. 203–13). In all this, Barabas and Ithamore are plausibly motivated by revenge and yet also inspired by a kind of pure comic delight in evil. As Barabas puts it, 'we are villains both. | Both circumcisèd, we hate Christians both' (ll. 219–20). The duality of motive and motivelessness gives a remarkable ambivalent energy to these artists in evil.

This theatrical pleasure in cunning expands in Barabas until the historically motivated Jew is ultimately lost sight of. He revels in his ability to look innocent when he is about to bite, to trade on his nominal Jewishness by fawning and grinning, to 'Heave up my shoulders when they call me dog, | And duck as low as any barefoot friar' (2.3.20–5). When Abigail, stung by the death of Mathias, gives incriminating evidence against her father to two friars, Jacomo and Barnardine, Barabas devises 'such a plot for both their lives | As never Jew nor Christian knew the like' (4.1.120–1). To get rid of Abigail he poisons the whole convent to which she is attached, using a powder he once bought in Italy. Though he professes to love Ithamore and claims to adopt him for his heir (3.4.43), he is in fact mistrustful from the start and soon falls out with him when Ithamore takes up with a whore (Bellamira) and a pimp (Pilia-Borza). Flamboyantly disguised as a French musician, Barabas has no trouble finding 'a means to rid 'em all' (4.3.62) by the use of a poisoned nosegay. At the acme of his career in villainy, he secretly allows the Turkish Calymath to enter Malta, in order that Barabas, with foreign help, may 'slay their children and their wives . . . fire the churches, pull their houses down', and still more (5.1.63–4). Made governor by Calymath but unsure of popular support, he bargains with Ferneze to rid Malta of the Turks and proceeds to devise a cunning trap-door device for the purpose, but falls himself into the waiting cauldron when Ferneze turns on him. His last words are defiantly all-encompassing in evil intent: 'Had I but escaped this stratagem | I would have brought confusion on you all, | Damned Christians, dogs, and Turkish infidels!' (5.5.83–5).

Why is such a death not an edifying illustration of villainy receiving its just reward? The answer lies partly in Barabas's sympathetic role as persecuted alien in earlier scenes, but also in the studiously ambiguous role of Ferneze. The Governor of Malta is both a sanctimonious hypocrite and a man with a job to do. Tiny Malta is surrounded by powerful enemies, not only Turkey but Spain. To play off these superpowers against each other, the ruler of a small island has to face realities. Ferneze taxes the Jewish minority on Malta 'To save the ruin of a multitude' (1.2.98). Since 'desire of gold' is 'the wind that bloweth all the world' (3.5.3–4), it behoves Ferneze to be as secure in wealth as possible. Ferneze is motivated to track down Barabas partly out of revenge for the death of his son Lodowick but also to demonstrate that 'the heavens are just' (5.1.54). Ferneze is, it would seem, the very model of a Machiavellian prince. Using lofty pieties as a good prince should do, publicly giving praise to heaven for the providential overthrow of Barabas, Ferneze knows when to bargain with Barabas and when to betray him. He is the Nemesis figure and the play's survivor, one who exemplifies the success of the Machiavellian 'policy' that the Prologue proclaims and that the figure of Barabas seems to embody in caricature. Perhaps what is most subversive about Marlowe's play is its readiness to punish Barabas for the same sort of 'kingly treachery' and deceit that enable Ferneze to triumph. Marlowe conjures up a jarring sympathy for both the misunderstood stranger and the amoral prince.

Political life in Marlowe's plays thus far, whether in the Middle East and eastern Europe, in papal Rome, or in the Mediterranean, is amoral, ruthlessly competitive, and usually corrupt; government is perennially unstable, tyrannical, and vulnerable to challenge by self-assertive men. Marlowe chooses in all these cases to portray a world distant from England, in exotic and unfamiliar locations where

Catholicism or pagan creeds prevail. In what may be his last major play, *Edward II* (*c*.1592), Marlowe centres on the English political scene and finds it essentially the same. He selects as his protagonist one of England's most notoriously weak kings, as did Shakespeare in the *Henry VI* plays, *King John*, and *Richard II*. But whereas Shakespeare allows dignified spokesmen in his plays to express their belief in the divine right of kings and the importance of regular succession in reply to challengers of royal authority (whose point of view is no less cogently presented), Marlowe gives us conflict in which neither side lays claim to moral advantage. Instead, a political struggle is driven by the expression of sexual and self-interested desires that defy norms of social evaluation.

From the start, our impressions of King Edward derive from his relationship to his favourite, Gaveston. The play begins as Gaveston returns from exile, reading an amorous letter from Edward inviting him to 'share the kingdom with thy dearest friend'. Gaveston speaks convincingly as one who is prepared to die in the King's arms, setting the world at enmity in the enjoyment of their love (1.1.1–15). At the same time, Gaveston makes no attempt to conceal from us, in soliloquy, the manipulative nature of his scheme to 'draw the pliant king which way I please': he will devise erotic masques featuring 'a lovely boy in Dian's shape | ... And in his sportful hands an olive tree | To hide those parts which men delight to see', for such things 'best please his majesty' (ll. 52–70). Gaveston will practise upon the king's homosexuality for his own advantage. Whether Gaveston enjoys sleeping with the king is perhaps beside the point. Gaveston is no less candid about his exploitation of three poor men who wish to be employed by him; since it costs him nothing 'to speak men fair', he will 'flatter these and make them live in hope', even though he has already decided that 'These are not men for me' (ll. 41–9). Such is the man for whom Edward is ready to lose a kingdom if necessary.

Edward's love for Gaveston may be touching and even noble, but it is also gullible and petulant. He never perceives self-interest in Gaveston's need to be protected from the nobles who loathe him as a parvenu and rival for influence with the Crown. Edward has his own reasons for hating the aristocrats who nominally serve him, and enlists Gaveston as an ally in his war on baronial privilege, but his own emotional vulnerability leads Edward to misjudge motive. He is too ready to believe that Gaveston's love is as unmaterialistic as his own. The sentiment does Edward credit, but the person upon whom it is so recklessly lavished is, by his own wry admission, no less self-interested and calculating than the barons who oppose him. The king of England is a victim of his own emotional fantasy. He may not even know his own motives in the case; his devotion for Gaveston may well be prompted to some degree by a desire to snub the barons and repudiate Isabella, his queen.

Ironies of this kind invite us to look into the barons' position. Chief among them is Mortimer junior, the kind of self-asserting rebel who, in earlier plays, is the Marlovian overreacher. Mortimer does indeed assume such a role in *Edward II*, albeit less centrally than do earlier protagonists. At first, as with Faustus, his impatience and ambition seem directed against real targets of corrupt authority. Edward's conduct as king leaves ample room for patriotic complaint. Mortimer can justly complain that 'one so basely born' as Gaveston 'Should by his sovereign's favour grow so pert | And riot it with the treasure of the realm'. The financial extravagance is indeed great, and at the expense of national defence: 'While soldiers mutiny for want of pay | He wears a lord's revenue on his back' (1.4.403–7). The commoners of England groan under their burden of oppression; the Irish are up in arms; the Scots make inroads with no military resistance; 'The haughty Dane commands the narrow seas'; foreign princes snub Edward by refusing to send ambassadors; ballads and rhymes are made in hope of Edward's overthrow (2.2.156 ff.). Lancaster and other nobles join in the litany of protest against a king who never shows himself in the field.

Yet Mortimer's motives are as suspect as Gaveston's or Edward's. A sense of personal animosity towards an uppity social inferior prompts Mortimer to rave against one who, 'Midas-like', 'jets it in the court | With base outlandish cullions at his heels . . . I have not seen a dapper jack so brisk' (1.4.408–12). Mortimer's own influence and autonomy are hampered when the king bestows the major portion of his wealth and attention on a favourite. More tellingly, perhaps, Mortimer's solicitude for Queen Isabel soon turns out to be a sexual and political interest in what this attractive and neglected consort can do for him as partner in a bid for the throne. In light of this development, we are invited to ask whether Mortimer's ire at Edward's defence policy has not been merely an excuse for him to make his move. Indeed, he is frank enough to admit to his fellow peers that Gaveston's baleful prominence may be of use to them after all by offering a justification for armed resistance: 'Then may we with some colour rise in arms'. He knows well enough that ''Tis treason to be up against the king' (1.4.279–81).

Certainly the portrait of Mortimer and Isabel as lovers affords increasingly dark intimations of conspiracy in deposition and secret murder. Isabel is at first the wronged wife who can protest to her faithless husband, 'Heavens can witness I love none but you', and lament in soliloquy, 'From my embracements thus he breaks away' (2.4.15–16). Yet her subsequent treachery is so calculating—as when she privately urges the murder of her husband 'so it were not by my means' and then publicly sends a ring to Edward as 'witness of my love' (5.2.45–72)—that our sympathies are mixed. 'Finely dissembled', murmurs her admiring partner in the art of deception. Was Edward wrong to suspect that Mortimer was her lover? Mortimer, for his part, increasingly becomes the practised dissembler who can rig matters so that the gullible lords will thrust upon him the protectorship that he desires but pretends not to want, or order the murder of Edward by means of an ambiguously worded letter that will afford him deniability (5.4.6–71). He deals with villains like Lightborn, who has 'learned in Naples how to poison flowers' or blow a little powder in his victim's ears (ll. 31–6). In Marlowe's dark portrayal, political rebellion uncovers much that is dismaying in human ambition and desire.

Edward's brother, the earl of Kent, is a pivotal figure through whose eyes these unsettling transformations assume a kind of clarity, though without much sense of how the conflict might be satisfactorily resolved. He responds as we do to Edward's infantile dependence on Gaveston and his choosing new and corrupt favourites like Spencer and Baldock once Gaveston is gone (3.2.143–7). Edward's failure to listen to his well-meaning brother is a sure sign of his pathetic lack of judgement. When, on the other hand, the barons go to the extreme of military rebellion, Kent's sympathies veer back towards the beleaguered king. He condemns what he sees as an 'unnatural revolt' and an adulterous love 'that hatcheth death and hate' (4.6.9–15). Yet however well he analyses political motive and sees through deception, Kent is condemned to vacillate between extremes and at last to be martyred in his attempt to rescue Edward. The middle ground offers no comfort in a history of stalemate and polarization.

Edward is rehabilitated for us in the play's ending as he becomes the victim of brutal oppressors and is stripped of his favourites. In one sense, his homosexuality is no longer an issue; even the barons are ready to concede numerous examples of 'the mightiest kings' and 'the wisest men', including Alexander, Hercules, Achilles, Cicero, and Socrates, who 'have had their minions' (1.4.391–7). And yet, this seeming pattern of history does not prevent Mortimer and his cohorts from choosing a form of execution that mocks Edward for his sexuality and represents an appalling violation of the sacred person of the king.

In suffering, Edward is compassionate and dauntless of mind, like Shakespeare's Richard II. His son, the young King Edward III, brings Edward's tormentors to account and gives every promise of future greatness on the throne; indeed, Marlowe's audience would have known that Edward III was to be as much a success as his father was a failure. Even in this note of resolution, however, Marlowe's play offers little assurance of providential harmony. The Crown is not a sacred institution but an object of contention for the possession of which human beings will use any means, however ignoble. *Edward II* is Marlowe's last look at the self-destructiveness and inevitability of human striving after power and pleasure.

NOTE ON THE TEXTS

EACH play in this edition has been edited afresh from the original text of best authority with modernized spelling and punctuation. Following the principles set forth by Stanley Wells in *Re-editing Shakespeare for the Modern Reader* (1984), we have modernized 'mushrump' to 'mushroom', 'porpentine' to 'porcupine', 'renowmd' to 'renowned', 'vilde' to 'vile', 'wrackes' to 'wrecks', 'swowns' to 'swounds', 'burladie' to 'By'r lady', 'and' to 'an' (where it means 'if'), 'enow' to 'enough', and the like. On the other hand, we preserve original words that are historically separate from the more recognizable modern cognates, as in 'bewray' (not 'betray') and 'beholding' (not 'beholden'). We retain strong forms of verbs such as 'gat' ('got') and 'loaden' ('loaded'). We retain archaic forms when the metre requires them: for example, 'accurst' rather than 'accursed', 'blest' rather than 'blessed', 'conster' rather than 'construe'. We spell out -ed endings to words like 'loved' (usually 'lov'd' in the original texts) even when the final -ed is not sounded in a separate syllable; when the metre requires that such a syllable be sounded (usually indicated in the original as 'loved'), we provide an accent mark: 'lovèd'. We expand normal abbreviations like 'Mr' ('Master') and '24' ('twenty-four'). We have emended readings in the original only in those instances where error is manifest and the correction persuasive. All six plays have been edited in five acts (the early texts of *Tamburlaine* provide act and scene divisions in Latin; only act divisions appear in *The Jew of Malta*; no acts or scenes are marked in *Edward II* or in either version of *Doctor Faustus*). Speech prefixes are silently expanded and normalized. Latin stage directions are translated. Added stage directions, intended to give concreteness to implied gestures and stage movements where they seem clearly intended to be performed, are supplied in square brackets; stage directions not in square brackets are from the original texts.

Most abbreviations are, we hope, self-explanatory. We use the following:

Q   quarto (printed four leaves or eight pages to a sheet)
Q1   the first quarto
Q2   the second quarto
A1   the first quarto of the A-text of *Doctor Faustus*, 1604

B1   the first quarto of the B-text of *Doctor Faustus*, 1616

octavo an early edition printed with eight leaves or sixteen pages to
a sheet

Tamburlaine

The two parts of *Tamburlaine*—the only of Marlowe's plays to be
printed in his lifetime—were entered in the Stationers' Register, the
official record book of the London Company of Stationers (printers
and booksellers), by Richard Jones in 1590 as 'The twooe commicall
discourses of Tomberlein the Cithian shepparde', and were published
together in octavo form that year. The title-page advertises the plays
as 'Tragicall Discourses'. The 'commicall' scenes were apparently
excised by the printer himself, who explains in an epistle to the
readers that he has 'omitted and left out some fond and frivolous
gestures, digressing, and, in my poor opinion, far unmeet for the
matter'.

The omission of necessary entrance and exit directions in the
octavo text (2.2.38, 2.3.48, 2.3.65, 2.6.40, 2.7.67, 3.2.106, 4.1.72,
4.4.144, and 5.1.195 in Part I; 2.2.64, 2.4.142, 3.3.40, 3.3.63, 4.1.59,
5.1.123, 5.1.126, 5.1.135, 5.1.200, 5.3.41, 5.3.101, and 5.3.253 in Part
II) indicates that the printer was not working from a theatrical
manuscript, in which such directions would probably have been
added by the bookkeeper. Moreover, the Latinate act and scene
headings along with the unusually formal conclusion of Part I, '*Finis
Actus quinti & ultimi huius primae partis*', suggest a manuscript
prepared in the study rather than the playhouse. The remarkably
clean 1590 text seems to derive from a carefully written manuscript,
perhaps a fair copy transcript made by Marlowe himself.

Doctor Faustus

Doctor Faustus exists in two considerably different early versions, the
A-text (1604) and the B-text (1616), both of which are provided in
full in this edition. The A-text contains a few short passages (totalling
36 lines) that do not appear in the B-text. For its part, the B-text
includes a number of episodes, totalling 676 lines, that are not found
in the A-text, and introduces thousands of minor changes throughout.
(See Introduction for a discussion of the significant thematic differen-
ces between the two versions.) In 1602 the owner of the Rose theatre,
Philip Henslowe, recorded a payment of £4 made to William Birde

and Samuel Rowley 'for ther adicyones in docter fostes'. The possibility that the new B-text episodes represent the additions written by Birde and Rowley was rejected in 1950 by W. W. Greg, who insisted instead that the A-text was a so-called 'bad quarto' put together from memory, in which the missing passages could be explained as memory lapses, and that the B-text is Marlowe's original play. Our recent studies of the A-text, however, have established (1) that the A-text was, in fact, set in type from an original authorial manuscript composed of interleaved scenes written by Marlowe and a collaborating playwright, and (2) that the B-text represents a version of the play that had been extensively revised more than a decade after Marlowe's death.

A-text

In January of 1601, the publisher Thomas Bushell entered in the Stationers' Register for his copy of 'a booke called the plaie of Doctor ffaustus'. The first edition is a quarto, known as A1, printed by Valentine Simmes for Bushell in 1604. Because the A1 quarto is based upon a 'foul paper' manuscript, it exhibits a number of imperfections and anomalies that one would expect to find in a dramatist's working draft. The indefinite stage direction at 5.1.8, '*Enter Faustus with two or three Scholars*', suggests that when Marlowe began writing the fifth act, he was still shaping the scene in his mind and was as yet undecided about how many scholars he would need. A1 also preserves an apparent false start at the conclusion of 3.2 where Mephistopheles enters twice (without exiting) and twice transforms the clowns into beasts. Apparently, the playwright had cancelled his original ending and rewrote the ending of the scene, but the printer, faced with a foul paper manuscript, failed to notice (or to understand) the playwright's deletion markings, and accidentally set the rejected passage along with the revised version.

A certain amount of shuffling and reshuffling of the manuscript seems to have occurred, as a result of which several scenes are out of place. Some scenes appear to be lost; the play in this A-text version is uncharacteristically short. The two comic scenes featuring Robin and Rafe (2.2 and 3.2 in this edition), which follow one immediately after the other in A1, are clearly not in their proper positions. The extraordinarily long scene in Act 2 involving an extensive discussion between Faustus and Mephistopheles and then the show of the Seven Deadly Sins seems to require division into two separated scenes (and indeed is so divided in the B-text). The present edition corrects this textual corruption by moving the first comic scene to the middle of Act 2. The Act 4 Chorus, which is obviously intended to introduce the Emperor Carolus scene but comes two scenes too early in the A-text, is also certainly misplaced and has been moved to its correct position in this edition.

B-text

In 1616, John Wright published a new quarto edition of *Doctor Faustus* known as B1 (advertised in 1619 as 'With new Additions'). The B1 quarto apparently derives from a composite manuscript with various layers of addition, revision, playhouse annotation, and censorship. A copy of the A-text version of the play (the A3 quarto of 1611) was also used in the printing of B1. Although the B-text straightens out some of the A-text tangles, it creates others. The Chorus that introduces Act 4 in the A-text is missing entirely from the B-text, while the other internal Chorus appears in two versions: Wagner's Chorus, copied verbatim from the A3 quarto, appears between 2.1 and 2.2 in the B-text; a revised and expanded version of this Chorus then appears in its correct position at the opening of Act 3. The B-text also attempts to sort out the misplaced scenes in the A-text, but its placement of the first comic scene after 2.3 is unpersuasive. The present edition relocates this scene to 2.2.

Further Reading

W. W. Greg, *Marlowe's 'Doctor Faustus' 1604–1616: Parallel Texts* (1950); Fredson T. Bowers, 'Marlowe's *Doctor Faustus*: The 1602 Additions', *Studies in Bibliography*, 26 (1973), 1–18; Constance Brown Kuriyama, 'Dr. Greg and *Doctor Faustus*: The Supposed Originality of the 1616 Text', *English Literary Renaissance*, 5 (1975), 171–97; Michael J. Warren, '*Doctor Faustus*: The Old Man and the Text', *English Literary Renaissance*, 11 (1981), 111–47; Eric Rasmussen, *A Textual Companion to 'Doctor Faustus'* (1993).

The Jew of Malta

In May of 1594, Nicholas Ling and Thomas Millington entered for publication in the Stationers' Register 'the famous tragedie of the Riche Jewe of Malta', but no copy of Ling and Millington's contemplated edition is extant and it may never have appeared. The earliest text is a 1633 quarto printed by John Beale with a dedication by the playwright Thomas Heywood. It has been argued that the quarto represents Heywood's revision of Marlowe's play. Calymath's followers are called 'Bassoes' in 1.2 (the spelling used in both parts of

Tamburlaine) and 'Bashaws' in 3.5 and 5.1, suggesting perhaps that someone other than Marlowe reworked the second half of the play. Similarly, Barabas has the speech-prefix '*Iew.*' in 1.1, but from then on it is '*Bar.*' (except for two reappearances of '*Iew.*' in 5.1.31 and 95). These inconsistencies may, of course, be Marlowe's own. (Compare the alternation between '*Iew.*' and '*Shylock.*' in the Q1 speech-prefixes of *The Merchant of Venice* printed from Shakespeare's foul papers.) The 1633 quarto's curious use of the plural 'governors' throughout the dialogue of the second scene may represent a false start. In his Revels edition, N. W. Bawcutt suggests that when Marlowe began writing the play he intended that a body of governors would rule Malta, but later decided upon a single governor, Ferneze, and did not make the necessary adjustments in the earlier scene.

However, Bawcutt's conclusion that the quarto derives from Marlowe's own fair copy of his foul papers does not account for the salient corruption in the 1633 text, such as the lacunae at 3.2.34 and 4.3.63, and the widespread misattribution of speeches: Ferneze's line at 1.2.137 is erroneously assigned to the First Officer; the Abbess's speeches at 1.2.307 and 313 are assigned to a nun; the anonymous slave's remarks at 2.3.115, 117, 120, and 124 are given to Ithamore; speeches for Lodowick and Mathias are interchanged at 3.2.3–4; speeches evidently intended for Barabas at 4.1.103 and for Friar Jacomo at 4.1.104 are assigned to Ithamore; Bellamira's line at 4.4.5 is given to Pilia-Borza. The 1633 printer may have had an authoritative manuscript, but it had clearly been subjected to some sort of intentional revision or accidental alteration in the more than four decades that had elapsed since Marlowe wrote his play.

Further Reading

J. C. Maxwell, 'How Bad is the Text of *The Jew of Malta*?', *Modern Language Review*, 48 (1953), 435–8; Richard W. Van Fossen (ed.), *The Jew of Malta*, Regents Renaissance Drama ed. (1964), pp. xxvi–xxviii; N. W. Bawcutt (ed.), *The Jew of Malta*, The Revels Plays (1978), pp. 37–58.

Edward II

On 6 July 1593, a little over a month after Marlowe's death, William Jones registered *Edward II* in the Stationers' Register: 'A booke Intituled The troublesom Reign and Lamentable Death of Edward the Second, king of England, with the tragicall fall of proud Mortymer.' A manuscript transcription of an early printed title-page suggests that the play may have been published in 1593, but the first extant edition is an octavo (albeit with the shape and size of a quarto, and thus often referred to as a quarto) printed by Jones in 1594.

Although W. W. Greg and some subsequent editors have argued that the text is based on a playhouse manuscript which had undergone some kind of revision for the stage, the present editors join with Fredson Bowers in holding that the anomalies, inconsistencies, and missing stage directions in the 1594 text suggest that it was printed from Marlowe's working manuscript or foul papers. It is unlikely, for instance, that a playbook prepared for use in the theatre would have left out a legion of necessary entrance and exit directions (1.2.38, 1.4.34, 2.1.82, 2.2.86, 2.2.137, 2.4.58, 3.2.88, 3.2.147, 3.2.180, 3.4.12, 3.4.29, 4.2.82, 4.3.52, 4.5.9, 4.7.116, 5.1.125, 5.1.127, 5.2.27, 5.2.37, 5.2.113, 5.2.117, 5.4.22, 5.4.47, 5.5.38, 5.5.41, 5.5.107, 5.6.10, 5.6.67, 5.6.92, 5.6.97, 5.6.102). The speech prefixes for Edmund earl of Kent, which alternate randomly between '*Edm.*' and '*Kent.*', display a characteristically authorial casualness about names that a bookkeeper would have found intolerable. Other textual oddities include the character 'Trussell' who suddenly appears in 5.1 without an entry direction, and is given the speech-prefix '*Tru.*', the full form of which is never used in the play and has to be supplied by editors. Moreover, there is a tendency in the 1594 text to confuse the earl of Arundel, one of the barons, with Matrevis, one of Edward's murderers who appears late in the play. Perhaps the same actor doubled the two parts. If Marlowe had indeed intended for the roles to be doubled, he might well have temporarily confused the two as he composed his play. (Compare the confusion of Peter and Balthasar in the foul paper Q2 text of *Romeo and Juliet*.)

Further Reading

W. W. Greg (ed.), *Edward II*, Malone Society (1925); W. Moelwyn Merchant (ed.), *Edward II*, New Mermaids (1967); Fredson Bowers (ed.), *The Complete Works of Christopher Marlowe* (1973), ii. 8–11.

SELECT BIBLIOGRAPHY

THE landmark studies in the history of Marlowe criticism engage in a fundamental debate over how to view the playwright and his creations. Una Ellis-Fermor, *Christopher Marlowe* (1927), Paul H. Kocher, *Christopher Marlowe: A Study of His Thought, Learning, and Character* (1946), and Harry Levin, *The Overreacher: A Study of Christopher Marlowe* (1952), present Marlowe as a frustrated idealist and rebellious free-thinker who shared and endorsed the iconoclastic attitudes of his heroes. On the other hand, Roy W. Battenhouse, *Marlowe's 'Tamburlaine': A Study in Renaissance Moral Philosophy* (1941), and Douglas Cole, *Suffering and Evil in the Plays of Christopher Marlowe* (1962), regard Marlowe as an orthodox Christian moralist whose plays are essentially didactic. In *Poetry and Humanism* (1950), M. M. Mahood suggests that Marlowe's attitude may be one of ironic detachment rather than explicit moral comment. Extracts from most of the above titles are conveniently available in Clifford Leech, *Marlowe: A Collection of Critical Essays* (1964). Irving Ribner provides a useful survey of the debate in 'Marlowe and the Critics', *Tulane Drama Review*, 8 (1964), 211–24. Ribner sides with those who see Marlowe as heterodox.

The biographical material on Marlowe set forth in encyclopaedic detail by John Bakeless, *The Tragicall History of Christopher Marlowe* (2 vols., 1942), has been supplemented and superseded to a certain extent by the careful archival research of William Urry, *Christopher Marlowe and Canterbury* (1988). Significant studies of Marlowe's debt to both classical and native English dramatic traditions have been made by Eugene M. Waith, *The Herculean Hero in Marlowe, Chapman, Shakespeare and Dryden* (1962), David Bevington, *From 'Mankind' to Marlowe: Growth of Structure in the Popular Drama of Tudor England* (1962), and Jan Kott, *The Bottom Translation: Marlowe and Shakespeare and the Carnival Tradition* (1987).

Valuable comparisons of Marlowe with other Elizabethan playwrights can be found in F. P. Wilson, *Marlowe and the Early Shakespeare* (1953), Wilbur Sanders, *The Dramatist and the Received Idea: Studies in the Plays of Marlowe and Shakespeare* (1968), E. A. J. Honigmann (ed.), *Shakespeare and His Contemporaries: Essays in Comparison* (1986), and James Shapiro, *Rival Playwrights: Marlowe, Jonson, Shakespeare* (1991). The most useful discussions of the staging of the plays are those by David Hard Zucker, *Stage and Image in the Plays of Christopher Marlowe* (1972), Felix Bosonnet, *The Function of Stage Properties in Christopher Marlowe's Plays* (1978), and Clifford Leech, *Christopher Marlowe, Poet for the Stage* (1986).

Recent developments in new historicist, cultural materialist, post-structuralist, feminist, and psychoanalytic methodologies have been fruitfully applied to Marlowe by Stephen Greenblatt, *Renaissance Self-Fashioning: From More to Shakespeare* (1980), Constance Brown Kuriyama, *Hammer or Anvil: Psychological Patterns in Christopher Marlowe's Plays* (1980), Simon Shepherd, *Marlowe and the Politics of the Elizabethan Theatre* (1986), and C. L. Barber, *Creating Elizabethan Tragedy: The Theatre of Marlowe and Kyd* (1988).

A number of editions of Marlowe's complete works and of individual plays contain much useful information. See various editions of *Tamburlaine* Parts I and II by J. W. Harper (1971) and J. S. Cunningham (1981); of *Doctor Faustus* by W. W. Greg (1950), Irving Ribner (1963), David Ormerod and Christopher Wortham (1985), Roma Gill (1990), Michael Keefer (1991), and David Bevington and Eric Rasmussen (1993); of *The Jew of Malta* by N. W. Bawcutt (1978); and of *Edward II* by H. B. Charlton and R. D. Waller (1955), W. Moelwyn Merchant (1967), and Charles Forker (1994).

The following list of recommended articles, which includes classic essays on the individual plays as well as some provocative recent studies, demonstrates the full range and depth of contemporary critical approaches to Christopher Marlowe.

Tamburlaine

Burnett, Mark Thornton, '*Tamburlaine* and the Body', *Criticism*, 33 (1991), 31–47.

Duthie, G. I., 'The Dramatic Structure of Marlowe's *Tamburlaine the Great, Parts I and II*', *Essays and Studies*, 1 (1948), 101–26.

Gardner, Helen, 'The Second Part of *Tamburlaine the Great*', *Modern Language Review*, 37 (1942), 18–24.

Hardin, Richard F., 'Irony and Privilege in Marlowe', *The Centennial Review*, 33 (1989), 207–27.

Kocher, Paul H., 'Marlowe's Art of War', *Studies in Philology*, 39 (1942), 207–25.

Ribner, Irving, 'The Idea of History in Marlowe's *Tamburlaine*', *English Literary History*, 20 (1953), 251–66.

Seaton, Ethel, 'Marlowe's Map', *Essays and Studies*, 10 (1924), 13–35.

Waith, Eugene M., 'Marlowe and the Jades of Asia', *Studies in English Literature*, 5 (1965), 229–45.

Doctor Faustus

Barber, C. L., 'The Form of Faustus' Fortunes Good or Bad', *Tulane Drama Review*, 8 (1964), 92–119.

Brooke, Nicholas, 'The Moral Tragedy of *Dr Faustus*', *Cambridge Journal*, 7 (1952), 662–87.

Greg, W. W., 'The Damnation of Faustus', *Modern Language Review*, 41 (1946), 97–107.

Ornstein, Robert, 'Marlowe and God: The Tragic Theology of *Dr. Faustus*', *PMLA*, 83 (1968), 1378–85.

Palmer, D. J., 'Magic and Poetry in *Doctor Faustus*', *Critical Quarterly*, 6 (1964), 56–67.

Ribner, Irving, 'Marlowe's "Tragicke Glass" ', in Richard Hosley (ed.), *Essays on Shakespeare and Elizabethan Drama in Honor of Hardin Craig* (1962), 91–114.

Stockholder, Kay, ' "Within the massy entrailes of the earth": Faustus's Relation to Women', in Kenneth Friedenreich *et al.* (eds.), *'A Poet and a Filthy Play-Maker': New Essays on Christopher Marlowe* (1988), 203–19.

Waswo, Richard, 'Damnation, Protestant Style: Macbeth, Faustus, and Christian Tragedy', *Journal of Medieval and Renaissance Studies*, 4 (1974), 63–99.

The Jew of Malta

Babb, Howard S., ' "Policy" in Marlowe's *The Jew of Malta*', *English Literary History*, 24 (1957), 85–94.

Bowers, Fredson T., 'The Audience and the Poisoner of Elizabethan Tragedy', *JEGP*, 36 (1937), 491–504.

Cartelli, Thomas, 'Shakespeare's Merchant, Marlowe's Jew: The Problem of Cultural Difference', *Shakespeare Studies*, 20 (1987), 255–68.

D'Andrea, Antonio, 'Studies on Machiavelli and his Reputation in the Sixteenth Century: Marlowe's Prologue to *The Jew of Malta*', *Medieval and Renaissance Studies* (Warburg Institute), 5 (1961), 214–48.

Freer, Coburn, 'Lies and Lying in *The Jew of Malta*', in Kenneth Friedenreich *et al.* (eds.), *'A Poet and a Filthy Play-Maker': New Essays on Christopher Marlowe* (1988), 143–65.

Lindley, David, 'The Unbeing of the Overreacher: Proteanism and the Marlovian Hero', *Modern Language Review*, 84 (1989), 1–17.

Tambling, Jeremy, 'Abigail's Party: "The Difference of Things" in *The Jew of Malta*', in Dorothea Kehler and Susan Baker (eds.), *Another Country: Feminist Perspectives on Renaissance Drama* (1991), 95–112.

Edward II

Bevington, David and Shapiro, James, ' "What are Kings, when Regiment is Gone?" The Decay of Ceremony in *Edward II*', in Kenneth Friedenreich *et al.* (eds.), *'A Poet and a Filthy Play-Maker': New Essays on Christopher Marlowe* (1988), 263–78.

Guy-Bray, Stephen, 'Homophobia and the Depoliticizing of *Edward II*', *English Studies in Canada*, 17 (1991), 125–33.

Leech, Clifford, 'Marlowe's *Edward II*: Power and Suffering', *Critical Quarterly*, 1 (1959), 181–96.

Mills, Laurens J., 'The Meaning of *Edward II*', *Modern Philology*, 33 (1934), 11–32.

Thurn, David H., 'Sovereignty, Disorder, and Fetishism in Marlowe's *Edward II*', *Renaissance Drama*, 21 (1990), 115–41.

A CHRONOLOGY OF
CHRISTOPHER MARLOWE

1564   Marlowe baptized on 26 February in Canterbury

1579   Enters as a scholar at King's School, Canterbury .

1580   Enters Corpus Christi College, Cambridge

1581–6   Apparently engages in secret government service.

1584   Receives Cambridge BA.

1586   Writes *Dido, Queen of Carthage*, possibly with Thomas Nashe.

1587   Receives Cambridge MA; writes both parts of *Tamburlaine*.

1588–9   Imprisoned in Newgate for a street brawl; writes *Doctor Faustus*.

c.1590   Writes *The Jew of Malta*; two parts of *Tamburlaine* published.

c.1592   Writes *Edward II* and *The Massacre at Paris*.

1593   Theatres closed on account of plague; writes *Hero and Leander*; summoned to appear before the Privy Council on a charge of atheism, 18 May; murdered by Ingram Frizer in a tavern at Deptford, 30 May.

1594   *Dido* and *Edward II* published.

1598   *Hero and Leander* published.

1604   The A-text of *Doctor Faustus* published.

1616   The B-text of *Doctor Faustus* published.

1633   *The Jew of Malta* published.

TAMBURLAINE
THE GREAT
Part I

DRAMATIS PERSONAE

The Prologue

Mycetes, King of Persia

Cosroe

Meander

Theridamas

Ortygius

Ceneus

Menaphon

Tamburlaine

Zenocrate

Techelles

Usumcasane

Magnetes

Agydas

Lords

Soldiers

A Spy

A Messenger

Bajazeth, Emperor of
  Turkey

King of Fez

King of Morocco

King of Argier

Bassoes

Anippe

Zabina

Ebea

The Sultan of Egypt

Capolin

Two Moors

King of Arabia

Governor of Damascus

Citizens

Four Virgins

Attendants

Philemus

Tamburlaine the Great, Part I

[Enter] the Prologue

PROLOGUE From jigging veins of rhyming mother-wits°
And such conceits as clownage keeps in pay
We'll lead you to the stately tent of War,
Where you shall hear the Scythian Tamburlaine
Threat'ning the world with high astounding terms   5
And scourging kingdoms with his conquering sword.
View but his picture in this tragic glass,°
And then applaud his fortunes as you please.

[Exit]

[1.1]

[Enter] Mycetes, Cosroe, Meander, Theridamas, Ortygius,
Ceneus, [Menaphon,] with others

MYCETES Brother Cosroe, I find myself aggrieved,
Yet insufficient to express the same,
For it requires a great and thund'ring speech.
Good brother, tell the cause unto my lords;
I know you have a better wit than I.   5

COSROE Unhappy Persia, that in former age
Hast been the seat of mighty conquerors
That in their prowess and their policies
Have triumphed over Afric, and the bounds
Of Europe where the sun dares scarce appear   10
For freezing meteors and congealèd cold—°
Now to be ruled and governed by a man
At whose birthday Cynthia with Saturn joined,
And Jove, the sun, and Mercury denied
To shed their influence in his fickle brain!°   15
Now Turks and Tartars shake their swords at thee,
Meaning to mangle all thy provinces.

MYCETES Brother, I see your meaning well enough,
And through your planets I perceive you think°
I am not wise enough to be a king.   20
But I refer me to my noblemen
That know my wit and can be witnesses.
I might command you to be slain for this.
Meander, might I not?

MEANDER Not for so small a fault, my sovereign lord.   25

MYCETES I mean it not, but yet I know I might.
Yet live, yea, live, Mycetes wills it so.
Meander, thou my faithful counsellor,
Declare the cause of my conceivèd grief,°
Which is, God knows, about that Tamburlaine,   30
That like a fox in midst of harvest time
Doth prey upon my flocks of passengers,
And, as I hear, doth mean to pull my plumes.
Therefore 'tis good and meet for to be wise.

MEANDER Oft have I heard your majesty complain   35

4

Of Tamburlaine, that sturdy Scythian thief,
That robs your merchants of Persepolis
Trading by land unto the Western Isles,°
And in your confines with his lawless train°
Daily commits incivil outrages,   40
Hoping, misled by dreaming prophecies,
To reign in Asia and with barbarous arms
To make himself the monarch of the East.
But ere he march in Asia or display
His vagrant ensign in the Persian fields,°   45
Your grace hath taken order by Theridamas,°
Charged with a thousand horse, to apprehend°
And bring him captive to your highness' throne.
MYCETES Full true thou speak'st, and like thyself, my lord,°
Whom I may term a Damon for thy love.°   50
Therefore 'tis best, if so it like you all,
To send my thousand horse incontinent
To apprehend that paltry Scythian.
How like you this, my honourable lords?
Is it not a kingly resolution?   55
COSROE It cannot choose, because it comes from you.°
MYCETES Then hear thy charge, valiant Theridamas,
The chiefest captain of Mycetes' host,
The hope of Persia, and the very legs
Whereon our state doth lean, as on a staff   60
That holds us up and foils our neighbour foes:
Thou shalt be leader of this thousand horse,
Whose foaming gall with rage and high disdain°
Have sworn the death of wicked Tamburlaine.
Go frowning forth, but come thou smiling home,   65
As did Sir Paris with the Grecian dame.°
Return with speed! Time passeth swift away.
Our life is frail, and we may die today.
THERIDAMAS Before the moon renew her borrowed light,°
Doubt not, my lord and gracious sovereign,   70
But Tamburlaine and that Tartarian rout°
Shall either perish by our warlike hands
Or plead for mercy at your highness' feet.
MYCETES Go, stout Theridamas. Thy words are swords,
And with thy looks thou conquerest all thy foes.   75
I long to see thee back return from thence,

That I may view these milk-white steeds of mine
All loaden with the heads of killèd men,
And from their knees ev'n to their hoofs below
Besmeared with blood, that makes a dainty show.   80
THERIDAMAS Then now, my lord, I humbly take my leave.
     Exit [Theridamas]
MYCETES Theridamas, farewell ten thousand times!
Ah, Menaphon, why stayest thou thus behind
When other men press forward for renown?
Go, Menaphon, go into Scythia,   85
And foot by foot follow Theridamas.
COSROE Nay, pray you, let him stay; a greater task°
Fits Menaphon than warring with a thief.
Create him prorex of Assyria,°
That he may win the Babylonians' hearts,   90
Which will revolt from Persian government
Unless they have a wiser king than you.
MYCETES 'Unless they have a wiser king than you'!
These are his words, Meander. Set them down.
COSROE And add this to them, that all Asia   95
Lament to see the folly of their king.
MYCETES Well, here I swear by this my royal seat—°
COSROE You may do well to kiss it, then.
MYCETES —Embossed with silk as best beseems my state,°
To be revenged for these contemptuous words.   100
O, where is duty and allegiance now?
Fled to the Caspian or the ocean main?
What, shall I call thee brother? No, a foe,
Monster of Nature, shame unto thy stock,
That dar'st presume thy sovereign for to mock.   105
Meander, come. I am abused, Meander.
     Exeunt [all, except] Cosroe and Menaphon
MENAPHON How now, my lord, what, mated and amazed
To hear the king thus threaten like himself?°
COSROE Ah, Menaphon, I pass not for his threats.
The plot is laid by Persian noblemen   110
And captains of the Median garrisons
To crown me emperor of Asia.
But this it is that does excruciate
The very substance of my vexèd soul:
To see our neighbours, that were wont to quake   115

6

And tremble at the Persian monarch's name,
Now sits and laughs our regiment to scorn;°
And that which might resolve me into tears,
Men from the farthest equinoctial line°
Have swarmed in troops into the Eastern India,   120
Lading their ships with gold and precious stones,
And made their spoils from all our provinces.
MENAPHON This should entreat your highness to rejoice,
Since Fortune gives you opportunity
To gain the title of a conqueror   125
By curing of this maimèd empery.°
Afric and Europe bordering on your land
And continent to your dominions,°
How easily may you with a mighty host
Pass into Graecia, as did Cyrus once,°   130
And cause them to withdraw their forces home
Lest you subdue the pride of Christendom!
     [A trumpet sounds]
COSROE But Menaphon, what means this trumpet's sound?
MENAPHON Behold, my lord, Ortygius and the rest,
Bringing the crown to make you emperor.   135
     Enter Ortygius and Ceneus, bearing a crown, with others
ORTYGIUS Magnificent and mighty prince Cosroe,
We, in the name of other Persian states
And commons of this mighty monarchy,
Present thee with th'imperial diadem.
CENEUS The warlike soldiers and the gentlemen   140
That heretofore have filled Persepolis
With Afric captains taken in the field,
Whose ransom made them march in coats of gold°
With costly jewels hanging at their ears
And shining stones upon their lofty crests,   145
Now living idle in the wallèd towns,
Wanting both pay and martial discipline,
Begin in troops to threaten civil war
And openly exclaim against the king.
Therefore, to stay all sudden mutinies,   150
We will invest your highness emperor;
Whereat the soldiers will conceive more joy
Than did the Macedonians at the spoil
Of great Darius and his wealthy host.°

7

COSROE Well, since I see the state of Persia droop   155
   And languish in my brother's government,
   I willingly receive th'imperial crown
   And vow to wear it for my country's good,
   In spite of them shall malice my estate.°
ORTYGIUS [*crowning Cosroe*] And in assurance of desired success   160
   We here do crown thee monarch of the East,
   Emperor of Asia and of Persia,
   Great lord of Media and Armenia,
   Duke of Assyria and Albania,
   Mesopotamia and of Parthia,   165
   East India and the late-discovered isles,
   Chief lord of all the wide vast Euxine Sea°
   And of the ever-raging Caspian lake.
   Long live Cosroë, mighty emperor!
COSROE And Jove may never let me longer live°   170
   Than I may seek to gratify your love
   And cause the soldiers that thus honour me
   To triumph over many provinces!
   By whose desires of discipline in arms
   I doubt not shortly but to reign sole king,   175
   And with the army of Theridamas,
   Whither we presently will fly, my lords,
   To rest secure against my brother's force.
ORTYGIUS We knew, my lord, before we brought the crown,
   Intending your investion so near   180
   The residence of your despisèd brother,
   The lords would not be too exasperate°
   To injure or suppress your worthy title.
   Or if they would, there are in readiness
   Ten thousand horse to carry you from hence   185
   In spite of all suspected enemies.
COSROE I know it well, my lord, and thank you all.
ORTYGIUS Sound up the trumpets, then. God save the king!
   [*The trumpets sound.*] *Exeunt*

[1.2]

[Enter] Tamburlaine, leading Zenocrate; Techelles,
Usumcasane, other lords, [among whom are Magnetes and
Agydas,] and Soldiers loaden with treasure

TAMBURLAINE Come, lady, let not this appal your thoughts.
    The jewels and the treasure we have ta'en
    Shall be reserved, and you in better state
    Than if you were arrived in Syria,
    Even in the circle of your father's arms,   5
    The mighty Sultan of Egyptia.
ZENOCRATE Ah, shepherd, pity my distressèd plight,
    If, as thou seem'st, thou art so mean a man,
    And seek not to enrich thy followers
    By lawless rapine from a silly maid   10
    Who, travelling with these Median lords
    To Memphis, from my uncle's country of Media,
    Where all my youth I have been governèd,°
    Have passed the army of the mighty Turk,
    Bearing his privy signet and his hand°   15
    To safe conduct us thorough Africa.°
MAGNETES And, since we have arrived in Scythia,
    Besides rich presents from the puissant Cham°
    We have his highness' letters to command
    Aid and assistance if we stand in need.   20
TAMBURLAINE But now you see these letters and commands
    Are countermanded by a greater man,
    And through my provinces you must expect
    Letters of conduct from my mightiness
    If you intend to keep your treasure safe.°   25
    But since I love to live at liberty,
    As easily may you get the Sultan's crown
    As any prizes out of my precinct;
    For they are friends that help to wean my state°
    Till men and kingdoms help to strengthen it,   30
    And must maintain my life exempt from servitude.
    But tell me, madam, is your grace betrothed?
ZENOCRATE I am, my lord—for so you do import.°
TAMBURLAINE I am a lord, for so my deeds shall prove,
    And yet a shepherd by my parentage.   35

But lady, this fair face and heavenly hue
Must grace his bed that conquers Asia°
And means to be a terror to the world,
Measuring the limits of his empery
By east and west as Phoebus doth his course.   40
Lie here, ye weeds that I disdain to wear!
This complete armour and this curtle-axe°
Are adjuncts more beseeming Tamburlaine.°
And, madam, whatsoever you esteem
Of this success, and loss unvaluèd,   45
Both may invest you empress of the East;
And these that seem but silly country swains°
May have the leading of so great an host
As with their weight shall make the mountains quake,
Even as when windy exhalations,   50
Fighting for passage, tilt within the earth.°
TECHELLES As princely lions when they rouse themselves,
Stretching their paws and threat'ning herds of beasts,
So in his armour looketh Tamburlaine.
Methinks I see kings kneeling at his feet,   55
And he with frowning brows and fiery looks
Spurning their crowns from off their captive heads.
USUMCASANE And making thee and me, Techelles, kings,
That even to death will follow Tamburlaine.
TAMBURLAINE Nobly resolved, sweet friends and followers.   60
These lords, perhaps, do scorn our estimates,°
And think we prattle with distempered spirits;°
But since they measure our deserts so mean
That in conceit bear empires on our spears,
Affecting thoughts coequal with the clouds,°   65
They shall be kept our forcèd followers
Till with their eyes they view us emperors.
ZENOCRATE The gods, defenders of the innocent,
Will never prosper your intended drifts
That thus oppress poor friendless passengers.   70
Therefore at least admit us liberty,
Even as thou hop'st to be eternized
By living Asia's mighty emperor.
AGYDAS I hope our lady's treasure and our own
May serve for ransom to our liberties.   75
Return our mules and empty camels back,

That we may travel into Syria,
Where her betrothèd, Lord Alcidamus,
Expects th' arrival of her highness' person.

MAGNETES And wheresoever we repose ourselves   80
We will report but well of Tamburlaine.

TAMBURLAINE Disdains Zenocrate to live with me?
Or you, my lords, to be my followers?
Think you I weigh this treasure more than you?
Not all the gold in India's wealthy arms   85
Shall buy the meanest soldier in my train.
Zenocrate, lovelier than the love of Jove,°
Brighter than is the silver Rhodope,°
Fairer than whitest snow on Scythian hills,
Thy person is more worth to Tamburlaine   90
Than the possession of the Persian crown,
Which gracious stars have promised at my birth.
A hundred Tartars shall attend on thee,
Mounted on steeds swifter than Pegasus;°
Thy garments shall be made of Median silk,   95
Enchased with precious jewels of mine own,
More rich and valurous than Zenocrate's;
With milk-white harts upon an ivory sled
Thou shalt be drawn amidst the frozen pools
And scale the icy mountains' lofty tops,   100
Which with thy beauty will be soon resolved;
My martial prizes, with five hundred men,
Won on the fifty-headed Volga's waves,°
Shall all we offer to Zenocrate,°
And then myself to fair Zenocrate.   105

TECHELLES [to Tamburlaine] What now? In love?

TAMBURLAINE Techelles, women must be flatterèd.
But this is she with whom I am in love.°
        Enter a Soldier

SOLDIER News, news!

TAMBURLAINE How now, what's the matter?   110

SOLDIER A thousand Persian horsemen are at hand,
Sent from the king to overcome us all.

TAMBURLAINE How now, my lords of Egypt and Zenocrate?
Now must your jewels be restored again
And I that triumphed so be overcome.   115
How say you, lordings, is not this your hope?

AGYDAS We hope yourself will willingly restore them.

TAMBURLAINE Such hope, such fortune, have the thousand horse.°
    Soft ye, my lords and sweet Zenocrate:
    You must be forcèd from me ere you go.   120
    A thousand horsemen! We, five hundred foot!
    An odds too great for us to stand against.°
    But are they rich? And is their armour good?

SOLDIER Their plumèd helms are wrought with beaten gold,
    Their swords enamelled, and about their necks   125
    Hangs massy chains of gold down to the waist,°
    In every part exceeding brave and rich.

TAMBURLAINE Then shall we fight courageously with them.
    Or look you I should play the orator?°

TECHELLES No. Cowards and faint-hearted runaways   130
    Look for orations when the foe is near.
    Our swords shall play the orators for us.

USUMCASANE Come, let us meet them at the mountain top,
    And with a sudden and an hot alarm
    Drive all their horses headlong down the hill.   135

TECHELLES Come, let us march.

TAMBURLAINE Stay, Techelles, ask a parley first.
    The Soldiers [of Tamburlaine] enter
    Open the mails, yet guard the treasure sure.°
    Lay out our golden wedges to the view,
    That their reflections may amaze the Persians.   140
    [The Soldiers lay out gold bars]
    And look we friendly on them when they come;
    But if they offer word or violence
    We'll fight five hundred men-at-arms to one
    Before we part with our possession.°
    And 'gainst the general we will lift our swords   145
    And either lance his greedy thirsting throat
    Or take him prisoner, and his chain shall serve°
    For manacles till he be ransomed home.

TECHELLES I hear them come. Shall we encounter them?

TAMBURLAINE Keep all your standings, and not stir a foot.°   150
    Myself will bide the danger of the brunt.
    Enter Theridamas with others

THERIDAMAS Where is this Scythian Tamburlaine?

TAMBURLAINE Whom seek'st thou, Persian? I am Tamburlaine.

THERIDAMAS *[aside]* Tamburlaine?

A Scythian shepherd, so embellishèd   155
With nature's pride and richest furniture?
His looks do menace heaven and dare the gods;
His fiery eyes are fixed upon the earth,
As if he now devised some stratagem,
Or meant to pierce Avernus' darksome vaults   160
And pull the triple-headed dog from hell.°

TAMBURLAINE [*to Techelles*] Noble and mild this Persian seems to be,
If outward habit judge the inward man.

TECHELLES [*to Tamburlaine*] His deep affections make him passionate.

TAMBURLAINE [*to Techelles*] With what a majesty he rears his looks!   165
[*To Theridamas*] In thee, thou valiant man of Persia,
I see the folly of thy emperor.
Art thou but captain of a thousand horse,
That by characters graven in thy brows°
And by thy martial face and stout aspect°   170
Deserv'st to have the leading of an host?
Forsake thy king, and do but join with me,
And we will triumph over all the world.
I hold the Fates bound fast in iron chains°
And with my hand turn Fortune's wheel about,   175
And sooner shall the sun fall from his sphere
Than Tamburlaine be slain or overcome.
Draw forth thy sword, thou mighty man-at-arms,
Intending but to raze my charmèd skin,
And Jove himself will stretch his hand from heaven   180
To ward the blow and shield me safe from harm.
See how he rains down heaps of gold in showers
As if he meant to give my soldiers pay!
     [*He indicates the gold bars*]
And, as a sure and grounded argument
That I shall be the monarch of the East,   185
He sends this Sultan's daughter, rich and brave,
To be my queen and portly emperess.
If thou wilt stay with me, renownèd man,
And lead thy thousand horse with my conduct,°
Besides thy share of this Egyptian prize   190
Those thousand horse shall sweat with martial spoil
Of conquered kingdoms and of cities sacked.
Both we will walk upon the lofty clifts,
And Christian merchants that with Russian stems°

Plough up huge furrows in the Caspian Sea   195
Shall vail to us as lords of all the lake.
Both we will reign as consuls of the earth,
And mighty kings shall be our senators.
Jove sometime maskèd in a shepherd's weed,
And by those steps that he hath scaled the heavens°   200
May we become immortal like the gods.
Join with me now in this my mean estate
(I call it mean, because, being yet obscure,
The nations far removed admire me not),
And when my name and honour shall be spread   205
As far as Boreas claps his brazen wings°
Or fair Boötes sends his cheerful light,°
Then shalt thou be competitor with me
And sit with Tamburlaine in all his majesty.
THERIDAMAS Not Hermes, prolocutor to the gods,°   210
Could use persuasions more pathetical.
TAMBURLAINE Nor are Apollo's oracles more true
Than thou shalt find my vaunts substantial.
TECHELLES We are his friends, and if the Persian king
Should offer present dukedoms to our state,°   215
We think it loss to make exchange for that°
We are assured of by our friend's success.
USUMCASANE And kingdoms at the least we all expect,
Besides the honour in assurèd conquests
Where kings shall crouch unto our conquering swords   220
And hosts of soldiers stand amazed at us,
When with their fearful tongues they shall confess,
'These are the men that all the world admires.'
THERIDAMAS What strong enchantments 'tice my yielding soul?
Are these resolvèd noble Scythians?°   225
But shall I prove a traitor to my king?
TAMBURLAINE No, but the trusty friend of Tamburlaine.
THERIDAMAS Won with thy words and conquered with thy looks,
I yield myself, my men, and horse to thee,
To be partaker of thy good or ill   230
As long as life maintains Theridamas.
TAMBURLAINE Theridamas, my friend, take here my hand,
Which is as much as if I swore by heaven
And called the gods to witness of my vow.
Thus shall my heart be still combined with thine   235

Until our bodies turn to elements
And both our souls aspire celestial thrones.
Techelles and Casane, welcome him.

TECHELLES Welcome, renownèd Persian, to us all!

USUMCASANE Long may Theridamas remain with us!   240

TAMBURLAINE These are my friends, in whom I more rejoice
Than doth the king of Persia in his crown.
And by the love of Pylades and Orestes,°
Whose statues we adore in Scythia,
Thyself and them shall never part from me°   245
Before I crown you kings in Asia.
Make much of them, gentle Theridamas,
And they will never leave thee till the death.

THERIDAMAS Nor thee nor them, thrice-noble Tamburlaine,
Shall want my heart to be with gladness pierced   250
To do you honour and security.°

TAMBURLAINE A thousand thanks, worthy Theridamas.
And now, fair madam, and my noble lords,
If you will willingly remain with me
You shall have honours as your merits be—°   255
Or else you shall be forced with slavery.

AGYDAS We yield unto thee, happy Tamburlaine.

TAMBURLAINE For you, then, madam, I am out of doubt.°

ZENOCRATE I must be pleased perforce. Wretched Zenocrate!
        Exeunt

[2.1]

[*Enter*] *Cosroe, Menaphon, Ortygius, Ceneus, with other*
Soldiers

COSROE Thus far are we towards Theridamas°
  And valiant Tamburlaine, the man of fame,
  The man that in the forehead of his fortune
  Bears figures of renown and miracle.°
  But tell me, that hast seen him, Menaphon,°   5
  What stature wields he, and what personage?
MENAPHON Of stature tall, and straightly fashionèd,
  Like his desire, lift upwards and divine;°
  So large of limbs, his joints so strongly knit,
  Such breadth of shoulders as might mainly bear   10
  Old Atlas' burden. 'Twixt his manly pitch°
  A pearl more worth than all the world is placed,°
  Wherein by curious sovereignty of art°
  Are fixed his piercing instruments of sight,
  Whose fiery circles bear encompassèd°   15
  A heaven of heavenly bodies in their spheres
  That guides his steps and actions to the throne
  Where honour sits invested royally;
  Pale of complexion—wrought in him with passion,
  Thirsting with sovereignty, with love of arms.   20
  His lofty brows in folds do figure death,°
  And in their smoothness amity and life.°
  About them hangs a knot of amber hair
  Wrappèd in curls, as fierce Achilles' was,°
  On which the breath of heaven delights to play,   25
  Making it dance with wanton majesty.
  His arms and fingers long and sinewy,
  Betokening valour and excess of strength;
  In every part proportioned like the man
  Should make the world subdued to Tamburlaine.°   30
COSROE Well hast thou portrayed in thy terms of life°
  The face and personage of a wondrous man.
  Nature doth strive with Fortune and his stars°
  To make him famous in accomplished worth,
  And well his merits show him to be made   35

His fortune's master and the king of men,
That could persuade at such a sudden pinch,
With reasons of his valour and his life,
A thousand sworn and overmatching foes.°
Then, when our powers in points of swords are joined   40
And closed in compass of the killing bullet,
Though strait the passage and the port be made
That leads to palace of my brother's life,
Proud is his fortune if we pierce it not.°
And when the princely Persian diadem   45
Shall overweigh his weary witless head
And fall like mellowed fruit, with shakes of death,
In fair Persia noble Tamburlaine
Shall be my regent and remain as king.

ORTYGIUS In happy hour we have set the crown   50
Upon your kingly head, that seeks our honour
In joining with the man ordained by heaven
To further every action to the best.

CENEUS He that with shepherds and a little spoil
Durst, in disdain of wrong and tyranny,   55
Defend his freedom 'gainst a monarchy,
What will he do supported by a king,
Leading a troop of gentlemen and lords,
And stuffed with treasure for his highest thoughts?°

COSROE And such shall wait on worthy Tamburlaine.°   60
Our army will be forty thousand strong
When Tamburlaine and brave Theridamas
Have met us by the river Araris,
And all conjoined to meet the witless king
That now is marching near to Parthia,   65
And with unwilling soldiers faintly armed,
To seek revenge on me and Tamburlaine.—
To whom, sweet Menaphon, direct me straight.

MENAPHON I will, my lord.
          Exeunt

[2.2]

[Enter] Mycetes, Meander, with other Lords and Soldiers

MYCETES Come, my Meander, let us to this gear.
   I tell you true, my heart is swoll'n with wrath
   On this same thievish villain Tamburlaine,
   And of that false Cosroe, my traitorous brother.
   Would it not grieve a king to be so abused   5
   And have a thousand horsemen ta'en away?
   And, which is worst, to have his diadem
   Sought for by such scald knaves as love him not?
   I think it would. Well then, by heavens I swear,
   Aurora shall not peep out of her doors°   10
   But I will have Cosroë by the head
   And kill proud Tamburlaine with point of sword.
   Tell you the rest, Meander; I have said.°
MEANDER Then, having passed Armenian deserts now
   And pitched our tents under the Georgian hills   15
   Whose tops are covered with Tartarian thieves
   That lie in ambush waiting for a prey,
   What should we do but bid them battle straight
   And rid the world of those detested troops,
   Lest, if we let them linger here a while,   20
   They gather strength by power of fresh supplies?
   This country swarms with vile outrageous men
   That live by rapine and by lawless spoil,
   Fit soldiers for the wicked Tamburlaine.
   And he that could with gifts and promises   25
   Inveigle him that led a thousand horse°
   And make him false his faith unto his king
   Will quickly win such as are like himself.
   Therefore cheer up your minds; prepare to fight.
   He that can take or slaughter Tamburlaine   30
   Shall rule the province of Albania.
   Who brings that traitor's head, Theridamas',
   Shall have a government in Media,
   Beside the spoil of him and all his train.
   But if Cosroë (as our spials say,   35
   And as we know) remains with Tamburlaine,
   His highness' pleasure is that he should live

And be reclaimed with princely lenity.
    [Enter a Scout or Spy]
SPY An hundred horsemen of my company,
    Scouting abroad upon these champian plains,   40
    Have viewed the army of the Scythians,
    Which make reports it far exceeds the king's.°
MEANDER Suppose they be in number infinite,
    Yet being void of martial discipline,
    All running headlong after greedy spoils   45
    And more regarding gain than victory,
    Like to the cruel brothers of the earth
    Sprung of the teeth of dragons venomous,°
    Their careless swords shall lance their fellows' throats
    And make us triumph in their overthrow.   50
MYCETES Was there such brethren, sweet Meander, say,
    That sprung of teeth of dragons venomous?
MEANDER So poets say, my lord.
MYCETES And 'tis a pretty toy to be a poet.
    Well, well, Meander, thou art deeply read,   55
    And having thee I have a jewel sure.
    Go on, my lord, and give your charge, I say;°
    Thy wit will make us conquerors today.
MEANDER Then, noble soldiers, to entrap these thieves
    That live confounded in disordered troops,   60
    If wealth or riches may prevail with them,
    We have our camels laden all with gold
    Which you that be but common soldiers
    Shall fling in every corner of the field,
    And while the base-born Tartars take it up,   65
    You, fighting more for honour than for gold,
    Shall massacre those greedy-minded slaves;
    And when their scattered army is subdued
    And you march on their slaughtered carcasses,
    Share equally the gold that bought their lives   70
    And live like gentlemen in Persia.
    Strike up the drum, and march courageously!
    Fortune herself doth sit upon our crests.
MYCETES He tells you true, my masters, so he does.
    Drums, why sound ye not when Meander speaks?°   75
    Exeunt

[2.3]

[Enter] Cosroe, Tamburlaine, Theridamas, Techelles,
Usumcasane, Ortygius, with others

COSROE Now, worthy Tamburlaine, have I reposed
  In thy approvèd fortunes all my hope.
  What think'st thou, man, shall come of our attempts?
  For even as from assurèd oracle
  I take thy doom for satisfaction.°   5
TAMBURLAINE And so mistake you not a whit, my lord,
  For fates and oracles of heaven have sworn
  To royalize the deeds of Tamburlaine,
  And make them blest that share in his attempts.
  And doubt you not but, if you favour me   10
  And let my fortunes and my valour sway
  To some direction in your martial deeds,°
  The world will strive with hosts of men-at-arms
  To swarm unto the ensign I support.
  The host of Xerxes, which by fame is said   15
  To drink the mighty Parthian Araris,°
  Was but a handful to that we will have.°
  Our quivering lances shaking in the air
  And bullets like Jove's dreadful thunderbolts
  Enrolled in flames and fiery smouldering mists   20
  Shall threat the gods more than Cyclopian wars;°
  And with our sun-bright armour as we march
  We'll chase the stars from heaven and dim their eyes
  That stand and muse at our admirèd arms.
THERIDAMAS *[to Cosroe]*
  You see, my lord, what working words he hath.   25
  But when you see his actions top his speech,
  Your speech will stay, or so extol his worth
  As I shall be commended and excused
  For turning my poor charge to his direction.
  And these his two renownèd friends, my lord,   30
  Would make one thrust and strive to be retained
  In such a great degree of amity.
TECHELLES With duty and with amity we yield
  Our utmost service to the fair Cosroe.
COSROE Which I esteem as portion of my crown.°   35

Usumcasane and Techelles both,
When she that rules in Rhamnus' golden gates°
And makes a passage for all prosperous arms
Shall make me solely emperor of Asia,
Then shall your meeds and valours be advanced   40
To rooms of honour and nobility.
TAMBURLAINE Then haste, Cosroë, to be king alone,
That I with these my friends and all my men
May triumph in our long-expected fate.
The king your brother is now hard at hand.   45
Meet with the fool, and rid your royal shoulders
Of such a burden as outweighs the sands
And all the craggy rocks of Caspia.
       [*Enter a Messenger*]
MESSENGER My lord, we have discoverèd the enemy
Ready to charge you with a mighty army.   50
COSROE Come, Tamburlaine, now whet thy wingèd sword
And lift thy lofty arm into the clouds,
That it may reach the king of Persia's crown
And set it safe on my victorious head.
TAMBURLAINE [*flourishing his sword*]
See where it is, the keenest curtle-axe   55
That e'er made passage thorough Persian arms.
These are the wings shall make it fly as swift°
As doth the lightning or the breath of heaven,
And kill as sure as it swiftly flies.
COSROE Thy words assure me of kind success.°   60
Go, valiant soldier, go before, and charge
The fainting army of that foolish king.
TAMBURLAINE Usumcasane and Techelles, come.
We are enough to scare the enemy
And more than needs to make an emperor.
       [*Exeunt*]

[2.4]

[Enter the armies] to the battle [and exeunt], and Mycetes
comes out alone with his crown in his hand, offering to hide it

MYCETES Accurst be he that first invented war!
　They knew not, ah, they knew not, simple men,
　How those were hit by pelting cannon shot°
　Stand staggering like a quivering aspen leaf
　Fearing the force of Boreas' boist'rous blasts.　　　　　　　5
　In what a lamentable case were I
　If nature had not given me wisdom's lore!
　For kings are clouts that every man shoots at,°
　Our crown the pin that thousands seek to cleave.
　Therefore in policy I think it good　　　　　　　　　　　10
　To hide it close—a goodly stratagem,
　And far from any man that is a fool.°
　So shall not I be known, or if I be,
　They cannot take away my crown from me.
　Here will I hide it in this simple hole.　　　　　　　　15
　　　[He starts to hide the crown.] Enter Tamburlaine
TAMBURLAINE What, fearful coward, straggling from the camp,
　When kings themselves are present in the field?
MYCETES Thou liest.
TAMBURLAINE　　　Base villain, dar'st thou give the lie?°
MYCETES Away, I am the king. Go, touch me not.
　Thou break'st the law of arms unless thou kneel　　　　20
　And cry me, 'Mercy, noble king!'
TAMBURLAINE Are you the witty king of Persia?
MYCETES Ay, marry, am I. Have you any suit to me?
TAMBURLAINE I would entreat you to speak but three wise words.
MYCETES So I can, when I see my time.　　　　　　　　25
TAMBURLAINE [*finding the crown*] Is this your crown?
MYCETES Ay. Didst thou ever see a fairer?
TAMBURLAINE You will not sell it, will ye?
MYCETES Such another word, and I will have thee executed. Come,
　give it me.　　　　　　　　　　　　　　　　　　30
TAMBURLAINE No. I took it prisoner.
MYCETES You lie. I gave it you.
TAMBURLAINE Then 'tis mine.
MYCETES No, I mean I let you keep it.

TAMBURLAINE Well, I mean you shall have it again.   35
    [*Giving the crown*]
  Here, take it for a while. I lend it thee
  Till I may see thee hemmed with armèd men.
  Then shalt thou see me pull it from thy head.
  Thou art no match for mighty Tamburlaine.
    [*Exit Tamburlaine*]
MYCETES O gods, is this Tamburlaine the thief?   40
  I marvel much he stole it not away.
    Sound trumpets to° the battle, and he runs in

[2.5]

    [*Enter*] *Cosroe* [*crowned*], *Tamburlaine, Theridamas,*
    Menaphon, Meander, Ortygius, Techelles, Usumcasane,
    with others

TAMBURLAINE [*presenting Cosroe with Mycetes's crown*]
  Hold thee, Cosroe, wear two imperial crowns.
  Think thee invested now as royally,
  Even by the mighty hand of Tamburlaine,
  As if as many kings as could encompass thee
  With greatest pomp had crowned thee emperor.   5
COSROE So do I, thrice-renownèd man-at-arms,
  And none shall keep the crown but Tamburlaine.°
  Thee do I make my regent of Persia
  And general lieutenant of my armies.
  Meander, you that were our brother's guide   10
  And chiefest counsellor in all his acts,
  Since he is yielded to the stroke of war,
  On your submission we with thanks excuse
  And give you equal place in our affairs.
MEANDER [*kneeling*]
  Most happy emperor, in humblest terms   15
  I vow my service to your majesty,
  With utmost virtue of my faith and duty.
COSROE Thanks, good Meander.
    [*Meander rises*]
               Then, Cosroë, reign,
  And govern Persia in her former pomp.

Now send embassage to thy neighbour kings   20
And let them know the Persian king is changed
From one that knew not what a king should do
To one that can command what 'longs thereto.
And now we will to fair Persepolis
With twenty thousand expert soldiers.   25
The lords and captains of my brother's camp
With little slaughter take Meander's course
And gladly yield them to my gracious rule.
Ortygius and Menaphon, my trusty friends,
Now will I gratify your former good°   30
And grace your calling with a greater sway.°
ORTYGIUS And as we ever aimed at your behoof
And sought your state all honour it deserved,°
So will we with our powers and our lives
Endeavour to preserve and prosper it.   35
COSROE I will not thank thee, sweet Ortygius;°
Better replies shall prove my purposes.
And now, Lord Tamburlaine, my brother's camp
I leave to thee and to Theridamas,
To follow me to fair Persepolis.   40
Then will we march to all those Indian mines
My witless brother to the Christians lost,
And ransom them with fame and usury.°
And till thou overtake me, Tamburlaine,
Staying to order all the scattered troops,   45
Farewell, lord regent and his happy friends!
I long to sit upon my brother's throne.
MENAPHON Your majesty shall shortly have your wish,
And ride in triumph through Persepolis.
       *Exeunt [all except] Tamburlaine, Techelles, Theridamas,
       Usumcasane*
TAMBURLAINE 'And ride in triumph through Persepolis'?   50
Is it not brave to be a king, Techelles?
Usumcasane and Theridamas,
Is it not passing brave to be a king°
And ride in triumph through Persepolis?
TECHELLES O my lord, 'tis sweet and full of pomp.   55
USUMCASANE To be a king is half to be a god.
THERIDAMAS A god is not so glorious as a king.
I think the pleasure they enjoy in heaven

Cannot compare with kingly joys in earth:
To wear a crown enchased with pearl and gold,   60
Whose virtues carry with it life and death;
To ask, and have; command, and be obeyed;
When looks breed love, with looks to gain the prize—
Such power attractive shines in princes' eyes.

TAMBURLAINE Why, say, Theridamas, wilt thou be a king?   65
THERIDAMAS Nay, though I praise it, I can live without it.
TAMBURLAINE What says my other friends? Will you be kings?
TECHELLES Ay, if I could, with all my heart, my lord.
TAMBURLAINE Why, that's well said, Techelles. So would I.
And so would you, my masters, would you not?   70
USUMCASANE What then, my lord?
TAMBURLAINE Why then, Casane, shall we wish for aught
The world affords in greatest novelty,
And rest attemptless, faint and destitute?
Methinks we should not. I am strongly moved   75
That if I should desire the Persian crown
I could attain it with a wondrous ease.
And would not all our soldiers soon consent
If we should aim at such a dignity?
THERIDAMAS I know they would, with our persuasions.   80
TAMBURLAINE Why then, Theridamas, I'll first essay
To get the Persian kingdom to myself;
Then thou for Parthia, they for Scythia and Media.°
And if I prosper, all shall be as sure
As if the Turk, the pope, Afric, and Greece°   85
Came creeping to us with their crowns apace.
TECHELLES Then shall we send to this triumphing king
And bid him battle for his novel crown?°
USUMCASANE Nay, quickly then, before his room be hot.°
TAMBURLAINE 'Twill prove a pretty jest, in faith, my friends. 90
THERIDAMAS A jest, to charge on twenty thousand men?
I judge the purchase more important far.°
TAMBURLAINE Judge by thyself, Theridamas, not me,
For presently Techelles here shall haste
To bid him battle ere he pass too far   95
And lose more labour than the gain will quite.°
Then shalt thou see the Scythian Tamburlaine
Make but a jest to win the Persian crown.
Techelles, take a thousand horse with thee

And bid him turn him back to war with us   100
That only made him king to make us sport.°
We will not steal upon him cowardly,
But give him warning and more warriors.°
Haste thee, Techelles. We will follow thee.
        [*Exit Techelles*]
What saith Theridamas?
THERIDAMAS   Go on, for me.°   105
        Exeunt

[2.6]

[*Enter*] *Cosroe, Meander, Ortygius, Menaphon, with other
Soldiers*

COSROE What means this devilish shepherd to aspire
    With such a giantly presumption,
    To cast up hills against the face of heaven
    And dare the force of angry Jupiter?
    But as he thrust them underneath the hills   5
    And pressed out fire from their burning jaws,°
    So will I send this monstrous slave to hell
    Where flames shall ever feed upon his soul.
MEANDER Some powers divine, or else infernal, mixed
    Their angry seeds at his conception;   10
    For he was never sprung of human race,
    Since with the spirit of his fearful pride
    He dares so doubtlessly resolve of rule°
    And by profession be ambitious.°
ORTYGIUS What god, or fiend, or spirit of the earth,°   15
    Or monster turnèd to a manly shape,
    Or of what mould or mettle he be made,°
    What star or state soever govern him,
    Let us put on our meet encount'ring minds,°
    And, in detesting such a devilish thief,   20
    In love of honour and defence of right
    Be armed against the hate of such a foe,
    Whether from earth, or hell, or heaven he grow.
COSROE Nobly resolved, my good Ortygius.
    And since we all have sucked one wholesome air,   25

And with the same proportion of elements
Resolve, I hope we are resembled,
Vowing our loves to equal death and life.°
Let's cheer our soldiers to encounter him,
That grievous image of ingratitude,   30
That fiery thirster after sovereignty,
And burn him in the fury of that flame°
That none can quench but blood and empery.°
Resolve, my lords and loving soldiers, now
To save your king and country from decay.   35
Then strike up drum! [*Sound drum*] And all the stars that make
The loathsome circle of my dated life,°
Direct my weapon to his barbarous heart
That thus opposeth him against the gods
And scorns the powers that govern Persia!   40
    [*Exeunt*]

[2.7]

Enter [the armies] to the battle, and after the battle enter
Cosroe wounded, Theridamas, Tamburlaine, Techelles,
Usumcasane, with others

COSROE Barbarous and bloody Tamburlaine,
  Thus to deprive me of my crown and life!
  Treacherous and false Theridamas,
  Even at the morning of my happy state,
  Scarce being seated in my royal throne,   5
  To work my downfall and untimely end!
  An uncouth pain torments my grievèd soul,
  And death arrests the organ of my voice,
  Who, ent'ring at the breach thy sword hath made,°
  Sacks every vein and artier of my heart.   10
  Bloody and insatiate Tamburlaine!
TAMBURLAINE The thirst of reign and sweetness of a crown,
  That caused the eldest son of heavenly Ops°
  To thrust his doting father from his chair
  And place himself in th'empyreal heaven,°   15
  Moved me to manage arms against thy state.
  What better precedent than mighty Jove?

Nature, that framed us of four elements
Warring within our breasts for regiment,
Doth teach us all to have aspiring minds.   20
Our souls, whose faculties can comprehend
The wondrous architecture of the world
And measure every wand'ring planet's course,
Still climbing after knowledge infinite
And always moving as the restless spheres,   25
Wills us to wear ourselves and never rest
Until we reach the ripest fruit of all,
That perfect bliss and sole felicity,
The sweet fruition of an earthly crown.
THERIDAMAS And that made me to join with Tamburlaine,   30
For he is gross and like the massy earth°
That moves not upwards nor by princely deeds
Doth mean to soar above the highest sort.
TECHELLES And that made us, the friends of Tamburlaine,
To lift our swords against the Persian king.   35
USUMCASANE For as when Jove did thrust old Saturn down,°
Neptune and Dis gained each of them a crown,°
So do we hope to reign in Asia
If Tamburlaine be placed in Persia.
COSROE The strangest men that ever nature made!   40
I know not how to take their tyrannies.
My bloodless body waxeth chill and cold,
And with my blood my life slides through my wound.
My soul begins to take her flight to hell,
And summons all my senses to depart.   45
The heat and moisture, which did feed each other,
For want of nourishment to feed them both
Is dry and cold, and now doth ghastly death
With greedy talons gripe my bleeding heart
And like a harpy tires on my life.°   50
Theridamas and Tamburlaine, I die,
And fearful vengeance light upon you both!
    [*Cosroe dies. Tamburlaine*] *takes the crown and puts it on*
TAMBURLAINE Not all the curses which the Furies breathe
Shall make me leave so rich a prize as this.
Theridamas, Techelles, and the rest,   55
Who think you now is king of Persia?
ALL Tamburlaine! Tamburlaine!

TAMBURLAINE Though Mars himself, the angry god of arms,
    And all the earthly potentates conspire
    To dispossess me of this diadem,   60
    Yet will I wear it in despite of them
    As great commander of this eastern world,
    If you but say that Tamburlaine shall reign.
ALL Long live Tamburlaine, and reign in Asia!
TAMBURLAINE So, now it is more surer on my head   65
    Than if the gods had held a parliament
    And all pronounced me king of Persia.
       [*Exeunt*]

[3.1]

[Enter] Bajazeth, the kings of Fez, Morocco, and Argier,
[Basso,] with others, in great pomp

BAJAZETH Great kings of Barbary, and my portly bassoes,
We hear the Tartars and the eastern thieves,
Under the conduct of one Tamburlaine,
Presume a bickering with your emperor°
And thinks to rouse us from our dreadful siege   5
Of the famous Grecian Constantinople.
You know our army is invincible;
As many circumcisèd Turks we have
And warlike bands of Christians renied
As hath the ocean or the Terrene Sea   10
Small drops of water when the moon begins
To join in one her semicircled horns.°
Yet would we not be braved with foreign power,°
Nor raise our siege before the Grecians yield
Or breathless lie before the city walls.   15
FEZ Renownèd emperor and mighty general,
What if you sent the bassoes of your guard
To charge him to remain in Asia,
Or else to threaten death and deadly arms
As from the mouth of mighty Bajazeth?   20
BAJAZETH Hie thee, my basso, fast to Persia.°
Tell him thy lord the Turkish emperor,
Dread lord of Afric, Europe, and Asia,
Great king and conqueror of Graecia,
The ocean Terrene, and the coal-black sea,°   25
The high and highest monarch of the world,
Wills and commands (for say not I entreat)
Not once to set his foot in Africa
Or spread his colours in Graecia,
Lest he incur the fury of my wrath.   30
Tell him I am content to take a truce
Because I hear he bears a valiant mind.
But if, presuming on his silly power,
He be so mad to manage arms with me,°
Then stay thou with him; say I bid thee so.   35

And if before the sun have measured heaven
With triple circuit thou regreet us not,
We mean to take his morning's next arise
For messenger he will not be reclaimed,°
And mean to fetch thee in despite of him.   40

BASSO Most great and puissant monarch of the earth,
Your basso will accomplish your behest
And show your pleasure to the Persian,
As fits the legate of the stately Turk.
   Exit Basso

ARGIER They say he is the king of Persia;°   45
But if he dare attempt to stir your siege,
'Twere requisite he should be ten times more,°
For all flesh quakes at your magnificence.

BAJAZETH True, Argier, and tremble at my looks.

MOROCCO The spring is hindered by your smothering host,   50
For neither rain can fall upon the earth
Nor sun reflex his virtuous beams thereon,
The ground is mantled with such multitudes.

BAJAZETH All this is true as holy Mahomet,
And all the trees are blasted with our breaths.   55

FEZ What thinks your greatness best to be achieved°
In pursuit of the city's overthrow?°

BAJAZETH I will the captive pioners of Argier°
Cut off the water that by leaden pipes
Runs to the city from the mountain Carnon;   60
Two thousand horse shall forage up and down,
That no relief or succour come by land;
And all the sea my galleys countermand.°
Then shall our footmen lie within the trench,
And with their cannons mouthed like Orcus' gulf°   65
Batter the walls, and we will enter in;
And thus the Grecians shall be conquerèd.
   Exeunt

[3.2]

[Enter] Agydas, Zenocrate, Anippe, with others

AGYDAS Madam Zenocrate, may I presume
　　To know the cause of these unquiet fits
　　That work such trouble to your wonted rest?
　　'Tis more than pity such a heavenly face
　　Should by heart's sorrow wax so wan and pale,　　　　5
　　When your offensive rape by Tamburlaine
　　(Which of your whole displeasures should be most)°
　　Hath seemed to be digested long ago.

ZENOCRATE Although it be digested long ago,
　　As his exceeding favours have deserved,　　　　　　10
　　And might content the queen of heaven as well°
　　As it hath changed my first-conceived disdain,
　　Yet, since, a farther passion feeds my thoughts°
　　With ceaseless and disconsolate conceits,
　　Which dyes my looks so lifeless as they are　　　　15
　　And might, if my extremes had full events,°
　　Make me the ghastly counterfeit of death.

AGYDAS Eternal heaven sooner be dissolved,
　　And all that pierceth Phoebe's silver eye,°
　　Before such hap fall to Zenocrate!　　　　　　　　20

ZENOCRATE Ah, life and soul still hover in his breast
　　And leave my body senseless as the earth,
　　Or else unite you to his life and soul,°
　　That I may live and die with Tamburlaine!
　　　　Enter [behind] Tamburlaine with Techelles and others

AGYDAS With Tamburlaine? Ah, fair Zenocrate,　　　　25
　　Let not a man so vile and barbarous,
　　That holds you from your father in despite
　　And keeps you from the honours of a queen—
　　Being supposed his worthless concubine—
　　Be honoured with your love but for necessity.°　　　30
　　So now the mighty Sultan hears of you,°
　　Your highness needs not doubt but in short time
　　He will, with Tamburlaine's destruction,
　　Redeem you from this deadly servitude.

ZENOCRATE Agydas, leave to wound me with these words,　35
　　And speak of Tamburlaine as he deserves.

The entertainment we have had of him
Is far from villainy or servitude,
And might in noble minds be counted princely.

AGYDAS How can you fancy one that looks so fierce,   40
Only disposed to martial stratagems?
Who, when he shall embrace you in his arms,
Will tell how many thousand men he slew,
And when you look for amorous discourse
Will rattle forth his facts of war and blood—°   45
Too harsh a subject for your dainty ears.

ZENOCRATE As looks the sun through Nilus' flowing stream,
Or when the morning holds him in her arms,°
So looks my lordly love, fair Tamburlaine;
His talk much sweeter than the Muses' song   50
They sung for honour 'gainst Pierides,°
Or when Minerva did with Neptune strive;°
And higher would I rear my estimate°
Than Juno, sister to the highest god,
If I were matched with mighty Tamburlaine.   55

AGYDAS Yet be not so inconstant in your love,
But let the young Arabian live in hope°
After your rescue to enjoy his choice.
You see, though first the king of Persia,
Being a shepherd, seemed to love you much,°   60
Now in his majesty he leaves those looks,
Those words of favour, and those comfortings,
And gives no more than common courtesies.

ZENOCRATE Thence rise the tears that so distain my cheeks,
Fearing his love through my unworthiness.°   65

*Tamburlaine goes to her, and takes her away lovingly by the
hand, looking wrathfully on Agydas, and says nothing.*
[*Exeunt all except Agydas*]

AGYDAS Betrayed by fortune and suspicious love,
Threatened with frowning wrath and jealousy,
Surprised with fear of hideous revenge,
I stand aghast, but most astonièd
To see his choler shut in secret thoughts   70
And wrapped in silence of his angry soul.
Upon his brows was portrayed ugly death,°
And in his eyes the fury of his heart,
That shine as comets, menacing revenge,

And casts a pale complexion on his cheeks.   75
As when the seaman sees the Hyades°
Gather an army of Cimmerian clouds°
(Auster and Aquilon, with wingèd steeds°
All sweating, tilt about the watery heavens°
With shivering spears enforcing thunderclaps,   80
And from their shields strike flames of lightning),
All fearful folds his sails, and sounds the main,°
Lifting his prayers to the heavens for aid
Against the terror of the winds and waves,
So fares Agydas for the late-felt frowns   85
That sent a tempest to my daunted thoughts
And makes my soul divine her overthrow.
    Enter Techelles with a naked dagger
TECHELLES [*giving the dagger*]
See you, Agydas, how the king salutes you.
He bids you prophesy what it imports.
    Exit [*Techelles*]
AGYDAS I prophesied before, and now I prove,   90
The killing frowns of jealousy and love.
He needed not with words confirm my fear,
For words are vain where working tools present
The naked action of my threatened end.
It says, Agydas, thou shalt surely die,   95
And of extremities elect the least:
More honour and less pain it may procure
To die by this resolvèd hand of thine
Than stay the torments he and heaven have sworn.
Then haste, Agydas, and prevent the plagues   100
Which thy prolongèd fates may draw on thee.
Go wander free from fear of tyrant's rage,
Removèd from the torments and the hell
Wherewith he may excruciate thy soul,
And let Agydas by Agydas die,   105
And with this stab slumber eternally.
    [*Agydas stabs himself and dies. Enter Techelles and*
    Usumcascane]
TECHELLES Usumcasane, see how right the man
Hath hit the meaning of my lord the king.
USUMCASANE Faith, and, Techelles, it was manly done;
And since he was so wise and honourable,   110

34

Let us afford him now the bearing hence
And crave his triple-worthy burial.
TECHELLES Agreed, Casane. We will honour him.
    [*Exeunt, bearing out Agydas's body*]

[3.3]

    [*Enter*] *Tamburlaine, Techelles, Usumcasane, Theridamas,*
    Basso, Zenocrate, [*Anippe,*] *with others,* [*with a throne*]

TAMBURLAINE Basso, by this thy lord and master knows
  I mean to meet him in Bithynia.°
  See how he comes! Tush, Turks are full of brags°
  And menace more than they can well perform.
  He meet me in the field and fetch thee hence!°   5
  Alas, poor Turk, his fortune is too weak
  T'encounter with the strength of Tamburlaine.
  View well my camp, and speak indifferently:
  Do not my captains and my soldiers look
  As if they meant to conquer Africa?   10
BASSO Your men are valiant, but their number few,
  And cannot terrify his mighty host.
  My lord, the great commander of the world,
  Besides fifteen contributory kings
  Hath now in arms ten thousand janizaries   15
  Mounted on lusty Mauritanian steeds
  Brought to the war by men of Tripoli;
  Two hundred thousand footmen that have served
  In two set battles fought in Graecia;
  And for the expedition of this war,°   20
  If he think good, can from his garrisons
  Withdraw as many more to follow him.
TECHELLES The more he brings, the greater is the spoil;
  For, when they perish by our warlike hands,
  We mean to seat our footmen on their steeds   25
  And rifle all those stately janizars.
TAMBURLAINE But will those kings accompany your lord?
BASSO Such as his highness please, but some must stay
  To rule the provinces he late subdued.
TAMBURLAINE [*to his followers*]

Then fight courageously, their crowns are yours.   30
This hand shall set them on your conquering heads
That made me emperor of Asia.

USUMCASANE Let him bring millions infinite of men,
Unpeopling western Africa and Greece,
Yet we assure us of the victory.   35

THERIDAMAS Even he, that in a trice vanquished two kings
More mighty than the Turkish emperor,
Shall rouse him out of Europe and pursue
His scattered army till they yield or die.

TAMBURLAINE Well said, Theridamas! Speak in that mood,   40
For 'will' and 'shall' best fitteth Tamburlaine,
Whose smiling stars gives him assurèd hope
Of martial triumph ere he meet his foes.
I that am termed the scourge and wrath of God,
The only fear and terror of the world,   45
Will first subdue the Turk and then enlarge
Those Christian captives which you keep as slaves,
Burd'ning their bodies with your heavy chains
And feeding them with thin and slender fare
That naked row about the Terrene Sea,   50
And when they chance to breathe and rest a space
Are punished with bastones so grievously°
That they lie panting on the galley's side
And strive for life at every stroke they give.
These are the cruel pirates of Argier,   55
That damnèd train, the scum of Africa,
Inhabited with straggling runagates,
That make quick havoc of the Christian blood.
But, as I live, that town shall curse the time
That Tamburlaine set foot in Africa.   60
        Enter Bajazeth with his Bassoes and contributory kings [of
        Fez, Morocco, and Argier; Zabina and Ebea. A throne is
        brought on]

BAJAZETH Bassoes and janizaries of my guard,
Attend upon the person of your lord,
The greatest potentate of Africa.

TAMBURLAINE Techelles and the rest, prepare your swords.
I mean t'encounter with that Bajazeth.   65

BAJAZETH Kings of Fez, Moroccus, and Argier,
He calls me Bajazeth, whom you call lord!

Note the presumption of this Scythian slave.—
I tell thee, villain, those that lead my horse
Have to their names titles of dignity;   70
And dar'st thou bluntly call me Bajazeth?
TAMBURLAINE And know thou, Turk, that those which lead my horse
    Shall lead thee captive thorough Africa;
    And dar'st thou bluntly call me Tamburlaine?
BAJAZETH By Mahomet my kinsman's sepulchre,   75
    And by the holy Alcoran, I swear
    He shall be made a chaste and lustless eunuch
    And in my sarell tend my concubines,°
    And all his captains that thus stoutly stand
    Shall draw the chariot of my emperess,   80
    Whom I have brought to see their overthrow.
TAMBURLAINE By this my sword that conquered Persia,
    Thy fall shall make me famous through the world.
    I will not tell thee how I'll handle thee,
    But every common soldier of my camp   85
    Shall smile to see thy miserable state.
FEZ [to Bajazeth] What means the mighty Turkish emperor
    To talk with one so base as Tamburlaine?
MOROCCO Ye Moors and valiant men of Barbary,
    How can ye suffer these indignities?   90
ARGIER Leave words and let them feel your lances' points,
    Which glided through the bowels of the Greeks.
BAJAZETH Well said, my stout contributory kings!
    Your threefold army and my hugy host
    Shall swallow up these base-born Persians.   95
TECHELLES Puissant, renowned, and mighty Tamburlaine,
    Why stay we thus prolonging all their lives?
THERIDAMAS I long to see those crowns won by our swords,
    That we may reign as kings of Africa.
USUMCASANE What coward would not fight for such a prize?   100
TAMBURLAINE Fight all courageously, and be you kings!
    I speak it, and my words are oracles.
BAJAZETH Zabina, mother of three braver boys
    Than Hercules, that in his infancy
    Did pash the jaws of serpents venomous,°   105
    Whose hands are made to gripe a warlike lance,
    Their shoulders broad, for complete armour fit,
    Their limbs more large and of a bigger size

Than all the brats y-sprung from Typhon's loins,°
Who, when they come unto their father's age,   110
Will batter turrets with their manly fists:
Sit here upon this royal chair of state
And on thy head wear my imperial crown,
Until I bring this sturdy Tamburlaine
And all his captains bound in captive chains.   115

ZABINA [*sitting in the Turkish throne and putting on the crown*]
Such good success happen to Bajazeth!

TAMBURLAINE Zenocrate, the loveliest maid alive,
Fairer than rocks of pearl and precious stone,
The only paragon of Tamburlaine,
Whose eyes are brighter than the lamps of heaven,   120
And speech more pleasant than sweet harmony,
That with thy looks canst clear the darkened sky
And calm the rage of thund'ring Jupiter:
Sit down by her, adornèd with my crown,
As if thou wert the empress of the world.   125
Stir not, Zenocrate, until thou see
Me march victoriously with all my men,
Triumphing over him and these his kings,
Which I will bring as vassals to thy feet.
Till then, take thou my crown, vaunt of my worth,   130
And manage words with her as we will arms.

ZENOCRATE [*sitting in the Persian throne and putting on the crown*]
And may my love, the king of Persia,
Return with victory and free from wound!

BAJAZETH Now shalt thou feel the force of Turkish arms
Which lately made all Europe quake for fear.   135
I have of Turks, Arabians, Moors, and Jews
Enough to cover all Bithynia.
Let thousands die, their slaughtered carcasses
Shall serve for walls and bulwarks to the rest;
And as the heads of Hydra, so my power,°   140
Subdued, shall stand as mighty as before.
If they should yield their necks unto the sword,°
Thy soldiers' arms could not endure to strike
So many blows as I have heads for thee.
Thou know'st not, foolish-hardy Tamburlaine,   145
What 'tis to meet me in the open field,
That leave no ground for thee to march upon.

TAMBURLAINE Our conquering swords shall marshal us the way
　　We use to march upon the slaughtered foe,
　　Trampling their bowels with our horses' hoofs—　　　　150
　　Brave horses, bred on the white Tartarian hills.
　　My camp is like to Julius Caesar's host,
　　That never fought but had the victory;°
　　Nor in Pharsalia was there such hot war°
　　As these my followers willingly would have.　　　　155
　　Legions of spirits fleeting in the air
　　Direct our bullets and our weapons' points
　　And make your strokes to wound the senseless air;
　　And when she sees our bloody colours spread,
　　Then Victory begins to take her flight,°　　　　160
　　Resting herself upon my milk-white tent.°
　　But come, my lords, to weapons let us fall!
　　The field is ours, the Turk, his wife, and all.
　　　　Exit [Tamburlaine,] with his followers
BAJAZETH Come, kings and bassoes, let us glut our swords
　　That thirst to drink the feeble Persians' blood!　　　　165
　　　　Exit [Bajazeth,] with his followers
ZABINA Base concubine, must thou be placed by me
　　That am the empress of the mighty Turk?
ZENOCRATE Disdainful Turkess and unreverend boss,°
　　Call'st thou me concubine, that am betrothed
　　Unto the great and mighty Tamburlaine?　　　　170
ZABINA To Tamburlaine, the great Tartarian thief!
ZENOCRATE Thou wilt repent these lavish words of thine
　　When thy great basso-master and thyself°
　　Must plead for mercy at his kingly feet
　　And sue to me to be your advocates.°　　　　175
ZABINA And sue to thee? I tell thee, shameless girl,
　　Thou shalt be laundress to my waiting-maid.—
　　How lik'st thou her, Ebea? Will she serve?
EBEA Madam, she thinks perhaps she is too fine.
　　But I shall turn her into other weeds　　　　180
　　And make her dainty fingers fall to work.
ZENOCRATE Hear'st thou, Anippe, how thy drudge doth talk,
　　And how my slave, her mistress, menaceth?
　　Both, for their sauciness, shall be employed
　　To dress the common soldiers' meat and drink,　　　　185
　　For we will scorn they should come near ourselves.

ANIPPE Yet sometimes let your highness send for them
　　To do the work my chambermaid disdains.
　　　　　They sound [to] the battle within, and stay°
ZENOCRATE Ye gods and powers that govern Persia
　　And made my lordly love her worthy king,　　　　　　　190
　　Now strengthen him against the Turkish Bajazeth,
　　And let his foes, like flocks of fearful roes
　　Pursued by hunters, fly his angry looks,
　　That I may see him issue conqueror.
ZABINA Now, Mahomet, solicit God himself,　　　　　　　195
　　And make him rain down murdering shot from heaven
　　To dash the Scythians' brains, and strike them dead
　　That dare to manage arms with him
　　That offered jewels to thy sacred shrine
　　When first he warred against the Christians.　　　　　200
　　　　　[They sound within] to the battle again
ZENOCRATE By this the Turks lie welt'ring in their blood,
　　And Tamburlaine is lord of Africa.
ZABINA Thou art deceived. I heard the trumpets sound
　　As when my emperor overthrew the Greeks
　　And led them captive into Africa.　　　　　　　　　205
　　Straight will I use thee as thy pride deserves;
　　Prepare thyself to live and die my slave.
ZENOCRATE If Mahomet should come from heaven and swear
　　My royal lord is slain or conquerèd,
　　Yet should he not persuade me otherwise　　　　　　210
　　But that he lives and will be conqueror.
　　　　　Bajazeth flies [across the stage], and [Tamburlaine] pursues
　　　　　him [offstage]. The battle short, and they [re-]enter. Bajazeth
　　　　　is overcome
TAMBURLAINE Now, king of bassoes, who is conqueror?
BAJAZETH Thou, by the fortune of this damnèd foil.
TAMBURLAINE Where are your stout contributory kings?
　　　　　Enter Techelles, Theridamas, Usumcasane, [each with
　　　　　a crown]
TECHELLES We have their crowns; their bodies strew the field.　215
TAMBURLAINE Each man a crown? Why, kingly fought, i'faith.
　　Deliver them into my treasury.
　　　　　[Techelles, Theridamas, and Usumcasane deliver over their
　　　　　crowns]
ZENOCRATE Now let me offer to my gracious lord

His royal crown again, so highly won.

TAMBURLAINE Nay, take the Turkish crown from her, Zenocrate,   220
And crown me emperor of Africa.°

ZABINA No, Tamburlaine, though now thou gat the best,°
Thou shalt not yet be lord of Africa.

THERIDAMAS [to Zabina] Give her the crown, Turkess, you were best.
    [Theridamas] takes it from her and gives it Zenocrate

ZABINA Injurious villains, thieves, runagates!   225
How dare you thus abuse my majesty?

THERIDAMAS Here, madam, you are empress, she is none.

TAMBURLAINE [as Zenocrate crowns him]
Not now, Theridamas. Her time is past.
The pillars that have bolstered up those terms°
Are fall'n in clusters at my conquering feet.   230

ZABINA Though he be prisoner, he may be ransomed.

TAMBURLAINE Not all the world shall ransom Bajazeth.

BAJAZETH Ah, fair Zabina, we have lost the field,
And never had the Turkish emperor
So great a foil by any foreign foe.   235
Now will the Christian miscreants be glad,°
Ringing with joy their superstitious bells
And making bonfires for my overthrow.
But ere I die, those foul idolaters
Shall make me bonfires with their filthy bones;   240
For, though the glory of this day be lost,
Afric and Greece have garrisons enough
To make me sovereign of the earth again.

TAMBURLAINE Those wallèd garrisons will I subdue,
And write myself great lord of Africa.   245
So from the east unto the furthest west
Shall Tamburlaine extend his puissant arm.
The galleys and those pilling brigantines°
That yearly sail to the Venetian gulf
And hover in the straits for Christians' wrack°   250
Shall lie at anchor in the Isle Asant°
Until the Persian fleet and men-of-war,
Sailing along the oriental sea,°
Have fetched about the Indian continent,°
Even from Persepolis to Mexico,   255
And thence unto the Straits of Jubalter,°
Where they shall meet and join their force in one,

Keeping in awe the Bay of Portingale
And all the ocean by the British shore.°
And by this means I'll win the world at last.   260
BAJAZETH Yet set a ransom on me, Tamburlaine.
TAMBURLAINE What, think'st thou Tamburlaine esteems thy gold?
I'll make the kings of India, ere I die,
Offer their mines, to sue for peace, to me,
And dig for treasure to appease my wrath.—   265
Come, bind them both, and one lead in the Turk.
The Turkess let my love's maid lead away.
        They bind them
BAJAZETH Ah, villains, dare ye touch my sacred arms?
O Mahomet, O sleepy Mahomet!
ZABINA O cursèd Mahomet, that makest us thus   270
The slaves to Scythians rude and barbarous!
TAMBURLAINE Come, bring them in, and for this happy conquest
Triumph, and solemnize a martial feast.
        Exeunt, [*leading in Bajazeth and Zabina captive*]

[4.1]

[Enter the] Sultan of Egypt with three or four Lords,
Capolin, [and a Messenger]

SULTAN Awake, ye men of Memphis! Hear the clang
    Of Scythian trumpets! Hear the basilisks
    That, roaring, shake Damascus' turrets down!°
    The rogue of Volga holds Zenocrate,
    The Sultan's daughter, for his concubine,   5
    And with a troop of thieves and vagabonds
    Hath spread his colours to our high disgrace,
    While you faint-hearted base Egyptians
    Lie slumbering on the flow'ry banks of Nile,
    As crocodiles that unaffrighted rest   10
    While thund'ring cannons rattle on their skins.

MESSENGER Nay, mighty Sultan, did your greatness see
    The frowning looks of fiery Tamburlaine,
    That with his terror and imperious eyes
    Commands the hearts of his associates,   15
    It might amaze your royal majesty.

SULTAN Villain, I tell thee, were that Tamburlaine
    As monstrous as Gorgon, prince of hell,°
    The Sultan would not start a foot from him.
    But speak, what power hath he?

MESSENGER   Mighty lord,   20
    Three hundred thousand men in armour clad
    Upon their prancing steeds, disdainfully
    With wanton paces trampling on the ground;
    Five hundred thousand footmen threat'ning shot,
    Shaking their swords, their spears, and iron bills,   25
    Environing their standard round, that stood
    As bristle-pointed as a thorny wood.°
    Their warlike engines and munition
    Exceed the forces of their martial men.

SULTAN Nay, could their numbers countervail the stars,   30
    Or ever-drizzling drops of April showers,
    Or withered leaves that Autumn shaketh down,
    Yet would the Sultan by his conquering power
    So scatter and consume them in his rage

That not a man should live to rue their fall.   35
CAPOLIN So might your highness, had you time to sort
    Your fighting men and raise your royal host.
    But Tamburlaine by expedition
    Advantage takes of your unreadiness.
SULTAN Let him take all th'advantages he can.   40
    Were all the world conspired to fight for him,
    Nay, were he devil—as he is no man—
    Yet in revenge of fair Zenocrate,
    Whom he detaineth in despite of us,
    This arm should send him down to Erebus°   45
    To shroud his shame in darkness of the night.
MESSENGER Pleaseth your mightiness to understand,
    His resolution far exceedeth all.
    The first day when he pitcheth down his tents,°
    White is their hue, and on his silver crest   50
    A snowy feather spangled white he bears,
    To signify the mildness of his mind
    That, satiate with spoil, refuseth blood.
    But when Aurora mounts the second time,
    As red as scarlet is his furniture;   55
    Then must his kindled wrath be quenched with blood,
    Not sparing any that can manage arms.
    But if these threats move not submission,
    Black are his colours—black pavilion,
    His spear, his shield, his horse, his armour, plumes,   60
    And jetty feathers menace death and hell.
    Without respect of sex, degree, or age,
    He razeth all his foes with fire and sword.
SULTAN Merciless villain, peasant ignorant
    Of lawful arms or martial discipline!°   65
    Pillage and murder are his usual trades;
    The slave usurps the glorious name of war.
    See, Capolin, the fair Arabian king,°
    That hath been disappointed by this slave
    Of my fair daughter and his princely love,   70
    May have fresh warning to go war with us°
    And be revenged for her disparagement.
      [*Exeunt*]

[4.2]

[A throne is brought on. Enter] Tamburlaine [all in white],
Techelles, Theridamas, Usumcasane, Zenocrate, Anippe, two
Moors drawing Bajazeth in his cage, and his wife [Zabina]
following him

TAMBURLAINE Bring out my footstool.
    [The two Moors] take [Bajazeth] out of the cage
BAJAZETH Ye holy priests of heavenly Mahomet,
  That, sacrificing, slice and cut your flesh,
  Staining his altars with your purple blood,
  Make heaven to frown, and every fixèd star   5
  To suck up poison from the moorish fens
  And pour it in this glorious tyrant's throat!
TAMBURLAINE The chiefest God, first mover of that sphere
  Enchased with thousands ever-shining lamps,°
  Will sooner burn the glorious frame of heaven   10
  Than it should so conspire my overthrow.
  But, villain, thou that wishest this to me,
  Fall prostrate on the low, disdainful earth
  And be the footstool of great Tamburlaine,
  That I may rise into my royal throne.   15
BAJAZETH First shalt thou rip my bowels with thy sword
  And sacrifice my heart to death and hell
  Before I yield to such a slavery.
TAMBURLAINE Base villain, vassal, slave to Tamburlaine,
  Unworthy to embrace or touch the ground   20
  That bears the honour of my royal weight,
  Stoop, villain, stoop, stoop, for so he bids
  That may command thee piecemeal to be torn
  Or scattered like the lofty cedar trees
  Struck with the voice of thund'ring Jupiter.   25
BAJAZETH Then, as I look down to the damnèd fiends,
  Fiends, look on me, and, thou dread god of hell,
  With ebon sceptre strike this hateful earth
  And make it swallow both of us at once!
    [Tamburlaine] gets up upon [Bajazeth] to his chair
TAMBURLAINE Now clear the triple region of the air°   30
  And let the majesty of heaven behold
  Their scourge and terror tread on emperors.

Smile, stars that reigned at my nativity,
And dim the brightness of their neighbour lamps!
Disdain to borrow light of Cynthia.   35
For I, the chiefest lamp of all the earth,
First rising in the east with mild aspect°
But fixèd now in the meridian line,°
Will send up fire to your turning spheres
And cause the sun to borrow light of you.   40
My sword struck fire from his coat of steel
Even in Bithynia, when I took this Turk,
As when a fiery exhalation
Wrapped in the bowels of a freezing cloud,
Fighting for passage, makes the welkin crack,   45
And casts a flash of lightning to the earth.
But ere I march to wealthy Persia
Or leave Damascus and th'Egyptian fields,
As was the fame of Clymene's brainsick son°
That almost brent the axletree of heaven,°   50
So shall our swords, our lances, and our shot
Fill all the air with fiery meteors.
Then, when the sky shall wax as red as blood,
It shall be said I made it red myself,
To make me think of naught but blood and war.   55

ZABINA Unworthy king, that by thy cruelty
Unlawfully usurp'st the Persian seat,
Dar'st thou, that never saw an emperor
Before thou met my husband in the field,
Being thy captive, thus abuse his state,   60
Keeping his kingly body in a cage
That roofs of gold and sun-bright palaces
Should have prepared to entertain his grace,
And treading him beneath thy loathsome feet
Whose feet the kings of Africa have kissed?   65

TECHELLES [to Tamburlaine]
You must devise some torment worse, my lord,
To make these captives rein their lavish tongues.

TAMBURLAINE Zenocrate, look better to your slave.

ZENOCRATE She is my handmaid's slave, and she shall look°
That these abuses flow not from her tongue.—   70
Chide her, Anippe.

ANIPPE [to Zabina] Let these be warnings for you, then, my slave,

How you abuse the person of the king,
Or else I swear to have you whipped stark naked.

BAJAZETH Great Tamburlaine, great in my overthrow,   75
Ambitious pride shall make thee fall as low
For treading on the back of Bajazeth,
That should be horsèd on four mighty kings.

TAMBURLAINE Thy names and titles and thy dignities
Are fled from Bajazeth and remain with me,   80
That will maintain it 'gainst a world of kings.—
Put him in again.

[*The two Moors put Bajazeth back in the cage*]

BAJAZETH Is this a place for mighty Bajazeth?
Confusion light on him that helps thee thus!

TAMBURLAINE There, whiles he lives, shall Bajazeth be kept,   85
And where I go be thus in triumph drawn;°
And thou, his wife, shalt feed him with the scraps
My servitors shall bring thee from my board.
For he that gives him other food than this
Shall sit by him and starve to death himself.   90
This is my mind, and I will have it so.
Not all the kings and emperors of the earth,
If they would lay their crowns before my feet,
Shall ransom him or take him from his cage.
The ages that shall talk of Tamburlaine,   95
Even from this day to Plato's wondrous year,°
Shall talk how I have handled Bajazeth.
These Moors that drew him from Bithynia
To fair Damascus, where we now remain,
Shall lead him with us wheresoe'er we go.   100
Techelles and my loving followers,
Now may we see Damascus' lofty towers,
Like to the shadows of Pyramides°
That with their beauties graced the Memphian fields.
The golden statue of their feathered bird°   105
That spreads her wings upon the city walls
Shall not defend it from our battering shot.
The townsmen mask in silk and cloth of gold,°
And every house is as a treasury.
The men, the treasure, and the town is ours.   110

THERIDAMAS Your tents of white now pitched before the gates,
And gentle flags of amity displayed,

I doubt not but the governor will yield,
Offering Damascus to your majesty.

TAMBURLAINE So shall he have his life, and all the rest.°   115
But if he stay until the bloody flag
Be once advanced on my vermilion tent,
He dies, and those that kept us out so long.
And when they see me march in black array,
With mournful streamers hanging down their heads,°   120
Were in that city all the world contained,
Not one should 'scape, but perish by our swords.

ZENOCRATE Yet would you have some pity for my sake,
Because it is my country's, and my father's.

TAMBURLAINE Not for the world, Zenocrate, if I have sworn.—   125
Come, bring in the Turk.

>   *Exeunt, [the two Moors drawing off Bajazeth in his cage]*

[4.3]

*[Enter the] Sultan, [the king of] Arabia, Capolin, with
streaming colours, and Soldiers*

SULTAN Methinks we march as Meleager did,°
Environèd with brave Argolian knights,°
To chase the savage Calydonian boar;
Or Cephalus with lusty Theban youths,°
Against the wolf that angry Themis sent   5
To waste and spoil the sweet Aonian fields.
A monster of five hundred thousand heads,
Compact of rapine, piracy, and spoil,
The scum of men, the hate and scourge of God,
Raves in Egyptia and annoyeth us.°   10
My lord, it is the bloody Tamburlaine,
A sturdy felon and a base-bred thief
By murder raisèd to the Persian crown,
That dares control us in our territories.
To tame the pride of this presumptuous beast,   15
Join your Arabians with the Sultan's power;
Let us unite our royal bands in one
And hasten to remove Damascus' siege.
It is a blemish to the majesty

And high estate of mighty emperors   20
That such a base, usurping vagabond
Should brave a king or wear a princely crown.

ARABIA Renownèd Sultan, have ye lately heard
The overthrow of mighty Bajazeth
About the confines of Bithynia?°   25
The slavery wherewith he persecutes
The noble Turk and his great emperess?

SULTAN I have, and sorrow for his bad success.
But, noble lord of great Arabia,
Be so persuaded that the Sultan is   30
No more dismayed with tidings of his fall
Than in the haven when the pilot stands
And views a stranger's ship rent in the winds
And shiverèd against a craggy rock.
Yet, in compassion of his wretched state,   35
A sacred vow to heaven and him I make,
Confirming it with Ibis' holy name,
That Tamburlaine shall rue the day, the hour,
Wherein he wrought such ignominious wrong
Unto the hallowed person of a prince,   40
Or kept the fair Zenocrate so long
As concubine, I fear, to feed his lust.

ARABIA Let grief and fury hasten on revenge!
Let Tamburlaine for his offences feel
Such plagues as heaven and we can pour on him.   45
I long to break my spear upon his crest
And prove the weight of his victorious arm,
For Fame, I fear, hath been too prodigal
In sounding through the world his partial praise.°

SULTAN Capolin, hast thou surveyed our powers?   50

CAPOLIN Great emperors of Egypt and Arabia,
The number of your hosts united is
A hundred and fifty thousand horse,
Two hundred thousand foot, brave men-at-arms,
Courageous and full of hardiness,   55
As frolic as the hunters in the chase
Of savage beasts amid the desert woods.

ARABIA My mind presageth fortunate success.
And, Tamburlaine, my spirit doth foresee
The utter ruin of thy men and thee.   60

SULTAN Then rear your standards! Let your sounding drums
   Direct our soldiers to Damascus' walls.
   Now, Tamburlaine, the mighty Sultan comes
   And leads with him the great Arabian king
   To dim thy baseness and obscurity,   65
   Famous for nothing but for theft and spoil,
   To raze and scatter thy inglorious crew
   Of Scythians and slavish Persians.
       [*Sound drums.*] *Exeunt*

[4.4]

> *The banquet [is brought on], and to it cometh Tamburlaine*
> *all in scarlet, [Zenocrate,] Theridamas, Techelles,*
> *Usumcasane, the Turk [Bajazeth, drawn in his cage*
> *by two Moors, Zabina], with others*

TAMBURLAINE Now hang our bloody colours by Damascus,
   Reflexing hues of blood upon their heads
   While they walk quivering on their city walls,
   Half dead for fear before they feel my wrath.
   Then let us freely banquet and carouse   5
   Full bowls of wine unto the god of war,
   That means to fill your helmets full of gold
   And make Damascus' spoils as rich to you
   As was to Jason Colchis' golden fleece.°
   And now, Bajazeth, hast thou any stomach?°   10
BAJAZETH Ay, such a stomach, cruel Tamburlaine, as I could
   willingly feed upon thy blood-raw heart.
TAMBURLAINE Nay, thine own is easier to come by; pluck out that,
   and 'twill serve thee and thy wife. Well, Zenocrate, Techelles, and
   the rest, fall to your victuals.   15
BAJAZETH Fall to, and never may your meat digest!
   Ye Furies, that can mask invisible,°
   Dive to the bottom of Avernus' pool°
   And in your hands bring hellish poison up
   And squeeze it in the cup of Tamburlaine!   20
   Or, wingèd snakes of Lerna, cast your stings,°
   And leave your venoms in this tyrant's dish!
ZABINA And may this banquet prove as ominous
   As Procne's to th'adulterous Thracian king

That fed upon the substance of his child!°   25
ZENOCRATE My lord, how can you suffer these outrageous curses by
these slaves of yours?
TAMBURLAINE To let them see, divine Zenocrate,
I glory in the curses of my foes,
Having the power from th'empyreal heaven°   30
To turn them all upon their proper heads.
TECHELLES I pray you, give them leave, madam. This speech is a
goodly refreshing to them.
THERIDAMAS But if his highness would let them be fed, it would do
them more good.   35
TAMBURLAINE [to Bajazeth] Sirrah, why fall you not to? Are you so
daintily brought up you cannot eat your own flesh?
BAJAZETH First, legions of devils shall tear thee in pieces.
USUMCASANE Villain, knowest thou to whom thou speakest?
TAMBURLAINE O, let him alone.—Here, eat, sir. Take it from my   40
sword's point, or I'll thrust it to thy heart.
          [Bajazeth] takes [the meat offered him] and stamps upon it
THERIDAMAS He stamps it under his feet, my lord.
TAMBURLAINE [to Bajazeth] Take it up, villain, and eat it, or I will
make thee slice the brawns of thy arms into carbonadoes and
eat them.   45
USUMCASANE Nay, 'twere better he killed his wife, and then she
shall be sure not to be starved, and he be provided for a month's
victual beforehand.
TAMBURLAINE [to Bajazeth] Here is my dagger. Dispatch her while
she is fat, for if she live but a while longer, she will fall into a   50
consumption with fretting, and then she will not be worth the
eating.
THERIDAMAS [to Bajazeth] Dost thou think that Mahomet will
suffer this?
TECHELLES 'Tis like he will, when he cannot let it.   55
TAMBURLAINE [to Bajazeth] Go to, fall to your meat.—What, not
a bit? Belike he hath not been watered° today. Give him some
drink.
          [The Moors] give him water to drink, and he flings it on the
          ground
Fast, and welcome, sir, while° hunger make you eat.—How now,
Zenocrate, doth not the Turk and his wife make a goodly show at   60
a banquet?
ZENOCRATE Yes, my lord.

THERIDAMAS Methinks 'tis a great deal better than a consort° of
    music.
TAMBURLAINE Yet music would do well to cheer up Zenocrate.   65
    [*To Zenocrate*] Pray thee, tell: why art thou so sad? If thou wilt
    have a song, the Turk shall strain his voice. But why is it?
ZENOCRATE My lord, to see my father's town besieged,
    The country wasted where myself was born—
    How can it but afflict my very soul?   70
    If any love remain in you, my lord,
    Or if my love unto your majesty
    May merit favour at your highness' hands,
    Then raise your siege from fair Damascus' walls
    And with my father take a friendly truce.   75
TAMBURLAINE Zenocrate, were Egypt Jove's own land,
    Yet would I with my sword make Jove to stoop.
    I will confute those blind geographers
    That make a triple region in the world,°
    Excluding regions which I mean to trace,°   80
    And with this pen reduce them to a map,°
    Calling the provinces, cities, and towns
    After my name and thine, Zenocrate.
    Here at Damascus will I make the point
    That shall begin the perpendicular.°   85
    And wouldst thou have me buy thy father's love
    With such a loss? Tell me, Zenocrate.
ZENOCRATE Honour still wait on happy Tamburlaine!
    Yet give me leave to plead for him, my lord.
TAMBURLAINE Content thyself. His person shall be safe,   90
    And all the friends of fair Zenocrate,
    If with their lives they will be pleased to yield
    Or may be forced to make me emperor;
    For Egypt and Arabia must be mine.
    [*To Bajazeth*] Feed, you slave. Thou mayst think thyself happy to   95
    be fed from my trencher.
BAJAZETH My empty stomach, full of idle heat,
    Draws bloody humours from my feeble parts,°
    Preserving life by hasting cruel death.°
    My veins are pale, my sinews hard and dry,   100
    My joints benumbed. Unless I eat, I die.
ZABINA Eat, Bajazeth. Let us live in spite of them, looking° some
    happy power will pity and enlarge us.

TAMBURLAINE [*offering Bajazeth an empty plate*] Here, Turk, wilt
thou have a clean trencher?   105

BAJAZETH Ay, tyrant, and more meat.

TAMBURLAINE Soft, sir, you must be dieted; too much eating will
make you surfeit.

THERIDAMAS [*to Tamburlaine*] So it would, my lord, specially having
so small a walk and so little exercise.   110

    Enter a second course of crowns°

TAMBURLAINE Theridamas, Techelles, and Casane, here are the
cates you desire to finger, are they not?

THERIDAMAS Ay, my lord, but none save kings must feed with these.

TECHELLES 'Tis enough for us to see them and for Tamburlaine
only to enjoy them.   115

TAMBURLAINE [*offering a toast*] Well, here is now to the Sultan of
Egypt, the king of Arabia, and the governor of Damascus. Now
take these three crowns, and pledge me, my contributory kings.
[*He presents the crowns in turn*] I crown you here, Theridamas, king
of Argier; Techelles, king of Fez; and Usumcasane, king of   120
Moroccus.—How say you to this, Turk? These are not your
contributory kings.

BAJAZETH Nor shall they long be thine, I warrant them.

TAMBURLAINE [*to his followers*]
    Kings of Argier, Moroccus, and of Fez,
    You that have marched with happy Tamburlaine   125
    As far as from the frozen plage of heaven°
    Unto the wat'ry morning's ruddy bower°
    And thence by land unto the torrid zone,
    Deserve these titles I endow you with
    By valour and by magnanimity.   130
    Your births shall be no blemish to your fame,°
    For virtue is the fount whence honour springs,
    And they are worthy she investeth kings.°

THERIDAMAS And since your highness hath so well vouchsafed,°
    If we deserve them not with higher meeds   135
    Than erst our states and actions have retained,
    Take them away again and make us slaves.

TAMBURLAINE Well said, Theridamas! When holy Fates
    Shall 'stablish me in strong Egyptia,
    We mean to travel to th'Antarctic Pole,   140
    Conqu'ring the people underneath our feet,°
    And be renowned as never emperors were.

Zenocrate, I will not crown thee yet,
Until with greater honours I be graced.

[*Exeunt, the two Moors drawing off Bajazeth in his cage*]

[5.1]

GOVERNOR Still doth this man, or rather god of war,
    Batter our walls and beat our turrets down;
    And to resist with longer stubbornness
    Or hope of rescue from the Sultan's power
    Were but to bring our wilful overthrow   5
    And make us desperate of our threatened lives.
    We see his tents have now been alterèd
    With terrors to the last and cruell'st hue;°
    His coal-black colours everywhere advanced
    Threaten our city with a general spoil;   10
    And if we should with common rites of arms
    Offer our safeties to his clemency,
    I fear the custom proper to his sword,
    Which he observes as parcel of his fame,
    Intending so to terrify the world,   15
    By any innovation or remorse
    Will never be dispensed with till our deaths.°
    Therefore, for these our harmless virgins' sakes,
    Whose honours and whose lives rely on him,
    Let us have hope that their unspotted prayers,   20
    Their blubbered cheeks, and hearty humble moans
    Will melt his fury into some remorse,
    And use us like a loving conqueror.°
FIRST VIRGIN If humble suits or imprecations—
    Uttered with tears of wretchedness and blood   25
    Shed from the heads and hearts of all our sex,°
    Some made your wives, and some your children—°
    Might have entreated your obdurate breasts°
    To entertain some care of our securities
    Whiles only danger beat upon our walls,°   30
    These more than dangerous warrants of our death
    Had never been erected as they be,
    Nor you depend on such weak helps as we.
GOVERNOR Well, lovely virgins, think our country's care,°

Our love of honour, loath to be enthralled   35
To foreign powers and rough imperious yokes,
Would not with too much cowardice or fear,
Before all hope of rescue were denied,
Submit yourselves and us to servitude.
Therefore, in that your safeties and our own,°   40
Your honours, liberties, and lives, were weighed
In equal care and balance with our own,
Endure as we the malice of our stars,
The wrath of Tamburlaine and power of wars;
Or be the means the overweighing heavens   45
Have kept to qualify these hot extremes,
And bring us pardon in your cheerful looks.
SECOND VIRGIN Then here, before the majesty of heaven
    And holy patrons of Egyptia,
    With knees and hearts submissive we entreat   50
    Grace to our words and pity to our looks,
    That this device may prove propitious,
    And through the eyes and ears of Tamburlaine
    Convey events of mercy to his heart.°
    Grant that these signs of victory we yield   55
    May bind the temples of his conquering head
    To hide the folded furrows of his brows
    And shadow his displeasèd countenance
    With happy looks of ruth and lenity.°
    Leave us, my lord, and loving countrymen;   60
    What simple virgins may persuade, we will.
GOVERNOR Farewell, sweet virgins, on whose safe return
    Depends our city, liberty, and lives!
            Exeunt [all except the Virgins. Enter] Tamburlaine, Techelles,
            Theridamas, Usumcasane, with others; Tamburlaine all in
            black, and very melancholy. [The Virgins make obeisance]
TAMBURLAINE What, are the turtles frayed out of their nests?
    Alas, poor fools, must you be first shall feel°   65
    The sworn destruction of Damascus?
    They know my custom. Could they not as well
    Have sent ye out when first my milk-white flags
    Through which sweet mercy threw her gentle beams,
    Reflexing them on your disdainful eyes,°   70
    As now when fury and incensèd hate
    Flings slaughtering terror from my coal-black tents

And tells for truth submissions comes too late?°
FIRST VIRGIN Most happy king and emperor of the earth,
　　Image of honour and nobility,   75
　　For whom the powers divine have made the world
　　And on whose throne the holy Graces sit,
　　In whose sweet person is comprised the sum
　　Of nature's skill and heavenly majesty:
　　Pity our plights, O, pity poor Damascus!   80
　　Pity old age, within whose silver hairs
　　Honour and reverence evermore have reigned!
　　Pity the marriage bed, where many a lord,
　　In prime and glory of his loving joy,
　　Embraceth now with tears of ruth and blood   85
　　The jealous body of his fearful wife,°
　　Whose cheeks and hearts—so punished with conceit°
　　To think thy puissant never-stayèd arm°
　　Will part their bodies and prevent their souls
　　From heavens of comfort yet their age might bear—°   90
　　Now wax all pale and withered to the death,
　　As well for grief our ruthless governor
　　Have thus refused the mercy of thy hand
　　(Whose sceptre angels kiss and Furies dread)
　　As for their liberties, their loves, or lives.   95
　　O then, for these, and such as we ourselves,
　　For us, for infants, and for all our bloods,°
　　That never nourished thought against thy rule,
　　Pity, O, pity, sacred emperor,
　　The prostrate service of this wretched town;   100
　　And take in sign thereof this gilded wreath
　　Whereto each man of rule hath given his hand°
　　And wished, as worthy subjects, happy means
　　To be investors of thy royal brows,°
　　Even with the true Egyptian diadem.   105
　　　　[*She offers a laurel wreath*]
TAMBURLAINE Virgins, in vain ye labour to prevent
　　That which mine honour swears shall be performed.
　　Behold my sword. What see you at the point?
VIRGINS Nothing but fear and fatal steel, my lord.
TAMBURLAINE Your fearful minds are thick and misty, then,   110
　　For there sits Death, there sits imperious Death,°
　　Keeping his circuit by the slicing edge.°

But I am pleased you shall not see him there;
He now is seated on my horsemen's spears,
And on their points his fleshless body feeds.   115
Techelles, straight go charge a few of them
To charge these dames, and show my servant Death,°
Sitting in scarlet on their armèd spears.
ALL THE VIRGINS O, pity us!
TAMBURLAINE Away with them, I say, and show them Death!   120
        [*Techelles and others*] *take them away*
I will not spare these proud Egyptians
Nor change my martial observations°
For all the wealth of Gihon's golden waves,°
Or for the love of Venus, would she leave
The angry god of arms and lie with me.°   125
They have refused the offer of their lives,
And know my customs are as peremptory°
As wrathful planets, death, or destiny.
        Enter Techelles
What, have your horsemen shown the virgins Death?
TECHELLES They have, my lord, and on Damascus' walls   130
Have hoisted up their slaughtered carcasses.
TAMBURLAINE A sight as baneful to their souls, I think,
As are Thessalian drugs or mithridate.°
But go, my lords. Put the rest to the sword.
        Exeunt [*all except Tamburlaine*]
Ah, fair Zenocrate, divine Zenocrate!   135
Fair is too foul an epithet for thee
That, in thy passion for thy country's love
And fear to see thy kingly father's harm,
With hair dishevelled wip'st thy watery cheeks,
And like to Flora in her morning's pride,°   140
Shaking her silver tresses in the air,
Rain'st on the earth resolvèd pearl in showers
And sprinklest sapphires on thy shining face°
Where Beauty, mother to the Muses, sits
And comments volumes with her ivory pen,°   145
Taking instructions from thy flowing eyes—
Eyes, when that Ebena steps to heaven
In silence of thy solemn evening's walk,
Making the mantle of the richest night,
The moon, the planets, and the meteors, light.°   150

There angels in their crystal armours fight
A doubtful battle with my tempted thoughts
For Egypt's freedom and the Sultan's life—
His life that so consumes Zenocrate,
Whose sorrows lay more siege unto my soul   155
Than all my army to Damascus' walls;
And neither Persians' sovereign nor the Turk
Troubled my senses with conceit of foil°
So much by much as doth Zenocrate.
What is beauty, saith my sufferings, then?°   160
If all the pens that ever poets held
Had fed the feeling of their masters' thoughts
And every sweetness that inspired their hearts,
Their minds and muses on admirèd themes;°
If all the heavenly quintessence they still°   165
From their immortal flowers of poesy,
Wherein as in a mirror we perceive
The highest reaches of a human wit;
If these had made one poem's period°
And all combined in beauty's worthiness,°   170
Yet should there hover in their restless heads
One thought, one grace, one wonder at the least,
Which into words no virtue can digest.°
But how unseemly is it for my sex,
My discipline of arms and chivalry,   175
My nature, and the terror of my name,
To harbour thoughts effeminate and faint!
Save only that in beauty's just applause,
With whose instinct the soul of man is touched—
And every warrior that is rapt with love   180
Of fame, of valour, and of victory,
Must needs have beauty beat on his conceits—
I thus conceiving and subduing, both,
That which hath stopped the tempest of the gods,
Even from the fiery spangled veil of heaven,   185
To feel the lovely warmth of shepherds' flames
And march in cottages of strewèd weeds,
Shall give the world to note, for all my birth,
That virtue solely is the sum of glory
And fashions men with true nobility.—°   190
Who's within there?

Enter two or three [Attendants]
Hath Bajazeth been fed today?

ATTENDANT Ay, my lord.

TAMBURLAINE Bring him forth, and let us know if the town be
ransacked.   195
*[Exeunt Attendants.] Enter Techelles, Theridamas, Usumcasane,
and others*

TECHELLES The town is ours, my lord, and fresh supply
Of conquest and of spoil is offered us.

TAMBURLAINE That's well, Techelles. What's the news?

TECHELLES The Sultan and the Arabian king together
March on us with such eager violence   200
As if there were no way but one with us.°

TAMBURLAINE No more there is not, I warrant thee, Techelles.
*[The two Moors] bring in the Turk [Bajazeth, in his cage,
and Zabina]*

THERIDAMAS We know the victory is ours, my lord.
But let us save the reverend Sultan's life
For fair Zenocrate that so laments his state.   205

TAMBURLAINE That will we chiefly see unto, Theridamas,
For sweet Zenocrate, whose worthiness
Deserves a conquest over every heart.—
And now, my footstool, if I lose the field,
You hope of liberty and restitution.—   210
Here let him stay, my masters, from the tents,
Till we have made us ready for the field.—
Pray for us, Bajazeth. We are going.
Exeunt [all except Bajazeth and Zabina]

BAJAZETH Go, never to return with victory!
Millions of men encompass thee about   215
And gore thy body with as many wounds!
Sharp, forkèd arrows light upon thy horse!
Furies from the black Cocytus lake°
Break up the earth, and with their firebrands
Enforce thee run upon the baneful pikes!   220
Volleys of shot pierce through thy charmèd skin,
And every bullet dipped in poisoned drugs!
Or roaring cannons sever all thy joints,
Making thee mount as high as eagles soar!

ZABINA Let all the swords and lances in the field   225
Stick in his breast as in their proper rooms!°

At every pore let blood come dropping forth,
That ling'ring pains may massacre his heart
And madness send his damnèd soul to hell!

BAJAZETH Ah, fair Zabina, we may curse his power,   230
The heavens may frown, the earth for anger quake,
But such a star hath influence in his sword
As rules the skies, and countermands the gods
More than Cimmerian Styx or Destiny.°
And then shall we in this detested guise,   235
With shame, with hunger, and with horror aye
Griping our bowels with retorquèd thoughts,°
And have no hope to end our ecstasies.

ZABINA Then is there left no Mahomet, no God,
No fiend, no Fortune, nor no hope of end°   240
To our infamous, monstrous slaveries?°
Gape, earth, and let the fiends infernal view
A hell as hopeless and as full of fear
As are the blasted banks of Erebus,°
Where shaking ghosts with ever-howling groans   245
Hover about the ugly ferryman°
To get a passage to Elysium!
Why should we live, O, wretches, beggars, slaves,
Why live we, Bajazeth, and build up nests°
So high within the region of the air,   250
By living long in this oppression,
That all the world will see and laugh to scorn
The former triumphs of our mightiness
In this obscure infernal servitude?

BAJAZETH O life more loathsome to my vexèd thoughts   255
Than noisome parbreak of the Stygian snakes°
Which fills the nooks of hell with standing air,°
Infecting all the ghosts with cureless griefs!
O dreary engines of my loathèd sight°
That sees my crown, my honour, and my name   260
Thrust under yoke and thraldom of a thief,
Why feed ye still on day's accursèd beams
And sink not quite into my tortured soul?
You see my wife, my queen and emperess,
Brought up and proppèd by the hand of fame,   265
Queen of fifteen contributory queens,
Now thrown to rooms of black abjection,

Smearèd with blots of basest drudgery,
And villeiness to shame, disdain, and misery.
Accursèd Bajazeth, whose words of ruth,   270
That would with pity cheer Zabina's heart
And make our souls resolve in ceaseless tears,
Sharp hunger bites upon and gripes the root
From whence the issues of my thoughts do break.°
O poor Zabina, O my queen, my queen,   275
Fetch me some water for my burning breast,
To cool and comfort me with longer date,°
That, in the shortened sequel of my life,
I may pour forth my soul into thine arms
With words of love, whose moaning intercourse   280
Hath hitherto been stayed with wrath and hate
Of our expressless, banned inflictions.°
ZABINA Sweet Bajazeth, I will prolong thy life
As long as any blood or spark of breath
Can quench or cool the torments of my grief.   285
      She goes out
BAJAZETH Now, Bajazeth, abridge thy baneful days
And beat thy brains out of thy conquered head,
Since other means are all forbidden me
That may be ministers of my decay.
O highest lamp of ever-living Jove,   290
Accursèd day, infected with my griefs,
Hide now thy stainèd face in endless night
And shut the windows of the lightsome heavens!
Let ugly Darkness with her rusty coach,
Engirt with tempests wrapped in pitchy clouds,   295
Smother the earth with never-fading mists,
And let her horses from their nostrils breathe
Rebellious winds and dreadful thunderclaps,
That in this terror Tamburlaine may live,
And my pined soul, resolved in liquid air,   300
May still excruciate his tormented thoughts!
Then let the stony dart of senseless cold
Pierce through the centre of my withered heart
And make a passage for my loathèd life!
      He brains himself against the cage. Enter Zabina
ZABINA What do mine eyes behold? My husband dead!   305
His skull all riven in twain, his brains dashed out!

The brains of Bajazeth, my lord and sovereign!
O Bajazeth, my husband and my lord,
O Bajazeth, O Turk, O emperor—give him his liquor? Not I.
Bring milk and fire, and my blood I bring him again; tear me in   310
pieces, give me the sword with a ball of wildfire° upon it. Down
with him, down with him! Go to my child. Away, away, away! Ah,
save that infant, save him, save him! I, even I, speak to her. The
sun was down. Streamers white, red, black, here, here, here. Fling
the meat in his face. Tamburlaine, Tamburlaine! Let the soldiers   315
be buried. Hell, death, Tamburlaine, hell! Make ready my coach,
my chair, my jewels. I come, I come, I come!
     She runs against the cage and brains herself. [Enter]
     Zenocrate with Anippe
ZENOCRATE Wretched Zenocrate, that liv'st to see
Damascus' walls dyed with Egyptian blood,
Thy father's subjects and thy countrymen,°   320
Thy streets strewed with disseverèd joints of men
And wounded bodies gasping yet for life,
But most accurst to see the sun-bright troop
Of heavenly virgins and unspotted maids,
Whose looks might make the angry god of arms   325
To break his sword and mildly treat of love,
On horsemen's lances to be hoisted up
And guiltlessly endure a cruel death!
For every fell and stout Tartarian steed,
That stamped on others with their thund'ring hoofs,   330
When all their riders charged their quivering spears,°
Began to check the ground and rein themselves,°
Gazing upon the beauty of their looks.
Ah, Tamburlaine, wert thou the cause of this,
That term'st Zenocrate thy dearest love—   335
Whose lives were dearer to Zenocrate°
Than her own life, or aught save thine own love?
     [She sees the dead Bajazeth and Zabina]
But see, another bloody spectacle!
Ah, wretched eyes, the enemies of my heart,
How are ye glutted with these grievous objects,   340
And tell my soul more tales of bleeding ruth!
See, see, Anippe, if they breathe or no.
ANIPPE *[examining the bodies]*
No breath, nor sense, nor motion in them both.

Ah, madam, this their slavery hath enforced,
And ruthless cruelty of Tamburlaine.   345
ZENOCRATE Earth, cast up fountains from thy entrails,
And wet thy cheeks for their untimely deaths;°
Shake with their weight in sign of fear and grief;
Blush, heaven, that gave them honour at their birth,
And let them die a death so barbarous!   350
Those that are proud of fickle empery
And place their chiefest good in earthly pomp,
Behold the Turk and his great emperess!
Ah, Tamburlaine my love, sweet Tamburlaine,
That fight'st for sceptres and for slippery crowns,   355
Behold the Turk and his great emperess!
Thou that in conduct of thy happy stars°
Sleep'st every night with conquest on thy brows
And yet wouldst shun the wavering turns of war,
In fear and feeling of the like distress   360
Behold the Turk and his great emperess!
Ah, mighty Jove and holy Mahomet,
Pardon my love, O, pardon his contempt
Of earthly fortune and respect of pity,°
And let not conquest ruthlessly pursued   365
Be equally against his life incensed
In this great Turk and hapless emperess!°
And pardon me that was not moved with ruth
To see them live so long in misery.
Ah, what may chance to thee, Zenocrate?   370
ANIPPE Madam, content yourself, and be resolved
Your love hath Fortune so at his command
That she shall stay, and turn her wheel no more
As long as life maintains his mighty arm
That fights for honour to adorn your head.   375
        Enter [Philemus,] a Messenger
ZENOCRATE What other heavy news now brings Philemus?
PHILEMUS Madam, your father and th'Arabian king,
The first affecter of your excellence,°
Comes now as Turnus 'gainst Aeneas did,°
Armèd with lance into th'Egyptian fields,   380
Ready for battle 'gainst my lord the king.
ZENOCRATE Now shame and duty, love and fear, presents
A thousand sorrows to my martyred soul.

Whom should I wish the fatal victory,
When my poor pleasures are divided thus   385
And racked by duty from my cursèd heart?°
My father and my first betrothèd love
Must fight against my life and present love,
Wherein the change I use condemns my faith°
And makes my deeds infamous through the world.   390
But as the gods, to end the Trojans' toil,
Prevented Turnus of Lavinia°
And fatally enriched Aeneas' love,°
So, for a final issue to my griefs,°
To pacify my country and my love,   395
Must Tamburlaine, by their resistless powers,°
With virtue of a gentle victory°
Conclude a league of honour to my hope;°
Then, as the powers divine have preordained,
With happy safety of my father's life   400
Send like defence of fair Arabia.°

> *They sound to the battle,° and Tamburlaine enjoys the*
> *victory. After, [the king of] Arabia enters wounded*

ARABIA What cursèd power guides the murdering hands
Of this infamous tyrant's soldiers,
That no escape may save their enemies
Nor fortune keep themselves from victory?   405
Lie down, Arabia, wounded to the death,
And let Zenocrate's fair eyes behold
That, as for her thou bear'st these wretched arms,
Even so for her thou diest in these arms,
Leaving thy blood for witness of thy love.   410

ZENOCRATE Too dear a witness for such love, my lord.°
Behold Zenocrate, the cursèd object
Whose fortunes never masterèd her griefs!°
Behold her wounded in conceit for thee,
As much as thy fair body is for me.   415

ARABIA Then shall I die with full contented heart,
Having beheld divine Zenocrate,
Whose sight with joy would take away my life—
As now it bringeth sweetness to my wound—
If I had not been wounded as I am.   420
Ah, that the deadly pangs I suffer now
Would lend an hour's licence to my tongue

To make discourse of some sweet accidents
Have chanced thy merits in this worthless bondage,°
And that I might be privy to the state   425
Of thy deserved contentment and thy love!
But, making now a virtue of thy sight
To drive all sorrow from my fainting soul,
Since death denies me further cause of joy,
Deprived of care, my heart with comfort dies   430
Since thy desirèd hand shall close mine eyes.
> [*He dies.*] *Enter Tamburlaine leading the Sultan; Techelles,*
> *Theridamas, Usumcasane [bearing a crown for Zenocrate],*
> *with others*

TAMBURLAINE Come, happy father of Zenocrate—
A title higher than thy Sultan's name.
Though my right hand have thus enthrallèd thee,
Thy princely daughter here shall set thee free—   435
She that hath calmed the fury of my sword,
Which had ere this been bathed in streams of blood
As vast and deep as Euphrates or Nile.°

ZENOCRATE O, sight thrice welcome to my joyful soul,
To see the king my father issue safe   440
From dangerous battle of my conquering love!°

SULTAN Well met, my only dear Zenocrate,
Though with the loss of Egypt and my crown.

TAMBURLAINE 'Twas I, my lord, that gat the victory.
And therefore grieve not at your overthrow,   445
Since I shall render all into your hands
And add more strength to your dominions
Than ever yet confirmed th'Egyptian crown.°
The god of war resigns his room to me,
Meaning to make me general of the world.   450
Jove, viewing me in arms, looks pale and wan,
Fearing my power should pull him from his throne.
Where'er I come, the Fatal Sisters sweat,°
And grisly Death, by running to and fro
To do their ceaseless homage to my sword;   455
And here in Afric, where it seldom rains,
Since I arrived with my triumphant host
Have swelling clouds, drawn from wide gasping wounds,
Been oft resolved in bloody purple showers—°
A meteor that might terrify the earth   460

And make it quake at every drop it drinks.
Millions of souls sit on the banks of Styx,
Waiting the back return of Charon's boat;
Hell and Elysium swarm with ghosts of men
That I have sent from sundry foughten fields   465
To spread my fame through hell and up to heaven.
And see, my lord, a sight of strange import:
Emperors and kings lie breathless at my feet.
The Turk and his great empress, as it seems,
Left to themselves while we were at the fight,   470
Have desperately dispatched their slavish lives.
With them Arabia too hath left his life—
All sights of power to grace my victory.°
And such are objects fit for Tamburlaine,
Wherein as in a mirror may be seen   475
His honour, that consists in shedding blood
When men presume to manage arms with him.

SULTAN Mighty hath God and Mahomet made thy hand,
Renownèd Tamburlaine, to whom all kings
Of force must yield their crowns and emperies.°   480
And I am pleased with this my overthrow
If, as beseems a person of thy state,
Thou hast with honour used Zenocrate.

TAMBURLAINE Her state and person wants no pomp, you see;
And for all blot of foul inchastity,°   485
I record heaven, her heavenly self is clear.°
Then let me find no further time to grace°
Her princely temples with the Persian crown;
But here these kings, that on my fortunes wait
And have been crowned for provèd worthiness   490
Even by this hand that shall establish them,
Shall now, adjoining all their hands with mine,
Invest her here my queen of Persia.
What saith the noble Sultan and Zenocrate?

SULTAN I yield with thanks and protestations   495
Of endless honour to thee for her love.°

TAMBURLAINE Then doubt I not but fair Zenocrate
Will soon consent to satisfy us both.

ZENOCRATE Else should I much forget myself, my lord.

THERIDAMAS Then let us set the crown upon her head   500
That long hath lingered for so high a seat.

TECHELLES My hand is ready to perform the deed,
  For now her marriage time shall work us rest.
USUMCASANE And here's the crown, my lord. Help set it on.
TAMBURLAINE Then sit thou down, divine Zenocrate.   505
    [*She sits in her throne for her coronation*]
  And here we crown thee queen of Persia
  And all the kingdoms and dominions
  That late the power of Tamburlaine subdued.
  As Juno, when the giants were suppressed
  That darted mountains at her brother Jove,°   510
  So looks my love, shadowing in her brows°
  Triumphs and trophies for my victories;
  Or, as Latona's daughter, bent to arms,°
  Adding more courage to my conquering mind.
  To gratify thee, sweet Zenocrate,   515
  Egyptians, Moors, and men of Asia,
  From Barbary unto the Western Indie,
  Shall pay a yearly tribute to thy sire,
  And from the bounds of Afric to the banks
  Of Ganges shall his mighty arm extend.   520
  And now, my lords and loving followers,
  That purchased kingdoms by your martial deeds,
  Cast off your armour, put on scarlet robes,
  Mount up your royal places of estate,
  Environèd with troops of noble men,   525
  And there make laws to rule your provinces.
  Hang up your weapons on Alcides' post,°
  For Tamburlaine takes truce with all the world.
  [*To Zenocrate*] Thy first betrothèd love, Arabia,
  Shall we with honour, as beseems, entomb,   530
  With this great Turk and his fair emperess.
  Then after all these solemn exequies
  We will our celebrated rites of marriage solemnize.
    [*Exeunt, bearing the dead bodies in stately procession*]

TAMBURLAINE
THE GREAT
Part II

DRAMATIS PERSONAE

The Prologue
Orcanes, King of Natolia
Gazellus, Viceroy of Byron
Uribassa
Attendants
Sigismond, King of Hungary
Frederick
Baldwin
Callapine
Almeda
Tamburlaine
Zenocrate
Calyphas ⎱
Amyras ⎬ *Tamburlaine's sons*
Celebinus ⎰
Theridamas
Techelles
Usumcasane

A Messenger
Three Physicians
King of Trebizond
King of Soria
King of Jerusalem
Soldiers
Pioners
A Captain, *Olympia's husband*
Olympia
The Captain's Son
Perdicas
Concubines
Governor of Babylon
Maximus
Citizens
King of Amasia
A Captain *serving under Callapine*

Tamburlaine the Great, Part II

[Enter] the Prologue

PROLOGUE The general welcome Tamburlaine received
 When he arrivèd last upon our stage
 Hath made our poet pen his second part,
 Where death cuts off the progress of his pomp
 And murd'rous Fates throws all his triumphs down.°   5
 But what became of fair Zenocrate,
 And with how many cities' sacrifice
 He celebrated her sad funeral,
 Himself in presence shall unfold at large.
  [Exit]

[1.1]

[Enter] Orcanes king of Natolia, Gazellus viceroy of Byron,
Uribassa, and their train, with drums and trumpets

ORCANES Egregious viceroys of these eastern parts,
 Placed by the issue of great Bajazeth°
 And sacred lord, the mighty Callapine,
 Who lives in Egypt prisoner to that slave
 Which kept his father in an iron cage: 5
 Now have we marched from fair Natolia°
 Two hundred leagues, and on Danubius' banks
 Our warlike host in complete armour rest,
 Where Sigismond the king of Hungary
 Should meet our person to conclude a truce.   10
 What, shall we parley with the Christian,
 Or cross the stream and meet him in the field?
GAZELLUS King of Natolia, let us treat of peace.
 We all are glutted with the Christians' blood,
 And have a greater foe to fight against: 15
 Proud Tamburlaine, that now in Asia
 Near Guyron's head doth set his conquering feet°
 And means to fire Turkey as he goes.
 'Gainst him, my lord, must you address your power.
URIBASSA Besides, King Sigismond hath brought from Christendom   20
 More than his camp of stout Hungarians,
 Slavonians, Almains, rutters, Muffs, and Danes,°
 That with the halberd, lance, and murdering axe
 Will hazard that we might with surety hold.°
ORCANES Though from the shortest northern parallel,°   25
 Vast Gruntland, compassed with the frozen sea,°
 Inhabited with tall and sturdy men,
 Giants as big as hugy Polypheme,°
 Millions of soldiers cut the Arctic line,°
 Bringing the strength of Europe to these arms,°   30
 Our Turkey blades shall glide through all their throats
 And make this champian mead a bloody fen.°
 Danubius' stream, that runs to Trebizond,
 Shall carry wrapped within his scarlet waves,°
 As martial presents to our friends at home,   35

The slaughtered bodies of these Christians.
The Terrene main, wherein Danubius falls,°
Shall by this battle be the bloody sea.
The wand'ring sailors of proud Italy
Shall meet those Christians fleeting with the tide,   40
Beating in heaps against their argosies,
And make fair Europe, mounted on her bull,°
Trapped with the wealth and riches of the world,°
Alight and wear a woeful mourning weed.

GAZELLUS Yet, stout Orcanes, prorex of the world,   45
Since Tamburlaine hath mustered all his men,
Marching from Cairon northward with his camp°
To Alexandria and the frontier towns,
Meaning to make a conquest of our land,
'Tis requisite to parley for a peace   50
With Sigismond the king of Hungary,
And save our forces for the hot assaults
Proud Tamburlaine intends Natolia.

ORCANES Viceroy of Byron, wisely hast thou said.
My realm, the centre of our empery,   55
Once lost, all Turkey would be overthrown;
And for that cause the Christians shall have peace.
Slavonians, Almains, rutters, Muffs, and Danes
Fear not Orcanes, but great Tamburlaine—°
Nor he, but Fortune that hath made him great.   60
We have revolted Grecians, Albanese,
Sicilians, Jews, Arabians, Turks, and Moors,
Natolians, Sorians, black Egyptians,
Illyrians, Thracians, and Bithynians,
Enough to swallow forceless Sigismond,   65
Yet scarce enough t'encounter Tamburlaine.
He brings a world of people to the field.
From Scythia to the oriental plage
Of India, where raging Lantchidol°
Beats on the regions with his boisterous blows,   70
That never seaman yet discoverèd,
All Asia is in arms with Tamburlaine.
Ev'n from the midst of fiery Cancer's tropic
To Amazonia under Capricorn,
And thence as far as Archipelago,   75
All Afric is in arms with Tamburlaine.

Therefore, viceroys, the Christians must have peace.
[Enter] Sigismond, Frederick, Baldwin, and their train, with
drums and trumpets

SIGISMOND Orcanes, as our legates promised thee,
We with our peers have crossed Danubius' stream
To treat of friendly peace or deadly war.   80
Take which thou wilt, for as the Romans used°
I here present thee with a naked sword.
[He presents his sword to Orcanes]
Wilt thou have war, then shake this blade at me;
If peace, restore it to my hands again,
And I will sheathe it to confirm the same.   85

ORCANES Stay, Sigismond. Forgett'st thou I am he
That with the cannon shook Vienna walls
And made it dance upon the continent,
As when the massy substance of the earth
Quiver about the axletree of heaven?°   90
Forgett'st thou that I sent a shower of darts
Mingled with powdered shot and feathered steel°
So thick upon the blink-eyed burghers' heads
That thou thyself, then County Palatine,
The king of Boheme, and the Austric duke   95
Sent heralds out, which basely on their knees
In all your names desired a truce of me?
Forgett'st thou that, to have me raise my siege,
Wagons of gold were set before my tent,
Stamped with the princely fowl that in her wings°   100
Carries the fearful thunderbolts of Jove?
How canst thou think of this and offer war?

SIGISMOND Vienna was besieged, and I was there,
Then County Palatine, but now a king;
And what we did was in extremity.   105
But now, Orcanes, view my royal host
That hides these plains, and seems as vast and wide
As doth the desert of Arabia
To those that stand on Baghdad's lofty tower,
Or as the ocean to the traveller   110
That rests upon the snowy Apennines;
And tell me whether I should stoop so low,
Or treat of peace with the Natolian king.

GAZELLUS Kings of Natolia and of Hungary,

We came from Turkey to confirm a league,   115
And not to dare each other to the field.
A friendly parley might become ye both.
FREDERICK And we from Europe to the same intent,
Which if your general refuse or scorn,°
Our tents are pitched, our men stand in array,   120
Ready to charge you ere you stir your feet.
ORCANES So prest are we. But yet if Sigismond
Speak as a friend and stand not upon terms,°
Here is his sword; let peace be ratified
On these conditions specified before,   125
Drawn with advice of our ambassadors.
SIGISMOND [*receiving back his sword*]
Then here I sheathe it, and give thee my hand
Never to draw it out or manage arms
Against thyself or thy confederates,
But, whilst I live, will be at truce with thee.   130
ORCANES But, Sigismond, confirm it with an oath
And swear in sight of heaven and by thy Christ.
SIGISMOND By Him that made the world and saved my soul,
The son of God and issue of a maid,
Sweet Jesus Christ, I solemnly protest   135
And vow to keep this peace inviolable.
ORCANES By sacred Mahomet, the friend of God,
Whose holy Alcoran remains with us,
Whose glorious body, when he left the world,
Closed in a coffin, mounted up the air   140
And hung on stately Mecca's temple roof,
I swear to keep this truce inviolable,
Of whose conditions and our solemn oaths
Signed with our hands, each shall retain a scroll
As memorable witness of our league.   145
Now, Sigismond, if any Christian king
Encroach upon the confines of thy realm,
Send word Orcanes of Natolia
Confirmed this league beyond Danubius' stream,
And they will, trembling, sound a quick retreat—   150
So am I feared among all nations.
SIGISMOND If any heathen potentate or king
Invade Natolia, Sigismond will send
A hundred thousand horse trained to the war

And backed by stout lancers of Germany,°   155
The strength and sinews of th'imperial seat.
ORCANES I thank thee, Sigismond; but when I war,
All Asia Minor, Africa, and Greece
Follow my standard and my thund'ring drums.
Come, let us go and banquet in our tents.   160
I will dispatch chief of my army hence
To fair Natolia and to Trebizond,
To stay my coming 'gainst proud Tamburlaine.
Friend Sigismond, and peers of Hungary,
Come banquet and carouse with us a while   165
And then depart we to our territories.
    Exeunt

[1.2]

[Enter] Callapine with Almeda, his keeper
CALLAPINE Sweet Almeda, pity the ruthful plight
Of Callapine, the son of Bajazeth,
Born to be monarch of the western world,°
Yet here detained by cruel Tamburlaine.°
ALMEDA My lord, I pity it, and with my heart   5
Wish your release. But he whose wrath is death,
My sovereign lord, renownèd Tamburlaine,
Forbids you further liberty than this.
CALLAPINE Ah, were I now but half so eloquent
To paint in words what I'll perform in deeds,   10
I know thou wouldst depart from hence with me.
ALMEDA Not for all Afric. Therefore move me not.
CALLAPINE Yet hear me speak, my gentle Almeda.
ALMEDA No speech to that end, by your favour, sir.
CALLAPINE By Cairo runs—°   15
ALMEDA No talk of running, I tell you, sir.
CALLAPINE A little further, gentle Almeda.
ALMEDA Well, sir, what of this?
CALLAPINE By Cairo runs to Alexandria Bay
Darote's streams, wherein at anchor lies°   20
A Turkish galley of my royal fleet,
Waiting my coming to the river side,

Hoping by some means I shall be released,
Which, when I come aboard, will hoist up sail
And soon put forth into the Terrene Sea,   25
Where 'twixt the isles of Cyprus and of Crete
We quickly may in Turkish seas arrive.
Then shalt thou see a hundred kings and more,
Upon their knees, all bid me welcome home.
Amongst so many crowns of burnished gold   30
Choose which thou wilt; all are at thy command.
A thousand galleys manned with Christian slaves
I freely give thee, which shall cut the Straits°
And bring armadoes from the coasts of Spain,
Freighted with gold of rich America.   35
The Grecian virgins shall attend on thee,
Skilful in music and in amorous lays,
As fair as was Pygmalion's ivory girl°
Or lovely Io metamorphosèd.°
With naked negroes shall thy coach be drawn,   40
And as thou rid'st in triumph through the streets,
The pavement underneath thy chariot wheels
With Turkey carpets shall be coverèd,
And cloth of arras hung about the walls,
Fit objects for thy princely eye to pierce.   45
A hundred bassoes, clothed in crimson silk,
Shall ride before thee on Barbarian steeds;
And when thou goest, a golden canopy
Enchased with precious stones which shine as bright
As that fair veil that covers all the world°   50
When Phoebus, leaping from his hemisphere,°
Descendeth downward to th'Antipodes—°
And more than this, for all I cannot tell.
ALMEDA How far hence lies the galley, say you?
CALLAPINE Sweet Almeda, scarce half a league from hence.   55
ALMEDA But need we not be spied going aboard?°
CALLAPINE Betwixt the hollow hanging of a hill
      And crooked bending of a craggy rock,
      The sails wrapped up, the mast and tacklings down,
      She lies so close that none can find her out.   60
ALMEDA I like that well. But tell me, my lord, if I should let you go,
      would you be as good as your word? Shall I be made a king for
      my labour?

77

CALLAPINE As I am Callapine the emperor,
And by the hand of Mahomet, I swear   65
Thou shalt be crowned a king and be my mate.
ALMEDA Then here I swear, as I am Almeda,
Your keeper under Tamburlaine the Great—
For that's the style and title I have yet—
Although he sent a thousand armèd men   70
To intercept this haughty enterprise,
Yet would I venture to conduct your grace
And die before I brought you back again.
CALLAPINE Thanks, gentle Almeda. Then let us haste,
Lest time be past and, ling'ring, let us both.   75
ALMEDA When you will, my lord. I am ready.
CALLAPINE Even straight. And farewell, cursèd Tamburlaine!
Now go I to revenge my father's death.
            Exeunt

[1.3]

[Enter] Tamburlaine with Zenocrate, and his three sons,
Calyphas, Amyras, and Celebinus, with drums and trumpets

TAMBURLAINE Now, bright Zenocrate, the world's fair eye,
Whose beams illuminate the lamps of heaven,
Whose cheerful looks do clear the cloudy air
And clothe it in a crystal livery,
Now rest thee here on fair Larissa plains°   5
Where Egypt and the Turkish empire parts,°
Between thy sons that shall be emperors
And every one commander of a world.
ZENOCRATE Sweet Tamburlaine, when wilt thou leave these arms
And save thy sacred person free from scathe   10
And dangerous chances of the wrathful war?
TAMBURLAINE When heaven shall cease to move on both the poles,°
And when the ground whereon my soldiers march
Shall rise aloft and touch the hornèd moon,
And not before, my sweet Zenocrate.   15
Sit up and rest thee like a lovely queen.
            [She sits in her throne]
So, now she sits in pomp and majesty

When these my sons, more precious in mine eyes
Than all the wealthy kingdoms I subdued,
Placed by her side, look on their mother's face.   20
But yet methinks their looks are amorous,
Not martial as the sons of Tamburlaine;°
Water and air, being symbolized in one,
Argue their want of courage and of wit;°
Their hair as white as milk and soft as down,   25
Which should be like the quills of porcupines,
As black as jet, and hard as iron or steel,
Bewrays they are too dainty for the wars.
Their fingers made to quaver on a lute,
Their arms to hang about a lady's neck,   30
Their legs to dance and caper in the air,
Would make me think them bastards, not my sons,
But that I know they issued from thy womb,
That never looked on man but Tamburlaine.

ZENOCRATE My gracious lord, they have their mother's looks,   35
But when they list, their conquering father's heart.
This lovely boy, the youngest of the three,
Not long ago bestrid a Scythian steed,
Trotting the ring and tilting at a glove,°
Which when he tainted with his slender rod°   40
He reined him straight and made him so curvet°
As I cried out for fear he should have fall'n.°

TAMBURLAINE [to Celebinus]
Well done, my boy. Thou shalt have shield and lance,
Armour of proof, horse, helm, and curtle-axe,°
And I will teach thee how to charge thy foe   45
And harmless run among the deadly pikes.
If thou wilt love the wars and follow me,
Thou shalt be made a king and reign with me,
Keeping in iron cages emperors.
If thou exceed thy elder brothers' worth   50
And shine in complete virtue more than they,°
Thou shalt be king before them, and thy seed
Shall issue crownèd from their mother's womb.

CELEBINUS Yes, father, you shall see me, if I live,
Have under me as many kings as you   55
And march with such a multitude of men
As all the world shall tremble at their view.

TAMBURLAINE These words assure me, boy, thou art my son.
　　When I am old and cannot manage arms,
　　Be thou the scourge and terror of the world.　　　　　　　　60
AMYRAS Why may not I, my lord, as well as he,
　　Be termed the scourge and terror of the world?
TAMBURLAINE Be all a scourge and terror to the world,
　　Or else you are not sons of Tamburlaine.
CALYPHAS But while my brothers follow arms, my lord,　　　65
　　Let me accompany my gracious mother.
　　They are enough to conquer all the world,
　　And you have won enough for me to keep.
TAMBURLAINE Bastardly boy, sprung from some coward's loins
　　And not the issue of great Tamburlaine,　　　　　　　　70
　　Of all the provinces I have subdued,
　　Thou shalt not have a foot, unless thou bear
　　A mind courageous and invincible.
　　For he shall wear the crown of Persia
　　Whose head hath deepest scars, whose breast most wounds,　　75
　　Which, being wroth, sends lightning from his eyes,
　　And in the furrows of his frowning brows
　　Harbours revenge, war, death, and cruelty.
　　For in a field, whose superficies
　　Is covered with a liquid purple veil　　　　　　　　80
　　And sprinkled with the brains of slaughtered men,
　　My royal chair of state shall be advanced;
　　And he that means to place himself therein
　　Must armèd wade up to the chin in blood.
ZENOCRATE My lord, such speeches to our princely sons　　85
　　Dismays their minds before they come to prove
　　The wounding troubles angry war affords.
CELEBINUS No, madam, these are speeches fit for us.
　　For if his chair were in a sea of blood,
　　I would prepare a ship and sail to it　　　　　　　　90
　　Ere I would lose the title of a king.
AMYRAS And I would strive to swim through pools of blood
　　Or make a bridge of murdered carcasses,
　　Whose arches should be framed with bones of Turks,
　　Ere I would lose the title of a king.　　　　　　　　95
TAMBURLAINE Well, lovely boys, you shall be emperors both,
　　Stretching your conquering arms from east to west.
　　[To Calyphas] And, sirrah, if you mean to wear a crown,

When we shall meet the Turkish deputy
And all his viceroys, snatch it from his head,   100
And cleave his pericranion with thy sword.
CALYPHAS If any man will hold him, I will strike,
And cleave him to the channel with my sword.°
TAMBURLAINE Hold him and cleave him, too, or I'll cleave thee,
For we will march against them presently.   105
Theridamas, Techelles, and Casane
Promised to meet me on Larissa plains
With hosts apiece against this Turkish crew,
For I have sworn by sacred Mahomet
To make it parcel of my empery.   110
The trumpets sound, Zenocrate. They come.
          Enter Theridamas and his train, with drums and trumpets
Welcome, Theridamas, king of Argier!
THERIDAMAS My lord the great and mighty Tamburlaine,
Arch-monarch of the world, I offer here
My crown, myself, and all the power I have,   115
In all affection at thy kingly feet.
          [*He lays his crown at Tamburlaine's feet*]
TAMBURLAINE Thanks, good Theridamas.
THERIDAMAS Under my colours march ten thousand Greeks,
And of Argier and Afric's frontier towns
Twice twenty thousand valiant men-at-arms,   120
All which have sworn to sack Natolia.
Five hundred brigantines are under sail,
Meet for your service on the sea, my lord,
That, launching from Argier to Tripoli,
Will quickly ride before Natolia   125
And batter down the castles on the shore.
TAMBURLAINE Well said, Argier. Receive thy crown again.
          [*He returns Theridamas's crown. Enter Techelles and
          Usumcasane together*]
Kings of Moroccus and of Fez, welcome.
USUMCASANE [*laying his crown before Tamburlaine*]
Magnificent and peerless Tamburlaine,
I and my neighbour king of Fez have brought,°   130
To aid thee in this Turkish expedition,
A hundred thousand expert soldiers.
From Azamor to Tunis near the sea
Is Barbary unpeopled for thy sake,

And all the men in armour under me,   135
Which with my crown I gladly offer thee.
TAMBURLAINE [*returning Usumcasane's crown*]
Thanks, king of Moroccus. Take your crown again.
TECHELLES [*laying his crown before Tamburlaine*]
And, mighty Tamburlaine, our earthly god,
Whose looks make this inferior world to quake,
I here present thee with the crown of Fez   140
And with an host of Moors trained to the war,
Whose coal-black faces make their foes retire
And quake for fear, as if infernal Jove,°
Meaning to aid thee in these Turkish arms,
Should pierce the black circumference of hell   145
With ugly Furies bearing fiery flags
And millions of his strong tormenting spirits.
From strong Tesella unto Biledull
All Barbary is unpeopled for thy sake.
TAMBURLAINE [*returning Techelles's crown*]
Thanks, king of Fez. Take here thy crown again.   150
Your presence, loving friends and fellow kings,
Makes me to surfeit in conceiving joy.°
If all the crystal gates of Jove's high court
Were opened wide, and I might enter in
To see the state and majesty of heaven,   155
It could not more delight me than your sight.
Now will we banquet on these plains a while
And after march to Turkey with our camp,
In number more than are the drops that fall
When Boreas rends a thousand swelling clouds;   160
And proud Orcanes of Natolia
With all his viceroys shall be so afraid
That though the stones, as at Deucalion's flood,
Were turned to men, he should be overcome.°
Such lavish will I make of Turkish blood°   165
That Jove shall send his wingèd messenger°
To bid me sheathe my sword and leave the field.
The sun, unable to sustain the sight,
Shall hide his head in Thetis' watery lap°
And leave his steeds to fair Boötes' charge;°   170
For half the world shall perish in this fight.
But now, my friends, let me examine ye.

How have ye spent your absent time from me?
USUMCASANE My lord, our men of Barbary have marched
    Four hundred miles with armour on their backs   175
    And lain in leaguer fifteen months and more.°
    For since we left you at the Sultan's court,
    We have subdued the southern Guallatia°
    And all the land unto the coast of Spain.
    We kept the narrow Strait of Gibraltar°   180
    And made Canarea call us kings and lords,°
    Yet never did they recreate themselves°
    Or cease one day from war and hot alarms;
    And therefore let them rest a while, my lord.
TAMBURLAINE They shall, Casane, and 'tis time, i'faith.   185
TECHELLES And I have marched along the river Nile
    To Machda, where the mighty Christian priest
    Called John the Great sits in a milk-white robe,°
    Whose triple mitre I did take by force°
    And made him swear obedience to my crown.   190
    From thence unto Cazates did I march,°
    Where Amazonians met me in the field,
    With whom, being women, I vouchsafed a league;
    And with my power did march to Zanzibar,
    The western part of Afric, where I viewed   195
    The Ethiopian sea, rivers and lakes,
    But neither man nor child in all the land.
    Therefore I took my course to Manico,
    Where, unresisted, I removed my camp.
    And by the coast of Byather at last   200
    I came to Cubar, where the negroes dwell,
    And, conquering that, made haste to Nubia.°
    There, having sacked Borno, the kingly seat,
    I took the king and led him bound in chains
    Unto Damasco, where I stayed before.°   205
TAMBURLAINE Well done, Techelles. What saith Theridamas?
THERIDAMAS I left the confines and the bounds of Afric
    And made a voyage into Europe,
    Where by the river Tyros I subdued
    Stoka, Podalia, and Codemia,°   210
    Then crossed the sea and came to Oblia,
    And Nigra Silva, where the devils dance,°
    Which in despite of them I set on fire.

From thence I crossed the gulf called by the name
Mare Maggiore of th'inhabitants.°   215
Yet shall my soldiers make no period
Until Natolia kneel before your feet.
TAMBURLAINE   Then will we triumph, banquet, and carouse;
Cooks shall have pensions to provide us cates°
And glut us with the dainties of the world.   220
Lachryma Christi and Calabrian wines°
Shall common soldiers drink in quaffing bowls—
Ay, liquid gold when we have conquered him,
Mingled with coral and with orient pearl.
Come, let us banquet and carouse the whiles.   225

    Exeunt

[2.1]

[Enter] Sigismond, Frederick, Baldwin, with their train

SIGISMOND Now say, my lords of Buda and Bohemia,
    What motion is it that inflames your thoughts
    And stirs your valours to such sudden arms?

FREDERICK Your majesty remembers, I am sure,
    What cruel slaughter of our Christian bloods°   5
    These heathenish Turks and pagans lately made
    Betwixt the city Zula and Danubius,
    How through the midst of Varna and Bulgaria
    And almost to the very walls of Rome
    They have, not long since, massacred our camp.   10
    It resteth now, then, that your majesty
    Take all advantages of time and power,
    And work revenge upon these infidels.
    Your highness knows for Tamburlaine's repair,°
    That strikes a terror to all Turkish hearts,   15
    Natolia hath dismissed the greatest part°
    Of all his army, pitched against our power
    Betwixt Cutheia and Orminius' mount,
    And sent them marching up to Belgasar,
    Acantha, Antioch, and Caesaria,   20
    To aid the kings of Soria and Jerusalem.
    Now then, my lord, advantage take hereof,
    And issue suddenly upon the rest,
    That, in the fortune of their overthrow,
    We may discourage all the pagan troop   25
    That dare attempt to war with Christians.

SIGISMOND But calls not, then, your grace to memory
    The league we lately made with King Orcanes,
    Confirmed by oath and articles of peace,
    And calling Christ for record of our truths?   30
    This should be treachery and violence°
    Against the grace of our profession.°

BALDWIN No whit, my lord. For with such infidels,
    In whom no faith nor true religion rests,
    We are not bound to those accomplishments°   35
    The holy laws of Christendom enjoin;

But as the faith which they profanely plight
Is not by necessary policy°
To be esteemed assurance for ourselves,
So what we vow to them should not infringe   40
Our liberty of arms and victory.

SIGISMOND Though I confess the oaths they undertake
Breed little strength to our security,
Yet those infirmities that thus defame
Their faiths, their honours, and their religion   45
Should not give us presumption to the like.
Our faiths are sound and must be consummate,
Religious, righteous, and inviolate.

FREDERICK Assure your grace, 'tis superstition
To stand so strictly on dispensive faith.°   50
And should we lose the opportunity
That God hath given to venge our Christians' death
And scourge their foul blasphemous paganism?
As fell to Saul, to Balaam, and the rest°
That would not kill and curse at God's command,   55
So surely will the vengeance of the Highest,
And jealous anger of His fearful arm,
Be poured with rigour on our sinful heads
If we neglect this offered victory.

SIGISMOND Then arm, my lords, and issue suddenly,   60
Giving commandment to our general host
With expedition to assail the pagan
And take the victory our God hath given.
          Exeunt

[2.2]

          [*Enter*] *Orcanes, Gazellus, Uribassa, with their train*
ORCANES Gazellus, Uribassa, and the rest,
Now will we march from proud Orminius' mount
To fair Natolia, where our neighbour kings
Expect our power and our royal presence,
T'encounter with the cruel Tamburlaine   5
That nigh Larissa sways a mighty host
And with the thunder of his martial tools

Makes earthquakes in the hearts of men and heaven.
GAZELLUS And now come we to make his sinews shake
   With greater power than erst his pride hath felt.   10
   An hundred kings by scores will bid him arms,°
   And hundred thousands subjects to each score—°
   Which, if a shower of wounding thunderbolts
   Should break out of the bowels of the clouds
   And fall as thick as hail upon our heads   15
   In partial aid of that proud Scythian,
   Yet should our courages and steelèd crests
   And numbers more than infinite of men
   Be able to withstand and conquer him.
URIBASSA Methinks I see how glad the Christian king   20
   Is made for joy of your admitted truce,
   That could not but before be terrified
   With unacquainted power of our host.
      Enter a Messenger
MESSENGER Arm, dread sovereign, and my noble lords!
   The treacherous army of the Christians,   25
   Taking advantage of your slender power,
   Comes marching on us and determines straight
   To bid us battle for our dearest lives.
ORCANES Traitors, villains, damnèd Christians!
   Have I not here the articles of peace   30
   And solemn covenants we have both confirmed,
   He by his Christ and I by Mahomet?
GAZELLUS Hell and confusion light upon their heads
   That with such treason seek our overthrow
   And cares so little for their prophet, Christ!   35
ORCANES Can there be such deceit in Christians,
   Or treason in the fleshly heart of man,
   Whose shape is figure of the highest god?
   Then if there be a Christ, as Christians say
   (But in their deeds deny him for their Christ),   40
   If he be son to everliving Jove
   And hath the power of his outstretched arm,
   If he be jealous of his name and honour
   As is our holy prophet Mahomet,
   Take here these papers as our sacrifice°   45
   And witness of Thy servant's perjury!
      [*He tears to pieces the articles of peace*]

87

Open, thou shining veil of Cynthia,°
And make a passage from th'empyreal heaven,
That He that sits on high and never sleeps
Nor in one place is circumscriptible,°   50
But everywhere fills every continent°
With strange infusion of His sacred vigour,
May in His endless power and purity
Behold and venge this traitor's perjury!
Thou Christ, that art esteemed omnipotent,   55
If thou wilt prove thyself a perfect God
Worthy the worship of all faithful hearts,
Be now revenged upon this traitor's soul,
And make the power I have left behind
(Too little to defend our guiltless lives)   60
Sufficient to discomfort and confound
The trustless force of those false Christians.
To arms, my lords! On Christ still let us cry.
If there be Christ, we shall have victory.
    [*Exeunt*]

[2.3]

Sound to the battle, and Sigismond comes out wounded
SIGISMOND Discomfited is all the Christian host,
    And God hath thundered vengeance from on high
    For my accurst and hateful perjury.
    O just and dreadful punisher of sin,
    Let the dishonour of the pains I feel   5
    In this my mortal well-deservèd wound
    End all my penance in my sudden death,
    And let this death, wherein to sin I die,°
    Conceive a second life in endless mercy!°
        [*He dies.*] *Enter Orcanes, Gazellus, Uribassa, with others*
ORCANES Now lie the Christians bathing in their bloods,   10
    And Christ or Mahomet hath been my friend.
GAZELLUS See here the perjured traitor, Hungary,
    Bloody and breathless for his villainy.
ORCANES Now shall his barbarous body be a prey
    To beasts and fowls, and all the winds shall breathe   15

Through shady leaves of every senseless tree
Murmurs and hisses for his heinous sin.
Now scalds his soul in the Tartarian streams
And feeds upon the baneful tree of hell,
That Zoacum, that fruit of bitterness,°   20
That in the midst of fire is engraft,
Yet flourisheth as Flora in her pride,
With apples like the heads of damnèd fiends.
The devils there in chains of quenchless flame
Shall lead his soul through Orcus' burning gulf°   25
From pain to pain, whose change shall never end.
What sayest thou yet, Gazellus, to his foil,
Which we referred to justice of his Christ
And to His power, which here appears as full
As rays of Cynthia to the clearest sight?   30
GAZELLUS 'Tis but the fortune of the wars, my lord,
     Whose power is often proved a miracle.°
ORCANES Yet in my thoughts shall Christ be honourèd,
     Not doing Mahomet an injury,
     Whose power had share in this our victory.   35
     And since this miscreant hath disgraced his faith
     And died a traitor both to heaven and earth,
     We will both watch and ward shall keep his trunk°
     Amidst these plains for fowls to prey upon.°
     Go, Uribassa, give it straight in charge.°   40
URIBASSA I will, my lord.
          Exit Uribassa [and others, with the body]
ORCANES And now, Gazellus, let us haste and meet
     Our army, and our brother of Jerusalem,°
     Of Soria, Trebizond, and Amasia,
     And happily, with full Natolian bowls   45
     Of Greekish wine, now let us celebrate
     Our happy conquest and his angry fate.°
          Exeunt

[2.4]

The arras is drawn,° and Zenocrate lies in her bed of state,
Tamburlaine sitting by her; three Physicians about her bed,
tempering potions. Theridamas, Techelles, Usumcasane, and
the three sons [Calyphas, Amyras, Celebinus]

TAMBURLAINE Black is the beauty of the brightest day!
The golden ball of heaven's eternal fire,
That danced with glory on the silver waves,
Now wants the fuel that inflamed his beams,
And all with faintness and for foul disgrace   5
He binds his temples with a frowning cloud,
Ready to darken earth with endless night.
Zenocrate, that gave him light and life,
Whose eyes shot fire from their ivory bowers°
And tempered every soul with lively heat,   10
Now by the malice of the angry skies,
Whose jealousy admits no second mate,
Draws in the comfort of her latest breath°
All dazzled with the hellish mists of death.°
Now walk the angels on the walls of heaven,   15
As sentinels to warn th'immortal souls
To entertain divine Zenocrate.
Apollo, Cynthia, and the ceaseless lamps°
That gently looked upon this loathsome earth
Shine downwards now no more, but deck the heavens   20
To entertain divine Zenocrate.
The crystal springs whose taste illuminates
Refinèd eyes with an eternal sight,
Like trièd silver, runs through Paradise
To entertain divine Zenocrate.   25
The cherubins and holy seraphins
That sing and play before the King of Kings
Use all their voices and their instruments
To entertain divine Zenocrate.
And in this sweet and curious harmony   30
The god that tunes this music to our souls
Holds out his hand in highest majesty
To entertain divine Zenocrate.
Then let some holy trance convey my thoughts

Up to the palace of th'empyreal heaven,   35
That this my life may be as short to me
As are the days of sweet Zenocrate.
Physicians, will no physic do her good?
PHYSICIAN My lord, your majesty shall soon perceive;
An if she pass this fit, the worst is past.°   40
TAMBURLAINE Tell me, how fares my fair Zenocrate?
ZENOCRATE I fare, my lord, as other empresses,
That, when this frail and transitory flesh
Hath sucked the measure of that vital air
That feeds the body with his dated health,   45
Wanes with enforced and necessary change.
TAMBURLAINE May never such a change transform my love,
In whose sweet being I repose my life,
Whose heavenly presence, beautified with health,
Gives light to Phoebus and the fixèd stars,   50
Whose absence make the sun and moon as dark
As when, opposed in one diameter,°
Their spheres are mounted on the Serpent's head
Or else descended to his winding train.
Live still, my love, and so conserve my life,   55
Or, dying, be the author of my death.
ZENOCRATE Live still, my lord, O, let my sovereign live,
And sooner let the fiery element
Dissolve and make your kingdom in the sky°
Than this base earth should shroud your majesty!   60
For, should I but suspect your death by mine,°
The comfort of my future happiness
And hope to meet your highness in the heavens,
Turned to despair, would break my wretched breast,
And fury would confound my present rest.   65
But let me die, my love, yet let me die;
With love and patience let your true love die.
Your grief and fury hurts my second life.
Yet let me kiss my lord before I die,
And let me die with kissing of my lord.   70
But since my life is lengthened yet a while,
Let me take leave of these my loving sons
And of my lords, whose true nobility
Have merited my latest memory.—°
Sweet sons, farewell! In death resemble me,   75

And in your lives your father's excellency.—
Some music, and my fit will cease, my lord.
   They call [for] music
TAMBURLAINE Proud fury and intolerable fit,
That dares torment the body of my love
And scourge the scourge of the immortal God!   80
Now are those spheres where Cupid used to sit,°
Wounding the world with wonder and with love,
Sadly supplied with pale and ghastly death°
Whose darts do pierce the centre of my soul.°
Her sacred beauty hath enchanted heaven,   85
And, had she lived before the siege of Troy,
Helen, whose beauty summoned Greece to arms
And drew a thousand ships to Tenedos,
Had not been named in Homer's *Iliads*;
Her name had been in every line he wrote.°   90
Or, had those wanton poets, for whose birth
Old Rome was proud, but gazed a while on her,°
Nor Lesbia nor Corinna had been named;°
Zenocrate had been the argument
Of every epigram or elegy.   95
   The music sounds, and she dies
What, is she dead? Techelles, draw thy sword,
And wound the earth, that it may cleave in twain,
And we descend into th'infernal vaults
To hale the Fatal Sisters by the hair°
And throw them in the triple moat of hell°   100
For taking hence my fair Zenocrate.
Casane and Theridamas, to arms!
Raise cavalieros higher than the clouds,°
And with the cannon break the frame of heaven,
Batter the shining palace of the sun   105
And shiver all the starry firmament,
For amorous Jove hath snatched my love from hence,
Meaning to make her stately queen of heaven.
What god soever holds thee in his arms,
Giving thee nectar and ambrosia,   110
Behold me here, divine Zenocrate,
Raving, impatient, desperate, and mad,
Breaking my steelèd lance with which I burst
The rusty beams of Janus' temple doors,

Letting out death and tyrannizing war°   115
To march with me under this bloody flag;
And if thou pitiest Tamburlaine the Great,°
Come down from heaven and live with me again!

THERIDAMAS Ah, good my lord, be patient. She is dead,
And all this raging cannot make her live.   120
If words might serve, our voice hath rent the air;
If tears, our eyes have watered all the earth;
If grief, our murdered hearts have strained forth blood.°
Nothing prevails, for she is dead, my lord.

TAMBURLAINE 'For she is dead'! Thy words do pierce my soul.   125
Ah, sweet Theridamas, say so no more.
Though she be dead, yet let me think she lives
And feed my mind that dies for want of her.
Where'er her soul be [*turning to address Zenocrate's body*], thou
    shalt stay with me,
Embalmed with cassia, ambergris, and myrrh,   130
Not lapped in lead but in a sheet of gold;
And till I die thou shalt not be interred.
Then in as rich a tomb as Mausolus'°
We both will rest and have one epitaph
Writ in as many several languages   135
As I have conquered kingdoms with my sword.
This cursèd town will I consume with fire
Because this place bereft me of my love.
The houses, burnt, will look as if they mourned,
And here will I set up her stature°   140
And march about it with my mourning camp,
Drooping and pining for Zenocrate.
    The arras is drawn. [*Exeunt*]

[3.1]

*Enter the kings of Trebizond and Soria, one bringing a
sword, and another a sceptre; next, [Orcanes king of] Natolia
and [the king of] Jerusalem with the imperial crown; after,
Callapine, and after him other Lords [and Almeda]. Orcanes
and Jerusalem crown [Callapine,] and the other[s] give him
the sceptre*

ORCANES Callapinus Cyricelibes, otherwise Cybelius, son and suc-
cessive heir to the late mighty emperor Bajazeth, by the aid of God
and his friend Mahomet emperor of Natolia, Jerusalem, Trebizond,
Soria, Amasia, Thracia, Illyria, Carmonia, and all the hundred and
thirty kingdoms late contributory to his mighty father: long live   5
Callapinus, emperor of Turkey!

CALLAPINE Thrice worthy kings of Natolia, and the rest,
   I will requite your royal gratitudes
   With all the benefits my empire yields.
   And, were the sinews of th'imperial seat   10
   So knit and strengthened as when Bajazeth,
   My royal lord and father, filled the throne,
   Whose cursèd fate hath so dismembered it,
   Then should you see this thief of Scythia,
   This proud usurping king of Persia,   15
   Do us such honour and supremacy,
   Bearing the vengeance of our father's wrongs,
   As all the world should blot our dignities
   Out of the book of baseborn infamies.°
   And now I doubt not but your royal cares   20
   Hath so provided for this cursèd foe
   That, since the heir of mighty Bajazeth—
   An emperor so honoured for his virtues—
   Revives the spirit of true Turkish hearts
   In grievous memory of his father's shame,   25
   We shall not need to nourish any doubt
   But that proud Fortune, who hath followed long
   The martial sword of mighty Tamburlaine,
   Will not retain her old inconstancy,
   And raise our honours to as high a pitch°   30
   In this our strong and fortunate encounter.

For so hath heaven provided my escape
From all the cruelty my soul sustained,
By this my friendly keeper's happy means,
That Jove, surcharged with pity of our wrongs,   35
Will pour it down in showers on our heads,
Scourging the pride of cursèd Tamburlaine.

ORCANES I have a hundred thousand men in arms,
Some that, in conquest of the perjured Christian
Being a handful to a mighty host,   40
Think them in number yet sufficient°
To drink the river Nile or Euphrates,
And, for their power, enough to win the world.

JERUSALEM And I as many from Jerusalem,
Judaea, Gaza, and Scalonia's bounds,   45
That on Mount Sinai with their ensigns spread
Look like the parti-coloured clouds of heaven
That show fair weather to the neighbour morn.

TREBIZOND And I as many bring from Trebizond,
Chio, Famastro, and Amasia,   50
All bord'ring on the Mare-Major Sea,°
Riso, Sancina, and the bordering towns
That touch the end of famous Euphrates,
Whose courages are kindled with the flames
The cursèd Scythian sets on all their towns,°   55
And vow to burn the villain's cruel heart.

SORIA From Soria with seventy thousand strong,
Ta'en from Aleppo, Soldino, Tripoli,
And so unto my city of Damasco,
I march to meet and aid my neighbour kings,   60
All which will join against this Tamburlaine
And bring him captive to your highness' feet.

ORCANES Our battle, then, in martial manner pitched,°
According to our ancient use, shall bear
The figure of the semicircled moon,   65
Whose horns shall sprinkle through the tainted air
The poisoned brains of this proud Scythian.

CALLAPINE Well then, my noble lords, for this my friend°
That freed me from the bondage of my foe,
I think it requisite and honourable   70
To keep my promise and to make him king,
That is a gentleman, I know, at least.

ALMEDA That's no matter, sir, for being a king,°
　　For Tamburlaine came up of nothing.

JERUSALEM Your majesty may choose some 'pointed time,　　75
　　Performing all your promise to the full.
　　'Tis nought for your majesty to give a kingdom.

CALLAPINE Then will I shortly keep my promise, Almeda.

ALMEDA Why, I thank your majesty.
　　　　Exeunt

[3.2]

[Enter] Tamburlaine [bearing a picture of Zenocrate] with
Usumcasane, and his three sons [Calyphas, Amyras,
Celebinus, bearing a memorial pillar, a funerary pennon, and
a tablet]; four [Soldiers] bearing the hearse of Zenocrate,
and the drums sounding a doleful march, the town burning

TAMBURLAINE So, burn the turrets of this cursèd town.°
　　Flame to the highest region of the air
　　And kindle heaps of exhalations
　　That, being fiery meteors, may presage
　　Death and destruction to th'inhabitants;　　　　　　5
　　Over my zenith hang a blazing star
　　That may endure till heaven be dissolved,
　　Fed with the fresh supply of earthly dregs,
　　Threat'ning a death and famine to this land!
　　Flying dragons, lightning, fearful thunderclaps,　　10
　　Singe these fair plains, and make them seem as black
　　As is the island where the Furies mask°
　　Compassed with Lethe, Styx, and Phlegethon,°
　　Because my dear Zenocrate is dead!

CALYPHAS This pillar placed in memory of her,　　　　15
　　Where in Arabian, Hebrew, Greek, is writ:
　　'This town, being burnt by Tamburlaine the Great,
　　Forbids the world to build it up again.'

AMYRAS And here this mournful streamer shall be placed,
　　Wrought with the Persian and Egyptian arms°　　　20
　　To signify she was a princess born
　　And wife unto the monarch of the East.

CELEBINUS And here this table, as a register

96

Of all her virtues and perfections.

TAMBURLAINE And here the picture of Zenocrate   25
To show her beauty which the world admired—
Sweet picture of divine Zenocrate
That, hanging here, will draw the gods from heaven
And cause the stars fixed in the southern arc,°
Whose lovely faces never any viewed   30
That have not passed the centre's latitude,
As pilgrims travel to our hemisphere
Only to gaze upon Zenocrate.
[*To her hearse*] Thou shalt not beautify Larissa plains,
But keep within the circle of mine arms!   35
At every town and castle I besiege
Thou shalt be set upon my royal tent,°
And when I meet an army in the field
Those looks will shed such influence in my camp
As if Bellona, goddess of the war,   40
Threw naked swords and sulphur balls of fire
Upon the heads of all our enemies.—
And now, my lords, advance your spears again.
Sorrow no more, my sweet Casane, now.
Boys, leave to mourn. This town shall ever mourn,   45
Being burnt to cinders for your mother's death.

CALYPHAS If I had wept a sea of tears for her,
It would not ease the sorrow I sustain.

AMYRAS As is that town, so is my heart consumed
With grief and sorrow for my mother's death.   50

CELEBINUS My mother's death hath mortified my mind,
And sorrow stops the passage of my speech.

TAMBURLAINE But now, my boys, leave off, and list to me
That mean to teach you rudiments of war.
I'll have you learn to sleep upon the ground,   55
March in your armour thorough watery fens,
Sustain the scorching heat and freezing cold,
Hunger and thirst—right adjuncts of the war;
And after this to scale a castle wall,
Besiege a fort, to undermine a town,   60
And make whole cities caper in the air.°
Then next, the way to fortify your men,
In champian grounds what figure serves you best;°
For which the quinque-angle form is meet,°

Because the corners there may fall more flat   65
Whereas the fort may fittest be assailed,
And sharpest where th'assault is desperate.
The ditches must be deep, the counterscarps°
Narrow and steep, the walls made high and broad,
The bulwarks and the rampires large and strong,°   70
With cavalieros and thick counterforts,°
And room within to lodge six thousand men.
It must have privy ditches, countermines,°
And secret issuings to defend the ditch;°
It must have high argins and covered ways°   75
To keep the bulwark fronts from battery,
And parapets to hide the musketeers,
Casemates to place the great artillery,°
And store of ordnance, that from every flank
May scour the outward curtains of the fort,°   80
Dismount the cannon of the adverse part,°
Murder the foe, and save the walls from breach.
When this is learned for service on the land,
By plain and easy demonstration
I'll teach you how to make the water mount,°   85
That you may dry-foot march through lakes and pools,°
Deep rivers, havens, creeks, and little seas,
And make a fortress in the raging waves,
Fenced with the concave of a monstrous rock,
Invincible by nature of the place.   90
When this is done, then are ye soldiers,
And worthy sons of Tamburlaine the Great.
CALYPHAS My lord, but this is dangerous to be done.
We may be slain or wounded ere we learn.
TAMBURLAINE Villain, art thou the son of Tamburlaine   95
And fear'st to die, or with a curtle-axe
To hew thy flesh and make a gaping wound?
Hast thou beheld a peal of ordnance strike
A ring of pikes, mingled with shot and horse,°
Whose shattered limbs, being tossed as high as heaven,   100
Hang in the air as thick as sunny motes,
And canst thou, coward, stand in fear of death?
Hast thou not seen my horsemen charge the foe,
Shot through the arms, cut overthwart the hands,°
Dyeing their lances with their streaming blood,   105

And yet at night carouse within my tent,
Filling their empty veins with airy wine
That, being concocted, turns to crimson blood,°
And wilt thou shun the field for fear of wounds?
View me, thy father, that hath conquered kings   110
And with his host marched round about the earth
Quite void of scars and clear from any wound,
That by the wars lost not a dram of blood,
And see him lance his flesh to teach you all.
    He cuts his arm
A wound is nothing, be it ne'er so deep;   115
Blood is the god of war's rich livery.
Now look I like a soldier, and this wound
As great a grace and majesty to me
As if a chair of gold enamellèd,
Enchased with diamonds, sapphires, rubies,   120
And fairest pearl of wealthy India,
Were mounted here under a canopy,
And I sat down, clothed with the massy robe
That late adorned the Afric potentate°
Whom I brought bound unto Damascus' walls.   125
Come, boys, and with your fingers search my wound
And in my blood wash all your hands at once,
While I sit smiling to behold the sight.
    [*They probe his wound with their fingers*]
Now, my boys, what think you of a wound?
CALYPHAS I know not what I should think of it. Methinks 'tis a   130
pitiful sight.
CELEBINUS 'Tis nothing. Give me a wound, father.
AMYRAS And me another, my lord.
TAMBURLAINE [*to Celebinus*] Come, sirrah, give me your arm.
CELEBINUS [*offering his arm*] Here, father, cut it bravely as you did   135
your own.
TAMBURLAINE It shall suffice thou dar'st abide a wound.
My boy, thou shalt not lose a drop of blood
Before we meet the army of the Turk.
But then run desperate through the thickest throngs,   140
Dreadless of blows, of bloody wounds and death.
And let the burning of Larissa walls,
My speech of war, and this my wound you see,
Teach you, my boys, to bear courageous minds

Fit for the followers of great Tamburlaine.   145
Usumcasane, now come let us march
Towards Techelles and Theridamas,
That we have sent before to fire the towns,
The towers and cities of these hateful Turks,
And hunt that coward, faint-heart runaway,°   150
With that accursèd traitor Almeda,
Till fire and sword have found them at a bay.°
USUMCASANE I long to pierce his bowels with my sword,
That hath betrayed my gracious sovereign,
That curst and damnèd traitor Almeda.   155
TAMBURLAINE Then let us see if coward Callapine
Dare levy arms against our puissance,
That we may tread upon his captive neck
And treble all his father's slaveries.
        Exeunt

[3.3]

[Enter] Techelles, Theridamas, and their train [Soldiers and
Pioners]

THERIDAMAS Thus have we marched northward from Tamburlaine
Unto the frontier point of Soria;
And this is Balsera, their chiefest hold,
Wherein is all the treasure of the land.
TECHELLES Then let us bring our light artillery,   5
Minions, falc'nets, and sakers, to the trench,°
Filling the ditches with the walls' wide breach,°
And enter in to seize upon the gold.
How say ye, soldiers, shall we not?
SOLDIERS Yes, my lord, yes! Come, let's about it.   10
THERIDAMAS But stay a while. Summon a parley, drum.
It may be they will yield it quietly,
Knowing two kings, the friends to Tamburlaine,
Stand at the walls with such a mighty power.
        [Drums] summon the battle.° [Enter above] Captain with his
        wife [Olympia] and Son
CAPTAIN What require you, my masters?   15
THERIDAMAS Captain, that thou yield up thy hold to us.

CAPTAIN To you? Why, do you think me weary of it?

TECHELLES Nay, captain, thou art weary of thy life
  If thou withstand the friends of Tamburlaine.

THERIDAMAS These pioners of Argier in Africa   20
  Even in the cannon's face shall raise a hill
  Of earth and faggots higher than thy fort,
  And over thy argins and covered ways
  Shall play upon the bulwarks of thy hold
  Volleys of ordnance till the breach be made   25
  That with his ruin fills up all the trench;°
  And when we enter in, not heaven itself
  Shall ransom thee, thy wife, and family.

TECHELLES Captain, these Moors shall cut the leaden pipes
  That bring fresh water to thy men and thee,   30
  And lie in trench before thy castle walls,
  That no supply of victual shall come in,
  Nor any issue forth but they shall die.
  And therefore, captain, yield it quietly.

CAPTAIN Were you, that are the friends of Tamburlaine,   35
  Brothers to holy Mahomet himself,
  I would not yield it. Therefore do your worst.
  Raise mounts, batter, entrench, and undermine,°
  Cut off the water, all convoys that can,°
  Yet I am resolute. And so, farewell.   40
     [Exeunt above]

THERIDAMAS Pioners, away! And where I stuck the stake
  Entrench with those dimensions I prescribed.
  Cast up the earth towards the castle wall,
  Which, till it may defend you, labour low,
  And few or none shall perish by their shot.°   45

PIONERS We will, my lord.
     Exeunt [Pioners]

TECHELLES A hundred horse shall scout about the plains
  To spy what force comes to relieve the hold.
  Both we, Theridamas, will entrench our men,
  And with the Jacob's staff measure the height°   50
  And distance of the castle from the trench,
  That we may know if our artillery
  Will carry full point-blank unto their walls.°

THERIDAMAS Then see the bringing of our ordinance°
  Along the trench into the battery,°   55

Where we will have gabions of six foot broad°
To save our cannoneers from musket shot,
Betwixt which shall our ordnance thunder forth,
And with the breach's fall, smoke, fire, and dust,
The crack, the echo, and the soldiers' cry,°   60
Make deaf the air and dim the crystal sky.
TECHELLES Trumpets and drums, alarum presently!
   And, soldiers, play the men. The hold is yours!
        [*Trumpets and drums sound the alarm. Exeunt*]

[3.4]

Enter the Captain with his wife [Olympia] and Son
OLYMPIA Come, good my lord, and let us haste from hence
   Along the cave that leads beyond the foe.
   No hope is left to save this conquered hold.
CAPTAIN A deadly bullet gliding through my side
   Lies heavy on my heart. I cannot live.   5
   I feel my liver pierced, and all my veins
   That there begin and nourish every part
   Mangled and torn, and all my entrails bathed
   In blood that straineth from their orifex.
   Farewell, sweet wife! Sweet son, farewell! I die.   10
        [*He dies*]
OLYMPIA Death, whither art thou gone, that both we live?
   Come back again, sweet Death, and strike us both!
   One minute end our days, and one sepulchre
   Contain our bodies! Death, why com'st thou not?
        [*She draws a dagger*]
   Well, this must be the messenger for thee.   15
   Now, ugly Death, stretch out thy sable wings,
   And carry both our souls where his remains.—
   Tell me, sweet boy, art thou content to die?
   These barbarous Scythians, full of cruelty,
   And Moors in whom was never pity found,   20
   Will hew us piecemeal, put us to the wheel,
   Or else invent some torture worse than that.
   Therefore, die by thy loving mother's hand,
   Who gently now will lance thy ivory throat

And quickly rid thee both of pain and life.   25
SON Mother, dispatch me, or I'll kill myself.
   For think ye I can live, and see him dead?
   Give me your knife, good mother, or strike home.
   The Scythians shall not tyrannize on me.
   Sweet mother, strike, that I may meet my father!   30
       She stabs him
OLYMPIA Ah, sacred Mahomet, if this be sin,
   Entreat a pardon of the God of heaven,
   And purge my soul before it come to thee!
       [*She burns the bodies.*]° *Enter Theridamas, Techelles, and all
       their train. [Olympia attempts to kill herself but is restrained]*
THERIDAMAS How now, madam, what are you doing?
OLYMPIA Killing myself, as I have done my son,   35
   Whose body with his father's I have burnt,
   Lest cruel Scythians should dismember him.
TECHELLES 'Twas bravely done, and like a soldier's wife.
   Thou shalt with us to Tamburlaine the Great,
   Who, when he hears how resolute thou wert,   40
   Will match thee with a viceroy or a king.
OLYMPIA My lord deceased was dearer unto me
   Than any viceroy, king, or emperor,
   And for his sake here will I end my days.
THERIDAMAS But lady, go with us to Tamburlaine,   45
   And thou shalt see a man greater than Mahomet,
   In whose high looks is much more majesty
   Than from the concave superficies
   Of Jove's vast palace, the empyreal orb,
   Unto the shining bower where Cynthia sits   50
   Like lovely Thetis in a crystal robe;°
   That treadeth Fortune underneath his feet
   And makes the mighty god of arms his slave;
   On whom Death and the Fatal Sisters wait
   With naked swords and scarlet liveries;   55
   Before whom, mounted on a lion's back,
   Rhamnusia bears a helmet full of blood°
   And strews the way with brains of slaughtered men;
   By whose proud side the ugly Furies run,
   Heark'ning when he shall bid them plague the world;   60
   Over whose zenith, clothed in windy air°
   And eagle's wings joined to her feathered breast,

103

Fame hovereth, sounding of her golden trump,°
That to the adverse poles of that straight line
Which measureth the glorious frame of heaven°   65
The name of mighty Tamburlaine is spread—
And him, fair lady, shall thy eyes behold.
Come.

OLYMPIA [*kneeling*] Take pity of a lady's ruthful tears,
That humbly craves upon her knees to stay   70
And cast her body in the burning flame
That feeds upon her son's and husband's flesh.

TECHELLES [*raising her*]
Madam, sooner shall fire consume us both
Than scorch a face so beautiful as this,
In frame of which Nature hath showed more skill°   75
Than when she gave eternal chaos form,
Drawing from it the shining lamps of heaven.

THERIDAMAS Madam, I am so far in love with you
That you must go with us. No remedy.

OLYMPIA Then carry me I care not where you will,   80
And let the end of this my fatal journey
Be likewise end to my accursèd life.

TECHELLES No madam, but the beginning of your joy.
Come willingly, therefore.

THERIDAMAS Soldiers, now let us meet the general,   85
Who by this time is at Natolia,
Ready to charge the army of the Turk.
The gold, the silver, and the pearl ye got
Rifling this fort, divide in equal shares.
This lady shall have twice so much again   90
Out of the coffers of our treasury.
    Exeunt

[3.5]

[*Enter*] Callapine, Orcanes; [*the kings of*] Jerusalem,
Trebizond, [*and*] Soria; [*and*] Almeda, with their train. [*To
them a Messenger*]

MESSENGER Renownèd emperor, mighty Callapine,
God's great lieutenant over all the world,

Here at Aleppo with an host of men°
Lies Tamburlaine, this king of Persia—
In number more than are the quivering leaves   5
Of Ida's forest, where your highness' hounds°
With open cry pursues the wounded stag—
Who means to girt Natolia's walls with siege,
Fire the town, and overrun the land.

CALLAPINE My royal army is as great as his,   10
That from the bounds of Phrygia to the sea°
Which washeth Cyprus with his brinish waves°
Covers the hills, the valleys, and the plains.
Viceroys and peers to Turkey, play the men!
Whet all your swords to mangle Tamburlaine,   15
His sons, his captains, and his followers.
By Mahomet, not one of them shall live!
The field wherein this battle shall be fought
For ever term the Persians' sepulchre
In memory of this our victory.   20

ORCANES Now he that calls himself the scourge of Jove,
The emperor of the world, and earthly god,
Shall end the warlike progress he intends
And travel headlong to the lake of hell
Where legions of devils, knowing he must die   25
Here in Natolia by your highness' hands,
All brandishing their brands of quenchless fire,
Stretching their monstrous paws, grin with their teeth
And guard the gates to entertain his soul.

CALLAPINE Tell me, viceroys, the number of your men, 30
And what our army royal is esteemed.

JERUSALEM From Palestina and Jerusalem,
Of Hebrews three score thousand fighting men
Are come since last we showed your majesty.°

ORCANES So from Arabia desert, and the bounds   35
Of that sweet land whose brave metropolis
Re-edified the fair Semiramis,°
Came forty thousand warlike foot and horse
Since last we numbered to your majesty.°

TREBIZOND From Trebizond in Asia the Less,   40
Naturalized Turks and stout Bithynians
Came to my bands full fifty thousand more
That, fighting, knows not what retreat doth mean,

Nor e'er return but with the victory,
Since last we numbered to your majesty.   45
SORIA Of Sorians from Halla is repaired,
And neighbour cities of your highness' land,
Ten thousand horse and thirty thousand foot°
Since last we numbered to your majesty;
So that the army royal is esteemed   50
Six hundred thousand valiant fighting men.
CALLAPINE Then welcome, Tamburlaine, unto thy death.
Come, puissant viceroys, let us to the field—
The Persians' sepulchre—and sacrifice
Mountains of breathless men to Mahomet,   55
Who now with Jove opens the firmament
To see the slaughter of our enemies.
> [*Enter*] *Tamburlaine with his three sons* [*Calyphas, Amyras,*
> *Celebinus*], *Usumcasane, with other* [*Soldiers*]
TAMBURLAINE How now, Casane? See, a knot of kings,
Sitting as if they were a-telling riddles.
USUMCASANE My lord, your presence makes them pale and wan.   60
Poor souls, they look as if their deaths were near.
TAMBURLAINE Why, so he is, Casane. I am here.
But yet I'll save their lives and make them slaves.—
Ye petty kings of Turkey, I am come
As Hector did into the Grecian camp   65
To overdare the pride of Graecia
And set his warlike person to the view
Of fierce Achilles, rival of his fame.°
I do you honour in the simile;
For if I should, as Hector did Achilles   70
(The worthiest knight that ever brandished sword)
Challenge in combat any of you all,
I see how fearfully ye would refuse
And fly my glove as from a scorpion.°
ORCANES Now thou art fearful of thy army's strength,   75
Thou wouldst with overmatch of person fight.°
But, shepherd's issue, baseborn Tamburlaine,
Think of thy end. This sword shall lance thy throat.
TAMBURLAINE Villain, the shepherd's issue, at whose birth
Heaven did afford a gracious aspect   80
And joined those stars that shall be opposite
Even till the dissolution of the world,°

And never meant to make a conqueror
So famous as is mighty Tamburlaine,
Shall so torment thee and that Callapine   85
That like a roguish runaway suborned
That villain there, that slave, that Turkish dog,°
To false his service to his sovereign,
As ye shall curse the birth of Tamburlaine.

CALLAPINE Rail not, proud Scythian. I shall now revenge   90
My father's vile abuses and mine own.

JERUSALEM By Mahomet, he shall be tied in chains,
Rowing with Christians in a brigantine
About the Grecian isles to rob and spoil
And turn him to his ancient trade again.   95
Methinks the slave should make a lusty thief.

CALLAPINE Nay, when the battle ends, all we will meet
And sit in council to invent some pain
That most may vex his body and his soul.

TAMBURLAINE Sirrah Callapine, I'll hang a clog about your neck   100
for° running away again. You shall not trouble me thus to come
and fetch you.
But as for you, viceroy, you shall have bits°
And, harnessed like my horses, draw my coach,
And, when ye stay, be lashed with whips of wire.   105
I'll have you learn to feed on provender
And in a stable lie upon the planks.

ORCANES But, Tamburlaine, first thou shalt kneel to us
And humbly crave a pardon for thy life.

TREBIZOND The common soldiers of our mighty host   110
Shall bring thee bound unto the general's tent.

SORIA And all have jointly sworn thy cruel death,
Or bind thee in eternal torment's wrath.

TAMBURLAINE Well, sirs, diet yourselves.° You know I shall have
occasion shortly to journey° you.   115

CELEBINUS See, father, how Almeda the gaoler looks upon us!

TAMBURLAINE [to Almeda] Villain, traitor, damnèd fugitive,
I'll make thee wish the earth had swallowed thee.
See'st thou not death within my wrathful looks?
Go, villain, cast thee headlong from a rock,   120
Or rip thy bowels and rend out thy heart
T'appease my wrath, or else I'll torture thee,
Searing thy hateful flesh with burning irons

And drops of scalding lead, while all thy joints
Be racked and beat asunder with the wheel.   125
For, if thou livest, not any element°
Shall shroud thee from the wrath of Tamburlaine.
CALLAPINE Well, in despite of thee he shall be king.
Come, Almeda, receive this crown of me.
I here invest thee king of Ariadan,   130
Bord'ring on Mare Rosso near to Mecca.°
          [*Callapine offers Almeda a crown, but Almeda hesitates,
          looking fearfully at Tamburlaine*]
ORCANES [*to Almeda*] What, take it, man!
ALMEDA [*to Tamburlaine*] Good my lord, let me take it.
CALLAPINE [*to Almeda*] Dost thou ask him leave? Here, take it.
TAMBURLAINE [*to Almeda*] Go to, sirrah, take your crown, and make   135
up the half dozen.°
          [*Almeda takes the crown*]
So, sirrah, now you are a king you must give arms.°
ORCANES [*to Tamburlaine*] So he shall, and wear thy head in his
scutcheon.
TAMBURLAINE No, let him hang a bunch of keys on his standard, to   140
put him in remembrance he was a gaoler, that, when I take him, I
may knock out his brains with them, and lock you in the stable
when you shall come sweating from my chariot.
TREBIZOND Away! Let us to the field, that the villain may be slain.
TAMBURLAINE [*to a soldier*] Sirrah, prepare whips, and bring my   145
chariot to my tent. For as soon as the battle is done, I'll ride in
triumph through the camp.
          Enter Theridamas, Techelles, and their train
How now, ye petty kings, lo, here are bugs°
Will make the hair stand upright on your heads
And cast your crowns in slavery at their feet.—   150
Welcome, Theridamas and Techelles both.
See ye this rout, and know ye this same king?
THERIDAMAS Ay, my lord. He was Callapine's keeper.
TAMBURLAINE Well, now you see he is a king, look to him,
Theridamas, when we are fighting, lest he hide his crown as the   155
foolish king of Persia did.
SORIA No, Tamburlaine, he shall not be put to that exigent, I
warrant thee.
TAMBURLAINE You know not, sir.°
But now, my followers and my loving friends,   160

Fight as you ever did, like conquerors.
The glory of this happy day is yours.
My stern aspect shall make fair Victory,
Hovering betwixt our armies, light on me,
Loaden with laurel wreaths to crown us all.   165
TECHELLES I smile to think how, when the field is fought
 And rich Natolia ours, our men shall sweat
 With carrying pearl and treasure on their backs.
TAMBURLAINE You shall be princes all immediately.
 Come fight, ye Turks, or yield us victory.   170
ORCANES No, we will meet thee, slavish Tamburlaine.
  Exeunt [in two separate armies]

[4.1]

*Alarm. Amyras and Celebinus issue from the tent° where
Calyphas sits asleep*

AMYRAS Now in their glories shine the golden crowns
Of these proud Turks, much like so many suns
That half dismay the majesty of heaven.
Now, brother, follow we our father's sword
That flies with fury swifter than our thoughts   5
And cuts down armies with his conquering wings.

CELEBINUS Call forth our lazy brother from the tent,
For, if my father miss him in the field,
Wrath kindled in the furnace of his breast
Will send a deadly lightning to his heart.   10

AMYRAS [*calling into the tent*]
Brother, ho! What, given so much to sleep
You cannot leave it when our enemies' drums
And rattling cannons thunder in our ears
Our proper ruin and our father's foil?

CALYPHAS Away, ye fools! My father needs not me,   15
Nor you, in faith, but that you will be thought
More childish-valorous than manly-wise.
If half our camp should sit and sleep with me,
My father were enough to scare the foe.
You do dishonour to his majesty   20
To think our helps will do him any good.

AMYRAS What, dar'st thou then be absent from the fight,
Knowing my father hates thy cowardice
And oft hath warned thee to be still in field
When he himself amidst the thickest troops   25
Beats down our foes, to flesh our taintless swords?°

CALYPHAS I know, sir, what it is to kill a man.
It works remorse of conscience in me.
I take no pleasure to be murderous,
Nor care for blood when wine will quench my thirst.   30

CELEBINUS O cowardly boy! Fie, for shame, come forth.
Thou dost dishonour manhood and thy house.

CALYPHAS Go, go, tall stripling, fight you for us both,
And take my other toward brother here,

For person like to prove a second Mars.   35
'Twill please my mind as well to hear both you
Have won a heap of honour in the field
And left your slender carcasses behind
As if I lay with you for company.
AMYRAS You will not go, then?   40
CALYPHAS You say true.
AMYRAS Were all the lofty mounts of Zona Mundi°
    That fill the midst of farthest Tartary
    Turned into pearl and proffered for my stay,
    I would not bide the fury of my father   45
    When, made a victor in these haughty arms,
    He comes and finds his sons have had no shares
    In all the honours he proposed for us.
CALYPHAS Take you the honour. I will take my ease;
    My wisdom shall excuse my cowardice.   50
    I go into the field before I need?
        Alarm, and Amyras and Celebinus run in°
    The bullets fly at random where they list,
    And, should I go and kill a thousand men,
    I were as soon rewarded with a shot,
    And sooner far than he that never fights.   55
    And, should I go and do nor harm nor good,
    I might have harm, which all the good I have,
    Joined with my father's crown, would never cure.
    I'll to cards.—Perdicas!
        [*Enter Perdicas*]
PERDICAS Here, my lord.   60
CALYPHAS Come, thou and I will go to cards to drive away the time.
PERDICAS Content, my lord. But what shall we play for?
CALYPHAS Who shall kiss the fairest of the Turks' concubines first,
    when my father hath conquered them.
PERDICAS Agreed, i'faith.   65
        They play [*in the open tent*]
CALYPHAS They say I am a coward, Perdicas, and I fear as little their
    taratantaras,° their swords, or their cannons as I do a naked lady
    in a net° of gold, and,° for fear I should be afraid, would put it off
    and come to bed with me.
PERDICAS Such a fear, my lord, would never make ye retire.   70
CALYPHAS I would my father would let me be put in the front of
    such a battle once, to try my valour.

Alarm
What a coil they keep! I believe there will be some hurt done anon
amongst them.

    Enter Tamburlaine, Theridamas, Techelles, Usumcasane,
    Amyras, Celebinus, leading the Turkish kings [Orcanes of
    Natolia, Jerusalem, Trebizond, Soria; and Soldiers]

TAMBURLAINE See now, ye slaves, my children stoops your pride°   75
And leads your glories sheeplike to the sword.
Bring them, my boys, and tell me if the wars
Be not a life that may illustrate gods°
And tickle not your spirits with desire
Still to be trained in arms and chivalry?   80

AMYRAS Shall we let go these kings again, my lord,
To gather greater numbers 'gainst our power,
That they may say it is not chance doth this
But matchless strength and magnanimity?

TAMBURLAINE No, no, Amyras, tempt not Fortune so.   85
Cherish thy valour still with fresh supplies,°
And glut it not with stale and daunted foes.
But where's this coward—villain, not my son,
But traitor to my name and majesty?

    He goes in [the tent] and brings [Calyphas] out
Image of sloth and picture of a slave,   90
The obloquy and scorn of my renown,
How may my heart, thus firèd with mine eyes,°
Wounded with shame and killed with discontent,
Shroud any thought may hold my striving hands°
From martial justice on thy wretched soul?   95

    [Tamburlaine's lieutenants kneel]

THERIDAMAS Yet pardon him, I pray your majesty.

TECHELLES AND USUMCASANE
Let all of us entreat your highness' pardon.

TAMBURLAINE Stand up, ye base, unworthy soldiers!
Know ye not yet the argument of arms?°

    [They stand. Amyras and Celebinus kneel]

AMYRAS Good my lord, let him be forgiven for once,   100
And we will force him to the field hereafter.

TAMBURLAINE Stand up, my boys, and I will teach ye arms°
And what the jealousy of wars must do.°

    [They stand]
O Samarcanda, where I breathèd first

And joyed the fire of this martial flesh,°   105
Blush, blush, fair city, at thine honour's foil
And shame of nature, which Jaertis' stream,
Embracing thee with deepest of his love,°
Can never wash from thy distainèd brows!
Here, Jove, receive his fainting soul again—   110
    [*He stabs Calyphas*]
A form not meet to give that subject essence
Whose matter is the flesh of Tamburlaine,
Wherein an incorporeal spirit moves,
Made of the mould whereof thyself consists,°
Which makes me valiant, proud, ambitious,   115
Ready to levy power against thy throne,
That I might move the turning spheres of heaven;
For earth and all this airy region
Cannot contain the state of Tamburlaine.
By Mahomet, thy mighty friend, I swear,°   120
In sending to my issue such a soul,°
Created of the massy dregs of earth,
The scum and tartar of the elements,°
Wherein was neither courage, strength, or wit,
But folly, sloth, and damnèd idleness,   125
Thou hast procured a greater enemy
Than he that darted mountains at thy head,°
Shaking the burden mighty Atlas bears,
Whereat thou, trembling, hidd'st thee in the air,
Clothed with a pitchy cloud for being seen.—°   130
And now, ye cankered curs of Asia,
That will not see the strength of Tamburlaine°
Although it shine as brightly as the sun,
Now you shall feel the strength of Tamburlaine,
And by the state of his supremacy   135
Approve the difference 'twixt himself and you.
ORCANES Thou showest the difference 'twixt ourselves and thee
    In this thy barbarous damnèd tyranny.
JERUSALEM Thy victories are grown so violent
    That shortly heaven, filled with the meteors   140
    Of blood and fire thy tyrannies have made,
    Will pour down blood and fire on thy head,
    Whose scalding drops will pierce thy seething brains
    And with our bloods revenge our bloods on thee.°

TAMBURLAINE Villains, these terrors and these tyrannies—   145
　　If tyrannies war's justice ye repute—°
　　I execute, enjoined me from above,
　　To scourge the pride of such as heaven abhors;
　　Nor am I made arch-monarch of the world,
　　Crowned and invested by the hand of Jove,   150
　　For deeds of bounty or nobility.
　　But since I exercise a greater name,
　　The scourge of God and terror of the world,
　　I must apply myself to fit those terms,
　　In war, in blood, in death, in cruelty,   155
　　And plague such peasants as resist in me
　　The power of heaven's eternal majesty.
　　Theridamas, Techelles, and Casane,
　　Ransack the tents and the pavilions
　　Of these proud Turks, and take their concubines.   160
　　Make them bury this effeminate brat,
　　For not a common soldier shall defile
　　His manly fingers with so faint a boy.
　　Then bring those Turkish harlots to my tent,
　　And I'll dispose them as it likes me best.   165
　　Meanwhile, take him in.
SOLDIERS We will, my lord.
　　　　　[Exeunt Tamburlaine's Lieutenants and some Soldiers with
　　　　　the body of Calyphas]
JERUSALEM O damnèd monster, nay, a fiend of hell,
　　Whose cruelties are not so harsh as thine,
　　Nor yet imposed with such a bitter hate!   170
ORCANES Revenge it, Rhadamanth and Aeacus,°
　　And let your hates, extended in his pains,
　　Expel the hate wherewith he pains our souls!
TREBIZOND May never day give virtue to his eyes,
　　Whose sight, composed of fury and of fire,   175
　　Doth send such stern affections to his heart!
SORIA May never spirit, vein, or artier feed
　　The cursèd substance of that cruel heart,
　　But, wanting moisture and remorseful blood,
　　Dry up with anger and consume with heat!   180
TAMBURLAINE Well, bark, ye dogs. I'll bridle all your tongues
　　And bind them close with bits of burnished steel
　　Down to the channels of your hateful throats,

And with the pains my rigour shall inflict
I'll make ye roar, that earth may echo forth 185
The far-resounding torments ye sustain,
As when an herd of lusty Cimbrian bulls°
Run mourning round about the females' miss,°
And, stung with fury of their following,°
Fill all the air with troublous bellowing. 190
I will, with engines never exercised,
Conquer, sack, and utterly consume
Your cities and your golden palaces,
And with the flames that beat against the clouds
Incense the heavens and make the stars to melt, 195
As if they were the tears of Mahomet
For hot consumption of his country's pride.°
And, till by vision or by speech I hear
Immortal Jove say 'Cease, my Tamburlaine',
I will persist a terror to the world,° 200
Making the meteors that, like armèd men,
Are seen to march upon the towers of heaven,
Run tilting round about the firmament,
And break their burning lances in the air
For honour of my wondrous victories. 205
Come, bring them in to our pavilion.
                Exeunt, [*the captive Lords led under guard*]

[4.2]

[*Enter*]° *Olympia alone,* [*holding a vial of ointment*]
OLYMPIA Distressed Olympia, whose weeping eyes
Since thy arrival here beheld no sun,
But, closed within the compass of a tent,
Hath stained thy cheeks and made thee look like death,
Devise some means to rid thee of thy life 5
Rather than yield to his detested suit
Whose drift is only to dishonour thee.
And since this earth, dewed with thy brinish tears,
Affords no herbs whose taste may poison thee,
Nor yet this air, beat often with thy sighs, 10
Contagious smells and vapours to infect thee,

Nor thy close cave a sword to murder thee,
Let this invention be the instrument.
    Enter Theridamas
THERIDAMAS Well met, Olympia. I sought thee in my tent,
But, when I saw the place obscure and dark   15
Which with thy beauty thou wast wont to light,
Enraged, I ran about the fields for thee,
Supposing amorous Jove had sent his son,
The wingèd Hermes, to convey thee hence.
But now I find thee, and that fear is past.   20
Tell me, Olympia, wilt thou grant my suit?
OLYMPIA My lord and husband's death, with my sweet son's,
With whom I buried all affections
Save grief and sorrow, which torment my heart,
Forbids my mind to entertain a thought   25
That tends to love, but meditate on death—
A fitter subject for a pensive soul.
THERIDAMAS Olympia, pity him in whom thy looks
Have greater operation and more force
Than Cynthia's in the watery wilderness,°   30
For with thy view my joys are at the full,°
And ebb again as thou depart'st from me.
OLYMPIA Ah, pity me, my lord, and draw your sword,
Making a passage for my troubled soul,
Which beats against this prison to get out   35
And meet my husband and my loving son.
THERIDAMAS Nothing but still thy husband and thy son?
Leave this, my love, and listen more to me.
Thou shalt be stately queen of fair Argier,
And, clothed in costly cloth of massy gold,   40
Upon the marble turrets of my court°
Sit like to Venus in her chair of state,
Commanding all thy princely eye desires;
And I will cast off arms and sit with thee,
Spending my life in sweet discourse of love.   45
OLYMPIA No such discourse is pleasant in mine ears
But that where every period ends with death
And every line begins with death again.
I cannot love to be an empress.°
THERIDAMAS Nay, lady, then if nothing will prevail   50
I'll use some other means to make you yield.

Such is the sudden fury of my love,
I must and will be pleased, and you shall yield.
Come to the tent again.
OLYMPIA Stay, good my lord! And, will you save my honour,°   55
I'll give your grace a present of such price
As all the world cannot afford the like.
THERIDAMAS What is it?
OLYMPIA An ointment which a cunning alchemist
Distillèd from the purest balsamum   60
And simplest extracts of all minerals,
In which the essential form of marble stone,
Tempered by science metaphysical°
And spells of magic from the mouths of spirits,
With which if you but 'noint your tender skin,   65
Nor pistol, sword, nor lance can pierce your flesh.
THERIDAMAS Why, madam, think ye to mock me thus palpably?
OLYMPIA To prove it, I will 'noint my naked throat,
Which when you stab, look on your weapon's point,
And you shall see't rebated with the blow.   70
THERIDAMAS Why gave you not your husband some of it,
If you loved him, and it so precious?
OLYMPIA My purpose was, my lord, to spend it so,
But was prevented by his sudden end.
And for a present easy proof hereof,   75
That I dissemble not, try it on me.
THERIDAMAS I will, Olympia, and will keep it for
The richest present of this eastern world.
    She 'noints her throat
OLYMPIA Now stab, my lord, and mark your weapon's point,
That will be blunted if the blow be great.°   80
THERIDAMAS [*stabbing her throat*] Here then, Olympia.
What, have I slain her? Villain, stab thyself!
Cut off this arm that murderèd my love,
In whom the learned rabbis of this age
Might find as many wondrous miracles   85
As in the theoria of the world!°
Now hell is fairer than Elysium;
A greater lamp than that bright eye of heaven
From whence the stars do borrow all their light
Wanders about the black circumference,   90
And now the damnèd souls are free from pain,

For every Fury gazeth on her looks.
Infernal Dis is courting of my love,
Inventing masques and stately shows for her,
Opening the doors of his rich treasury   95
To entertain this queen of chastity,
Whose body shall be tombed with all the pomp
The treasure of my kingdom may afford.
     Exit, taking her away

[4.3]

[Enter] Tamburlaine, drawn in his chariot by [the kings of]
Trebizond and Soria with bits in their mouths, reins in his
left hand, in his right hand a whip, with which he scourgeth
them. Techelles, Theridamas, Usumcasane, Amyras,
Celebinus; [Orcanes of] Natolia and [the king of] Jerusalem
led by° with five or six common Soldiers

TAMBURLAINE Holla, ye pampered jades of Asia!
What, can ye draw but twenty miles a day
And have so proud a chariot at your heels
And such a coachman as great Tamburlaine,
But from Asphaltis, where I conquered you,   5
To Byron here where thus I honour you?°
The horse that guide the golden eye of heaven
And blow the morning from their nosterils,°
Making their fiery gait above the clouds,
Are not so honoured in their governor°   10
As you, ye slaves, in mighty Tamburlaine.
The headstrong jades of Thrace Alcides tamed,°
That King Aegeus fed with human flesh
And made so wanton that they knew their strengths,
Were not subdued with valour more divine   15
Than you by this unconquered arm of mine.
To make you fierce, and fit my appetite,
You shall be fed with flesh as raw as blood
And drink in pails the strongest muscatel.
If you can live with it, then live, and draw   20
My chariot swifter than the racking clouds.°
If not, then die like beasts and fit for nought

But perches for the black and fatal ravens.
Thus am I right the scourge of highest Jove,°
And see the figure of my dignity°   25
By which I hold my name and majesty.
AMYRAS Let me have coach, my lord, that I may ride
And thus be drawn with these two idle kings.°
TAMBURLAINE Thy youth forbids such ease, my kingly boy.
They shall tomorrow draw my chariot   30
While these their fellow kings may be refreshed.
ORCANES O thou that swayest the region under earth,
And art a king as absolute as Jove,
Come as thou didst in fruitful Sicily,
Surveying all the glories of the land!   35
And as thou took'st the fair Proserpina,
Joying the fruit of Ceres' garden plot,
For love, for honour, and to make her queen,°
So for just hate, for shame, and to subdue
This proud contemner of thy dreadful power,   40
Come once in fury and survey his pride,°
Haling him headlong to the lowest hell!
THERIDAMAS [to Tamburlaine]
Your majesty must get some bits for these,
To bridle their contemptuous cursing tongues
That like unruly never-broken jades
Break through the hedges of their hateful mouths°   45
And pass their fixèd bounds exceedingly.
TECHELLES Nay, we will break the hedges of their mouths
And pull their kicking colts out of their pastures.°
USUMCASANE Your majesty already hath devised   50
A mean as fit as may be to restrain
These coltish coach-horse tongues from blasphemy.
          [Celebinus bridles Orcanes]°
CELEBINUS How like you that, sir king? Why speak you not?
JERUSALEM Ah, cruel brat, sprung from a tyrant's loins,
How like his cursèd father he begins   55
To practise taunts and bitter tyrannies!
TAMBURLAINE Ay, Turk, I tell thee, this same boy is he
That must, advanced in higher pomp than this,
Rifle the kingdoms I shall leave unsacked
If Jove, esteeming me too good for earth,   60
Raise me to match the fair Aldebaran°

Above the threefold astracism of heaven°
Before I conquer all the triple world.°
Now fetch me out the Turkish concubines.
I will prefer them for the funeral   65
They have bestowed on my abortive son.°
        The Concubines are brought in
Where are my common soldiers now that fought
So lion-like upon Asphaltis' plains?
SOLDIERS Here, my lord.
TAMBURLAINE Hold ye, tall soldiers. Take ye queens apiece—°   70
I mean such queens as were kings' concubines.
Take them. Divide them and their jewels too,
And let them equally serve all your turns.°
SOLDIERS We thank your majesty.
TAMBURLAINE Brawl not, I warn you, for your lechery,°   75
For every man that so offends shall die.
ORCANES Injurious tyrant, wilt thou so defame
The hateful fortunes of thy victory
To exercise upon such guiltless dames
The violence of thy common soldiers' lust?   80
TAMBURLAINE Live continent, then, ye slaves, and meet not me
With troops of harlots at your slothful heels.°
CONCUBINES O, pity us, my lord, and save our honours!
TAMBURLAINE Are ye not gone, ye villains, with your spoils?
        [*The Soldiers*] *run away with the Ladies*
JERUSALEM O, merciless, infernal cruelty!   85
TAMBURLAINE 'Save your honours'! 'Twere but time indeed,°
Lost long before you knew what honour meant.
THERIDAMAS It seems they meant to conquer us, my lord,
And make us jesting pageants for their trulls.
TAMBURLAINE And now themselves shall make our pageant,   90
And common soldiers jest with all their trulls.°
Let them take pleasure soundly in their spoils°
Till we prepare our march to Babylon,
Whither we next make expedition.
TECHELLES Let us not be idle, then, my lord,   95
But presently be prest to conquer it.
TAMBURLAINE We will, Techelles.—Forward, then, ye jades!
Now crouch, ye kings of greatest Asia,
And tremble when ye hear this scourge will come
That whips down cities and controlleth crowns,°   100

Adding their wealth and treasure to my store.
The Euxine Sea north to Natolia,
The Terrene west, the Caspian north-north-east,
And on the south Sinus Arabicus,°
Shall all be loaden with the martial spoils   105
We will convey with us to Persia.
Then shall my native city Samarcanda
And crystal waves of fresh Jaertis' stream,°
The pride and beauty of her princely seat,
Be famous through the furthest continents;   110
For there my palace royal shall be placed,
Whose shining turrets shall dismay the heavens
And cast the fame of Ilion's tower to hell.°
Thorough the streets with troops of conquered kings
I'll ride in golden armour like the sun,   115
And in my helm a triple plume shall spring,
Spangled with diamonds dancing in the air,
To note me emperor of the threefold world,
Like to an almond tree ymounted high
Upon the lofty and celestial mount   120
Of ever-green Selinus, quaintly decked°
With blooms more white than Erycina's brows,°
Whose tender blossoms tremble every one
At ev'ry little breath that thorough heaven is blown.
Then in my coach, like Saturn's royal son,°   125
Mounted his shining chariot gilt with fire°
And drawn with princely eagles through the path°
Paved with bright crystal and enchased with stars
When all the gods stand gazing at his pomp,
So will I ride through Samarcanda streets,   130
Until my soul, dissevered from this flesh,
Shall mount the milk-white way and meet him there.
To Babylon, my lords, to Babylon!
          Exeunt, [Tamburlaine in his chariot drawn by the kings of
          Trebizond and Soria]

[5.1]

Enter the Governor of Babylon upon the walls° with
[Maximus and] others

GOVERNOR What saith Maximus?

MAXIMUS My lord, the breach the enemy hath made
Gives such assurance of our overthrow
That little hope is left to save our lives
Or hold our city from the conqueror's hands.   5
Then hang out flags, my lord, of humble truce,
And satisfy the people's general prayers
That Tamburlaine's intolerable wrath
May be suppressed by our submission.

GOVERNOR Villain, respects thou more thy slavish life   10
Than honour of thy country or thy name?
Is not my life and state as dear to me,
The city and my native country's weal,
As any thing of price with thy conceit?°
Have we not hope, for all our battered walls,°   15
To live secure and keep his forces out,
When this our famous lake of Limnasphaltis
Makes walls afresh with every thing that falls
Into the liquid substance of his stream,
More strong than are the gates of death or hell?°   20
What faintness should dismay our courages
When we are thus defenced against our foe
And have no terror but his threat'ning looks?

Enter another [Citizen above], kneeling to the Governor

CITIZEN My lord, if ever you did deed of ruth
And now will work a refuge to our lives,   25
Offer submission, hang up flags of truce,
That Tamburlaine may pity our distress
And use us like a loving conqueror.
Though this be held his last day's dreadful siege
Wherein he spareth neither man nor child,   30
Yet are there Christians of Georgia here,
Whose state he ever pitied and relieved,
Will get his pardon if your grace would send.°

GOVERNOR How is my soul environèd,

And this eternized city Babylon   35
Filled with a pack of faint-heart fugitives
That thus entreat their shame and servitude!
    [*Enter another Citizen, above, kneeling to the Governor*]
SECOND CITIZEN My lord, if ever you will win our hearts,
Yield up the town, save our wives and children!
For I will cast myself from off these walls   40
Or die some death of quickest violence
Before I bide the wrath of Tamburlaine.
GOVERNOR Villains, cowards, traitors to our state!
Fall to the earth and pierce the pit of hell,
That legions of tormenting spirits may vex   45
Your slavish bosoms with continual pains!
I care not, nor the town will never yield
As long as any life is in my breast.
    Enter Theridamas and Techelles, with other Soldiers
THERIDAMAS Thou desperate governor of Babylon,
To save thy life, and us a little labour,   50
Yield speedily the city to our hands,
Or else be sure thou shalt be forced with pains
More exquisite than ever traitor felt.
GOVERNOR Tyrant, I turn the traitor in thy throat,°
And will defend it in despite of thee.—   55
Call up the soldiers to defend these walls.
TECHELLES Yield, foolish governor. We offer more
Than ever yet we did to such proud slaves
As durst resist us till our third day's siege.
Thou seest us prest to give the last assault,   60
And that shall bide no more regard of parley.°
GOVERNOR Assault and spare not. We will never yield.
    Alarm, and [Tamburlaine's forces] scale the walls. [Exeunt
    Citizens and Governor above, followed in by Theridamas,
    Techelles, and their Soldiers.] Enter Tamburlaine [all in
    black, on the main stage, drawn in his chariot by the kings of
    Trebizond and Soria], with Usumcasane, Amyras, and
    Celebinus, with others; the two spare kings [Orcanes of
    Natolia, and Jerusalem]°
TAMBURLAINE The stately buildings of fair Babylon,
Whose lofty pillars, higher than the clouds,
Were wont to guide the seaman in the deep,°   65
Being carried thither by the cannon's force,°

Now fill the mouth of Limnasphaltis' lake
And make a bridge unto the battered walls.
Where Belus, Ninus, and great Alexander°
Have rode in triumph, triumphs Tamburlaine,   70
Whose chariot wheels have burst th'Assyrians' bones,
Drawn with these kings on heaps of carcasses.°
Now in the place where fair Semiramis,
Courted by kings and peers of Asia,
Hath trod the measures, do my soldiers march;°   75
And in the streets, where brave Assyrian dames
Have rid in pomp like rich Saturnia,°
With furious words and frowning visages
My horsemen brandish their unruly blades.

> *Enter Theridamas and Techelles, bringing the Governor of*
> *Babylon*

Who have ye there, my lords?   80

THERIDAMAS The sturdy governor of Babylon,
That made us all the labour for the town
And used such slender reck'ning of your majesty.°

TAMBURLAINE Go bind the villain. He shall hang in chains
Upon the ruins of this conquered town.—   85
Sirrah, the view of our vermilion tents,°
Which threatened more than if the region
Next underneath the element of fire°
Were full of comets and of blazing stars
Whose flaming trains should reach down to the earth,   90
Could not affright you; no, nor I myself,
The wrathful messenger of mighty Jove,
That with his sword hath quailed all earthly kings,°
Could not persuade you to submission,
But still the ports were shut. Villain, I say,   95
Should I but touch the rusty gates of hell,
The triple-headed Cerberus would howl°
And wake black Jove to crouch and kneel to me;°
But I have sent volleys of shot to you,
Yet could not enter till the breach was made.   100

GOVERNOR Nor, if my body could have stopped the breach,
Shouldst thou have entered, cruel Tamburlaine.
'Tis not thy bloody tents can make me yield,
Nor yet thyself, the anger of the Highest,°
For, though thy cannon shook the city walls,   105

My heart did never quake, or courage faint.
TAMBURLAINE Well, now I'll make it quake.—Go draw him up.
Hang him in chains upon the city walls,
And let my soldiers shoot the slave to death.
GOVERNOR Vile monster, born of some infernal hag,   110
And sent from hell to tyrannize on earth,
Do all thy worst. Nor death, nor Tamburlaine,
Torture, or pain can daunt my dreadless mind.
TAMBURLAINE Up with him, then; his body shall be scarred.
GOVERNOR But Tamburlaine, in Limnasphaltis' lake   115
There lies more gold than Babylon is worth,
Which when the city was besieged I hid.
Save but my life, and I will give it thee.
TAMBURLAINE Then, for all your valour, you would save your life?
Whereabout lies it?   120
GOVERNOR Under a hollow bank, right opposite
Against the western gate of Babylon.
TAMBURLAINE Go thither, some of you, and take his gold.°
          [*Exeunt some Soldiers*]
The rest, forward with execution!
Away with him hence; let him speak no more.—   125
I think I make your courage something quail.
          [*Exit Governor,° led off by Soldiers*]
When this is done, we'll march from Babylon
And make our greatest haste to Persia.
These jades are broken-winded and half tired;
Unharness them, and let me have fresh horse.   130
          [*Soldiers unharness Trebizond and Soria*]
So, now their best is done to honour me,°
Take them and hang them both up presently.
TREBIZOND Vile tyrant, barbarous, bloody Tamburlaine!
TAMBURLAINE Take them away, Theridamas. See them dispatched.
THERIDAMAS I will, my lord.   135
          [*Exit Theridamas with the kings of Trebizond and Soria,
          guarded*]
TAMBURLAINE Come, Asian viceroys, to your tasks a while,
And take such fortune as your fellows felt.
ORCANES First let thy Scythian horse tear both our limbs
Rather than we should draw thy chariot
And like base slaves abject our princely minds   140
To vile and ignominious servitude.

125

JERUSALEM Rather lend me thy weapon, Tamburlaine,
  That I may sheathe it in this breast of mine.
  A thousand deaths could not torment our hearts
  More than the thought of this doth vex our souls.   145
AMYRAS They will talk still, my lord, if you do not bridle them.
TAMBURLAINE Bridle them, and let me to my coach.
      *They bridle [and harness] them. [The Governor of Babylon
      is discovered hanging in chains. Re-enter Theridamas.°
      Tamburlaine mounts his chariot]*
AMYRAS See now, my lord, how brave the captain hangs!
TAMBURLAINE 'Tis brave indeed, my boy. Well done!
  Shoot first, my lord, and then the rest shall follow.   150
THERIDAMAS Then have at him to begin withal.
      Theridamas shoots [and hits the Governor]
GOVERNOR Yet save my life, and let this wound appease
  The mortal fury of great Tamburlaine.
TAMBURLAINE No, though Asphaltis' lake were liquid gold
  And offered me as ransom for thy life,   155
  Yet shouldst thou die.—Shoot at him all at once.
      They shoot
  So, now he hangs like Baghdad's governor,°
  Having as many bullets in his flesh
  As there be breaches in her battered wall.
  Go now and bind the burghers hand and foot,   160
  And cast them headlong in the city's lake;
  Tartars and Persians shall inhabit there,
  And, to command the city, I will build
  A citadel, that all Africa,
  Which hath been subject to the Persian king,   165
  Shall pay me tribute for, in Babylon.
TECHELLES What shall be done with their wives and children, my lord?
TAMBURLAINE Techelles, drown them all, man, woman, and child.
  Leave not a Babylonian in the town.
TECHELLES I will about it straight. Come, soldiers.   170
      Exit [Techelles with Soldiers]
TAMBURLAINE Now, Casane, where's the Turkish Alcoran
  And all the heaps of superstitious books
  Found in the temples of that Mahomet
  Whom I have thought a god? They shall be burnt.
USUMCASANE [*presenting the books*] Here they are, my lord.   175
TAMBURLAINE Well said. Let there be a fire presently.

[Soldiers light a fire]°
In vain, I see, men worship Mahomet.
My sword hath sent millions of Turks to hell,
Slew all his priests, his kinsmen, and his friends,
And yet I live untouched by Mahomet.   180
There is a God full of revenging wrath,
From whom the thunder and the lightning breaks,
Whose scourge I am, and him will I obey.
So, Casane, fling them in the fire.
        [The books are burnt]
Now, Mahomet, if thou have any power,   185
Come down thyself and work a miracle.
Thou art not worthy to be worshippèd
That suffers flames of fire to burn the writ
Wherein the sum of thy religion rests.
Why send'st thou not a furious whirlwind down   190
To blow thy Alcoran up to thy throne
Where men report thou sitt'st by God himself,
Or vengeance on the head of Tamburlaine,°
That shakes his sword against thy majesty
And spurns the abstracts of thy foolish laws?°   195
Well, soldiers, Mahomet remains in hell;
He cannot hear the voice of Tamburlaine.
Seek out another godhead to adore,
The God that sits in heaven, if any god,
For he is God alone, and none but he.   200
        [Re-enter Techelles]
TECHELLES I have fulfilled your highness' will, my lord.
    Thousands of men, drowned in Asphaltis' lake,
    Have made the water swell above the banks,
    And fishes, fed by human carcasses,
    Amazed, swim up and down upon the waves   205
    As when they swallow asafoetida,
    Which makes them fleet aloft and gasp for air.
TAMBURLAINE Well, then, my friendly lords, what now remains
    But that we leave sufficient garrison
    And presently depart to Persia   210
    To triumph after all our victories?
THERIDAMAS Ay, good my lord. Let us in haste to Persia,
    And let this captain be removed the walls°
    To some high hill about the city here.

TAMBURLAINE Let it be so. About it, soldiers.   215
   But stay. I feel myself distempered suddenly.
TECHELLES What is it dares distemper Tamburlaine?
TAMBURLAINE Something, Techelles, but I know not what.
   But forth, ye vassals! Whatsoe'er it be,
   Sickness or death can never conquer me.   220
       Exeunt, [Tamburlaine drawn in his chariot by Orcanes and
       the king of Jerusalem. The Governor's body is removed from
       the wall or hidden from view]

[5.2]

       Enter Callapine, [the king of] Amasia, [a Captain, Soldiers,]
       with drums and trumpets
CALLAPINE King of Amasia, now our mighty host
   Marcheth in Asia Major, where the streams
   Of Euphrates and Tigris swiftly runs,
   And here may we behold great Babylon,
   Circled about with Limnasphaltis' lake,   5
   Where Tamburlaine with all his army lies—
   Which being faint and weary with the siege,
   We may lie ready to encounter him
   Before his host be full from Babylon,°
   And so revenge our latest grievous loss,   10
   If God or Mahomet send any aid.
AMASIA Doubt not, my lord, but we shall conquer him.
   The monster that hath drunk a sea of blood
   And yet gapes still for more to quench his thirst,
   Our Turkish swords shall headlong send to hell;   15
   And that vile carcass drawn by warlike kings
   The fowls shall eat, for never sepulchre
   Shall grace that baseborn tyrant Tamburlaine.
CALLAPINE When I record my parents' slavish life,
   Their cruel death, mine own captivity,   20
   My viceroys' bondage under Tamburlaine,
   Methinks I could sustain a thousand deaths
   To be revenged of all his villainy.
   Ah, sacred Mahomet! Thou that hast seen
   Millions of Turks perish by Tamburlaine,   25
   Kingdoms made waste, brave cities sacked and burnt,

And but one host is left to honour thee,
Aid thy obedient servant Callapine,
And make him, after all these overthrows,
To triumph over cursèd Tamburlaine! 30
AMASIA Fear not, my lord. I see great Mahomet
Clothèd in purple clouds, and on his head
A chaplet brighter than Apollo's crown,
Marching about the air with armèd men
To join with you against this Tamburlaine. 35
CAPTAIN Renownèd general, mighty Callapine,
Though God himself and holy Mahomet
Should come in person to resist your power,
Yet might your mighty host encounter all
And pull proud Tamburlaine upon his knees 40
To sue for mercy at your highness' feet.
CALLAPINE Captain, the force of Tamburlaine is great,
His fortune greater, and the victories
Wherewith he hath so sore dismayed the world
Are greatest to discourage all our drifts. 45
Yet when the pride of Cynthia is at full
She wanes again, and so shall his, I hope,
For we have here the chief selected men
Of twenty several kingdoms at the least.
Nor ploughman, priest, nor merchant stays at home; 50
All Turkey is in arms with Callapine,
And never will we sunder camps and arms
Before himself or his be conquerèd.
This is the time that must eternize me
For conquering the tyrant of the world. 55
Come, soldiers, let us lie in wait for him,
And if we find him absent from his camp
Or that it be rejoined again at full,°
Assail it and be sure of victory.
    Exeunt

[5.3]

[Enter] Theridamas, Techelles, Usumcasane

THERIDAMAS Weep, heavens, and vanish into liquid tears!
    Fall, stars that govern his nativity,
    And summon all the shining lamps of heaven
    To cast their bootless fires to the earth
    And shed their feeble influence in the air!   5
    Muffle your beauties with eternal clouds,
    For hell and darkness pitch their pitchy tents,
    And Death with armies of Cimmerian spirits°
    Gives battle 'gainst the heart of Tamburlaine.
    Now, in defiance of that wonted love   10
    Your sacred virtues poured upon his throne
    And made his state an honour to the heavens,
    These cowards invisibly assail his soul
    And threaten conquest on our sovereign;
    But if he die, your glories are disgraced,   15
    Earth droops and says that hell in heaven is placed.
TECHELLES O then, ye powers that sway eternal seats
    And guide this massy substance of the earth,
    If you retain desert of holiness,°
    As your supreme estates instruct our thoughts,   20
    Be not inconstant, careless of your fame;
    Bear not the burden of your enemies' joys,°
    Triumphing in his fall whom you advanced;
    But as his birth, life, health, and majesty
    Were strangely blest and governèd by heaven,   25
    So honour, heaven, till heaven dissolvèd be,
    His birth, his life, his health, and majesty.
USUMCASANE Blush, heaven, to lose the honour of thy name,
    To see thy footstool set upon thy head,
    And let no baseness in thy haughty breast   30
    Sustain a shame of such inexcellence,°
    To see the devils mount in angels' thrones
    And angels dive into the pools of hell.
    And though they think their painful date is out°
    And that their power is puissant as Jove's,   35
    Which makes them manage arms against thy state,°
    Yet make them feel the strength of Tamburlaine,°

Thy instrument and note of majesty,°
Is greater far than they can thus subdue;
For if he die, thy glory is disgraced,   40
Earth droops and says that hell in heaven is placed.
> [*Enter Tamburlaine in his chariot, drawn by Orcanes of
> Natolia and the king of Jerusalem, and attended by Amyras,
> Celebinus, and Physicians*]

TAMBURLAINE What daring god torments my body thus
And seeks to conquer mighty Tamburlaine?
Shall sickness prove me now to be a man,°
That have been termed the terror of the world?   45
Techelles and the rest, come take your swords
And threaten him whose hand afflicts my soul.
Come let us march against the powers of heaven
And set black streamers in the firmament
To signify the slaughter of the gods.   50
Ah, friends, what shall I do? I cannot stand.
Come, carry me to war against the gods,
That thus envy the health of Tamburlaine.°

THERIDAMAS Ah, good my lord, leave these impatient words,
Which add much danger to your malady.   55

TAMBURLAINE Why shall I sit and languish in this pain?
No! Strike the drums, and, in revenge of this,
Come, let us charge our spears and pierce his breast°
Whose shoulders bear the axis of the world,
That if I perish, heaven and earth may fade.   60
Theridamas, haste to the court of Jove.
Will him to send Apollo hither straight
To cure me, or I'll fetch him down myself.

TECHELLES Sit still, my gracious lord. This grief will cease
And cannot last, it is so violent.   65

TAMBURLAINE Not last, Techelles? No, for I shall die.
See where my slave, the ugly monster Death,
Shaking and quivering, pale and wan for fear,
Stands aiming at me with his murdering dart,
Who flies away at every glance I give,   70
And when I look away comes stealing on.—
Villain, away, and hie thee to the field!
I and mine army come to load thy bark
With souls of thousand mangled carcasses.—
Look where he goes! But see, he comes again   75

Because I stay. Techelles, let us march,
And weary Death with bearing souls to hell.

PHYSICIAN [*offering medicine*]
Pleaseth your majesty to drink this potion,
Which will abate the fury of your fit
And cause some milder spirits govern you.°   80

TAMBURLAINE Tell me, what think you of my sickness now?

PHYSICIAN I viewed your urine, and the hypostasis,°
Thick and obscure, doth make your danger great;
Your veins are full of accidental heat°
Whereby the moisture of your blood is dried.   85
The humidum and calor, which some hold°
Is not a parcel of the elements
But of a substance more divine and pure,
Is almost clean extinguishèd and spent,
Which, being the cause of life, imports your death.   90
Besides, my lord, this day is critical,°
Dangerous to those whose crisis is as yours.
Your artiers, which alongst the veins convey°
The lively spirits which the heart engenders,
Are parched and void of spirit, that the soul,   95
Wanting those organons by which it moves,°
Cannot endure by argument of art.°
Yet if your majesty may escape this day,
No doubt but you shall soon recover all.

TAMBURLAINE Then will I comfort all my vital parts   100
And live in spite of Death above a day.
        Alarm within. [*Enter a Messenger*]

MESSENGER My lord, young Callapine, that lately fled from your
majesty, hath now gathered a fresh army, and, hearing your
absence in the field, offers to set upon us presently.

TAMBURLAINE See, my physicians, now, how Jove hath sent   105
A present medicine to recure my pain!
My looks shall make them fly, and, might I follow,
There should not one of all the villain's power
Live to give offer of another fight.

USUMCASANE I joy, my lord, your highness is so strong,   110
That can endure so well your royal presence°
Which only will dismay the enemy.°

TAMBURLAINE I know it well, Casane.—Draw, you slaves!
In spite of Death I will go show my face.

Alarm. Tamburlaine goes in [in his chariot], and comes out
again with all the rest

TAMBURLAINE Thus are the villains, cowards, fled for fear,   115
Like summer's vapours vanished by the sun.°
And could I but a while pursue the field,
That Callapine should be my slave again.
But I perceive my martial strength is spent;
In vain I strive and rail against those powers   120
That mean t'invest me in a higher throne,
As much too high for this disdainful earth.
Give me a map, then, let me see how much
Is left for me to conquer all the world,
That these my boys may finish all my wants.   125

One brings a map

Here I began to march towards Persia,
Along Armenia and the Caspian Sea,
And thence unto Bythinia, where I took
The Turk and his great empress prisoners;
Then marched I into Egypt and Arabia,   130
And here, not far from Alexandria,
Whereas the Terrene and the Red Sea meet,
Being distant less than full a hundred leagues,
I meant to cut a channel to them both,
That men might quickly sail to India.°   135
From thence to Nubia, near Borno lake,
And so along the Ethiopian sea,
Cutting the tropic line of Capricorn,
I conquered all as far as Zanzibar.
Then by the northern part of Africa   140
I came at last to Graecia, and from thence
To Asia, where I stay against my will,
Which is from Scythia, where I first began,
Backward and forwards, near five thousand leagues.
Look here, my boys, see what a world of ground   145
Lies westward from the midst of Cancer's line
Unto the rising of this earthly globe,
Whereas the sun, declining from our sight,
Begins the day with our Antipodes;°
And shall I die, and this unconquerèd?   150
Lo, here, my sons, are all the golden mines,°
Inestimable drugs, and precious stones,

More worth than Asia and the world beside;
And from th'Antarctic Pole eastward behold
As much more land, which never was descried,°   155
Wherein are rocks of pearl that shine as bright
As all the lamps that beautify the sky;
And shall I die, and this unconquerèd?
Here, lovely boys: what Death forbids my life,
That let your lives command in spite of Death.   160

AMYRAS Alas, my lord, how should our bleeding hearts,
Wounded and broken with your highness' grief,
Retain a thought of joy or spark of life?
Your soul gives essence to our wretched subjects,
Whose matter is incorporate in your flesh.°   165

CELEBINUS Your pains do pierce our souls; no hope survives,
For by your life we entertain our lives.

TAMBURLAINE But sons, this subject, not of force enough°
To hold the fiery spirit it contains,
Must part, imparting his impressions°   170
By equal portions into both your breasts;
My flesh, divided in your precious shapes,
Shall still retain my spirit though I die,
And live in all your seeds immortally.
Then now remove me, that I may resign   175
My place and proper title to my son.
[To Amyras] First take my scourge and my imperial crown,°
And mount my royal chariot of estate,
That I may see thee crowned before I die.
Help me, my lords, to make my last remove.   180
        [Tamburlaine is helped down from his chariot into a chair]

THERIDAMAS A woeful change, my lord, that daunts our thoughts
More than the ruin of our proper souls.

TAMBURLAINE Sit up, my son. Let me see how well
Thou wilt become thy father's majesty.
        They crown [Amyras, but he refuses to ascend the royal
        chariot]

AMYRAS With what a flinty bosom should I joy   185
The breath of life and burden of my soul,
If not resolved into resolvèd pains
My body's mortifièd lineaments
Should exercise the motions of my heart,
Pierced with the joy of any dignity!°   190

O father, if the unrelenting ears
Of Death and hell be shut against my prayers,
And that the spiteful influence of heaven
Deny my soul fruition of her joy,
How should I step or stir my hateful feet   195
Against the inward powers of my heart,
Leading a life that only strives to die,
And plead in vain unpleasing sovereignty?°
TAMBURLAINE Let not thy love exceed thine honour, son,°
Nor bar thy mind that magnanimity   200
That nobly must admit necessity.
Sit up, my boy, and with those silken reins
Bridle the steelèd stomachs of those jades.°
THERIDAMAS [to Amyras] My lord, you must obey his majesty,
Since fate commands, and proud necessity.   205
AMYRAS [as he ascends the chariot]
Heavens witness me, with what a broken heart
And damnèd spirit I ascend this seat,°
And send my soul, before my father die,
His anguish and his burning agony!°
TAMBURLAINE Now fetch the hearse of fair Zenocrate.   210
Let it be placed by this my fatal chair°
And serve as parcel of my funeral.
        [Exeunt some]
USUMCASANE Then feels your majesty no sovereign ease,
Nor may our hearts, all drowned in tears of blood,
Joy any hope of your recovery?   215
TAMBURLAINE Casane, no. The monarch of the earth
And eyeless monster that torments my soul
Cannot behold the tears ye shed for me,
And therefore still augments his cruelty.
TECHELLES Then let some god oppose his holy power   220
Against the wrath and tyranny of Death,
That his tear-thirsty and unquenchèd hate
May be upon himself reverberate.
        They bring in the hearse [of Zenocrate]
TAMBURLAINE Now, eyes, enjoy your latest benefit,
And when my soul hath virtue of your sight,°   225
Pierce through the coffin and the sheet of gold
And glut your longings with a heaven of joy.
So, reign, my son! Scourge and control those slaves,

Guiding thy chariot with thy father's hand.
As precious is the charge thou undertak'st   230
As that which Clymene's brainsick son did guide
When wand'ring Phoebe's ivory cheeks were scorched°
And all the earth, like Etna, breathing fire.°
Be warned by him, then; learn with awful eye
To sway a throne as dangerous as his.   235
For if thy body thrive not full of thoughts
As pure and fiery as Phyteus' beams,°
The nature of these proud rebelling jades°
Will take Occasion by the slenderest hair°
And draw thee piecemeal like Hippolytus°   240
Through rocks more steep and sharp than Caspian clifts.
The nature of thy chariot will not bear
A guide of baser temper than myself,
More than heaven's coach the pride of Phaethon.
Farewell, my boys; my dearest friends, farewell!   245
My body feels, my soul doth weep to see
Your sweet desires deprived of company;
For Tamburlaine, the scourge of God, must die.
        [*He dies*]
AMYRAS Meet heaven and earth, and here let all things end!
For earth hath spent the pride of all her fruit,   250
And heaven consumed his choicest living fire.°
Let earth and heaven his timeless death deplore,
For both their worths will equal him no more.
        [*Exeunt in funeral procession, bearing in the hearse of
        Zenocrate and the body of Tamburlaine, Orcanes and the
        king of Jerusalem drawing in the chariot of Amyras*]

DOCTOR FAUSTUS
A–Text

DRAMATIS PERSONAE

The Chorus
Doctor John Faustus
Wagner
Good Angel
Evil Angel
Valdes
Cornelius
Three Scholars
Mephistopheles
Robin, *the Clown*
Devils
Rafe
Lucifer
Beelzebub
Pride
Covetousness } *The Seven*
Wrath   *Deadly Sins*
Envy

Gluttony } *The Seven*
Sloth   *Deadly Sins*
Lechery
The Pope
The Cardinal of Lorraine
Friars
A Vintner
The Emperor of Germany,
    Charles V
A Knight
Attendants
Alexander the Great } *Spirits*
His Paramour
A Horse-Courser
The Duke of Vanholt
The Duchess of Vanholt
Helen of Troy, *a spirit*
An Old Man

The Tragical History of Doctor Faustus (A-Text)

[PROLOGUE]

Enter Chorus

CHORUS Not marching now in fields of Trasimene°
    Where Mars did mate the Carthaginians,°
    Nor sporting in the dalliance of love
    In courts of kings where state is overturned,°
    Nor in the pomp of proud audacious deeds,   5
    Intends our muse to daunt his heavenly verse.°
    Only this, gentlemen: we must perform
    The form of Faustus' fortunes, good or bad.
    To patient judgements we appeal our plaud,°
    And speak for Faustus in his infancy.   10
    Now is he born, his parents base of stock,
    In Germany, within a town called Rhode.
    Of riper years to Wittenberg he went,°
    Whereas his kinsmen chiefly brought him up.
    So soon he profits in divinity,   15
    The fruitful plot of scholarism graced,°
    That shortly he was graced with doctor's name,
    Excelling all whose sweet delight disputes°
    In heavenly matters of theology;
    Till, swoll'n with cunning of a self-conceit,   20
    His waxen wings did mount above his reach,°
    And melting heavens conspired his overthrow.
    For, falling to a devilish exercise,
    And glutted more with learning's golden gifts,
    He surfeits upon cursed necromancy;   25
    Nothing so sweet as magic is to him,
    Which he prefers before his chiefest bliss.°
    And this the man that in his study sits.
    Exit

[1.1]

Enter Faustus in his study°

FAUSTUS Settle thy studies, Faustus, and begin
To sound the depth of that thou wilt profess.°
Having commenced, be a divine in show,°
Yet level at the end of every art,
And live and die in Aristotle's works.   5
Sweet *Analytics*, 'tis thou hast ravished me!
[*He reads*] '*Bene disserere est finis logices*.'°
Is to dispute well logic's chiefest end?
Affords this art no greater miracle?
Then read no more; thou hast attained the end.   10
A greater subject fitteth Faustus' wit.
Bid *On kai me on* farewell. Galen, come!°
Seeing *ubi desinit philosophus, ibi incipit medicus*,°
Be a physician, Faustus. Heap up gold,
And be eternized for some wondrous cure.   15
[*He reads*] '*Summum bonum medicinae sanitas*':°
The end of physic is our body's health.
Why Faustus, hast thou not attained that end?
Is not thy common talk sound aphorisms?
Are not thy bills hung up as monuments,°   20
Whereby whole cities have escaped the plague
And thousand desp'rate maladies been eased?
Yet art thou still but Faustus, and a man.
Wouldst thou make man to live eternally,
Or, being dead, raise them to life again,°   25
Then this profession were to be esteemed.
Physic, farewell. Where is Justinian?°
[*He reads*] '*Si una eademque res legatur duobus,*
Alter rem, alter valorem rei', etc.°
A pretty case of paltry legacies!   30
[*He reads*] '*Exhaereditare filium non potest pater nisi*—'°
Such is the subject of the Institute
And universal body of the Church.°
His study fits a mercenary drudge°
Who aims at nothing but external trash—   35
Too servile and illiberal for me.

When all is done, divinity is best.°
Jerome's Bible, Faustus, view it well.°
[*He reads*] '*Stipendium peccati mors est.*' Ha!
'*Stipendium*', etc.   40
The reward of sin is death. That's hard.
[*He reads*] '*Si peccasse negamus, fallimur*
Et nulla est in nobis veritas.'
If we say that we have no sin,
We deceive ourselves, and there's no truth in us.   45
Why then belike we must sin,
And so consequently die.°
Ay, we must die an everlasting death.
What doctrine call you this? *Che serà, serà,*
What will be, shall be? Divinity, adieu!   50
        [*He picks up a book of magic*]
These metaphysics of magicians°
And necromantic books are heavenly,
Lines, circles, signs, letters, and characters—
Ay, these are those that Faustus most desires.
O, what a world of profit and delight,   55
Of power, of honour, of omnipotence
Is promised to the studious artisan!
All things that move between the quiet poles°
Shall be at my command. Emperors and kings
Are but obeyed in their several provinces,   60
Nor can they raise the wind or rend the clouds;
But his dominion that exceeds in this°
Stretcheth as far as doth the mind of man.
A sound magician is a mighty god.
Here, Faustus, try thy brains to gain a deity.°   65
Wagner!
        Enter Wagner
            Commend me to my dearest friends,
The German Valdes and Cornelius.
Request them earnestly to visit me.
WAGNER I will, sir.
        Exit [*Wagner*]
FAUSTUS Their conference will be a greater help to me   70
Than all my labours, plod I ne'er so fast.
        Enter the Good Angel and the Evil Angel
GOOD ANGEL O Faustus, lay that damnèd book aside

And gaze not on it, lest it tempt thy soul
And heap God's heavy wrath upon thy head!
Read, read the Scriptures. That is blasphemy.°   75
EVIL ANGEL Go forward, Faustus, in that famous art
Wherein all nature's treasury is contained.
Be thou on earth as Jove is in the sky,
Lord and commander of these elements.
          Exeunt [*Angels*]
FAUSTUS How am I glutted with conceit of this!°   80
Shall I make spirits fetch me what I please,
Resolve me of all ambiguities,°
Perform what desperate enterprise I will?
I'll have them fly to India for gold,
Ransack the ocean for orient pearl,   85
And search all corners of the new-found world
For pleasant fruits and princely delicates.
I'll have them read me strange philosophy
And tell the secrets of all foreign kings.
I'll have them wall all Germany with brass   90
And make swift Rhine circle fair Wittenberg.°
I'll have them fill the public schools with silk,°
Wherewith the students shall be bravely clad.
I'll levy soldiers with the coin they bring°
And chase the Prince of Parma from our land,°   95
And reign sole king of all our provinces;
Yea, stranger engines for the brunt of war
Than was the fiery keel at Antwerp's bridge
I'll make my servile spirits to invent.°
Come, German Valdes and Cornelius,   100
And make me blest with your sage conference!
          Enter Valdes and Cornelius
Valdes, sweet Valdes, and Cornelius,
Know that your words have won me at the last
To practise magic and concealèd arts.
Yet not your words only, but mine own fantasy,   105
That will receive no object, for my head°
But ruminates on necromantic skill.°
Philosophy is odious and obscure;
Both law and physic are for petty wits;
Divinity is basest of the three,   110
Unpleasant, harsh, contemptible, and vile.

'Tis magic, magic that hath ravished me.
Then, gentle friends, aid me in this attempt,
And I, that have with concise syllogisms
Gravelled the pastors of the German Church°   115
And made the flow'ring pride of Wittenberg
Swarm to my problems as the infernal spirits
On sweet Musaeus when he came to hell,°
Will be as cunning as Agrippa was,°
Whose shadows made all Europe honour him.°   120

VALDES Faustus, these books, thy wit, and our experience
Shall make all nations to canonize us.°
As Indian Moors obey their Spanish lords,°
So shall the subjects of every element°
Be always serviceable to us three.   125
Like lions shall they guard us when we please,
Like Almaine rutters with their horsemen's staves,°
Or Lapland giants, trotting by our sides;
Sometimes like women, or unwedded maids,
Shadowing more beauty in their airy brows°   130
Than in the white breasts of the Queen of Love.°
From Venice shall they drag huge argosies,
And from America the golden fleece
That yearly stuffs old Philip's treasury,°
If learnèd Faustus will be resolute.   135

FAUSTUS Valdes, as resolute am I in this
As thou to live. Therefore object it not.°

CORNELIUS The miracles that magic will perform
Will make thee vow to study nothing else.
He that is grounded in astrology,   140
Enriched with tongues, well seen in minerals,°
Hath all the principles magic doth require.
Then doubt not, Faustus, but to be renowned
And more frequented for this mystery°
Than heretofore the Delphian oracle.°   145
The spirits tell me they can dry the sea
And fetch the treasure of all foreign wrecks—
Ay, all the wealth that our forefathers hid
Within the massy entrails of the earth.
Then tell me, Faustus, what shall we three want?   150

FAUSTUS Nothing, Cornelius. O, this cheers my soul!
Come, show me some demonstrations magical,

That I may conjure in some lusty grove
And have these joys in full possession.
VALDES Then haste thee to some solitary grove,   155
And bear wise Bacon's and Albanus' works,°
The Hebrew Psalter, and New Testament;
And whatsoever else is requisite
We will inform thee ere our conference cease.
CORNELIUS Valdes, first let him know the words of art,   160
And then, all other ceremonies learned,
Faustus may try his cunning by himself.
VALDES First I'll instruct thee in the rudiments,
And then wilt thou be perfecter than I.
FAUSTUS Then come and dine with me, and after meat   165
We'll canvass every quiddity thereof,°
For ere I sleep I'll try what I can do.
This night I'll conjure, though I die therefore.
        Exeunt

[1.2]

        Enter two Scholars
FIRST SCHOLAR I wonder what's become of Faustus, that was wont
to make our schools ring with '*sic probo*'.°
SECOND SCHOLAR That shall we know, for see, here comes his boy.
        Enter Wagner, [*carrying wine*]
FIRST SCHOLAR How now, sirrah, where's thy master?
WAGNER God in heaven knows.   5
SECOND SCHOLAR Why, dost not thou know?
WAGNER Yes, I know, but that follows not.°
FIRST SCHOLAR Go to, sirrah! Leave your jesting, and tell us where
he is.
WAGNER That follows not necessary by force of argument that you,   10
being licentiate, should stand upon't.° Therefore, acknowledge
your error, and be attentive.
SECOND SCHOLAR Why, didst thou not say thou knew'st?
WAGNER Have you any witness on't?
FIRST SCHOLAR Yes, sirrah, I heard you.   15
WAGNER Ask my fellow if I be a thief.°
SECOND SCHOLAR Well, you will not tell us.

WAGNER Yes, sir, I will tell you. Yet if you were not dunces, you
would never ask me such a question. For is not he *corpus naturale*?
And is not that *mobile*?° Then, wherefore should you ask me such   20
a question? But that° I am by nature phlegmatic, slow to wrath,
and prone to lechery—to love, I would say—it were not for you to
come within forty foot of the place of execution,° although I do
not doubt to see you both hanged the next sessions. Thus, having
triumphed over you, I will set my countenance like a precisian°   25
and begin to speak thus: Truly, my dear brethren, my master is
within at dinner with Valdes and Cornelius, as this wine, if it could
speak, it would inform your worships. And so the Lord bless you,
preserve you, and keep you, my dear brethren, my dear brethren.
    Exit [Wagner]
FIRST SCHOLAR Nay, then, I fear he is fall'n into that damned art   30
    for which they two are infamous through the world.
SECOND SCHOLAR Were he a stranger, and not allied° to me, yet
    should I grieve for him. But come, let us go and inform the
    Rector,° and see if he, by his grave counsel, can reclaim him.
FIRST SCHOLAR O, but I fear me nothing can reclaim him.   35
SECOND SCHOLAR Yet let us try what we can do.
    Exeunt

[1.3]

Enter Faustus to conjure
FAUSTUS Now that the gloomy shadow of the earth,
    Longing to view Orion's drizzling look,
    Leaps from th'Antarctic world unto the sky
    And dims the welkin with her pitchy breath,°
    Faustus, begin thine incantations,   5
    And try if devils will obey thy hest,
    Seeing thou hast prayed and sacrificed to them.
    Within this circle is Jehovah's name,
    Forward and backward anagrammatized,
    The breviated names of holy saints,   10
    Figures of every adjunct to the heavens,
    And characters of signs and erring stars,°
    By which the spirits are enforced to rise.
    Then fear not, Faustus, but be resolute,

And try the uttermost magic can perform.   15
Sint mihi dei Acherontis propitii! Valeat numen triplex Jehovae! Ignei,
aerii, aquatici, terreni, spiritus, salvete! Orientis princeps Lucifer,
Beelzebub, inferni ardentis monarcha, et Demogorgon, propitiamus vos,
ut appareat et surgat Mephistopheles. Quid tu moraris? Per Jehovam,
Gehennam, et consecratam aquam quam nunc spargo, signumque crucis   20
quod nunc facio, et per vota nostra, ipse nunc surgat nobis dicatus
Mephistopheles!°

    [*Faustus sprinkles holy water and makes a sign of the cross.*]
    Enter a Devil [*Mephistopheles*]

I charge thee to return and change thy shape.
Thou art too ugly to attend on me.
Go, and return an old Franciscan friar;   25
That holy shape becomes a devil best.
    Exit Devil [*Mephistopheles*]
I see there's virtue in my heavenly words.
Who would not be proficient in this art?
How pliant is this Mephistopheles,
Full of obedience and humility!   30
Such is the force of magic and my spells.
Now, Faustus, thou art conjurer laureate,
That canst command great Mephistopheles.
Quin redis, Mephistopheles, fratris imagine!°
    Enter Mephistopheles [*dressed as a friar*]

MEPHISTOPHELES Now, Faustus, what wouldst thou have me do?   35
FAUSTUS I charge thee wait upon me whilst I live,
    To do whatever Faustus shall command,
    Be it to make the moon drop from her sphere
    Or the ocean to overwhelm the world.
MEPHISTOPHELES I am a servant to great Lucifer   40
    And may not follow thee without his leave.
    No more than he commands must we perform.
FAUSTUS Did not he charge thee to appear to me?
MEPHISTOPHELES No, I came now hither of mine own accord.
FAUSTUS Did not my conjuring speeches raise thee? Speak.   45
MEPHISTOPHELES That was the cause, but yet *per accidens.°*
    For when we hear one rack the name of God,
    Abjure the Scriptures and his Saviour Christ,
    We fly in hope to get his glorious soul,°
    Nor will we come unless he use such means   50
    Whereby he is in danger to be damned.

Therefore, the shortest cut for conjuring
Is stoutly to abjure the Trinity
And pray devoutly to the prince of hell.

FAUSTUS So Faustus hath   55
Already done, and holds this principle:
There is no chief but only Beelzebub,
To whom Faustus doth dedicate himself.
This word 'damnation' terrifies not him,
For he confounds hell in Elysium.°   60
His ghost be with the old philosophers!°
But leaving these vain trifles of men's souls,
Tell me what is that Lucifer thy lord?

MEPHISTOPHELES Arch-regent and commander of all spirits.

FAUSTUS Was not that Lucifer an angel once?   65

MEPHISTOPHELES Yes, Faustus, and most dearly loved of God.

FAUSTUS How comes it then that he is prince of devils?

MEPHISTOPHELES O, by aspiring pride and insolence,
For which God threw him from the face of heaven.

FAUSTUS And what are you that live with Lucifer?   70

MEPHISTOPHELES Unhappy spirits that fell with Lucifer,
Conspired against our God with Lucifer,
And are for ever damned with Lucifer.

FAUSTUS Where are you damned?

MEPHISTOPHELES In hell.   75

FAUSTUS How comes it then that thou art out of hell?

MEPHISTOPHELES Why, this is hell, nor am I out of it.
Think'st thou that I, who saw the face of God
And tasted the eternal joys of heaven,
Am not tormented with ten thousand hells   80
In being deprived of everlasting bliss?
O Faustus, leave these frivolous demands,
Which strike a terror to my fainting soul!

FAUSTUS What, is great Mephistopheles so passionate
For being deprivèd of the joys of heaven?   85
Learn thou of Faustus manly fortitude,
And scorn those joys thou never shalt possess.
Go bear these tidings to great Lucifer:
Seeing Faustus hath incurred eternal death
By desp'rate thoughts against Jove's deity,   90
Say he surrenders up to him his soul,
So he will spare him four-and-twenty years,

Letting him live in all voluptuousness,
Having thee ever to attend on me,
To give me whatsoever I shall ask,   95
To tell me whatsoever I demand,
To slay mine enemies and aid my friends,
And always be obedient to my will.
Go and return to mighty Lucifer,
And meet me in my study at midnight,   100
And then resolve me of thy master's mind.°
MEPHISTOPHELES I will, Faustus.
        Exit [Mephistopheles]
FAUSTUS Had I as many souls as there be stars,
I'd give them all for Mephistopheles.
By him I'll be great emperor of the world   105
And make a bridge through the moving air
To pass the ocean with a band of men;
I'll join the hills that bind the Afric shore
And make that land continent to Spain,°
And both contributory to my crown.   110
The emperor shall not live but by my leave,
Nor any potentate of Germany.
Now that I have obtained what I desire,
I'll live in speculation of this art°
Till Mephistopheles return again.   115
        Exit

[1.4]

Enter Wagner and [Robin] the Clown
WAGNER Sirrah boy, come hither.
ROBIN How, 'boy'? 'Swounds, 'boy'! I hope you have seen many
    boys with such pickedevants° as I have. 'Boy', quotha?
WAGNER Tell me, sirrah, hast thou any comings in?°
ROBIN Ay, and goings out° too, you may see else.°   5
WAGNER Alas, poor slave, see how poverty jesteth in his nakedness!
    The villain is bare and out of service,° and so hungry that I know
    he would give his soul to the devil for a shoulder of mutton,
    though it were blood raw.

ROBIN How? My soul to the devil for a shoulder of mutton, though   10
'twere blood raw? Not so, good friend. By'r Lady, I had need have
it well roasted, and good sauce to it, if I pay so dear.

WAGNER Well, wilt thou serve me, and I'll make thee go like *Qui
mihi discipulus?*°

ROBIN How, in verse?   15

WAGNER No, sirrah, in beaten° silk and stavesacre.°

ROBIN How, how, knave's acre? [*Aside*] Aye, I thought that was all
the land his father left him. [*To Wagner*] Do ye hear? I would be
sorry to rob you of your living.

WAGNER Sirrah, I say in stavesacre.   20

ROBIN Oho, oho, 'stavesacre'! Why then, belike, if I were your man,
I should be full of vermin.

WAGNER So thou shalt, whether thou beest with me or no. But
sirrah, leave your jesting, and bind° yourself presently unto me for
seven years, or I'll turn all the lice about thee into familiars,° and   25
they shall tear thee in pieces.

ROBIN Do you hear, sir? You may save that labour. They are too
familiar with me already. 'Swounds, they are as bold with my flesh
as if they had paid for my meat and drink.

WAGNER Well, do you hear, sirrah? [*Offering money*] Hold, take these   30
guilders.°

ROBIN Gridirons? What be they?

WAGNER Why, French crowns.

ROBIN Mass, but for the name of° French crowns a man were as good
have as many English counters.° And what should I do with these?   35

WAGNER Why now, sirrah, thou art at an hour's warning whensoever
or wheresoever the devil shall fetch thee.

ROBIN No, no, here, take your gridirons again.
[*He attempts to return the money*]

WAGNER Truly, I'll none of them.

ROBIN Truly, but you shall.   40

WAGNER [*to the audience*] Bear witness I gave them him.

ROBIN Bear witness I give them you again.

WAGNER Well, I will cause two devils presently to fetch thee away.—
Balioll and Belcher!

ROBIN Let your Balio and your Belcher come here and I'll knock   45
them. They were never so knocked since they were devils. Say I
should kill one of them, what would folks say? 'Do ye see yonder
tall fellow in the round slop?° He has killed the devil.' So I should
be called 'Kill devil'° all the parish over.

Enter two Devils, and [Robin] the Clown runs up and down
crying

WAGNER Balioll and Belcher! Spirits, away!   50
    Exeunt [Devils]

ROBIN What, are they gone? A vengeance on them! They have vile
long nails. There was a he devil and a she devil. I'll tell you how
you shall know them: all he devils has horns,° and all she devils
has clefts° and cloven feet.

WAGNER Well, sirrah, follow me.   55

ROBIN But do you hear? If I should serve you, would you teach me
to raise up Banios and Belcheos?

WAGNER I will teach thee to turn thyself to anything, to a dog, or a
cat, or a mouse, or a rat, or anything.

ROBIN How? A Christian fellow to a dog or a cat, a mouse or a rat?   60
No, no, sir. If you turn me into anything, let it be in the likeness
of a little, pretty, frisking flea, that I may be here and there and
everywhere. O, I'll tickle the pretty wenches' plackets!° I'll be
amongst them, i'faith!

WAGNER Well, sirrah, come.   65

ROBIN But do you hear, Wagner?

WAGNER How?—Balioll and Belcher!

ROBIN O Lord, I pray sir, let Banio and Belcher go sleep.

WAGNER Villain, call me Master Wagner, and let thy left eye be
diametarily° fixed upon my right heel, with *quasi vestigiis nostris*   70
insistere.°
    Exit [Wagner]

ROBIN God forgive me, he speaks Dutch fustian.° Well, I'll follow
him, I'll serve him, that's flat.
    Exit

[2.1]

Enter Faustus in his study

FAUSTUS Now, Faustus, must thou needs be damned,
And canst thou not be saved.
What boots it then to think of God or heaven?
Away with such vain fancies and despair!
Despair in God and trust in Beelzebub.   5
Now go not backward. No, Faustus, be resolute.
Why waverest thou? O, something soundeth in mine ears:
'Abjure this magic, turn to God again!'
Ay, and Faustus will turn to God again.
To God? He loves thee not.   10
The god thou servest is thine own appetite,
Wherein is fixed the love of Beelzebub.
To him I'll build an altar and a church,
And offer lukewarm blood of new-born babes.
Enter Good Angel and Evil [Angel]
GOOD ANGEL Sweet Faustus, leave that execrable art.   15
FAUSTUS Contrition, prayer, repentance—what of them?
GOOD ANGEL O, they are means to bring thee unto heaven.
EVIL ANGEL Rather illusions, fruits of lunacy,
That makes men foolish that do trust them most.
GOOD ANGEL Sweet Faustus, think of heaven and heavenly things.   20
EVIL ANGEL No, Faustus, think of honour and wealth.
Exeunt [Angels]
FAUSTUS Of wealth?
Why, the seigniory of Emden shall be mine.°
When Mephistopheles shall stand by me,
What god can hurt thee, Faustus? Thou art safe;   25
Cast no more doubts. Come, Mephistopheles,°
And bring glad tidings from great Lucifer.
Is't not midnight? Come, Mephistopheles!
Veni, veni, Mephistophile!°
Enter Mephistopheles
Now tell, what says Lucifer thy lord?   30
MEPHISTOPHELES That I shall wait on Faustus whilst he lives,°
So he will buy my service with his soul.
FAUSTUS Already Faustus hath hazarded that for thee.

MEPHISTOPHELES But, Faustus, thou must bequeath it solemnly
   And write a deed of gift with thine own blood,   35
   For that security craves great Lucifer.
   If thou deny it, I will back to hell.
FAUSTUS Stay, Mephistopheles, and tell me, what good will my soul
   do thy lord?
MEPHISTOPHELES Enlarge his kingdom.   40
FAUSTUS Is that the reason he tempts us thus?
MEPHISTOPHELES *Solamen miseris socios habuisse doloris.*°
FAUSTUS Have you any pain, that tortures others?°
MEPHISTOPHELES As great as have the human souls of men.
   But tell me, Faustus, shall I have thy soul?   45
   And I will be thy slave, and wait on thee,
   And give thee more than thou hast wit to ask.
FAUSTUS Ay, Mephistopheles, I give it thee.
MEPHISTOPHELES Then stab thine arm courageously,
   And bind thy soul that at some certain day   50
   Great Lucifer may claim it as his own,
   And then be thou as great as Lucifer.
FAUSTUS [*cutting his arm*]
   Lo, Mephistopheles, for love of thee
   I cut mine arm, and with my proper blood
   Assure my soul to be great Lucifer's,   55
   Chief lord and regent of perpetual night.
   View here the blood that trickles from mine arm,
   And let it be propitious for my wish.
MEPHISTOPHELES But Faustus, thou must write it in manner of a
   deed of gift.   60
FAUSTUS Ay, so I will. [*He writes*] But Mephistopheles,
   My blood congeals, and I can write no more.
MEPHISTOPHELES I'll fetch thee fire to dissolve it straight.
      Exit [*Mephistopheles*]
FAUSTUS What might the staying of my blood portend?
   Is it unwilling I should write this bill?   65
   Why streams it not, that I may write afresh?
   'Faustus gives to thee his soul'—ah, there it stayed!
   Why shouldst thou not? Is not thy soul thine own?
   Then write again: 'Faustus gives to thee his soul.'
      Enter Mephistopheles with a chafer° *of coals*
MEPHISTOPHELES Here's fire. Come Faustus, set it on.°   70
FAUSTUS So. Now the blood begins to clear again.

Now will I make an end immediately.
    [*He writes*]
MEPHISTOPHELES [*aside*]
    O, what will not I do to obtain his soul?
FAUSTUS *Consummatum est*. This bill is ended,°
    And Faustus hath bequeathed his soul to Lucifer.   75
    But what is this inscription on mine arm?
    '*Homo, fuge!*' Whither should I fly?°
    If unto God, he'll throw thee down to hell.—
    My senses are deceived; here's nothing writ.—
    I see it plain. Here in this place is writ   80
    '*Homo, fuge!*' Yet shall not Faustus fly.
MEPHISTOPHELES [*aside*]
    I'll fetch him somewhat to delight his mind.
        Exit [Mephistopheles, then re-]enter with Devils, giving
        crowns and rich apparel to Faustus, and dance and then depart
FAUSTUS Speak, Mephistopheles. What means this show?
MEPHISTOPHELES
    Nothing, Faustus, but to delight thy mind withal
    And to show thee what magic can perform.   85
FAUSTUS But may I raise up spirits when I please?
MEPHISTOPHELES Ay, Faustus, and do greater things than these.
FAUSTUS Then there's enough for a thousand souls.°
    Here, Mephistopheles, receive this scroll,
    A deed of gift of body and of soul—   90
    But yet conditionally that thou perform
    All articles prescribed between us both.
MEPHISTOPHELES Faustus, I swear by hell and Lucifer
    To effect all promises between us made.
FAUSTUS Then hear me read them.   95
    'On these conditions following:
    First, that Faustus may be a spirit in form and substance.
    Secondly, that Mephistopheles shall be his servant, and at his
    command.
    Thirdly, that Mephistopheles shall do for him and bring him   100
    whatsoever.
    Fourthly, that he shall be in his chamber or house invisible.
    Lastly, that he shall appear to the said John Faustus at all times in
    what form or shape soever he please.
    I, John Faustus of Wittenberg, Doctor, by these presents° do give   105
    both body and soul to Lucifer, Prince of the East, and his minister

Mephistopheles; and furthermore grant unto them that, four-and-twenty years being expired, the articles above written inviolate,° full power to fetch or carry the said John Faustus, body and soul, flesh, blood, or goods, into their habitation wheresoever.   110
                        By me, John Faustus.'

MEPHISTOPHELES Speak, Faustus. Do you deliver this as your deed?
FAUSTUS [*giving the deed*] Ay. Take it, and the devil give thee good on't.
MEPHISTOPHELES Now, Faustus, ask what thou wilt.   115
FAUSTUS First will I question with thee about hell.
    Tell me, where is the place that men call hell?
MEPHISTOPHELES Under the heavens.
FAUSTUS   Ay, but whereabout?
MEPHISTOPHELES Within the bowels of these elements,°
    Where we are tortured and remain for ever.   120
    Hell hath no limits, nor is circumscribed
    In one self place, for where we are is hell,°
    And where hell is must we ever be.
    And, to conclude, when all the world dissolves,
    And every creature shall be purified,   125
    All places shall be hell that is not heaven.
FAUSTUS Come, I think hell's a fable.
MEPHISTOPHELES
    Ay, think so still, till experience change thy mind.
FAUSTUS Why, think'st thou then that Faustus shall be damned?
MEPHISTOPHELES Ay, of necessity, for here's the scroll   130
    Wherein thou hast given thy soul to Lucifer.
FAUSTUS Ay, and body too. But what of that?
    Think'st thou that Faustus is so fond
    To imagine that after this life there is any pain?
    Tush, these are trifles and mere old wives' tales.   135
MEPHISTOPHELES
    But, Faustus, I am an instance to prove the contrary,
    For I am damnèd and am now in hell.
FAUSTUS How? Now in hell? Nay, an this be hell, I'll willingly be damned here. What? Walking, disputing, etc.? But leaving off this, let me have a wife, the fairest maid in Germany, for I am wanton   140
and lascivious and cannot live without a wife.
MEPHISTOPHELES How, a wife? I prithee, Faustus, talk not of a wife.
FAUSTUS Nay, sweet Mephistopheles, fetch me one, for I will have one.

MEPHISTOPHELES Well, thou wilt have one. Sit there till I come. I'll   145
    fetch thee a wife, in the devil's name.°
        [*Exit Mephistopheles, then re-*]*enter with a Devil dressed like*
        a woman, with fireworks
MEPHISTOPHELES Tell, Faustus, how dost thou like thy wife?
FAUSTUS A plague on her for a hot whore!
MEPHISTOPHELES Tut, Faustus, marriage is but a ceremonial toy.
    If thou lovest me, think no more of it.°   150
        [*Exit Devil*]
    I'll cull thee out the fairest courtesans
    And bring them ev'ry morning to thy bed.
    She whom thine eye shall like, thy heart shall have,
    Be she as chaste as was Penelope,
    As wise as Saba, or as beautiful   155
    As was bright Lucifer before his fall.°
        [*Presenting a book*]
    Hold, take this book. Peruse it thoroughly.
    The iterating of these lines brings gold;
    The framing of this circle on the ground
    Brings whirlwinds, tempests, thunder, and lightning.   160
    Pronounce this thrice devoutly to thyself,
    And men in armour shall appear to thee,
    Ready to execute what thou desir'st.
FAUSTUS Thanks, Mephistopheles. Yet fain would I have a book
    wherein I might behold all spells and incantations, that I might   165
    raise up spirits when I please.
MEPHISTOPHELES Here they are in this book. (*There turn to them*)°
FAUSTUS Now would I have a book where I might see all characters
    and planets of the heavens, that I might know their motions and
    dispositions.   170
MEPHISTOPHELES Here they are too. (*Turn to them*)
FAUSTUS Nay, let me have one book more—and then I have
    done—wherein I might see all plants, herbs, and trees that grow
    upon the earth.
MEPHISTOPHELES Here they be.   175
FAUSTUS O, thou art deceived.
MEPHISTOPHELES Tut, I warrant thee.° (*Turn to them*)
        [*Exeunt*]

[2.2]

Enter Robin the ostler with a book in his hand

ROBIN O, this is admirable! Here I ha' stol'n one of Doctor Faustus' conjuring books, and, i'faith, I mean to search some circles° for my own use. Now will I make all the maidens in our parish dance at my pleasure stark naked before me, and so by that means I shall see more than e'er I felt or saw yet.   5

Enter Rafe, calling Robin

RAFE Robin, prithee, come away.° There's a gentleman tarries to have his horse, and he would have his things rubbed and made clean; he keeps such a chafing° with my mistress about it, and she has sent me to look thee out. Prithee, come away.

ROBIN Keep out, keep out, or else you are blown up, you are dis-   10
membered, Rafe! Keep out, for I am about a roaring piece of work.

RAFE Come, what dost thou with that same book? Thou canst not read.

ROBIN Yes, my master and mistress shall find that I can read—he for his forehead, she for her private study. She's born to bear with me,   15
or else my art fails.

RAFE Why, Robin, what book is that?

ROBIN What book? Why the most intolerable° book for conjuring that e'er was invented by any brimstone devil.

RAFE Canst thou conjure with it?   20

ROBIN I can do all these things easily with it: first, I can make thee drunk with hippocras at any tavern in Europe for nothing. That's one of my conjuring works.

RAFE Our Master Parson says that's nothing.°

ROBIN True, Rafe; and more, Rafe, if thou hast any mind to Nan   25
Spit, our kitchen maid, then turn her and wind her to thy own use as often as thou wilt, and at midnight.°

RAFE O brave Robin! Shall I have Nan Spit, and to mine own use? On that condition I'll feed thy devil with horse-bread as long as he lives, of free cost.   30

ROBIN No more, sweet Rafe. Let's go and make clean our boots, which lie foul upon our hands, and then to our conjuring, in the devil's name.°

Exeunt

[2.3]

[Enter Faustus in his study, and Mephistopheles]

FAUSTUS When I behold the heavens, then I repent
  And curse thee, wicked Mephistopheles,
  Because thou hast deprived me of those joys.
MEPHISTOPHELES Why Faustus,
  Think'st thou heaven is such a glorious thing?   5
  I tell thee, 'tis not half so fair as thou
  Or any man that breathes on earth.
FAUSTUS How provest thou that?
MEPHISTOPHELES
  It was made for man; therefore is man more excellent.
FAUSTUS If it were made for man, 'twas made for me.   10
  I will renounce this magic and repent.
     Enter Good Angel and Evil Angel
GOOD ANGEL Faustus, repent yet, God will pity thee.
EVIL ANGEL Thou art a spirit. God cannot pity thee.
FAUSTUS Who buzzeth in mine ears I am a spirit?
  Be I a devil, yet God may pity me;°   15
  Ay, God will pity me if I repent.
EVIL ANGEL Ay, but Faustus never shall repent.
     Exeunt [Angels]
FAUSTUS My heart's so hardened I cannot repent.
  Scarce can I name salvation, faith, or heaven
  But fearful echoes thunders in mine ears: 20
  'Faustus, thou art damned!' Then swords and knives,
  Poison, guns, halters, and envenomed steel°
  Are laid before me to dispatch myself;
  And long ere this I should have slain myself
  Had not sweet pleasure conquered deep despair.   25
  Have not I made blind Homer sing to me
  Of Alexander's love and Oenone's death?°
  And hath not he that built the walls of Thebes°
  With ravishing sound of his melodious harp
  Made music with my Mephistopheles?   30
  Why should I die, then, or basely despair?
  I am resolved Faustus shall ne'er repent.
  Come, Mephistopheles, let us dispute again
  And argue of divine astrology.

Tell me, are there many heavens above the moon?°   35
Are all celestial bodies but one globe,
As is the substance of this centric earth?°
MEPHISTOPHELES As are the elements, such are the spheres,
Mutually folded in each other's orb;°
And, Faustus, all jointly move upon one axletree,   40
Whose terminine is termed the world's wide pole.°
Nor are the names of Saturn, Mars, or Jupiter
Feigned, but are erring stars.°
FAUSTUS But tell me, have they all one motion, both *situ et tempore*?°
MEPHISTOPHELES All jointly move from east to west in four-and-   45
twenty hours upon the poles of the world, but differ in their
motion upon the poles of the zodiac.°
FAUSTUS Tush, these slender trifles Wagner can decide.
Hath Mephistopheles no greater skill?
Who knows not the double motion of the planets?   50
The first is finished in a natural day,
The second thus, as Saturn in thirty years,
Jupiter in twelve, Mars in four, the sun, Venus, and Mercury in a
year, the moon in twenty-eight days.° Tush, these are freshmen's
suppositions. But tell me, hath every sphere a dominion or   55
intelligentia?°
MEPHISTOPHELES Ay.
FAUSTUS How many heavens or spheres are there?
MEPHISTOPHELES Nine: the seven planets, the firmament,° and the
empyreal heaven.°   60
FAUSTUS Well, resolve me in this question: why have we not
conjunctions, oppositions, aspects, eclipses all at one time, but in
some years we have more, in some less?°
MEPHISTOPHELES *Per inaequalem motum respectu totius.*°
FAUSTUS Well, I am answered. Tell me who made the world.   65
MEPHISTOPHELES I will not.
FAUSTUS Sweet Mephistopheles, tell me.
MEPHISTOPHELES Move° me not, for I will not tell thee.
FAUSTUS Villain, have I not bound thee to tell me anything?
MEPHISTOPHELES Ay, that is not against our kingdom, but this is.   70
Think thou on hell, Faustus, for thou art damned.
FAUSTUS Think, Faustus, upon God, that made the world.
MEPHISTOPHELES Remember this.°
        Exit [*Mephistopheles*]
FAUSTUS Ay, go, accursèd spirit, to ugly hell!

'Tis thou hast damned distressèd Faustus' soul.   75
Is't not too late?
    Enter Good Angel and Evil [Angel]
EVIL ANGEL Too late.
GOOD ANGEL Never too late, if Faustus can repent.
EVIL ANGEL If thou repent, devils shall tear thee in pieces.
GOOD ANGEL Repent, and they shall never raze thy skin.   80
    Exeunt [Angels]
FAUSTUS Ah, Christ, my Saviour,
Seek to save distressèd Faustus' soul!°
    Enter Lucifer, Beelzebub, and Mephistopheles
LUCIFER Christ cannot save thy soul, for he is just.
There's none but I have int'rest in the same.
FAUSTUS O, who art thou that look'st so terrible?   85
LUCIFER I am Lucifer,
And this is my companion prince in hell.
FAUSTUS O Faustus, they are come to fetch away thy soul!
LUCIFER We come to tell thee thou dost injure us.
Thou talk'st of Christ, contrary to thy promise.   90
Thou shouldst not think of God. Think of the devil,
And of his dame, too.°
FAUSTUS Nor will I henceforth. Pardon me in this,
And Faustus vows never to look to heaven,
Never to name God or to pray to him,   95
To burn his Scriptures, slay his ministers,
And make my spirits pull his churches down.
LUCIFER Do so, and we will highly gratify thee.
Faustus, we are come from hell to show thee some pastime. Sit
down, and thou shalt see all the Seven Deadly Sins appear in their   100
proper shapes.
FAUSTUS That sight will be as pleasing unto me as paradise was to
Adam the first day of his creation.
LUCIFER Talk not of paradise nor creation, but mark this show. Talk
of the devil, and nothing else.—Come away!   105
    [Faustus sits.] Enter the Seven Deadly Sins
Now, Faustus, examine them of their several names and dispositions.
FAUSTUS What art thou, the first?
PRIDE I am Pride. I disdain to have any parents. I am like to Ovid's
flea:° I can creep into every corner of a wench. Sometimes like a
periwig I sit upon her brow, or like a fan of feathers I kiss her lips.   110
Indeed I do. What do I not? But fie, what a scent is here! I'll not

speak another word except the ground were perfumed and covered
with cloth of arras.

FAUSTUS What art thou, the second?

COVETOUSNESS I am Covetousness, begotten of an old churl in an   115
old leathern bag; and might I have my wish, I would desire that
this house and all the people in it were turned to gold, that I might
lock you up in my good chest. O my sweet gold!

FAUSTUS What art thou, the third?

WRATH I am Wrath. I had neither father nor mother. I leaped   120
out of a lion's mouth when I was scarce half an hour old, and
ever since I have run up and down the world with this case° of
rapiers, wounding myself when I had nobody to fight withal. I
was born in hell, and look to it,° for some of you shall be° my
father.   125

FAUSTUS What art thou, the fourth?

ENVY I am Envy, begotten of a chimney-sweeper and an oyster-wife.
I cannot read, and therefore wish all books were burnt. I am lean
with seeing others eat. O, that there would come a famine through
all the world, that all might die, and I live alone! Then thou   130
shouldst see how fat I would be. But must thou sit and I stand?
Come down, with a vengeance!°

FAUSTUS Away, envious rascal!—What art thou, the fifth?

GLUTTONY Who, I, sir? I am Gluttony. My parents are all dead, and
the devil a penny° they have left me but a bare pension, and that   135
is thirty meals a day, and ten bevers—° a small trifle to suffice
nature.° O, I come of a royal parentage. My grandfather was a
gammon of bacon,° my grandmother a hogshead of claret wine.
My godfathers were these: Peter Pickle-herring and Martin
Martlemas-beef.° O, but my godmother, she was a jolly gentle-   140
woman, and well beloved in every good town and city; her name
was Mistress Margery March-beer. Now, Faustus, thou° hast
heard all my progeny, wilt thou bid me to supper?

FAUSTUS No, I'll see thee hanged. Thou wilt eat up all my victuals.

GLUTTONY Then the devil choke thee!   145

FAUSTUS Choke thyself, glutton!—What art thou, the sixth?

SLOTH I am Sloth. I was begotten on a sunny bank, where I have
lain ever since, and you have done me great injury to bring me
from thence. Let me be carried thither again by Gluttony and
Lechery. I'll not speak another word for a king's ransom.   150

FAUSTUS What are you, Mistress Minx, the seventh and last?

LECHERY Who, I, sir? I am one that loves an inch of raw mut-

ton° better than an ell° of fried stockfish,° and the first letter of
my name begins with lechery.

LUCIFER Away, to hell, to hell!   155

    Exeunt the Sins

Now, Faustus, how dost thou like this?

FAUSTUS O, this feeds my soul!

LUCIFER Tut, Faustus, in hell is all manner of delight.

FAUSTUS O, might I see hell and return again, how happy were I
then!   160

LUCIFER Thou shalt. I will send for thee at midnight. [*Presenting a
book*] In meantime, take this book. Peruse it throughly, and thou
shalt turn thyself into what shape thou wilt.

FAUSTUS [*taking the book*] Great thanks, mighty Lucifer. This will I
keep as chary as my life.   165

LUCIFER Farewell, Faustus, and think on the devil.

FAUSTUS Farewell, great Lucifer. Come, Mephistopheles.

    Exeunt omnes, [Faustus and Mephistopheles by one way,
    Lucifer and Beelzebub by another]

[3. CHORUS]

Enter Wagner solus

WAGNER Learnèd Faustus,
  To know the secrets of astronomy
  Graven in the book of Jove's high firmament,
  Did mount himself to scale Olympus' top,°
  Being seated in a chariot burning bright   5
  Drawn by the strength of yoky dragons' necks.°
  He now is gone to prove cosmography,°
  And, as I guess, will first arrive at Rome
  To see the pope and manner of his court
  And take some part of holy Peter's feast°   10
  That to this day is highly solemnized.
      Exit Wagner

[3.1]

Enter Faustus and Mephistopheles

FAUSTUS Having now, my good Mephistopheles,
　　Passed with delight the stately town of Trier,
　　Environed round with airy mountaintops,
　　With walls of flint and deep intrenchèd lakes,
　　Not to be won by any conquering prince;   5
　　From Paris next, coasting the realm of France,°
　　We saw the river Maine fall into Rhine,
　　Whose banks are set with groves of fruitful vines.
　　Then up to Naples, rich Campania,°
　　Whose buildings, fair and gorgeous to the eye,   10
　　The streets straight forth and paved with finest brick,°
　　Quarters the town in four equivalents,°
　　There saw we learnèd Maro's golden tomb,
　　The way he cut an English mile in length
　　Thorough a rock of stone in one night's space.°   15
　　From thence to Venice, Padua, and the rest,
　　In midst of which a sumptuous temple stands°
　　That threats the stars with her aspiring top.°
　　Thus hitherto hath Faustus spent his time.
　　But tell me now, what resting place is this?   20
　　Hast thou, as erst I did command,
　　Conducted me within the walls of Rome?
MEPHISTOPHELES Faustus, I have. And because° we will not be un-
　　provided, I have taken up his holiness' privy chamber° for our
　　use.   25
FAUSTUS I hope his holiness will bid us welcome.
MEPHISTOPHELES Tut, 'tis no matter, man. We'll be bold with his
　　good cheer.
　　And now, my Faustus, that thou mayst perceive
　　What Rome containeth to delight thee with,   30
　　Know that this city stands upon seven hills
　　That underprops the groundwork of the same.
　　Just through the midst runs flowing Tiber's stream,
　　With winding banks that cut it in two parts,°
　　Over the which four stately bridges lean,   35
　　That makes safe passage to each part of Rome.

        Upon the bridge called Ponte Angelo
        Erected is a castle passing strong,
        Within whose walls such store of ordnance are,
        And double cannons, framed of carvèd brass,   40
        As match the days within one complete year—°
        Besides the gates and high pyramides°
        Which Julius Caesar brought from Africa.
FAUSTUS   Now, by the kingdoms of infernal rule,
        Of Styx, Acheron, and the fiery lake   45
        Of ever-burning Phlegethon, I swear°
        That I do long to see the monuments
        And situation of bright splendent Rome.
        Come, therefore, let's away!
MEPHISTOPHELES
        Nay, Faustus, stay. I know you'd fain see the pope   50
        And take some part of holy Peter's feast,°
        Where thou shalt see a troupe of bald-pate friars
        Whose *summum bonum* is in belly cheer.°
FAUSTUS   Well, I am content to compass then some sport,
        And by their folly make us merriment.   55
        Then charm° me that I may be invisible, to do what I please
        unseen of any whilst I stay in Rome.
MEPHISTOPHELES [*placing a robe on Faustus*] So, Faustus, now do
        what thou wilt, thou shalt not be discerned.
                Sound a sennet. Enter the Pope and the Cardinal of Lorraine
                to the banquet, with Friars attending
POPE   My lord of Lorraine, will't please you draw near?   60
FAUSTUS   Fall to, and the devil choke you an you spare.°
POPE   How now, who's that which spake? Friars, look about.
                [*Some Friars attempt to search*]
FRIAR   Here's nobody, if it like your holiness.
POPE   [*presenting a dish*] My lord, here is a dainty dish was sent me
        from the bishop of Milan.   65
FAUSTUS   I thank you, sir. (*Snatch it*)°
POPE   How now, who's that which snatched the meat from me? Will
        no man look?
                [*Some Friars search about*]
        My lord, this dish was sent me from the cardinal of Florence.
FAUSTUS   [*snatching the dish*] You say true. I'll ha't.   70
POPE   What again?—My lord, I'll drink to your grace.
FAUSTUS   [*snatching the cup*] I'll pledge your grace.

LORRAINE My lord, it may be some ghost, newly crept out of
purgatory, come to beg a pardon° of your holiness.

POPE It may be so. Friars, prepare a dirge to lay the fury of this   75
ghost. Once again, my lord, fall to.

    The Pope crosseth himself

FAUSTUS What, are you crossing of yourself?
Well, use that trick no more, I would advise you.

    [*The Pope*] *cross[es himself] again*

Well, there's a second time. Aware the third,°
I give you fair warning.   80

    [*The Pope*] *cross[es himself] again, and Faustus hits him a
    box of the ear, and they all [except Faustus and Mephistopheles]
    run away*

Come on, Mephistopheles. What shall we do?

MEPHISTOPHELES Nay, I know not. We shall be cursed with bell,
book, and candle.

FAUSTUS How? Bell, book, and candle, candle, book, and bell,
Forward and backward, to curse Faustus to hell.   85
Anon you shall hear a hog grunt, a calf bleat, and an ass bray,
Because it is Saint Peter's holy day.

    Enter all the Friars to sing the dirge

FRIAR Come, brethren, let's about our business with good devotion.

    [*The Friars*] *sing this*

Cursèd be he that stole away his holiness' meat from the table.

    Maledicat Dominus!°   90

Cursèd be he that struck his holiness a blow on the face.

    Maledicat Dominus!

Cursèd be he that took Friar Sandelo a blow on the pate.°

    Maledicat Dominus!

Cursèd be he that disturbeth our holy dirge.   95

    Maledicat Dominus!

Cursèd be he that took away his holiness' wine.

    Maledicat Dominus!

Et omnes sancti. Amen.°

    [*Faustus and Mephistopheles*] *beat the Friars, and fling
    fireworks among them, and so exeunt*

[3.2]

Enter Robin [with a conjuring book] and Rafe with a silver goblet

ROBIN Come, Rafe, did not I tell thee we were for ever made° by this Doctor Faustus' book? *Ecce signum!*° Here's a simple purchase for horse-keepers.° Our horses shall eat no hay° as long as this lasts.

Enter the Vintner°

RAFE But Robin, here comes the Vintner.   5

ROBIN Hush, I'll gull him supernaturally.—Drawer,° I hope all is paid. God be with you. Come, Rafe.

[They start to go]

VINTNER *[to Robin]* Soft, sir, a word with you. I must yet have a goblet paid from you ere you go.

ROBIN I, a goblet? Rafe, I, a goblet? I scorn you, and you are but a   10
etc.° I, a goblet? Search me.

VINTNER I mean so, sir, with your favour.°

[The Vintner searches Robin]

ROBIN How say you now?

VINTNER I must say somewhat° to your fellow—you, sir.

RAFE Me, sir? Me, sir? Search your fill.   15

[He tosses the goblet to Robin; then the Vintner searches Rafe]

Now, sir, you may be ashamed to burden honest men with a matter of truth.

VINTNER Well, t'one of you hath this goblet about you.

ROBIN You lie, drawer, 'tis afore me.° Sirrah, you, I'll teach ye to impeach honest men. Stand by. I'll scour° you for a goblet. Stand   20
aside, you had best, I charge you in the name of Beelzebub.

[He tosses the goblet to Rafe]

Look to the goblet, Rafe.

VINTNER What mean you, sirrah?

ROBIN I'll tell you what I mean. *(He reads)*

'Sanctobulorum Periphrasticon!' Nay, I'll tickle you, Vintner. Look   25
to the goblet, Rafe. 'Polypragmos Belseborams framanto pacostiphos
tostu Mephistopheles!'° etc.

Enter to them Mephistopheles.° *[Exit the Vintner, running]*

MEPHISTOPHELES Monarch of hell, under whose black survey
Great potentates do kneel with awful fear,
Upon whose altars thousand souls do lie,   30

How am I vexèd with these villains' charms!
From Constantinople am I hither come
Only for pleasure of these damnèd slaves.

ROBIN How, from Constantinople? You have had a great journey.
Will you take sixpence in your purse to pay for your supper and   35
be gone?

MEPHISTOPHELES Well, villains, for your presumption I transform
thee [*to Robin*] into an ape and thee [*to Rafe*] into a dog. And so,
begone!

        [*They are transformed in shape.*] *Exit* [*Mephistopheles*]

ROBIN How, into an ape? That's brave. I'll have fine sport with the   40
boys; I'll get nuts and apples enough.

RAFE And I must be a dog.

ROBIN I'faith, thy head will never be out of the pottage pot.

        Exeunt

[4. CHORUS]

Enter Chorus

CHORUS When Faustus had with pleasure ta'en the view
    Of rarest things and royal courts of kings,
    He stayed his course and so returnèd home,°
    Where such as bear his absence but with grief—
    I mean his friends and nearest companions—   5
    Did gratulate his safety with kind words.°
    And in their conference of what befell,
    Touching his journey through the world and air,
    They put forth questions of astrology,
    Which Faustus answered with such learnèd skill   10
    As they admired and wondered at his wit.°
    Now is his fame spread forth in every land.
    Amongst the rest the emperor is one,
    Carolus the Fifth, at whose palace now°
    Faustus is feasted 'mongst his noblemen.   15
    What there he did in trial of his art
    I leave untold, your eyes shall see performed.°
        Exit

[4.1]

Enter Emperor, Faustus, [Mephistopheles,] and a Knight,
with Attendants

EMPEROR Master Doctor Faustus, I have heard strange report of thy
knowledge in the black art—how that none in my empire, nor in
the whole world, can compare with thee for the rare effects of
magic. They say thou hast a familiar spirit by whom thou canst
accomplish what thou list. This, therefore, is my request: that thou   5
let me see some proof of thy skill, that mine eyes may be witnesses
to confirm what mine ears have heard reported. And here I swear
to thee, by the honour of mine imperial crown, that whatever thou
dost, thou shalt be no ways prejudiced or endamaged.

KNIGHT (*aside*) I'faith, he looks much like a conjurer.°   10

FAUSTUS My gracious sovereign, though I must confess myself far
inferior to the report men have published, and nothing answerable
to° the honour of your imperial majesty, yet, for that° love and
duty binds me thereunto, I am content to do whatsoever your
majesty shall command me.   15

EMPEROR Then, Doctor Faustus, mark what I shall say.
As I was sometime solitary set
Within my closet, sundry thoughts arose
About the honour of mine ancestors—
How they had won by prowess such exploits,   20
Got such riches, subdued so many kingdoms
As we that do succeed or they that shall°
Hereafter possess our throne shall,
I fear me, never attain to that degree
Of high renown and great authority.   25
Amongst which kings is Alexander the Great,
Chief spectacle of the world's pre-eminence,°
The bright shining of whose glorious acts
Lightens the world with his reflecting beams—°
As when I hear but motion made of him,°   30
It grieves my soul I never saw the man.
If, therefore, thou by cunning of thine art
Canst raise this man from hollow vaults below
Where lies entombed this famous conqueror,
And bring with him his beauteous paramour,   35

Both in their right shapes, gesture, and attire
They used to wear during their time of life,
Thou shalt both satisfy my just desire
And give me cause to praise thee whilst I live.

FAUSTUS My gracious lord, I am ready to accomplish your request,   40
so far forth as by art and power of my spirit I am able to perform.

KNIGHT (*aside*) I'faith, that's just nothing at all.

FAUSTUS But if it like your grace, it is not in my ability to present
before your eyes the true substantial bodies of those two deceased
princes, which long since are consumed to dust.   45

KNIGHT (*aside*) Ay, marry, Master Doctor, now there's a sign of
grace in you, when you will confess the truth.

FAUSTUS But such spirits as can lively° resemble Alexander and his
paramour shall appear before your grace in that manner that they
best lived in, in their most flourishing estate—which I doubt not   50
shall sufficiently content your imperial majesty.

EMPEROR Go to, Master Doctor. Let me see them presently.

KNIGHT Do you hear, Master Doctor? You bring Alexander and his
paramour before the emperor?

FAUSTUS How then, sir?   55

KNIGHT I'faith, that's as true as Diana turned me to a stag.

FAUSTUS No, sir, but when Actaeon° died, he left the horns for you.
[*Aside to Mephistopheles*] Mephistopheles, begone!
        Exit Mephistopheles

KNIGHT Nay, an you go to conjuring, I'll be gone.
        Exit Knight

FAUSTUS [*aside*] I'll meet with° you anon for interrupting me so.—   60
Here they are, my gracious lord.
        Enter Mephistopheles with Alexander and his Paramour

EMPEROR Master Doctor, I heard this lady while she lived had a wart
or mole in her neck. How shall I know whether it be so or no?

FAUSTUS Your highness may boldly go and see.
        [*The Emperor makes an inspection, and then*] *exeunt*
        Alexander [*and his Paramour*]

EMPEROR Sure these are no spirits, but the true substantial bodies of   65
those two deceased princes.

FAUSTUS Will't please your highness now to send for the knight that
was so pleasant with me here of late?

EMPEROR One of you call him forth.
        [*An Attendant goes to summon the Knight.*] *Enter the Knight*
        with a pair of horns on his head

How now, sir knight? Why, I had thought thou hadst been a   70
bachelor,° but now I see thou hast a wife, that not only gives thee
horns but makes thee wear them.° Feel on thy head.

KNIGHT [to Faustus] Thou damnèd wretch and execrable dog,
Bred in the concave of some monstrous rock,°
How dar'st thou thus abuse a gentleman?   75
Villain, I say, undo what thou hast done.

FAUSTUS O, not so fast, sir. There's no haste but good.°
Are you remembered how you crossed me in my conference with
the emperor? I think I have met with you for it.

EMPEROR Good Master Doctor, at my entreaty release him. He hath   80
done penance sufficient.

FAUSTUS My gracious lord, not so much for the injury he offered
me here in your presence as to delight you with some mirth
hath Faustus worthily requited this injurious knight; which being
all I desire, I am content to release him of his horns.—And, sir   85
knight, hereafter speak well of scholars. [Aside to Mephistopheles]
Mephistopheles, transform him straight. [The horns are removed]
Now, my good lord, having done my duty, I humbly take my
leave.

EMPEROR Farewell, Master Doctor. Yet, ere you go,   90
Expect from me a bounteous reward.
          Exeunt Emperor, [Knight, and Attendants]

FAUSTUS Now, Mephistopheles, the restless course
That time doth run with calm and silent foot,
Short'ning my days and thread of vital life,
Calls for the payment of my latest years.°   95
Therefore, sweet Mephistopheles, let us make haste
To Wittenberg.°

MEPHISTOPHELES What, will you go on horseback or on foot?

FAUSTUS Nay, till I am past this fair and pleasant green,
I'll walk on foot.   100
          Enter a Horse-courser°

HORSE-COURSER I have been all this day seeking one Master Fustian.° Mass, see where he is.—God save you, Master Doctor.

FAUSTUS What, Horse-courser! You are well met.

HORSE-COURSER [offering money] Do you hear, sir? I have brought
you forty dollars for your horse.   105

FAUSTUS I cannot sell him so. If thou lik'st him for fifty, take him.

HORSE-COURSER Alas, sir, I have no more. [To Mephistopheles]° I
pray you, speak for me.

171

MEPHISTOPHELES [*to Faustus*] I pray you, let him have him. He is
    an honest fellow, and he has a great charge, neither wife nor   110
    child.°
FAUSTUS Well, come, give me your money. [*He takes the money*] My
    boy will deliver him to you. But I must tell you one thing before
    you have him: ride him not into the water, at any hand.°
HORSE-COURSER Why, sir, will he not drink of all waters?°   115
FAUSTUS O, yes, he will drink of all waters. But ride him not into
    the water. Ride him over hedge, or ditch, or where thou wilt, but
    not into the water.
HORSE-COURSER Well, sir. [*Aside*] Now am I made man° for ever.
    I'll not leave° my horse for forty. If he had but the quality of hey,   120
    ding, ding, hey, ding, ding, I'd make a brave living on him; he has
    a buttock as slick as an eel.° [*To Faustus*] Well, goodbye, sir. Your
    boy will deliver him me? But hark ye, sir: if my horse be sick or
    ill at ease, if I bring his water° to you, you'll tell me what it is?
FAUSTUS Away, you villain! What, dost think I am a horse-doctor?   125
        Exit Horse-courser
    What art thou, Faustus, but a man condemned to die?
    Thy fatal time doth draw to final end.°
    Despair doth drive distrust unto my thoughts.
    Confound these passions with a quiet sleep.°
    Tush! Christ did call the thief upon the cross;   130
    Then rest thee, Faustus, quiet in conceit.
        [*Faustus*] *sleep*[*s*] *in his chair. Enter Horse-courser all wet,*
        crying
HORSE-COURSER Alas, alas! 'Doctor' Fustian, quotha! Mass, Doctor
    Lopus° was never such a doctor. H'as given me a purgation,° h'as
    purged me of forty dollars. I shall never see them more. But yet,
    like an ass as I was, I would not be ruled by him, for he bade me   135
    I should ride him into no water. Now I, thinking my horse had
    had some rare quality that he would not have had me known of,° I,
    like a venturous youth, rid him into the deep pond at the town's
    end. I was no sooner in the middle of the pond but my horse
    vanished away and I sat upon a bottle° of hay, never so near   140
    drowning in my life. But I'll seek out my doctor and have my forty
    dollars again, or I'll make it the dearest horse! O, yonder is his
    snipper-snapper.° —Do you hear? You, hey-pass,° where's your
    master?
MEPHISTOPHELES Why, sir, what would you? You cannot speak   145
    with him.

HORSE-COURSER But I will speak with him.

MEPHISTOPHELES Why, he's fast asleep. Come some other time.

HORSE-COURSER I'll speak with him now, or I'll break his glass windows° about his ears.   150

MEPHISTOPHELES I tell thee he has not slept this eight nights.

HORSE-COURSER An he have not slept this eight weeks, I'll speak with him.

MEPHISTOPHELES See where he is, fast asleep.

HORSE-COURSER Ay, this is he.—God save ye, Master Doctor.   155
Master Doctor, Master Doctor Fustian! Forty dollars, forty dollars for a bottle of hay!

MEPHISTOPHELES Why, thou seest he hears thee not.

HORSE-COURSER (holler[s] in his ear) So-ho, ho! So-ho, ho! No, will you not wake? I'll make you wake ere I go.   160
   [The Horse-courser] pull[s] him by the leg, and pull[s] it away
Alas, I am undone! What shall I do?

FAUSTUS O my leg, my leg! Help, Mephistopheles! Call the officers! My leg, my leg!

MEPHISTOPHELES [seizing the Horse-courser] Come, villain, to the constable.   165

HORSE-COURSER O Lord, sir, let me go, and I'll give you forty dollars more.

MEPHISTOPHELES Where be they?

HORSE-COURSER I have none about me. Come to my hostry, and I'll give them you.   170

MEPHISTOPHELES Begone, quickly.
   Horse-courser runs away

FAUSTUS What, is he gone? Farewell, he!° Faustus has his leg again, and the horse-courser, I take it, a bottle of hay for his labour. Well, this trick shall cost him forty dollars more.
   Enter Wagner
How now, Wagner, what's the news with thee?   175

WAGNER Sir, the duke of Vanholt° doth earnestly entreat your company.

FAUSTUS The duke of Vanholt! An honourable gentleman, to whom I must be no niggard of my cunning. Come, Mephistopheles, let's away to him.   180
   Exeunt

[4.2]

*[Enter Faustus with Mephistopheles.] Enter to them the Duke
[of Vanholt] and the [pregnant] Duchess. The Duke speaks*

DUKE Believe me, Master Doctor, this merriment hath much pleased
me.

FAUSTUS My gracious lord, I am glad it contents you so well.—But
it may be, madam, you take no delight in this. I have heard that
great-bellied° women do long for some dainties or other. What is   5
it, madam? Tell me, and you shall have it.

DUCHESS Thanks, good Master Doctor. And, for I see your courteous intent to pleasure me, I will not hide from you the thing my
heart desires. And were it now summer, as it is January and the
dead time of the winter, I would desire no better meat than a dish   10
of ripe grapes.

FAUSTUS Alas, madam, that's nothing. *[Aside to Mephistopheles]*
Mephistopheles, begone!

Exit Mephistopheles

Were it a greater thing than this, so it would content you, you
should have it.   15

Enter Mephistopheles with the grapes

Here they be, madam. Will't please you taste on them?

[The Duchess tastes the grapes]

DUKE Believe me, Master Doctor, this makes me wonder above the
rest, that, being in the dead time of winter and in the month of
January, how you should come by these grapes.

FAUSTUS If it like your grace, the year is divided into two circles over   20
the whole world, that when it is here winter with us, in the
contrary circle° it is summer with them, as in India, Saba, and
farther countries in the East; and by means of a swift spirit that I
have, I had them brought hither, as ye see.—How do you like
them, madam? Be they good?   25

DUCHESS Believe me, Master Doctor, they be the best grapes that
e'er I tasted in my life before.

FAUSTUS I am glad they content you so, madam.

DUKE Come, madam, let us in,
Where you must well reward this learnèd man   30
For the great kindness he hath showed to you.

DUCHESS And so I will, my lord, and whilst I live
Rest beholding for this courtesy.

FAUSTUS I humbly thank your grace.
DUKE Come, Master Doctor, follow us and receive your reward.   35
    Exeunt

[5.1]

Enter Wagner solus

WAGNER I think my master means to die shortly,
  For he hath given to me all his goods.
  And yet methinks if that death were near
  He would not banquet and carouse and swill
  Amongst the students, as even now he doth,   5
  Who are at supper with such belly-cheer
  As Wagner ne'er beheld in all his life.
  See where they come. Belike the feast is ended.
    [Exit Wagner.] Enter Faustus with two or three Scholars
    [and Mephistopheles]

FIRST SCHOLAR Master Doctor Faustus, since our conference about
fair ladies—which was the beautifull'st in all the world—we have   10
determined with ourselves that Helen of Greece was the admir-
ablest lady that ever lived. Therefore, Master Doctor, if you will
do us that favour as to let us see that peerless dame of Greece,
whom all the world admires for majesty, we should think ourselves
much beholding unto you.   15

FAUSTUS Gentlemen,
  For that I know your friendship is unfeigned,°
  And Faustus' custom is not to deny
  The just requests of those that wish him well,
  You shall behold that peerless dame of Greece,   20
  No otherways for pomp and majesty°
  Than when Sir Paris crossed the seas with her
  And brought the spoils to rich Dardania.°
  Be silent then, for danger is in words.
    Music sounds and Helen, [led in by Mephistopheles,] passeth
    over the stage°

SECOND SCHOLAR Too simple is my wit to tell her praise,   25
  Whom all the world admires for majesty.

THIRD SCHOLAR No marvel though the angry Greeks pursued
  With ten years' war the rape of such a queen,
  Whose heavenly beauty passeth all compare.

FIRST SCHOLAR Since we have seen the pride of nature's works   30
  And only paragon of excellence,
    Enter an Old Man

176

Let us depart; and for this glorious deed
Happy and blest be Faustus evermore.°
FAUSTUS Gentlemen, farewell. The same I wish to you.
    Exeunt Scholars
OLD MAN Ah, Doctor Faustus, that I might prevail   35
To guide thy steps unto the way of life,
By which sweet path thou mayst attain the goal
That shall conduct thee to celestial rest!
Break heart, drop blood, and mingle it with tears—
Tears falling from repentant heaviness   40
Of thy most vile and loathsome filthiness,
The stench whereof corrupts the inward soul
With such flagitious crimes of heinous sins°
As no commiseration may expel
But mercy, Faustus, of thy Saviour sweet,   45
Whose blood alone must wash away thy guilt.
FAUSTUS Where art thou, Faustus? Wretch, what hast thou done?
Damned art thou, Faustus, damned! Despair and die!
Hell calls for right, and with a roaring voice
Says, 'Faustus, come! Thine hour is come.'   50
    Mephistopheles gives him a dagger
And Faustus will come to do thee right.
    [*Faustus prepares to stab himself*]
OLD MAN Ah, stay, good Faustus, stay thy desperate steps!
I see an angel hovers o'er thy head,
And with a vial full of precious grace
Offers to pour the same into thy soul.
Then call for mercy and avoid despair.   55
FAUSTUS Ah, my sweet friend, I feel thy words
To comfort my distressèd soul.
Leave me a while to ponder on my sins.
OLD MAN I go, sweet Faustus, but with heavy cheer,   60
Fearing the ruin of thy hopeless soul.
    [*Exit the Old Man*]
FAUSTUS Accursèd Faustus, where is mercy now?
I do repent, and yet I do despair.
Hell strives with grace for conquest in my breast.
What shall I do to shun the snares of death?   65
MEPHISTOPHELES Thou traitor, Faustus, I arrest thy soul
For disobedience to my sovereign lord.
Revolt, or I'll in piecemeal tear thy flesh.°

FAUSTUS Sweet Mephistopheles, entreat thy lord
　　To pardon my unjust presumption,　　　　　　　　　　　　70
　　And with my blood again I will confirm
　　My former vow I made to Lucifer.
MEPHISTOPHELES Do it then quickly, with unfeignèd heart,
　　Lest greater danger do attend thy drift.°
　　　　　[*Faustus cuts his arm and writes with his blood*]
FAUSTUS Torment, sweet friend, that base and crooked age°　　75
　　That durst dissuade me from thy Lucifer,
　　With greatest torments that our hell affords.
MEPHISTOPHELES His faith is great. I cannot touch his soul.
　　But what I may afflict his body with
　　I will attempt, which is but little worth.　　　　　　　　80
FAUSTUS One thing, good servant, let me crave of thee
　　To glut the longing of my heart's desire:
　　That I might have unto my paramour°
　　That heavenly Helen which I saw of late,
　　Whose sweet embracings may extinguish clean　　　　　　85
　　These thoughts that do dissuade me from my vow,
　　And keep mine oath I made to Lucifer.
MEPHISTOPHELES Faustus, this, or what else thou shalt desire,
　　Shall be performed in twinkling of an eye.
　　　　　Enter Helen [*brought in by Mephistopheles*]
FAUSTUS Was this the face that launched a thousand ships　　90
　　And burnt the topless towers of Ilium?°
　　Sweet Helen, make me immortal with a kiss.
　　　　　[*They kiss*]
　　Her lips sucks forth my soul. See where it flies!
　　Come, Helen, come, give me my soul again.
　　　　　[*They kiss again*]
　　Here will I dwell, for heaven be in these lips,　　　　　95
　　And all is dross that is not Helena.
　　　　　Enter [*the*] *Old Man*
　　I will be Paris, and for love of thee
　　Instead of Troy shall Wittenberg be sacked,
　　And I will combat with weak Menelaus,°
　　And wear thy colours on my plumèd crest.　　　　　　　100
　　Yea, I will wound Achilles in the heel°
　　And then return to Helen for a kiss.
　　O, thou art fairer than the evening air,
　　Clad in the beauty of a thousand stars.

Brighter art thou than flaming Jupiter   105
When he appeared to hapless Semele,°
More lovely than the monarch of the sky
In wanton Arethusa's azured arms;°
And none but thou shalt be my paramour.
              Exeunt [Faustus and Helen, with Mephistopheles]
OLD MAN Accursèd Faustus, miserable man,   110
    That from thy soul exclud'st the grace of heaven
    And fliest the throne of His tribunal seat!
              *Enter the Devils, [with Mephistopheles. They menace the
              Old Man]*
    Satan begins to sift me with his pride.
    As in this furnace God shall try my faith,
    My faith, vile hell, shall triumph over thee.   115
    Ambitious fiends, see how the heavens smiles
    At your repulse and laughs your state to scorn!
    Hence, hell! For hence I fly unto my God.
              Exeunt

[5.2]

              Enter Faustus with the Scholars
FAUSTUS Ah, gentlemen!
FIRST SCHOLAR What ails Faustus?
FAUSTUS Ah, my sweet chamber-fellow! Had I lived with thee, then
    had I lived still, but now I die eternally. Look, comes he not?
    Comes he not?   5
              [The Scholars speak among themselves]
SECOND SCHOLAR What means Faustus?
THIRD SCHOLAR Belike he is grown into some sickness by being
    over-solitary.
FIRST SCHOLAR If it be so, we'll have physicians to cure him. *[To
    Faustus]* 'Tis but a surfeit. Never fear, man.   10
FAUSTUS A surfeit of deadly sin that hath damned both body and soul.
SECOND SCHOLAR Yet, Faustus, look up to heaven. Remember
    God's mercies are infinite.
FAUSTUS But Faustus' offence can ne'er be pardoned. The serpent
    that tempted Eve may be saved, but not° Faustus. Ah, gentlemen, 15
    hear me with patience, and tremble not at my speeches. Though

my heart pants and quivers to remember that I have been a student here these thirty years, O, would I had never seen Wittenberg, never read book! And what wonders I have done, all Germany can witness, yea, all the world, for which Faustus hath lost both 20 Germany and the world, yea, heaven itself—heaven, the seat of God, the throne of the blessed, the kingdom of joy—and must remain in hell for ever. Hell, ah, hell for ever! Sweet friends, what shall become of Faustus, being in hell for ever?

THIRD SCHOLAR Yet, Faustus, call on God.   25

FAUSTUS On God, whom Faustus hath abjured? On God, whom Faustus hath blasphemed? Ah, my God, I would weep, but the devil draws in my tears. Gush forth blood instead of tears, yea, life and soul. O, he stays my tongue! I would lift up my hands, but see, they hold them, they hold them.   30

ALL Who, Faustus?

FAUSTUS Lucifer and Mephistopheles. Ah, gentlemen! I gave them my soul for my cunning.

ALL God forbid!

FAUSTUS God forbade it indeed, but Faustus hath done it.° For vain 35 pleasure of four-and-twenty years hath Faustus lost eternal joy and felicity. I writ them a bill with mine own blood. The date is expired, the time will come, and he will fetch me.

FIRST SCHOLAR Why did not Faustus tell us of this before, that divines might have prayed for thee?   40

FAUSTUS Oft have I thought to have done so, but the devil threatened to tear me in pieces if I named God, to fetch both body and soul if I once gave ear to divinity. And now 'tis too late. Gentlemen, away, lest you perish with me.

SECOND SCHOLAR O, what shall we do to save° Faustus?   45

FAUSTUS Talk not of me, but save yourselves and depart.

THIRD SCHOLAR God will strengthen me. I will stay with Faustus.

FIRST SCHOLAR [to the Third Scholar] Tempt not God, sweet friend, but let us into the next room and there pray for him.

FAUSTUS Ay, pray for me, pray for me! And what noise soever ye 50 hear, come not unto me, for nothing can rescue me.

SECOND SCHOLAR Pray thou, and we will pray that God may have mercy upon thee.

FAUSTUS Gentlemen, farewell. If I live till morning, I'll visit you; if not, Faustus is gone to hell.   55

ALL Faustus, farewell.

　　　Exeunt Scholars. The clock strikes eleven

FAUSTUS Ah, Faustus,
   Now hast thou but one bare hour to live,
   And then thou must be damned perpetually.
   Stand still, you ever-moving spheres of heaven,   60
   That time may cease and midnight never come!
   Fair nature's eye, rise, rise again, and make°
   Perpetual day; or let this hour be but
   A year, a month, a week, a natural day,
   That Faustus may repent and save his soul!   65
   O lente, lente currite noctis equi!°
   The stars move still; time runs; the clock will strike;
   The devil will come, and Faustus must be damned.
   O, I'll leap up to my God! Who pulls me down?
   See, see where Christ's blood streams in the firmament!   70
   One drop would save my soul, half a drop. Ah, my Christ!
   Ah, rend not my heart for naming of my Christ!
   Yet will I call on him. O, spare me, Lucifer!
   Where is it now? 'Tis gone; and see where God
   Stretcheth out his arm and bends his ireful brows!   75
   Mountains and hills, come, come and fall on me,
   And hide me from the heavy wrath of God!
   No, no!
   Then will I headlong run into the earth.
   Earth, gape! O, no, it will not harbour me.   80
   You stars that reigned at my nativity,
   Whose influence hath allotted death and hell,
   Now draw up Faustus like a foggy mist
   Into the entrails of yon labouring cloud,
   That when you vomit forth into the air,   85
   My limbs may issue from your smoky mouths,
   So that my soul may but ascend to heaven.°
      The watch strikes.
   Ah, half the hour is past!
   'Twill all be past anon.
   O God,   90
   If thou wilt not have mercy on my soul,
   Yet for Christ's sake, whose blood hath ransomed me,
   Impose some end to my incessant pain.
   Let Faustus live in hell a thousand years,
   A hundred thousand, and at last be saved.   95
   O, no end is limited to damnèd souls.

Why wert thou not a creature wanting soul?
Or why is this immortal that thou hast?
Ah, Pythagoras' *metempsychosis*, were that true,°
This soul should fly from me and I be changed   100
Unto some brutish beast.
All beasts are happy, for, when they die,
Their souls are soon dissolved in elements;
But mine must live still to be plagued in hell.
Curst be the parents that engendered me!   105
No, Faustus, curse thyself. Curse Lucifer,
That hath deprived thee of the joys of heaven.
    The clock striketh twelve
O, it strikes, it strikes! Now, body, turn to air,
Or Lucifer will bear thee quick to hell.°
    Thunder and lightning
O soul, be changed into little waterdrops,   110
And fall into the ocean, ne'er be found!
My God, my God, look not so fierce on me!
    Enter [Lucifer, Mephistopheles, and other] Devils
Adders and serpents, let me breathe a while!
Ugly hell, gape not. Come not, Lucifer!
I'll burn my books. Ah, Mephistopheles!   115
    [*The Devils*] *exeunt with him*

[EPILOGUE]

Enter Chorus

CHORUS Cut is the branch that might have grown full straight,
And burnèd is Apollo's laurel bough
That sometime grew within this learnèd man.
Faustus is gone. Regard his hellish fall,
Whose fiendful fortune may exhort the wise   5
Only to wonder at unlawful things,
Whose deepness doth entice such forward wits
To practise more than heavenly power permits.
        [*Exit*]
        Terminat hora diem; terminat author opus.°

DOCTOR FAUSTUS
B-Text

DRAMATIS PERSONAE

The Chorus
Doctor John Faustus
Wagner
Good Angel
Bad Angel
Valdes
Cornelius
Three Scholars
Lucifer
Devils
Mephistopheles
Robin, *the Clown*
A Woman Devil
Dick
Beelzebub
Pride ⎫
Covetousness ⎪
Envy ⎪
Wrath ⎬ *The Seven Deadly Sins*
Gluttony ⎪
Sloth ⎪
Lechery ⎭
Pope Adrian
Raymond, King of Hungary
Bruno, *the rival pope*
The Cardinal of France
The Cardinal of Padua
The Archbishop of Rheims

The Bishop of Lorraine
Monks
Friars
A Vintner
Martino
Frederick
Officers
Gentlemen
Benvolio
The Emperor of Germany, Charles V
The Duke of Saxony
Alexander the Great ⎫
His Paramour ⎬ *Spirits*
Darius ⎭
Belimoth ⎫
Argiron ⎬ *Devils*
Ashtaroth ⎭
Soldiers
A Horse-Courser
A Carter
A Hostess
The Duke of Vanholt
The Duchess of Vanholt
A Servant
Helen of Troy, *a spirit*
An Old Man
Two Cupids

The Tragedy of Doctor Faustus (B-Text)

[PROLOGUE]

Enter Chorus

CHORUS Not marching in the fields of Trasimene
    Where Mars did mate the warlike Carthagens,
    Nor sporting in the dalliance of love
    In courts of kings where state is overturned,
    Nor in the pomp of proud audacious deeds,   5
    Intends our muse to vaunt his heavenly verse.°
    Only this, gentles: we must now perform
    The form of Faustus' fortunes, good or bad.
    And now to patient judgements we appeal,
    And speak for Faustus in his infancy.   10
    Now is he born, of parents base of stock,
    In Germany, within a town called Rhode.
    At riper years to Wittenberg he went,
    Whereas his kinsmen chiefly brought him up.
    So much he profits in divinity   15
    That shortly he was graced with doctor's name,
    Excelling all, and sweetly can dispute
    In th'heavenly matters of theology;
    Till, swoll'n with cunning of a self-conceit,
    His waxen wings did mount above his reach,   20
    And, melting, heavens conspired his overthrow.
    For, falling to a devilish exercise,
    And glutted now with learning's golden gifts,
    He surfeits upon cursèd necromancy;
    Nothing so sweet as magic is to him,   25
    Which he prefers before his chiefest bliss.
    And this the man that in his study sits.
        [Exit]

[1.1]

Faustus in his study

FAUSTUS Settle thy studies, Faustus, and begin
    To sound the depth of that thou wilt profess.
    Having commenced, be a divine in show,
    Yet level at the end of every art,
    And live and die in Aristotle's works.   5
    Sweet *Analytics*, 'tis thou hast ravished me!
    [*He reads*] '*Bene disserere est finis logices.*'
    Is to dispute well logic's chiefest end?
    Affords this art no greater miracle?
    Then read no more; thou hast attained that end.   10
    A greater subject fitteth Faustus' wit.
    Bid *Oeconomy* farewell, and Galen, come!°
    Be a physician, Faustus. Heap up gold,
    And be eternized for some wondrous cure.
    [*He reads*] '*Summum bonum medicinae sanitas*':   15
    The end of physic is our body's health.
    Why Faustus, hast thou not attained that end?
    Are not thy bills hung up as monuments,
    Whereby whole cities have escaped the plague
    And thousand desperate maladies been cured?   20
    Yet art thou still but Faustus, and a man.
    Couldst thou make men to live eternally,
    Or, being dead, raise them to life again,
    Then this profession were to be esteemed.
    Physic, farewell! Where is Justinian?   25
    [*He reads*] '*Si una eademque res legatur duobus,*
    Alter rem, alter valorem rei', etc.
    A petty case of paltry legacies!
    [*He reads*] '*Exhaereditare filium non potest pater nisi*—'
    Such is the subject of the Institute   30
    And universal body of the law.
    This study fits a mercenary drudge
    Who aims at nothing but external trash—
    Too servile and illiberal for me.
    When all is done, divinity is best.   35
    Jerome's Bible, Faustus, view it well.

[*He reads*] '*Stipendium peccati mors est.*' Ha!
'*Stipendium*', etc.
The reward of sin is death? That's hard.
[*He reads*] '*Si peccasse negamus, fallimur*   40
Et nulla est in nobis veritas.'
If we say that we have no sin,
We deceive ourselves, and there is no truth in us.
Why then belike we must sin,
And so consequently die.   45
Ay, we must die an everlasting death.
What doctrine call you this? *Che serà, serà*:
What will be, shall be. Divinity, adieu!
    [*He picks up a book of magic*]
These metaphysics of magicians
And necromantic books are heavenly,   50
Lines, circles, letters, characters—
Ay, these are those that Faustus most desires.
O, what a world of profit and delight,
Of power, of honour, and omnipotence
Is promised to the studious artisan!   55
All things that move between the quiet poles
Shall be at my command. Emperors and kings
Arc but obeyed in their several provinces,
But his dominion that exceeds in this
Stretcheth as far as doth the mind of man.   60
A sound magician is a demigod.
Here tire my brains to get a deity.°
Wagner!
    Enter Wagner
      Commend me to my dearest friends,
The German Valdes and Cornelius.
Request them earnestly to visit me.   65
WAGNER I will, sir.
    Exit [*Wagner*]
FAUSTUS Their conference will be a greater help to me
Than all my labours, plod I ne'er so fast.
    Enter the [*Good*] *Angel and Spirit,* [*i.e. the Bad Angel*]
GOOD ANGEL O Faustus, lay that damnèd book aside
And gaze not on it, lest it tempt thy soul   70
And heap God's heavy wrath upon thy head!
Read, read the Scriptures. That is blasphemy.

BAD ANGEL Go forward, Faustus, in that famous art
   Wherein all nature's treasure is contained.
   Be thou on earth as Jove is in the sky,   75
   Lord and commander of these elements.
     Exeunt Angels
FAUSTUS How am I glutted with conceit of this!
   Shall I make spirits fetch me what I please?
   Resolve me of all ambiguities?
   Perform what desperate enterprise I will?   80
   I'll have them fly to India for gold,
   Ransack the ocean for orient pearl,
   And search all corners of the new-found world
   For pleasant fruits and princely delicates.
   I'll have them read me strange philosophy   85
   And tell the secrets of all foreign kings.
   I'll have them wall all Germany with brass
   And make swift Rhine circle fair Wittenberg.
   I'll have them fill the public schools with silk,
   Wherewith the students shall be bravely clad.   90
   I'll levy soldiers with the coin they bring
   And chase the Prince of Parma from our land,
   And reign sole king of all the provinces;
   Yea, stranger engines for the brunt of war
   Than was the fiery keel at Antwerp bridge   95
   I'll make my servile spirits to invent.
   Come, German Valdes and Cornelius,
   And make me blest with your sage conference!
    Enter Valdes and Cornelius
   Valdes, sweet Valdes, and Cornelius,
   Know that your words have won me at the last   100
   To practise magic and concealèd arts.
   Philosophy is odious and obscure;
   Both law and physic are for petty wits;
   'Tis magic, magic that hath ravished me.
   Then, gentle friends, aid me in this attempt,   105
   And I, that have with subtle syllogisms
   Gravelled the pastors of the German Church
   And made the flow'ring pride of Wittenberg
   Swarm to my problems as th'infernal spirits
   On sweet Musaeus when he came to hell,   110
   Will be as cunning as Agrippa was,

Whose shadow made all Europe honour him.
VALDES Faustus, these books, thy wit, and our experience
    Shall make all nations to canonize us.
    As Indian Moors obey their Spanish lords,   115
    So shall the spirits of every element
    Be always serviceable to us three.
    Like lions shall they guard us when we please,
    Like Almaine rutters with their horsemen's staves,
    Or Lapland giants, trotting by our sides;   120
    Sometimes like women, or unwedded maids,
    Shadowing more beauty in their airy brows
    Than has the white breasts of the Queen of Love.
    From Venice shall they drag huge argosies,
    And from America the golden fleece   125
    That yearly stuffed old Philip's treasury,
    If learnèd Faustus will be resolute.
FAUSTUS Valdes, as resolute am I in this
    As thou to live. Therefore object it not.
CORNELIUS The miracles that magic will perform   130
    Will make thee vow to study nothing else.
    He that is grounded in astrology,
    Enriched with tongues, well seen in minerals,
    Hath all the principles magic doth require.
    Then doubt not, Faustus, but to be renowned   135
    And more frequented for this mystery
    Than heretofore the Delphian oracle.
    The spirits tell me they can dry the sea
    And fetch the treasure of all foreign wrecks—
    Yea, all the wealth that our forefathers hid   140
    Within the massy entrails of the earth.
    Then tell me, Faustus, what shall we three want?
FAUSTUS Nothing, Cornelius. O, this cheers my soul!
    Come, show me some demonstrations magical,
    That I may conjure in some bushy grove   145
    And have these joys in full possession.
VALDES Then haste thee to some solitary grove,
    And bear wise Bacon's and Albanus' works,
    The Hebrew Psalter, and New Testament;
    And whatsoever else is requisite   150
    We will inform thee ere our conference cease.
CORNELIUS Valdes, first let him know the words of art,

And then, all other ceremonies learned,
Faustus may try his cunning by himself.
VALDES First I'll instruct thee in the rudiments,   155
And then wilt thou be perfecter than I.
FAUSTUS Then come and dine with me, and after meat
We'll canvass every quiddity thereof,
For ere I sleep I'll try what I can do.
This night I'll conjure, though I die therefore.   160
          Exeunt

[1.2]

          Enter two Scholars
FIRST SCHOLAR I wonder what's become of Faustus, that was wont
to make our schools ring with '*sic probo*'.
          Enter Wagner, [*carrying wine*]
SECOND SCHOLAR That shall we presently know. Here comes his
boy.
FIRST SCHOLAR How now, sirrah, where's thy master?   5
WAGNER God in heaven knows.
SECOND SCHOLAR Why, dost not thou know, then?
WAGNER Yes, I know, but that follows not.
FIRST SCHOLAR Go to, sirrah! Leave your jesting, and tell us where
he is.   10
WAGNER That follows not by force of argument, which you, being
licentiates, should stand upon. Therefore, acknowledge your error,
and be attentive.
SECOND SCHOLAR Then you will not tell us?
WAGNER You are deceived, for I will tell you. Yet if you were not   15
dunces, you would never ask me such a question. For is he not
corpus naturale? And is not that *mobile*? Then, wherefore should
you ask me such a question? But that I am by nature phlegmatic,
slow to wrath, and prone to lechery—to love, I would say—it were
not for you to come within forty foot of the place of execution,   20
although I do not doubt but to see you both hanged the next
sessions. Thus, having triumphed over you, I will set my countenance like a precisian and begin to speak thus: Truly, my dear
brethren, my master is within at dinner with Valdes and Cornelius,
as this wine, if it could speak, would inform your worships. And   25

so the Lord bless you, preserve you, and keep you, my dear
brethren.
    Exit [Wagner]
FIRST SCHOLAR O Faustus,
  Then I fear that which I have long suspected,
  That thou art fall'n into that damnèd art   30
  For which they two are infamous through the world.
SECOND SCHOLAR Were he a stranger, not allied to me,
  The danger of his soul would make me mourn.
  But come, let us go and inform the Rector.
  It may be his grave counsel may reclaim him.   35
FIRST SCHOLAR I fear me nothing will reclaim him now.
SECOND SCHOLAR Yet let us see what we can do.
    Exeunt

[1.3]

Thunder. Enter Lucifer and four Devils [above].° [Enter]
Faustus to them with this speech. [He holds a book, unaware
of their presence]
FAUSTUS Now that the gloomy shadow of the night,
  Longing to view Orion's drizzling look,
  Leaps from th'Antarctic world unto the sky
  And dims the welkin with her pitchy breath,
  Faustus, begin thine incantations,   5
  And try if devils will obey thy hest,
  Seeing thou hast prayed and sacrificed to them.
    [He draws a circle]
  Within this circle is Jehovah's name
  Forward and backward anagrammatized,
  Th'abbreviated names of holy saints,   10
  Figures of every adjunct to the heavens,
  And characters of signs and erring stars,°
  By which the spirits are enforced to rise.
  Then fear not, Faustus, to be resolute,
  And try the utmost magic can perform.   15
    Thunder
Sint mihi dei Acherontis propitii! Valeat numen triplex Jehovae! Ignei,
aerii, aquatici, terreni, spiritus, salvete! Orientis princeps Lucifer,

Beelzebub, inferni ardentis monarcha, et Demogorgon, propitiamus vos,
ut appareat et surgat Mephistopheles. Quid tu moraris? Per Jehovam,
Gehennam, et consecratam aquam quam nunc spargo, signumque crucis   20
quod nunc facio, et per vota nostra, ipse nunc surgat nobis dicatus
Mephistopheles!
  [*Faustus sprinkles holy water and makes a sign of the cross.*]
  Enter a Devil [*Mephistopheles, in the shape of a*] *dragon*
I charge thee to return and change thy shape.
Thou art too ugly to attend on me.
Go, and return an old Franciscan friar;   25
That holy shape becomes a devil best.
  Exit Devil [*Mephistopheles*]
I see there's virtue in my heavenly words.
Who would not be proficient in this art?
How pliant is this Mephistopheles,
Full of obedience and humility!   30
Such is the force of magic and my spells.
  Enter Mephistopheles [*dressed as a friar*]
MEPHISTOPHELES Now, Faustus, what wouldst thou have me do?
FAUSTUS I charge thee wait upon me whilst I live,
To do whatever Faustus shall command,
Be it to make the moon drop from her sphere   35
Or the ocean to overwhelm the world.
MEPHISTOPHELES I am a servant to great Lucifer
And may not follow thee without his leave.
No more than he commands must we perform.
FAUSTUS Did not he charge thee to appear to me?   40
MEPHISTOPHELES No, I came now hither of mine own accord.
FAUSTUS Did not my conjuring raise thee? Speak.
MEPHISTOPHELES That was the cause, but yet *per accidens*.
For when we hear one rack the name of God,
Abjure the Scriptures and his Saviour Christ,   45
We fly in hope to get his glorious soul,
Nor will we come unless he use such means
Whereby he is in danger to be damned.
Therefore, the shortest cut for conjuring
Is stoutly to abjure all godliness   50
And pray devoutly to the prince of hell.
FAUSTUS So Faustus hath
Already done, and holds this principle:
There is no chief but only Beelzebub,

To whom Faustus doth dedicate himself.   55
This word 'damnation' terrifies not me,
For I confound hell in Elysium.
My ghost be with the old philosophers!
But leaving these vain trifles of men's souls,
Tell me, what is that Lucifer thy lord?   60
MEPHISTOPHELES Arch-regent and commander of all spirits.
FAUSTUS Was not that Lucifer an angel once?
MEPHISTOPHELES Yes, Faustus, and most dearly loved of God.
FAUSTUS How comes it then that he is prince of devils?
MEPHISTOPHELES O, by aspiring pride and insolence,   65
For which God threw him from the face of heaven.
FAUSTUS And what are you that live with Lucifer?
MEPHISTOPHELES Unhappy spirits that fell with Lucifer,°
Conspired against our God with Lucifer,
And are for ever damned with Lucifer.   70
FAUSTUS Where are you damned?
MEPHISTOPHELES In hell.
FAUSTUS How comes it then that thou art out of hell?
MEPHISTOPHELES Why, this is hell, nor am I out of it.
Think'st thou that I, that saw the face of God   75
And tasted the eternal joys of heaven,
Am not tormented with ten thousand hells
In being deprived of everlasting bliss?
O Faustus, leave these frivolous demands,
Which strikes a terror to my fainting soul!   80
FAUSTUS What, is great Mephistopheles so passionate
For being deprivèd of the joys of heaven?
Learn thou of Faustus manly fortitude,
And scorn those joys thou never shalt possess.
Go bear these tidings to great Lucifer: 85
Seeing Faustus hath incurred eternal death
By desperate thoughts against Jove's deity,
Say he surrenders up to him his soul,
So he will spare him four-and-twenty years,
Letting him live in all voluptuousness,   90
Having thee ever to attend on me,
To give me whatsoever I shall ask,
To tell me whatsoever I demand,
To slay mine enemies and to aid my friends,
And always be obedient to my will,   95

Go and return to mighty Lucifer,
And meet me in my study at midnight,
And then resolve me of thy master's mind.
MEPHISTOPHELES I will, Faustus.
          Exit [Mephistopheles]
FAUSTUS Had I as many souls as there be stars,   100
I'd give them all for Mephistopheles.
By him I'll be great emperor of the world
And make a bridge through the moving air
To pass the ocean; with a band of men
I'll join the hills that bind the Afric shore   105
And make that country continent to Spain,
And both contributory to my crown.
The emperor shall not live but by my leave,
Nor any potentate of Germany.
Now that I have obtained what I desired,   110
I'll live in speculation of this art
Till Mephistopheles return again.
          Exit [Faustus below; exeunt Lucifer and other Devils
          above]

[1.4]

          Enter Wagner and [Robin] the Clown
WAGNER Come hither, sirrah boy.
ROBIN 'Boy'? O, disgrace to my person! Zounds, 'boy' in your face!
     You have seen many boys with beards, I am sure.
WAGNER Sirrah, hast thou no comings in?
ROBIN Yes, and goings out too, you may see, sir.   5
WAGNER Alas, poor slave, see how poverty jests in his nakedness! I
     know the villain's out of service, and so hungry that I know he
     would give his soul to the devil for a shoulder of mutton, though
     it were blood raw.
ROBIN Not so, neither. I had need to have it well roasted, and good 10
     sauce to it, if I pay so dear, I can tell you.
WAGNER Sirrah, wilt thou be my man and wait on me? And I will
     make these go like *Qui mihi discipulus.*
ROBIN What, in verse?
WAGNER No, slave, in beaten silk and stavesacre.   15

ROBIN Stavesacre? That's good to kill vermin. Then belike if I serve you, I shall be lousy.°

WAGNER Why, so thou shalt be, whether thou dost it or no; for, sirrah, if thou dost not presently bind thyself to me for seven years, I'll turn all the lice about thee into familiars and make them tear thee in pieces.   20

ROBIN Nay, sir, you may save yourself a labour, for they are as familiar with me as if they paid for their meat and drink, I can tell you.

WAGNER [*offering money*] Well, sirrah, leave your jesting, and take these guilders.   25

ROBIN Yes, marry, sir, and I thank you, too.

WAGNER So, now thou art to be at an hour's warning whensoever and wheresoever the devil shall fetch thee.

ROBIN Here, take your guilders. I'll none of 'em.   30
        [*He attempts to return the money*]

WAGNER Not I. Thou art pressed.° Prepare thyself, for I will presently raise up two devils to carry thee away.—Banio! Belcher!

ROBIN Belcher? An Belcher come here, I'll belch him. I am not afraid of a devil.
        Enter two Devils

WAGNER [*to Robin*] How now, sir, will you serve me now?   35

ROBIN Ay, good Wagner. Take away the devil, then.

WAGNER Spirits, away!
        [*Exeunt Devils*]
        Now, sirrah, follow me.

ROBIN I will, sir. But hark you, master, will you teach me this conjuring occupation?   40

WAGNER Ay, sirrah, I'll teach thee to turn thyself to a dog, or a cat, or a mouse, or a rat, or anything.

ROBIN A dog, or a cat, or a mouse, or a rat? O brave, Wagner!

WAGNER Villain, call me Master Wagner, and see that you walk attentively, and let your right eye be always diametrally fixed upon   45 my left heel, that thou mayst *quasi vestigiis nostris insistere.*

ROBIN Well, sir, I warrant you.
        Exeunt

[2.1]

Enter Faustus in his study

FAUSTUS Now, Faustus, must thou needs be damned?
  Canst thou not be saved?
  What boots it then to think on God or heaven?
  Away with such vain fancies, and despair!
  Despair in God and trust in Beelzebub.   5
  Now go not backward, Faustus, be resolute.
  Why waver'st thou? O, something soundeth in mine ear:
  'Abjure this magic, turn to God again!'
  Why, he loves thee not.
  The god thou serv'st is thine own appetite,   10
  Wherein is fixed the love of Beelzebub.
  To him I'll build an altar and a church,
  And offer lukewarm blood of new-born babes.
      Enter the two Angels
BAD ANGEL Go forward, Faustus, in that famous art.
GOOD ANGEL Sweet Faustus, leave that execrable art.   15
FAUSTUS Contrition, prayer, repentance—what of these?
GOOD ANGEL O, they are means to bring thee unto heaven.
BAD ANGEL Rather illusions, fruits of lunacy,
  That make them foolish that do use them most.°
GOOD ANGEL
  Sweet Faustus, think of heaven and heavenly things.   20
BAD ANGEL No, Faustus, think of honour and of wealth.
      Exeunt Angels
FAUSTUS Wealth?
  Why, the seigniory of Emden shall be mine.
  When Mephistopheles shall stand by me,
  What power can hurt me? Faustus, thou art safe;   25
  Cast no more doubts. Mephistopheles, come,
  And bring glad tidings from great Lucifer.
  Is't not midnight? Come, Mephistopheles!
  Veni, veni, Mephistophile!
      Enter Mephistopheles
  Now tell me what saith Lucifer thy lord?   30
MEPHISTOPHELES That I shall wait on Faustus whilst he lives,
  So he will buy my service with his soul.

FAUSTUS Already Faustus hath hazarded that for thee.
MEPHISTOPHELES But now thou must bequeath it solemnly
  And write a deed of gift with thine own blood,   35
  For that security craves Lucifer.
  If thou deny it, I must back to hell.
FAUSTUS Stay, Mephistopheles, and tell me,
  What good will my soul do thy lord?
MEPHISTOPHELES Enlarge his kingdom.   40
FAUSTUS Is that the reason why he tempts us thus?
MEPHISTOPHELES *Solamen miseris socios habuisse doloris.*
FAUSTUS Why, have you any pain, that torture other?
MEPHISTOPHELES As great as have the human souls of men.
  But tell me, Faustus, shall I have thy soul?   45
  And I will be thy slave, and wait on thee,
  And give thee more than thou hast wit to ask.
FAUSTUS Ay, Mephistopheles, I'll give it him.
MEPHISTOPHELES Then, Faustus, stab thy arm courageously,
  And bind thy soul that at some certain day   50
  Great Lucifer may claim it as his own,
  And then be thou as great as Lucifer.
FAUSTUS [*cutting his arm*]
  Lo, Mephistopheles, for love of thee
  Faustus hath cut his arm, and with his proper blood
  Assures his soul to be great Lucifer's,   55
  Chief lord and regent of perpetual night.
  View here this blood that trickles from mine arm,
  And let it be propitious for my wish.
MEPHISTOPHELES But Faustus,
  Write it in manner of a deed of gift.   60
FAUSTUS Ay, so I do. [*He writes*] But Mephistopheles,
  My blood congeals, and I can write no more.
MEPHISTOPHELES I'll fetch thee fire to dissolve it straight.
     Exit [*Mephistopheles*]
FAUSTUS What might the staying of my blood portend?
  Is it unwilling I should write this bill?   65
  Why streams it not, that I may write afresh?
  'Faustus gives to thee his soul'—O, there it stayed!
  Why shouldst thou not? Is not thy soul thine own?
  Then write again: 'Faustus gives to thee his soul.'
     Enter Mephistopheles with the chafer of fire
MEPHISTOPHELES See, Faustus, here is fire. Set it on.   70

FAUSTUS So. Now the blood begins to clear again.
  Now will I make an end immediately.
    [*He writes*]
MEPHISTOPHELES [*aside*]
  What will not I do to obtain his soul?
FAUSTUS *Consummatum est.* This bill is ended,
  And Faustus hath bequeathed his soul to Lucifer.   75
  But what is this inscription on mine arm?
  'Homo, fuge!' Whither should I fly?
  If unto heaven, he'll throw me down to hell.—
  My senses are deceived; here's nothing writ.—
  O, yes, I see it plain. Even here is writ   80
  'Homo, fuge!' Yet shall not Faustus fly.
MEPHISTOPHELES [*aside*]
  I'll fetch him somewhat to delight his mind.
      Exit [Mephistopheles]. Enter Devils, giving crowns and rich
      apparel to Faustus; they dance, and then depart. Enter
      Mephistopheles
FAUSTUS What means this show? Speak, Mephistopheles.
MEPHISTOPHELES Nothing, Faustus, but to delight thy mind
  And let thee see what magic can perform.   85
FAUSTUS But may I raise such spirits when I please?
MEPHISTOPHELES Ay, Faustus, and do greater things than these.
FAUSTUS Then Mephistopheles, receive this scroll,
  A deed of gift of body and of soul—
  But yet conditionally that thou perform   90
  All covenants and articles between us both.
MEPHISTOPHELES Faustus, I swear by hell and Lucifer
  To effect all promises between us both.
FAUSTUS Then hear me read it, Mephistopheles.
  'On these conditions following: 95
  First, that Faustus may be a spirit in form and substance.
  Secondly, that Mephistopheles shall be his servant, and be by him
  commanded.
  Thirdly, that Mephistopheles shall do for him and bring him
  whatsoever.   100
  Fourthly, that he shall be in his chamber or house invisible.
  Lastly, that he shall appear to the said John Faustus at all times in
  what shape and form soever he please.
  I, John Faustus of Wittenberg, Doctor, by these presents, do give
  both body and soul to Lucifer, Prince of the East, and his min- 105

ister Mephistopheles; and furthermore grant unto them that four-
and-twenty years being expired, and these articles above written
being inviolate, full power to fetch or carry the said John Faustus,
body and soul, flesh, blood, into their habitation wheresoever.

By me, John Faustus.' 110

MEPHISTOPHELES Speak, Faustus. Do you deliver this as your deed?

FAUSTUS [*giving the deed*] Ay. Take it, and the devil give thee good
of it.

MEPHISTOPHELES So. Now, Faustus, ask me what thou wilt.

FAUSTUS First I will question thee about hell. 115
Tell me, where is the place that men call hell?

MEPHISTOPHELES Under the heavens.

FAUSTUS Ay, so are all things else. But whereabouts?

MEPHISTOPHELES Within the bowels of these elements,
Where we are tortured and remain for ever. 120
Hell hath no limits, nor is circumscribed
In one self place, but where we are is hell,
And where hell is there must we ever be.
And, to be short, when all the world dissolves,
And every creature shall be purified, 125
All places shall be hell that is not heaven.

FAUSTUS I think hell's a fable.

MEPHISTOPHELES
Ay, think so still, till experience change thy mind.

FAUSTUS
Why, dost thou think that Faustus shall be damned?

MEPHISTOPHELES Ay, of necessity, for here's the scroll 130
In which thou hast given thy soul to Lucifer.

FAUSTUS Ay, and body too. But what of that?
Think'st thou that Faustus is so fond to imagine
That after this life there is any pain?
No, these are trifles and mere old wives' tables. 135

MEPHISTOPHELES But I am an instance to prove the contrary,
For I tell thee I am damned and now in hell.

FAUSTUS Nay, an this be hell, I'll willingly be damned.
What? Sleeping, eating, walking, and disputing?
But leaving this, let me have a wife, the fairest maid in Germany, 140
for I am wanton and lascivious and cannot live without a wife.

MEPHISTOPHELES Well, Faustus, thou shalt have a wife.
He fetches in a woman Devil

FAUSTUS What sight is this?

MEPHISTOPHELES Now, Faustus, wilt thou have a wife?
FAUSTUS Here's a hot whore indeed! No, I'll no wife.   145
MEPHISTOPHELES Marriage is but a ceremonial toy.
    An if thou lovest me, think no more of it.
        [*Exit Devil*]
    I'll cull thee out the fairest courtesans
    And bring them every morning to thy bed.
    She whom thine eye shall like, thy heart shall have,°   150
    Were she as chaste as was Penelope,
    As wise as Saba, or as beautiful
    As was bright Lucifer before his fall.
        [*Presenting a book*]
    Here, take this book and peruse it well.
    The iterating of these lines brings gold;   155
    The framing of this circle on the ground
    Brings thunder, whirlwinds, storm, and lightning.
    Pronounce this thrice devoutly to thyself,
    And men in harness shall appear to thee
    Ready to execute what thou command'st.   160
FAUSTUS Thanks, Mephistopheles, for this sweet book.
    This will I keep as chary as my life.
        Exeunt

[2.2]

Enter [Robin] the Clown [with a conjuring book]
ROBIN [*calling offstage*] What, Dick, look to the horses there till I
    come again.—I have gotten one of Doctor Faustus' conjuring
    books, and now we'll have such knavery as't passes.°
        Enter Dick
DICK What, Robin, you must come away and walk the horses.
ROBIN I walk the horses? I scorn't, 'faith. I have other matters   5
    in hand. Let the horses walk themselves an they will. [*He reads*]
    'A' *per se* 'a'; 't', 'h', 'e', 'the'; 'o' *per se* 'o'; 'deny orgon,
    gorgon'.° —Keep further from me, O thou illiterate and unlearned
    ostler.
DICK 'Snails, what hast thou got there, a book? Why, thou canst not   10
    tell ne'er a word on't.°

ROBIN That thou shalt see presently. [*He draws a circle*] Keep out of
the circle, I say, lest I send you into the hostry, with a vengeance.°

DICK That's like,° 'faith! You had best leave your foolery, for an my
master° come he'll conjure° you, 'faith.   15

ROBIN My master conjure me? I'll tell thee what: an my master come
here, I'll clap as fair a pair of horns° on's head as e'er thou sawest
in thy life.

DICK Thou need'st not do that, for my mistress° hath done it.

ROBIN Ay, there be of us here that have waded as deep into matters   20
as other men, if they were disposed to talk.°

DICK A plague take you! I thought you did not sneak up and down
after her for nothing. But I prithee tell me in good sadness, Robin,
is that a conjuring book?

ROBIN Do but speak what thou'lt have me to do, and I'll do't. If   25
thou'lt dance naked, put off thy clothes, and I'll conjure thee about
presently. Or if thou'lt go but to the tavern with me, I'll give thee
white wine, red wine, claret wine, sack, muscadine, malmsey,
and whippincrust, hold belly hold,° and we'll not pay one penny
for it.

DICK O brave! Prithee let's to it presently, for I am as dry as a   30
dog.

ROBIN Come, then, let's away.
        Exeunt

[2.3]

Enter Faustus in his study, and Mephistopheles

FAUSTUS When I behold the heavens, then I repent
    And curse thee, wicked Mephistopheles,
    Because thou hast deprived me of those joys.

MEPHISTOPHELES 'Twas thine own seeking, Faustus. Thank thyself.
    But think'st thou heaven is such a glorious thing?   5
    I tell thee, Faustus, it is not half so fair
    As thou or any man that breathes on earth.

FAUSTUS How prov'st thou that?

MEPHISTOPHELES 'Twas made for man; then he's more excellent.

FAUSTUS If heaven was made for man, 'twas made for me.   10
    I will renounce this magic and repent.
        Enter the two Angels

GOOD ANGEL Faustus, repent! Yet God will pity thee.
BAD ANGEL Thou art a spirit. God cannot pity thee.
FAUSTUS Who buzzeth in mine ears I am a spirit?
    Be I a devil, yet God may pity me;   15
    Yea, God will pity me if I repent.
BAD ANGEL Ay, but Faustus never shall repent.
        Exeunt Angels
FAUSTUS My heart is hardened; I cannot repent.
    Scarce can I name salvation, faith, or heaven.
    Swords, poison, halters, and envenomed steel   20
    Are laid before me to dispatch myself;
    And long ere this I should have done the deed,
    Had not sweet pleasure conquered deep despair.
    Have not I made blind Homer sing to me
    Of Alexander's love and Oenone's death?   25
    And hath not he that built the walls of Thebes
    With ravishing sound of his melodious harp
    Made music with my Mephistopheles?
    Why should I die, then, or basely despair?
    I am resolved, Faustus shall not repent.   30
    Come, Mephistopheles, let us dispute again
    And reason of divine astrology.
    Speak. Are there many spheres above the moon?
    Are all celestial bodies but one globe,
    As is the substance of this centric earth?   35
MEPHISTOPHELES As are the elements, such are the heavens,
    Even from the moon unto the empyreal orb,°
    Mutually folded in each other's spheres,
    And jointly move upon one axletree,
    Whose terminè is termed the world's wide pole.°   40
    Nor are the names of Saturn, Mars, or Jupiter
    Feigned, but are erring stars.
FAUSTUS But have they all one motion, both *situ et tempore*?
MEPHISTOPHELES All move from east to west in four-and-twenty
    hours upon the poles of the world, but differ in their motions upon   45
    the poles of the zodiac.
FAUSTUS These slender questions Wagner can decide.
    Hath Mephistopheles no greater skill?
    Who knows not the double motion of the planets?
    That the first is finished in a natural day,   50
    The second thus: Saturn in thirty years,

Jupiter in twelve, Mars in four, the sun, Venus, and Mercury in a
year, the moon in twenty-eight days. These are freshmen's questions. But tell me, hath every sphere a dominion or *intelligentia*?

MEPHISTOPHELES Ay.   55

FAUSTUS How many heavens or spheres are there?

MEPHISTOPHELES Nine: the seven planets, the firmament, and the
empyreal heaven.

FAUSTUS But is there not *coelum igneum et crystallinum*?°

MEPHISTOPHELES No, Faustus, they be but fables.   60

FAUSTUS Resolve me then in this one question: why are not conjunctions, oppositions, aspects, eclipses all at one time, but in some
years we have more, in some less?

MEPHISTOPHELES *Per inaequalem motum respectu totius.*

FAUSTUS Well, I am answered. Now tell me who made the world.   65

MEPHISTOPHELES I will not.

FAUSTUS Sweet Mephistopheles, tell me.

MEPHISTOPHELES Move me not, Faustus.

FAUSTUS Villain, have not I bound thee to tell me anything?

MEPHISTOPHELES Ay, that is not against our kingdom.   70
This is. Thou art damned. Think thou of hell.

FAUSTUS Think, Faustus, upon God, that made the world.

MEPHISTOPHELES Remember this.
          Exit [Mephistopheles]

FAUSTUS Ay, go, accursèd spirit, to ugly hell!
'Tis thou hast damned distressèd Faustus' soul.   75
Is't not too late?
          Enter the two Angels

BAD ANGEL Too late.

GOOD ANGEL Never too late, if Faustus will repent.°

BAD ANGEL If thou repent, devils will tear thee in pieces.

GOOD ANGEL Repent, and they shall never raze thy skin.   80
          Exeunt Angels

FAUSTUS O Christ, my Saviour, my Saviour,
Help to save distressèd Faustus' soul!°
          Enter Lucifer, Beelzebub, and Mephistopheles

LUCIFER Christ cannot save thy soul, for he is just.
There's none but I have int'rest in the same.

FAUSTUS O, what art thou that look'st so terribly?   85

LUCIFER I am Lucifer,
And this is my companion prince in hell.

FAUSTUS O, Faustus, they are come to fetch thy soul!

BEELZEBUB We are come to tell thee thou dost injure us.

LUCIFER Thou call'st on Christ, contrary to thy promise. 90

BEELZEBUB Thou shouldst not think on God.

LUCIFER Think on the devil.

BEELZEBUB And his dam, too.

FAUSTUS Nor will Faustus henceforth. Pardon him for this, and Faustus vows never to look to heaven. 95

LUCIFER So shalt thou show thyself an obedient servant, and we will highly gratify thee for it.

BEELZEBUB Faustus, we are come from hell in person to show thee some pastime. Sit down, and thou shalt behold the Seven Deadly Sins appear to thee in their own proper shapes and likeness. 100

FAUSTUS That sight will be as pleasant to me as paradise was to Adam the first day of his creation.

LUCIFER Talk not of paradise or creation, but mark the show. Go, Mephistopheles, fetch them in.

[*Faustus sits, and Mephistopheles fetches the Sins.*] *Enter the Seven Deadly Sins*

BEELZEBUB Now, Faustus, question them of their names and dis- 105 positions.

FAUSTUS That shall I soon.—What art thou, the first?

PRIDE I am Pride. I disdain to have any parents. I am like to Ovid's flea: I can creep into every corner of a wench. Sometimes like a periwig I sit upon her brow; next, like a necklace I hang about her 110 neck; then, like a fan of feathers I kiss her, and then, turning myself to a wrought° smock, do what I list. But fie, what a smell is here! I'll not speak a word more for a king's ransom, unless the ground be perfumed and covered with cloth of arras.

FAUSTUS Thou art a proud knave, indeed.—What are thou, the 115 second?

COVETOUSNESS I am Covetousness, begotten of an old churl in a leather bag; and might I now obtain my wish, this house, you, and all should turn to gold, that I might lock you safe into my chest. O my sweet gold! 120

FAUSTUS And what art thou, the third?

ENVY I am Envy, begotten of a chimney-sweeper and an oyster-wife. I cannot read, and therefore wish all books burnt. I am lean with seeing others eat. O, that there would come a famine over all the world, that all might die and I live alone! Then thou shouldst see 125 how fat I'd be. But must thou sit and I stand? Come down, with a vengeance!

FAUSTUS Out, envious wretch!—But what art thou, the fourth?

WRATH I am Wrath. I had neither father nor mother. I leaped out of a lion's mouth when I was scarce an hour old, and ever since have run up and down the world with these case° of rapiers, wounding myself when I could get none to fight withal. I was born in hell, and look to it, for some of you shall be my father.   130

FAUSTUS And what art thou, the fifth?

GLUTTONY I am Gluttony. My parents are all dead, and the devil a penny they have left me but a small pension, and that buys me thirty meals a day, and ten bevers—a small trifle to suffice nature. I come of a royal pedigree. My father was a gammon of bacon, and my mother was a hogshead of claret wine. My godfathers were these: Peter Pickled-herring and Martin Martlemas-beef. But my godmother, O, she was an ancient gentlewoman; her name was Margery March-beer. Now, Faustus, thou hast heard all my progeny, wilt thou bid me to supper?   135

FAUSTUS Not I.

GLUTTONY Then the devil choke thee!   145

FAUSTUS Choke thyself, glutton!—What art thou, the sixth?

SLOTH Heigh-ho. I am Sloth. I was begotten on a sunny bank. Heigh-ho. I'll not speak a word more for a king's ransom.

FAUSTUS And what are you, Mistress Minx, the seventh and last?

LECHERY Who, I? I, sir? I am one that loves an inch of raw mutton better than an ell of fried stockfish, and the first letter of my name begins with lechery.   150

LUCIFER Away, to hell, away! On, piper!°
    Exeunt the Seven Sins

FAUSTUS O, how this sight doth delight my soul!

LUCIFER But Faustus, in hell is all manner of delight.   155

FAUSTUS O, might I see hell and return again safe, how happy were I then!

LUCIFER Faustus, thou shalt. At midnight I will send for thee. [*Presenting a book*] Meanwhile, peruse this book, and view it throughly, and thou shalt turn thyself into what shape thou wilt.   160

FAUSTUS [*taking the book*] Thanks, mighty Lucifer. This will I keep as chary as my life.

LUCIFER Now, Faustus, farewell.

FAUSTUS Farewell, great Lucifer. Come, Mephistopheles.
    Exeunt, several ways

[3. Chorus]

Enter the Chorus
CHORUS Learnèd Faustus,
  To find the secrets of astronomy
  Graven in the book of Jove's high firmament,
  Did mount him up to scale Olympus' top,
  Where, sitting in a chariot burning bright   5
  Drawn by the strength of yokèd dragons' necks,
  He views the clouds, the planets, and the stars,
  The tropics, zones, and quarters of the sky,°
  From the bright circle of the hornèd moon°
  Even to the height of *Primum Mobile*;°   10
  And, whirling round with this circumference
  Within the concave compass of the pole,°
  From east to west his dragons swiftly glide
  And in eight days did bring him home again.
  Not long he stayed within his quiet house   15
  To rest his bones after his weary toil,
  But new exploits do hale him out again,
  And, mounted then upon a dragon's back,
  That with his wings did part the subtle air,°
  He now is gone to prove cosmography,   20
  That measures coasts and kingdoms of the earth,
  And, as I guess, will first arrive at Rome
  To see the pope and manner of his court
  And take some part of holy Peter's feast,
  The which this day is highly solemnized.   25
        Exit

[3.1]

Enter Faustus and Mephistopheles

FAUSTUS Having now, my good Mephistopheles,
  Passed with delight the stately town of Trier,
  Environed round with airy mountaintops,
  With walls of flint and deep intrenchèd lakes,
  Not to be won by any conquering prince;   5
  From Paris next, coasting the realm of France,
  We saw the river Maine fall into Rhine,
  Whose banks are set with groves of fruitful vines.
  Then up to Naples, rich Campania,
  Whose buildings, fair and gorgeous to the eye,   10
  The streets straight forth and paved with finest brick.
  There saw we learnèd Maro's golden tomb,
  The way he cut an English mile in length
  Through a rock of stone in one night's space.
  From thence to Venice, Padua, and the east,°   15
  In one of which a sumptuous temple stands°
  That threats the stars with her aspiring top,
  Whose frame is paved with sundry coloured stones,
  And roofed aloft with curious work in gold.
  Thus hitherto hath Faustus spent his time.   20
  But tell me now, what resting place is this?
  Hast thou, as erst I did command,
  Conducted me within the walls of Rome?
MEPHISTOPHELES I have, my Faustus, and for proof thereof
  This is the goodly palace of the pope;   25
  And 'cause we are no common guests
  I choose his privy chamber for our use.
FAUSTUS I hope his holiness will bid us welcome.
MEPHISTOPHELES All's one, for we'll be bold with his venison.
  But now, my Faustus, that thou mayst perceive   30
  What Rome contains for to delight thine eyes,
  Know that this city stands upon seven hills
  That underprop the groundwork of the same.
  Just through the midst runs flowing Tiber's stream,
  With winding banks that cut it in two parts,   35
  Over the which two stately bridges lean,°

That make safe passage to each part of Rome.
Upon the bridge called Ponte Angelo
Erected is a castle passing strong,
Where thou shalt see such store of ordinance   40
As that the double cannons, forged of brass,°
Do match the number of the days contained
Within the compass of one complete year—
Beside the gates and high pyramides
That Julius Caesar brought from Africa.   45
FAUSTUS Now, by the kingdoms of infernal rule,
Of Styx, of Acheron, and the fiery lake
Of ever-burning Phlegethon, I swear
That I do long to see the monuments
And situation of bright splendent Rome.   50
Come, therefore, let's away!
MEPHISTOPHELES
Nay stay, my Faustus. I know you'd see the pope
And take some part of holy Peter's feast,
The which this day with high solemnity
This day is held through Rome and Italy   55
In honour of the pope's triumphant victory.°
FAUSTUS Sweet Mephistopheles, thou pleasest me.
Whilst I am here on earth, let me be cloyed
With all things that delight the heart of man.
My four-and-twenty years of liberty   60
I'll spend in pleasure and in dalliance,
That Faustus' name, whilst this bright frame doth stand,°
May be admirèd through the furthest land.
MEPHISTOPHELES
'Tis well said, Faustus. Come, then, stand by me,
And thou shalt see them come immediately.   65
FAUSTUS Nay, stay, my gentle Mephistopheles,
And grant me my request, and then I go.
Thou know'st within the compass of eight days
We viewed the face of heaven, of earth, and hell.
So high our dragons soared into the air   70
That, looking down, the earth appeared to me
No bigger than my hand in quantity.
There did we view the kingdoms of the world,
And what might please mine eye I there beheld.
Then in this show let me an actor be,   75

That this proud pope may Faustus' cunning see.
MEPHISTOPHELES Let it be so, my Faustus. But first stay
And view their triumphs as they pass this way,
And then devise what best contents thy mind,
By cunning in thine art, to cross the pope   80
Or dash the pride of this solemnity—
To make his monks and abbots stand like apes
And point like antics at his triple crown,°
To beat the beads about the friars' pates°
Or clap huge horns upon the cardinals' heads,   85
Or any villainy thou canst devise,
And I'll perform it, Faustus. Hark, they come.
This day shall make thee be admired in Rome.
> [*They stand aside.*]° *Enter the Cardinals* [*of France and
> Padua*] *and Bishops* [*of Lorraine and Rheims*], *some bearing
> crosiers, some the pillars;*° *Monks and Friars singing their
> procession. Then the Pope* [*Adrian*] *and Raymond, King of
> Hungary, with Bruno* [*the rival Pope*] *led in chains.* [*The
> papal throne and Bruno's crown are borne in*]

POPE Cast down our footstool.
RAYMOND   Saxon Bruno, stoop,
Whilst on thy back his holiness ascends   90
Saint Peter's chair and state pontifical.
BRUNO Proud Lucifer, that state belongs to me!
But thus I fall to Peter, not to thee.°
> [*He kneels in front of the throne*]
POPE To me and Peter shalt thou grovelling lie
And crouch before the papal dignity.   95
Sound trumpets, then, for thus Saint Peter's heir
From Bruno's back ascends Saint Peter's chair.
> *A flourish while he ascends*
Thus, as the gods creep on with feet of wool°
Long ere with iron hands they punish men,
So shall our sleeping vengeance now arise   100
And smite with death thy hated enterprise.
Lord Cardinals of France and Padua,
Go forthwith to our holy consistory°
And read amongst the statutes decretal°
What, by the holy council held at Trent,°   105
The sacred synod hath decreed for him
That doth assume the papal government

Without election and a true consent.°
Away, and bring us word with speed.
FIRST CARDINAL We go, my lord.   110
    Exeunt Cardinals
POPE Lord Raymond—
    [*Pope Adrian and Raymond converse apart*]
FAUSTUS [*aside*] Go haste thee, gentle Mephistopheles.
    Follow the cardinals to the consistory,
    And as they turn their superstitious books
    Strike them with sloth and drowsy idleness,   115
    And make them sleep so sound that in their shapes
    Thyself and I may parley with this pope,
    This proud confronter of the emperor,
    And in despite of all his holiness°
    Restore this Bruno to his liberty   120
    And bear him to the states of Germany.
MEPHISTOPHELES Faustus, I go.
FAUSTUS Dispatch it soon.
    The pope shall curse that Faustus came to Rome.
    Exeunt Faustus and Mephistopheles
BRUNO Pope Adrian, let me have some right of law.   125
    I was elected by the emperor.
POPE We will depose the emperor for that deed
    And curse the people that submit to him.
    Both he and thou shalt stand excommunicate
    And interdict from Church's privilege   130
    And all society of holy men.
    He grows too proud in his authority,
    Lifting his lofty head above the clouds,
    And like a steeple overpeers the Church.°
    But we'll pull down his haughty insolence.   135
    And as Pope Alexander, our progenitor,
    Trod on the neck of German Frederick,°
    Adding this golden sentence to our praise,
    'That Peter's heirs should tread on emperors
    And walk upon the dreadful adder's back,   140
    Treading the lion and the dragon down,
    And fearless spurn the killing basilisk',
    So will we quell that haughty schismatic
    And by authority apostolical
    Depose him from his regal government.   145

BRUNO Pope Julius swore to princely Sigismond,
    For him and the succeeding popes of Rome,
    To hold the emperors their lawful lords.°
POPE Pope Julius did abuse the Church's rights,
    And therefore none of his decrees can stand.   150
    Is not all power on earth bestowed on us?
    And therefore, though we would, we cannot err.°
    Behold this silver belt, whereto is fixed
    Seven golden keys fast sealed with seven seals
    In token of our sevenfold power from heaven,   155
    To bind or loose, lock fast, condemn, or judge,
    Resign, or seal, or whatso pleaseth us.°
    Then he and thou and all the world shall stoop,
    Or be assurèd of our dreadful curse
    To light as heavy as the pains of hell.°   160
       Enter Faustus and Mephistopheles, [dressed] like the cardinals
MEPHISTOPHELES [*aside to Faustus*]
    Now tell me, Faustus, are we not fitted well?
FAUSTUS [*aside to Mephistopheles*]
    Yes, Mephistopheles, and two such cardinals
    Ne'er served a holy pope as we shall do.°
    But whilst they sleep within the consistory,
    Let us salute his reverend fatherhood.   165
RAYMOND [*to the Pope*]
    Behold, my lord, the cardinals are returned.
POPE Welcome, grave fathers. Answer presently:
    What have our holy council there decreed
    Concerning Bruno and the emperor,
    In quittance of their late conspiracy   170
    Against our state and papal dignity?
FAUSTUS Most sacred patron of the Church of Rome,
    By full consent of all the synod
    Of priests and prelates, it is thus decreed:
    That Bruno and the German emperor   175
    Be held as Lollards and bold schismatics°
    And proud disturbers of the Church's peace.
    And if that Bruno by his own assent,°
    Without enforcement of the German peers,°
    Did seek to wear the triple diadem   180
    And by your death to climb Saint Peter's chair,
    The statutes decretal have thus decreed:

He shall be straight condemned of heresy
And on a pile of faggots burnt to death.
POPE It is enough. Here, take him to your charge,   185
And bear him straight to Ponte Angelo,
And in the strongest tower enclose him fast.
Tomorrow, sitting in our consistory
With all our college of grave cardinals,
We will determine of his life or death.   190
Here, take his triple crown along with you
And leave it in the Church's treasury.
  [*Bruno's papal crown is given to Faustus and Mephistopheles*]
Make haste again, my good lord cardinals,°
And take our blessing apostolical.
MEPHISTOPHELES [*aside*]
So, so, was never devil thus blessed before!   195
FAUSTUS [*aside*] Away, sweet Mephistopheles, begone.
The cardinals will be plagued for this anon.
        Exeunt Faustus and Mephistopheles [*with Bruno*]
POPE Go presently and bring a banquet forth,
That we may solemnize Saint Peter's feast
And with Lord Raymond, king of Hungary,   200
Drink to our late and happy victory.
        Exeunt

[3.2]

*A sennet while the banquet is brought in. [Seats are provided
at the banquet. Exeunt Attendants,] and then enter Faustus
and Mephistopheles in their own shapes*

MEPHISTOPHELES Now, Faustus, come, prepare thyself for mirth.
The sleepy cardinals are hard at hand
To censure Bruno, that is posted hence
And on a proud-paced steed, as swift as thought,
Flies o'er the Alps to fruitful Germany,   5
There to salute the woeful emperor.
FAUSTUS The pope will curse them for their sloth today,
That slept both Bruno and his crown away.
But now, that Faustus may delight his mind
And by their folly make some merriment,   10

Sweet Mephistopheles, so charm me here
That I may walk invisible to all
And do whate'er I please, unseen of any.
MEPHISTOPHELES Faustus, thou shalt. Then kneel down presently,
     [*Faustus kneels*]
Whilst on thy head I lay my hand   15
And charm thee with this magic wand.
     [*Presenting a magic girdle*]
First wear this girdle, then appear
Invisible to all are here.°
The planets seven, the gloomy air,
Hell, and the Furies' forkèd hair,°   20
Pluto's blue fire, and Hecate's tree°
With magic spells so compass thee
That no eye may thy body see.
     [*Faustus rises*]
So, Faustus, now, for all their holiness,
Do what thou wilt, thou shalt not be discerned.   25
FAUSTUS Thanks, Mephistopheles. Now, friars, take heed
Lest Faustus make your shaven crowns to bleed.
MEPHISTOPHELES
Faustus, no more. See where the cardinals come.
     Enter Pope and all the lords: [*Raymond, King of Hungary,*
     the Archbishop of Rheims, etc., Friars and Attendants.] *Enter*
     the [*two*] *Cardinals* [*of France and Padua*] *with a book*
POPE Welcome, lord cardinals. Come, sit down.
Lord Raymond, take your seat.
     [*They sit*]
                          Friars, attend,   30
And see that all things be in readiness,
As best beseems this solemn festival.
FIRST CARDINAL First, may it please your sacred holiness
To view the sentence of the reverend synod
Concerning Bruno and the emperor?   35
POPE What needs this question? Did I not tell you
Tomorrow we would sit i'th'consistory
And there determine of his punishment?
You brought us word even now, it was decreed
That Bruno and the cursèd emperor   40
Were by the holy council both condemned
For loathèd Lollards and base schismatics.

Then wherefore would you have me view that book?
FIRST CARDINAL
    Your grace mistakes. You gave us no such charge.
RAYMOND Deny it not. We all are witnesses   45
    That Bruno here was late delivered you,
    With his rich triple crown to be reserved
    And put into the Church's treasury.
BOTH CARDINALS By holy Paul, we saw them not.
POPE By Peter, you shall die   50
    Unless you bring them forth immediately.—
    Hale them to prison. Lade their limbs with gyves!—
    False prelates, for this hateful treachery
    Curst be your souls to hellish misery.
            [*Exeunt Attendants with the two Cardinals*]
FAUSTUS [*aside*]
    So, they are safe. Now, Faustus, to the feast.°   55
    The pope had never such a frolic guest.
POPE Lord Archbishop of Rheims, sit down with us.
ARCHBISHOP [*sitting*] I thank your holiness.
FAUSTUS Fall to. The devil choke you an you spare.
POPE Who's that spoke? Friars, look about.   60
            [*Some Friars attempt to search*]
    Lord Raymond, pray fall to. I am beholding
    To the bishop of Milan for this so rare a present.
FAUSTUS [*snatching the meat*] I thank you, sir.
POPE How now? Who snatched the meat from me?
    Villains, why speak you not?—   65
    My good Lord Archbishop, here's a most dainty dish
    Was sent me from a cardinal in France.°
FAUSTUS [*snatching the dish*] I'll have that, too.
POPE What Lollards do attend our holiness,
    That we receive such great indignity?   70
    Fetch me some wine.
            [*Wine is brought*]
FAUSTUS [*aside*] Ay, pray do, for Faustus is adry.
POPE Lord Raymond, I drink unto your grace.
FAUSTUS [*snatching the cup*] I pledge your grace.
POPE My wine gone, too? Ye lubbers, look about   75
    And find the man that doth this villainy,
    Or by our sanctitude you all shall die!—
            [*Some Friars search about*]

I pray, my lords, have patience at this troublesome banquet.

ARCHBISHOP Please it your holiness, I think it be some ghost crept
out of purgatory and now is come unto your holiness for his   80
pardon.

POPE It may be so.
Go, then, command our priests to sing a dirge
To lay the fury of this same troublesome ghost.
    [Exit one. The Pope crosses himself]

FAUSTUS How now? Must every bit be spicèd with a cross?   85
    [The Pope crosses himself again]
Nay, then, take that!
    [Faustus gives the Pope a blow on the head]

POPE O, I am slain! Help me, my lords.
O, come and help to bear my body hence.
Damned be this soul for ever for this deed!
    Exeunt the Pope and his train

MEPHISTOPHELES Now, Faustus, what will you do now? For I can   90
tell you you'll be cursed with bell, book, and candle.

FAUSTUS Bell, book, and candle; candle, book, and bell,
Forward and backward, to curse Faustus to hell.
    Enter the Friars with bell, book, and candle, for the dirge

FIRST FRIAR Come, brethren, let's about our business with good
devotion.   95
    [The Friars chant]
Cursèd be he that stole his holiness' meat from the table.
    Maledicat Dominus!
Cursèd be he that struck his holiness a blow on the face.
    Maledicat Dominus!
Cursèd be he that struck Friar Sandelo a blow on the pate.   100
    Maledicat Dominus!
Cursèd be he that disturbeth our holy dirge.
    Maledicat Dominus!
Cursèd be he that took away his holiness' wine.
    Maledicat Dominus!   105
    [Faustus and Mephistopheles] beat the Friars, fling firework[s]
    among them, and exeunt

[3.3]

Enter Clown [Robin], and Dick with a cup

DICK Sirrah Robin, we were best look° that your devil can
answer° the stealing of this same cup, for the Vintner's boy follows
us at the hard heels.°

ROBIN 'Tis no matter. Let him come. An he follow us, I'll so conjure
him as he was never conjured in his life, I warrant him. Let me   5
see the cup.

Enter Vintner

DICK [*giving the cup to Robin*] Here 'tis. Yonder he comes. Now,
Robin, now or never show thy cunning.

VINTNER O, are you here? I am glad I have found you. You are a
couple of fine companions! Pray, where's the cup you stole from   10
the tavern?

ROBIN How, how? We steal a cup? Take heed what you say.
We look not like cup-stealers, I can tell you.

VINTNER Never deny't, for I know you have it, and I'll search you.

ROBIN Search me? Ay, and spare not. [*Aside to Dick, tossing him the*   15
cup] Hold the cup, Dick. [*To the Vintner*] Come, come, search me,
search me.

[*The Vintner searches Robin*]

VINTNER [*to Dick*] Come on, sirrah, let me search you now.

DICK Ay, ay, do, do. [*Aside to Robin, tossing him the cup*] Hold the
cup, Robin. [*To the Vintner*] I fear not your searching. We scorn   20
to steal your cups, I can tell you.

[*The Vintner searches Dick*]

VINTNER Never outface me for the matter, for sure the cup is
between you two.

ROBIN [*brandishing the cup*] Nay, there you lie. 'Tis beyond° us both.

VINTNER A plague take you! I thought 'twas your knavery to take it   25
away. Come, give it me again.

ROBIN Ay, much! When, can you tell?° Dick, make me a circle, and
stand close at my back, and stir not for thy life. [*Dick makes a*
circle] Vintner, you shall have your cup anon. Say nothing, Dick.
'O' *per se* 'o', Demogorgon, Belcher, and Mephistopheles!   30

Enter Mephistopheles. [Exit the Vintner, running]

MEPHISTOPHELES You princely legions of infernal rule,
How am I vexèd by these villains' charms!
From Constantinople have they brought me now

Only for pleasure of these damnèd slaves.

ROBIN By Lady, sir, you have had a shrewd journey of it. Will it   35
please you to take a shoulder of mutton to supper and a tester in
your purse, and go back again?

DICK Ay, I pray you heartily, sir, for we called you but in jest, I
promise you.

MEPHISTOPHELES To purge the rashness of this cursèd deed,   40
First, [*To Dick*] be thou turnèd to this ugly shape,
For apish deeds transformèd to an ape.
        [*Dick is transformed in shape*]

ROBIN O brave, an ape! I pray, sir, let me have the carrying of him
about to show some tricks.

MEPHISTOPHELES And so thou shalt. Be thou transformed to a dog,   45
and carry him upon thy back. Away, begone!
        [*Robin is transformed in shape*]

ROBIN A dog? That's excellent. Let the maids look well to their
porridge pots, for I'll into the kitchen presently. Come, Dick,
come.
        Exeunt the two Clowns [*with Dick on Robin's back*]

MEPHISTOPHELES Now with the flames of ever-burning fire   50
I'll wing myself and forthwith fly amain
Unto my Faustus, to the Great Turk's court.
        Exit

[4.1]

Enter Martino and Frederick at several doors

MARTINO What ho, officers, gentlemen!°
Hie to the presence to attend the emperor.
Good Frederick, see the rooms be voided straight;
His majesty is coming to the hall.
Go back, and see the state in readiness.°   5

FREDERICK But where is Bruno, our elected pope,
That on a Fury's back came post from Rome?
Will not his grace consort the emperor?

MARTINO O, yes, and with him comes the German conjurer,
The learnèd Faustus, fame of Wittenberg,   10
The wonder of the world for magic art;
And he intends to show great Carolus°
The race of all his stout progenitors,
And bring in presence of his majesty
The royal shapes and warlike semblances   15
Of Alexander and his beauteous paramour.

FREDERICK Where is Benvolio?

MARTINO Fast asleep, I warrant you.
He took his rouse with stoups of Rhenish wine°
So kindly yesternight to Bruno's health   20
That all this day the sluggard keeps his bed.

FREDERICK See, see, his window's ope. We'll call to him.

MARTINO What ho, Benvolio!
      Enter Benvolio above at a window, in his nightcap, buttoning

BENVOLIO What a devil ail you two?

MARTINO Speak softly, sir, lest the devil hear you;   25
For Faustus at the court is late arrived,
And at his heels a thousand Furies wait
To accomplish whatsoever the doctor please.

BENVOLIO What of this?

MARTINO Come, leave thy chamber first, and thou shalt see   30
This conjurer perform such rare exploits
Before the pope and royal emperor°
As never yet was seen in Germany.

BENVOLIO Has not the pope enough of conjuring yet?
He was upon the devil's back late enough;   35

And if he be so far in love with him,
I would he would post with him to Rome again.

FREDERICK Speak, wilt thou come and see this sport?
BENVOLIO   Not I.
MARTINO Wilt thou stand in thy window and see it, then?
BENVOLIO Ay, an I fall not asleep i'th'meantime.   40
MARTINO The emperor is at hand, who comes to see
What wonders by black spells may compassed be.
BENVOLIO Well, go you attend the emperor. I am content for this
once to thrust my head out at a window, for they say if a man be
drunk overnight the devil cannot hurt him in the morning. If that   45
be true, I have a charm in my head shall control him as well as the
conjurer, I warrant you.

> *Exeunt [Frederick and Martino. Benvolio remains at his*
> *window.] A sennet. [Enter] Charles the German Emperor,*
> *Bruno, [the Duke of] Saxony, Faustus, Mephistopheles,*
> *Frederick, Martino, and Attendants. [The Emperor sits in his*
> *throne]*°

EMPEROR Wonder of men, renowned magician,
Thrice-learnèd Faustus, welcome to our court.
This deed of thine, in setting Bruno free   50
From his and our professèd enemy,
Shall add more excellence unto thine art
Than if by powerful necromantic spells
Thou couldst command the world's obedience.
For ever be beloved of Carolus.   55
And if this Bruno thou hast late redeemed
In peace possess the triple diadem
And sit in Peter's chair, despite of chance,°
Thou shalt be famous through all Italy
And honoured of the German emperor.   60
FAUSTUS These gracious words, most royal Carolus,
Shall make poor Faustus to his utmost power
Both love and serve the German emperor
And lay his life at holy Bruno's feet.
For proof whereof, if so your grace be pleased,   65
The doctor stands prepared by power of art
To cast his magic charms, that shall pierce through
The ebon gates of ever-burning hell
And hale the stubborn Furies from their caves
To compass whatsoe'er your grace commands.   70

BENVOLIO [*aside, at the window*]° Blood, he speaks terribly. But for all that, I do not greatly believe him. He looks as like a conjurer as the pope to a costermonger.

EMPEROR Then, Faustus, as thou late didst promise us,
We would behold that famous conqueror   75
Great Alexander and his paramour
In their true shapes and state majestical,
That we may wonder at their excellence.

FAUSTUS Your majesty shall see them presently.—
[*Aside to Mephistopheles*] Mephistopheles, away,   80
And with a solemn noise of trumpet's sound
Present before this royal emperor
Great Alexander and his beauteous paramour.

MEPHISTOPHELES [*aside to Faustus*] Faustus, I will.
[*Exit Mephistopheles*]

BENVOLIO [*at the window*] Well, Master Doctor, an your devils come   85
not away quickly, you shall have me asleep presently. Zounds, I
could eat myself for anger to think I have been such an ass all this
while, to stand gaping after the devil's governor° and can see
nothing.

FAUSTUS [*aside*] I'll make you feel something anon, if my art fail me   90
not.—
[*To Emperor*] My lord, I must forewarn your majesty
That when my spirits present the royal shapes
Of Alexander and his paramour,
Your grace demand no questions of the king,   95
But in dumb silence let them come and go.

EMPEROR Be it as Faustus please. We are content.

BENVOLIO [*at the window*] Ay, ay, and I am content too. An thou
bring Alexander and his paramour before the emperor, I'll be
Actaeon and turn myself to a stag.   100

FAUSTUS [*aside*] And I'll play Diana and send you the horns presently.
[*Enter Mephistopheles. A*] sennet. *Enter at one [door] the
Emperor Alexander, at the other Darius.° They meet; Darius
is thrown down. Alexander kills him, takes off his crown, and,
offering to go out, his Paramour meets him. He embraceth her
and sets Darius' crown upon her head; and, coming back,
both salute the [German] Emperor, who, leaving his state,
offers to embrace them, which Faustus seeing suddenly stays
him. Then trumpets cease and music sounds*
My gracious lord, you do forget yourself.

These are but shadows, not substantial.

EMPEROR O, pardon me. My thoughts are so ravishèd
 With sight of this renownèd emperor   105
 That in mine arms I would have compassed him.
 But Faustus, since I may not speak to them
 To satisfy my longing thoughts at full,
 Let me this tell thee: I have heard it said
 That this fair lady, whilst she lived on earth,   110
 Had on her neck a little wart or mole.
 How may I prove that saying to be true?

FAUSTUS Your majesty may boldly go and see.

EMPEROR [*making an inspection*] Faustus, I see it plain,
 And in this sight thou better pleasest me   115
 Than if I gained another monarchy.

FAUSTUS [*to the spirits*] Away, begone!
  Exit Show
 See, see, my gracious lord, what strange beast is yon, that thrusts
 his head out at window.
  [*Benvolio is seen to have sprouted horns*]

EMPEROR O wondrous sight! See, Duke of Saxony,   120
 Two spreading horns most strangely fastenèd
 Upon the head of young Benvolio.

SAXONY What, is he asleep, or dead?

FAUSTUS He sleeps, my lord, but dreams not of his horns.

EMPEROR This sport is excellent. We'll call and wake him.— 125
 What ho, Benvolio!

BENVOLIO A plague upon you! Let me sleep a while.

EMPEROR I blame thee not to sleep much, having such a head of
 thine own.

SAXONY Look up, Benvolio. 'Tis the emperor calls.°   130

BENVOLIO The emperor? Where? O, zounds, my head!

EMPEROR Nay, an thy horns hold, 'tis no matter for thy head, for
 that's armed sufficiently.

FAUSTUS Why, how now, sir knight? What, hanged by the horns?
 This is most horrible. Fie, fie, pull in your head, for shame. Let 135
 not all the world wonder at you.

BENVOLIO Zounds, doctor, is this your villainy?

FAUSTUS O, say not so, sir. The doctor has no skill,
 No art, no cunning to present these lords
 Or bring before this royal emperor   140
 The mighty monarch, warlike Alexander.

If Faustus do it, you are straight resolved
In bold Actaeon's shape to turn a stag.—
And therefore, my lord, so please your majesty,
I'll raise a kennel of hounds shall hunt him so   145
As all his footmanship shall scarce prevail
To keep his carcass from their bloody fangs.
Ho, Belimoth, Argiron, Ashtaroth!

BENVOLIO Hold, hold! Zounds, he'll raise up a kennel of devils, I
think, anon. Good my lord, entreat for me. 'Sblood, I am never   150
able to endure these torments.°

EMPEROR Then, good Master Doctor,
Let me entreat you to remove his horns.
He has done penance now sufficiently.

FAUSTUS My gracious lord, not so much for injury done to me as to   155
delight your majesty with some mirth hath Faustus justly requited
this injurious knight; which being all I desire, I am content to remove his horns.—Mephistopheles, transform him. [*Mephistopheles
removes the horns*] And hereafter, sir, look you speak well of scholars.

BENVOLIO Speak well of ye?° 'Sblood, an scholars be such cuckold-   160
makers to clap horns of° honest men's heads o' this order,° I'll
ne'er trust smooth faces and small ruffs° more. But, an I be not
revenged for this, would I might be turned to a gaping oyster and
drink nothing but salt water.
   [*Exit Benvolio from the window*]

EMPEROR Come, Faustus. While the emperor lives,   165
In recompense of this thy high desert
Thou shalt command the state of Germany
And live beloved of mighty Carolus.
   Exeunt

[4.2]

Enter Benvolio, Martino, Frederick, and Soldiers
MARTINO Nay, sweet Benvolio, let us sway thy thoughts
From this attempt against the conjurer.
BENVOLIO Away! You love me not, to urge me thus.
Shall I let slip so great an injury
When every servile groom jests at my wrongs   5
And in their rustic gambols proudly say,

'Benvolio's head was graced with horns today'?
O, may these eyelids never close again
Till with my sword I have that conjurer slain!
If you will aid me in this enterprise,   10
Then draw your weapons and be resolute.
If not, depart. Here will Benvolio die
But Faustus' death shall quit my infamy.°
FREDERICK Nay, we will stay with thee, betide what may,
And kill that doctor if he come this way.   15
BENVOLIO Then, gentle Frederick, hie thee to the grove,
And place our servants and our followers
Close in an ambush there behind the trees.
By this, I know, the conjurer is near;°
I saw him kneel and kiss the emperor's hand   20
And take his leave, laden with rich rewards.
Then, soldiers, boldly fight. If Faustus die,
Take you the wealth; leave us the victory.
FREDERICK Come, soldiers, follow me unto the grove.
Who kills him shall have gold and endless love.°   25
        Exit Frederick with the Soldiers
BENVOLIO My head is lighter than it was by th'horns,
But yet my heart's more ponderous than my head
And pants until I see that conjurer dead.
MARTINO Where shall we place ourselves, Benvolio?
BENVOLIO Here will we stay to bide the first assault.   30
O, were that damnèd hellhound but in place,°
Thou soon shouldst see me quit my foul disgrace.
        Enter Frederick
FREDERICK Close, close! The conjurer is at hand
And all alone comes walking in his gown.
Be ready, then, and strike the peasant down.   35
BENVOLIO Mine be that honour, then. Now, sword, strike home!
For horns he gave, I'll have his head anon.
        Enter Faustus, with the false head
MARTINO See, see, he comes.
BENVOLIO   No words. This blow ends all.
Hell take his soul! His body thus must fall.
        [*He strikes Faustus*]
FAUSTUS [*falling*] O!   40
FREDERICK Groan you, Master Doctor?
BENVOLIO Break may his heart with groans! Dear Frederick, see,

Thus will I end his griefs immediately.
MARTINO Strike with a willing hand.
        [*Benvolio strikes off Faustus's false head*]
                                His head is off!
BENVOLIO The devil's dead. The Furies now may laugh.   45
FREDERICK Was this that stern aspect, that awful frown,
    Made the grim monarch of infernal spirits°
    Tremble and quake at his commanding charms?
MARTINO Was this that damnèd head whose heart conspired
    Benvolio's shame before the emperor?   50
BENVOLIO Ay, that's the head, and here the body lies,
    Justly rewarded for his villainies.
FREDERICK Come, let's devise how we may add more shame
    To the black scandal of his hated name.
BENVOLIO First, on his head, in quittance of my wrongs,   55
    I'll nail huge forkèd horns and let them hang
    Within the window where he yoked me first,
    That all the world may see my just revenge.
MARTINO What use shall we put his beard to?
BENVOLIO We'll sell it to a chimney-sweeper. It will wear out ten   60
    birchen brooms, I warrant you.
FREDERICK What shall his eyes do?
BENVOLIO We'll put out his eyes, and they shall serve for buttons to
    his lips to keep his tongue from catching cold.
MARTINO An excellent policy. And now, sirs, having divided him,   65
    what shall the body do?
        [*Faustus rises*]
BENVOLIO Zounds, the devil's alive again!
FREDERICK Give him his head, for God's sake!
FAUSTUS Nay, keep it. Faustus will have heads and hands,
    Ay, all your hearts, to recompense this deed.   70
    Knew you not, traitors, I was limited
    For four-and-twenty years to breathe on earth?°
    And had you cut my body with your swords,
    Or hewed this flesh and bones as small as sand,
    Yet in a minute had my spirit returned,   75
    And I had breathed a man made free from harm.
    But wherefore do I dally my revenge?
    Ashtaroth, Belimoth, Mephistopheles!
        Enter Mephistopheles and other Devils [*Belimoth and
        Ashtaroth*]

Go horse these traitors on your fiery backs,°
And mount aloft with them as high as heaven;   80
Thence pitch them headlong to the lowest hell.
Yet stay. The world shall see their misery,
And hell shall after plague their treachery.°
Go, Belimoth, and take this caitiff hence,
And hurl him in some lake of mud and dirt.   85
    [*To Ashtaroth*]
Take thou this other; drag him through the woods
Amongst the pricking thorns and sharpest briers,
Whilst with my gentle Mephistopheles
This traitor flies unto some steepy rock°
That, rolling down, may break the villain's bones   90
As he intended to dismember me.
Fly hence. Dispatch my charge immediately.

FREDERICK Pity us, gentle Faustus. Save our lives!

FAUSTUS Away!

FREDERICK   He must needs go that the devil drives.
    Exeunt Spirits with the Knights [*on their backs*].
    Enter the ambushed° *Soldiers*

FIRST SOLDIER Come, sirs. Prepare yourselves in readiness; 95
Make haste to help these noble gentlemen.
I heard them parley with the conjurer.

SECOND SOLDIER
See where he comes. Dispatch, and kill the slave.

FAUSTUS What's here? An ambush to betray my life?
Then, Faustus, try thy skill. Base peasants, stand!   100
For lo, these trees remove at my command°
And stand as bulwarks 'twixt yourselves and me
To shield me from your hated treachery.
Yet to encounter this your weak attempt,
Behold an army comes incontinent.   105
    Faustus strikes the door, and enter a Devil playing on a
    drum, after him another bearing an ensign, and divers with
    weapons; Mephistopheles with fireworks. They set upon the
    Soldiers and drive them out. [*Exit Faustus*]

[4.3]

Enter at several doors Benvolio, Frederick, and Martino,
their heads and faces bloody and besmeared with mud and
dirt, all having horns on their heads

MARTINO What ho, Benvolio!
BENVOLIO   Here. What, Frederick, ho!
FREDERICK O, help me, gentle friend. Where is Martino?
MARTINO Dear Frederick, here,
  Half smothered in a lake of mud and dirt
  Through which the Furies dragged me by the heels.   5
FREDERICK Martino, see! Benvolio's horns again.
MARTINO O misery! How now, Benvolio?
BENVOLIO Defend me, heaven. Shall I be haunted still?
MARTINO Nay, fear not, man. We have no power to kill.
BENVOLIO My friends transformèd thus! O hellish spite!   10
  Your heads are all set with horns.
FREDERICK   You hit it right.
  It is your own you mean. Feel on your head.
BENVOLIO [*feeling his head*] Zounds, horns again!°
MARTINO Nay, chafe not, man, we all are sped.
BENVOLIO What devil attends this damned magician,   15
  That, spite of spite, our wrongs are doublèd?°
FREDERICK What may we do, that we may hide our shames?
BENVOLIO If we should follow him to work revenge,
  He'd join long asses' ears to these huge horns
  And make us laughing-stocks to all the world.   20
MARTINO What shall we then do, dear Benvolio?
BENVOLIO I have a castle joining near these woods,
  And thither we'll repair and live obscure
  Till time shall alter this our brutish shapes.
  Sith black disgrace hath thus eclipsed our fame,   25
  We'll rather die with grief than live with shame.
     Exeunt

[4.4]

Enter Faustus, and the Horse-courser, and Mephistopheles

HORSE-COURSER [*offering money*] I beseech your worship, accept of these forty dollars.

FAUSTUS Friend, thou canst not buy so good a horse for so small a price. I have no great need to sell him, but if thou likest him for ten dollars more, take him, because I see thou hast a good mind to him.   5

HORSE-COURSER I beseech you, sir, accept of this. I am a very poor man and have lost very much of late by horseflesh, and this bargain will set me up again.

FAUSTUS Well, I will not stand° with thee. Give me the money. [*He takes the money*] Now, sirrah, I must tell you that you may ride   10 him o'er hedge and ditch, and spare him not. But do you hear? In any case ride him not into the water.

HORSE-COURSER How, sir, not into the water? Why, will he not drink of all waters?

FAUSTUS Yes, he will drink of all waters. But ride him not into the   15 water. O'er hedge and ditch, or where thou wilt, but not into the water. Go bid the ostler deliver him unto you, and remember what I say.

HORSE-COURSER I warrant you, sir.—O, joyful day! Now am I a made man for ever.   20

> *Exit [Horse-courser]*

FAUSTUS What art thou, Faustus, but a man condemned to die?
Thy fatal time draws to a final end.
Despair doth drive distrust into my thoughts.
Confound these passions with a quiet sleep.
Tush! Christ did call the thief upon the cross;   25
Then rest thee, Faustus, quiet in conceit.

> *He sits to sleep. Enter the Horse-courser, wet*

HORSE-COURSER O, what a cozening doctor was this! I, riding my horse into the water, thinking some hidden mystery had been in the horse, I had nothing under me but a little straw and had much ado to escape drowning. Well, I'll go rouse him and make him give   30 me my forty dollars again.—Ho, sirrah doctor, you cozening scab! Master Doctor, awake, and rise, and give me my money again, for your horse is turned to a bottle of hay. Master Doctor! (*He pulls off his leg*) Alas, I am undone! What shall I do? I have pulled off his leg.   35

FAUSTUS O, help, help! The villain hath murdered me.

HORSE-COURSER Murder or not murder, now he has but one leg I'll outrun him and cast this leg into some ditch or other.

    [Exit Horse-courser with the leg]

FAUSTUS Stop him, stop him, stop him!—Ha, ha, ha! Faustus hath his leg again, and the Horse-courser a bundle of hay for his forty 40 dollars.

    Enter Wagner

How now, Wagner, what news with thee?

WAGNER If it please you, the duke of Vanholt doth earnestly entreat your company and hath sent some of his men to attend you with provision fit for your journey. 45

FAUSTUS The duke of Vanholt's an honourable gentleman, and one to whom I must be no niggard of my cunning. Come away.

    Exeunt

[4.5]

    Enter Clown [Robin], Dick, Horse-courser, and a Carter

CARTER Come, my masters, I'll bring you to the best beer in Europe.—What ho, Hostess!—Where be these whores?

    Enter Hostess

HOSTESS How now, what lack you? What, my old guests, welcome!

ROBIN *[aside to Dick]* Sirrah Dick, dost thou know why I stand so mute? 5

DICK *[aside to Robin]* No, Robin, why is't?

ROBIN *[aside to Dick]* I am eighteen pence on the score.° But say nothing. See if she have forgotten me.

HOSTESS *[seeing Robin]* Who's this that stands so solemnly by himself? *[To Robin]* What, my old guest? 10

ROBIN O, Hostess, how do you? I hope my score stands still.°

HOSTESS Ay, there's no doubt of that,° for methinks you make no haste to wipe it out.

DICK Why, Hostess, I say, fetch us some beer.

HOSTESS You shall, presently.—Look up into th' hall there, ho!° 15

    Exit [Hostess]

DICK Come, sirs, what shall we do now till mine Hostess comes?

CARTER Marry, sir, I'll tell you the bravest tale how a conjurer served° me. You know Doctor Fauster?

HORSE-COURSER Ay, a plague take him! Here's some on's° have
cause to know him. Did he conjure thee, too?   20

CARTER I'll tell you how he served me. As I was going to Wittenberg
t'other day with a load of hay, he met me and asked me what he
should give me for as much hay as he could eat. Now, sir, I
thinking that a little would serve his turn, bade him take as much
as he would for three farthings. So he presently gave me my money   25
and fell to eating; and, as I am a cursen° man, he never left eating
till he had eat° up all my load of hay.

ALL O monstrous! Eat a whole load of hay!

ROBIN Yes, yes, that may be, for I have heard of one that has eat a
load of logs.°   30

HORSE-COURSER Now, sirs, you shall hear how villainously he
served me. I went to him yesterday to buy a horse of him, and he
would by no means sell him under forty dollars. So, sir, because I
knew him to be such a horse as would run over hedge and ditch
and never tire, I gave him his money. So when I had my horse,   35
Doctor Fauster bade me ride him night and day and spare him no
time. 'But', quoth he, 'in any case ride him not into the water.'
Now, sir, I, thinking the horse had had some quality that he would
not have me know of, what did I but rid him into a great river?
And when I came just in the midst, my horse vanished away, and   40
I sat straddling upon a bottle of hay.

ALL O brave doctor!

HORSE-COURSER But you shall hear how bravely I served him for it.
I went me° home to his house, and there I found him asleep. I
kept a halloing and whooping in his ears, but all could not wake   45
him. I, seeing that, took him by the leg and never rested pulling
till I had pulled me his leg quite off, and now 'tis at home in mine
hostry.

ROBIN And has the doctor but one leg, then? That's excellent, for
one of his devils turned me into the likeness of an ape's face.   50

CARTER Some more drink, Hostess!

ROBIN Hark you, we'll into another room and drink a while, and then
we'll go seek out the doctor.

     Exeunt

[4.6]

Enter the Duke of Vanholt, his [pregnant] Duchess, Faustus,
and Mephistopheles [and Servants]

DUKE Thanks, Master Doctor, for these pleasant sights. Nor know I
how sufficiently to recompense your great deserts in erecting that
enchanted castle in the air, the sight whereof so delighted me as
nothing in the world could please me more.

FAUSTUS I do think myself, my good lord, highly recompensed in   5
that it pleaseth your grace to think but well of that which Faustus
hath performed.—But, gracious lady, it may be that you have
taken no pleasure in those sights. Therefore, I pray you tell me
what is the thing you most desire to have; be it in the world, it
shall be yours. I have heard that great-bellied women do long for   10
things are° rare and dainty.

DUCHESS True, Master Doctor, and, since I find you so kind, I will
make known unto you what my heart desires to have. And were it
now summer, as it is January, a dead time of the winter, I would
request no better meat than a dish of ripe grapes.   15

FAUSTUS This is but a small matter. [*Aside to Mephistopheles*] Go,
Mephistopheles, away!

Exit Mephistopheles

Madam, I will do more than this for your content.

Enter Mephistopheles again with the grapes

Here. Now taste ye these. They should be good, for they come
from a far country, I can tell you.   20

[*The Duchess tastes the grapes*]

DUKE This makes me wonder more than all the rest, that at this time
of the year, when every tree is barren of his fruit, from whence
you had these ripe grapes.

FAUSTUS Please it your grace, the year is divided into two circles over
the whole world, so that, when it is winter with us, in the contrary 25
circle it is likewise summer with them, as in India, Saba, and such
countries that lie far east, where they have fruit twice a year. From
whence, by means of a swift spirit that I have, I had these grapes
brought, as you see.

DUCHESS And, trust me, they are the sweetest grapes that e'er I   30
tasted.

The Clown[s] bounce° at the gate, within

DUKE What rude disturbers have we at the gate?

Go pacify their fury. Set it ope,
And then demand of them what they would have.
        They knock again and call out to talk with Faustus
SERVANT [*calling offstage*]
    Why, how now, masters, what a coil is there!   35
    What is the reason you disturb the duke?
DICK [*offstage*] We have no reason for it. Therefore, a fig for him!
SERVANT Why, saucy varlets, dare you be so bold?
HORSE-COURSER [*offstage*] I hope, sir, we have wit enough to be
    more bold than welcome.   40
SERVANT It appears so. Pray be bold elsewhere, and trouble not the
    duke.
DUKE [*to the Servant*] What would they have?
SERVANT They all cry out to speak with Doctor Faustus.
CARTER [*offstage*] Ay, and we will speak with him.   45
DUKE Will you, sir?—Commit° the rascals.
DICK [*offstage*] Commit with us? He were as good commit with his
    father as commit with us.
FAUSTUS I do beseech your grace, let them come in.
    They are good subject for a merriment.   50
DUKE Do as thou wilt, Faustus. I give thee leave.
FAUSTUS I thank your grace.
        [*The Servant opens the gate.*] *Enter the Clown [Robin], Dick,*
        Carter, and Horse-courser
                        Why, how now, my good friends?
    'Faith, you are too outrageous. But come near;
    I have procured your pardons. Welcome all!
ROBIN Nay, sir, we will be welcome for our money, and we will pay 55
    for what we take.—What ho! Give's half a dozen of beer here, and
    be hanged.°
FAUSTUS Nay, hark you, can you tell me where you are?
CARTER Ay, marry, can I. We are under heaven.
SERVANT Ay, but, sir saucebox, know you in what place?   60
HORSE-COURSER Ay, ay, the house is good enough to drink in.
    Zounds, fill us some beer, or we'll break all the barrels in the house
    and dash out all your brains with your bottles.°
FAUSTUS Be not so furious. Come, you shall have beer.—
    My lord, beseech you give me leave a while.   65
    I'll gage my credit 'twill content your grace.°
DUKE With all my heart, kind doctor. Please thyself.
    Our servants and our court's at thy command.

FAUSTUS I humbly thank your grace.—Then fetch some beer.

HORSE-COURSER Ay, marry, there spake a doctor indeed, and, 'faith,   70
I'll drink a health to thy wooden leg for that word.

FAUSTUS My wooden leg? What dost thou mean by that?

CARTER Ha, ha, ha! Dost hear him, Dick? He has forgot his leg.

HORSE-COURSER Ay, ay. He does not stand much upon that.°

FAUSTUS No, 'faith, not much upon a wooden leg.   75

CARTER Good Lord, that flesh and blood° should be so frail with
your worship! Do not you remember a horse-courser you sold a
horse to?

FAUSTUS Yes, I remember I sold one a horse.

CARTER And do you remember you bid he should not ride into the   80
water?

FAUSTUS Yes, I do very well remember that.

CARTER And do you remember nothing of your leg?

FAUSTUS No, in good sooth.

CARTER Then, I pray, remember your curtsy.°   85

FAUSTUS [*making a curtsy*] I thank you, sir.

CARTER 'Tis not so much worth.° I pray you tell me one thing.

FAUSTUS What's that?

CARTER Be both your legs bedfellows every night together?°

FAUSTUS Wouldst thou make a Colossus° of me, that thou askest me   90
such questions?

CARTER No, truly, sir, I would make nothing of you.° But I would
fain know that.

    Enter Hostess with drink

FAUSTUS Then, I assure thee, certainly they are.

CARTER I thank you. I am fully satisfied.   95

FAUSTUS But wherefore dost thou ask?

CARTER For nothing, sir. But methinks you should have a wooden
bedfellow of one of 'em.

HORSE-COURSER Why, do you hear, sir? Did not I pull off one of
your legs when you were asleep?   100

FAUSTUS But I have it again now I am awake. Look you here, sir.
    [*He shows them his legs*]°

ALL O, horrible! Had the doctor three legs?

CARTER Do you remember, sir, how you cozened me and eat up my
load of—
    Faustus charms him dumb

DICK Do you remember how you made me wear an ape's—   105
    [*Faustus charms him dumb*]

HORSE-COURSER You whoreson conjuring scab, do you remember
    how you cozened me with a ho—
        [*Faustus charms him dumb*]
ROBIN Ha' you forgotten me? You think to carry it away° with your
    'hey-pass' and 'repass'.° Do you remember the dog's fa—
        [*Faustus charms him dumb*.] *Exeunt Clowns*
HOSTESS Who pays for the ale? Hear you, Master Doctor, now you   110
    have sent away my guests, I pray, who shall pay me for my a—
        [*Faustus charms her dumb*.] *Exit Hostess*
DUCHESS [*to the Duke*] My lord,
    We are much beholding to this learnèd man.
DUKE So are we, madam, which we will recompense
    With all the love and kindness that we may.   115
    His artful sport drives all sad thoughts away.
        Exeunt

[5.1]

Thunder and lightning. Enter Devils with covered dishes.
Mephistopheles leads them into Faustus's study. Then enter
Wagner

WAGNER I think my master means to die shortly.
He has made his will and given me his wealth:
His house, his goods, and store of golden plate,
Besides two thousand ducats ready coined.
I wonder what he means. If death were nigh,   5
He would not frolic thus. He's now at supper
With the scholars, where there's such belly-cheer
As Wagner in his life ne'er saw the like.
And see where they come. Belike the feast is done.
      Exit [Wagner.] Enter Faustus, Mephistopheles, and two or
      three Scholars

FIRST SCHOLAR Master Doctor Faustus, since our conference about   10
fair ladies—which was the beautifullest in all the world—we have
determined with ourselves that Helen of Greece was the admir-
ablest lady that ever lived. Therefore, Master Doctor, if you will
do us so much favour as to let us see that peerless dame of Greece,
whom all the world admires for majesty, we should think ourselves   15
much beholding unto you.

FAUSTUS Gentlemen,
For that I know your friendship is unfeigned,
It is not Faustus' custom to deny
The just request of those that wish him well: 20
You shall behold that peerless dame of Greece,
No otherwise for pomp or majesty
Than when Sir Paris crossed the seas with her
And brought the spoils to rich Dardania.
Be silent then, for danger is in words.   25
      [Mephistopheles goes to the door.] Music sound[s].
      Mephistopheles brings in Helen. She passeth over the
      stage

SECOND SCHOLAR Was this fair Helen, whose admirèd worth
Made Greece with ten years' wars afflict poor Troy?

THIRD SCHOLAR Too simple is my wit to tell her worth,
Whom all the world admires for majesty.

FIRST SCHOLAR
    Now we have seen the pride of nature's work,   30
    We'll take our leaves, and for this blessed sight
    Happy and blest be Faustus evermore.
FAUSTUS Gentlemen, farewell. The same wish I to you.
        Exeunt Scholars. Enter an Old Man
OLD MAN O gentle Faustus, leave this damnèd art,
    This magic, that will charm thy soul to hell   35
    And quite bereave thee of salvation!
    Though thou hast now offended like a man,
    Do not persever in it like a devil.
    Yet, yet thou hast an amiable soul,
    If sin by custom grow not into nature.°   40
    Then, Faustus, will repentance come too late;
    Then thou art banished from the sight of heaven.
    No mortal can express the pains of hell.
    It may be this my exhortation
    Seems harsh and all unpleasant. Let it not,   45
    For, gentle son, I speak it not in wrath
    Or envy of thee, but in tender love°
    And pity of thy future misery;
    And so have hope that this my kind rebuke,
    Checking thy body, may amend thy soul.°   50
FAUSTUS
    Where art thou, Faustus? Wretch, what hast thou done?
    Hell claims his right, and with a roaring voice
    Says, 'Faustus, come! Thine hour is almost come.'
        Mephistopheles gives him a dagger
    And Faustus now will come to do thee right.
        [*Faustus prepares to stab himself*]
OLD MAN O, stay, good Faustus, stay thy desperate steps!   55
    I see an angel hover o'er thy head,
    And with a vial full of precious grace
    Offers to pour the same into thy soul.
    Then call for mercy and avoid despair.
FAUSTUS
    O friend, I feel thy words to comfort my distressèd soul.   60
    Leave me a while to ponder on my sins.
OLD MAN Faustus, I leave thee, but with grief of heart,
    Fearing the enemy of thy hapless soul.
        Exit [*Old Man*]

FAUSTUS Accursèd Faustus, wretch, what hast thou done?
I do repent, and yet I do despair.   65
Hell strives with grace for conquest in my breast.
What shall I do to shun the snares of death?
MEPHISTOPHELES Thou traitor, Faustus, I arrest thy soul
For disobedience to my sovereign lord.
Revolt, or I'll in piecemeal tear thy flesh.   70
FAUSTUS I do repent I e'er offended him.
Sweet Mephistopheles, entreat thy lord
To pardon my unjust presumption,
And with my blood again I will confirm
The former vow I made to Lucifer.   75
MEPHISTOPHELES Do it then, Faustus, with unfeignèd heart,
Lest greater dangers do attend thy drift.
      [*Faustus cuts his arm and writes with his blood*]
FAUSTUS Torment, sweet friend, that base and agèd man
That durst dissuade me from thy Lucifer,
With greatest torment that our hell affords.   80
MEPHISTOPHELES His faith is great. I cannot touch his soul.
But what I may afflict his body with
I will attempt, which is but little worth.
FAUSTUS One thing, good servant, let me crave of thee
To glut the longing of my heart's desire: 85
That I may have unto my paramour
That heavenly Helen, which I saw of late,
Whose sweet embraces may extinguish clear
Those thoughts that do dissuade me from my vow,
And keep my vow I made to Lucifer.   90
MEPHISTOPHELES This, or what else my Faustus shall desire,
Shall be performed in twinkling of an eye.
      Enter Helen again [*brought in by Mephistopheles*], *passing*
      over between two Cupids
FAUSTUS Was this the face that launched a thousand ships
And burnt the topless towers of Ilium?
Sweet Helen, make me immortal with a kiss.   95
      [*They kiss*]
Her lips suck forth my soul. See where it flies!
Come, Helen, come, give me my soul again.
      [*They kiss again*]
Here will I dwell, for heaven is in these lips,
And all is dross that is not Helena.

I will be Paris, and for love of thee   100
Instead of Troy shall Wittenberg be sacked,
And I will combat with weak Menelaus,
And wear thy colours on my plumèd crest.
Yea, I will wound Achilles in the heel
And then return to Helen for a kiss.   105
O, thou art fairer than the evening's air,
Clad in the beauty of a thousand stars.
Brighter art thou than flaming Jupiter
When he appeared to hapless Semele,
More lovely than the monarch of the sky   110
In wanton Arethusa's azure arms;
And none but thou shalt be my paramour.
    Exeunt

[5.2]

Thunder. Enter Lucifer, Beelzebub, and Mephistopheles [*above*]

LUCIFER Thus from infernal Dis do we ascend
To view the subjects of our monarchy,
Those souls which sin seals the black sons of hell,
'Mong which as chief, Faustus, we come to thee,
Bringing with us lasting damnation   5
To wait upon thy soul. The time is come°
Which makes it forfeit.

MEPHISTOPHELES   And this gloomy night
Here in this room will wretched Faustus be.

BEELZEBUB And here we'll stay
To mark him how he doth demean himself.°   10

MEPHISTOPHELES How should he, but in desperate lunacy?
Fond worldling, now his heart-blood dries with grief;
His conscience kills it, and his labouring brain
Begets a world of idle fantasies
To overreach the devil. But all in vain.   15
His store of pleasures must be sauced with pain.
He and his servant Wagner are at hand,
Both come from drawing Faustus' latest will.°
See where they come.

    Enter Faustus and Wagner

FAUSTUS Say, Wagner. Thou hast perused my will;   20
How dost thou like it?
WAGNER   Sir, so wondrous well
As in all humble duty I do yield
My life and lasting service for your love.
          Enter the Scholars
FAUSTUS Gramercies, Wagner.—Welcome, gentlemen.
          [*Exit Wagner*]
FIRST SCHOLAR Now, worthy Faustus, methinks your looks are   25
changed.
FAUSTUS O gentlemen!
SECOND SCHOLAR What ails Faustus?
FAUSTUS Ah, my sweet chamber-fellow! Had I lived with thee, then
had I lived still, but now must die eternally. Look, sirs, comes he   30
not? Comes he not?
FIRST SCHOLAR O my dear Faustus, what imports this fear?
SECOND SCHOLAR Is all our pleasure turned to melancholy?
THIRD SCHOLAR[*to the other Scholars*] He is not well with being
over-solitary.   35
SECOND SCHOLAR If it be so, we'll have physicians, and Faustus
shall be cured.
THIRD SCHOLAR [*to Faustus*] 'Tis but a surfeit, sir. Fear nothing.
FAUSTUS A surfeit of deadly sin, that hath damned both body and
soul.   40
SECOND SCHOLAR Yet, Faustus, look up to heaven, and remember
mercy is infinite.
FAUSTUS But Faustus' offence can ne'er be pardoned. The serpent
that tempted Eve may be saved, but not Faustus. O gentlemen,
hear with patience, and tremble not at my speeches. Though my   45
heart pant and quiver to remember that I have been a student here
these thirty years, O, would I had never seen Wittenberg, never
read book! And what wonders I have done, all Germany can
witness, yea, all the world, for which Faustus hath lost both
Germany and the world, yea, heaven itself—heaven, the seat of   50
God, the throne of the blessed, the kingdom of joy—and must
remain in hell for ever. Hell, O, hell for ever! Sweet friends, what
shall become of Faustus, being in hell for ever?
SECOND SCHOLAR Yet, Faustus, call on God.
FAUSTUS On God, whom Faustus hath abjured? On God, whom   55
Faustus hath blasphemed? O my God, I would weep, but the devil
draws in my tears. Gush forth blood instead of tears, yea, life and

soul. O, he stays my tongue! I would lift up my hands, but see,
they° hold 'em, they hold 'em.

ALL Who, Faustus?   60

FAUSTUS Why, Lucifer and Mephistopheles. O gentlemen, I gave
them my soul for my cunning.

ALL O, God forbid!

FAUSTUS God forbade it indeed, but Faustus hath done it. For the
vain pleasure of four-and-twenty years hath Faustus lost eternal   65
joy and felicity. I writ them a bill with mine own blood. The date
is expired. This is the time, and he will fetch me.

FIRST SCHOLAR Why did not Faustus tell us of this before, that
divines might have prayed for thee?

FAUSTUS Oft have I thought to have done so, but the devil threat-   70
ened to tear me in pieces if I named God, to fetch me body and
soul if I once gave ear to divinity. And now 'tis too late. Gentlemen,
away, lest you perish with me.

SECOND SCHOLAR O, what may we do to save Faustus?

FAUSTUS Talk not of me, but save yourselves and depart.   75

THIRD SCHOLAR God will strengthen me. I will stay with Faustus.

FIRST SCHOLAR [to the Third Scholar] Tempt not God, sweet friend,
but let us into the next room and pray for him.

FAUSTUS Ay, pray for me, pray for me! And what noise soever you   80
hear, come not unto me, for nothing can rescue me.

SECOND SCHOLAR Pray thou, and we will pray that God may have
mercy upon thee.

FAUSTUS Gentlemen, farewell. If I live till morning,
I'll visit you; if not, Faustus is gone to hell.

ALL Faustus, farewell.   85
      Exeunt Scholars

MEPHISTOPHELES Ay, Faustus, now thou hast no hope of heaven;°
Therefore despair. Think only upon hell,
For that must be thy mansion, there to dwell.

FAUSTUS O thou bewitching fiend, 'twas thy temptation
Hath robbed me of eternal happiness.°   90

MEPHISTOPHELES I do confess it, Faustus, and rejoice.
'Twas I that, when thou wert i'the way to heaven,
Dammed up thy passage. When thou took'st the book
To view the Scriptures, then I turned the leaves
And led thine eye.   95
What, weep'st thou? 'Tis too late. Despair, farewell!
Fools that will laugh on earth must weep in hell.

Exit [Mephistopheles]. Enter the Good Angel and the Bad
Angel at several doors

GOOD ANGEL O Faustus, if thou hadst given ear to me,
Innumerable joys had followed thee.
But thou didst love the world.
BAD ANGEL   Gave ear to me,°   100
And now must taste hell's pains perpetually.
GOOD ANGEL O, what will all thy riches, pleasures, pomps
Avail thee now?
BAD ANGEL   Nothing but vex thee more,
To want in hell, that had on earth such store.
    Music while the throne descends°
GOOD ANGEL O, thou hast lost celestial happiness,   105
Pleasures unspeakable, bliss without end.
Hadst thou affected sweet divinity,
Hell or the devil had had no power on thee.
Hadst thou kept on that way, Faustus, behold
In what resplendent glory thou hadst set°   110
In yonder throne, like those bright shining saints,
And triumphed over hell. That hast thou lost.
And now, poor soul, must thy good angel leave thee.
The jaws of hell are open to receive thee.
    [The throne ascends.] Exit [Good Angel]. Hell is discovered°
BAD ANGEL Now, Faustus, let thine eyes with horror stare   115
Into that vast perpetual torture-house.
There are the Furies tossing damnèd souls
On burning forks; their bodies boil in lead.
There are live quarters broiling on the coals,°
That ne'er can die. This ever-burning chair   120
Is for o'er-tortured souls to rest them in.
These that are fed with sops of flaming fire
Were gluttons, and loved only delicates,
And laughed to see the poor starve at their gates.
But yet all these are nothing. Thou shalt see   125
Ten thousand tortures that more horrid be.
FAUSTUS O, I have seen enough to torture me!
BAD ANGEL Nay, thou must feel them, taste the smart of all.
He that loves pleasure must for pleasure fall.
And so I leave thee, Faustus, till anon;   130
Then wilt thou tumble in confusion.
    Exit [Bad Angel]. The clock strikes eleven

FAUSTUS O Faustus,
    Now hast thou but one bare hour to live,
    And then thou must be damned perpetually.
    Stand still, you ever-moving spheres of heaven,   135
    That time may cease and midnight never come!
    Fair nature's eye, rise, rise again, and make
    Perpetual day; or let this hour be but
    A year, a month, a week, a natural day,
    That Faustus may repent and save his soul!   140
    O lente, lente currite noctis equi!
    The stars move still; time runs; the clock will strike;
    The devil will come, and Faustus must be damned.
    O, I'll leap up to heaven! Who pulls me down?
    One drop of blood will save me. O, my Christ!   145
    Rend not my heart for naming of my Christ!
    Yet will I call on him. O, spare me, Lucifer!
    Where is it now? 'Tis gone;
    And see a threat'ning arm, an angry brow.
    Mountains and hills, come, come and fall on me,   150
    And hide me from the heavy wrath of heaven!
    No? Then will I headlong run into the earth.
    Gape, earth! O, no, it will not harbour me.
    You stars that reigned at my nativity,
    Whose influence hath allotted death and hell,   155
    Now draw up Faustus like a foggy mist
    Into the entrails of yon labouring cloud,
    That when you vomit forth into the air,
    My limbs may issue from your smoky mouths,
    But let my soul mount and ascend to heaven.   160
        The watch strikes
    O, half the hour is past! 'Twill all be past anon.
    O, if my soul must suffer for my sin,
    Impose some end to my incessant pain.
    Let Faustus live in hell a thousand years,
    A hundred thousand, and at last be saved.   165
    No end is limited to damnèd souls.
    Why wert thou not a creature wanting soul?
    Or why is this immortal that thou hast?
    O, Pythagoras' *metempsychosis*, were that true,
    This soul should fly from me and I be changed   170
    Into some brutish beast.

All beasts are happy, for, when they die,
Their souls are soon dissolved in elements;
But mine must live still to be plagued in hell.
Curst be the parents that engendered me!   175
No, Faustus, curse thyself. Curse Lucifer,
That hath deprived thee of the joys of heaven.
          The clock strikes twelve
It strikes, it strikes! Now, body, turn to air,
Or Lucifer will bear thee quick to hell.
O soul, be changed into small waterdrops,   180
And fall into the ocean, ne'er be found!
          Thunder, and enter the Devils
O, mercy, heaven, look not so fierce on me!
Adders and serpents, let me breathe a while!
Ugly hell, gape not. Come not, Lucifer!
I'll burn my books. O, Mephistopheles!   185
          Exeunt°

[5.3]

          Enter the Scholars
FIRST SCHOLAR Come, gentlemen, let us go visit Faustus,
     For such a dreadful night was never seen
     Since first the world's creation did begin.
     Such fearful shrieks and cries were never heard.
     Pray heaven the doctor have escaped the danger.   5
SECOND SCHOLAR
     O, help us, heaven! See, here are Faustus' limbs,
     All torn asunder by the hand of death.
THIRD SCHOLAR
     The devils whom Faustus served have torn him thus.
     For, 'twixt the hours of twelve and one, methought
     I heard him shriek and call aloud for help,   10
     At which self time the house seemed all on fire°
     With dreadful horror of these damnèd fiends.
SECOND SCHOLAR Well, gentlemen, though Faustus' end be such
     As every Christian heart laments to think on,
     Yet, for he was a scholar, once admired°   15
     For wondrous knowledge in our German schools,

We'll give his mangled limbs due burial;
And all the students, clothed in mourning black,
Shall wait upon his heavy funeral.°
    Exeunt

[EPILOGUE]

Enter Chorus

CHORUS Cut is the branch that might have grown full straight,
And burnèd is Apollo's laurel bough
That sometime grew within this learnèd man.
Faustus is gone. Regard his hellish fall,
Whose fiendful fortune may exhort the wise   5
Only to wonder at unlawful things,
Whose deepness doth entice such forward wits
To practise more than heavenly power permits.
    [Exit]
    Terminat hora diem; terminat author opus.

THE JEW OF MALTA

DRAMATIS PERSONAE

Machiavel
Barabas
Two Merchants
Three Jews
Ferneze, Governor of Malta
Knights of Malta
Officers
Callapine
Bashaws
Calymath
Abigail, *Barabas's daughter*
Friar Jacomo
Friar Barnardine
An Abbess

Two Nuns
Mathias
Lodowick, *Ferneze's son*
Martin del Bosco
Ithamore
Slaves
Katherine, *Mathias's mother*
Bellamira
Pilia-Borza
Attendants
Servants
Turkish Janizaries
A Messenger
Carpenters

The Epistle Dedicatory to My Worthy Friend, Master Thomas Hammon, of Gray's Inn, etc.

This play, composed by so worthy an author as Master Marlowe, and the part of the Jew presented by so unimitable an actor as Master Alleyn,° being in this later age commended to the stage, as I ushered it unto the court, and presented it to the Cock-pit,° with these prologues and epilogues here inserted, so now being newly brought   5
to the press, I was loath it should be published without the ornament of an epistle, making choice of you unto whom to devote it, than whom (of all those gentlemen and acquaintance within the compass of my long knowledge) there is none more able to tax ignorance or attribute right to merit. Sir, you have been pleased to grace some of   10
mine own works with your courteous patronage. I hope this will not be the worse accepted because commended by me, over whom none can claim more power or privilege than yourself. I had no better a New Year's gift to present you with. Receive it therefore as a continuance of that inviolable obligement by which he rests still   15
engaged, who, as he ever hath, shall always remain,

Tuissimus,°

Thomas Heywood

THE PROLOGUE SPOKEN AT COURT

Gracious and great, that we so boldly dare°
('Mongst other plays that now in fashion are)
To present this, writ many years agone,
And in that age thought second unto none,
We humbly crave your pardon. We pursue   5
The story of a rich and famous Jew
Who lived in Malta. You shall find him still,
In all his projects, a sound Machevill;°
And that's his character. He that hath passed
So many censures is now come at last   10
To have your princely ears. Grace you him; then
You crown the action and renown the pen.

THE PROLOGUE TO THE STAGE,
AT THE COCK-PIT

We know not how our play may pass this stage;
But by the best of poets in that age°
The *Malta Jew* had being, and was made,
And he then by the best of actors played.°
In *Hero and Leander*, one did gain°   5
A lasting memory; in *Tamburlaine*,
This *Jew*, with others many, th' other wan°
The attribute of peerless, being a man
Whom we may rank with (doing no one wrong)
Proteus for shapes and Roscius for a tongue,°   10
So could he speak, so vary; nor is't hate
To merit in him who doth personate
Our Jew this day, nor is it his ambition°
To exceed, or equal, being of condition
More modest. This is all that he intends,   15
And that, too, at the urgence of some friends:
To prove his best, and if none here gainsay it,
The part he hath studied, and intends to play it.

The Jew of Malta

[PROLOGUE]

[*Enter*] *Machiavel*°

MACHIAVEL Albeit the world think Machiavel is dead,
Yet was his soul but flown beyond the Alps,
And, now the Guise is dead, is come from France°
To view this land and frolic with his friends.°
To some perhaps my name is odious,   5
But such as love me guard me from their tongues,
And let them know that I am Machiavel,
And weigh not men, and therefore not men's words.°
Admired I am of those that hate me most.
Though some speak openly against my books,   10
Yet will they read me and thereby attain
To Peter's chair, and, when they cast me off,
Are poisoned by my climbing followers.°
I count religion but a childish toy
And hold there is no sin but ignorance.   15
Birds of the air will tell of murders past!°
I am ashamed to hear such fooleries.°
Many will talk of title to a crown;
What right had Caesar to the empery?°
Might first made kings, and laws were then most sure   20
When, like the Draco's, they were writ in blood.°
Hence comes it that a strong-built citadel
Commands much more than letters can import—°
Which maximé had Phalaris observed,°
He'd never bellowed in a brazen bull   25
Of great ones' envy. O'th'poor petty wits°
Let me be envied and not pitièd!°
But whither am I bound? I come not, I,
To read a lecture here in Britainy,°
But to present the tragedy of a Jew,   30
Who smiles to see how full his bags are crammed,
Which money was not got without my means.
I crave but this: grace him as he deserves,

And let him not be entertained the worse
Because he favours me.   35
    [*Exit*]

[1.1]

*Enter Barabas in his counting-house, with heaps of gold
before him°*

BARABAS So that of thus much that return was made,
And, of the third part of the Persian ships,
There was the venture summed and satisfied.°
As for those Samnites and the men of Uz,°
That bought my Spanish oils and wines of Greece,   5
Here have I pursed their paltry silverlings.°
Fie, what a trouble 'tis to count this trash!
Well fare the Arabians, who so richly pay
The things they traffic for with wedge of gold,
Whereof a man may easily in a day   10
Tell that which may maintain him all his life.
The needy groom that never fingered groat
Would make a miracle of thus much coin;°
But he whose steel-barred coffers are crammed full,
And all his lifetime hath been tired,   15
Wearying his fingers' ends with telling it,
Would in his age be loath to labour so,
And for a pound to sweat himself to death.
Give me the merchants of the Indian mines,
That trade in metal of the purest mould;   20
The wealthy Moor, that in the eastern rocks°
Without control can pick his riches up,
And in his house heap pearl like pebble-stones,
Receive them free, and sell them by the weight—°
Bags of fiery opals, sapphires, amethysts,   25
Jacinths, hard topaz, grass-green emeralds,
Beauteous rubies, sparkling diamonds,
And seld-seen costly stones of so great price
As one of them, indifferently rated°
And of a carat of this quantity,   30
May serve in peril of calamity°
To ransom great kings from captivity.
This is the ware wherein consists my wealth;
And thus methinks should men of judgement frame
Their means of traffic from the vulgar trade,°   35

And as their wealth increaseth, so enclose
Infinite riches in a little room.
But now, how stands the wind?
Into what corner peers my halcyon's bill?°
Ha, to the east? Yes. See, how stands the vanes?°   40
East and by south. Why then, I hope my ships
I sent for Egypt and the bordering isles°
Are gotten up by Nilus' winding banks;°
Mine argosy from Alexandria,
Loaden with spice and silks, now under sail,   45
Are smoothly gliding down by Candy shore°
To Malta, through our Mediterranean Sea.
But who comes here?
                Enter a [First] Merchant
                        How now?
FIRST MERCHANT   Barabas,
Thy ships are safe, riding in Malta road;
And all the merchants with other merchandise   50
Are safe arrived, and have sent me to know
Whether yourself will come and custom them.°
BARABAS The ships are safe, thou say'st, and richly fraught?
FIRST MERCHANT They are.
BARABAS   Why then, go bid them come ashore
And bring with them their bills of entry.   55
I hope our credit in the custom-house
Will serve as well as I were present there.°
Go send 'em threescore camels, thirty mules,
And twenty wagons to bring up the ware.
But art thou master in a ship of mine,   60
And is thy credit not enough for that?
FIRST MERCHANT The very custom barely comes to more°
Than many merchants of the town are worth,
And therefore far exceeds my credit, sir.
BARABAS Go tell 'em the Jew of Malta sent thee, man.   65
Tush, who amongst 'em knows not Barabas?
FIRST MERCHANT I go.
                [He starts to leave]
BARABAS So then, there's somewhat come.—°
Sirrah, which of my ships art thou master of?
FIRST MERCHANT Of the *Speranza*, sir.
BARABAS.   And saw'st thou not   70

Mine argosy at Alexandria?
Thou couldst not come from Egypt or by Caire°
But at the entry there into the sea
Where Nilus pays his tribute to the main°
Thou needs must sail by Alexandria.   75
FIRST MERCHANT I neither saw them nor inquired of them.
But this we heard some of our seamen say:
They wondered how you durst with so much wealth
Trust such a crazèd vessel, and so far.
BARABAS
Tush, they are wise! I know her and her strength.°   80
But go, go thou thy ways; discharge thy ship,
And bid my factor bring his loading in.°
    [*Exit First Merchant*]
And yet I wonder at this argosy.°
    Enter a Second Merchant
SECOND MERCHANT Thine argosy from Alexandria,
Know, Barabas, doth ride in Malta road,   85
Laden with riches and exceeding store
Of Persian silks, of gold, and orient pearl.
BARABAS How chance you came not with those other ships°
That sailed by Egypt?
SECOND MERCHANT   Sir, we saw 'em not.
BARABAS Belike they coasted round by Candy shore   90
About their oils, or other businesses.°
But 'twas ill done of you to come so far
Without the aid or conduct of their ships.°
SECOND MERCHANT Sir, we were wafted by a Spanish fleet°
That never left us till within a league,°   95
That had the galleys of the Turk in chase.°
BARABAS O, they were going up to Sicily. Well, go°
And bid the merchants and my men dispatch
And come ashore, and see the fraught discharged.
SECOND MERCHANT I go.   100
    Exit [*Second Merchant*]
BARABAS Thus trolls our fortune in by land and sea,°
And thus are we on every side enriched.
These are the blessings promised to the Jews,
And herein was old Abram's happiness.°
What more may heaven do for earthly man   105
Than thus to pour out plenty in their laps,

Ripping the bowels of the earth for them,
Making the sea their servant, and the winds
To drive their substance with successful blasts?°
Who hateth me but for my happiness?   110
Or who is honoured now but for his wealth?
Rather had I, a Jew, be hated thus
Than pitied in a Christian poverty;
For I can see no fruits in all their faith°
But malice, falsehood, and excessive pride,   115
Which methinks fits not their profession.°
Haply some hapless man hath conscience,°
And for his conscience lives in beggary.
They say we are a scattered nation;
I cannot tell, but we have scambled up°   120
More wealth by far than those that brag of faith.
There's Kirriah Jairim, the great Jew of Greece,°
Obed in Bairseth, Nones in Portugal,
Myself in Malta, some in Italy,
Many in France, and wealthy every one—   125
Ay, wealthier far than any Christian.
I must confess we come not to be kings.°
That's not our fault. Alas, our number's few,
And crowns come either by succession
Or urged by force; and nothing violent,   130
Oft have I heard tell, can be permanent.
Give us a peaceful rule; make Christians kings,
That thirst so much for principality.
I have no charge, nor many children,
But one sole daughter, whom I hold as dear   135
As Agamemnon did his Iphigen;°
And all I have is hers. But who comes here?
        Enter three Jews [speaking to one another]
FIRST JEW Tush, tell not me, 'twas done of policy.°
SECOND JEW Come, therefore, let us go to Barabas,
For he can counsel best in these affairs;   140
And here he comes.
BARABAS   Why, how now, countrymen?
Why flock you thus to me in multitudes?
What accident's betided to the Jews?
FIRST JEW A fleet of warlike galleys, Barabas,
Are come from Turkey, and lie in our road;   145

And they this day sit in the council-house°
To entertain them and their embassy.
BARABAS Why, let 'em come, so they come not to war;
Or let 'em war, so we be conquerors.
    (*Aside*) Nay, let 'em combat, conquer, and kill all,   150
So they spare me, my daughter, and my wealth.
FIRST JEW Were it for confirmation of a league,
They would not come in warlike manner thus.
SECOND JEW I fear their coming will afflict us all.
BARABAS Fond men, what dream you of their multitudes?   155
What need they treat of peace that are in league?°
The Turks and those of Malta are in league.
Tut, tut, there is some other matter in't.
FIRST JEW Why, Barabas, they come for peace or war.
BARABAS Haply for neither, but to pass along   160
Towards Venice by the Adriatic Sea,
With whom they have attempted many times,°
But never could effect their stratagem.
THIRD JEW And very wisely said; it may be so.
SECOND JEW But there's a meeting in the senate-house,   165
And all the Jews in Malta must be there.
BARABAS Umh. All the Jews in Malta must be there?
Ay, like enough. Why then, let every man
Provide him, and be there for fashion sake.°
If anything shall there concern our state,°   170
Assure yourselves I'll look—(*aside*) unto myself.
FIRST JEW I know you will. Well, brethren, let us go.
SECOND JEW Let's take our leaves. Farewell, good Barabas.
BARABAS Do so. Farewell, Zaareth, farewell, Tcmainte.
    [*Exeunt the three Jews*]
And, Barabas, now search this secret out.   175
Summon thy senses; call thy wits together.
These silly men mistake the matter clean.
Long to the Turk did Malta contribute,°
Which tribute—all in policy, I fear—
The Turks have let increase to such a sum   180
As all the wealth of Malta cannot pay,
And now by that advantage thinks, belike,
To seize upon the town. Ay, that he seeks.
Howe'er the world go, I'll make sure for one,°
And seek in time to intercept the worst,   185

Warily guarding that which I ha' got.
Ego mihimet sum semper proximus.°
Why, let 'em enter, let 'em take the town.
[*Exit*]

[1.2]

Enter [Ferneze] Governor° of Malta, Knights, [and Officers],
met by [Callapine and other] Bashaws of the Turk [and]
Calymath

FERNEZE Now, bashaws, what demand you at our hands?
CALLAPINE Know, Knights of Malta, that we came from Rhodes,°
From Cyprus, Candy, and those other isles
That lie betwixt the Mediterranean seas.
FERNEZE What's Cyprus, Candy, and those other isles   5
To us, or Malta? What at our hands demand ye?
CALYMATH The ten years' tribute that remains unpaid.
FERNEZE Alas, my lord, the sum is over-great.
I hope your highness will consider us.
CALYMATH I wish, grave governor, 'twere in my power   10
To favour you, but 'tis my father's cause,°
Wherein I may not, nay, I dare not dally.
FERNEZE Then give us leave, great Selim Calymath.°
      [*Ferneze consults with his Knights*]
CALYMATH [*to his Bashaws*]
Stand all aside, and let the knights determine,
And send to keep our galleys under sail,°   15
For happily we shall not tarry here.
[*To Ferneze*] Now, governor, how are you resolved?
FERNEZE Thus: since your hard conditions are such
That you will needs have ten years' tribute past,
We may have time to make collection°   20
Amongst the inhabitants of Malta for't.
CALLAPINE That's more than is in our commission.
CALYMATH What, Callapine, a little courtesy!
Let's know their time; perhaps it is not long,°
And 'tis more kingly to obtain by peace   25
Than to enforce conditions by constraint.—
What respite ask you, governor?

FERNEZE   But a month.

CALYMATH We grant a month, but see you keep your promise.
    Now launch our galleys back again to sea,
    Where we'll attend the respite you have ta'en,   30
    And for the money send our messenger.
    Farewell, great governor, and brave Knights of Malta.

FERNEZE And all good fortune wait on Calymath!
        Exeunt [Calymath, Callapine, and other Bashaws]
    Go, one, and call those Jews of Malta hither.
        [An Officer goes to the door]
    Were they not summoned to appear today?   35

OFFICER They were, my lord, and here they come.
        Enter Barabas and three Jews

FIRST KNIGHT Have you determined what to say to them?

FERNEZE Yes, give me leave; and Hebrews, now come near.
    From the emperor of Turkey is arrived
    Great Selim Calymath, his highness' son,   40
    To levy of us ten years' tribute past.
    Now then, here know that it concerneth us.

BARABAS Then, good my lord, to keep your quiet still,
    Your lordship shall do well to let them have it.

FERNEZE Soft, Barabas, there's more 'longs to't than so.°   45
    To what this ten years' tribute will amount,
    That we have cast, but cannot compass it
    By reason of the wars, that robbed our store;
    And therefore are we to request your aid.

BARABAS Alas, my lord, we are no soldiers;   50
    And what's our aid against so great a prince?°

FIRST KNIGHT Tut, Jew, we know thou art no soldier;
    Thou art a merchant and a moneyed man,
    And 'tis thy money, Barabas, we seek.

BARABAS How, my lord, my money?

FERNEZE   Thine and the rest.   55
    For, to be short, amongst you 't must be had.

FIRST JEW Alas, my lord, the most of us are poor!

FERNEZE Then let the rich increase your portions.

BARABAS Are strangers with your tribute to be taxed?°

SECOND KNIGHT
    Have strangers leave with us to get their wealth?   60
    Then let them with us contribute.

BARABAS How, equally?

FERNEZE   No, Jew, like infidels.
    For through our sufferance of your hateful lives,
    Who stand accursèd in the sight of heaven,
    These taxes and afflictions are befall'n,   65
    And therefore thus we are determinèd.—
    Read there the articles of our decrees.
OFFICER (*reads*) 'First, the tribute money of the Turks shall all be
    levied amongst the Jews, and each of them to pay one half of his
    estate.'   70
BARABAS
    How, half his estate? [*Aside*] I hope you mean not mine.
FERNEZE Read on.
OFFICER (*reads*) 'Secondly, he that denies to pay shall straight
    become a Christian.'
BARABAS How, a Christian? [*Aside*] Hum, what's here to do?   75
OFFICER (*reads*) 'Lastly, he that denies this shall absolutely lose all
    he has.'
ALL THREE JEWS O my lord, we will give half!
BARABAS O earth-mettled villains, and no Hebrews born!
    And will you basely thus submit yourselves   80
    To leave your goods to their arbitrament?
FERNEZE Why, Barabas, wilt thou be christenèd?
BARABAS No, governor, I will be no convertite.
FERNEZE Then pay thy half.
BARABAS Why, know you what you did by this device?   85
    Half of my substance is a city's wealth.
    Governor, it was not got so easily,
    Nor will I part so slightly therewithal.
FERNEZE Sir, half is the penalty of our decree.
    Either pay that, or we will seize on all.   90
BARABAS *Corpo di Dio!* Stay, you shall have half.°
    Let me be used but as my brethren are.
FERNEZE No, Jew, thou hast denied the articles,
    And now it cannot be recalled.
        [*Exeunt Officers on a signal from Ferneze*]
BARABAS Will you then steal my goods?   95
    Is theft the ground of your religion?
FERNEZE No, Jew, we take particularly thine
    To save the ruin of a multitude;
    And better one want for a common good°
    Than many perish for a private man.   100

Yet, Barabas, we will not banish thee,
But here in Malta, where thou got'st thy wealth,
Live still; and, if thou canst, get more.
BARABAS Christians, what or how can I multiply?
Of naught is nothing made.   105
FIRST KNIGHT
From naught at first thou cam'st to little wealth,
From little unto more, from more to most.
If your first curse fall heavy on thy head°
And make thee poor and scorned of all the world,
'Tis not our fault, but thy inherent sin.   110
BARABAS What? Bring you scripture to confirm your wrongs?
Preach me not out of my possessions.
Some Jews are wicked, as all Christians are;
But say the tribe that I descended of
Were all in general cast away for sin,   115
Shall I be tried by their transgression?
The man that dealeth righteously shall live;°
And which of you can charge me otherwise?
FERNEZE Out, wretched Barabas,
Sham'st thou not thus to justify thyself,   120
As if we knew not thy profession?°
If thou rely upon thy righteousness,
Be patient, and thy riches will increase.
Excess of wealth is cause of covetousness,
And covetousness, O, 'tis a monstrous sin.   125
BARABAS
Ay, but theft is worse. Tush, take not from me then,°
For that is theft; and if you rob me thus,
I must be forced to steal and compass more.
FIRST KNIGHT Grave governor, list not to his exclaims.
Convert his mansion to a nunnery;   130
His house will harbour many holy nuns.
FERNEZE It shall be so.
          Enter Officers
                      Now, officers, have you done?
AN OFFICER Ay, my lord, we have seized upon the goods
And wares of Barabas, which, being valued,
Amount to more than all the wealth in Malta.   135
And of the other we have seizèd half.°
FERNEZE Then we'll take order for the residue.°

BARABAS Well then, my lord, say, are you satisfied?
    You have my goods, my money, and my wealth,
    My ships, my store, and all that I enjoyed;   140
    And having all, you can request no more,
    Unless your unrelenting flinty hearts
    Suppress all pity in your stony breasts
    And now shall move you to bereave my life.
FERNEZE No, Barabas, to stain our hands with blood   145
    Is far from us and our profession.
BARABAS Why, I esteem the injury far less
    To take the lives of miserable men
    Than be the causers of their misery.
    You have my wealth, the labour of my life,   150
    The comfort of mine age, my children's hope;
    And therefore ne'er distinguish of the wrong.°
FERNEZE Content thee, Barabas. Thou hast naught but right.°
BARABAS Your extreme right does me exceeding wrong.°
    But take it to you, i'th'devil's name!   155
FERNEZE Come, let us in, and gather of these goods
    The money for this tribute of the Turk.
FIRST KNIGHT 'Tis necessary that be looked unto;
    For if we break our day, we break the league,°
    And that will prove but simple policy.   160
        Exeunt [Ferneze, Knights, and Officers]
BARABAS Ay, policy! That's their profession,
    And not simplicity, as they suggest.
    The plagues of Egypt, and the curse of heaven,
    Earth's barrenness, and all men's hatred
    Inflict upon them, thou great Primus Motor!°   165
    And here upon my knees, striking the earth,°
    I ban their souls to everlasting pains
    And extreme tortures of the fiery deep,
    That thus have dealt with me in my distress.
FIRST JEW O, yet be patient, gentle Barabas.   170
BARABAS O silly brethren, born to see this day!
    Why stand you thus unmoved with my laments?
    Why weep you not to think upon my wrongs?
    Why pine not I and die in this distress?
FIRST JEW Why, Barabas, as hardly can we brook   175
    The cruel handling of ourselves in this.
    Thou seest they have taken half our goods.

BARABAS Why did you yield to their extortion?
 You were a multitude, and I but one,
 And of me only have they taken all.   180
FIRST JEW Yet, brother Barabas, remember Job.
BARABAS What tell you me of Job? I wot his wealth
 Was written thus: he had seven thousand sheep,°
 Three thousand camels, and two hundred yoke
 Of labouring oxen, and five hundred   185
 She-asses; but for every one of those,
 Had they been valued at indifferent rate,
 I had at home, and in mine argosy
 And other ships that came from Egypt last,°
 As much as would have bought his beasts and him, 190
 And yet have kept enough to live upon;
 So that not he, but I, may curse the day,
 Thy fatal birthday, forlorn Barabas,°
 And henceforth wish for an eternal night,
 That clouds of darkness may enclose my flesh 195
 And hide these extreme sorrows from mine eyes.°
 For only I have toiled to inherit here
 The months of vanity and loss of time,°
 And painful nights have been appointed me.
SECOND JEW Good Barabas, be patient.
BARABAS   Ay, ay;   200
 Pray leave me in my patience. You that°
 Were ne'er possessed of wealth are pleased with want.°
 But give him liberty at least to mourn
 That in a field amidst his enemies
 Doth see his soldiers slain, himself disarmed, 205
 And knows no means of his recovery.
 Ay, let me sorrow for this sudden chance;
 'Tis in the trouble of my spirit I speak.
 Great injuries are not so soon forgot.
FIRST JEW Come, let us leave him in his ireful mood. 210
 Our words will but increase his ecstasy.
SECOND JEW On, then. But trust me, 'tis a misery
 To see a man in such affliction.
 Farewell, Barabas.
    Exeunt [*the three Jews, weeping*]
BARABAS   Ay, fare you well.
 See the simplicity of these base slaves,   215

Who, for the villains have no wit themselves,°
Think me to be a senseless lump of clay
That will with every water wash to dirt.
No, Barabas is born to better chance
And framed of finer mould than common men°   220
That measure naught but by the present time.
A reaching thought will search his deepest wits°
And cast with cunning for the time to come,
For evils are apt to happen every day.
>   *Enter Abigail, the Jew's daughter,* [*weeping*]
But whither wends my beauteous Abigail?   225
O, what has made my lovely daughter sad?—
What, woman, moan not for a little loss.
Thy father has enough in store for thee.

ABIGAIL Not for myself, but agèd Barabas,
Father, for thee lamenteth Abigail.   230
But I will learn to leave these fruitless tears,
And, urged thereto with my afflictions,°
With fierce exclaims run to the senate-house,
And in the senate reprehend them all,
And rend their hearts with tearing of my hair,   235
Till they reduce the wrongs done to my father.

BARABAS No, Abigail, things past recovery
Are hardly cured with exclamations.
Be silent, daughter; sufferance breeds ease,
And time may yield us an occasion   240
Which on the sudden cannot serve the turn.°
Besides, my girl, think me not all so fond
As negligently to forgo so much
Without provision for thyself and me.
Ten thousand portagues, besides great pearls,   245
Rich, costly jewels, and stones infinite,
Fearing the worst of this before it fell,
I closely hid.

ABIGAIL Where, father?

BARABAS In my house, my girl.   250

ABIGAIL Then shall they ne'er be seen of Barabas,
For they have seized upon thy house and wares.

BARABAS But they will give me leave once more, I trow,
To go into my house.

ABIGAIL   That may they not,

For there I left the governor placing nuns,   255
Displacing me; and of thy house they mean
To make a nunnery, where none but their own sect
Must enter in, men generally barred.
BARABAS My gold, my gold, and all my wealth is gone!
You partial heavens, have I deserved this plague?   260
What, will you thus oppose me, luckless stars,
To make me desperate in my poverty,
And, knowing me impatient in distress,
Think me so mad as I will hang myself,
That I may vanish o'er the earth in air   265
And leave no memory that e'er I was?
No, I will live, nor loathe I this my life;
And since you leave me in the ocean thus
To sink or swim, and put me to my shifts,
I'll rouse my senses and awake myself.   270
Daughter, I have it! Thou perceiv'st the plight
Wherein these Christians have oppressèd me.
Be ruled by me, for in extremity
We ought to make bar of no policy.
ABIGAIL Father, whate'er it be, to injure them   275
That have so manifestly wrongèd us,
What will not Abigail attempt?
BARABAS   Why, so.
Then thus: thou told'st me they have turned my house
Into a nunnery, and some nuns are there.
ABIGAIL I did.
BARABAS   Then, Abigail, there must my girl   280
Entreat the Abbess to be entertained.
ABIGAIL How, as a nun?
BARABAS   Ay, daughter, for religion
Hides many mischiefs from suspicion.
ABIGAIL Ay, but father, they will suspect me there.
BARABAS Let 'em suspect, but be thou so precise   285
As they may think it done of holiness.
Entreat 'em fair, and give them friendly speech,°
And seem to them as if thy sins were great,
Till thou hast gotten to be entertained.
ABIGAIL Thus, father, shall I much dissemble.°
BARABAS   Tush,   290
As good dissemble that thou never mean'st

As first mean truth and then dissemble it.
A counterfeit profession is better
Than unseen hypocrisy.°
ABIGAIL Well, father, say I be entertained,   295
What then shall follow?
BARABAS   This shall follow then:
There have I hid, close underneath the plank
That runs along the upper-chamber floor,
The gold and jewels which I kept for thee.
But here they come. Be cunning, Abigail.   300
ABIGAIL Then, father, go with me.
BARABAS   No, Abigail, in this
It is not necessary I be seen,°
For I will seem offended with thee for't.°
Be close, my girl, for this must fetch my gold.
      [*Barabas stands aside.*] *Enter two Friars* [*Jacomo and*
      Barnardine] *and* [*an Abbess and*] *two Nuns*
FRIAR JACOMO Sisters,   305
We now are almost at the new-made nunnery.
ABBESS The better; for we love not to be seen.
'Tis thirty winters long since some of us
Did stray so far amongst the multitude.
FRIAR JACOMO But, madam, this house   310
And waters of this new-made nunnery°
Will much delight you.
ABBESS It may be so. But who comes here?
ABIGAIL [*coming forward*]
Grave Abbess, and you, happy virgins' guide,°
Pity the state of a distressèd maid!   315
ABBESS What art thou, daughter?
ABIGAIL The hopeless daughter of a hapless Jew,°
The Jew of Malta, wretched Barabas,
Sometimes the owner of a goodly house
Which they have now turned to a nunnery.   320
ABBESS Well, daughter, say, what is thy suit with us?
ABIGAIL Fearing the afflictions which my father feels
Proceed from sin or want of faith in us,°
I'd pass away my life in penitence
And be a novice in your nunnery   325
To make atonement for my labouring soul.

FRIAR JACOMO [*to Barnardine*] No doubt, brother, but this pro-
ceedeth of the spirit.
FRIAR BARNARDINE [*to Jacomo*] Ay, and of a moving spirit° too,
brother. But come,   330
Let us entreat she may be entertained.
ABBESS Well, daughter, we admit you for a nun.
ABIGAIL First let me as a novice learn to frame
My solitary life to your strait laws,
And let me lodge where I was wont to lie.   335
I do not doubt, by your divine precepts
And mine own industry, but to profit much.
BARABAS (*aside*) As much, I hope, as all I hid is worth.°
ABBESS Come, daughter, follow us.
BARABAS [*coming forward*]
Why, how now, Abigail? What mak'st thou°   340
Amongst these hateful Christians?
FRIAR JACOMO Hinder her not, thou man of little faith,
For she has mortified herself.°
BARABAS   How, mortified?
FRIAR JACOMO And is admitted to the sisterhood.
BARABAS Child of perdition, and thy father's shame,   345
What wilt thou do among these hateful fiends?
I charge thee on my blessing that thou leave
These devils and their damnèd heresy.
ABIGAIL Father, give me—
BARABAS   Nay, back, Abigail!°
    (*Whispers to her*)
And think upon the jewels and the gold;   350
The board is markèd thus [*making the sign of the cross*] that
covers it.
[*Aloud*] Away, accursèd, from thy father's sight!
FRIAR JACOMO Barabas, although thou art in misbelief
And wilt not see thine own afflictions,
Yet let thy daughter be no longer blind.°   355
BARABAS Blind, friar? I reck not thy persuasions.°
    [*Aside to Abigail*]
The board is markèd thus [*making the sign of the cross*] that
covers it.
[*Aloud*] For I had rather die than see her thus.—
Wilt thou forsake me too in my distress,

Seducèd daughter? (*Aside to her*) Go, forget not.   360
[*Aloud*] Becomes it Jews to be so credulous?
(*Aside to her*) Tomorrow early I'll be at the door.
[*Aloud*] No, come not at me! If thou wilt be damned,
Forget me, see me not, and so begone.
(*Aside* [*to her*]) Farewell. Remember tomorrow morning.   365
[*Aloud*] Out, out, thou wretch!
        [*Exeunt Abigail, Abbess, Friars, and Nuns one way, Barabas
        another. As they are leaving,*] *enter Mathias*
MATHIAS [*to himself*]
    Who's this? Fair Abigail, the rich Jew's daughter,
    Become a nun? Her father's sudden fall
    Has humbled her and brought her down to this.
    Tut, she were fitter for a tale of love   370
    Than to be tired out with orisons;
    And better would she far become a bed,
    Embracèd in a friendly lover's arms,
    Than rise at midnight to a solemn mass.
        Enter Lodowick
LODOWICK Why, how now, Don Mathias, in a dump?°   375
MATHIAS Believe me, noble Lodowick, I have seen
    The strangest sight, in my opinion,
    That ever I beheld.
LODOWICK   What was't, I prithee?
MATHIAS A fair young maid, scarce fourteen years of age,
    The sweetest flower in Cytherea's field,°   380
    Cropped from the pleasures of the fruitful earth
    And strangely metamorphized nun.
LODOWICK But say, what was she?
MATHIAS   Why, the rich Jew's daughter.
LODOWICK What, Barabas, whose goods were lately seized?
    Is she so fair?
MATHIAS   And matchless beautiful,   385
    As, had you seen her, 'twould have moved your heart,
    Though countermined with walls of brass, to love,°
    Or at the least to pity.
LODOWICK An if she be so fair as you report,
    'Twere time well spent to go and visit her.   390
    How say you, shall we?
MATHIAS I must and will, sir; there's no remedy.°
LODOWICK [*aside*] And so will I too, or it shall go hard.—°

Farewell, Mathias.
MATHIAS   Farewell, Lodowick.
  Exeunt [separately]

[2.1]

Enter Barabas, with a light°

BARABAS Thus like the sad presaging raven, that tolls°
 The sick man's passport in her hollow beak,°
 And in the shadow of the silent night
 Doth shake contagion from her sable wings,°
 Vexed and tormented runs poor Barabas   5
 With fatal curses towards these Christians.
 The incertain pleasures of swift-footed time
 Have ta'en their flight and left me in despair,
 And of my former riches rests no more
 But bare remembrance—like a soldier's scar,   10
 That has no further comfort for his maim.
 O Thou, that with a fiery pillar led'st
 The sons of Israel through the dismal shades,
 Light Abraham's offspring, and direct the hand°
 Of Abigail this night! Or let the day   15
 Turn to eternal darkness after this.
 No sleep can fasten on my watchful eyes
 Nor quiet enter my distempered thoughts
 Till I have answer of my Abigail.
   *Enter Abigail, above, [with gold and jewels. She and Barabas
   do not see each other at first]*
ABIGAIL Now have I happily espied a time   20
 To search the plank my father did appoint.
 And here, behold, unseen, where I have found
 The gold, the pearls, and jewels which he hid!
BARABAS Now I remember those old women's words,
 Who in my wealth would tell me winter's tales,°   25
 And speak of spirits and ghosts that glide by night
 About the place where treasure hath been hid.
 And now methinks that I am one of those,
 For whilst I live here lives my soul's sole hope,
 And when I die here shall my spirit walk.   30
ABIGAIL Now that my father's fortune were so good
 As but to be about this happy place!°
 'Tis not so happy; yet when we parted last,
 He said he would attend me in the morn.

Then, gentle sleep, where'er his body rests,   35
Give charge to Morpheus that he may dream°
A golden dream, and of the sudden wake,°
Come, and receive the treasure I have found.
BARABAS *Bueno para todos mi ganado no era.*°
  As good go on as sit so sadly thus.   40
  But stay, what star shines yonder in the east?°
  The lodestar of my life, if Abigail.—
  Who's there?
ABIGAIL   Who's that?
BARABAS   Peace, Abigail, 'tis I.
ABIGAIL Then, father, here receive thy happiness.
BARABAS Hast thou't?   45
ABIGAIL Here. (*Throws down bags*) Hast thou't?
  There's more, and more, and more.
BARABAS   O my girl,
  My gold, my fortune, my felicity,
  Strength to my soul, death to mine enemy!
  Welcome, the first beginner of my bliss!   50
  O Abigail, Abigail, that I had thee here too!
  Then my desires were fully satisfied.
  But I will practise thy enlargement thence.°
  O girl, O gold, O beauty, O my bliss! (*Hugs his bags*)°
ABIGAIL Father, it draweth towards midnight now,   55
  And 'bout this time the nuns begin to wake;
  To shun suspicion, therefore, let us part.
BARABAS Farewell, my joy, and by my fingers take
  A kiss from him that sends it from his soul.
      [*He blows her a kiss.*° *Exit Abigail above*]
  Now, Phoebus, ope the eyelids of the day,   60
  And for the raven wake the morning lark,°
  That I may hover with her in the air,
  Singing o'er these, as she does o'er her young,°
  [*sings*] *Hermoso placer de los dineros.*°
      Exit

[2.2]

Enter Ferneze, Martin del Bosco, the Knights, [and Officers]

FERNEZE Now, captain, tell us whither thou art bound,°
 Whence is thy ship that anchors in our road,
 And why thou cam'st ashore without our leave.

DEL BOSCO Governor of Malta, hither am I bound;
 My ship, the *Flying Dragon*, is of Spain,   5
 And so am I. Del Bosco is my name,
 Vice-admiral unto the Catholic king.

FIRST KNIGHT [*to Ferneze*]
 'Tis true, my lord. Therefore entreat him well.

DEL BOSCO Our fraught is Grecians, Turks, and Afric Moors.
 For, late upon the coast of Corsica,   10
 Because we vailed not to the Turkish fleet,°
 Their creeping galleys had us in the chase;°
 But suddenly the wind began to rise,
 And then we luffed and tacked, and fought at ease.°
 Some have we fired, and many have we sunk, 15
 But one amongst the rest became our prize.
 The captain's slain, the rest remain our slaves,
 Of whom we would make sale in Malta here.

FERNEZE Martin del Bosco, I have heard of thee.
 Welcome to Malta, and to all of us.   20
 But to admit a sale of these thy Turks
 We may not, nay, we dare not give consent,
 By reason of a tributary league.

FIRST KNIGHT Del Bosco, as thou lov'st and honour'st us,
 Persuade our governor against the Turk.   25
 This truce we have is but in hope of gold,
 And with that sum he craves might we wage war.

DEL BOSCO Will Knights of Malta be in league with Turks,
 And buy it basely too for sums of gold?
 My lord, remember that, to Europe's shame, 30
 The Christian isle of Rhodes, from whence you came,°
 Was lately lost, and you were stated here°
 To be at deadly enmity with Turks.

FERNEZE Captain, we know it, but our force is small.

DEL BOSCO What is the sum that Calymath requires? 35

FERNEZE A hundred thousand crowns.

DEL BOSCO My lord and king hath title to this isle,
      And he means quickly to expel them hence;
      Therefore be ruled by me, and keep the gold.
      I'll write unto his majesty for aid,   40
      And not depart until I see you free.
FERNEZE On this condition shall thy Turks be sold.
      Go, officers, and set them straight in show.
            [*Exeunt Officers*]
      Bosco, thou shalt be Malta's general;
      We and our warlike knights will follow thee   45
      Against these barbarous, misbelieving Turks.
DEL BOSCO So shall you imitate those you succeed;°
      For when their hideous force environed Rhodes,°
      Small though the number was that kept the town,
      They fought it out, and not a man survived   50
      To bring the hapless news to Christendom.
FERNEZE So will we fight it out. Come, let's away.
      Proud-daring Calymath, instead of gold
      We'll send thee bullets wrapped in smoke and fire.
      Claim tribute where thou wilt, we are resolved;   55
      Honour is bought with blood and not with gold.
            Exeunt

[2.3]

            Enter Officers with [*Ithamore and other*] *Slaves*
FIRST OFFICER This is the marketplace. Here let 'em stand.
      Fear not their sale, for they'll be quickly bought.°
SECOND OFFICER Every one's price is written on his back,
      And so much must they yield or not be sold.
            Enter Barabas
FIRST OFFICER
      Here comes the Jew. Had not his goods been seized,   5
      He'd give us present money for them all.
BARABAS [*aside*] In spite of these swine-eating Christians—
      Unchosen nation, never circumcised,
      Such as, poor villains, were ne'er thought upon
      Till Titus and Vespasian conquered us—°   10
      Am I become as wealthy as I was.

They hoped my daughter would ha' been a nun,
But she's at home, and I have bought a house
As great and fair as is the governor's;
And there in spite of Malta will I dwell,   15
Having Ferneze's hand, whose heart I'll have—°
Ay, and his son's, too, or it shall go hard.
I am not of the tribe of Levi, I,°
That can so soon forget an injury.
We Jews can fawn like spaniels when we please,   20
And when we grin, we bite; yet are our looks
As innocent and harmless as a lamb's.
I learned in Florence how to kiss my hand,°
Heave up my shoulders when they call me dog,°
And duck as low as any barefoot friar,   25
Hoping to see them starve upon a stall,°
Or else be gathered for in our synagogue,°
That when the offering basin comes to me,
Even for charity I may spit into't.°
Here comes Don Lodowick, the governor's son,   30
One that I love for his good father's sake.°
    Enter Lodowick, [*not seeing Barabas at first*]
LODOWICK I hear the wealthy Jew walked this way.
    I'll seek him out and so insinuate°
    That I may have a sight of Abigail,
    For Don Mathias tells me she is fair.   35
BARABAS [*aside*] Now will I show myself to have more of the serpent
    than the dove—that is, more knave than fool.
LODOWICK Yond walks the Jew. Now for fair Abigail.
BARABAS [*aside*] Ay, ay, no doubt but she's at your command.°
LODOWICK Barabas, thou know'st I am the governor's son.   40
BARABAS I would you were his father too, sir; that's all the harm I
    wish you.° [*Aside*] The slave looks like a hog's cheek new
    singed.°
    [*Barabas turns away from Lodowick*]
LODOWICK Whither walk'st thou, Barabas?
BARABAS No further. 'Tis a custom held with us   45
    That, when we speak with gentiles like to you,
    We turn into the air to purge ourselves;°
    For unto us the promise doth belong.°
LODOWICK Well, Barabas, canst help me to a diamond?
BARABAS O, sir, your father had my diamonds.   50

Yet I have one left that will serve your turn.°
(*Aside*) I mean my daughter—but ere he shall have her,
I'll sacrifice her on a pile of wood.°
I ha' the poison of the city for him,°
And the white leprosy.°   55
LODOWICK What sparkle does it give without a foil?
BARABAS The diamond that I talk of ne'er was foiled.
[*Aside*] But when he touches it, it will be foiled.°
[*To him*] Lord Lodowick, it sparkles bright and fair.
LODOWICK Is it square or pointed? Pray let me know.   60
BARABAS Pointed it is, good sir—(*aside*) but not for you.°
LODOWICK I like it much the better.
BARABAS   So do I, too.
LODOWICK How shows it by night?
BARABAS   Outshines Cynthia's rays.°
(*Aside*) You'll like it better far a-nights than days.
LODOWICK And what's the price?
BARABAS [*aside*]   Your life, an if you have it.°   65
[*To him*] O, my lord, we will not jar about the price; come to my
house and I will give't your honour—° (*aside*) with a vengeance.
LODOWICK No, Barabas, I will deserve it first.
BARABAS Good sir,
  Your father has deserved it at my hands,°   70
  Who, of mere charity and Christian ruth,
  To bring me to religious purity,
  And as it were in catechizing sort,°
  To make me mindful of my mortal sins,
  Against my will, and whether I would or no,   75
  Seized all I had, and thrust me out o' doors,
  And made my house a place for nuns most chaste.
LODOWICK No doubt your soul shall reap the fruit of it.
BARABAS Ay, but, my lord, the harvest is far off;
  And yet I know the prayers of those nuns   80
  And holy friars, having money for their pains,
  Are wondrous—(*aside*) and indeed do no man good.
  [*To him*] And seeing they are not idle, but still doing,
  'Tis likely they in time may reap some fruit—°
  I mean in fullness of perfection.   85
LODOWICK Good Barabas, glance not at our holy nuns.°
BARABAS No, but I do it through a burning zeal,°
  (*Aside*) Hoping ere long to set the house afire;

For though they do a while increase and multiply,
I'll have a saying to that nunnery.°   90
[*To him*] As for the diamond, sir, I told you of,
Come home, and there's no price shall make us part,°
Even for your honourable father's sake.
(*Aside*) It shall go hard but I will see your death.
[*To him*] But now I must be gone to buy a slave.   95
LODOWICK And, Barabas, I'll bear thee company.
BARABAS Come then, here's the marketplace.
        [*They inspect the slaves*]
    What's the price of this slave? Two hundred crowns? Do the
    Turks weigh so much?
FIRST OFFICER Sir, that's his price.   100
BARABAS What, can he steal, that you demand so much?
    Belike he has some new trick for a purse.°
    An if he has, he is worth three hundred plates,
    So that, being bought, the town seal might be got°
    To keep him for his lifetime from the gallows.°   105
    The sessions day is critical to thieves,°
    And few or none 'scape but by being purged.°
LODOWICK [*examining another slave*] Ratest thou this Moor but at
    two hundred plates?
FIRST OFFICER No more, my lord.   110
BARABAS Why should this Turk be dearer than that Moor?
FIRST OFFICER Because he is young and has more qualities.
BARABAS [*to the Turkish slave*] What, hast the philosopher's stone?°
    An thou hast, break my head with it; I'll forgive thee.
FIRST SLAVE No, sir, I can cut and shave.°   115
BARABAS Let me see, sirrah. Are you not an old shaver?°
FIRST SLAVE Alas, sir, I am a very youth.
BARABAS A youth? I'll buy you, and marry you to Lady Vanity° if
    you do well.
FIRST SLAVE I will serve you, sir.   120
BARABAS Some wicked trick or other.° It may be under colour of
    shaving thou'lt cut my throat for my goods. Tell me, hast thou thy
    health well?
FIRST SLAVE Ay, passing well.
BARABAS So much the worse; I must have one that's sickly, an't be 125
    but for sparing victuals. 'Tis not a stone of beef a day will maintain
    you in these chops.° —Let me see one that's somewhat leaner.
FIRST OFFICER [*indicating Ithamore*] Here's a leaner. How like you him?

BARABAS [*to Ithamore*] Where was thou born?

ITHAMORE In Thrace. Brought up in Arabia.   130

BARABAS So much the better. Thou art for my turn.—°
  An hundred crowns? I'll have him; there's the coin.
          [*He gives money*]

FIRST OFFICER Then mark him, sir, and take him hence.

BARABAS [*aside*] Ay, mark him, you were best, for this is he°
  That by my help shall do much villainy.   135
  [*To Lodowick*] My lord, farewell. [*To Ithamore*] Come, sirrah, you
    are mine.
  [*To Lodowick*] As for the diamond, it shall be yours.
  I pray, sir, be no stranger at my house;
  All that I have shall be at your command.
          Enter Mathias [and his] Mother [Katherine]

MATHIAS [*aside*] What makes the Jew and Lodowick so private?   140
  I fear me 'tis about fair Abigail.
          [*Exit Lodowick*]

BARABAS [*aside to Ithamore*]
  Yonder comes Don Mathias; let us stay.°
  He loves my daughter, and she holds him dear,
  But I have sworn to frustrate both their hopes
  And be revenged upon the governor.°   145
          [*Katherine and Mathias inspect the slaves*]

KATHERINE This Moor is comeliest, is he not? Speak, son.

MATHIAS No, this is the better, mother. View this well.
          [*Barabas approaches Mathias while Katherine arranges to
          purchase a slave*]

BARABAS [*aside to Mathias*]
  Seem not to know me here before your mother,
  Lest she mistrust the match that is in hand.
  When you have brought her home, come to my house.   150
  Think of me as thy father. Son, farewell.

MATHIAS [*aside to Barabas*]
  But wherefore talked Don Lodowick with you?

BARABAS [*aside to Mathias*]
  Tush, man, we talked of diamonds, not of Abigail.

KATHERINE [*having made her purchase*]
  Tell me, Mathias, is not that the Jew?

BARABAS [*aloud to Mathias, as though continuing a conversation*]
  As for the comment on the Maccabees,°   155
  I have it, sir, and 'tis at your command.

MATHIAS [*to Katherine*]
  Yes, madam, and my talk with him was but
  About the borrowing of a book or two.
KATHERINE
  Converse not with him; he is cast off from heaven.
  [*To Officer*] Thou hast thy crowns, fellow.—Come, let's away.   160
MATHIAS Sirrah Jew, remember the book.
BARABAS Marry will I, sir.
     Exeunt [*Mathias, Katherine, and a Slave*]
FIRST OFFICER
  Come, I have made a reasonable market; let's away.
     [*Exeunt Officers with the rest of the Slaves. Barabas and
     Ithamore remain*]
BARABAS Now let me know thy name, and therewithal
  Thy birth, condition, and profession.   165
ITHAMORE Faith, sir, my birth is but mean, my name's Ithamore,
  my profession what you please.
BARABAS Hast thou no trade? Then listen to my words,
  And I will teach thee that shall stick by thee.°
  First, be thou void of these affections: 170
  Compassion, love, vain hope, and heartless fear.
  Be moved at nothing; see thou pity none,
  But to thyself smile when the Christians moan.
ITHAMORE O brave, master, I worship your nose for this!°
BARABAS As for myself, I walk abroad a-nights   175
  And kill sick people groaning under walls;
  Sometimes I go about and poison wells;
  And now and then, to cherish Christian thieves,
  I am content to lose some of my crowns,
  That I may, walking in my gallery,   180
  See 'em go pinioned along by my door.
  Being young, I studied physic, and began
  To practise first upon the Italian;°
  There I enriched the priests with burials,
  And always kept the sexton's arms in ure   185
  With digging graves and ringing dead men's knells.
  And after that was I an engineer,
  And in the wars 'twixt France and Germany,
  Under pretence of helping Charles the Fifth,
  Slew friend and enemy with my stratagems.   190
  Then after that was I an usurer,

And with extorting, cozening, forfeiting,
And tricks belonging unto brokery,
I filled the gaols with bankrupts in a year,
And with young orphans planted hospitals,° 195
And every moon made some or other mad,°
And now and then one hang himself for grief,°
Pinning upon his breast a long great scroll°
How I with interest tormented him.°
But mark how I am blest for plaguing them: 200
I have as much coin as will buy the town.
But tell me now, how hast thou spent thy time?
ITHAMORE Faith, master,
In setting Christian villages on fire,
Chaining of eunuchs, binding galley slaves. 205
One time I was an ostler in an inn,
And in the night-time secretly would I steal
To travellers' chambers and there cut their throats.
Once at Jerusalem, where the pilgrims kneeled,
I strewèd powder on the marble stones, 210
And therewithal their knees would rankle, so
That I have laughed a-good to see the cripples
Go limping home to Christendom on stilts.
BARABAS Why, this is something. Make account of me
As of thy fellow; we are villains both. 215
Both circumcisèd, we hate Christians both.
Be true and secret, thou shalt want no gold.
But stand aside, here comes Don Lodowick.
          [*Ithamore stands aside.*] *Enter Lodowick*
LODOWICK O, Barabas, well met.
Where is the diamond you told me of? 220
BARABAS
I have it for you, sir; please you walk in with me.—°
What ho, Abigail! Open the door, I say.
          Enter Abigail [*with letters*]
ABIGAIL In good time, father, here are letters come
From Ormuz, and the post stays here within.°
BARABAS Give me the letters. Daughter, do you hear? 225
Entertain Lodowick, the governor's son,
With all the courtesy you can afford—
(*Aside* [*to her*]) Provided that you keep your maidenhead.
Use him as if he were a Philistine.°

Dissemble, swear, protest, vow to love him;   230
He is not of the seed of Abraham.
[*Aloud*] I am a little busy, sir; pray pardon me.
Abigail, bid him welcome for my sake.
ABIGAIL For your sake and his own he's welcome hither.
BARABAS Daughter, a word more. [*Aside to her*] Kiss him, speak him
    fair,   235
And like a cunning Jew so cast about
That ye be both made sure ere you come out.°
ABIGAIL [*aside to Barabas*] O, father, Don Mathias is my love!
BARABAS [*aside to her*]
    I know it; yet, I say, make love to him.
    Do, it is requisite it should be so.   240
    [*Aloud*] Nay, on my life, it is my factor's hand.°
    But go you in; I'll think upon the account.
        [*Exeunt Lodowick and Abigail*]
    The account is made, for Lodowick dies.°
    My factor sends me word a merchant's fled
    That owes me for a hundred tun of wine.   245
    I weigh it thus much. [*He snaps his fingers*] I have wealth enough.
    For now by this has he kissed Abigail,
    And she vows love to him, and he to her.
    As sure as heaven rained manna for the Jews,°
    So sure shall he and Don Mathias die.   250
    His father was my chiefest enemy.
        Enter Mathias
    Whither goes Don Mathias? Stay a while.
MATHIAS Whither but to my fair love Abigail?
BARABAS Thou know'st, and heaven can witness it is true,
    That I intend my daughter shall be thine.   255
MATHIAS Ay, Barabas, or else thou wrong'st me much.
BARABAS [*pretending to weep*]
    O, heaven forbid I should have such a thought!
    Pardon me though I weep. The governor's son
    Will, whether I will or no, have Abigail.
    He sends her letters, bracelets, jewels, rings.   260
MATHIAS Does she receive them?
BARABAS She? No, Mathias, no, but sends them back,
    And when he comes she locks herself up fast;
    Yet through the keyhole will he talk to her,
    While she runs to the window, looking out   265

When you should come and hale him from the door.°
MATHIAS O, treacherous Lodowick!
BARABAS Even now, as I came home, he slipped me in,°
  And I am sure he is with Abigail.
MATHIAS [*drawing his sword*] I'll rouse him thence.   270
BARABAS Not for all Malta. Therefore sheathe your sword.
  If you love me, no quarrels in my house.
  But steal you in, and seem to see him not.°
  I'll give him such a warning ere he goes
  As he shall have small hopes of Abigail.°   275
  Away, for here they come.
        Enter Lodowick [with] Abigail, [who pretends affection for
        him. Mathias stands aside]
MATHIAS What, hand in hand? I cannot suffer this.
BARABAS Mathias, as thou lov'st me, not a word.
MATHIAS Well, let it pass. Another time shall serve.
        Exit [Mathias]
LODOWICK Barabas, is not that the widow's son?   280
BARABAS Ay, and take heed, for he hath sworn your death.
LODOWICK My death? What, is the baseborn peasant mad?
BARABAS No, no; but happily he stands in fear
  Of that which you, I think, ne'er dream upon:°
  My daughter here, a paltry, silly girl.   285
LODOWICK Why, loves she Don Mathias?
BARABAS Doth she not with her smiling answer you?
ABIGAIL [*aside*] He has my heart; I smile against my will.°
LODOWICK
  Barabas, thou know'st I have loved thy daughter long.
BARABAS And so has she done you, even from a child.   290
LODOWICK And now I can no longer hold my mind.°
BARABAS Nor I the affection that I bear to you.
LODOWICK This is thy diamond. Tell me, shall I have it?
BARABAS Win it and wear it. It is yet unfoiled.°
  O, but I know your lordship would disdain   295
  To marry with the daughter of a Jew;
  And yet I'll give her many a golden cross,°
  With Christian posies round about the ring.°
LODOWICK 'Tis not thy wealth, but her that I esteem,
  Yet crave I thy consent.   300
BARABAS And mine you have; yet let me talk to her.
        [Barabas speaks] aside [with Abigail]

This offspring of Cain, this Jebusite,°
That never tasted of the Passover,
Nor e'er shall see the land of Canaan
Nor our Messias that is yet to come,°   305
This gentle maggot—Lodowick, I mean—°
Must be deluded. Let him have thy hand,
But keep thy heart till Don Mathias comes.
ABIGAIL   What, shall I be betrothed to Lodowick?
BARABAS   It is no sin to deceive a Christian,   310
For they themselves hold it a principle
Faith is not to be held with heretics.°
But all are heretics that are not Jews;
This follows well, and therefore, daughter, fear not.
[To Lodowick] I have entreated her, and she will grant.   315
LODOWICK   Then, gentle Abigail, plight thy faith to me.
ABIGAIL   [aside] I cannot choose, seeing my father bids.°
[Aloud] Nothing but death shall part my love and me.°
LODOWICK   Now have I that for which my soul hath longed.
BARABAS   (aside) So have not I, but yet I hope I shall.   320
ABIGAIL   [aside] O wretched Abigail, what hast thou done?
LODOWICK   Why on the sudden is your colour changed?
ABIGAIL   I know not; but farewell, I must be gone.
BARABAS   [to Lodowick]
    Stay her; [aside, for Abigail's ears] but let her not speak one word
    more.
LODOWICK   Mute o' the sudden? Here's a sudden change.   325
BARABAS   O, muse not at it. 'Tis the Hebrews' guise
That maidens new-betrothed should weep a while.
Trouble her not, sweet Lodowick, depart.
She is thy wife, and thou shalt be mine heir.
LODOWICK   O, is't the custom? Then I am resolved.   330
But rather let the brightsome heavens be dim,
And nature's beauty choke with stifling clouds,
Than my fair Abigail should frown on me.
        Enter Mathias
There comes the villain. Now I'll be revenged.
BARABAS   Be quiet, Lodowick. It is enough   335
That I have made thee sure to Abigail.
LODOWICK   Well, let him go.
        Exit [Lodowick]
BARABAS   [to Mathias]

Well, but for me, as you went in at doors
You had been stabbed; but not a word on't now.
Here must no speeches pass, nor swords be drawn.   340
MATHIAS Suffer me, Barabas, but to follow him.°
BARABAS No. So shall I, if any hurt be done,
Be made an accessory of your deeds.°
Revenge it on him when you meet him next.
MATHIAS For this I'll have his heart.   345
BARABAS Do so. Lo, here I give thee Abigail.
     [Barabas joins their hands]
MATHIAS What greater gift can poor Mathias have?
Shall Lodowick rob me of so fair a love?
My life is not so dear as Abigail.
BARABAS My heart misgives me, that, to cross your love,   350
He's with your mother; therefore after him.
MATHIAS What, is he gone unto my mother?
BARABAS Nay, if you will, stay till she comes herself.°
MATHIAS I cannot stay, for if my mother come,
She'll die with grief.°   355
     Exit [Mathias]
ABIGAIL I cannot take my leave of him for tears.°
Father, why have you thus incensed them both?
BARABAS What's that to thee?
ABIGAIL I'll make 'em friends again.
BARABAS You'll make 'em friends?   360
Are there not Jews enough in Malta
But thou must dote upon a Christian?
ABIGAIL I will have Don Mathias; he is my love.
BARABAS Yes, you shall have him. *[To Ithamore]* Go put her in.
ITHAMORE Ay, I'll put her in.   365
     [He pushes Abigail into the house]
BARABAS Now tell me, Ithamore, how lik'st thou this?
ITHAMORE Faith, master, I think by this
You purchase both their lives. Is it not so?
BARABAS True; and it shall be cunningly performed.
ITHAMORE O, master, that I might have a hand in this!   370
BARABAS Ay, so thou shalt; 'tis thou must do the deed.
     [Giving a letter]
Take this and bear it to Mathias straight,
And tell him that it comes from Lodowick.
ITHAMORE 'Tis poisoned, is it not?°

BARABAS No, no; and yet it might be done that way.   375
   It is a challenge feigned from Lodowick.
ITHAMORE Fear not; I'll so set his heart afire
   That he shall verily think it comes from him.
BARABAS I cannot choose but like thy readiness.
   Yet be not rash, but do it cunningly.   380
ITHAMORE As I behave myself in this, employ me hereafter.
BARABAS Away, then.
         Exit [Ithamore]
   So, now will I go in to Lodowick,
   And like a cunning spirit feign some lie,
   Till I have set 'em both at enmity.   385
         Exit

[3.1]

Enter [Bellamira,] a Courtesan°

BELLAMIRA Since this town was besieged, my gain grows cold.°
The time has been that but for one bare night°
A hundred ducats have been freely given;
But now against my will I must be chaste.
And yet I know my beauty doth not fail.   5
From Venice merchants, and from Padua
Were wont to come rare-witted gentlemen,
Scholars, I mean, learnèd and liberal;°
And now, save Pilia-Borza, comes there none,
And he is very seldom from my house.°   10
And here he comes.
    Enter Pilia-Borza
PILIA-BORZA Hold thee, wench; there's something for thee to spend.
    [*He gives her money from a bag*]
BELLAMIRA 'Tis silver; I disdain it.
PILIA-BORZA Ay, but the Jew has gold,
And I will have it, or it shall go hard.   15
BELLAMIRA Tell me, how cam'st thou by this?
PILIA-BORZA Faith, walking the back lanes through the gardens I
chanced to cast mine eye up to the Jew's counting-house, where
I saw some bags of money, and in the night I clambered up with
my hooks,° and as I was taking my choice, I heard a rumbling   20
in the house; so I took only this and run my way. But here's the
Jew's man.
    Enter Ithamore
BELLAMIRA Hide the bag.
PILIA-BORZA Look not towards him; let's away. Zounds, what a
looking thou keep'st! Thou'lt betray's anon.°   25
    [*Exeunt Bellamira and Pilia-Borza*]
ITHAMORE O, the sweetest face that ever I beheld! I know she is a
courtesan by her attire.° Now would I give a hundred of the Jew's
crowns that I had such a concubine.
Well, I have delivered the challenge in such sort°
As meet they will, and fighting die. Brave sport!   30
    Exit

[3.2]

Enter Mathias

MATHIAS This is the place. Now Abigail shall see°
Whether Mathias holds her dear or no.
      Enter Lodowick, reading,° [not seeing Mathias at first]
LODOWICK What, dares the villain write in such base terms?
MATHIAS [*to Lodowick*] I did it; and revenge it if thou dar'st.
      [*They*] *fight. Enter Barabas above*
BARABAS O, bravely fought! And yet they thrust not home.   5
Now, Lodowick! Now, Mathias! So.
      [*Both fall dead*]
So, now they have showed themselves to be tall fellows.
VOICES WITHIN Part 'em, part 'em!°
BARABAS Ay, part 'em now they are dead. Farewell, farewell.
      Exit [Barabas.] Enter Ferneze, Katherine, [and Attendants]
FERNEZE What sight is this? My Lodowick slain!   10
These arms of mine shall be thy sepulchre.
      [*Ferneze and Katherine tend the bodies of their dead sons*]
KATHERINE Who is this? My son Mathias slain!
FERNEZE O Lodowick, hadst thou perished by the Turk,
Wretched Ferneze might have venged thy death.°
KATHERINE Thy son slew mine, and I'll revenge his death.   15
FERNEZE Look, Katherine, look, thy son gave mine these wounds.
KATHERINE O, leave to grieve me! I am grieved enough.
FERNEZE O, that my sighs could turn to lively breath,
And these my tears to blood, that he might live!
KATHERINE Who made them enemies?   20
FERNEZE I know not, and that grieves me most of all.
KATHERINE My son loved thine.
FERNEZE   And so did Lodowick him.
KATHERINE Lend me that weapon that did kill my son,
And it shall murder me.°
FERNEZE Nay, madam, stay. That weapon was my son's,   25
And on that rather should Ferneze die.
KATHERINE Hold. Let's inquire the causers of their deaths,
That we may venge their blood upon their heads.°
FERNEZE Then take them up, and let them be interred
Within one sacred monument of stone,   30
Upon which altar I will offer up

My daily sacrifice of sighs and tears,
And with my prayers pierce th'impartial heavens,
Till they reveal the causers of our smarts°
Which forced their hands divide united hearts.°   35
Come, Katherine, our losses equal are;
Then of true grief let us take equal share.
          Exeunt [with the bodies]

[3.3]

          Enter Ithamore
ITHAMORE Why, was there ever seen such villainy,
    So neatly plotted and so well performed?
    Both held in hand, and flatly both beguiled?°
          Enter Abigail
ABIGAIL Why, how now, Ithamore, why laugh'st thou so?
ITHAMORE O mistress, ha, ha, ha!   5
ABIGAIL Why, what ail'st thou?
ITHAMORE O, my master!
ABIGAIL Ha!
ITHAMORE O mistress, I have the bravest, gravest, secret, subtle,
    bottle-nosed° knave to° my master that ever gentleman had. 10
ABIGAIL Say, knave, why rail'st upon my father thus?
ITHAMORE O, my master has the bravest policy.
ABIGAIL Wherein?
ITHAMORE Why, know you not?
ABIGAIL Why, no.   15
ITHAMORE Know you not of Mathias' and Don Lodowick's disaster?
ABIGAIL No, what was it?
ITHAMORE Why, the devil invented a challenge, my master writ it,
    and I carried it, first to Lodowick and *imprimis*° to Mathias.
    And then they met, and as the story says,   20
    In doleful wise they ended both their days.°
ABIGAIL And was my father furtherer of their deaths?
ITHAMORE Am I Ithamore?
ABIGAIL Yes.
ITHAMORE So sure did your father write, and I carry, the challenge. 25
ABIGAIL Well, Ithamore, let me request thee this:
    Go to the new-made nunnery, and inquire

For any of the friars of Saint Jacques,°
And say I pray them come and speak with me.°

ITHAMORE I pray, mistress, will you answer me to one question?   30
ABIGAIL Well, sirrah, what is't?
ITHAMORE A very feeling° one: have not the nuns fine sport with the
friars now and then?
ABIGAIL Go to, sirrah sauce,° is this your question? Get ye gone.
ITHAMORE I will forsooth, mistress.   35

    Exit [Ithamore]

ABIGAIL Hard-hearted father, unkind Barabas,
Was this the pursuit of thy policy,°
To make me show them favour severally,
That by my favour they should both be slain?°
Admit thou loved'st not Lodowick for his sire,°   40
Yet Don Mathias ne'er offended thee.
But thou wert set upon extreme revenge
Because the sire dispossessed thee once,°
And couldst not venge it but upon his son,
Nor on his son but by Mathias' means,   45
Nor on Mathias but by murdering me.
But I perceive there is no love on earth,
Pity in Jews, nor piety in Turks.
But here comes cursèd Ithamore with the friar.

    Enter Ithamore [and] *Friar* [*Jacomo*]

FRIAR JACOMO *Virgo, salve!*°   50
ITHAMORE When, duck you?°
ABIGAIL Welcome, grave friar. Ithamore, begone.

    Exit [*Ithamore*]

Know, holy sir, I am bold to solicit thee.
FRIAR JACOMO Wherein?
ABIGAIL To get me be admitted for a nun.°   55
FRIAR JACOMO Why, Abigail, it is not yet long since
That I did labour thy admission,°
And then thou didst not like that holy life.
ABIGAIL Then were my thoughts so frail and unconfirmed,
And I was chained to follies of the world;   60
But now experience, purchasèd with grief,
Has made me see the difference of things.
My sinful soul, alas, hath paced too long
The fatal labyrinth of misbelief,
Far from the Son that gives eternal life.   65

FRIAR JACOMO Who taught thee this?
ABIGAIL   The abbess of the house,
  Whose zealous admonition I embrace.
  O therefore, Jacomo, let me be one,
  Although unworthy, of that sisterhood.
FRIAR JACOMO Abigail, I will, but see thou change no more,   70
  For that will be most heavy to thy soul.
ABIGAIL That was my father's fault.
FRIAR JACOMO   Thy father's? How?
ABIGAIL Nay, you shall pardon me. [*Aside*] O Barabas,°
  Though thou deservest hardly at my hands,
  Yet never shall these lips bewray thy life.   75
FRIAR JACOMO Come, shall we go?
ABIGAIL   My duty waits on you.
        Exeunt

[3.4]

        Enter Barabas, reading a letter
BARABAS What, Abigail become a nun again?
  False and unkind! What, hast thou lost thy father,
  And, all unknown and unconstrained of me,
  Art thou again got to the nunnery?
  Now here she writes, and wills me to repent.   5
  Repentance? *Spurca!* What pretendeth this?°
  I fear she knows—'tis so—of my device
  In Don Mathias' and Lodovico's deaths.
  If so, 'tis time it be seen into,
  For she that varies from me in belief   10
  Gives great presumption that she loves me not,
  Or, loving, doth dislike of something done.
        [*Enter Ithamore*]
  But who comes here? O Ithamore, come near.
  Come near, my love, come near, thy master's life,
  My trusty servant, nay, my second self!°   15
  For I have now no hope but even in thee,
  And on that hope my happiness is built.
  When saw'st thou Abigail?
ITHAMORE Today.

BARABAS With whom?   20
ITHAMORE A friar.
BARABAS A friar? False villain, he hath done the deed.
ITHAMORE How, sir?
BARABAS Why, made mine Abigail a nun.
ITHAMORE That's no lie, for she sent me for him.   25
BARABAS O, unhappy day!
    False, credulous, inconstant Abigail!
    But let 'em go; and Ithamore, from hence
    Ne'er shall she grieve me more with her disgrace;
    Ne'er shall she live to inherit aught of mine,   30
    Be blest of me, nor come within my gates,
    But perish underneath my bitter curse,
    Like Cain by Adam, for his brother's death.
ITHAMORE O, master!
BARABAS Ithamore, entreat not for her; I am moved,   35
    And she is hateful to my soul and me.
    And lest thou yield to this that I entreat,°
    I cannot think but that thou hat'st my life.
ITHAMORE Who, I, master? Why, I'll run to some rock and throw
    myself headlong into the sea. Why, I'll do anything for your sweet   40
    sake.
BARABAS O trusty Ithamore, no servant, but my friend!
    I here adopt thee for mine only heir.
    All that I have is thine when I am dead,
    And, whilst I live, use half; spend as myself.   45
    Here, take my keys. I'll give 'em thee anon.
    Go buy thee garments. But thou shalt not want.
    Only know this, that thus thou art to do.
    But first go fetch me in the pot of rice
    That for our supper stands upon the fire.°   50
ITHAMORE [aside] I hold my head my master's hungry.°
    [To him] I go, sir.
            Exit [Ithamore]
BARABAS Thus every villain ambles after wealth,
    Although he ne'er be richer than in hope.
    But husht.   55
            Enter Ithamore with the pot
ITHAMORE Here 'tis, master.
BARABAS Well said, Ithamore.
    What, hast thou brought the ladle with thee too?

ITHAMORE Yes, sir; the proverb says, he that eats with the devil had
 need of a long spoon. I have brought you a ladle.   60
BARABAS Very well, Ithamore, then now be secret,
 And for thy sake, whom I so dearly love,
 Now shalt thou see the death of Abigail,
 That thou mayst freely live to be my heir.
ITHAMORE Why, master, will you poison her with a mess of rice 65
 porridge? That will preserve life, make her round and plump, and
 batten more than you are aware.
BARABAS Ay, but Ithamore, seest thou this?
   [*He shows a poison*]
 It is a precious powder that I bought
 Of an Italian in Ancona once,   70
 Whose operation is to bind, infect,
 And poison deeply, yet not appear
 In forty hours after it is ta'en.
ITHAMORE How, master?
BARABAS Thus, Ithamore: 75
 This even they use in Malta here—'tis called°
 Saint Jacques' Even—and then, I say, they use
 To send their alms unto the nunneries.
 Among the rest bear this and set it there.°
 There's a dark entry where they take it in,   80
 Where they must neither see the messenger
 Nor make inquiry who hath sent it them.
ITHAMORE How so?
BARABAS Belike there is some ceremony in't.
 There, Ithamore, must thou go place this pot.   85
 Stay, let me spice it first.
ITHAMORE Pray do, and let me help you, master. Pray let me taste
 first.
BARABAS Prithee do. [*Ithamore tastes*] What say'st thou now?
ITHAMORE Troth, master, I'm loath such a pot of pottage should be 90
 spoiled.
BARABAS [*putting in poison*]
 Peace, Ithamore, 'tis better so than spared.°
 Assure thyself thou shalt have broth by the eye.°
 My purse, my coffer, and myself is thine.
ITHAMORE Well, master, I go.   95
BARABAS Stay, first let me stir it, Ithamore.
   [*He stirs the pot as he pronounces a curse*]

As fatal be it to her as the draught
Of which great Alexander drunk and died,°
And with her let it work like Borgia's wine,
Whereof his sire, the Pope, was poisonèd!°   100
In few, the blood of Hydra, Lerna's bane,°
The juice of hebon, and Cocytus' breath,°
And all the poisons of the Stygian pool,°
Break from the fiery kingdom, and in this°
Vomit your venom and envenom her   105
That like a fiend hath left her father thus!

ITHAMORE   What a blessing has he given't! Was ever pot of rice
porridge so sauced?—What shall I do with it?

BARABAS   O my sweet Ithamore, go set it down,
And come again so soon as thou hast done,   110
For I have other business for thee.

ITHAMORE   Here's a drench° to poison a whole stable of Flanders
mares!° I'll carry't to the nuns with a powder.°

BARABAS   And the horse-pestilence to boot. Away!°

ITHAMORE   I am gone.   115
Pay me my wages, for my work is done.
            Exit [Ithamore, with the poisoned pot]

BARABAS   I'll pay thee with a vengeance, Ithamore.°
            Exit

[3.5]

*Enter Ferneze, [Martin Del] Bosco, Knights, [and Callapine,
the] bashaw, [with his entourage]*

FERNEZE   Welcome, great bashaws. How fares Calymath?
What wind drives you thus into Malta road?

CALLAPINE   The wind that bloweth all the world besides:
Desire of gold.

FERNEZE   Desire of gold, great sir?
That's to be gotten in the Western Inde;   5
In Malta are no golden minerals.

CALLAPINE   To you of Malta thus saith Calymath:
The time you took for respite is at hand
For the performance of your promise passed,°
And for the tribute-money I am sent.   10

FERNEZE Bashaw, in brief, shalt have no tribute here,
　　Nor shall the heathens live upon our spoil.
　　First will we raze the city walls ourselves,
　　Lay waste the island, hew the temples down,
　　And, shipping off our goods to Sicily,   15
　　Open an entrance for the wasteful sea,
　　Whose billows, beating the resistless banks,
　　Shall overflow it with their refluence.°
CALLAPINE Well, governor, since thou hast broke the league
　　By flat denial of the promised tribute,   20
　　Talk not of razing down your city walls;
　　You shall not need trouble yourselves so far.
　　For Selim Calymath shall come himself,
　　And with brass bullets batter down your towers
　　And turn proud Malta to a wilderness   25
　　For these intolerable wrongs of yours.
　　And so farewell.
　　　　[Exeunt Callapine and his entourage]
FERNEZE Farewell.
　　And now, you men of Malta, look about,
　　And let's provide to welcome Calymath.   30
　　Close your portcullis, charge your basilisks,
　　And as you profitably take up arms,°
　　So now courageously encounter them;
　　For by this answer broken is the league,
　　And naught is to be looked for now but wars,   35
　　And naught to us more welcome is than wars.
　　　　Exeunt

[3.6]

　　　　Enter [the] two Friars [Jacomo and Barnardine]
FRIAR JACOMO O brother, brother, all the nuns are sick,
　　And physic will not help them! They must die.
FRIAR BARNARDINE The abbess sent for me to be confessed.
　　O, what a sad confession will there be!
FRIAR JACOMO And so did fair Maria send for me.°   5
　　I'll to her lodging; hereabouts she lies.
　　　　Exit [Friar Jacomo.] Enter Abigail

FRIAR BARNARDINE What, all dead save only Abigail?
ABIGAIL And I shall die too, for I feel death coming.
  Where is the friar that conversed with me?
FRIAR BARNARDINE O, he is gone to see the other nuns.   10
ABIGAIL I sent for him, but seeing you are come,
  Be you my ghostly father; and first know
  That in this house I lived religiously,
  Chaste, and devout, much sorrowing for my sins.
  But ere I came—   15
FRIAR BARNARDINE What then?
ABIGAIL I did offend high heaven so grievously
  As I am almost desperate for my sins,
  And one offence torments me more than all.
  You knew Mathias and Don Lodowick?   20
FRIAR BARNARDINE Yes, what of them?
ABIGAIL My father did contract me to 'em both:
  First to Don Lodowick, him I never loved.
  Mathias was the man that I held dear,
  And for his sake did I become a nun.   25
FRIAR BARNARDINE So. Say, how was their end?
ABIGAIL Both, jealous of my love, envied each other,
  And by my father's practice, which is there
  Set down at large, the gallants were both slain.
     [*She gives him a paper*]
FRIAR BARNARDINE O, monstrous villainy!   30
ABIGAIL To work my peace, this I confess to thee.°
  Reveal it not, for then my father dies.
FRIAR BARNARDINE
  Know that confession must not be revealed;
  The canon law forbids it, and the priest
  That makes it known, being degraded first,°   35
  Shall be condemned and then sent to the fire.
ABIGAIL So I have heard; pray therefore keep it close.
  Death seizeth on my heart. Ah, gentle friar,
  Convert my father that he may be saved,
  And witness that I die a Christian.   40
     [*She dies*]
FRIAR BARNARDINE Ay, and a virgin, too; that grieves me most.
  But I must to the Jew and exclaim on him,
  And make him stand in fear of me.
     Enter Friar [*Jacomo*]

FRIAR JACOMO
O brother, all the nuns are dead! Let's bury them.

FRIAR BARNARDINE First help to bury this, then go with me 45
And help me to exclaim against the Jew.

FRIAR JACOMO Why? What has he done?

FRIAR BARNARDINE A thing that makes me tremble to unfold.

FRIAR JACOMO What, has he crucified a child?°

FRIAR BARNARDINE No, but a worse thing. 'Twas told me in shrift; 50
Thou know'st 'tis death an if it be revealed.
Come, let's away.
    Exeunt, [*bearing Abigail's body*]

[4.1]

Enter Barabas [and] Ithamore. Bells within

BARABAS There is no music to a Christian's knell.°
How sweet the bells ring, now the nuns are dead,
That sound at other times like tinkers' pans!
I was afraid the poison had not wrought,
Or, though it wrought, it would have done no good,   5
For every year they swell, and yet they live.°
Now all are dead; not one remains alive.

ITHAMORE That's brave, master. But think you it will not be
known?

BARABAS How can it, if we two be secret?   10

ITHAMORE For my part fear you not.

BARABAS I'd cut thy throat if I did.

ITHAMORE And reason, too.
But here's a royal monast'ry hard by;
Good master, let me poison all the monks.   15

BARABAS Thou shalt not need, for, now the nuns are dead,
They'll die with grief.

ITHAMORE Do you not sorrow for your daughter's death?

BARABAS No, but I grieve because she lived so long.
An Hebrew born, and would become a Christian!   20
Cazzo, diabole!°

Enter the two Friars [Jacomo and Barnardine]

ITHAMORE Look, look, master, here come two religious caterpillars.

BARABAS I smelt 'em ere they came.

ITHAMORE God-a-mercy, nose! Come, let's be gone.°

[Barabas and Ithamore start to leave]

FRIAR BARNARDINE Stay, wicked Jew! Repent, I say, and stay.   25

FRIAR JACOMO Thou hast offended, therefore must be damned.

BARABAS *[aside to Ithamore]*
I fear they know we sent the poisoned broth.

ITHAMORE *[aside to Barabas]*
And so do I, master. Therefore speak 'em fair.

FRIAR BARNARDINE Barabas, thou hast—

FRIAR JACOMO Ay, that thou hast—   30

BARABAS True, I have money. What though I have?

FRIAR BARNARDINE Thou art a—

296

FRIAR JACOMO Ay, that thou art, a—
BARABAS What needs all this? I know I am a Jew.
FRIAR BARNARDINE Thy daughter—   35
FRIAR JACOMO Ay, thy daughter—
BARABAS O, speak not of her; then I die with grief.
FRIAR BARNARDINE Remember that—
FRIAR JACOMO Ay, remember that—
BARABAS I must needs say that I have been a great usurer.   40
FRIAR BARNARDINE Thou has committed—
BARABAS Fornication? But that was in another country; and besides,
  the wench is dead.
FRIAR BARNARDINE Ay, but Barabas, remember Mathias and Don
  Lodowick.   45
BARABAS Why, what of them?
FRIAR BARNARDINE I will not say that by a forged challenge they
  met.
BARABAS (aside [to Ithamore])
  She has confessed, and we are both undone,
  My bosom inmate! But I must dissemble.   50
  [To them] O holy friars, the burden of my sins
  Lie heavy on my soul. Then pray you tell me,°
  Is't not too late now to turn Christian?
  I have been zealous in the Jewish faith,
  Hard-hearted to the poor, a covetous wretch,   55
  That would for lucre's sake have sold my soul.
  A hundred for a hundred I have ta'en,°
  And now for store of wealth may I compare
  With all the Jews in Malta. But what is wealth?
  I am a Jew, and therefore am I lost.   60
  Would penance serve for this my sin,
  I could afford to whip myself to death—
ITHAMORE [aside] And so could I; but penance will not serve.°
BARABAS To fast, to pray, and wear a shirt of hair,
  And on my knees creep to Jerusalem.   65
  Cellars of wine and sollars full of wheat,°
  Warehouses stuffed with spices and with drugs,
  Whole chests of gold, in bullion and in coin,
  Besides I know not how much weight in pearl,
  Orient and round, have I within my house;   70
  At Alexandria, merchandise unsold.
  But yesterday two ships went from this town;

Their voyage will be worth ten thousand crowns.
In Florence, Venice, Antwerp, London, Seville,
Frankfurt, Lubeck, Moscow, and where not,   75
Have I debts owing; and in most of these,
Great sums of money lying in the banco.
All this I'll give to some religious house,
So I may be baptized and live therein.
FRIAR JACOMO O good Barabas, come to our house!   80
FRIAR BARNARDINE O no, good Barabas, come to our house!
And Barabas, you know—
BARABAS [*to Friar Barnardine*]
    I know that I have highly sinned.
    You shall convert me; you shall have all my wealth.
FRIAR JACOMO O, Barabas, their laws are strict.   85
BARABAS [*to Friar Jacomo*]
    I know they are, and I will be with you.
FRIAR JACOMO They wear no shirts, and they go barefoot too.
BARABAS [*to Friar Jacomo*]
    Then 'tis not for me; and I am resolved
    You shall confess me and have all my goods.
FRIAR BARNARDINE Good Barabas, come to me.   90
BARABAS [*to Friar Jacomo*]
    You see I answer him, and yet he stays.
    Rid him away, and go you home with me.
FRIAR JACOMO [*to Barabas*] I'll be with you tonight.
BARABAS [*to Friar Jacomo*]
    Come to my house at one o'clock this night.
FRIAR JACOMO [*to Friar Barnardine*]
    You hear your answer, and you may be gone.   95
FRIAR BARNARDINE Why, go get you away.
FRIAR JACOMO I will not go for thee.
FRIAR BARNARDINE Not? Then I'll make thee, rogue.°
FRIAR JACOMO How, dost call me rogue?
        [*The Friars*] *fight*
ITHAMORE Part 'em, master, part 'em.   100
BARABAS This is mere frailty. Brethren, be content.
    Friar Barnardine, go you with Ithamore.
        [*Aside to Friar Barnardine*]
    You know my mind; let me alone with him.
FRIAR JACOMO
    Why does he go to thy house? Let him be gone.

BARABAS [*aside to Friar Jacomo*]
    I'll give him something, and so stop his mouth.   105
        Exit [Ithamore with Friar Barnardine]
    I never heard of any man but he
    Maligned the order of the Jacobins.°
    But do you think that I believe his words?
    Why, brother, you converted Abigail,
    And I am bound in charity to requite it;°   110
    And so I will. O Jacomo, fail not, but come.°

FRIAR JACOMO But, Barabas, who shall be your godfathers?
    For presently you shall be shrived.

BARABAS Marry, the Turk shall be one of my godfathers.°
    But not a word to any of your convent.   115

FRIAR JACOMO I warrant thee, Barabas.
        Exit [Jacomo]

BARABAS So, now the fear is past, and I am safe,
    For he that shrived her is within my house.°
    What if I murdered him ere Jacomo comes?
    Now I have such a plot for both their lives   120
    As never Jew nor Christian knew the like.
    One turned my daughter, therefore he shall die;°
    The other knows enough to have my life,°
    Therefore 'tis not requisite he should live.
    But are not both these wise men to suppose   125
    That I will leave my house, my goods, and all,
    To fast and be well whipped? I'll none of that.
    Now, Friar Barnardine, I come to you.
    I'll feast you, lodge you, give you fair words,
    And after that, I and my trusty Turk—   130
    No more but so. It must and shall be done.
        Enter Ithamore
    Ithamore, tell me, is the friar asleep?

ITHAMORE Yes, and I know not what the reason is,
    Do what I can, he will not strip himself
    Nor go to bed, but sleeps in his own clothes.   135
    I fear me he mistrusts what we intend.

BARABAS No, 'tis an order which the friars use.°
    Yet if he knew our meanings, could he 'scape?°

ITHAMORE No, none can hear him, cry he ne'er so loud.

BARABAS Why, true. Therefore did I place him there.   140
    The other chambers open towards the street.

ITHAMORE You loiter, master. Wherefore stay we thus?
  O, how I long to see him shake his heels!°
     [*A curtained discovery space*° *is disclosed, revealing Friar*
     Barnardine asleep]
BARABAS Come on, sirrah,
  Off with your girdle, make a handsome noose.   145
     [*They put the Friar's rope belt around his neck*]
  Friar, awake!
FRIAR BARNARDINE What, do you mean to strangle me?
ITHAMORE Yes, 'cause you use to confess.°
BARABAS
Blame not us but the proverb, 'Confess and be hanged.'—°
  Pull hard!°   150
FRIAR BARNARDINE What, will you have my life?°
BARABAS Pull hard, I say!—You would have had my goods.
ITHAMORE Ay, and our lives too.—Therefore, pull amain.°
     [*They strangle him*]
  'Tis neatly done, sir. Here's no print at all.°
BARABAS Then is it as it should be. Take him up.   155
ITHAMORE Nay, master, be ruled by me a little. So, let him lean
  upon his staff.
     [*He props up the body*]°
  Excellent! He stands as if he were begging of bacon.
BARABAS Who would not think but that this friar lived?
  What time o' night is't now, sweet Ithamore?   160
ITHAMORE Towards one.
BARABAS Then will not Jacomo be long from hence.
     [*They conceal themselves.*] *Enter* [*Friar*] *Jacomo*
FRIAR JACOMO This is the hour
  Wherein I shall proceed. O happy hour,°
  Wherein I shall convert an infidel   165
  And bring his gold into our treasury!
  But soft, is not this Barnardine? It is;
  And, understanding I should come this way,
  Stands here o' purpose, meaning me some wrong,
  And intercept my going to the Jew.—°   170
  Barnardine!
  Wilt thou not speak? Thou think'st I see thee not.
  Away, I'd wish thee, and let me go by.
  No, wilt thou not? Nay then, I'll force my way.
  And see, a staff stands ready for the purpose.   175

As thou lik'st that, stop me another time.
>   [*Friar Jacomo grabs Barnardine's staff and*] *strike*[*s*] *him;*
>   [*Barnardine*] *falls. Enter Barabas* [*and Ithamore from*
>   *concealment*]

BARABAS   Why, how now, Jacomo, what hast thou done?

FRIAR JACOMO   Why, stricken him that would have struck at me.

BARABAS   Who is it? Barnadine? Now out, alas, he is slain!

ITHAMORE   Ay, master, he's slain. Look how his brains drop out on's   180
nose.

FRIAR JACOMO   Good sirs, I have done't, but nobody knows it but
you two, I may escape.

BARABAS   So might my man and I hang with you for company.

ITHAMORE   No, let us bear him to the magistrates.   185
>   [*They seize Friar Jacomo*]

FRIAR JACOMO   Good Barabas, let me go.

BARABAS   No, pardon me, the law must have his course.°
I must be forced to give in evidence°
That, being importuned by this Barnardine
To be a Christian, I shut him out,   190
And there he sat. Now I, to keep my word,
And give my goods and substance to your house,
Was up thus early with intent to go
Unto your friary, because you stayed.°

ITHAMORE   Fie upon 'em, master, will you turn Christian,   195
When holy friars turn devils and murder one another?

BARABAS   No, for this example I'll remain a Jew.
Heaven bless me! What, a friar a murderer?
When shall you see a Jew commit the like?

ITHAMORE   Why, a Turk could ha' done no more.°   200

BARABAS   Tomorrow is the sessions; you shall to it.
Come, Ithamore, let's help to take him hence.

FRIAR JACOMO   Villains, I am a sacred person; touch me not.°

BARABAS   The law shall touch you; we'll but lead you, we.°
'Las, I could weep at your calamity.—   205
Take in the staff too, for that must be shown;
Law wills that each particular be known.
>   *Exeunt*

[4.2]

Enter [Bellamira the] Courtesan and Pilia-Borza

BELLAMIRA Pilia-Borza, didst thou meet with Ithamore?

PILIA-BORZA I did.

BELLAMIRA And didst thou deliver my letter?

PILIA-BORZA I did.

BELLAMIRA And what think'st thou, will he come?   5

PILIA-BORZA I think so, and yet I cannot tell, for at the reading of
the letter he looked like a man of another world.

BELLAMIRA Why so?

PILIA-BORZA That such a base slave as he should be saluted by such
a tall man as I am, from such a beautiful dame as you.   10

BELLAMIRA And what said he?

PILIA-BORZA Not a wise word; only gave me a nod, as who should
say, 'Is it even so?'° And so I left him, being driven to a
nonplus° at the critical aspect of my terrible countenance.

BELLAMIRA And where didst meet him?   15

PILIA-BORZA Upon mine own freehold,° within forty foot of the
gallows, conning his neck-verse,° I take it, looking of a friar's
execution,° whom I saluted with an old hempen° proverb, '*Hodie
tibi, cras mihi*',° and so I left him to the mercy of the hangman.
But the exercise° being done, see where he comes.   20

Enter Ithamore

ITHAMORE [*to himself*] I never knew a man take his death so patiently
as this friar. He was ready to leap off ere the halter was about his
neck, and when the hangman had put on his hempen tippet° he
made such haste to his prayers as if he had had another cure° to
serve. Well, go whither he will, I'll be none of his followers in   25
haste. And now I think on't, going to the execution, a fellow met
me with a muschatoes° like a raven's wing and a dagger with a hilt
like a warming-pan,° and he gave me a letter from one Madam
Bellamira, saluting me in such sort as if he had meant to make
clean my boots with his lips; the effect° was that I should come to   30
her house. I wonder what the reason is. It may be she sees more
in me than I can find in myself, for she writes further that she
loves me ever since she saw me, and who would not requite
such love? Here's her house, and here she comes, and now would
I were gone. I am not worthy to look upon her.   35

PILIA-BORZA [*presenting Ithamore*] This is the gentleman you writ to.

ITHAMORE [*aside*] 'Gentleman'! He flouts me. What gentry can be in a poor Turk of tenpence? I'll be gone.

BELLAMIRA Is't not a sweet-faced youth, Pilia?

ITHAMORE [*aside*] Again, 'sweet youth'! [*To Pilia-Borza*] Did not   40
you, sir, bring the 'sweet youth' a letter?

PILIA-BORZA I did, sir, and from this gentlewoman, who, as myself and the rest of the family, stand or fall° at your service.

BELLAMIRA Though woman's modesty should hale me back,
I can withhold no longer. Welcome, sweet love.   45
[*She kisses him*]

ITHAMORE [*aside*] Now am I clean, or rather foully, out of the way.°
[*He starts to leave*]

BELLAMIRA Whither so soon?

ITHAMORE [*aside*] I'll go steal some money from my master, to make me handsome. [*Aloud*] Pray pardon me, I must go see a ship discharged.   50

BELLAMIRA Canst thou be so unkind to leave me thus?

PILIA-BORZA An ye did but know how she loves you, sir!

ITHAMORE Nay, I care not how much she loves me.—Sweet Bellamira, would I had my master's wealth for thy sake.

PILIA-BORZA And you can have it, sir, an if you please.   55

ITHAMORE If 'twere above ground I could and would have it, but he hides and buries it up as partridges do their eggs, under the earth.

PILIA-BORZA And is't not possible to find it out?

ITHAMORE By no means possible.

BELLAMIRA [*aside to Pilia-Borza*]
What shall we do with this base villain, then?   60

PILIA-BORZA [*aside to Bellamira*]
Let me alone, do but you speak him fair.
[*To Ithamore*] But you know some secrets of the Jew,
Which if they were revealed would do him harm.

ITHAMORE Ay, and such as—Go to, no more, I'll make him send me   65
half he has, and glad he 'scapes so too. Pen and ink! I'll write unto him; we'll have money straight.

PILIA-BORZA [*providing pen and ink*] Send for a hundred crowns at least.

ITHAMORE Ten hundred thousand crowns. (*He writes*) 'Master   70
Barabas—'

PILIA-BORZA Write not so submissively, but threatening him.

ITHAMORE 'Sirrah Barabas, send me a hundred crowns.'

PILIA-BORZA Put in two hundred at least.

ITHAMORE 'I charge thee send me three hundred by this bearer, and   75
this shall be your warrant. If you do not, no more but so.'
PILIA-BORZA Tell him you will confess.
ITHAMORE 'Otherwise I'll confess all.' Vanish, and return in a
twinkle.
PILIA-BORZA Let me alone. I'll use him in his kind.°   80
[*Exit Pilia-Borza*]
ITHAMORE Hang him, Jew!
BELLAMIRA Now, gentle Ithamore, lie in my lap.
[*Calling offstage, as Ithamore luxuriates in her embrace*]
Where are my maids? Provide a running banquet;°
Send to the merchant, bid him bring me silks.
Shall Ithamore my love go in such rags?   85
ITHAMORE And bid the jeweller come hither too.
BELLAMIRA I have no husband, sweet, I'll marry thee.
ITHAMORE Content, but we will leave this paltry land°
And sail from hence to Greece, to lovely Greece.
I'll be thy Jason, thou my golden fleece;°   90
Where painted carpets o'er the meads are hurled,°
And Bacchus' vineyards overspread the world,
Where woods and forests go in goodly green,
I'll be Adonis, thou shalt be Love's queen.°
The meads, the orchards, and the primrose lanes,   95
Instead of sedge and reed, bear sugar-canes.
Thou in those groves, by Dis above,°
Shalt live with me and be my love.°
BELLAMIRA Whither will I not go with gentle Ithamore?
Enter Pilia-Borza [with a moneybag]
ITHAMORE How now? Hast thou the gold?   100
PILIA-BORZA Yes.
[*He delivers the money*]
ITHAMORE But came it freely? Did the cow give down her milk
freely?
PILIA-BORZA At reading of the letter, he stared and stamped, and
turned aside. I took him by the beard and looked upon him   105
thus, told him he were best to send it; then he hugged and
embraced me.
ITHAMORE Rather for fear than love.
PILIA-BORZA Then like a Jew he laughed and jeered, and told me he
loved me for your sake, and said what a faithful servant you had   110
been.

ITHAMORE The more villain he to keep me thus. Here's goodly
'parel, is there not?°

PILIA-BORZA To conclude, he gave me ten crowns.°

ITHAMORE But ten? I'll not leave him worth a grey groat. Give me   115
a ream° of paper. We'll have a kingdom of gold for't.

PILIA-BORZA [*providing paper*] Write for five hundred crowns.

ITHAMORE [*writing*] 'Sirrah Jew, as you love your life, send me five
hundred crowns, and give the bearer one hundred.' Tell him I
must have't.   120

PILIA-BORZA I warrant your worship shall have't.

ITHAMORE And if he ask why I demand so much, tell him I scorn
to write a line under a hundred crowns.

PILIA-BORZA You'd make a rich poet, sir. I am gone.
       Exit [Pilia-Borza]

ITHAMORE [*giving Bellamira the money*]
Take thou the money. Spend it for my sake.   125

BELLAMIRA 'Tis not thy money but thyself I weigh.
Thus Bellamira esteems of gold;
       [*She throws it aside*]
But thus of thee.
       [*She*] *kiss[es] him*

ITHAMORE [*aside*] That kiss again! She runs division of° my lips.
What an eye she casts on me! It twinkles like a star.   130

BELLAMIRA Come, my dear love, let's in and sleep together.

ITHAMORE O, that ten thousand nights were put in one, that we
might sleep seven years together afore we wake!

BELLAMIRA Come, amorous wag, first banquet and then sleep.
       [*Exeunt*]

[4.3]

       Enter Barabas, reading [Ithamore's first] letter°

BARABAS 'Barabas, send me three hundred crowns.'
Plain 'Barabas'? O, that wicked courtesan!
He was not wont to call me 'Barabas'.
'Or else I will confess.' Ay, there it goes.
But if I get him, *coupe de gorge* for that.°   5
He sent a shaggy, tottered, staring slave
That, when he speaks, draws out his grisly beard

And winds it twice or thrice about his ear;
Whose face has been a grindstone for men's swords;
His hands are hacked, some fingers cut quite off;   10
Who, when he speaks, grunts like a hog and looks
Like one that is employed in catzerie°
And crossbiting—such a rogue°
As is the husband to a hundred whores.°
And I by him must send three hundred crowns!°   15
Well, my hope is he will not stay there still;°
And when he comes—O, that he were but here!
      Enter Pilia-Borza
PILIA-BORZA Jew, I must ha' more gold.
BARABAS Why, want'st thou any of thy tale?°
PILIA-BORZA No; but three hundred will not serve his turn.   20
BARABAS Not serve his turn, sir?
PILIA-BORZA No, sir, and therefore I must have five hundred more.
BARABAS I'll rather—
PILIA-BORZA O, good words, sir, and send it, you were best; see,
      there's his letter.   25
      [*He presents Ithamore's second letter*]
BARABAS Might he not as well come as send? Pray bid him come and
      fetch it; what he writes for you,° ye shall have straight.
PILIA-BORZA Ay, and the rest too, or else—
BARABAS [*aside*] I must make this villain away.° [*To him*] Please you
      dine with me, sir, (*aside*) and you shall be most heartily poisoned. 30
PILIA-BORZA No, God-a-mercy. Shall I have these crowns?
BARABAS I cannot do it. I have lost my keys.
PILIA-BORZA O, if that be all, I can pick ope your locks.
BARABAS Or climb up to my counting-house window? You know my
      meaning.°   35
PILIA-BORZA I know enough, and therefore talk not to me of your
      counting-house. The gold! or know, Jew, it is in my power to hang
      thee.
BARABAS [*aside*] I am betrayed.
      [*To him*] 'Tis not five hundred crowns that I esteem;   40
      I am not moved at that. This angers me,
      That he who knows I love him as myself
      Should write in this imperious vein.—Why, sir,
      You know I have no child, and unto whom
      Should I leave all but unto Ithamore?   45
PILIA-BORZA Here's many words but no crowns. The crowns!

BARABAS Commend me to him, sir, most humbly,
And unto your good mistress as unknown.°
PILIA-BORZA Speak, shall I have 'em, sir?
BARABAS Sir, here they are. [*He gives money*]   50
[*Aside*] O, that I should part with so much gold!
[*To him*] Here, take 'em, fellow, with as good a will—
[*Aside*] As I would see thee hanged. [*To him*] O, love stops my breath.
Never loved man servant as I do Ithamore.
PILIA-BORZA I know it, sir.   55
BARABAS Pray, when, sir, shall I see you at my house?
PILIA-BORZA Soon enough, to your cost, sir. Fare you well.
          Exit [*Pilia-Borza*]
BARABAS Nay, to thine own cost, villain, if thou com'st.
Was ever Jew tormented as I am?
To have a shag-rag knave to come demand°   60
Three hundred crowns, and then five hundred crowns?
Well, I must seek a means to rid 'em all,
And presently, for in his villainy
He will tell all he knows, and I shall die for't.
I have it!   65
I will in some disguise go see the slave,
And how the villain revels with my gold.
          Exit

[4.4]

Enter Courtesan [*Bellamira*], *Ithamore, Pilia-Borza* [*and
Servants with wine. The revellers drink repeatedly*]

BELLAMIRA I'll pledge thee, love, and therefore drink it off.°
ITHAMORE Say'st thou me so? Have at it! And do you hear?
          [*He whispers° to her*]
BELLAMIRA Go to, it shall be so.
ITHAMORE Of° that condition I will drink it up. Here's to thee.
BELLAMIRA Nay, I'll have all or none.°   5
ITHAMORE There. If thou lov'st me, do not leave a drop.°
BELLAMIRA Love thee?—Fill me three glasses!
ITHAMORE Three-and-fifty dozen I'll pledge thee.
PILIA-BORZA Knavely spoke, and like a knight at arms.
ITHAMORE Hey, *Rivo Castiliano*! A man's a man.°   10

BELLAMIRA Now to the Jew.°
ITHAMORE Ha, to the Jew! And send me money, you were best.°
PILIA-BORZA What wouldst thou do if he should send thee none?
ITHAMORE Do? Nothing. But I know what I know. He's a murderer.
BELLAMIRA I had not thought he had been so brave a man.   15
ITHAMORE You knew Mathias and the governor's son? He and I
   killed 'em both, and yet never touched 'em.
PILIA-BORZA O, bravely done!
ITHAMORE I carried the broth that poisoned the nuns, and he and
   I—snickle, hand to! fast!°—strangled a friar.   20
BELLAMIRA You two alone?
ITHAMORE We two; and 'twas never known, nor never shall be for
   me.°
PILIA-BORZA [aside to Bellamira]
   This shall with me unto the governor.
BELLAMIRA [aside to Pilia-Borza]
   And fit it should; but first let's ha' more gold.   25
   [To Ithamore] Come, gentle Ithamore, lie in my lap.
ITHAMORE Love me little, love me long. Let music rumble,°
   Whilst I in thy incony lap do tumble.°
     Enter Barabas with a lute, disguised, [and a nosegay in his
     hat]
BELLAMIRA A French musician! Come, let's hear your skill.
BARABAS Must tuna my lute for sound, twang, twang, first.   30
ITHAMORE Wilt drink, Frenchman? Here's to thee with a—Pox on
   this drunken hiccup!
BARABAS [accepting a drink] Gramercy, monsieur.
BELLAMIRA Prithee, Pilia-Borza, bid the fiddler give me the posy in
   his hat there.   35
PILIA-BORZA Sirrah, you must give my mistress your posy.
BARABAS A vôtre commandement,° madame.
   [He presents his nosegay, from which they all inhale]
BELLAMIRA How sweet, my Ithamore, the flowers smell!
ITHAMORE Like thy breath, sweetheart; no violet like 'em.
PILIA-BORZA Foh, methinks they stink like a hollyhock.   40
BARABAS [aside] So, now I am revenged upon 'em all.
   The scent thereof was death; I poisoned it.
ITHAMORE Play, fiddler, or I'll cut your cat's guts into chitterlings.
BARABAS Pardonnez-moi, be no in tune yet. [He tunes] So now, now
   all be in.   45
ITHAMORE Give him a crown, and fill° me out more wine.

PILIA-BORZA [*giving money*] There's two crowns for thee. Play.
BARABAS (*aside*) How liberally the villain gives me mine own gold!
    [*He plays the lute*]
PILIA-BORZA Methinks he fingers very well.
BARABAS (*aside*) So did you when you stole my gold.°   50
PILIA-BORZA How swift he runs!
BARABAS (*aside*) You run° swifter when you threw my gold out of
    my window.
BELLAMIRA Musician, hast been in Malta long?
BARABAS Two, three, four month, madame.   55
ITHAMORE Dost not know a Jew, one Barabas?
BARABAS Very mush, monsieur. You no be his man?
PILIA-BORZA His man?
ITHAMORE I scorn the peasant. Tell him so.
BARABAS [*aside*] He knows it already.   60
ITHAMORE 'Tis a strange thing of that Jew: he lives upon pickled
    grasshoppers and sauced mushrooms.
BARABAS (*aside*) What a slave's this! The governor feeds not as I do.
ITHAMORE He never put on clean shirt since he was circumcised.
BARABAS (*aside*) O, rascal! I change myself twice a day.   65
ITHAMORE The hat he wears, Judas left under the elder° when he
    hanged himself.
BARABAS (*aside*) 'Twas sent me for a present from the Great Cham.°
PILIA-BORZA A masty° slave he is.
    [*Barabas starts to go*]
  Whither now, fiddler?   70
BARABAS *Pardonnez-moi*, monsieur, me be no well.
    Exit [*Barabas*]
PILIA-BORZA Farewell, fiddler.—One letter more to the Jew.
BELLAMIRA Prithee, sweet love, one more, and write it sharp.
ITHAMORE No, I'll send by word of mouth now. [*To Pilia-Borza*]
    Bid him deliver thee a thousand crowns, by the same token that   75
    the nuns loved rice,° that Friar Barnardine slept in his own
    clothes—any of 'em will do it.
PILIA-BORZA Let me alone to urge it, now I know the meaning.
ITHAMORE The meaning has a meaning.°
    [*Exit Pilia-Borza*]
                           Come, let's in.
  To undo a Jew is charity, and not sin.°   80
    Exeunt

[5.1]

Enter Governor [Ferneze], Knights, Martin del Bosco, [and Officers]

FERNEZE Now, gentlemen, betake you to your arms,
And see that Malta be well fortified.
And it behoves you to be resolute,
For Calymath, having hovered here so long,
Will win the town or die before the walls.   5

FIRST KNIGHT And die he shall, for we will never yield.
Enter Courtesan [Bellamira, and] Pilia-Borza

BELLAMIRA [*to an Officer*] O, bring us to the governor.

FERNEZE Away with her! She is a courtesan.

BELLAMIRA Whate'er I am, yet, governor, hear me speak.
I bring thee news by whom thy son was slain: 10
Mathias did it not, it was the Jew.

PILIA-BORZA Who, besides the slaughter of these gentlemen, poisoned his own daughter and the nuns, strangled a friar, and I know
not what mischief beside.

FERNEZE Had we but proof of this!   15

BELLAMIRA
Strong proof, my lord. His man's now at my lodging
That was his agent; he'll confess it all.

FERNEZE Go fetch him straight.
   [*Exeunt Officers*]
                                    I always feared that Jew.°
Enter [Officers roughly escorting Barabas the] Jew [and] Ithamore°

BARABAS I'll go alone, dogs, do not hale me thus.

ITHAMORE Nor me neither. I cannot outrun you, constable. O, my   20
belly!°

BARABAS [*aside*] One dram of powder more had made all sure.
What a damned slave was I!

FERNEZE Make fires, heat irons, let the rack be fetched.

FIRST KNIGHT Nay, stay, my lord, 't may be he will confess.   25

BARABAS Confess? What mean you, lords, who should confess?

FERNEZE Thou and thy Turk. 'Twas you that slew my son.

ITHAMORE Guilty, my lord, I confess. Your son and Mathias were
both contracted unto Abigail; he forged a counterfeit challenge.

BARABAS Who carried that challenge?   30
ITHAMORE I carried it, I confess, but who writ it? Marry, even he
    that strangled Barnardine, poisoned the nuns, and his own
    daughter.
FERNEZE Away with him! His sight is death to me.°
BARABAS For what? You men of Malta, hear me speak.   35
    She is a courtesan, and he a thief,
    And he my bondman. Let me have law,
    For none of this can prejudice my life.
FERNEZE Once more, away with him! You shall have law.°
BARABAS Devils, do your worst, I'll live in spite of you.   40
    As these have spoke, so be it to their souls.°
    [*Aside*] I hope the poisoned flowers will work anon.
        Exeunt [Officers with Barabas, Ithamore, Bellamira, and
        Pilia-Borza]. Enter Katherine
KATHERINE Was my Mathias murdered by the Jew?
    Ferneze, 'twas thy son that murdered him.
FERNEZE Be patient, gentle madam; it was he.   45
    He forged the daring challenge made them fight.°
KATHERINE Where is the Jew? Where is that murderer?
FERNEZE In prison, till the law has passed on him.
        Enter [an] Officer
OFFICER My lord, the courtesan and her man are dead;
    So is the Turk, and Barabas the Jew.   50
FERNEZE Dead?
OFFICER   Dead, my lord, and here they bring his body.
        [*Enter Officers, carrying Barabas as dead*]
DEL BOSCO This sudden death of his is very strange.
FERNEZE Wonder not at it, sir, the heavens are just.
    Their deaths were like their lives; then think not of 'em.
    Since they are dead, let them be buried.°   55
    For the Jew's body, throw that o'er the walls°
    To be a prey for vultures and wild beasts.
        [*Officers toss the body aside*]°
    So, now away, and fortify the town.
        Exeunt [all but Barabas]
BARABAS [*rising*] What, all alone? Well fare, sleepy drink!°
    I'll be revenged on this accursèd town,   60
    For by my means Calymath shall enter in.
    I'll help to slay their children and their wives,
    To fire the churches, pull their houses down,

Take my goods too, and seize upon my lands.°
I hope to see the governor a slave,   65
And, rowing in a galley, whipped to death.
    Enter Calymath, Bashaws, [and] Turks
CALYMATH Whom have we there, a spy?
BARABAS Yes, my good lord, one that can spy a place
Where you may enter and surprise the town.
My name is Barabas; I am a Jew.   70
CALYMATH Art thou that Jew whose goods we heard were sold
For tribute-money?
BARABAS   The very same, my lord;
And since that time they have hired a slave, my man,
To accuse me of a thousand villainies.
I was imprisoned, but escaped their hands.   75
CALYMATH Didst break prison?
BARABAS No, no,
I drank of poppy and cold mandrake juice,
And, being asleep, belike they thought me dead
And threw me o'er the walls. So, or how else,°   80
The Jew is here, and rests at your command.
CALYMATH 'Twas bravely done. But tell me, Barabas,
Canst thou, as thou reportest, make Malta ours?
BARABAS Fear not, my lord; for here, against the sluice,°
The rock is hollow and of purpose digged   85
To make a passage for the running streams
And common channels of the city.
Now, whilst you give assault unto the walls,
I'll lead five hundred soldiers through the vault,°
And rise with them i'th'middle of the town,°   90
Open the gates for you to enter in,
And by this means the city is your own.
CALYMATH If this be true, I'll make thee governor.
BARABAS And if it be not true, then let me die.°
CALYMATH Thou'st doomed thyself. Assault it presently.   95
    Exeunt

[5.2]

Alarms. Enter [Calymath,] Turks, [and] Barabas, [with]
Ferneze and Knights prisoners

CALYMATH Now vail your pride, you captive Christians,
And kneel for mercy to your conquering foe.
Now where's the hope you had of haughty Spain?
Ferneze, speak. Had it not been much better
To've kept thy promise than be thus surprised?   5
FERNEZE What should I say? We are captives and must yield.
CALYMATH Ay, villains, you must yield, and under Turkish yokes
Shall groaning bear the burden of our ire.
And, Barabas, as erst we promised thee,
For thy desert we make thee governor.   10
Use them at thy discretion.°
BARABAS   Thanks, my lord.
FERNEZE O, fatal day, to fall into the hands
Of such a traitor and unhallowed Jew!
What greater misery could heaven inflict?
CALYMATH 'Tis our command; and Barabas, we give,   15
To guard thy person, these our janizaries;
Entreat them well, as we have usèd thee.
And now, brave bashaws, come, we'll walk about
The ruined town and see the wrack we made.
Farewell, brave Jew, farewell, great Barabas.   20
BARABAS May all good fortune follow Calymath!
        Exeunt [Calymath and Bashaws]
And now, as entrance to our safety,°
To prison with the governor and these
Captains, his consorts and confederates.
FERNEZE O villain, heaven will be revenged on thee!   25
BARABAS Away, no more! Let him not trouble me.
        Exeunt [Turkish Janizaries with Ferneze and Knights.
        Barabas remains alone]
Thus hast thou gotten, by thy policy,
No simple place, no small authority.
I now am governor of Malta. True,
But Malta hates me, and, in hating me,   30
My life's in danger; and what boots it thee,
Poor Barabas, to be the governor,

Whenas thy life shall be at their command?
No, Barabas, this must be looked into;
And since by wrong thou got'st authority,   35
Maintain it bravely by firm policy,
At least unprofitably lose it not.°
For he that liveth in authority,
And neither gets him friends nor fills his bags,
Lives like the ass that Aesop speaketh of,   40
That labours with a load of bread and wine
And leaves it off to snap on thistle tops.°
But Barabas will be more circumspect.
Begin betimes; Occasion's bald behind;°
Slip not thine opportunity, for fear too late   45
Thou seek'st for much but canst not compass it.
[*Calling offstage*] Within, there!
   Enter Ferneze, with a Guard° [*of janizaries*]
FERNEZE My lord?
BARABAS [*aside*] Ay, 'lord'; thus slaves will learn.
 [*To him*] Now, governor. [*To the Guard*] Stand by, there.
  Wait within.   50
   [*The Guard retires*]
 This is the reason that I sent for thee:
 Thou seest thy life and Malta's happiness
 Are at my arbitrament, and Barabas
 At his discretion may dispose of both.
 Now tell me, governor, and plainly too,   55
 What think'st thou shall become of it and thee?
FERNEZE This, Barabas: since things are in thy power,
 I see no reason but of Malta's wrack,°
 Nor hope of thee but extreme cruelty;
 Nor fear I death, nor will I flatter thee.   60
BARABAS Governor, good words; be not so furious.°
 'Tis not thy life which can avail me aught.
 Yet you do live, and live for me you shall;°
 And as for Malta's ruin, think you not
 'Twere slender policy for Barabas   65
 To dispossess himself of such a place?°
 For sith, as once you said, within this isle,
 In Malta here, that I have got my goods,°
 And in this city still have had success,
 And now at length am grown your governor,   70

Yourselves shall see it shall not be forgot.
For, as a friend not known but in distress,°
I'll rear up Malta, now remediless.
FERNEZE Will Barabas recover Malta's loss?
Will Barabas be good to Christians?   75
BARABAS What wilt thou give me, governor, to procure
A dissolution of the slavish bands
Wherein the Turk hath yoked your land and you?
What will you give me if I render you
The life of Calymath, surprise his men,   80
And in an outhouse of the city shut°
His soldiers till I have consumed 'em all with fire?
What will you give him that procureth this?
FERNEZE Do but bring this to pass which thou pretendest,
Deal truly with us as thou intimatest,   85
And I will send amongst the citizens
And by my letters privately procure
Great sums of money for thy recompense.
Nay, more: do this, and live thou governor still.
BARABAS Nay, do thou this, Ferneze, and be free.   90
Governor, I enlarge thee. Live with me,
Go walk about the city, see thy friends.
Tush, send not letters to 'em, go thyself,
And let me see what money thou canst make.°
Here is my hand that I'll set Malta free.   95
And thus we cast it: to a solemn feast°
I will invite young Selim Calymath,
Where be thou present only to perform
One stratagem that I'll impart to thee,
Wherein no danger shall betide thy life,   100
And I will warrant Malta free for ever.
FERNEZE Here is my hand.
      [*They shake hands*]
                          Believe me, Barabas,
I will be there and do as thou desirest.
When is the time?
BARABAS   Governor, presently.
For Calymath, when he hath viewed the town,   105
Will take his leave and sail toward Ottoman.°
FERNEZE Then will I, Barabas, about this coin,°
And bring it with me to thee in the evening.

BARABAS Do so, but fail not. Now farewell, Ferneze.
    [*Exit Ferneze*]
  And thus far roundly goes the business.   110
  Thus, loving neither, will I live with both,
  Making a profit of my policy;
  And he from whom my most advantage comes
  Shall be my friend.
  This is the life we Jews are used to lead,   115
  And reason, too, for Christians do the like.
  Well, now about effecting this device:
  First, to surprise great Selim's soldiers,
  And then to make provision for the feast,
  That at one instant all things may be done.   120
  My policy detests prevention.°
  To what event my secret purpose drives,
  I know, and they shall witness with their lives.°
    Exit

[5.3]

    Enter Calymath [and] Bashaws
CALYMATH Thus have we viewed the city, seen the sack,
  And caused the ruins to be new repaired,
  Which with our bombards' shot and basilisks
  We rent in sunder at our entry.
  And, now I see the situation,   5
  And how secure this conquered island stands—
  Environed with the Mediterranean Sea,
  Strong countermined with other petty isles,
  And, toward Calabria, backed by Sicily
  (Where Syracusian Dionysius reigned),   10
  Two lofty turrets that command the town—°
  I wonder how it could be conquered thus.
    Enter a Messenger
MESSENGER From Barabas, Malta's governor, I bring
  A message unto mighty Calymath.
  Hearing his sovereign was bound for sea   15
  To sail to Turkey, to great Ottoman,°
  He humbly would entreat your majesty

To come and see his homely citadel
And banquet with him ere thou leav'st the isle.
CALYMATH To banquet with him in his citadel?   20
   I fear me, messenger, to feast my train
   Within a town of war so lately pillaged
   Will be too costly and too troublesome.
   Yet would I gladly visit Barabas,
   For well has Barabas deserved of us.   25
MESSENGER Selim, for that, thus saith the governor:°
   That he hath in store a pearl so big,
   So precious, and withal so orient,
   As, be it valued but indifferently,
   The price thereof will serve to entertain   30
   Selim and all his soldiers for a month.
   Therefore he humbly would entreat your highness
   Not to depart till he has feasted you.
CALYMATH I cannot feast my men in Malta walls,
   Except he place his tables in the streets.   35
MESSENGER Know, Selim, that there is a monastery
   Which standeth as an outhouse to the town.
   There will he banquet them, but thee at home,
   With all thy bashaws and brave followers.
CALYMATH Well, tell the governor we grant his suit.   40
   We'll in this summer evening feast with him.
MESSENGER I shall, my lord.
      Exit [Messenger]
CALYMATH And now, bold bashaws, let us to our tents
   And meditate how we may grace us best
   To solemnize our governor's great feast.   45
      Exeunt

[5.4]

Enter Ferneze, Knights, [and Martin] del Bosco
FERNEZE In this, my countrymen, be ruled by me:
   Have special care that no man sally forth
   Till you shall hear a culverin discharged°
   By him that bears the linstock, kindled thus;°
   Then issue out and come to rescue me,   5

For happily I shall be in distress
Or you releasèd of this servitude.°
FIRST KNIGHT　Rather than thus to live as Turkish thralls,
What will we not adventure?
FERNEZE　On then, begone.
FIRST KNIGHT　　　　　　　Farewell, grave governor.　　　　　10
　　　[*Exeunt, separately*]

[5.5]

　　　Enter [Barabas] with a hammer above,° very busy, [and
　　　Carpenters to work with him]
BARABAS　How stand the cords? How hang these hinges, fast?
Are all the cranes and pulleys sure?
A CARPENTER　　　　　　　　　All fast.
BARABAS　Leave nothing loose, all levelled to my mind.°
Why, now I see that you have art indeed.
　　　[*He gives money*]
There, carpenters, divide that gold amongst you.　　　　　5
Go swill in bowls of sack and muscadine;
Down to the cellar, taste of all my wines.
A CARPENTER　We shall, my lord, and thank you.
　　　Exeunt [Carpenters]
BARABAS　And if you like them, drink your fill—and die;
For, so I live, perish may all the world.°　　　　　10
Now, Selim Calymath, return me word
That thou wilt come, and I am satisfied.
　　　Enter Messenger
Now, sirrah, what, will he come?
MESSENGER　He will, and has commanded all his men
To come ashore and march through Malta streets,　　　　　15
That thou mayst feast them in thy citadel.
　　　[*Exit Messenger*]
BARABAS　Then now are all things as my wish would have 'em.
There wanteth nothing but the governor's pelf—
　　　Enter Ferneze [to Barabas, with a bag of money]
And see, he brings it.—Now, governor, the sum?
FERNEZE　With free consent, a hundred thousand pounds.　　　　　20

BARABAS

    Pounds, say'st thou, governor? Well, since it is no more,
    I'll satisfy myself with that; nay, keep it still,
    For if I keep not promise, trust not me.
    And, governor, now partake my policy:
    First, for his army, they are sent before,°   25
    Entered the monastery, and underneath
    In several places are field-pieces pitched,
    Bombards, whole barrels full of gunpowder,
    That on the sudden shall dissever it
    And batter all the stones about their ears,   30
    Whence none can possibly escape alive.
    Now, as for Calymath and his consorts,
    Here have I made a dainty gallery,
    The floor whereof, this cable being cut,
    Doth fall asunder, so that it doth sink   35
    Into a deep pit past recovery.
        [Barabas gives Ferneze a knife]
    Here, hold that knife, and when thou seest he comes,
    And with his bashaws shall be blithely set,
    A warning-piece shall be shot off from the tower
    To give thee knowledge when to cut the cord   40
    And fire the house. Say, will not this be brave?°

FERNEZE O, excellent!
        [He offers the bag of money]
                Here, hold thee, Barabas.
    I trust thy word. Take what I promised thee.

BARABAS No, governor, I'll satisfy thee first.
    Thou shalt not live in doubt of anything.   45
    Stand close, for here they come.
        [Ferneze conceals himself]
                    Why, is not this
    A kingly kind of trade, to purchase towns
    By treachery and sell 'em by deceit?
    Now tell me, worldlings, underneath the sun°
    If greater falsehood ever has been done.   50
        Enter Calymath and Bashaws [on the main stage]

CALYMATH Come, my companion bashaws, see, I pray,
    How busy Barabas is there above
    To entertain us in his gallery.
    Let us salute him.—Save thee, Barabas!

BARABAS Welcome, great Calymath.   55
FERNEZE [*aside*] How the slave jeers at him!°
BARABAS Will't please thee, mighty Selim Calymath,
    To ascend our homely stairs?
CALYMATH   Ay, Barabas.
    Come, bashaws, attend.
FERNEZE [*coming forward*] Stay, Calymath!
    For I will show thee greater courtesy   60
    Than Barabas would have afforded thee.
FIRST KNIGHT [*within*] Sound a charge there!°
       A [trumpet] charge [sounded], the cable cut [by Ferneze], a
       cauldron discovered° [*into which Barabas falls through a trap*
       door. Enter Martin del Bosco and Knights]
CALYMATH How now, what means this?
BARABAS Help, help me, Christians, help!
FERNEZE See, Calymath, this was devised for thee.   65
CALYMATH Treason, treason! Bashaws, fly!
FERNEZE No, Selim, do not fly.
    See his end first, and fly then if thou canst.
BARABAS O, help me, Selim, help me, Christians!
    Governor, why stand you all so pitiless?   70
FERNEZE Should I, in pity of thy plaints or thee,
    Accursèd Barabas, base Jew, relent?
    No, thus I'll see thy treachery repaid,
    But wish thou hadst behaved thee otherwise.
BARABAS You will not help me, then?
FERNEZE   No, villain, no.   75
BARABAS And, villains, know you cannot help me now.°
    Then, Barabas, breathe forth thy latest fate,°
    And in the fury of thy torments strive
    To end thy life with resolution.
    Know, governor, 'twas I that slew thy son;   80
    I framed the challenge that did make them meet.
    Know, Calymath, I aimed thy overthrow,
    And had I but escaped this stratagem
    I would have brought confusion on you all,
    Damned Christians, dogs, and Turkish infidels!   85
    But now begins the extremity of heat
    To pinch me with intolerable pangs.
    Die, life! Fly, soul! Tongue, curse thy fill and die!
       [*He dies*]

CALYMATH Tell me, you Christians, what doth this portend?
FERNEZE This train he laid to have entrapped thy life.   90
  Now, Selim, note the unhallowed deeds of Jews:
  Thus he determined to have handled thee,
  But I have rather chose to save thy life.
CALYMATH Was this the banquet he prepared for us?
  Let's hence, lest further mischief be pretended.   95
FERNEZE Nay, Selim, stay, for since we have thee here
  We will not let thee part so suddenly.
  Besides, if we should let thee go, all's one,°
  For with thy galleys couldst thou not get hence
  Without fresh men to rig and furnish them.   100
CALYMATH Tush, governor, take thou no care for that.
  My men are all aboard,
  And do attend my coming there by this.
FERNEZE Why, heard'st thou not the trumpet sound a charge?
CALYMATH Yes, what of that?
FERNEZE   Why, then the house was fired,   105
  Blown up, and all thy soldiers massacred.
CALYMATH O, monstrous treason!
FERNEZE   A Jew's courtesy;
  For he that did by treason work our fall
  By treason hath delivered thee to us.
  Know, therefore, till thy father hath made good   110
  The ruins done to Malta and to us,
  Thou canst not part; for Malta shall be freed,
  Or Selim ne'er return to Ottoman.
CALYMATH Nay, rather, Christians, let me go to Turkey,
  In person there to mediate your peace.   115
  To keep me here will naught advantage you.
FERNEZE Content thee, Calymath, here thou must stay
  And live in Malta prisoner; for, come all the world°
  To rescue thee, so will we guard us now
  As sooner shall they drink the ocean dry   120
  Than conquer Malta or endanger us.
  So, march away, and let due praise be given
  Neither to fate nor fortune, but to heaven.
      [*Exeunt*]

EPILOGUE SPOKEN AT COURT

It is our fear, dread sovereign, we have been
Too tedious; neither can 't be less than sin
To wrong your princely patience. If we have,
Thus low dejected, we your pardon crave;°
And if aught here offend your ear or sight,   5
We only act, and speak, what others write.

EPILOGUE TO THE STAGE

In graving with Pygmalion to contend,°
Or painting with Apelles, doubtless the end°
Must be disgrace. Our actor did not so;
He only aimed to go, but not outgo.
Nor think that this day any prize was played;   5
Here were no bets at all, no wagers laid.
All the ambition that his mind doth swell
Is but to hear from you (by me) 'twas well.

EDWARD II

DRAMATIS PERSONAE

Gaveston
Three Poor Men
King Edward II
Earl of Lancaster
Mortimer Senior
Mortimer Junior
Edmund Earl of Kent
Guy Earl of Warwick
Attendants
The Bishop of Coventry
The Archbishop of Canterbury
Queen Isabella
Earl of Pembroke
Guards
Beaumont, *the Clerk of the Crown*
Spencer Junior
Baldock
The King's Niece
A Messenger
Two Ladies in Waiting
Earl of Arundel
Soldiers

James
A Horseboy
Spencer Senior
Prince Edward, *later* King Edward III
Levune
A Herald
Sir John of Hainault
A Post
Rice ap Howell
The Mayor of Bristol
An Abbot
Monks
A Mower
Earl of Leicester
The Bishop of Winchester
Sir William Trussell
Sir Thomas Berkeley
Matrevis
Gurney
Lightborn
A Champion
Lords

Edward II

[1.1]

*Enter Gaveston reading on a letter that was brought him from
the King*

GAVESTON [*reads*] 'My father is deceased; come, Gaveston,
And share the kingdom with thy dearest friend.'
Ah, words that make me surfeit with delight!
What greater bliss can hap to Gaveston
Than live and be the favourite of a king?   5
Sweet prince, I come; these, these thy amorous lines
Might have enforced me to have swum from France
And like Leander gasped upon the sand,°
So thou wouldst smile and take me in thy arms.
The sight of London to my exiled eyes   10
Is as Elysium to a new-come soul—
Not that I love the city or the men,
But that it harbours him I hold so dear,
The king, upon whose bosom let me die°
And with the world be still at enmity.   15
What need the arctic people love starlight,
To whom the sun shines both by day and night?
Farewell, base stooping to the lordly peers;
My knee shall bow to none but to the king.
As for the multitude, that are but sparks   20
Raked up in embers of their poverty,
Tanti; I'll fawn first on the wind°
That glanceth at my lips and flieth away.
But how now, what are these?
          Enter three Poor Men

POOR MEN Such as desire your worship's service.   25
GAVESTON [*to the first*] What canst thou do?
FIRST POOR MAN I can ride.
GAVESTON But I have no horses.—What art thou?
SECOND POOR MAN A traveller.
GAVESTON Let me see, thou wouldst do well to wait at my trencher   30
    and tell me lies at dinner time, and, as I like your discoursing, I'll
    have you.—And what art thou?

THIRD POOR MAN A soldier, that hath served against the Scot.°
GAVESTON Why, there are hospitals for such as you.
    I have no war, and therefore, sir, begone.   35
THIRD POOR MAN Farewell, and perish by a soldier's hand,
    That wouldst reward them with an hospital!
       [*The Poor Men start to go*]
GAVESTON [*aside*] Ay, ay, these words of his move me as much
    As if a goose should play the porcupine
    And dart her plumes, thinking to pierce my breast.°   40
    But yet it is no pain to speak men fair;
    I'll flatter these and make them live in hope.
    [*To them*] You know that I came lately out of France,
    And yet I have not viewed my lord the king;
    If I speed well, I'll entertain you all.   45
POOR MEN We thank your worship.
GAVESTON I have some business; leave me to myself.
POOR MEN We will wait here about the court.
GAVESTON Do.
      Exeunt [*Poor Men*]
         These are not men for me.
    I must have wanton poets, pleasant wits,   50
    Musicians that with touching of a string
    May draw the pliant king which way I please.
    Music and poetry is his delight;
    Therefore I'll have Italian masques by night,°
    Sweet speeches, comedies, and pleasing shows;   55
    And in the day, when he shall walk abroad,
    Like sylvan nymphs my pages shall be clad;
    My men, like satyrs grazing on the lawns,
    Shall with their goat feet dance an antic hay.°
    Sometime a lovely boy in Dian's shape,°   60
    With hair that gilds the water as it glides,
    Crownets of pearl about his naked arms,
    And in his sportful hands an olive tree
    To hide those parts which men delight to see,
    Shall bathe him in a spring, and there hard by   65
    One like Actaeon peeping through the grove°
    Shall by the angry goddess be transformed,
    And running in the likeness of an hart
    By yelping hounds pulled down and seem to die.
    Such things as these best please his majesty,   70

My lord. Here comes the king and the nobles
From the parliament. I'll stand aside.

Enter the King [Edward], Lancaster, Mortimer Senior,
Mortimer Junior, Edmund Earl of Kent, Guy Earl of
Warwick, [and Attendants]

EDWARD Lancaster!

LANCASTER My lord?

GAVESTON [*aside*] That earl of Lancaster do I abhor.   75

EDWARD Will you not grant me this? [*Aside*] In spite of them
I'll have my will, and these two Mortimers
That cross me thus shall know I am displeased.

MORTIMER SENIOR [*to Edward*]
If you love us, my lord, hate Gaveston.

GAVESTON [*aside*] That villain Mortimer! I'll be his death.   80

MORTIMER [*to Edward*] Mine uncle here, this earl, and I myself°
Were sworn to your father at his death
That he should ne'er return into the realm;
And know, my lord, ere I will break my oath,
This sword of mine that should offend your foes   85
Shall sleep within the scabbard at thy need,
And underneath thy banners march who will,
For Mortimer will hang his armour up.

GAVESTON [*aside*] *Mort Dieu!*°

EDWARD Well Mortimer, I'll make thee rue these words.   90
Beseems it thee to contradict thy king?
Frown'st thou thereat, aspiring Lancaster?
The sword shall plane the furrows of thy brows
And hew these knees that now are grown so stiff.°
I will have Gaveston, and you shall know   95
What danger 'tis to stand against your king.

GAVESTON [*aside*] Well done, Ned!

LANCASTER My lord, why do you thus incense your peers,
That naturally would love and honour you
But for that base and obscure Gaveston?°   100
Four earldoms have I besides Lancaster—
Derby, Salisbury, Lincoln, Leicester.
These will I sell to give my soldiers pay
Ere Gaveston shall stay within the realm.
Therefore, if he be come, expel him straight.   105

KENT Barons and earls, your pride hath made me mute,
But now I'll speak, and to the proof, I hope.°

I do remember in my father's days
Lord Percy of the north, being highly moved,
Braved Mowbray in presence of the king,   110
For which, had not his highness loved him well,
He should have lost his head; but with his look
The undaunted spirit of Percy was appeased,
And Mowbray and he were reconciled;
Yet dare you brave the king unto his face.   115
Brother, revenge it, and let these their heads
Preach upon poles for trespass of their tongues.°
WARWICK O, our heads?
EDWARD Ay, yours, and therefore I would wish you grant.°
WARWICK Bridle thy anger, gentle Mortimer.   120
MORTIMER I cannot, nor I will not; I must speak.
Cousin, our hands, I hope, shall fence our heads
And strike off his that makes you threaten us.
Come, uncle, let us leave the brainsick king
And henceforth parley with our naked swords.   125
MORTIMER SENIOR Wiltshire hath men enough to save our heads.
WARWICK All Warwickshire will love him for my sake.
LANCASTER And, northward, Gaveston hath many friends.°
Adieu, my lord, and either change your mind
Or look to see the throne where you should sit   130
To float in blood, and at thy wanton head
The glozing head of thy base minion thrown.
        *Exeunt nobles. [Kent, King Edward, and Gaveston remain
        onstage]*
EDWARD I cannot brook these haughty menaces!
Am I a king, and must be overruled?
Brother, display my ensigns in the field;   135
I'll bandy with the barons and the earls,
And either die or live with Gaveston.
GAVESTON [*coming forward*]
I can no longer keep me from my lord.
        [*He kneels and offers to kiss the King's hand*]
EDWARD [*raising him*]
What, Gaveston, welcome! Kiss not my hand;
Embrace me, Gaveston, as I do thee.   140
        [*They embrace*]
Why shouldst thou kneel? Knowest thou not who I am?
Thy friend, thy self, another Gaveston.

Not Hylas was more mourned of Hercules°
Than thou hast been of me since thy exile.°

GAVESTON And since I went from hence, no soul in hell   145
Hath felt more torment than poor Gaveston.

EDWARD I know it.—Brother, welcome home my friend.—
Now let the treacherous Mortimers conspire,
And that high-minded earl of Lancaster;
I have my wish, in that I joy thy sight,   150
And sooner shall the sea o'erwhelm my land
Than bear the ship that shall transport thee hence.
I here create thee Lord High Chamberlain,
Chief Secretary to the state and me,
Earl of Cornwall, King and Lord of Man.   155

GAVESTON My lord, these titles far exceed my worth.

KENT Brother, the least of these may well suffice
For one of greater birth than Gaveston.

EDWARD Cease, brother, for I cannot brook these words.—
Thy worth, sweet friend, is far above my gifts;   160
Therefore, to equal it, receive my heart.
If for these dignities thou be envied,°
I'll give thee more, for but to honour thee
Is Edward pleased with kingly regiment.
Fear'st thou thy person? Thou shalt have a guard.°   165
Wants thou gold? Go to my treasury.
Wouldst thou be loved and feared? Receive my seal,°
Save or condemn, and in our name command
Whatso thy mind affects or fancy likes.

GAVESTON It shall suffice me to enjoy your love,   170
Which whiles I have, I think myself as great
As Caesar riding in the Roman street
With captive kings at his triumphant car.
        Enter the Bishop of Coventry

EDWARD Whither goes my lord of Coventry so fast?

COVENTRY To celebrate your father's exequies.   175
But is that wicked Gaveston returned?

EDWARD Ay, priest, and lives to be revenged on thee
That wert the only cause of his exile.

GAVESTON 'Tis true, and, but for reverence of these robes,
Thou shouldst not plod one foot beyond this place.   180

COVENTRY I did no more than I was bound to do,
And, Gaveston, unless thou be reclaimed,°

329

As then I did incense the Parliament,
So will I now, and thou shalt back to France.
GAVESTON Saving your reverence, you must pardon me.°   185
    [*He lays hold of him*]
EDWARD Throw off his golden mitre, rend his stole,°
And in the channel christen him anew.°
KENT Ah, brother, lay not violent hands on him,
For he'll complain unto the see of Rome.
GAVESTON Let him complain unto the see of hell,   190
I'll be revenged on him for my exile.
EDWARD No, spare his life, but seize upon his goods;
Be thou lord bishop, and receive his rents,
And make him serve thee as thy chaplain.
I give him thee; here, use him as thou wilt.   195
GAVESTON He shall to prison, and there die in bolts.
EDWARD Ay, to the Tower, the Fleet, or where thou wilt.°
COVENTRY For this offence be thou accurst of God.
EDWARD [*calling to Attendants*]
    Who's there? Convey this priest to the Tower.
COVENTRY True, true.°   200
    [*Exit the Bishop of Coventry, guarded*]
EDWARD But in the meantime, Gaveston, away,
And take possession of his house and goods.
Come follow me, and thou shalt have my guard
To see it done and bring thee safe again.
GAVESTON What should a priest do with so fair a house?   205
A prison may beseem his holiness.
    [*Exeunt*]

[1.2]

    Enter both the Mortimers, Warwick, and Lancaster
WARWICK 'Tis true, the bishop is in the Tower,
And goods and body given to Gaveston.
LANCASTER What, will they tyrannize upon the Church?
Ah, wicked king! Accursèd Gaveston!
This ground, which is corrupted with their steps,   5
Shall be their timeless sepulchre or mine.
MORTIMER Well, let that peevish Frenchman guard him sure;
Unless his breast be sword-proof, he shall die.

MORTIMER SENIOR How now, why droops the earl of Lancaster?

MORTIMER Wherefore is Guy of Warwick discontent?   10

LANCASTER That villain Gaveston is made an earl.

MORTIMER SENIOR An earl!

WARWICK Ay, and besides, Lord Chamberlain of the realm,
  And Secretary too, and Lord of Man.

MORTIMER SENIOR We may not nor we will not suffer this.   15

MORTIMER Why post we not from hence to levy men?

LANCASTER 'My lord of Cornwall' now at every word!
  And happy is the man whom he vouchsafes,
  For vailing of his bonnet, one good look.°
  Thus, arm in arm, the king and he doth march;   20
  Nay more, the guard upon his lordship waits,
  And all the court begins to flatter him.

WARWICK Thus leaning on the shoulder of the king,
  He nods, and scorns, and smiles at those that pass.

MORTIMER SENIOR Doth no man take exceptions at the slave?°   25

LANCASTER All stomach him, but none dare speak a word.

MORTIMER Ah, that bewrays their baseness, Lancaster.
  Were all the earls and barons of my mind,
  We'll hale him from the bosom of the king
  And at the court-gate hang the peasant up,   30
  Who, swoll'n with venom of ambitious pride,
  Will be the ruin of the realm and us.

     Enter the [Arch]bishop of Canterbury [and an Attendant]

WARWICK Here comes my lord of Canterbury's grace.°

LANCASTER His countenance bewrays he is displeased.

CANTERBURY [*to his Attendant*]
  First were his sacred garments rent and torn,°   35
  Then laid they violent hands upon him, next
  Himself imprisoned and his goods asseized.
  This certify the pope. Away, take horse.
    [*Exit Attendant*]

LANCASTER [*to Canterbury*]
  My lord, will you take arms against the king?

CANTERBURY What need I? God himself is up in arms   40
  When violence is offered to the Church.

MORTIMER Then will you join with us that be his peers°
  To banish or behead that Gaveston?

CANTERBURY What else, my lords? For it concerns me near;
  The bishopric of Coventry is his.   45

Enter the Queen

MORTIMER Madam, whither walks your majesty so fast?
QUEEN Unto the forest, gentle Mortimer,°
  To live in grief and baleful discontent,
  For now my lord the king regards me not
  But dotes upon the love of Gaveston.   50
  He claps his cheeks and hangs about his neck,
  Smiles in his face and whispers in his ears,
  And when I come he frowns, as who should say,°
  'Go whither thou wilt, seeing I have Gaveston.'
MORTIMER SENIOR
  Is it not strange that he is thus bewitched?   55
MORTIMER Madam, return unto the court again.
  That sly, inveigling Frenchman we'll exile
  Or lose our lives; and yet ere that day come
  The king shall lose his crown, for we have power,
  And courage too, to be revenged at full.   60
CANTERBURY But yet lift not your swords against the king.
LANCASTER No, but we'll lift Gaveston from hence.°
WARWICK And war must be the means, or he'll stay still.
QUEEN Then let him stay, for, rather than my lord
  Shall be oppressed by civil mutinies,   65
  I will endure a melancholy life,
  And let him frolic with his minion.
CANTERBURY My lords, to ease all this, but hear me speak.°
  We and the rest that are his counsellors
  Will meet and with a general consent   70
  Confirm his banishment with our hands and seals.°
LANCASTER What we confirm the king will frustrate.
MORTIMER Then may we lawfully revolt from him.
WARWICK But say, my lord, where shall this meeting be?
CANTERBURY At the New Temple.°   75
MORTIMER Content.
CANTERBURY And in the meantime I'll entreat you all
  To cross to Lambeth and there stay with me.
LANCASTER Come then, let's away.
MORTIMER Madam, farewell.   80
QUEEN Farewell, sweet Mortimer, and for my sake
  Forbear to levy arms against the king.
MORTIMER Ay, if words will serve; if not, I must.
      [*Exeunt, the Queen one way and the rest another*]

[1.3]

Enter Gaveston and the Earl of Kent
GAVESTON Edmund, the mighty prince of Lancaster,
That hath more earldoms than an ass can bear,
And both the Mortimers, two goodly men,
With Guy of Warwick, that redoubted knight,
Are gone towards Lambeth. There let them remain.   5
Exeunt

[1.4]

*Enter nobles [Lancaster, Warwick, Pembroke, Mortimer
Senior, Mortimer Junior, the Archbishop of Canterbury,
attended by Guards. A throne and chair are brought on]*
LANCASTER *[presenting Canterbury a document]*
Here is the form of Gaveston's exile.
May it please your lordship to subscribe your name.
CANTERBURY Give me the paper.
          [He subscribes, as the others do after him]
LANCASTER Quick, quick, my lord, I long to write my name.
WARWICK But I long more to see him banished hence.   5
MORTIMER The name of Mortimer shall fright the king,
Unless he be declined from that base peasant.°
          *Enter the King and Gaveston [and Kent. The King sits on
          the throne with Gaveston at his side]*
EDWARD What, are you moved that Gaveston sits here?
It is our pleasure; we will have it so.
LANCASTER Your grace doth well to place him by your side,   10
For nowhere else the new earl is so safe.
MORTIMER SENIOR
What man of noble birth can brook this sight?
Quam male conveniunt!°
See what a scornful look the peasant casts.
PEMBROKE Can kingly lions fawn on creeping ants?   15
WARWICK Ignoble vassal, that like Phaethon°
Aspir'st unto the guidance of the sun!
MORTIMER Their downfall is at hand, their forces down;

We will not thus be faced and overpeered.°
EDWARD Lay hands on that traitor Mortimer!   20
MORTIMER SENIOR Lay hands on that traitor Gaveston!
     [*Gaveston is seized*]
KENT Is this the duty that you owe your king?
WARWICK We know our duties. Let him know his peers.
EDWARD Whither will you bear him? Stay, or ye shall die.
MORTIMER SENIOR
     We are no traitors; therefore threaten not.   25
GAVESTON [*to the King*]
     No, threaten not, my lord, but pay them home.
     Were I a king—
MORTIMER Thou villain, wherefore talks thou of a king,
     That hardly art a gentleman by birth?
EDWARD Were he a peasant, being my minion,   30
     I'll make the proudest of you stoop to him.
LANCASTER My lord, you may not thus disparage us.—
     Away, I say, with hateful Gaveston!
MORTIMER SENIOR
     And with the earl of Kent that favours him.
     [*Exeunt Kent and Gaveston, guarded*]
EDWARD Nay, then lay violent hands upon your king.   35
     Here, Mortimer, sit thou in Edward's throne;
     Warwick and Lancaster, wear you my crown.
     Was ever king thus overruled as I?
LANCASTER Learn then to rule us better, and the realm.
MORTIMER
     What we have done, our heart-blood shall maintain.   40
WARWICK Think you that we can brook this upstart pride?
EDWARD Anger and wrathful fury stops my speech.
CANTERBURY Why are you moved? Be patient, my lord,°
     And see what we your counsellors have done.
MORTIMER My lords, now let us all be resolute,   45
     And either have our wills or lose our lives.
EDWARD Meet you for this, proud overdaring peers?
     Ere my sweet Gaveston shall part from me,
     This isle shall fleet upon the ocean
     And wander to the unfrequented Inde.°   50
CANTERBURY You know that I am legate to the pope.
     On your allegiance to the see of Rome,
     Subscribe as we have done to his exile.

[*The King is offered the document to sign*]

MORTIMER [*to Canterbury*]
Curse him if he refuse, and then may we°
Depose him and elect another king.   55

EDWARD Ay, there it goes, but yet I will not yield,
Curse me, depose me, do the worst you can.°

LANCASTER Then linger not, my lord, but do it straight.

CANTERBURY Remember how the bishop was abused.
Either banish him that was the cause thereof,   60
Or I will presently discharge these lords
Of duty and allegiance due to thee.

EDWARD [*aside*]
It boots me not to threat; I must speak fair.
The legate of the pope will be obeyed.
     [*To Canterbury*]
My lord, you shall be Chancellor of the realm,   65
Thou, Lancaster, High Admiral of our fleet,
Young Mortimer and his uncle shall be earls,
And you, Lord Warwick, President of the North,
     [*To Pembroke*]
And thou of Wales. If this content you not,
Make several kingdoms of this monarchy   70
And share it equally amongst you all,
So I may have some nook or corner left
To frolic with my dearest Gaveston.

CANTERBURY Nothing shall alter us. We are resolved.

LANCASTER Come, come, subscribe.   75

MORTIMER
Why should you love him whom the world hates so?

EDWARD Because he loves me more than all the world.
Ah, none but rude and savage-minded men
Would seek the ruin of my Gaveston.
You that be noble born should pity him.   80

WARWICK You that are princely born should shake him off.
For shame, subscribe, and let the loon depart.

MORTIMER SENIOR [*to Canterbury*] Urge him, my lord.

CANTERBURY Are you content to banish him the realm?

EDWARD I see I must, and therefore am content.   85
Instead of ink, I'll write it with my tears.
     [*He writes*]

MORTIMER The king is lovesick for his minion.

335

EDWARD 'Tis done, and now, accursèd hand, fall off!
LANCASTER [*taking the document*]
　　Give it me. I'll have it published in the streets.
MORTIMER I'll see him presently dispatched away.　　　　　90
CANTERBURY Now is my heart at ease.
WARWICK　　　　　　　　　　　　　And so is mine.
PEMBROKE This will be good news to the common sort.°
MORTIMER SENIOR Be it or no, he shall not linger here.
　　Exeunt nobles. [King Edward alone remains]
EDWARD How fast they run to banish him I love!
　　They would not stir, were it to do me good.　　　　　95
　　Why should a king be subject to a priest?
　　Proud Rome, that hatchest such imperial grooms,°
　　For these thy superstitious taperlights,
　　Wherewith thy antichristian churches blaze,
　　I'll fire thy crazèd buildings and enforce°　　　　　100
　　The papal towers to kiss the lowly ground,
　　With slaughtered priests make Tiber's channel swell,°
　　And banks raised higher with their sepulchres.
　　As for the peers that back the clergy thus,
　　If I be king, not one of them shall live.　　　　　105
　　　Enter Gaveston
GAVESTON My lord, I hear it whispered everywhere
　　That I am banished and must fly the land.
EDWARD 'Tis true, sweet Gaveston. O, were it false!
　　The legate of the pope will have it so,
　　And thou must hence or I shall be deposed.　　　　　110
　　But I will reign to be revenged of them;
　　And therefore, sweet friend, take it patiently.
　　Live where thou wilt, I'll send thee gold enough;
　　And long thou shalt not stay, or, if thou dost,
　　I'll come to thee; my love shall ne'er decline.　　　　　115
GAVESTON Is all my hope turned to this hell of grief?
EDWARD Rend not my heart with thy too-piercing words;
　　Thou from this land, I from myself am banished.
GAVESTON To go from hence grieves not poor Gaveston,
　　But to forsake you, in whose gracious looks　　　　　120
　　The blessedness of Gaveston remains,
　　For nowhere else seeks he felicity.
EDWARD And only this torments my wretched soul,
　　That, whether I will or no, thou must depart.

Be governor of Ireland in my stead,   125
And there abide till fortune call thee home.
Here, take my picture and let me wear thine.
        [*They exchange lockets*]
O, might I keep thee here as I do this,
Happy were I, but now most miserable.
GAVESTON 'Tis something to be pitied of a king.   130
EDWARD Thou shalt not hence; I'll hide thee, Gaveston.
GAVESTON I shall be found, and then 'twill grieve me more.
EDWARD Kind words and mutual talk makes our grief greater;
    Therefore with dumb embracement let us part.
        [*They embrace. Gaveston starts to leave*]
    Stay, Gaveston, I cannot leave thee thus.   135
GAVESTON For every look, my lord, drops down a tear;
    Seeing I must go, do not renew my sorrow.
EDWARD The time is little that thou hast to stay,
    And therefore give me leave to look my fill.
    But come, sweet friend, I'll bear thee on thy way.°   140
GAVESTON The peers will frown.
EDWARD I pass not for their anger. Come, let's go.
    O, that we might as well return as go!
        Enter Queen Isabel
QUEEN Whither goes my lord?
EDWARD Fawn not on me, French strumpet; get thee gone.   145
QUEEN On whom but on my husband should I fawn?
GAVESTON On Mortimer, with whom, ungentle queen—
    I say no more; judge you the rest, my lord.
QUEEN In saying this, thou wrong'st me, Gaveston.
    Is't not enough that thou corrupts my lord   150
    And art a bawd to his affections,
    But thou must call mine honour thus in question?
GAVESTON I mean not so; your grace must pardon me.
EDWARD [*to the Queen*]
    Thou art too familiar with that Mortimer,
    And by thy means is Gaveston exiled;   155
    But I would wish thee reconcile the lords,
    Or thou shalt ne'er be reconciled to me.
QUEEN Your highness knows it lies not in my power.
EDWARD Away then, touch me not. Come, Gaveston.
QUEEN [*to Gaveston*]
    Villain, 'tis thou that robb'st me of my lord.   160

GAVESTON Madam, 'tis you that rob me of my lord.
EDWARD Speak not unto her; let her droop and pine.
QUEEN Wherein, my lord, have I deserved these words?
    Witness the tears that Isabella sheds,
    Witness this heart that, sighing for thee, breaks,   165
    How dear my lord is to poor Isabel.
EDWARD [pushing her away]
    And witness heaven how dear thou art to me.
    There weep, for, till my Gaveston be repealed,
    Assure thyself thou com'st not in my sight.
       Exeunt Edward and Gaveston
QUEEN O, miserable and distressèd queen!   170
    Would when I left sweet France and was embarked,
    That charming Circes, walking on the waves,°
    Had changed my shape, or at the marriage day
    The cup of Hymen had been full of poison,°
    Or with those arms that twined about my neck   175
    I had been stifled and not lived to see
    The king my lord thus to abandon me.
    Like frantic Juno will I fill the earth
    With ghastly murmur of my sighs and cries,
    For never doted Jove on Ganymede°   180
    So much as he on cursèd Gaveston.
    But that will more exasperate his wrath.
    I must entreat him, I must speak him fair,
    And be a means to call home Gaveston;
    And yet he'll ever dote on Gaveston,   185
    And so am I for ever miserable.
       Enter the nobles [Lancaster, Warwick, Pembroke, Mortimer
       Senior, and Mortimer Junior] to the Queen
LANCASTER Look where the sister of the king of France
    Sits wringing of her hands and beats her breast.
WARWICK The king, I fear, hath ill intreated her.
PEMBROKE Hard is the heart that injures such a saint.   190
MORTIMER I know 'tis long of Gaveston she weeps.
MORTIMER SENIOR Why? He is gone.
MORTIMER [to the Queen]   Madam, how fares your grace?
QUEEN Ah, Mortimer! Now breaks the king's hate forth,
    And he confesseth that he loves me not.
MORTIMER Cry quittance, madam, then, and love not him.°   195
QUEEN No, rather will I die a thousand deaths.

And yet I love in vain; he'll ne'er love me.

LANCASTER Fear ye not, madam. Now his minion's gone,
His wanton humour will be quickly left.

QUEEN O, never, Lancaster! I am enjoined   200
To sue unto you all for his repeal;
This wills my lord, and this must I perform,
Or else be banished from his highness' presence.

LANCASTER For his repeal, madam? He comes not back,
Unless the sea cast up his shipwrack body.   205

WARWICK And to behold so sweet a sight as that
There's none here but would run his horse to death.

MORTIMER But, madam, would you have us call him home?

QUEEN Ay, Mortimer, for till he be restored
The angry king hath banished me the court;   210
And therefore, as thou lovest and tend'rest me,
Be thou my advocate unto these peers.

MORTIMER What, would ye have me plead for Gaveston?

MORTIMER SENIOR Plead for him he that will, I am resolved.°

LANCASTER And so am I, my lord. Dissuade the queen.   215

QUEEN O Lancaster, let him dissuade the king,
For 'tis against my will he should return.

WARWICK Then speak not for him; let the peasant go.

QUEEN 'Tis for myself I speak, and not for him.

PEMBROKE No speaking will prevail, and therefore cease.   220

MORTIMER Fair queen, forbear to angle for the fish
Which, being caught, strikes him that takes it dead—
I mean that vile torpedo, Gaveston,°
That now, I hope, floats on the Irish seas.

QUEEN Sweet Mortimer, sit down by me a while,   225
And I will tell thee reasons of such weight
As thou wilt soon subscribe to his repeal.

MORTIMER [sitting beside her]
It is impossible; but speak your mind.

QUEEN Then thus, but none shall hear it but ourselves.
          [They talk apart]

LANCASTER My lords, albeit the queen win Mortimer,   230
Will you be resolute and hold with me?

MORTIMER SENIOR Not I against my nephew.

PEMBROKE Fear not, the queen's words cannot alter him.

WARWICK No? Do but mark how earnestly she pleads.

LANCASTER And see how coldly his looks make denial.   235

WARWICK She smiles. Now, for my life, his mind is changed.

LANCASTER I'll rather lose his friendship, I, than grant.

MORTIMER [*returning to the lords*]
    Well, of necessity it must be so.—
    My lords, that I abhor base Gaveston
    I hope your honours make no question,   240
    And therefore, though I plead for his repeal,
    'Tis not for his sake but for our avail—
    Nay, for the realm's behoof and for the king's.

LANCASTER Fie, Mortimer, dishonour not thyself.
    Can this be true, 'twas good to banish him,   245
    And is this true, to call him home again?
    Such reasons make white black and dark night day.

MORTIMER My lord of Lancaster, mark the respect.°

LANCASTER In no respect can contraries be true.

QUEEN Yet, good my lord, hear what he can allege.   250

WARWICK All that he speaks is nothing; we are resolved.

MORTIMER Do you not wish that Gaveston were dead?

PEMBROKE I would he were.

MORTIMER Why then, my lord, give me but leave to speak.

MORTIMER SENIOR But, nephew, do not play the sophister.   255

MORTIMER This which I urge is of a burning zeal
    To mend the king and do our country good.
    Know you not Gaveston hath store of gold
    Which may in Ireland purchase him such friends
    As he will front the mightiest of us all?   260
    And whereas he shall live and be beloved
    'Tis hard for us to work his overthrow.

WARWICK Mark you but that, my lord of Lancaster.

MORTIMER But were he here, detested as he is,
    How easily might some base slave be suborned   265
    To greet his lordship with a poniard,
    And none so much as blame the murderer,
    But rather praise him for that brave attempt
    And in the chronicle enrol his name
    For purging of the realm of such a plague.   270

PEMBROKE He saith true.

LANCASTER Ay, but how chance this was not done before?

MORTIMER Because, my lords, it was not thought upon.
    Nay, more, when he shall know it lies in us
    To banish him and then to call him home,   275

'Twill make him vail the top-flag of his pride°
And fear to offend the meanest nobleman.

MORTIMER SENIOR But how if he do not, nephew?

MORTIMER Then may we with some colour rise in arms;
For, howsoever we have borne it out,°   280
'Tis treason to be up against the king.°
So shall we have the people of our side,°
Which for his father's sake lean to the king
But cannot brook a night-grown mushroom,°
Such a one as my lord of Cornwall is,°   285
Should bear us down of the nobility.
And when the commons and the nobles join,
'Tis not the king can buckler Gaveston;°
We'll pull him from the strongest hold he hath.
My lords, if to perform this I be slack,   290
Think me as base a groom as Gaveston.

LANCASTER On that condition, Lancaster will grant.

WARWICK And so will Pembroke and I.

MORTIMER SENIOR And I.

MORTIMER In this I count me highly gratified,   295
And Mortimer will rest at your command.

QUEEN And when this favour Isabel forgets,
Then let her live abandoned and forlorn.
But see, in happy time, my lord the king,°
Having brought the earl of Cornwall on his way,   300
Is new returned. This news will glad him much,
Yet not so much as me. I love him more
Than he can Gaveston. Would he loved me
But half so much, then were I treble blest.

> *Enter King Edward, mourning° [and Attendants, including*
> *Beaumont, Clerk of the Crown]*

EDWARD He's gone, and for his absence thus I mourn.   305
Did never sorrow go so near my heart
As doth the want of my sweet Gaveston,
And, could my crown's revenue bring him back,°
I would freely give it to his enemies,
And think I gained, having bought so dear a friend.   310

QUEEN [*to the lords*] Hark, how he harps upon his minion.

EDWARD My heart is as an anvil unto sorrow,
Which beats upon it like the Cyclops' hammers,°
And with the noise turns up my giddy brain°

341

And makes me frantic for my Gaveston.   315
Ah, had some bloodless Fury rose from hell°
And with my kingly sceptre struck me dead,
When I was forced to leave my Gaveston!°
LANCASTER *Diablo!* What passions call you these?°
QUEEN [*to Edward*]   320
    My gracious lord, I come to bring you news.
EDWARD That you have parlèd with your Mortimer?
QUEEN That Gaveston, my lord, shall be repealed.
EDWARD Repealed! The news is too sweet to be true.
QUEEN But will you love me if you find it so?
EDWARD If it be so, what will not Edward do?   325
QUEEN For Gaveston, but not for Isabel.
EDWARD For thee, fair queen, if thou lovest Gaveston,
    I'll hang a golden tongue about thy neck,°
    Seeing thou hast pleaded with so good success.
QUEEN [*holding his arms around her*]
    No other jewels hang about my neck   330
    Than these, my lord, nor let me have more wealth°
    Than I may fetch from this rich treasury.
        [*They kiss*]
    O, how a kiss revives poor Isabel!
EDWARD Once more receive my hand, and let this be
    A second marriage 'twixt thyself and me.   335
QUEEN And may it prove more happy than the first.
        [*The lords kneel*]
    My gentle lord, bespeak these nobles fair,
    That wait attendance for a gracious look,
    And on their knees salute your majesty.
EDWARD [*raising and embracing them*]
    Courageous Lancaster, embrace thy king,   340
    And, as gross vapours perish by the sun,
    Even so let hatred with thy sovereign's smile.
    Live thou with me as my companion.
LANCASTER This salutation overjoys my heart.
EDWARD Warwick shall be my chiefest counsellor;   345
    These silver hairs will more adorn my court
    Than gaudy silks or rich embroidery.
    Chide me, sweet Warwick, if I go astray.
WARWICK Slay me, my lord, when I offend your grace.
EDWARD In solemn triumphs and in public shows   350

Pembroke shall bear the sword before the king.
PEMBROKE And with this sword Pembroke will fight for you.
EDWARD But wherefore walks young Mortimer aside?
   Be thou commander of our royal fleet,
   Or, if that lofty office like thee not,   355
   I make thee here Lord Marshal of the realm.
MORTIMER My lord, I'll marshal so your enemies°
   As England shall be quiet and you safe.
EDWARD And as for you, Lord Mortimer of Chirk,
   Whose great achievements in our foreign war   360
   Deserves no common place nor mean reward,
   Be you the general of the levied troops
   That now are ready to assail the Scots.
MORTIMER SENIOR In this your grace hath highly honoured me,
   For with my nature war doth best agree.   365
QUEEN Now is the king of England rich and strong,
   Having the love of his renownèd peers.
EDWARD Ay, Isabel, ne'er was my heart so light.—
   Clerk of the Crown, direct our warrant forth
   For Gaveston to Ireland; Beaumont, fly°   370
   As fast as Iris or Jove's Mercury.°
BEAUMONT It shall be done, my gracious lord.
    [*Exit Beaumont*]
EDWARD Lord Mortimer, we leave you to your charge.
   Now let us in and feast it royally.
   Against our friend the earl of Cornwall comes,   375
   We'll have a general tilt and tournament,
   And then his marriage shall be solemnized,
   For wot you not that I have made him sure°
   Unto our cousin, the earl of Gloucester's heir?°
LANCASTER Such news we hear, my lord.   380
EDWARD That day, if not for him, yet for my sake,
   Who in the triumph will be challenger,
   Spare for no cost; we will requite your love.°
WARWICK In this, or aught, your highness shall command us.
EDWARD Thanks, gentle Warwick. Come, let's in and revel.   385
    Exeunt all except the Mortimers, who remain
MORTIMER SENIOR
   Nephew, I must to Scotland; thou stayest here.
   Leave now to oppose thyself against the king.
   Thou seest by nature he is mild and calm,

And, seeing his mind so dotes on Gaveston,
Let him without controlment have his will.   390
The mightiest kings have had their minions:
Great Alexander loved Hephaestion,
The conquering Hercules for Hylas wept,°
And for Patroclus stern Achilles drooped.
And not kings only, but the wisest men: 395
The Roman Tully loved Octavius,
Grave Socrates, wild Alcibiades.°
Then let his grace, whose youth is flexible,
And promiseth as much as we can wish,
Freely enjoy that vain, light-headed earl,   400
For riper years will wean him from such toys.

MORTIMER   Uncle, his wanton humour grieves not me,
But this I scorn, that one so basely born
Should by his sovereign's favour grow so pert
And riot it with the treasure of the realm.   405
While soldiers mutiny for want of pay
He wears a lord's revenue on his back,°
And Midas-like he jets it in the court°
With base outlandish cullions at his heels,°
Whose proud fantastic liveries make such show   410
As if that Proteus, god of shapes, appeared.°
I have not seen a dapper jack so brisk.
He wears a short Italian hooded cloak,
Larded with pearl, and in his Tuscan cap
A jewel of more value than the crown.   415
Whiles other walk below, the king and he°
From out a window laugh at such as we,
And flout our train, and jest at our attire.
Uncle, 'tis this that makes me impatient.

MORTIMER SENIOR
But, nephew, now you see the king is changed.   420

MORTIMER   Then so am I, and live to do him service.
But whiles I have a sword, a hand, a heart,
I will not yield to any such upstart.
You know my mind. Come, uncle, let's away.
            Exeunt

[2.1]

Enter Spencer [Junior] and Baldock

BALDOCK Spencer,
  Seeing that our lord th'earl of Gloucester's dead,
  Which of the nobles dost thou mean to serve?
SPENCER Not Mortimer, nor any of his side,
  Because the king and he are enemies.   5
  Baldock, learn this of me: a factious lord
  Shall hardly do himself good, much less us,
  But he that hath the favour of a king
  May with one word advance us while we live.
  The liberal earl of Cornwall is the man   10
  On whose good fortune Spencer's hope depends.
BALDOCK What, mean you then to be his follower?
SPENCER No, his companion, for he loves me well,
  And would have once preferred me to the king.
BALDOCK But he is banished; there's small hope of him.   15
SPENCER Ay, for a while. But, Baldock, mark the end:
  A friend of mine told me in secrecy
  That he's repealed and sent for back again,
  And even now a post came from the court
  With letters to our lady from the king,   20
  And as she read, she smiled, which makes me think
  It is about her lover Gaveston.
BALDOCK 'Tis like enough, for since he was exiled
  She neither walks abroad nor comes in sight.
  But I had thought the match had been broke off   25
  And that his banishment had changed her mind.
SPENCER Our lady's first love is not wavering.
  My life for thine, she will have Gaveston.°
BALDOCK Then hope I by her means to be preferred,
  Having read unto her since she was a child.°   30
SPENCER Then, Baldock, you must cast the scholar off
  And learn to court it like a gentleman.°
  'Tis not a black coat and a little band,°
  A velvet-caped cloak faced before with serge,°
  And smelling to a nosegay all the day,°   35
  Or holding of a napkin in your hand,

Or saying a long grace at a table's end,
Or making low legs to a nobleman,°
Or looking downward with your eyelids close,
And saying, 'Truly, an't may please your honour',   40
Can get you any favour with great men;
You must be proud, bold, pleasant, resolute,
And now and then stab as occasion serves.
BALDOCK Spencer, thou knowest I hate such formal toys,°
And use them but of mere hypocrisy.   45
Mine old lord, while he lived, was so precise
That he would take exceptions at my buttons,
And, being like pins' heads, blame me for the bigness,
Which made me curate-like in mine attire,
Though inwardly licentious enough   50
And apt for any kind of villainy.
I am none of these common pedants, I,
That cannot speak without '*propterea quod*'.°
SPENCER But one of those that saith '*quandoquidem*'
And hath a special gift to form a verb.°   55
BALDOCK Leave off this jesting; here my lady comes.
        Enter the Lady, [*niece to the King, with letters*]
NIECE [*to herself*] The grief for his exile was not so much
As is the joy of his returning home.
This letter came from my sweet Gaveston.
What need'st thou, love, thus to excuse thyself?   60
I know thou couldst not come and visit me.
        [*She reads*]
'I will not long be from thee, though I die.'
This argues the entire love of my lord.
        [*She reads*]
'When I forsake thee, death seize on my heart.'
But rest thee here where Gaveston shall sleep.   65
        [*She places the letter in her bosom*]
Now to the letter of my lord the king.
        [*She examines another letter*]
He wills me to repair unto the court
And meet my Gaveston. Why do I stay,
Seeing that he talks thus of my marriage day?—
Who's there? Baldock?   70
See that my coach be ready; I must hence.
BALDOCK It shall be done, madam.

NIECE And meet me at the park pale presently.
        Exit [Baldock]
    Spencer, stay you and bear me company,
    For I have joyful news to tell thee of: 75
    My lord of Cornwall is a-coming over
    And will be at the court as soon as we.
SPENCER I knew the king would have him home again.
NIECE If all things sort out as I hope they will,
    Thy service, Spencer, shall be thought upon.   80
SPENCER I humbly thank your ladyship.
NIECE Come, lead the way; I long till I am there.
        [Exeunt]

[2.2]

*Enter Edward, the Queen, Lancaster, Mortimer [Junior],
Warwick, Pembroke, Kent, [and] Attendants. [The lords bear
heraldic devices on their shields]*

EDWARD The wind is good. I wonder why he stays;
    I fear me he is wrecked upon the sea.
QUEEN [*aside to Lancaster*]
    Look, Lancaster, how passionate he is,
    And still his mind runs on his minion.
LANCASTER [*to the King*] My lord—   5
EDWARD How now, what news? Is Gaveston arrived?
MORTIMER Nothing but 'Gaveston'! What means your grace?
    You have matters of more weight to think upon;
    The king of France sets foot in Normandy.
EDWARD A trifle. We'll expel him when we please.   10
    But tell me, Mortimer, what's thy device°
    Against the stately triumph we decreed?
MORTIMER A homely one, my lord, not worth the telling.
EDWARD Prithee let me know it.
MORTIMER But seeing you are so desirous, thus it is: 15
    A lofty cedar tree, fair flourishing,
    On whose top branches kingly eagles perch,
    And by the bark a canker creeps me up°
    And gets unto the highest bough of all.
    The motto: *Aeque tandem.*°   20

EDWARD And what is yours, my lord of Lancaster?
LANCASTER My lord, mine's more obscure than Mortimer's.
   Pliny reports there is a flying fish°
   Which all the other fishes deadly hate,
   And therefore, being pursued, it takes the air;   25
   No sooner is it up, but there's a fowl
   That seizeth it. This fish, my lord, I bear;
   The motto this: *Undique mors est*.°
EDWARD Proud Mortimer! Ungentle Lancaster!
   Is this the love you bear your sovereign?   30
   Is this the fruit your reconcilement bears?
   Can you in words make show of amity,
   And in your shields display your rancorous minds?
   What call you this but private libelling
   Against the earl of Cornwall and my brother?°   35
QUEEN Sweet husband, be content. They all love you.
EDWARD They love me not that hate my Gaveston.
   I am that cedar. Shake me not too much.
       [*To the lords*]
   And you the eagles, soar ye ne'er so high,
   I have the jesses that will pull you down,   40
   And *Aeque tandem* shall that canker cry
   Unto the proudest peer of Britainy.°
       [*To Lancaster*]
   Though thou compar'st him to a flying fish,
   And threatenest death whether he rise or fall,
   'Tis not the hugest monster of the sea
   Nor foulest harpy that shall swallow him.°   45
MORTIMER [*to the lords*]
   If in his absence thus he favours him,
   What will he do whenas he shall be present?
LANCASTER That shall we see. Look where his lordship comes.
       Enter Gaveston
EDWARD My Gaveston!   50
   Welcome to Tynemouth, welcome to thy friend.
   Thy absence made me droop and pine away;
   For, as the lovers of fair Danaë,°
   When she was locked up in a brazen tower,
   Desired her more and waxed outrageous,   55
   So did it sure with me; and now thy sight
   Is sweeter far than was thy parting hence

Bitter and irksome to my sobbing heart.

GAVESTON Sweet lord and king, your speech preventeth mine,
   Yet have I words left to express my joy.   60
   The shepherd nipped with biting winter's rage
   Frolics not more to see the painted spring°
   Than I do to behold your majesty.

EDWARD Will none of you salute my Gaveston?

LANCASTER Salute him? Yes. Welcome, Lord Chamberlain.   65

MORTIMER Welcome is the good earl of Cornwall.

WARWICK Welcome, Lord Governor of the Isle of Man.

PEMBROKE Welcome, Master Secretary.

KENT Brother, do you hear them?

EDWARD Still will these earls and barons use me thus?   70

GAVESTON My lord, I cannot brook these injuries.

QUEEN Ay me, poor soul, when these begin to jar.

EDWARD [to Gaveston]
   Return it to their throats, I'll be thy warrant.°

GAVESTON Base leaden earls, that glory in your birth,°
   Go sit at home and eat your tenants' beef,   75
   And come not here to scoff at Gaveston,
   Whose mounting thoughts did never creep so low
   As to bestow a look on such as you.

LANCASTER Yet I disdain not to do this for you.
      [*He draws his sword; in the mêlée, Mortimer Junior and
      Gaveston draw also*]

EDWARD Treason, treason! Where's the traitor?°   80

PEMBROKE Here, here.°

EDWARD Convey hence Gaveston! They'll murder him.

GAVESTON [to Mortimer Junior]
   The life of thee shall salve this foul disgrace.

MORTIMER Villain, thy life, unless I miss mine aim.
      [*He wounds Gaveston*]

QUEEN Ah, furious Mortimer, what hast thou done?   85

MORTIMER No more than I would answer, were he slain.°
      [*Exit Gaveston, attended*]

EDWARD Yes, more than thou canst answer, though he live.
   Dear shall you both aby this riotous deed.°
   Out of my presence! Come not near the court!

MORTIMER I'll not be barred the court for Gaveston.   90

LANCASTER We'll hale him by the ears unto the block.

EDWARD Look to your own heads; his is sure enough.

WARWICK Look to your own crown, if you back him thus.
KENT Warwick, these words do ill beseem thy years.
EDWARD Nay, all of them conspire to cross me thus;   95
    But if I live, I'll tread upon their heads
    That think with high looks thus to tread me down.
    Come, Edmund, let's away and levy men.
    'Tis war that must abate these barons' pride.
      Exeunt the King, [Queen, and Kent, attended]
WARWICK Let's to our castles, for the king is moved.   100
MORTIMER Moved may he be, and perish in his wrath!°
LANCASTER Cousin, it is no dealing with him now.°
    He means to make us stoop by force of arms;
    And therefore let us jointly here protest
    To prosecute that Gaveston to the death.   105
MORTIMER By heaven, the abject villain shall not live.
WARWICK I'll have his blood or die in seeking it.
PEMBROKE The like oath Pembroke takes.
LANCASTER   And so doth Lancaster.
    Now send our heralds to defy the king,°
    And make the people swear to put him down.   110
      Enter a Post
MORTIMER Letters, from whence?
MESSENGER From Scotland, my lord.
      [Mortimer Junior takes and reads a letter]
LANCASTER Why, how now, cousin, how fares all our friends?
MORTIMER My uncle's taken prisoner by the Scots.
LANCASTER We'll have him ransomed, man; be of good cheer.   115
MORTIMER They rate his ransom at five thousand pound.
    Who should defray the money but the king,
    Seeing he is taken prisoner in his wars?
    I'll to the king.
LANCASTER Do, cousin, and I'll bear thee company.   120
WARWICK Meantime, my lord of Pembroke and myself
    Will to Newcastle here and gather head.°
MORTIMER About it then, and we will follow you.
LANCASTER Be resolute and full of secrecy.
WARWICK I warrant you.   125
      [Exeunt all but Mortimer Junior and Lancaster]
MORTIMER Cousin, an if he will not ransom him,
    I'll thunder such a peal into his ears
    As never subject did unto his king.

LANCASTER Content, I'll bear my part.—Holla! Who's there?
    [*Enter a Guard*]°
MORTIMER Ay, marry, such a guard as this doth well.°   130
LANCASTER Lead on the way.
GUARD Whither will your lordships?
MORTIMER Whither else but to the king?
GUARD His highness is disposed to be alone.
LANCASTER Why, so he may, but we will speak to him.   135
GUARD You may not in, my lord.
MORTIMER May we not?
    [*Enter the King and Kent*]
EDWARD How now, what noise is this?
  Who have we there? Is't you?
    [*He starts to go back*]
MORTIMER Nay, stay, my lord, I come to bring you news: 140
  Mine uncle's taken prisoner by the Scots.
EDWARD Then ransom him.
LANCASTER 'Twas in your wars; you should ransom him.
MORTIMER And you shall ransom him, or else.
KENT What, Mortimer, you will not threaten him?   145
EDWARD Quiet yourself. You shall have the broad seal,°
  To gather for him throughout the realm.
LANCASTER Your minion Gaveston hath taught you this.
MORTIMER My lord, the family of the Mortimers
  Are not so poor but, would they sell their land,   150
  Would levy men enough to anger you.
  We never beg, but use such prayers [*laying a hand on his sword*]
    as these.°
EDWARD Shall I still be haunted thus?
MORTIMER Nay, now you are here alone, I'll speak my mind.
LANCASTER And so will I, and then, my lord, farewell.   155
MORTIMER The idle triumphs, masques, lascivious shows,
  And prodigal gifts bestowed on Gaveston
  Have drawn thy treasure dry and made thee weak,
  The murmuring commons overstretchèd hath.°
LANCASTER Look for rebellion; look to be deposed.   160
  Thy garrisons are beaten out of France,
  And lame and poor lie groaning at the gates.
  The wild O'Neill, with swarms of Irish kerns,°
  Lives uncontrolled within the English pale.°
  Unto the walls of York the Scots made road,   165

And, unresisted, drave away rich spoils.°
MORTIMER The haughty Dane commands the narrow seas,°
  While in the harbour ride thy ships unrigged.
LANCASTER What foreign prince sends thee ambassadors?
MORTIMER Who loves thee but a sort of flatters?   170
LANCASTER Thy gentle queen, sole sister to Valois,°
  Complains that thou hast left her all forlorn.
MORTIMER Thy court is naked, being bereft of those
  That makes a king seem glorious to the world:
  I mean the peers, whom thou shouldst dearly love.   175
  Libels are cast again thee in the street;°
  Ballads and rhymes made of thy overthrow.
LANCASTER The northern borderers, seeing their houses burnt,
  Their wives and children slain, run up and down,
  Cursing the name of thee and Gaveston.   180
MORTIMER When wert thou in the field with banner spread?
  But once, and then thy soldiers marched like players,°
  With garish robes, not armour; and thyself,
  Bedaubed with gold, rode laughing at the rest,
  Nodding and shaking of thy spangled crest,   185
  Where women's favours hung like labels down.°
LANCASTER And thereof came it that the fleering Scots,
  To England's high disgrace, have made this jig:
      'Maids of England, sore may you mourn,
      For your lemans you have lost at Bannocksbourn,   190
        With a heave and a ho!
      What weeneth the king of England,
      So soon to have won Scotland?
        With a rumbelow.'
MORTIMER Wigmore shall fly, to set my uncle free.°   195
LANCASTER And when 'tis gone, our swords shall purchase more.°
  If ye be moved, revenge it as you can.
  Look next to see us with our ensigns spread.
    Exeunt nobles [Mortimer Junior and Lancaster]
EDWARD My swelling heart for very anger breaks.
  How oft have I been baited by these peers,   200
  And dare not be revenged, for their power is great!
  Yet shall the crowing of these cockerels
  Affright a lion? Edward, unfold thy paws,
  And let their lives' blood slake thy fury's hunger.
  If I be cruel and grow tyrannous,   205

Now let them thank themselves, and rue too late.
KENT My lord, I see your love to Gaveston
    Will be the ruin of the realm and you,
    For now the wrathful nobles threaten wars,
    And therefore, brother, banish him for ever.   210
EDWARD Art thou an enemy to my Gaveston?
KENT Ay, and it grieves me that I favoured him.
EDWARD Traitor, begone! Whine thou with Mortimer.
KENT So will I, rather than with Gaveston.
EDWARD Out of my sight, and trouble me no more.   215
KENT No marvel though thou scorn thy noble peers,
    When I thy brother am rejected thus.
EDWARD Away!
      Exit [Kent]
    Poor Gaveston, that hast no friend but me.
    Do what they can, we'll live in Tynemouth here,   220
    And, so I walk with him about the walls,°
    What care I though the earls begirt us round?
    Here comes she that's cause of all these jars.
      Enter the Queen, three Ladies [(the King's Niece and two
      Ladies-in-waiting), Gaveston,] Baldock, and Spencer
      [Junior]
QUEEN My lord, 'tis thought the earls are up in arms.
EDWARD Ay, and 'tis likewise thought you favour him.°   225
QUEEN Thus do you still suspect me without cause.
NIECE Sweet uncle, speak more kindly to the queen.
GAVESTON *[aside to Edward]*
    My lord, dissemble with her, speak her fair.
EDWARD *[to the Queen]*
    Pardon me, sweet, I forgot myself.
QUEEN Your pardon is quickly got of Isabel.   230
EDWARD The younger Mortimer is grown so brave
    That to my face he threatens civil wars.
GAVESTON Why do you not commit him to the Tower?
EDWARD I dare not, for the people love him well.
GAVESTON Why then, we'll have him privily made away.   235
EDWARD Would Lancaster and he had both caroused
    A bowl of poison to each other's health!
    But let them go, and tell me what are these.°
NIECE Two of my father's servants whilst he lived.
    May't please your grace to entertain them now?   240

EDWARD [*to Baldock*]
  Tell me, where wast thou born? What is thine arms?°
BALDOCK My name is Baldock, and my gentry°
  I fetched from Oxford, not from heraldry.
EDWARD The fitter art thou, Baldock, for my turn.
  Wait on me, and I'll see thou shalt not want.   245
BALDOCK I humbly thank your majesty.
EDWARD [*indicating Spencer Junior*]
  Knowest thou him, Gaveston?
GAVESTON   Ay, my lord,
  His name is Spencer; he is well allied.
  For my sake, let him wait upon your grace;
  Scarce shall you find a man of more desert.   250
EDWARD Then, Spencer, wait upon me; for his sake
  I'll grace thee with a higher style ere long.
SPENCER No greater titles happen unto me
  Than to be favoured of your majesty.
EDWARD [*to his Niece*]
  Cousin, this day shall be your marriage feast.   255
  And, Gaveston, think that I love thee well
  To wed thee to our niece, the only heir
  Unto the earl of Gloucester late deceased.
GAVESTON I know, my lord, many will stomach me,
  But I respect neither their love nor hate.   260
EDWARD The headstrong barons shall not limit me;
  He that I list to favour shall be great.
  Come, let's away, and when the marriage ends
  Have at the rebels and their complices.
        Exeunt

[2.3]

  Enter Lancaster, Mortimer [Junior], Warwick, Pembroke,
  [their followers, and] Kent
KENT My lords, of love to this our native land
  I come to join with you and leave the king,
  And in your quarrel and the realm's behoof
  Will be the first that shall adventure life.°
LANCASTER I fear me you are sent of policy,°   5

To undermine us with a show of love.

WARWICK He is your brother; therefore have we cause
     To cast the worst, and doubt of your revolt.°

KENT Mine honour shall be hostage of my truth.
     If that will not suffice, farewell, my lords.   10

MORTIMER Stay, Edmund. Never was Plantagenet
     False of his word, and therefore trust we thee.

PEMBROKE But what's the reason you should leave him now?

KENT I have informed the earl of Lancaster.

LANCASTER And it sufficeth. Now, my lords, know this,   15
     That Gaveston is secretly arrived
     And here in Tynemouth frolics with the king.°
     Let us with these our followers scale the walls
     And suddenly surprise them unawares.

MORTIMER I'll give the onset.

WARWICK   And I'll follow thee.   20

MORTIMER This tattered ensign of my ancestors,
     Which swept the desert shore of that Dead Sea
     Whereof we got the name of Mortimer,°
     Will I advance upon this castle walls.
     Drums, strike alarum! Raise them from their sport,   25
     And ring aloud the knell of Gaveston.

LANCASTER None be so hardy as to touch the king,
     But neither spare you Gaveston nor his friends.
               Exeunt. [*Drums are sounded*]

[2.4]

     [*Alarums.*]° *Enter the King and Spencer* [*Junior, meeting*]

EDWARD O tell me, Spencer, where is Gaveston?

SPENCER I fear me he is slain, my gracious lord.

EDWARD No, here he comes. Now let them spoil and kill.
     [*Enter*] *to them Gaveston,* [*the Queen, the King's Niece,
     and lords*]
     Fly, fly, my lords! The earls have got the hold.
     Take shipping and away to Scarborough;   5
     Spencer and I will post away by land.

GAVESTON O stay, my lord. They will not injure you.

EDWARD I will not trust them, Gaveston. Away!

GAVESTON Farewell, my lord.
EDWARD Lady, farewell.   10
NIECE Farewell, sweet uncle, till we meet again.
EDWARD Farewell, sweet Gaveston, and farewell, niece.
QUEEN No farewell to poor Isabel, thy queen?
EDWARD Yes, yes, for Mortimer, your lover's sake.
        Exeunt all but Queen Isabella
QUEEN Heavens can witness I love none but you.—   15
    From my embracements thus he breaks away.
    O, that mine arms could close this isle about,
    That I might pull him to me where I would,
    Or that these tears that drizzle from mine eyes
    Had power to mollify his stony heart,   20
    That when I had him we might never part!
        Enter the barons [Lancaster, Warwick, Mortimer Junior, and
        others]. Alarums
LANCASTER I wonder how he 'scaped.
MORTIMER   Who's this, the queen?
QUEEN Ay, Mortimer, the miserable queen,
    Whose pining heart her inward sighs have blasted
    And body with continual mourning wasted.   25
    These hands are tired with haling of my lord
    From Gaveston, from wicked Gaveston,
    And all in vain, for when I speak him fair
    He turns away and smiles upon his minion.
MORTIMER Cease to lament, and tell us where's the king?   30
QUEEN What would you with the king? Is't him you seek?
LANCASTER No, madam, but that cursèd Gaveston.
    Far be it from the thought of Lancaster
    To offer violence to his sovereign;
    We would but rid the realm of Gaveston.   35
    Tell us where he remains, and he shall die.
QUEEN He's gone by water unto Scarborough;
    Pursue him quickly, and he cannot 'scape.
    The king hath left him, and his train is small.
WARWICK Forslow no time, sweet Lancaster, let's march.°   40
MORTIMER How comes it that the king and he is parted?
QUEEN That this your army, going several ways,°
    Might be of lesser force, and with the power
    That he intendeth presently to raise
    Be easily suppressed; and therefore begone.°   45

MORTIMER Here in the river rides a Flemish hoy.
　　Let's all aboard and follow him amain.°
LANCASTER The wind that bears him hence will fill our sails.
　　Come, come, aboard. 'Tis but an hour's sailing.
MORTIMER Madam, stay you within this castle here.　　　　50
QUEEN No, Mortimer, I'll to my lord the king.
MORTIMER Nay, rather sail with us to Scarborough.
QUEEN You know the king is so suspicious
　　As, if he hear I have but talked with you,
　　Mine honour will be called in question;　　　　　　　　55
　　And therefore, gentle Mortimer, begone.
MORTIMER Madam, I cannot stay to answer you;
　　But think of Mortimer as he deserves.
　　　　[Exeunt all but the Queen]
QUEEN So well hast thou deserved, sweet Mortimer,
　　As Isabel could live with thee for ever.　　　　　　　　60
　　In vain I look for love at Edward's hand,
　　Whose eyes are fixed on none but Gaveston.
　　Yet once more I'll importune him with prayers.
　　If he be strange and not regard my words,
　　My son and I will over into France　　　　　　　　　　65
　　And to the king my brother there complain
　　How Gaveston hath robbed me of his love;
　　But yet I hope my sorrows will have end
　　And Gaveston this blessèd day be slain.
　　　　Exit

[2.5]

　　　　Enter Gaveston, pursued°
GAVESTON Yet, lusty lords, I have escaped your hands,
　　Your threats, your larums, and your hot pursuits;
　　And though divorcèd from King Edward's eyes,
　　Yet liveth Piers of Gaveston unsurprised,°
　　Breathing, in hope (*malgrado* all your beards,°　　　　5
　　That muster rebels thus against your king)
　　To see his royal sovereign once again.
　　　　Enter the nobles [*Warwick, Lancaster, Pembroke, Mortimer
　　　　Junior, with Soldiers and Attendants*]

WARWICK Upon him, soldiers. Take away his weapons.
MORTIMER [*as the Soldiers attack Gaveston*]
    Thou proud disturber of thy country's peace,
    Corrupter of thy king, cause of these broils,   10
    Base flatterer, yield! And were it not for shame,
    Shame and dishonour to a soldier's name,
    Upon my weapon's point here shouldst thou fall,
    And welter in thy gore.
LANCASTER   Monster of men,
    That, like the Greekish strumpet, trained to arms°   15
    And bloody wars so many valiant knights,
    Look for no other fortune, wretch, than death.
    King Edward is not here to buckler thee.°
WARWICK Lancaster, why talk'st thou to the slave?
    Go, soldiers, take him hence, for, by my sword,   20
    His head shall off. Gaveston, short warning
    Shall serve thy turn; it is our country's cause
    That here severely we will execute
    Upon thy person.—Hang him at a bough.
GAVESTON My lord!   25
WARWICK Soldiers, have him away.—
    But, for thou wert the favourite of a king,°
    Thou shalt have so much honour at our hands.°
GAVESTON I thank you all, my lords. Then I perceive
    That heading is one, and hanging is the other,   30
    And death is all.
        Enter Earl of Arundel
LANCASTER How now, my lord of Arundel?
ARUNDEL My lords, King Edward greets you all by me.
WARWICK Arundel, say your message.
ARUNDEL   His majesty,
    Hearing that you had taken Gaveston,   35
    Entreateth you by me yet but he may°
    See him before he dies, forwhy, he says,
    And sends you word, he knows that die he shall;
    And if you gratify his grace so far,
    He will be mindful of the courtesy.   40
WARWICK How now?
GAVESTON   Renownèd Edward, how thy name
    Revives poor Gaveston!
WARWICK   No, it needeth not.°

Arundel, we will gratify the king
In other matters; he must pardon us in this.
Soldiers, away with him.

GAVESTON   Why, my lord of Warwick,   45
Will not these delays beget my hopes?°
I know it, lords, it is this life you aim at;
Yet grant King Edward this.

MORTIMER   Shalt thou appoint
What we shall grant? Soldiers, away with him.
Thus we'll gratify the king: 50
We'll send his head by thee. Let him bestow
His tears on that, for that is all he gets
Of Gaveston, or else his senseless trunk.

LANCASTER Not so, my lord, lest he bestow more cost
In burying him than he hath ever earned.°   55

ARUNDEL My lords, it is his majesty's request,
And, in the honour of a king, he swears
He will but talk with him and send him back.

WARWICK When, can you tell? Arundel, no.°
We wot, he that the care of realm remits   60
And drives his nobles to these exigents
For Gaveston will, if he seize him once,°
Violate any promise to possess him.

ARUNDEL Then if you will not trust his grace in keep,°
My lords, I will be pledge for his return.   65

MORTIMER It is honourable in thee to offer this,
But, for we know thou art a noble gentleman,°
We will not wrong thee so
To make away a true man for a thief.

GAVESTON How mean'st thou, Mortimer? That is over-base.°   70

MORTIMER Away, base groom, robber of king's renown!
Question with thy companions and thy mates.°

PEMBROKE My lord Mortimer, and you my lords each one,
To gratify the king's request therein
Touching the sending of this Gaveston,   75
Because his majesty so earnestly
Desires to see the man before his death,
I will upon mine honour undertake
To carry him and bring him back again,
Provided this: that you, my lord of Arundel,   80
Will join with me.

WARWICK   Pembroke, what wilt thou do?
  Cause yet more bloodshed? Is it not enough
  That we have taken him, but must we now
  Leave him on 'had-I-wist' and let him go?°
PEMBROKE My lords, I will not over-woo your honours,   85
  But, if you dare trust Pembroke with the prisoner,
  Upon mine oath, I will return him back.
ARUNDEL My lord of Lancaster, what say you in this?
LANCASTER Why, I say let him go on Pembroke's word.
PEMBROKE And you, lord Mortimer?   90
MORTIMER How say you, my lord of Warwick?
WARWICK Nay, do your pleasures. I know how 'twill prove.
PEMBROKE Then give him me.
GAVESTON   Sweet sovereign, yet I come
  To see thee ere I die.
WARWICK [aside]   Yet not, perhaps,
  If Warwick's wit and policy prevail.   95
MORTIMER My lord of Pembroke, we deliver him you;
  Return him on your honour.—Sound, away!
      [Gaveston is delivered into Pembroke's custody. Trumpets
      sound. Then] exeunt all but Pembroke, Arundel, Gaveston,
      and Pembroke's men: four Soldiers, [one of them James, and
      a Horseboy]
PEMBROKE [to Arundel] My lord, you shall go with me.
  My house is not far hence, out of the way
  A little, but our men shall go along.   100
  We that have pretty wenches to our wives,°
  Sir, must not come so near and balk their lips.°
ARUNDEL 'Tis very kindly spoke, my lord of Pembroke.°
  Your honour hath an adamant of power
  To draw a prince.°
PEMBROKE   So, my lord.—Come hither, James.   105
  I do commit this Gaveston to thee.
  Be thou this night his keeper; in the morning
  We will discharge thee of thy charge. Begone.
GAVESTON Unhappy Gaveston, whither goest thou now?
      Exit [Gaveston] with [James and] Pembroke's [other] servants
HORSEBOY My lord, we'll quickly be at Cobham.   110
      Exeunt both [Pembroke and Arundel, the Horseboy leading]

[3.1]

Enter Gaveston mourning, and the Earl of Pembroke's Men
[James and three Soldiers]

GAVESTON O treacherous Warwick, thus to wrong thy friend!°

JAMES I see it is your life these arms pursue.

GAVESTON Weaponless must I fall, and die in bands?
O, must this day be period of my life?
Centre of all my bliss! An ye be men,°   5
Speed to the king.
        Enter Warwick and his company

WARWICK   My lord of Pembroke's men,
Strive you no longer; I will have that Gaveston.

JAMES Your lordship doth dishonour to yourself
And wrong our lord, your honourable friend.

WARWICK No, James, it is my country's cause I follow.—   10
Go, take the villain.
        [Gaveston is taken]
                        Soldiers, come away.
We'll make quick work. *[To James]* Commend me to your master,
My friend, and tell him that I watched it well.°
[To Gaveston] Come, let thy shadow parley with King Edward.

GAVESTON Treacherous earl, shall I not see the king?   15

WARWICK The king of heaven perhaps, no other king.—
Away!
        Exeunt Warwick and his men, with Gaveston. James remains
        with the others

JAMES Come, fellows, it booted not for us to strive.
We will in haste go certify our lord.
        Exeunt

[3.2]

Enter King Edward and Spencer [Junior, and Baldock,] with
drums and fifes

EDWARD I long to hear an answer from the barons
Touching my friend, my dearest Gaveston.

361

Ah, Spencer, not the riches of my realm
Can ransom him! Ah, he is marked to die.
I know the malice of the younger Mortimer,   5
Warwick I know is rough, and Lancaster
Inexorable, and I shall never see
My lovely Piers, my Gaveston again.
The barons overbear me with their pride.

SPENCER   Were I King Edward, England's sovereign,   10
Son to the lovely Eleanor of Spain,
Great Edward Longshanks' issue, would I bear°
These braves, this rage, and suffer uncontrolled
These barons thus to beard me in my land,
In mine own realm? My lord, pardon my speech.   15
Did you retain your father's magnanimity,°
Did you regard the honour of your name,
You would not suffer thus your majesty
Be counterbuffed of your nobility.°
Strike off their heads, and let them preach on poles.°   20
No doubt, such lessons they will teach the rest
As, by their preachments, they will profit much°
And learn obedience to their lawful king.

EDWARD   Yea, gentle Spencer, we have been too mild,
Too kind to them, but now have drawn our sword,   25
And if they send me not my Gaveston
We'll steel it on their crest and poll their tops.°

BALDOCK   This haught resolve becomes your majesty,
Not to be tied to their affection°
As though your highness were a schoolboy still   30
And must be awed and governed like a child.

> Enter Hugh Spencer (an old man, father to the young
> Spencer), with his truncheon, and Soldiers

SPENCER SENIOR   Long live my sovereign, the noble Edward,
In peace triumphant, fortunate in wars!

EDWARD   Welcome, old man. Com'st thou in Edward's aid?
Then tell thy prince of whence and what thou art.   35

SPENCER SENIOR   Lo, with a band of bowmen and of pikes,°
Brown bills and targeteers, four hundred strong,°
Sworn to defend King Edward's royal right,
I come in person to your majesty—
Spencer, the father of Hugh Spencer there,   40
Bound to your highness everlastingly

For favours done in him unto us all.°
EDWARD Thy father, Spencer?
SPENCER   True, an it like your grace,
   That pours, in lieu of all your goodness shown,°
   His life, my lord, before your princely feet.   45
EDWARD Welcome ten thousand times, old man, again.
   Spencer, this love, this kindness to thy king
   Argues thy noble mind and disposition.
   Spencer, I here create thee earl of Wiltshire,
   And daily will enrich thee with our favour,   50
   That, as the sunshine, shall reflect o'er thee.
   Beside, the more to manifest our love,
   Because we hear Lord Bruce doth sell his land,
   And that the Mortimers are in hand withal,°
   Thou shalt have crowns of us t'outbid the barons;   55
   And, Spencer, spare them not, but lay it on.—
   Soldiers, a largess, and thrice welcome all!°
SPENCER My lord, here comes the queen.
            Enter, [with a letter,] the Queen and her son [Prince
            Edward], and Levune, a Frenchman
EDWARD   Madam, what news?
QUEEN News of dishonour, lord, and discontent.
   Our friend Levune, faithful and full of trust,   60
   Informeth us, by letters and by words,
   That Lord Valois our brother, king of France,
   Because your highness hath been slack in homage,°
   Hath seizèd Normandy into his hands.
   These be the letters, this the messenger.   65
            [*She shows the letter to Edward*]
EDWARD Welcome, Levune.—Tush, Sib, if this be all,°
   Valois and I will soon be friends again.
   But to my Gaveston: shall I never see,
   Never behold thee now? Madam, in this matter
   We will employ you and your little son;   70
   You shall go parley with the king of France.
   Boy, see you bear you bravely to the king°
   And do your message with a majesty.
PRINCE Commit not to my youth things of more weight
   Than fits a prince so young as I to bear;   75
   And fear not, lord and father, heaven's great beams
   On Atlas' shoulder shall not lie more safe°

Than shall your charge committed to my trust.
QUEEN Ah, boy, this towardness makes thy mother fear°
    Thou art not marked to many days on earth.   80
EDWARD Madam, we will that you with speed be shipped,
    And this our son; Levune shall follow you
    With all the haste we can despatch him hence.
    Choose of our lords to bear you company,
    And go in peace; leave us in wars at home.°   85
QUEEN Unnatural wars, where subjects brave their king;
    God end them once! My lord, I take my leave°
    To make my preparation for France.°
      [*Exeunt Queen and Prince Edward.*] *Enter Lord Arundel*
EDWARD What, Lord Arundel, dost thou come alone?
ARUNDEL Yea, my good lord, for Gaveston is dead.   90
EDWARD Ah, traitors! Have they put my friend to death?
    Tell me, Arundel, died he ere thou cam'st,
    Or didst thou see my friend to take his death?
ARUNDEL Neither, my lord, for, as he was surprised,
    Begirt with weapons and with enemies round,   95
    I did your highness' message to them all,
    Demanding him of them—entreating rather—
    And said, upon the honour of my name,
    That I would undertake to carry him
    Unto your highness and to bring him back.   100
EDWARD And tell me, would the rebels deny me that?
SPENCER Proud recreants!
EDWARD   Yea, Spencer, traitors all.
ARUNDEL I found them at the first inexorable.
    The earl of Warwick would not bide the hearing;
    Mortimer hardly; Pembroke and Lancaster   105
    Spake least; and when they flatly had denied,
    Refusing to receive me pledge for him,°
    The earl of Pembroke mildly thus bespake:
    'My lords, because our sovereign sends for him,
    And promiseth he shall be safe returned,   110
    I will this undertake: to have him hence
    And see him re-delivered to your hands.'
EDWARD Well, and how fortunes that he came not?
SPENCER Some treason or some villainy was cause.
ARUNDEL The earl of Warwick seized him on his way;   115
    For, being delivered unto Pembroke's men,

Their lord rode home, thinking his prisoner safe;
But ere he came, Warwick in ambush lay
And bare him to his death, and in a trench
Strake off his head, and marched unto the camp.   120
SPENCER A bloody part, flatly against law of arms.°
EDWARD O, shall I speak, or shall I sigh and die?
SPENCER My lord, refer your vengeance to the sword
    Upon these barons; hearten up your men;
    Let them not unrevenged murder your friends.°   125
    Advance your standard, Edward, in the field,
    And march to fire them from their starting-holes.°
EDWARD (*kneels*) By earth, the common mother of us all,
    By heaven, and all the moving orbs thereof,°
    By this right hand, and by my father's sword,   130
    And all the honours 'longing to my crown,
    I will have heads and lives for him, as many
    As I have manors, castles, towns, and towers.
    Treacherous Warwick, traitorous Mortimer!
    If I be England's king, in lakes of gore   135
    Your headless trunks, your bodies will I trail,
    That you may drink your fill and quaff in blood,
    And stain my royal standard with the same,
    That so my bloody colours may suggest
    Remembrance of revenge immortally   140
    On your accursèd traitorous progeny,
    You villains that have slain my Gaveston.
        [*He rises*]
    And in this place of honour and of trust,
    Spencer, sweet Spencer, I adopt thee here,
    And merely of our love we do create thee°   145
    Earl of Gloucester and Lord Chamberlain,
    Despite of times, despite of enemies.
        [*Enter an Attendant who whispers to Spencer Junior*]
SPENCER My lord, here is a messenger from the barons
    Desires access unto your majesty.°
EDWARD Admit him near.   150
        [*One goes to the door.*] Enter the Herald from the barons,
        with his coat of arms°
HERALD Long live King Edward, England's lawful lord!
EDWARD So wish not they, iwis, that sent thee hither.
    Thou com'st from Mortimer and his complices.

A ranker rout of rebels never was.
Well, say thy message.   155
HERALD The barons up in arms by me salute
Your highness with long life and happiness,
And bid me say, as plainer to your grace,
That if without effusion of blood
You will this grief have ease and remedy,°   160
That from your princely person you remove
This Spencer, as a putrefying branch
That deads the royal vine whose golden leaves
Impale your princely head, your diadem,
Whose brightness such pernicious upstarts dim,°   165
Say they, and lovingly advise your grace
To cherish virtue and nobility,
And have old servitors in high esteem,
And shake off smooth dissembling flatterers.
This granted, they, their honours, and their lives   170
Are to your highness vowed and consecrate.
SPENCER Ah, traitors, will they still display their pride?
EDWARD Away! Tarry no answer, but begone.
Rebels, will they appoint their sovereign
His sports, his pleasures, and his company?   175
Yet ere thou go, see how I do divorce
Spencer from me. (*Embrace[s] Spencer*) Now get thee to thy lords,
And tell them I will come to chastise them
For murdering Gaveston. Hie thee, get thee gone.
Edward with fire and sword follows at thy heels.   180
      [*Exit the Herald*]
My lords, perceive you how these rebels swell?°
Soldiers, good hearts, defend your sovereign's right,
For now, even now, we march to make them stoop.
Away!
      Exeunt

[3.3]

Alarums, excursions, a great fight, and a retreat. Enter the
King, Spencer the father, Spencer the son, and the noblemen
of the King's side°

EDWARD Why do we sound retreat? Upon them, lords!
This day I shall pour vengeance with my sword
On those proud rebels that are up in arms
And do confront and countermand their king.

SPENCER I doubt it not, my lord, right will prevail.   5

SPENCER SENIOR 'Tis not amiss, my liege, for either part°
To breathe a while; our men, with sweat and dust
All choked well near, begin to faint for heat,
And this retire refresheth horse and man.

SPENCER Here come the rebels.   10
        Enter the barons: Mortimer [Junior], Lancaster, Warwick,
        Pembroke, and others

MORTIMER Look, Lancaster,
Yonder is Edward among his flatterers.

LANCASTER And there let him be,
Till he pay dearly for their company.

WARWICK And shall, or Warwick's sword shall smite in vain.   15

EDWARD What, rebels, do you shrink and sound retreat?

MORTIMER No, Edward, no. Thy flatterers faint and fly.

LANCASTER They'd best betimes forsake thee and their trains,
For they'll betray thee, traitors as they are.

SPENCER Traitor in thy face, rebellious Lancaster!°   20

PEMBROKE Away, base upstart. Brav'st thou nobles thus?

SPENCER SENIOR A noble attempt and honourable deed
Is it not, trow ye, to assemble aid
And levy arms against your lawful king?

EDWARD For which ere long their heads shall satisfy,   25
T'appease the wrath of their offended king.

MORTIMER Then, Edward, thou wilt fight it to the last,
And rather bathe thy sword in subjects' blood
Than banish that pernicious company?

EDWARD Ay, traitors all, rather than thus be braved,   30
Make England's civil towns huge heaps of stones,
And ploughs to go about our palace gates.

WARWICK A desperate and unnatural resolution.

Alarum! To the fight!°
Saint George for England and the barons' right!°   35
EDWARD Saint George for England and King Edward's right!
    [*Alarums. Exeunt on two sides*]

[3.4]

*Enter Edward [and his followers, including the Spencers,
Levune, and Baldock], with the barons° [including Warwick
and Lancaster] captives, [along with Kent]°*

EDWARD Now, lusty lords, now, not by chance of war,
    But justice of the quarrel and the cause,
    Vailed is your pride. Methinks you hang the heads,
    But we'll advance them, traitors. Now 'tis time°
    To be avenged on you for all your braves   5
    And for the murder of my dearest friend,
    To whom right well you knew our soul was knit:
    Good Piers of Gaveston, my sweet favourite.
    Ah, rebels, recreants, you made him away!°
KENT Brother, in regard of thee and of thy land   10
    Did they remove that flatterer from thy throne.
EDWARD So, sir, you have spoke. Away, avoid our presence.
    [*Exit Kent*]
    Accursèd wretches, was't in regard of us,
    When we had sent our messenger to request
    He might be spared to come to speak with us,   15
    And Pembroke undertook for his return,
    That thou, proud Warwick, watched the prisoner,°
    Poor Piers, and headed him against law of arms?
    For which thy head shall overlook the rest°
    As much as thou in rage outwent'st the rest.   20
WARWICK Tyrant, I scorn thy threats and menaces.
    'Tis but temporal that thou canst inflict.
LANCASTER The worst is death, and better die to live°
    Than live in infamy under such a king.
EDWARD Away with them, my lord of Winchester.°   25
    These lusty leaders, Warwick and Lancaster,
    I charge you roundly: off with both their heads.
    Away!
WARWICK Farewell, vain world.

LANCASTER   Sweet Mortimer, farewell.
    [Exeunt Warwick and Lancaster, guarded, led off by Spencer
    Senior]
MORTIMER England, unkind to thy nobility,   30
    Groan for this grief! Behold how thou art maimed.
EDWARD Go take that haughty Mortimer to the Tower.
    There see him safe bestowed, and, for the rest,
    Do speedy execution on them all.
    Begone!   35
MORTIMER What, Mortimer, can ragged stony walls
    Immure thy virtue that aspires to heaven?°
    No, Edward, England's scourge, it may not be;
    Mortimer's hope surmounts his fortune far.°
    [Exit Mortimer Junior, guarded]
EDWARD
    Sound drums and trumpets! March with me, my friends.   40
    Edward this day hath crowned him king anew.
    [Drums and trumpets sound.] Exeunt all except Spencer
    Junior, Levune, and Baldock
SPENCER Levune, the trust that we repose in thee
    Begets the quiet of King Edward's land.°
    Therefore begone in haste, and with advice°
    Bestow that treasure on the lords of France,°
    That therewith all enchanted, like the guard   45
    That suffered Jove to pass in showers of gold
    To Danaë, all aid may be denied°
    To Isabel the queen—that now in France
    Makes friends—to cross the seas with her young son   50
    And step into his father's regiment.
LEVUNE That's it these barons and the subtle queen
    Long levelled at.°
BALDOCK   Yea, but, Levune, thou seest
    These barons lay their heads on blocks together.°
    What they intend, the hangman frustrates clean.   55
LEVUNE Have you no doubts, my lords. I'll clap so close°
    Among the lords of France with England's gold
    That Isabel shall make her plaints in vain
    And France shall be obdurate with her tears.°
SPENCER Then make for France amain, Levune, away!   60
    Proclaim King Edward's wars and victories.
    Exeunt

[4.1]

Enter Edmund [the Earl of Kent]

KENT Fair blows the wind for France. Blow, gentle gale,
  Till Edmund be arrived for England's good.
  Nature, yield to my country's cause in this.°
  A brother, no, a butcher of thy friends,
  Proud Edward, dost thou banish me thy presence?   5
  But I'll to France, and cheer the wrongèd queen,
  And certify what Edward's looseness is.
  Unnatural king, to slaughter noble men
  And cherish flatterers!
  Mortimer, I stay thy sweet escape;   10
  Stand gracious, gloomy night, to his device!°

Enter Mortimer [Junior] disguised

MORTIMER Holla! Who walketh there? Is't you, my lord?

KENT Mortimer, 'tis I.
  But hath thy potion wrought so happily?°

MORTIMER It hath, my lord. The warders all asleep,   15
  I thank them, gave me leave to pass in peace.
  But hath your grace got shipping unto France?

KENT Fear it not.

Exeunt

[4.2]

Enter the Queen and her son [Prince Edward]

QUEEN Ah, boy, our friends do fail us all in France,
  The lords are cruel, and the king unkind.
  What shall we do?

PRINCE   Madam, return to England,
  And please my father well, and then a fig
  For all my uncle's friendship here in France.°   5
  I warrant you, I'll win his highness quickly;
  'A loves me better than a thousand Spencers.

QUEEN Ah, boy, thou art deceived, at least in this,
  To think that we can yet be tuned together.

No, no, we jar too far. Unkind Valois,°   10
Unhappy Isabel! When France rejects,°
Whither, O, whither dost thou bend thy steps?
    Enter Sir John of Hainault
SIR JOHN Madam, what cheer?
QUEEN   Ah, good Sir John of Hainault,
Never so cheerless nor so far distressed.
SIR JOHN I hear, sweet lady, of the king's unkindness.   15
But droop not, madam; noble minds contemn
Despair. Will your grace with me to Hainault
And there stay time's advantage with your son?—°
How say you, my lord, will you go with your friends
And shake off all our fortunes equally?°   20
PRINCE So pleaseth the queen my mother, me it likes.
The king of England nor the court of France
Shall have me from my gracious mother's side
Till I be strong enough to break a staff,°
And then have at the proudest Spencer's head.   25
SIR JOHN Well said, my lord.
QUEEN O, my sweet heart, how do I moan thy wrongs,
Yet triumph in the hope of thee, my joy.
Ah, sweet Sir John, even to the utmost verge
Of Europe, or the shore of Tanaïs,°   30
Will we with thee to Hainault, so we will.
The marquis is a noble gentleman;
His grace, I dare presume, will welcome me.
But who are these?
    Enter Edmund [Earl of Kent] and Mortimer [Junior]
KENT   Madam, long may you live,
Much happier than your friends in England do.   35
QUEEN Lord Edmund and Lord Mortimer alive?
Welcome to France. [*To Mortimer*] The news was here, my lord,
That you were dead, or very near your death.
MORTIMER Lady, the last was truest of the twain,
But Mortimer, reserved for better hap,°   40
Hath shaken off the thraldom of the Tower,
    [*To Prince Edward*]
And lives t'advance your standard, good my lord.
PRINCE How mean you, an the king my father lives?°
No, my Lord Mortimer, not I, I trow.
QUEEN Not, son? Why not? I would it were no worse.°   45

But, gentle lords, friendless we are in France.

MORTIMER Monsieur le Grand, a noble friend of yours,
Told us at our arrival all the news:
How hard the nobles, how unkind the king
Hath showed himself. But, madam, right makes room   50
Where weapons want; and, though a many friends
Are made away—as Warwick, Lancaster,
And others of our party and faction—
Yet have we friends, assure your grace, in England
Would cast up caps and clap their hands for joy°   55
To see us there appointed for our foes.°

KENT Would all were well, and Edward well reclaimed
For England's honour, peace, and quietness!

MORTIMER But by the sword, my lord, it must be deserved.°
The king will ne'er forsake his flatterers.   60

SIR JOHN My lords of England, sith the ungentle king
Of France refuseth to give aid of arms
To this distressèd queen his sister here,
Go you with her to Hainault. Doubt ye not
We will find comfort, money, men, and friends   65
Ere long to bid the English king a base.°
How say, young prince, what think you of the match?

PRINCE I think King Edward will outrun us all.

QUEEN Nay, son, not so, and you must not discourage
Your friends that are so forward in your aid.   70

KENT Sir John of Hainault, pardon us, I pray.
These comforts that you give our woeful queen
Bind us in kindness all at your command.

QUEEN Yea, gentle brother, and the God of heaven°
Prosper your happy motion, good Sir John!   75

MORTIMER This noble gentleman, forward in arms,°
Was born, I see, to be our anchor-hold.°
Sir John of Hainault, be it thy renown
That England's queen and nobles in distress
Have been by thee restored and comforted.   80

SIR JOHN Madam, along, and you, my lord, with me,
That England's peers may Hainault's welcome see.
      [*Exeunt*]

[4.3]

Enter the King, Arundel, the two Spencers, with others

EDWARD Thus after many threats of wrathful war
  Triumpheth England's Edward with his friends;
  And triumph Edward, with his friends uncontrolled.°
  My lord of Gloucester, do you hear the news?
SPENCER What news, my lord?   5
EDWARD Why, man, they say there is great execution
  Done through the realm. My lord of Arundel,
  You have the note, have you not?
ARUNDEL [*producing a note*]
  From the lieutenant of the Tower, my lord.
EDWARD I pray let us see it. What have we there?   10
  Read it, Spencer.
      Spencer reads the names [of those executed]°
  Why so, they barked apace a month ago;
  Now, on my life, they'll neither bark nor bite.
  Now, sirs, the news from France. Gloucester, I trow
  The lords of France love England's gold so well   15
  As Isabella gets no aid from thence.
  What now remains? Have you proclaimed, my lord,
  Reward for them can bring in Mortimer?
SPENCER My lord, we have, and if he be in England,
  'A will be had ere long, I doubt it not.   20
EDWARD 'If', dost thou say? Spencer, as true as death,
  He is in England's ground. Our port-masters
  Are not so careless of their king's command.
      Enter a Post [with a letter]
  How now, what news with thee? From whence come these?
POST Letters, my lord, and tidings forth of France,   25
  To you, my lord of Gloucester, from Levune.
EDWARD Read.
SPENCER (*reads the letter*) 'My duty to your honour premised,° etc.
  I have, according to instructions in that behalf, dealt with the king
  of France his° lords, and effected that the queen, all discontented   30
  and discomforted, is gone; whither, if you ask, with Sir John of
  Hainault, brother to the marquis, into Flanders. With them are
  gone Lord Edmund and the Lord Mortimer, having in their
  company divers of your nation and others; and, as constant report

goeth, they intend to give King Edward battle in England sooner   35
than he can look for them. This is all the news of import.
                              Your honour's in all service, Levune.'
EDWARD Ah, villains, hath that Mortimer escaped?
  With him is Edmund gone associate?
  And will Sir John of Hainault lead the round?   40
  Welcome, i' God's name, madam, and your son.
  England shall welcome you and all your rout.
  Gallop apace, bright Phoebus, through the sky,
  And dusky night, in rusty iron car,
  Between you both shorten the time, I pray,   45
  That I may see that most desirèd day
  When we may meet these traitors in the field.
  Ah, nothing grieves me but my little boy
  Is thus misled to countenance their ills.
  Come, friends, to Bristol, there to make us strong;   50
  And, winds, as equal be to bring them in
  As you injurious were to bear them forth.°
      [*Exeunt*]

[4.4]

  *Enter the Queen, her son [Prince Edward], Edmund [Earl of
  Kent], Mortimer [Junior], and Sir John [of Hainault]*
QUEEN Now, lords, our loving friends and countrymen,
  Welcome to England all with prosperous winds.
  Our kindest friends in Belgia have we left°
  To cope with friends at home—a heavy case,
  When force to force is knit, and sword and glaive°   5
  In civil broils makes kin and countrymen
  Slaughter themselves in others, and their sides
  With their own weapons gored. But what's the help?°
  Misgoverned kings are cause of all this wrack,
  And, Edward, thou art one among them all   10
  Whose looseness hath betrayed thy land to spoil
  And made the channels overflow with blood.
  Of thine own people patron shouldst thou be,
  But thou—
MORTIMER Nay, madam, if you be a warrior,   15

Ye must not grow so passionate in speeches.
Lords, sith that we are by sufferance of heaven
Arrived and armèd in this prince's right,
Here for our country's cause swear we to him
All homage, fealty, and forwardness;   20
And, for the open wrongs and injuries
Edward hath done to us, his queen, and land,
We come in arms to wreck it with the sword,
That England's queen in peace may repossess
Her dignities and honours, and withal   25
We may remove these flatterers from the king
That havocs England's wealth and treasury.
SIR JOHN Sound trumpets, my lord, and forward let us march.
Edward will think we come to flatter him.°
KENT I would he never had been flattered more.°   30
          [*Trumpets sound. Exeunt*]

[4.5]

          *Enter the King, Baldock, and Spencer the son, flying about
          the stage*
SPENCER Fly, fly, my lord! The queen is over-strong;
Her friends do multiply, and yours do fail.
Shape we our course to Ireland, there to breathe.°
EDWARD What, was I born to fly and run away,
And leave the Mortimers conquerors behind?
Give me my horse, and let's r'enforce our troops   5
And in this bed of honour die with fame.
BALDOCK O no, my lord, this princely resolution
Fits not the time. Away! We are pursued.
          [*Exeunt*]

[4.6]

          [*Enter*] *Edmund* [*Earl of Kent*] *alone, with a sword and target*
KENT This way he fled, but I am come too late.
Edward, alas, my heart relents for thee.

Proud traitor, Mortimer, why dost thou chase
Thy lawful king, thy sovereign, with thy sword?
Vile wretch, and why hast thou, of all unkind,°   5
Borne arms against thy brother and thy king?
Rain showers of vengeance on my cursèd head,
Thou God, to whom in justice it belongs
To punish this unnatural revolt!
Edward, this Mortimer aims at thy life;   10
O, fly him, then! But, Edmund, calm this rage.
Dissemble or thou diest, for Mortimer
And Isabel do kiss while they conspire;
And yet she bears a face of love, forsooth.
Fie on that love that hatcheth death and hate!   15
Edmund, away. Bristol to Longshanks' blood
Is false. Be not found single for suspect;°
Proud Mortimer pries near into thy walks.
        Enter the Queen, Mortimer [Junior], the young Prince
        [Edward], and Sir John of Hainault
QUEEN Successful battles gives the God of kings°
        To them that fight in right and fear his wrath.   20
        Since then successfully we have prevailed,
        Thanks be heaven's great architect and you.
        Ere farther we proceed, my noble lords,
        We here create our well-belovèd son,
        Of love and care unto his royal person,°   25
        Lord Warden of the realm; and sith the Fates°
        Have made his father so infortunate,
        Deal you, my lords, in this, my loving lords,°
        As to your wisdoms fittest seems in all.
KENT   Madam, without offence if I may ask,   30
        How will you deal with Edward in his fall?
PRINCE Tell me, good uncle, what Edward do you mean?
KENT   Nephew, your father; I dare not call him king.
MORTIMER My lord of Kent, what needs these questions?
        'Tis not in her controlment, nor in ours,   35
        But as the realm and Parliament shall please,
        So shall your brother be disposèd of.
            [Aside to the Queen]
        I like not this relenting mood in Edmund.
        Madam, 'tis good to look to him betimes.

QUEEN [*to Mortimer Junior*]
    My lord, the Mayor of Bristol knows our mind.°   40
MORTIMER Yea, madam, and they 'scape not easily
    That fled the field.
QUEEN   Baldock is with the king;
    A goodly chancellor, is he not, my lord?°
SIR JOHN So are the Spencers, the father and the son.
KENT [*aside*] This, Edward, is the ruin of the realm.°   45
        Enter Rice ap Howell° and the Mayor of Bristol, with
        Spencer the father [*prisoner, and guards*]
RICE God save Queen Isabel and her princely son!
    Madam, the mayor and citizens of Bristol,
    In sign of love and duty to this presence,°
    Present by me this traitor to the state:
    Spencer, the father to that wanton Spencer   50
    That like the lawless Catiline of Rome°
    Revelled in England's wealth and treasury.
QUEEN We thank you all.
MORTIMER   Your loving care in this
    Deserveth princely favours and rewards.
    But where's the king and the other Spencer fled?   55
RICE Spencer the son, created earl of Gloucester,
    Is with that smooth-tongued scholar Baldock gone
    And shipped but late for Ireland with the king.
MORTIMER Some whirlwind fetch them back or sink them all!°
    They shall be started thence, I doubt it not.°   60
PRINCE Shall I not see the king my father yet?
KENT [*aside*] Unhappy Edward, chased from England's bounds!
SIR JOHN Madam, what resteth? Why stand ye in a muse?°
QUEEN I rue my lord's ill fortune; but alas,
    Care of my country called me to this war.   65
MORTIMER Madam, have done with care and sad complaint;
    Your king hath wronged your country and himself,
    And we must seek to right it as we may.
    Meanwhile, have hence this rebel to the block.
        [*To Spencer Senior*]
    Your lordship cannot privilege your head.°   70
SPENCER SENIOR 'Rebel' is he that fights against his prince;°
    So fought not they that fought in Edward's right.
MORTIMER Take him away, he prates.

[Spencer Senior is led off]
                                    You, Rice ap Howell,
Shall do good service to her majesty,
Being of countenance in your country here,°   75
To follow these rebellious runagates.
We in mean while, madam, must take advice
How Baldock, Spencer, and their complices
May in their fall be followed to their end.
          Exeunt

[4.7]

*Enter the Abbot, Monks, [King] Edward, Spencer [Junior],
and Baldock [disguised in religious garb]*

ABBOT Have you no doubt, my lord, have you no fear.
    As silent and as careful will we be
    To keep your royal person safe with us,
    Free from suspect and fell invasion
    Of such as have your majesty in chase,   5
    Yourself, and those your chosen company,
    As danger of this stormy time requires.
EDWARD Father, thy face should harbour no deceit.
    O, hadst thou ever been a king, thy heart,
    Pierced deeply with sense of my distress,   10
    Could not but take compassion of my state.
    Stately and proud, in riches and in train,
    Whilom I was, powerful and full of pomp;
    But what is he whom rule and empery°
    Have not in life or death made miserable?   15
    Come, Spencer, come, Baldock, come sit down by me;
    Make trial now of that philosophy
    That in our famous nurseries of arts°
    Thou sucked'st from Plato and from Aristotle.
    Father, this life contemplative is heaven.   20
    O, that I might this life in quiet lead!
    But we, alas, are chased, and you my friends;
    Your lives and my dishonour they pursue.
    Yet, gentle monks, for treasure, gold, nor fee
    Do you betray us and our company.   25

A MONK Your grace may sit secure if none but we°
    Do wot of your abode.
SPENCER Not one alive; but shrewdly I suspect
    A gloomy fellow in a mead below.°
    'A gave a long look after us, my lord,   30
    And all the land, I know, is up in arms—
    Arms that pursue our lives with deadly hate.
BALDOCK We were embarked for Ireland, wretched we,
    With awkward winds and sore tempests driven,
    To fall on shore and here to pine in fear°   35
    Of Mortimer and his confederates.
EDWARD Mortimer! Who talks of Mortimer?
    Who wounds me with the name of Mortimer,
    That bloody man? Good father, on thy lap
    Lay I this head, laden with mickle care.   40
        [*He rests his head on the Abbot's lap*]
    O, might I never open these eyes again,
    Never again lift up this drooping head,
    O, never more lift up this dying heart!
SPENCER Look up, my lord. Baldock, this drowsiness
    Betides no good; here even we are betrayed.   45
        Enter, with Welsh hooks, [Soldiers,] Rice ap Howell, a
        Mower, and the Earl of Leicester
MOWER Upon my life, those be the men ye seek.
RICE Fellow, enough.—My lord, I pray be short.°
    A fair commission warrants what we do.
LEICESTER [*aside*]
    The queen's commission, urged by Mortimer.
    What cannot gallant Mortimer with the queen?   50
    Alas, see where he sits and hopes unseen°
    T'escape their hands that seek to reave his life.
    Too true it is, *Quem dies vidit veniens superbum,*
    Hunc dies vidit fugiens iacentem.°
    But, Leicester, leave to grow so passionate.°   55
        [*To Spencer Junior and Baldock*]
    Spencer and Baldock, by no other names°
    I arrest you of high treason here.
    Stand not on titles, but obey th'arrest;°
    'Tis in the name of Isabel the queen.—
    My lord, why droop you thus?   60
EDWARD O day, the last of all my bliss on earth,

Centre of all misfortune! O my stars!
Why do you lour unkindly on a king?
Comes Leicester, then, in Isabella's name
To take my life, my company from me? 65
Here, man, rip up this panting breast of mine
And take my heart in rescue of my friends.°

RICE Away with them.

SPENCER [*To Leicester*] It may become thee yet
To let us take our farewell of his grace.

ABBOT My heart with pity earns to see this sight—° 70
A king to bear these words and proud commands.

EDWARD Spencer, ah, sweet Spencer, thus then must we part?

SPENCER We must, my lord; so will the angry heavens.°

EDWARD Nay, so will hell and cruel Mortimer.
The gentle heavens have not to do in this. 75

BALDOCK My lord, it is in vain to grieve or storm.
Here humbly of your grace we take our leaves.
Our lots are cast; I fear me, so is thine.

EDWARD In heaven we may, in earth never shall we meet.
And, Leicester, say, what shall become of us? 80

LEICESTER Your majesty must go to Killingworth.°

EDWARD 'Must'! 'Tis somewhat hard when kings 'must' go.

LEICESTER Here is a litter ready for your grace
That waits your pleasure, and the day grows old.

RICE As good be gone as stay and be benighted. 85

EDWARD A litter hast thou? Lay me in a hearse,
And to the gates of hell convey me hence;
Let Pluto's bells ring out my fatal knell,
And hags howl for my death at Charon's shore,°
For friends hath Edward none, but these, and these,° 90
And these must die under a tyrant's sword.°

RICE My lord, be going. Care not for these,
For we shall see them shorter by the heads.

EDWARD Well, that shall be shall be. Part we must,°
Sweet Spencer; gentle Baldock, part we must. 95
    [*He throws aside his robes*]
Hence, feignèd weeds! Unfeignèd are my woes.
Father, farewell. Leicester, thou stay'st for me,
And go I must. Life, farewell, with my friends.°
    Exeunt Edward [*guarded*] *and Leicester*

SPENCER O, is he gone? Is noble Edward gone,

Parted from hence, never to see us more?   100
Rend, sphere of heaven, and fire, forsake thy orb;°
Earth, melt to air! Gone is my sovereign,
Gone, gone, alas, never to make return.
BALDOCK Spencer, I see our souls are fleeted hence;
We are deprived the sunshine of our life.   105
Make for a new life, man; throw up thy eyes
And heart and hand to heaven's immortal throne;
Pay nature's debt with cheerful countenance.
Reduce we all our lessons unto this:
To die, sweet Spencer, therefore live we all;   110
Spencer, all live to die, and rise to fall.°
RICE Come, come, keep these preachments till you come to the place
appointed.° You, and such as you are, have made wise work in
England.—Will your lordships° away?
MOWER Your worship, I trust, will remember me?°   115
RICE Remember thee, fellow? What else?° Follow me to the town.
    [*Exeunt, with Spencer Junior and Baldock under guard*]

Enter the King [wearing the crown], Leicester, with a Bishop
[of Winchester, and Trussell] for the crown, [with Attendants]

LEICESTER Be patient, good my lord; cease to lament.
  Imagine Killingworth Castle were your court,
  And that you lay for pleasure here a space,
  Not of compulsion or necessity.
EDWARD Leicester, if gentle words might comfort me,   5
  Thy speeches long ago had eased my sorrows,
  For kind and loving hast thou always been.
  The griefs of private men are soon allayed,
  But not of kings. The forest deer, being struck,
  Runs to an herb that closeth up the wounds,°   10
  But when the imperial lion's flesh is gored,
  He rends and tears it with his wrathful paw,
  And, highly scorning that the lowly earth
  Should drink his blood, mounts up into the air;°
  And so it fares with me, whose dauntless mind   15
  The ambitious Mortimer would seek to curb,
  And that unnatural queen, false Isabel,
  That thus hath pent and mewed me in a prison.°
  For such outrageous passions cloy my soul
  As with the wings of rancour and disdain°   20
  Full often am I soaring up to heaven,
  To plain me to the gods against them both;°
  But when I call to mind I am a king,
  Methinks I should revenge me of the wrongs
  That Mortimer and Isabel have done.   25
  But what are kings, when regiment is gone,
  But perfect shadows in a sunshine day?°
  My nobles rule, I bear the name of king;
  I wear the crown but am controlled by them,
  By Mortimer and my unconstant queen,   30
  Who spots my nuptial bed with infamy,
  Whilst I am lodged within this cave of care,
  Where sorrow at my elbow still attends
  To company my heart with sad laments
  That bleeds within me for this strange exchange.°   35

But tell me, must I now resign my crown
To make usurping Mortimer a king?
WINCHESTER Your grace mistakes; it is for England's good
And princely Edward's right we crave the crown.
EDWARD No, 'tis for Mortimer, not Edward's head,   40
For he's a lamb encompassèd by wolves
Which in a moment will abridge his life.
But if proud Mortimer do wear this crown,
Heavens turn it to a blaze of quenchless fire,°
Or, like the snaky wreath of Tisiphon,°   45
Engirt the temples of his hateful head!
So shall not England's vine be perishèd,°
But Edward's name survives, though Edward dies.
LEICESTER My lord, why waste you thus the time away?
They stay your answer. Will you yield your crown?   50
EDWARD Ah, Leicester, weigh how hardly I can brook°
To lose my crown and kingdom without cause,°
To give ambitious Mortimer my right,
That like a mountain overwhelms my bliss,°
In which extreme my mind here murdered is.   55
But what the heavens appoint, I must obey.
        [*He takes off the crown*]
Here, take my crown, the life of Edward too!
Two kings in England cannot reign at once.
But stay a while. Let me be king till night,
That I may gaze upon this glittering crown;   60
So shall my eyes receive their last content,
My head the latest honour due to it,
And jointly both yield up their wishèd right.°
Continue ever, thou celestial sun;
Let never silent night possess this clime;   65
Stand still, you watches of the element;°
All times and seasons, rest you at a stay,°
That Edward may be still fair England's king.
But day's bright beams doth vanish fast away,
And needs I must resign my wishèd crown.°   70
Inhuman creatures, nursed with tiger's milk,
Why gape you for your sovereign's overthrow?
My diadem, I mean, and guiltless life.
        [*He puts the crown back on*]
See, monsters, see, I'll wear my crown again.

What, fear you not the fury of your king?   75
But, hapless Edward, thou art fondly led;°
They pass not for thy frowns as late they did,
But seeks to make a new-elected king,
Which fills my mind with strange despairing thoughts,
Which thoughts are martyrèd with endless torments,   80
And in this torment comfort find I none
But that I feel the crown upon my head,
And therefore let me wear it yet a while.

TRUSSELL My lord, the Parliament must have present news,
And therefore say, will you resign or no?   85
      The King rageth

EDWARD I'll not resign, but whilst I live be king.°
Traitors, begone, and join you with Mortimer!
Elect, conspire, install, do what you will;
Their blood and yours shall seal these treacheries.°

WINCHESTER This answer we'll return, and so farewell.   90
    [Winchester and Trussell start to go]

LEICESTER *[to Edward]*
Call them again, my lord, and speak them fair,
For if they go the prince shall lose his right.

EDWARD Call thou them back. I have no power to speak.

LEICESTER *[to Winchester]*
My lord, the king is willing to resign.

WINCHESTER If he be not, let him choose.   95

EDWARD O, would I might! But heavens and earth conspire
To make me miserable. Here, receive my crown.
    [He starts to give them the crown]
Receive it? No, these innocent hands of mine
Shall not be guilty of so foul a crime.
He of you all that most desires my blood,   100
And will be called the murderer of a king,
Take it. What, are you moved? Pity you me?
Then send for unrelenting Mortimer,
And Isabel, whose eyes, being turned to steel,
Will sooner sparkle fire than shed a tear.   105
Yet stay, for rather than I will look on them,
Here, here.
    [He resigns the crown]
        Now, sweet God of heaven,
Make me despise this transitory pomp

And sit for aye enthronizèd in heaven!
Come, Death, and with thy fingers close my eyes, 110
Or if I live, let me forget myself.
WINCHESTER My lord—°
EDWARD Call me not lord. Away, out of my sight!
Ah, pardon me, grief makes me lunatic.
Let not that Mortimer protect my son;° 115
More safety is there in a tiger's jaws
Than his embracements. Bear this to the queen,
        [*He gives a handkerchief*]
Wet with my tears and dried again with sighs;
If with the sight thereof she be not moved,
Return it back and dip it in my blood. 120
Commend me to my son, and bid him rule
Better than I. Yet how have I transgressed,
Unless it be with too much clemency?
TRUSSELL And thus most humbly do we take our leave.
EDWARD Farewell.
        [*Exeunt Bishop of Winchester and Trussell*]
                        I know the next news that they bring 125
Will be my death, and welcome shall it be;
To wretched men death is felicity.
        Enter Berkeley, [who gives Leicester a letter]
LEICESTER Another post. What news bring he?°
        [*He reads the letter*]
EDWARD Such news as I expect. Come, Berkeley, come,
And tell thy message to my naked breast.° 130
BERKELEY My lord, think not a thought so villainous
Can harbour in a man of noble birth.
To do your highness service and devoir,
And save you from your foes, Berkeley would die.
LEICESTER My lord, the council of the queen commands 135
That I resign my charge.
EDWARD And who must keep me now? Must you, my lord?
BERKELEY Ay, my most gracious lord, so 'tis decreed.
        [*He shows the letter to the King*]
EDWARD By Mortimer, whose name is written here.
Well may I rend his name that rends my heart! 140
        [*He tears the letter*]
This poor revenge hath something eased my mind.
So may his limbs be torn, as is this paper!

Hear me, immortal Jove, and grant it too.
BERKELEY Your grace must hence with me to Berkeley straight.
EDWARD Whither you will; all places are alike,   145
And every earth is fit for burial.
LEICESTER [*to Berkeley*]
Favour him, my lord, as much as lieth in you.°
BERKELEY Even so betide my soul as I use him.
EDWARD Mine enemy hath pitied my estate,°
And that's the cause that I am now removed.   150
BERKELEY And thinks your grace that Berkeley will be cruel?
EDWARD I know not, but of this am I assured:
That death ends all, and I can die but once.
Leicester, farewell.
LEICESTER Not yet, my lord. I'll bear you on your way.   155
        Exeunt

[5.2]

Enter Mortimer [*Junior*] *and Queen Isabel*
MORTIMER Fair Isabel, now have we our desire:
The proud corrupters of the light-brained king
Have done their homage to the lofty gallows,
And he himself lies in captivity.
Be ruled by me, and we will rule the realm.°   5
In any case, take heed of childish fear,
For now we hold an old wolf by the ears
That, if he slip, will seize upon us both
And grip the sorer, being gripped himself.°
Think therefore, madam, that imports us much°   10
To erect your son with all the speed we may°
And that I be Protector over him,
For our behoof will bear the greater sway
Whenas a king's name shall be under writ.°
QUEEN Sweet Mortimer, the life of Isabel,   15
Be thou persuaded that I love thee well;
And therefore, so the prince my son be safe,°
Whom I esteem as dear as these mine eyes,
Conclude against his father what thou wilt
And I myself will willingly subscribe.   20

MORTIMER First would I hear news that he were deposed,
And then let me alone to handle him.
>*Enter Messenger [with a letter, and then the Bishop of*
>*Winchester° with the crown]*
Letters, from whence?
MESSENGER [*presenting the letter*]
>   From Killingworth, my lord.
QUEEN How fares my lord the king?
MESSENGER In health, madam, but full of pensiveness.   25
QUEEN Alas, poor soul, would I could ease his grief.—
Thanks, gentle Winchester. [*To the Messenger*]   Sirrah, begone.°
>*[Exit Messenger]*
WINCHESTER The king hath willingly resigned his crown.
QUEEN O happy news! Send for the prince my son.
WINCHESTER
Further, ere this letter was sealed, Lord Berkeley came,°   30
So that he now is gone from Killingworth,°
And we have heard that Edmund laid a plot
To set his brother free; no more but so.°
The lord of Berkeley is so pitiful°
As Leicester that had charge of him before.   35
QUEEN Then let some other be his guardian.
MORTIMER Let me alone. Here is the privy seal.°
>*[Exit the Bishop of Winchester. Mortimer calls offstage]*
Who's there? Call hither Gurney and Matrevis.—
To dash the heavy-headed Edmund's drift,°
Berkeley shall be discharged, the king removed,°   40
And none but we shall know where he lieth.
QUEEN But, Mortimer, as long as he survives,
What safety rests for us, or for my son?
MORTIMER Speak, shall he presently be dispatched and die?
QUEEN I would he were, so it were not by my means.   45
>*Enter Matrevis and Gurney*
MORTIMER Enough.
>*[He speaks out of the Queen's hearing]*
Matrevis, write a letter presently
Unto the lord of Berkeley from ourself,
That he resign the king to thee and Gurney,
And when 'tis done we will subscribe our name.   50
MATREVIS It shall be done, my lord.
>*[Matrevis writes the letter]*

MORTIMER   Gurney.
GURNEY   My lord.
MORTIMER As thou intendest to rise by Mortimer,
   Who now makes Fortune's wheel turn as he please,
   Seek all the means thou canst to make him droop,°
   And neither give him kind word nor good look.   55
GURNEY I warrant you, my lord.
MORTIMER And this above the rest: because we hear
   That Edmund casts to work his liberty,
   Remove him still from place to place by night
   Till at the last he come to Killingworth   60
   And then from thence to Berkeley back again;
   And by the way, to make him fret the more,
   Speak curstly to him, and in any case
   Let no man comfort him if he chance to weep,
   But amplify his grief with bitter words.   65
MATREVIS Fear not, my lord, we'll do as you command.
MORTIMER So now away. Post thitherwards amain.
QUEEN [*joining the conversation*]
   Whither goes this letter? To my lord the king?°
   Commend me humbly to his majesty,
   And tell him that I labour all in vain   70
   To ease his grief and work his liberty;
   And bear him this as witness of my love.
     [*She gives Matrevis a ring*]
MATREVIS I will, madam.
     Exeunt Matrevis and Gurney. Isabel and Mortimer remain.
     Enter the young Prince [Edward], and the earl of Kent
     talking with him. [Mortimer and the Queen speak apart]
MORTIMER Finely dissembled. Do so still, sweet queen.
   Here comes the young prince, with the Earl of Kent.   75
QUEEN Something he whispers in his childish ears.
MORTIMER If he have such access unto the prince,
   Our plots and stratagems will soon be dashed.
QUEEN Use Edmund friendly, as if all were well.
MORTIMER [*aloud to Kent*]
   How fares my honourable lord of Kent?   80
KENT In health, sweet Mortimer. How fares your grace?
QUEEN Well, if my lord your brother were enlarged.°
KENT I hear of late he hath deposed himself.
QUEEN The more my grief.

MORTIMER And mine.   85
KENT [*aside*] Ah, they do dissemble.
QUEEN Sweet son, come hither. I must talk with thee.
      [*She takes Prince Edward aside*]
MORTIMER [*to Kent*]
    Thou being his uncle and the next of blood,
    Do look to be Protector over the prince.
KENT Not I, my lord. Who should protect the son   90
    But she that gave him life, I mean the queen?
PRINCE Mother, persuade me not to wear the crown.
    Let him be king; I am too young to reign.°
QUEEN But be content, seeing 'tis his highness' pleasure.
PRINCE Let me but see him first, and then I will.   95
KENT Ay, do, sweet nephew.
QUEEN Brother, you know it is impossible.
PRINCE Why, is he dead?
QUEEN No, God forbid!
KENT I would those words proceeded from your heart.   100
MORTIMER Inconstant Edmund, dost thou favour him,
    That wast a cause of his imprisonment?°
KENT The more cause have I now to make amends.
MORTIMER I tell thee 'tis not meet that one so false
    Should come about the person of a prince.   105
      [*To Prince Edward*]
    My lord, he hath betrayed the king his brother,
    And therefore trust him not.
PRINCE But he repents and sorrows for it now.
QUEEN Come, son, and go with this gentle lord and me.
PRINCE With you I will, but not with Mortimer.   110
MORTIMER Why, youngling, 'sdain'st thou so of Mortimer?°
    [*Seizing him*] Then I will carry thee by force away.°
PRINCE Help, uncle Kent! Mortimer will wrong me.
      [*Exit Mortimer Junior with the Prince*]
QUEEN Brother Edmund, strive not; we are his friends.°
    Isabel is nearer than the earl of Kent.°   115
KENT Sister, Edward is my charge. Redeem him.°
QUEEN Edward is my son, and I will keep him.
      [*Exit the Queen*]
KENT Mortimer shall know that he hath wronged me.
    Hence will I haste to Killingworth Castle,
    And rescue agèd Edward from his foes,   120

To be revenged on Mortimer and thee.°
   Exit

[5.3]

Enter Matrevis and Gurney with the King [and Soldiers,
   with torches]

MATREVIS My lord, be not pensive; we are your friends.
   Men are ordained to live in misery;
   Therefore come. Dalliance dangereth our lives.
EDWARD Friends, whither must unhappy Edward go?
   Will hateful Mortimer appoint no rest?   5
   Must I be vexèd like the nightly bird°
   Whose sight is loathsome to all wingèd fowls?
   When will the fury of his mind assuage?
   When will his heart be satisfied with blood?
   If mine will serve, unbowel straight this breast°   10
   And give my heart to Isabel and him;
   It is the chiefest mark they level at.
GURNEY Not so, my liege. The queen hath given this charge
   To keep your grace in safety.
   Your passions make your dolours to increase.   15
EDWARD This usage makes my misery increase.
   But can my air of life continue long°
   When all my senses are annoyed with stench?
   Within a dungeon England's king is kept,
   Where I am starved for want of sustenance;   20
   My daily diet is heart-breaking sobs
   That almost rends the closet of my heart.°
   Thus lives old Edward, not relieved by any,
   And so must die, though pitièd by many.
   O, water, gentle friends, to cool my thirst   25
   And clear my body from foul excrements!
      [*Ditch water° is brought*]
MATREVIS Here's channel water, as our charge is given.
   Sit down, for we'll be barbers to your grace.
EDWARD Traitors, away! What, will you murder me,
   Or choke your sovereign with puddle water?   30
GURNEY No, but wash your face and shave away your beard,

Lest you be known and so be rescuèd.

MATREVIS Why strive you thus? Your labour is in vain.

EDWARD The wren may strive against the lion's strength,
But all in vain, so vainly do I strive   35
To seek for mercy at a tyrant's hand.

> *They wash him with puddle water and shave his beard away*

Immortal powers, that knows the painful cares
That waits upon my poor distressèd soul,
O, level all your looks upon these daring men
That wrongs their liege and sovereign, England's king.   40
O Gaveston, it is for thee that I am wronged;
For me, both thou and both the Spencers died,
And for your sakes a thousand wrongs I'll take.
The Spencers' ghosts, wherever they remain,°
Wish well to mine. Then, tush, for them I'll die.   45

MATREVIS 'Twixt theirs and yours shall be no enmity.°
Come, come, away. Now put the torches out;
We'll enter in by darkness to Killingworth.

> *[They put out their torches.] Enter Edmund [Earl of Kent]*

GURNEY How now, who comes there?

> *[They draw their weapons]*

MATREVIS Guard the king sure. It is the earl of Kent.°   50

EDWARD O gentle brother, help to rescue me!

MATREVIS Keep them asunder! Thrust in the king.°

KENT Soldiers, let me but talk to him one word.

GURNEY Lay hands upon the earl for this assault.

KENT Lay down your weapons, traitors. Yield the king.   55

MATREVIS Edmund, yield thou thyself, or thou shalt die.

> *[Kent is seized]*

KENT Base villains, wherefore do you grip me thus?

GURNEY *[to the Soldiers]*
Bind him and so convey him to the court.

KENT Where is the court but here? Here is the king,
And I will visit him. Why stay you me?   60

MATREVIS The court is where Lord Mortimer remains.
Thither shall your honour go, and so farewell.

> *Exeunt Matrevis and Gurney with the King. Edmund [Earl*
> *of Kent] and the Soldiers remain*

KENT O, miserable is that commonweal
Where lords keep courts and kings are locked in prison!

A SOLDIER Wherefore stay we? On, sirs, to the court.   65

KENT Ay, lead me whither you will, even to my death,
   Seeing that my brother cannot be released.
      Exeunt, [Kent under guard]

[5.4]

      Enter Mortimer [Junior] alone, [with a letter]
MORTIMER The king must die, or Mortimer goes down.
   The commons now begin to pity him;
   Yet he that is the cause of Edward's death
   Is sure to pay for it when his son is of age,
   And therefore will I do it cunningly.   5
   This letter, written by a friend of ours,
   Contains his death, yet bids them save his life.
   '*Edwardum occidere nolite timere, bonum est*',
   'Fear not to kill the king, 'tis good he die.'
   But read it thus, and that's another sense: 10
   '*Edwardum occidere nolite, timere bonum est*',
   'Kill not the king, 'tis good to fear the worst.'
   Unpointed as it is, thus shall it go,
   That, being dead, if it chance to be found,°
   Matrevis and the rest may bear the blame   15
   And we be quit that caused it to be done.
   Within this room is locked the messenger
   That shall convey it and perform the rest,
   And by a secret token that he bears
   Shall he be murdered when the deed is done.   20
      [He unlocks and opens a door]
   Lightborn,
   Come forth.
      [Enter Lightborn]
                  Art thou as resolute as thou wast?
LIGHTBORN What else, my lord? And far more resolute.
MORTIMER And hast thou cast how to accomplish it?
LIGHTBORN Ay, ay, and none shall know which way he died.   25
MORTIMER But at his looks, Lightborn, thou wilt relent.
LIGHTBORN Relent? Ha, ha! I use much to relent.°
MORTIMER Well, do it bravely and be secret.
LIGHTBORN You shall not need to give instructions;

'Tis not the first time I have killed a man.   30
I learned in Naples how to poison flowers,°
To strangle with a lawn thrust through the throat,°
To pierce the windpipe with a needle's point,
Or, whilst one is asleep, to take a quill
And blow a little powder in his ears,   35
Or open his mouth and pour quicksilver down;
But yet I have a braver way than these.
MORTIMER What's that?
LIGHTBORN Nay, you shall pardon me, none shall know my tricks.
MORTIMER I care not how it is, so it be not spied.   40
    [*Giving the letter*] Deliver this to Gurney and Matrevis.
    At every ten miles' end thou hast a horse.°
    [*Giving a token*] Take this. Away, and never see me more.°
LIGHTBORN No?
MORTIMER No,   45
    Unless thou bring me news of Edward's death.
LIGHTBORN That will I quickly do. Farewell, my lord.
        [*Exit Lightborn*]
MORTIMER The prince I rule; the queen do I command;
    And, with a lowly *congé* to the ground,
    The proudest lords salute me as I pass.   50
    I seal, I cancel, I do what I will.°
    Feared am I more than loved. Let me be feared,
    And when I frown, make all the court look pale.
    I view the prince with Aristarchus' eyes,°
    Whose looks were as a breeching to a boy.   55
    They thrust upon me the protectorship
    And sue to me for that that I desire,°
    While at the council table, grave enough,
    And not unlike a bashful Puritan,
    First I complain of imbecility,   60
    Saying it is *onus quam gravissimum*,°
    Till, being interrupted by my friends,
    Suscepi that *provinciam*, as they term it,°
    And, to conclude, I am Protector now.
    Now is all sure. The queen and Mortimer   65
    Shall rule the realm, the king, and none rule us;
    Mine enemies will I plague, my friends advance,
    And what I list command, who dare control?
    Maior sum quam cui possit fortuna nocere;°

And that this be the coronation day   70
It pleaseth me and Isabel the queen.
    [Trumpets are sounded offstage]
The trumpets sound. I must go take my place.
    Enter the young King, [Arch]bishop [of Canterbury],
    Champion,° nobles, Queen, [and Attendants]
CANTERBURY Long live King Edward, by the grace of God,
King of England and Lord of Ireland!
CHAMPION If any Christian, Heathen, Turk, or Jew   75
Dares but affirm that Edward's not true king,
And will avouch his saying with the sword,
I am the champion that will combat him.
MORTIMER None comes. Sound, trumpets!
    [The trumpets sound]
EDWARD III Champion, here's to thee.°   80
QUEEN Lord Mortimer, now take him to your charge.°
    Enter Soldiers with the Earl of Kent prisoner
MORTIMER What traitor have we there, with blades and bills?°
A SOLDIER Edmund, the earl of Kent.
EDWARD III   What hath he done?
A SOLDIER 'A would have taken the king away perforce
As we were bringing him to Killingworth.   85
MORTIMER Did you attempt his rescue, Edmund? Speak.
KENT Mortimer, I did; he is our king,
And thou compell'st this prince to wear the crown.
MORTIMER Strike off his head! He shall have martial law.
KENT Strike off my head? Base traitor, I defy thee.   90
EDWARD III *[to Mortimer Junior]*
My lord, he is my uncle and shall live.
MORTIMER My lord, he is your enemy and shall die.
    [The Soldiers start to remove Kent]
KENT Stay, villains!
EDWARD III Sweet mother, if I cannot pardon him,
Entreat my Lord Protector for his life.   95
QUEEN Son, be content. I dare not speak a word.
EDWARD III Nor I, and yet methinks I should command;
But seeing I cannot, I'll entreat for him.—
My lord, if you will let my uncle live,
I will requite it when I come of age.   100
MORTIMER 'Tis for your highness' good, and for the realm's.
    [To Soldiers] How often shall I bid you bear him hence?

KENT Art thou king? Must I die at thy command?

MORTIMER At our command.—Once more, away with him.

KENT Let me but stay and speak; I will not go.   105
   Either my brother or his son is king,
   And none of both them thirst for Edmund's blood.
   And therefore, soldiers, whither will you hale me?
       They hale Edmund [Earl of Kent] away and carry him to be
       beheaded. [The Queen and her son speak privately as the
       others leave the stage]

EDWARD III What safety may I look for at his hands
   If that my uncle shall be murdered thus?   110

QUEEN Fear not, sweet boy, I'll guard thee from thy foes.
   Had Edmund lived, he would have sought thy death.
   Come, son, we'll ride a-hunting in the park.

EDWARD III And shall my uncle Edmund ride with us?

QUEEN He is a traitor. Think not on him. Come.   115
   Exeunt

[5.5]

   Enter Matrevis and Gurney [with lights. A bed is thrust
   onstage]

MATREVIS Gurney, I wonder the king dies not,
   Being in a vault up to the knees in water
   To which the channels of the castle run,
   From whence a damp continually ariseth
   That were enough to poison any man—   5
   Much more a king brought up so tenderly.

GURNEY And so do I, Matrevis. Yesternight
   I opened but the door to throw him meat,
   And I was almost stifled with the savour.

MATREVIS He hath a body able to endure   10
   More than we can inflict, and therefore now
   Let us assail his mind another while.

GURNEY Send for him out thence, and I will anger him.

MATREVIS But stay, who's this?
     Enter Lightborn

LIGHTBORN [*giving them the letter*]
                   My Lord Protector greets you.

[Matrevis and Gurney read the letter]
GURNEY *[aside to Matrevis]*
    What's here? I know not how to conster it.   15
MATREVIS *[aside to Gurney]*
    Gurney, it was left unpointed for the nonce.°
    '*Edwardum occidere nolite timere*',
    That's his meaning.
LIGHTBORN *[showing them the token]*
    Know you this token? I must have the king.
MATREVIS
    Ay. Stay a while; thou shalt have answer straight.   20
    [Aside to Gurney] This villain's sent to make away the king.
GURNEY *[aside to Matrevis]*
    I thought as much.
MATREVIS *[aside to Gurney]*
                    And when the murder's done,
    See how he must be handled for his labour:
    '*Pereat iste*.' Let him have the king.°
    What else? *[To Lightborn]* Here is the keys; this is the lake.°   25
    [He indicates the door of Edward's dungeon]
    Do as you are commanded by my lord.
LIGHTBORN I know what I must do. Get you away.
    Yet be not far off; I shall need your help.
    See that in the next room I have a fire,
    And get me a spit, and let it be red hot.   30
MATREVIS Very well.
GURNEY Need you anything besides?
LIGHTBORN What else? A table and a featherbed.°
GURNEY That's all?
LIGHTBORN Ay, ay, so; when I call you, bring it in.   35
MATREVIS Fear not you that.°
GURNEY *[giving a light]*
    Here's a light to go into the dungeon.
LIGHTBORN So.
    [Exeunt Matrevis and Gurney]°
    Now must I about this gear. Ne'er was there any
    So finely handled as this king shall be.   40
    [Lightborn opens the door or trapdoor of Edward's dungeon]
    Foh! Here's a place indeed, with all my heart.°
    [Enter King Edward]
EDWARD Who's there? What light is that? Wherefore comes thou?

LIGHTBORN To comfort you and bring you joyful news.
EDWARD Small comfort finds poor Edward in thy looks.
   Villain, I know thou com'st to murder me.   45
LIGHTBORN To murder you, my most gracious lord?
   Far is it from my heart to do you harm.
   The queen sent me to see how you were used,
   For she relents at this your misery.
   And what eyes can refrain from shedding tears   50
   To see a king in this most piteous state?
EDWARD Weep'st thou already? List a while to me,
   And then thy heart, were it as Gurney's is,
   Or as Matrevis', hewn from the Caucasus,°
   Yet will it melt ere I have done my tale.   55
   The dungeon where they keep me is the sink
   Wherein the filth of all the castle falls.
LIGHTBORN O, villains!
EDWARD And there in mire and puddle have I stood
   This ten days' space, and, lest that I should sleep,   60
   One plays continually upon a drum.
   They give me bread and water, being a king,
   So that for want of sleep and sustenance
   My mind's distempered and my body's numbed,
   And whether I have limbs or no I know not.   65
   O, would my blood dropped out from every vein°
   As doth this water from my tattered robes!
   Tell Isabel the queen I looked not thus
   When for her sake I ran at tilt in France°
   And there unhorsed the duke of Cleremont.   70
LIGHTBORN O, speak no more, my lord! This breaks my heart.
   Lie on this bed and rest yourself a while.
EDWARD These looks of thine can harbour nought but death;
   I see my tragedy written in thy brows.
   Yet stay a while; forbear thy bloody hand,   75
   And let me see the stroke before it comes,
   That, even then when I shall lose my life,
   My mind may be more steadfast on my God.
LIGHTBORN What means your highness to mistrust me thus?
EDWARD What means thou to dissemble with me thus?   80
LIGHTBORN These hands were never stained with innocent blood,
   Nor shall they now be tainted with a king's.
EDWARD Forgive my thought for having such a thought.

One jewel have I left; receive thou this.
    [*He gives a jewel*]
Still fear I, and I know not what's the cause,   85
But every joint shakes as I give it thee.
O, if thou harbour'st murder in thy heart,
Let this gift change thy mind and save thy soul.
Know that I am a king. O, at that name
I feel a hell of grief. Where is my crown?   90
Gone, gone, and do I remain alive?
LIGHTBORN You're overwatched, my lord. Lie down and rest.
    [*The King lies down*]
EDWARD But that grief keeps me waking, I should sleep,
    For not these ten days have these eyes' lids closed;
    Now as I speak they fall, and yet with fear   95
    Open again.
    [*Lightborn sits on the bed*]
        O, wherefore sits thou here?
LIGHTBORN If you mistrust me, I'll be gone, my lord.
EDWARD No, no, for if thou mean'st to murder me
    Thou wilt return again, and therefore stay.
LIGHTBORN He sleeps.   100
EDWARD [*starting*]
    O, let me not die yet! Stay, O, stay a while!
LIGHTBORN How now, my lord?
EDWARD Something still buzzeth in mine ears
    And tells me if I sleep I never wake;°
    This fear is that which makes me tremble thus.   105
    And therefore tell me: wherefore art thou come?
LIGHTBORN To rid thee of thy life.—Matrevis, come!
    [*Enter Matrevis and Gurney*]
EDWARD I am too weak and feeble to resist.
    Assist me, sweet God, and receive my soul!
LIGHTBORN Run for the table.   110
EDWARD O, spare me, or dispatch me in a trice!
    [*Matrevis and Gurney bring in a table and a red-hot spit*]
LIGHTBORN So, lay the table down, and stamp on it,
    But not too hard, lest that you bruise his body.
    [*The King is murdered*]°
MATREVIS I fear me that this cry will raise the town,
    And therefore let us take horse and away.   115
LIGHTBORN Tell me, sirs, was it not bravely done?

GURNEY Excellent well. Take this for thy reward.
        Then Gurney stabs Lightborn
    Come, let us cast the body in the moat,
    And bear the king's to Mortimer, our lord.
    Away!   120
        Exeunt [with the bodies]

[5.6]

        Enter Mortimer [Junior] and Matrevis [at different doors]
MORTIMER Is't done, Matrevis, and the murderer dead?
MATREVIS Ay, my good lord. I would it were undone.
MORTIMER Matrevis, if thou now growest penitent,
    I'll be thy ghostly father. Therefore choose°
    Whether thou wilt be secret in this   5
    Or else die by the hand of Mortimer.
MATREVIS Gurney, my lord, is fled, and will, I fear,
    Betray us both; therefore let me fly.
MORTIMER Fly to the savages.°
MATREVIS I humbly thank your honour.   10
        [Exit Matrevis]
MORTIMER As for myself, I stand as Jove's huge tree,°
    And others are but shrubs compared to me;
    All tremble at my name, and I fear none.
    Let's see who dare impeach me for his death?
        Enter the Queen
QUEEN Ah, Mortimer, the king my son hath news   15
    His father's dead, and we have murdered him.
MORTIMER What if he have? The king is yet a child.
QUEEN Ay, ay, but he tears his hair, and wrings his hands,
    And vows to be revenged upon us both.
    Into the council chamber he is gone   20
    To crave the aid and succour of his peers.
    Ay me! See where he comes, and they with him.
    Now, Mortimer, begins our tragedy.
        Enter the King, with the lords [and Attendants]
FIRST LORD Fear not, my lord. Know that you are a king.°
EDWARD III *[to Mortimer Junior]* Villain!   25
MORTIMER How now, my lord?

EDWARD III Think not that I am frighted with thy words.
  My father's murdered through thy treachery,
  And thou shalt die, and on his mournful hearse
  Thy hateful and accursèd head shall lie,   30
  To witness to the world that by thy means
  His kingly body was too soon interred.
QUEEN Weep not, sweet son.
EDWARD III Forbid not me to weep. He was my father,
  And, had you loved him half so well as I,   35
  You could not bear his death thus patiently;
  But you, I fear, conspired with Mortimer.
FIRST LORD [to Mortimer Junior]
  Why speak you not unto my lord the king?
MORTIMER Because I think scorn to be accused.
  Who is the man dare say I murdered him?   40
EDWARD III Traitor, in me my loving father speaks
  And plainly saith 'twas thou that murdered'st him.
MORTIMER But hath your grace no other proof than this?
EDWARD III Yes, if this be the hand of Mortimer.
    [He shows the letter]
MORTIMER [aside] False Gurney hath betrayed me and himself.   45
QUEEN [aside] I feared as much. Murder cannot be hid.°
MORTIMER 'Tis my hand. What gather you by this?°
EDWARD III That thither thou didst send a murderer.
MORTIMER What murderer? Bring forth the man I sent.
EDWARD III Ah, Mortimer, thou knowest that he is slain,   50
  And so shalt thou be too.—Why stays he here?°
  Bring him unto a hurdle! Drag him forth,
  Hang him, I say, and set his quarters up,
  But bring his head back presently to me.°
QUEEN For my sake, sweet son, pity Mortimer.   55
MORTIMER Madam, entreat not. I will rather die
  Than sue for life unto a paltry boy.
EDWARD III Hence with the traitor, with the murderer!
MORTIMER Base Fortune, now I see that in thy wheel
  There is a point to which when men aspire   60
  They tumble headlong down. That point I touched,
  And, seeing there was no place to mount up higher,
  Why should I grieve at my declining fall?
  Farewell, fair queen. Weep not for Mortimer,
  That scorns the world, and as a traveller   65

    Goes to discover countries yet unknown.

EDWARD III [*to his lords and Attendants*]
    What, suffer you the traitor to delay?
        [*Exit Mortimer Junior, guarded, with the First Lord*]

QUEEN As thou received'st thy life from me,
    Spill not the blood of gentle Mortimer.

EDWARD III This argues that you spilt my father's blood,   70
    Else would you not entreat for Mortimer.

QUEEN I spill his blood? No.

EDWARD III Ay, madam, you, for so the rumour runs.

QUEEN That rumour is untrue; for loving thee
    Is this report raised on poor Isabel.   75

EDWARD III [*to his lords*] I do not think her so unnatural.°

SECOND LORD My lord, I fear me it will prove too true.

EDWARD III Mother, you are suspected for his death,
    And therefore we commit you to the Tower
    Till further trial may be made thereof.   80
    If you be guilty, though I be your son,
    Think not to find me slack or pitiful.

QUEEN Nay, to my death, for too long have I lived
    Whenas my son thinks to abridge my days.

EDWARD III [*weeping*]
    Away with her! Her words enforce these tears,   85
    And I shall pity her if she speak again.

QUEEN Shall I not mourn for my belovèd lord,
    And with the rest accompany him to his grave?

SECOND LORD Thus, madam: 'tis the king's will you shall hence.

QUEEN He hath forgotten me. Stay, I am his mother.   90

SECOND LORD That boots not. Therefore, gentle madam, go.

QUEEN Then come, sweet death, and rid me of this grief.
        [*Exit Queen, attended.° Enter the First Lord with Mortimer's
        head*]

FIRST LORD My lord, here is the head of Mortimer.

EDWARD III
    Go fetch my father's hearse, where it shall lie,°
    And bring my funeral robes. Accursèd head,   95
    Could I have ruled thee then as I do now,
    Thou hadst not hatched this monstrous treachery!
        [*Enter some with Edward II's hearse*]
    Here comes the hearse. Help me to mourn, my lords.
    Sweet father, here unto thy murdered ghost

I offer up this wicked traitor's head;
And let these tears distilling from mine eyes
Be witness of my grief and innocency!
    [*Exeunt, bearing in the hearse*]

EXPLANATORY NOTES

Tamburlaine Part I

Prologue 1 *jigging*: in doggerel style, suitable to a 'jig' or dancing interlude at the end of a play.

mother-wits: those who possess native common sense (here said condescendingly).

7 *tragic glass*: Marlowe contrasts the high seriousness of his mirror for princes with the doggerel style and 'clownage' of much popular theatre of his day.

1.1 This scene appears to take place at or near the court of Persia. See ll. 180–1.

11 *For . . . cold*: on account of sleet and snow. (Persia's former empire, says Cosroe, extended into the far north of Siberia.)

13–15 *At . . . brain*: according to Cosroe, Mycetes was born under Saturn (hence, sluggish, cold, and gloomy) and the Moon or Cynthia (hence, fickle and irresolute), with no qualities of Jove or Jupiter (majestic, jovial), the Sun (royal, sanguine), or Mercury (eloquent, ingenious).

19 *your planets*: your citing of astrological bodies.

29 *my conceivèd grief*: the grief I have conceived in my mind.

38 *Trading*: the original reading, *Treading*, is possible but unlikely.

the Western Isles: Britain, or the West Indies.

39 *in your confines*: within your borders.

45 *vagrant ensign*: nomadic banner.

46 *taken order by*: given order to.

47 *Charged . . . horse*: put in command of a thousand horsemen.

49 *like thyself*: as is worthy of you.

50 *Damon*: the friend of Pythias; a model of heroic friendship.

56 *choose*: be otherwise. (Said ironically.)

63 *gall*: rancour (literally, secretion of the liver).

66 *the Grecian dame*: Helen, abducted from the Greeks by Paris of Troy.

69 *Before . . . light*: i.e. within a month.

71 *Tartarian rout*: mob of Tartar thieves.

87 *task*: omitted in the octavo.

89 *prorex*: viceroy.

Assyria: the octavo reads 'Affrica' here and at l. 164.

97 *seat*: throne; but Cosroe, in the next line, puns on 'ass'.

99 *state*: (1) royal rank (2) raised chair of state, continuing the wordplay in ll. 97–8.

108 *like himself*: as a king should do.

117 *laughs . . . scorn*: laughs scornfully at our authority.

119 *from . . . line*: from the farthest equatorial regions.

126 *By . . . empery*: by restoring to health this wounded empire and authority.

128 *continent to*: being adjacent to.

130 *Cyrus*: Persian conqueror of the Greek cities of Asia Minor in the sixth century BC. It was Darius I and Xerxes who invaded Greece in the 490s and 480s.

143 *Whose . . . gold*: the ransom money obtained in previous campaigns for African prisoners of high rank has enabled their Persian captors to go about in coats of gold.

154 *Darius*: Darius III (not Darius I, mentioned in 130 note above), defeated by Alexander the Great of Macedon in 333 and 331 BC.

159 *them shall malice*: those who maliciously seek to injure.

167 *Euxine Sea*: Black Sea.

170 *Jove may*: may Jove.

182 *too exasperate*: so exasperated as. (Ortygius is not worried that Persia's aristocracy will defend Mycetes against this coup.)

1.2 This scene takes place somewhere in Scythia. See l. 17.

13 *governèd*: cared for and brought up.

15 *his privy . . . hand*: a document signed by him and to which is affixed his privy seal.

16 *thorough Africa*: i.e. through the Middle East to Egypt.

18 *puissant Cham*: mighty emperor of Tartary.

25 *treasure*: (1) wealth (2) chastity.

29 *they . . . state*: these prizes assist the growth of my power.

33 *so . . . import*: your bearing and speech imply that you are a lord.

37 *his bed that*: the bed of him who.

41–3 *Lie . . . Tamburlaine*: Tamburlaine evidently doffs at this point the shepherd's garb in which he and his followers are attired (see ll. 7–8, 47), putting on instead a suit of armour he has captured.

42 *complete*: stressed on the first syllable.

47 *these*: i.e. Techelles and Usumcasane.

50–1 *Even . . . earth*: Tamburlaine describes an earthquake, presumed to be caused by vapours attempting to escape from within the earth.

61 *estimates*: reputations.

62 *with distempered spirits*: intemperately, madly.

63–5 *measure . . . clouds*: have such a low regard for us who dream of hoisting many empires on our spears, daring to presume equality with the heavens themselves.

87 *the love of Jove*: Juno, or perhaps one of Jove's human lovers like Leda and Semele.

88 *Rhodope*: Mount Rhodope, famous for its silver mines, named supposedly for a queen of Thrace who preferred herself in beauty to Juno; also a celebrated Greek courtesan.

94 *Pegasus*: winged horse of classical mythology.

103 *fifty-headed*: fed by fifty tributary streams.

104 *Shall all we*: all of these we shall.

106–8 TECHELLES . . . *in love*: editors sometimes mark these speeches as *aside*, and perhaps plausibly, but *Tamburlaine*'s idiom is usually more direct.

118 *Such . . . horse*: i.e. the thousand Persian horsemen entertain the same vain hope as do Zenocrate, Agydas, and Magnetes.

122 *An . . . against*: said ironically.

126 *Hangs*: a singular form of the verb, often used with plural subjects in Elizabethan English.

129 *look . . . orator?*: are you waiting for me to make a speech?

138 *mails*: travelling packs, here containing booty.

144 *possession*: pronounced in four syllables, 'pos-séss-i-on'. The 'ion' suffix often receives two syllables, as in 'destruction' at 3.2.33 and 'expedition' at 4.1.38; in *Tamburlaine, Part II*, 'profession' at 2.1.32; and so on in other plays.

147 *chain*: chain of office.

150 *standings*: stations.

160–1 *Or . . . hell*: in the last of his twelve labours, Hercules descended to Hades (sometimes called 'Avernus' after a lake by that name near Naples where Aeneas entered a cave to the nether world) in order to capture and bring back Cerberus, the three-headed dog guarding Hades.

169 *characters*: distinctive marks (suggesting also the astrological symbols of the planets). Accented on the second syllable.

170 *stout aspect*: brave expression (suggesting also astrological influence and position). *Aspect* is accented on the second syllable, here and generally throughout Marlowe's plays.

174 *the Fates*: Clotho, Lachesis, and Atropos, who held the distaff, drew off the thread of destiny, and cut it short.

189 *with my conduct*: under my leadership.

194 *Christian . . . stems*: Christian-owned merchant ships that with their Russian timber prows.

200 *that*: by which.

206 *Boreas*: the north wind.

207 *Boötes*: the northern constellation of the Plough, following right behind the Big Dipper or Great Bear.

210 *Hermes*: messenger of the gods, here called *prolocutor*, i.e. spokesman.

215 *to our state*: in exchange for our present state.

216 *that*: that which.

225 *Are . . . Scythians?*: i.e. can Scythians be thus resolute and noble?

243 *Pylades and Orestes*: models of friendship, as portrayed in various accounts of the murder of Orestes' father Agamemnon.

245 *them*: i.e. they, Techelles and Usumcasane.

249–51 *Nor . . . security*: neither you nor they, thrice-noble Tamburlaine, shall fail to have in me a heart pierced with gladness to honour and protect you.

255 *as your merits be*: according to your deserving.

258 *I . . . doubt*: i.e. I consider the matter settled and offer you my assurances.

2.1.1 *Thus . . . we*: thus far have we advanced. Cosroe's plan is to rendezvous with Theridamas and Tamburlaine, whom he regards as allies, near the Araris River—probably the Araxes, flowing into the Caspian Sea; see l. 63.

4 *figures*: facial characteristics expressive of, as at 1.2.169–70, where the *characters* engraved in Theridamas' brow (by Allah, according to Muslim belief) are suggestive of the astrological influence of the planets.

5 *that hast*: you that have.

8 *lift*: lifted.

11 *Atlas*: the son of a Titan who was made to support the heavens.
pitch: highest point, shoulders.

12 *pearl*: i.e. head.

13 *curious . . . art*: intricately wrought excellence of Nature's skill.

15 *fiery circles*: (as though his eyes were planetary spheres encompassing or containing the *heavenly bodies* of l. 16).

21 *in folds do figure*: when furrowed, prefigure.

22 *in their smoothness*: when not frowning, (they prefigure).

24 *Achilles*: the fair hair of this famous Greek warrior is referred to in the *Iliad*, i. 197, and elsewhere.

30 *Should*: destined to.

31 *terms of life*: lifelike description.

33 *Nature . . . stars*: the gifts of Nature, chance, and the astrological power of the heavenly bodies all vie with each other.

37–9 *That . . . foes*: (a man) who could in such a critical situation, through the example of his own valour and conduct, win over a thousand powerful foes sworn to defeat him.

40–4 *Then . . . not*: then, when our armies are joined (the combined force of Cosroe, Tamburlaine, and Theridamas against Mycetes), swords' points against swords' points, and are at close range for firing, my brother will be lucky indeed if we do not kill him, finding the straight and narrow passage to his heart.

59 *And . . . thoughts?*: and handsomely provided with riches to encourage (or in proportion to) his aspiration?

60 *such*: i.e. troops of followers and rich rewards.

2.2 The unhistorical battle in the following scenes is depicted as taking place 'near to Parthia' (2.1.65), in the vicinity of the Caspian Sea.

10 *Aurora*: goddess of the dawn.

13 *have said*: have finished speaking.

26 *him*: i.e. Theridamas.

42 *Which*: who, i.e. the scouts.

47–8 *Like . . . venomous*: when Cadmus, founder of ancient Thebes, sowed dragon's teeth, armed warriors sprang up and attacked one another.

57 *charge*: exhortation to the troops.

75 *Drums*: the drums may or may not respond to Mycetes's ineffectual call.

2.3.5 *doom*: opinion (but with ironic suggestion of something portentous).

11–12 *sway . . . in*: have some authority over.

16 *To . . . Araris*: i.e. to have drunk dry a mighty river in Parthia (called the Araxes in Herodotus, book 7).

17 *that*: that which.

21 *Cyclopian wars*: the Cyclopes, one-eyed giants who made Zeus' or Jove's thunderbolts, are here conflated with the giants or Titans, both of whom warred against Zeus.

35 *Which . . . crown*: which service I esteem as dearly as I do my own crown, as an integral part of my authority.

37 *she*: i.e. Nemesis (to whom a temple stood at Rhamnus in Attica), a personification of the gods' resentment of, and ultimate punishment of, insolence or *hubris* towards themselves. Cosroe hubristically thinks Nemesis will favour him.

57 *the wings shall*: i.e. the arms (literally, the cross-piece of my cutlass) that shall.

60 *Thy words . . . success*: scansion suggests either that *assure* is to be pronounced in three syllables or that the text should read *of a kind success*.

2.4.3 *those were*: those who have been.

  8 *clouts*: marks shot at in archery. To cleave the *pin* (l. 9) used to fasten the clout is to hit the very centre of the target.

 12 *far from*: uncharacteristic of.

 18 *Thou liest*: Mycetes's jest is that kings are not in the field, since he himself has withdrawn.

   give the lie: accuse me to my face of lying (and thus invite a duel).

 41 S.D. *sound trumpets to*: the trumpets give the signal to resume.

2.5.7 *keep*: protect (?). Conceivably, Cosroe returns Mycetes's crown to Tamburlaine as his regent in Persia, but more probably Tamburlaine has no crown of his own until he takes Cosroe's at 2.7.52 S.D.

 30 *gratify . . . good*: repay your service.

 31 *calling*: present name and position.

 33 *sought your state*: sought on behalf of your royal authority.

 36 *thank thee*: i.e. gratify your service merely with words of thanks.

 43 *with fame and usury*: gaining acclaim and profit.

 53 *passing brave*: exceedingly fine and glorious.

 83 *they*: i.e. Techelles and Usumcasane, respectively.

 85 *the Turk*: the Turkish emperor, Bajazeth.

   Afric, and Greece: i.e. the Sultan of Egypt and the Grecian emperor.

 88 *novel*: newly acquired.

 89 *before . . . hot*: before he has had time to warm his throne by sitting in it.

 92 *purchase*: (1) endeavour (2) advantage gained, plunder.

 96 *lose*: cause us to lose; ere we lose.

   quite: requite.

101 *That . . . sport*: we who made him king only to amuse ourselves.

103 *more warriors*: i.e. a chance to amass more troops.

105 *for me*: as far as I am concerned.

2.6.5–6 *But . . . jaws*: Jupiter or Zeus thrust the giants beneath the mountains for their rebellion against the gods, whereupon their fire continued to erupt in volcanic fury.

 13 *so . . . rule*: so unhesitatingly to set his mind on political power.

 14 *by profession*: by vocation, avowedly.

 15 *What*: whatsoever.

 17 *mould or mettle*: earth or substance.

 19 *Let . . . minds*: let us prepare our thoughts for the encounter.

25–8 *And . . . life*: and since we breathe one common vital air, and resolve upon a course of action, having been made of the same four elements, I hope we are also in accord to pledge loyalty to one another whether for mutual death or shared victory. (Alternatively, 'And with . . . Resolve' in ll. 26–7 may mean, 'and are dissolved at death into the same four elements'.)

32 *that flame*: his own ambition.

33 *blood and empery*: slaughter and conquest.

36–7 *that make . . . life*: that dictate the extent of a life whose end is already cruelly predetermined.

2.7 Whether a scene break occurs here is unclear. Quite possibly Cosroe and his supporters exeunt only after having been attacked by the army of Tamburlaine and his allies, in the to-and-fro action of alarums and excursions.

9 *Who*: i.e. death.

13 *eldest . . . Ops*: Zeus, saved by his mother, Rhea (often identified with Ops), from being swallowed by his father Cronos, went on to fulfil Cronos' fear of overthrow by one of his own children.

15 *th'empyreal heaven*: the immovable highest heaven of light and fire enclosing the moving celestial spheres; with suggestion also of 'imperial' (spelled 'Emperiall' in the octavo.)

31 *he*: anyone.

36 *Saturn*: the husband of Ops, often identified with Cronos as the overthrown father of Zeus; see ll. 13–15.

37 *Neptune and Dis*: Poseidon (Neptune) and Hades (Dis), sons of Cronos and Rhea, ruled with their brother Zeus after the overthrow of Cronos (Saturn).

50 *harpy*: fabulous rapacious monster with a woman's face and body and a bird's wings and claws.

tires: tears with the beak.

3.1 The scene is imagined to take place at the siege of Constantinople; see ll. 5–15.

4 *Presume a bickering*: presume to quarrel or skirmish.

11–12 *when . . . horns*: i.e. when the moon is full and the tides are unusually high.

13 *Yet . . . power*: invincible as we are, I will not permit us to be menaced by a foreign army.

21 *Persia*: the new king of Persia, Tamburlaine.

25 *coal-black sea*: Black Sea.

34 *mad to*: insane as to.

38–9 *We . . . reclaimed*: we will interpret the rising of the next morning's sun as token that Tamburlaine refuses to be reclaimed to or restrained by the duty he owes.

45 *he*: i.e. Tamburlaine.

46–7 *to stir . . . more*: to disrupt your siege of Constantinople, he would need to be ten times more powerful than he is.

56 *your greatness*: an honorific term of address, like 'your majesty'.

57 *pursuit*: accented on the first syllable.

58 *will*: command that.

63 *countermand*: keep under command.

65 *Orcus' gulf*: the entrance to hell.

3.2.7 *of . . . displeasures*: of all the wrongs you have suffered.

11 *the queen of heaven*: Juno.

13 *since*: since then.

16 *if . . . events*: if my fears of catastrophe were to be fulfilled, or, if my extremity of feeling were to be fully manifested.

19 *all . . . eye*: all that the moon beholds, everything beneath the moon.

23 *you*: Zenocrate addresses her own life and soul.

30 *your . . . necessity*: your love except in so far as you are constrained (to show him duty); or, a love yielded by you under threat of force.

31 *So*: provided that. Or, Agydas may be saying, in effect, 'as long as the Sultan hears only of you as you are at present—i.e. resisting Tamburlaine, not compliant with his desires—you can rely on rescue. If, however, he heard you were damaged goods, he might abandon you to your fate.'

45 *facts*: deeds.

48 *the morning . . . arms*: Aurora, goddess of dawn, holds the sun god in her arms.

51 *Pierides*: the daughters of Pierus, who challenged the Muses in song and were turned into magpies for their presumption.

52 *Minerva . . . Neptune*: Athene (Minerva) won a contest with Poseidon (Neptune) for the land of Attica by presenting an olive tree (considered even more valuable than Poseidon's gift of a horse), and thereby gave her name to Athens.

53 *estimate*: sense of my own worth.

57 *the young Arabian*: Alcidamus, the young king of Arabia, to whom Zenocrate has been betrothed (1.2.33).

59–60 *You . . . much*: you see how Tamburlaine, though he seemed to love you much at first when he was a humble shepherd.

65 *Fearing*: doubting, fearing to lose.

72 *portrayed*: accented on the first syllable.

76 *the Hyades*: the daughters of Atlas, who supply moisture to the earth. They appear in the constellation of Taurus, in which the sun is ascendant during the wet season of spring.

77 *Cimmerian*: black. The Cimmerians inhabit the limits of the world where the sun never shines.

78 *Auster and Aquilon*: the south wind and the north or north-north-east wind.

79 *tilt*: joust (and thus produce thunder and lightning).

82 *sounds the main*: takes soundings for depth of water.

3.3.2 *Bithynia*: near Constantinople, from the siege of which Bajazeth comes to meet with Tamburlaine.

3 *See how he comes!*: i.e. I am ready; where is he? (Said caustically.)

5 *He . . . hence*: Tamburlaine sarcastically refers to the pledge made by Bajazeth at 3.1.40 to reclaim his hostage, the Basso.

20 *expedition*: expeditious waging.

52 *bastones*: cudgels.

78 *sarell*: seraglio, where Muslim wives and concubines are secluded.

104–5 *Hercules . . . venomous*: Hercules, according to legend, strangled two serpents that Hera or Juno had sent to kill him.

109 *Typhon*: this frightful monster, son of Tartarus and Ge (Earth), coupled with the monster Echidna to produce the Nemean lion, the dogs Orthrus and Cerberus, the Chimaera, the Theban Sphinx, and the Lernaean Hydra. In some accounts Echidna is the mother of Typhon.

140 *Hydra*: whenever any of the Lernaean Hydra's many heads were cut off, others grew in their place.

142 *If they*: even if my soldiers.

153 *but had*: without winning.

154 *Pharsalia*: the battle in which Julius Caesar defeated Pompey the Great, 48 BC.

160 *take her flight*: spread her wings (not flee in retreat).

161 *Resting herself*: coming to rest.

168 *boss*: fat woman.

173 *basso-master*: king of the pashas, as in l. 212. (Said derisively.)

175 *your advocates*: advocates for you both.

188 S.D. *They . . . stay*: trumpeters offstage give the trumpet-signal to begin, and then cease sounding.

221 *Africa*: here understood to be part of the Turkish empire.

222 *gat the best*: got the upper hand.

229 *terms*: statuary busts atop pillars (formerly honouring Bajazeth and Zabina).

236 *the Christian miscreants*: i.e. the Christians of Europe, faithless from a Muhammadan point of view, who will rejoice at the overthrow of the Turk as Europe's most dangerous foe.

248 *pilling brigantines*: small vessels used for plundering and piracy.

250 *for Christians' wrack*: to prey upon Christian shipping.

251 *Asant*: Zacynthus or Zaconthos, on the western coast of Greece.

253 *oriental sea*: i.e. Indian Ocean and Pacific.

254 *fetched about*: sailed around.

256 *Jubalter*: Gibraltar.

258–9 *Keeping . . . shore*: maintaining naval control over shipping in the Bay of Biscay, lying north from Portugal, and the English Channel.

4.1.2–3 *Hear . . . down*: perhaps Marlowe supposes Damascus (in Syria) to be near Memphis in lower Egypt; but the Sultan may also speak hyperbolically, asking his hearers to imagine Tamburlaine, at the siege of Damascus, as an imminent threat to Egypt. See 4.2.48, 102–4, and 124, and 4.4.68–77.

18 *Gorgon*: Demogorgon, 'prince of hell', with suggestion too of a monster capable of turning to stone anything that met its gaze; Medusa was a Gorgon.

26–7 *Environing . . . wood*: the spear-carrying soldiers, standing close together around their battle standard, create a bristle-pointed effect.

45 *Erebus*: primeval darkness, here associated with the underworld.

49 *pitcheth down*: pitches, sets up in place.

65 *lawful arms*: the law of arms.

68 *See*: see to it that.

71 *warning*: notification.

with: in alliance with.

4.2 Tamburlaine is at the siege of Damascus, having overcome Bajazeth at Bithynia; see ll. 42 and 98–102 below and 3.3.2, note.

8–9 *that . . . lamps*: that transparent sphere adorned with the fixed stars as they revolve eternally around the world.

30 *triple region*: divided into three regions: (1) the upper region of fire (2) the middle region of cold (3) the region at the surface of the earth, warmed by the sun.

37 *aspect*: (1) appearance (2) astrological disposition.

38 *meridian line*: line passing from pole to pole through the observer's zenith, hence the point of highest altitude.

49 *fame*: report, story.

Clymene's brainsick son: Phaethon, son of Clymene and the sun god Helios, managed his father's chariot so ineptly that he almost burned the earth and had to be destroyed by Zeus.

50 *the axletree of heaven*: the axis of the earth on which the heavens appear to revolve.

69 *she shall look*: Anippe shall look to it.

86 *in triumph*: as a captive in my triumphal procession.

96 *Plato's wondrous year*: the end of time, when the planets will return to their original positions in the celestial cycle (*Timaeus* 39 D).

103 *Like to the shadows*: like copies.
Pyramides is pronounced in four syllables, stressed on the second.

105 *bird*: i.e. the ibis. (See 4.3.37.)

108 *mask*: dress richly, as though for a masque.

115 *all the rest*: all the rest shall have their lives.

120 *their*: i.e. the *streamers'* or pennons'.

4.3.1 *Meleager*: King of Calydon who, accompanied by a band of Grecian warriors, attacked and killed the wild boar sent by Artemis to ravage the countryside, but then died when his mother Althaea threw into the fire the brand that prophetically determined the length of his life (Ovid, *Metamorphoses*, viii. 270 ff.).

2 *Argolian*: from Argolis, i.e. Greek.

4 *Cephalus*: Cephalus' wonderful hound named Lailaps, fated to catch whatever it pursued, was set to hunt an uncatchable fox (not wolf) which had been sent by the Titaness *Themis* to lay waste to the Theban (*Aonian*) fields in revenge for the death of the Sphinx. Zeus turned both hound and fox to stone, and Cephalus was later killed in error by his wife Procris (Ovid, *Metamorphoses*, vii. 762 ff.).

10 *Raves*: rages, roves.

25 *About . . . Bithynia*: in Bithynia.

49 *his partial praise*: praise that is partial to him.

4.4.9 *Jason*: Jason sailed from Greece to Colchis (at the eastern end of the Black Sea) with the argonauts to bring back the golden fleece.

10 *stomach*: (1) appetite (2) courage, anger.

17 *mask*: be concealed (in darkness).

18 *Avernus' pool*: a river of the underworld.

21 *snakes of Lerna*: the many-headed monster whose blood made the arrows of Hercules capable of inflicting incurable wounds.

24–5 *Procne's . . . child*: when Procne's husband, Tereus (king of Thrace), ravished Procne's sister Philomela and cut out her tongue, Procne revenged the deed by serving her own son Itys to Tereus in a stew (Ovid, *Metamorphoses*, vi. 433 ff.).

30 *th'empyreal heaven*: see note at 2.7.15.

57 *watered*: given water, as though he were an animal.

59 *while*: until.

63 *consort*: harmonious combination of singers or instrumentalists (with a pun on the idea of a spouse).

79 *triple region*: i.e. divided into Europe, Asia, and Africa.

80 *trace*: (1) travel (2) chart.

81 *this pen*: i.e. this sword. (The actor gestures.)

reduce them to: (1) bring them into the form of (2) subjugate them to.

85 *the perpendicular*: either (1) the vertical part of a capital 'T' inscribed inside a circle (the so-called 'T-in-O map') as a way of dividing the known world into the three areas of Europe, Asia, and Africa, or (2) the meridian, as at 4.2.38.

98 *bloody humours*: blood, one of the body's four humours or fluids.

99 *Preserving . . . death*: the stomach preserves itself at the expense of the rest of the body.

102 *looking*: hoping, expecting that.

110 S.D. *second course of crowns*: the first crowns given to Tamburlaine's three lieutenants were of Parthia, Scythia, and Media; see 2.5.83. Now they are to be kings in Africa. There may also be a play on sweetmeats and other *cates* or delicacies (l. 112) made in the shape of crowns.

126 *plage*: region (here in the far north).

127 *Unto . . . bower*: i.e. to the extreme east, where dawn comes up over the ocean.

131 *births*: humble origins.

133 *they*: those who.

134 *so well vouchsafed*: so graciously consented to bestow these honours on us.

141 *underneath our feet*: (1) living in the southern hemisphere (2) trampled by us.

5.1.8 *With terrors*: terrifyingly; accompanied with speeches or actions prophesying terrible ends for those in the city.

16–17 *By any . . . Will never*: by no alteration in his practice or exercise of pity will ever.

23 *use*: cause him to use.

25–6 *blood . . . hearts*: each sigh was thought to cost the heart a drop of blood.

27 *made*: being.

28 *obdurate*: accented on the second syllable.

30 *only danger*: danger but not the certainty of disaster.

34 *think . . . care*: consider that our concern for our country.

40 *in that*: in view of the fact that.

54 *Convey events of mercy*: prompt thoughts of a merciful resolution.

55–9 *Grant . . . lenity*: may the gods grant that these laurel boughs, placed on Tamburlaine's temples, will hide his frowns and screen or cover over his anger with propitious looks of pity and mercy.

65 *first*: the first who.

68–70 *when . . . eyes*: a verb seems to be missing, such as 'when first my white flags *appeared* through which . . .'

73 *for truth*: truly.

86 *jealous*: anxious (for the loved person's well-being).

87 *punished with conceit*: oppressed with anticipation.

88 *never-stayèd*: unstoppable, never halted.

89–90 *prevent . . . bear*: deprive them of the precious comforts that they might expect to enjoy still in their old age.

97 *bloods*: i.e. lives.

102 *of rule*: in a position of authority.

104 *investors*: those who clothe or invest.

111 *imperious*: (1) imperial (2) overmastering.

112 *circuit*: (1) judicial circuit (2) swath.

116–17 *charge . . . charge*: order . . . charge upon.

122 *observations*: rituals.

123 *Gihon*: a river flowing out of Eden and encompassing part of north-eastern Africa (Genesis 2: 13), i.e. the Nile.

125 *The angry god of arms*: Mars, the god of war and lover of Venus.

127 *peremptory*: accented on the first and third syllables.

133 *mithridate*: usually an antidote, but regarded here as a poison.

140 *Flora*: goddess of fertility and flowers.

142–3 *Rain'st . . . face*: Zenocrate's tears fall plentifully like dissolved pearls and shine like sapphires on her cheeks.

145 *comments*: expounds. Traditionally, the Muses are daughters of Mnemosyne or Memory; Marlowe instead personifies their mother as Beauty, and pictures her dwelling in Zenocrate's face where she can take notes on what she sees there.

147–50 *Eyes . . . light*: Zenocrate's eyes are here figuratively imagined as lighting up the moon and other celestial bodies as Ebena (Night) mounts the heavens in silence and the rich mantle of darkness.

158 *conceit of foil*: anticipation of overthrow.

160 *What . . . then?*: what strange power is in beauty, attested to by my troubled thoughts?

161–70 *If . . . worthiness*: Tamburlaine imagines what it would be like to gather in one poem all the feelings about beauty that have ever inspired poets to write.

164 *muses*: the poets' genius, inspiration.

165 *they still*: that poets' pens distil.

169 *period*: end to be attained; complete rhetorical structure.

170 *And . . . worthiness*: and if all these beautiful ideas were put together in a poem as perfectly as beauty deserves.

173 *Which . . . digest*: which the greatest poetic power imaginable cannot reduce into words.

178–90 *Save . . . nobility*: except that in justly applauding beauty—as we all must do, even the soldier in love with fame and victory—I, by both taking into my mind and subduing this strange power that subdues the gods themselves and teaches them to descend from heaven into the passionate world of shepherds and cottages, will show the world a model, despite my lowly birth, of true *virtú* and nobility. (In l. 179, *instinct* is accented on the second syllable.)

201 *no way but one*: the proverbial phrase implies, 'nothing but disaster', but Tamburlaine turns the phrase to his own account: 'If there can be only one outcome, let us be the winners.'

218 *Cocytus lake*: a river of Hades.

226 *in their proper rooms*: where they properly belong.

234 *Cimmerian Styx*: the principal river of Hades.

237 *retorquèd*: turned backwards on themselves.

240 *fiend*: i.e. infernal spirit to whom we might pray for help.

241 *infamous*: accented on the second syllable, as also at ll. 390 and 403 below.

244 *Erebus*: primeval darkness, hell.

246 *ferryman*: Charon, who conveyed the souls of the dead across the River Styx to Hades—or, as Zabina says, to *Elysium* (l. 247), here imagined to be in the underworld, as in Virgil.

249 *build up nests*: i.e. build false hopes.

256 *noisome parbreak*: offensive vomit.

257 *standing*: stagnant.

259 *engines*: i.e. eyes.

273–4 *Sharp . . . break*: sharp hunger cuts off at their source the thoughts of pity that Bajazeth would otherwise express to comfort Zabina.

277 *date*: duration.

282 *Of . . . inflictions*: of our inexpressible, cursed afflictions.

311 *wildfire*: inflammable substances used in warfare.

320 *Thy*: i.e. the blood of thy.

331 *charged*: levelled.

332 *check*: paw, strike.

336 *Whose*: this possessive pronoun refers to the Virgins.

346–7 *Earth . . . deaths*: Zenocrate exclaims that such momentous deaths should be accompanied by earthquakes and by geysers cast up as subterranean winds struggle to escape from within the earth. Compare 1.2.50–1.

357 *in conduct*: under the guidance.

364 *Of . . . pity*: for the inevitable turn of Fortune's wheel and for considerations of pity.

367 *In*: as in.

378 *affecter*: lover.

379 *Turnus*: the betrothed of Lavinia and defeated opponent of the marriage of Aeneas to Lavinia in Virgil's *Aeneid*. (See ll. 391–3.)

386 *racked*: pulled apart. Zenocrate's heart is pulled in two by her divided loyalties.

389 *change I use*: inconstancy I practise.

392 *Prevented*: deprived.

393 *fatally*: i.e. to Turnus (and, by analogy, to the king of Arabia).

394 *issue to*: outcome or resolution of.

396 *by . . . powers*: considering that both armies are irresistible (or, *their* may refer to the gods in l. 391).

397 *With virtue of*: by means of.

398 *to*: in accordance with.

399–401 *Then . . . Arabia*: Zenocrate prays that, if it be the gods' will, her father and the king of Arabia may both be saved.

401 S.D. *They . . . battle*: trumpeters (offstage) give the signal to begin.

411 *for such love*: for such an unworthy loved one.

413 *Whose . . . griefs*: whose apparent good fortune has never quieted her sorrow.

423–4 *sweet . . . merits*: unexpectedly good things that have happened to you, deserving as you are.

438 *Euphrates*: accented on the first syllable.

441 *of*: with.

448 *confirmed*: established firmly, or, was confirmed by.

453 *the Fatal Sisters*: the three Fates; see 1.2.174.

459 *resolved*: dissolved. (Tamburlaine imagines the sun drawing up the blood he has spilled and distilling it in bloody rain, creating the effect of a shower of bloody meteors.)

473 *of power*: able to.

480 *Of force*: of necessity.

485 *for*: as for.

486 *record*: call to witness. (Stressed on first syllable.)

487 *find . . . time*: seek for no further-off time.

496 *her love*: your love of her.

510–11 *As . . . Jove*: on Zeus' triumph over the giants (often confused by poets with the Titans) and his thrusting them beneath the mountains, see 2.3.21 and 2.6.5–6 above.

511 *shadowing*: harbouring; depicting.

513 *Latona's . . . arms*: Artemis or Diana, devoted to the hunt.

527 *on Alcides' post*: on the door-post of Hercules' temple.

Tamburlaine Part II

Prologue 5 *Fates*: see Part I, 1.2.174 and note.

1.1 The scene is set on the banks of the Danube.

2 *Placed . . . issue*: placed in authority close to the offspring.

6 *Natolia*: in Asia Minor, modern-day Turkey.

17 *Near Guyron's head*: Guiron is a town on the upper Euphrates, north-east of Aleppo.

22 *Almains, rutters, Muffs*: Germans, cavalry, Swiss.

24 *hazard . . . might*: put in hazard that which we might otherwise.

25 *parallel*: circle of latitude.

26 *Gruntland*: Greenland.

compassed with: surrounded by.

28 *Polypheme*: Polyphemus, one-eyed giant in the *Odyssey*.

29 *cut the Arctic line*: cross the Arctic circle heading southward.

30 *Bringing . . . arms*: bringing to Sigismond's army a military might equivalent to that of all Europe.

32 *champian mead*: open plain.

34 *his scarlet*: its bloodstained.

37 *Terrene main*: Mediterranean. (The Danube flows into the Black Sea and thence through the Bosporus and Dardanelles to the Aegean, where Italian merchant sailors will encounter the floating bodies of Christians.)

42 *Europe*: the European Christian merchants and warriors who ply the Middle East are compared to Europa, swimming across the Aegean on the back of the bull (Zeus in disguise) who has abducted her, except that this present 'Europe' will be humbled and beaten.

43 *Trapped*: adorned; but with suggestion also of 'entrapped'.

47 *Cairon*: Cairo.

59 *Fear*: frighten.

69 *Lantchidol*: the Indian Ocean.

81 *used*: made it their custom.

90 *the axletree of heaven*: the axis through the earth around which the heavens seem to rotate.

92 *feathered steel*: steel-tipped arrows.

100 *princely fowl*: eagle.

119 *your general*: Orcanes.

123 *stand not upon terms*: does not insist on unreasonable conditions.

155 *lancers*: presumably stressed on the second syllable, as though the word were 'lanciers'.

1.2.3 *the western world*: i.e. western Asia, Turkey.

4 *here*: i.e. in Egypt (1.1.4).

15 *runs*: flows; but with pun on *running*, escaping, in the next line.

20 *Darote's streams*: i.e. the Nile delta. *Darote's* is pronounced in three syllables.

33 *Straits*: straits of Gibraltar.

38 *Pygmalion*: legendary king who fell in love with a beautiful statue (made by himself, according to Ovid, *Metamorphoses*, x. 243 ff.).

39 *Io*: Io was transformed into a white heifer by Zeus to conceal her from the jealous Hera (Ovid, *Metamorphoses*, i. 588 ff.).

50 *fair veil*: i.e. moonlight and starlight.

51 *Phoebus*: the sun.

52 *th'Antipodes*: people dwelling on the opposite side of the globe, and the region where they dwell.

56 *need we not*: will we not inevitably.

1.3.5 *Larissa*: a seacoast town between Syria and Egypt.

6 *parts*: are divided.

12 *on both the poles*: on the axis passing through both poles.

22 *as*: as befits.

23–4 *Water . . . wit*: water (moist and cold) and air (moist and hot), mixed together in the absence of earth and fire, point to a humour that is overly phlegmatic and amorous, lacking in fierceness and determination (or bile and choler).

39 *Trotting the ring*: riding inside a ring designed for the *manège* or training of horses.

40 *tainted*: hit; a technical term from *tilting* or jousting.

41 *curvet*: raise the forelegs and then leap with the hindlegs before the forelegs touch the ground.

42 *As*: that.

44 *Armour of proof*: armour of tested strength.

51 *complete*: stressed on the first syllable.

103 *channel*: neck, channel-bone or collar-bone.

130 *my . . . Fez*: i.e. Techelles.

143 *infernal Jove*: Hades or Pluto.

152 *Makes . . . joy*: fills me to overflowing with the joy which I conceive, and which itself multiplies imaginings of all that these 'fellow kings' can achieve together.

163–4 *as at . . . men*: after the great flood, Deucalion and his wife Pyrrha threw stones over their shoulders from which sprang up men and women. (Ovid, *Metamorphoses*, i. 318 ff.).

165 *lavish*: profusion.

166 *his wingèd messenger*: Mercury.

169 *Thetis*: a Nereid or sea-maiden.

170 *Boötes*: see Part I, 1.2.207 and note.

176 *lain in leaguer*: lain in camp as the besieger.

178 *Guallatia*: a town in the Libyan desert.

180 *kept*: controlled; sailed through.

181 *Canarea*: the Canary islands.

182 *they*: i.e. our soldiers.

188 *John the Great*: Prester John, an alleged Christian priest or king who ruled Abyssinia (where Machda is located).

189 *triple mitre*: papal tiara.

191 *Cazates*: located near the source of the Nile.

202 *Nubia*: located between the Red Sea and the Nile.

205 *Damasco*: in Part I, 4.1, Marlowe imagines Damascus to be on the Nile.

210 *Podalia*: in southern Russia near Rumania.

212 *Nigra Silva*: the Black Forest, regarded at the time as huge and dangerous.

215 *Mare Maggiore*: the Black Sea.

219 *pensions*: payments.

221 *Lachryma Christi*: a strong, sweet wine of southern Italy. Literally, Christ's tears.

2.1.5 *bloods*: lives.

14 *repair*: imminent arrival.

16 *Natolia hath dismissed*: Orcanes has redeployed (from Eastern Europe to Turkey).

31 *should*: would.

32 *our profession*: our vows.

35 *accomplishments*: fulfilments of vows.

38 *Is . . . policy*: is, according to the dictates of prudent statecraft, not.

50 *dispensive faith*: an oath that can be dispensed with.

54 *Saul . . . Balaam*: Saul sinned by not utterly destroying the Amalekites as the Lord had commanded (1 Samuel 15); Balaam refused to curse Israel at Balak's behest, but only when the ass he was riding stopped him from going further (Numbers 22).

2.2.11 *by . . . arms*: in waves will challenge him to combat.

12 *And . . . score*: with 100,000 subjects in each wave of attack.

45 *our sacrifice*: a sacrifice we offer up to Thee.

47 *veil of Cynthia*: moonlit sky, as at 1.2.50 and note.

50 *in . . . circumscriptible*: is subject to limits of space.

51 *continent*: (1) thing to be filled (2) connected land mass.

2.3.8 *wherein . . . die*: in which death I end the possibility of sinning, end sin by dying.

9 *Conceive*: beget, institute.

20 *Zoacum*: a tree mentioned in the Koran, xxxvii. 60–4, with properties as described here in ll. 19–23.

25 *Orcus'*: hell's.

32 *proved*: urged as though proving.

38 *We . . . trunk*: I decree that a continuous watch be set to guard his body.

39 *fowls*: birds of prey.

40 *give . . . charge*: see that it be carried out immediately.

43 *brother*: fellow king(s).

47 *his angry fate*: Sigismond's bitter fate.

2.4 S.D. *The arras is drawn*: the curtain is withdrawn from before the discovery space or a removable curtained booth. The actors presumably come forward on to the stage during the scene. At the scene's end, the curtain is drawn once again.

9 *bowers*: i.e. eye-sockets.

13 *Draws . . . breath*: draws her last breaths, her last comfort.

14 *dazzled with*: overpowered by.

18 *Apollo . . . lamps*: the sun, moon, and other heavenly bodies.

40 *An if*: the original octavo reading, 'And if', should possibly be left unchanged in a modernized text. See note at l. 117 below.

52 *opposed . . . diameter*: diametrically opposed on two sides of the earth in a lunar eclipse. Lunar eclipses take place in the dark of night, when the

ascending moon crosses the ecliptic at the Serpent's head (*caput draconis*), or else in its descending node at the Serpent's tail (*cauda draconis*); see ll. 53–4. The moon must be on or near the ecliptic or plane of the solar system for an eclipse to occur. The 'Serpent' is probably the constellation Scorpio, in the Zodiac, but it could be Hydra or Serpens.

58–9 *And . . . sky*: and sooner let the outermost heavenly sphere of pure fire dissolve to fashion you a kingdom in the farthest region of the sky.

61 *suspect . . . mine*: imagine your death to follow as a consequence of mine.

74 *my latest memory*: my remembrance of them in this my last hour.

81 *spheres*: eyes like heavenly spheres.

83 *supplied*: filled up.

84 *Whose darts*: referring both to Death and to her eyes.

90 *Her*: Zenocrate's.

92 *but*: only.

93 *Lesbia . . . Corinna*: women addressed in the erotic poetry of Catullus, Horace, and Ovid.

99 *Fatal Sisters*: see note to Prologue, l. 5.

100 *triple moat*: comprising Lethe, Styx, and Phlegethon.

103 *cavalieros*: high earthen fortifications for cannon.

114–15 *The rusty . . . war*: the doors of the temple in the Roman Forum dedicated to Janus, god of beginnings, stood open in times of war and were closed in times of peace.

117 *And if*: the original text is ambiguous as to whether this means 'And if', continuing the thought of the previous lines, or 'An if', meaning 'if'. The same is true in reverse at l. 40 above.

123 *If . . . blood*: if grief might serve, our broken hearts have bled.

133 *Mausolus'*: the tomb of this king from Asia Minor (d. 353 BC), called the Mausoleum, was one of the seven wonders of the ancient world.

140 *stature*: statue.

3.1.16–19 *Do . . . infamies*: be forced to acknowledge and honour my supremacy, and suffer such vengeance for the wrongs he did my father, that the world would wipe out from the book of infamy the shameful blot on our noble names caused by my father's abusive treatment. (Or, 'Bearing . . . wrongs' in l. 17 may mean 'I, Callapine, who bear the sacred obligation to avenge my father's wrongs'. 'Baseborn infamies' in l. 19 suggests 'an infamy basely borne' by Orcanes, an imputation that he can wipe out with decisive military retaliation.)

30 *And . . . pitch*: and will raise our honours to as great a height as Fortune raised Tamburlaine. (*Pitch* is the highest point from which a falcon swoops down on its prey.)

39–41 *Some . . . sufficient*: soldiers who, being but a handful in comparison to the huge army of the perjured Christians they conquered, yet are confident that their own numbers are sufficient. (*Them* in l. 41 means 'themselves'.)

51 *Mare-Major Sea*: Black Sea.

54–5 *Whose . . . towns*: whose courage is kindled by Tamburlaine's having burned their towns.

63 *in martial manner pitched*: set in order for fighting. The armies will adopt a crescent formation.

68 *for*: as for.

73 *That's . . . king*: i.e. it is nothing to boast about, being promoted from gentleman to king.

3.2.1 *this cursèd town*: i.e. Larissa.

12 *mask*: lurk unseen.

13 *Compassed . . . Phlegethon*: surrounded by the three rivers of the underworld.

20 *Wrought*: decorated.

29 *arc*: i.e. hemisphere. The southern stars, never before seen in the north, will cross the equator (*the centre's latitude*, l. 31) as pilgrims to gaze worshipfully on Zenocrate's portrait (ll. 32–3).

37 *Thou*: i.e. your portrait.

61 *caper*: i.e. having been blown up.

63 *figure*: shape of fortification.

64 *For . . . meet*: and for what kind of terrain the quinque-angle is best suited. (This star-shaped or irregular pentagon fortification, with its obtuse and sharp angles, is appropriate not for the *champian* or flat terrain of l. 63 but for uneven ground, where its strong and weak points can be strategically fitted to points of greatest and least vulnerability, as ll. 65–7 go on to explain.)

68 *counterscarps*: steeply sloped walls of ditches at the outermost ring of fortification.

70 *bulwarks*: projecting earthworks at angles of the fort.

rampires: earthen ramparts supporting the walls from behind.

71 *cavalieros*: high earthen fortifications for cannon.

counterforts: braces strengthening walls from the inside.

73 *countermines*: tunnels used to intercept enemy mining operations.

74 *secret issuings*: small doorways permitting sallies to defend the fortifications.

75 *argins*: ramparts in front of a fort.

78 *Casemates*: bomb-proof vaults within the ramparts.

80 *curtains*: walls connecting the fortress towers.

81 *Dismount*: throw down from their carriages.

adverse part: adversary.

85 *mount*: rise (by means of damming).

86 *That*: in such a way that.

99 *A ring . . . horse*: a defensive ring of pikebearers, serving together with weapon-bearing infantry and cavalry.

104 *overthwart*: across.

107–8 *Filling . . . blood*: wine was thought to replenish the blood supply. Wine is *airy* because the element *air* is hot and moist, like blood.

concocted: digested.

124 *the Afric potentate*: Bajazeth, the Turkish emperor of Part I.

150 *runaway*: i.e. Callapine.

152 *at a bay*: at bay.

3.3.6 *Minions, falc'nets, and sakers*: various kinds of light artillery.

7 *Filling . . . breach*: breaching the enemy's fortifications so extensively that the rubble will fill up their ditches.

14 S.D. *[Drums] summon the battle*: Theridamas's drums summon the enemy troops (*the battle*) to a parley or negotiation about terms. The Captain and his family appear above on 'the walls' (l. 14) of the besieged Balsera, parleying with the besieging forces on the main stage in front of those walls.

20–6 *These . . . trench*: Theridamas's strategy is to raise earthworks in front of the besieged fortification so high that his cannon can shoot over the ramparts and outer walls with their hidden passageways on to the defences of the inner fortress (the *hold*).

26 *his ruin*: the falling in of the breached fortifications.

38 *mounts*: earthworks.

39 *all convoys that can*: and cut off all supply convoys that you can.

43–5 *Cast . . . shot*: the pioners or sappers are to dig trenches by throwing the earth forward as a defence for themselves, though they will have to keep down as much as they can at first. Compare ll. 20–1.

50 *Jacob's staff*: a surveying instrument used to find ranges for the guns. Named after a pilgrim's staff.

53 *full point-blank*: on a straight horizontal shot.

54 *see*: see to.

ordinance: ordnance, artillery. The old spelling is retained here for pronunciation in three syllables.

55 *battery*: artillery platform.

56 *gabions*: wicker cylindrical forms filled with earth, serving as fortifications.

60 *crack*: loud noise.

3.4.33 S.D. *[She burns the bodies]*: some sort of stage enactment seems necessary, in view of the following lines.

48–51 *Than . . . robe*: than is to be found throughout the entire universe, from the outermost sphere of fire that forms the concave surface of Jove's vast palace to the innermost sphere of the moon.

51 *Thetis*: one of the Nereids or sea-maidens. The moon is associated with the sea.

57 *Rhamnusia*: Nemesis, to whom a temple stood at Rhamnus in Attica. See Part I, 2.3.37 and note.

61 *zenith*: head; highest ascent.

63 *sounding . . . trump*: sounding her golden trumpet.

64–5 *That . . . heaven*: so that from one end of heaven's celestial axis to the other.

75 *In frame of which*: in the fashioning of which.

3.5.3 *Aleppo*: a city in modern-day Syria near the Turkish border and hence at the south-eastern corner of Natolia, Marlowe's usual name for Asia Minor—though in ll. 8–9 'Natolia' seems to refer to a walled town. Presumably Marlowe regards this town as the capital of the region.

6 *Ida*: Mount Ida, near Troy(?).

11 *Phrygia*: in central and western modern-day Turkey.

11–12 *the sea . . . Cyprus*: the eastern Mediterranean.

34 *showed*: displayed to, as in a military march of inspection before a commander or sovereign.

36–7 *Of that . . . Semiramis*: Semiramis, a queen of legendary beauty, is supposed to have built Babylon with its hanging gardens.

39 *numbered*: reckoned up the numbers.

46–8 *Of . . . foot*: from Halla and other neighbouring cities have come 10,000 Sorian cavalry and 30,000 footsoldiers.

65–8 *As Hector . . . fame*: this is a post-Homeric episode found for example in Lydgate's *Troy Book* and in Shakespeare's *Troilus and Cressida*.

overdare: surpass in daring.

74 *fly my glove*: flee from the gauntlet I throw down as challenge to combat.

75–6 *Now . . . fight*: now that you fear your army's weakness, you would rather rely on your superiority in single combat.

79–82 *Villain . . . world*: Tamburlaine attributes his uniqueness to the favourable aspects of Jupiter, Mars, Venus, etc., all uniquely in conjunction at his birth.

87 *That villain*: Almeda.

101 *for*: to prevent.

103 *viceroy*: Almeda(?). Tamburlaine scornfully alludes to his position as Callapine's favourite and seeming heir.

114 *diet yourselves*: Tamburlaine sardonically addresses his enemies as though they were work animals about to be fed and harnessed.

115 *journey*: drive.

126 *not any element*: i.e. nothing, not earth, water, fire, or air.

131 *Mare Rosso*: the Red Sea.

135–6 *make . . . dozen*: make it a nice even half dozen, i.e. swell the already absurd number of persons Callapine has crowned king.

137 *give arms*: (1) display a coat of arms (2) give alms.

148 *ye petty kings*: Callapine, Orcanes, Jerusalem, etc.
    bugs: bugbears, bogeys (who).

159 *You know not*: you never can tell.

4.1 S.D. *from the tent*: the tent is evidently arranged at a stage door, as with Zenocrate's bed at 2.4, or possibly as a movable structure. Calyphas is visible at the tent's mouth.

26 *to flesh . . . swords*: to initiate into battle our unstained swords, as though feeding them with flesh.

42 *Zona mundi*: mountains in Tartary in central Asia.

51 S.D. *run in*: i.e. run offstage, as though to the battle.

67 *taratantaras*: bugle calls.

68 *net*: fine mesh or veil (suggesting also the snare in which Mars and Venus were caught by Vulcan as they made love; *Odyssey*, viii. 300 ff.).
    and: i.e. and who.

75 *stoops*: force to stoop, humiliate.

78 *illustrate*: shed lustre upon, show to good advantage. Accented on the second syllable.

86 *Cherish . . . supplies*: nourish your valour continually with fresh supplies of enemies.

92 *thus . . . eyes*: set afire with fury at what I see.

94 *Shroud any thought*: harbour any thought that.

99 *argument of arms*: military code.

102 *arms*: the proper use of weapons.

103 *the jealousy of wars*: zealous devotion to the cause of war.

105 *joyed . . . flesh*: delighted in being born into this human flesh, ardent with vitality and aspiring to military deeds.

107–8 *Jaertis' . . . love*: the Jaertis (Iaxartes) is imagined to run through Samarkand as a deep river gently embracing the river bank.

113–14 *A form . . . consists*: the cowardly soul of Calyphas is not worthy to receive and embody the spiritual and Jove-like essence that resides in the flesh of Tamburlaine.

120 *thy*: i.e. Jove's.

121 *to my issue*: to my son, or, to be my son.

123 *tartar*: hard, crusty scum in the fermentation process.

127 *he*: i.e. one of the Titans. Atlas (l. 129), a Titan, was made to bear up the earth in punishment for his part in the revolt.

130 *for*: for fear of.

132 *will not see*: wilfully refuse to acknowledge.

144 *And . . . thee*: the Turkish blood previously shed by Tamburlaine will thus rain down on him in revenge.

146 *If . . . repute*: if, that is, you deem tyrannical the justice made manifest in my victories on the battlefield.

171 *Rhadamanth and Aeacus*: sons of Zeus who became judges of the dead as a consequence of their just lives on earth.

187 *Cimbrian*: Teutonic.

188 *the females' miss*: lacking or being separated from females.

189 *their following*: following them.

197 *For . . . pride*: shed for the burning of his country's cities and palaces.

200 *persist*: persist in being.

4.2 S.D. *[Enter]*: Olympia may come forward from a stage door as though from Theridamas's tent (see ll. 3 and 14), like Calyphas in the previous scene. A 'discovery' effect by means of a withdrawn curtain is possible but not necessary.

30 *Than . . . wilderness*: than the moon's effect on the ocean tides.

31 *thy view*: my viewing of you.

41 *turrets*: i.e. raised platforms.

49 *love to be*: (1) wish to be (2) fall in love even for the sake of becoming.

55 *will . . . honour*: if you agree not to assail my chastity.

62–3 *In . . . metaphysical*: containing the essential property of marble, brought to a proper consistency by means of supernatural knowledge.

80 *if*: even if.

86 *theoria*: contemplation, survey(?).

4.3 S.D. *led by*: the captive kings are paraded past. (Or perhaps *by* with states the same idea twice, in error.)

6 *Byron*: a town near Babylon and Asphaltis Lake (l. 5).

8 *nosterils*: nostrils (pronounced in three syllables).

10 *governor*: driver.

12 *Alcides*: Hercules, who, in one version of his eighth labour, must tame and drive off the horses that King Aegeus has fed on human flesh. In the more common version, the offending king is Diomedes of Thrace. Hercules feeds his body to the horses.

21 *racking*: being driven before the wind.

24 *right*: rightly, indeed.

25 *see the figure*: behold in me the very image.

28 *idle*: (1) unemployed—referring to Orcanes and Jerusalem (2) worthless.

32–8 *O thou . . . queen*: Dis or Hades, to whom Orcanes prays, carried off Persephone or Proserpina from Sicily and made her queen of the underworld, thus taking for his own pleasure the chief joy of Ceres or Demeter, Persephone's mother, and bringing winter to the world during Persephone's yearly absence (Ovid, *Metamorphoses*, v. 385 ff.).

41 *once*: once and for all.

46 *hedges*: barriers, teeth (and leading to sardonic wordplay about hedged-in animals in ll. 48–9).

49 *their kicking . . . pastures*: i.e. their frisky tongues out of their mouths.

52 S.D. *[Celebinus bridles Orcanes]*: the stage action is uncertain. If Orcanes is bridled, as the dialogue suggests, is not the king of Jerusalem also bridled after l. 56, as Theridamas threatens at ll. 43–7? Yet if both are bridled in order to rein their tongues, how do they manage to speak at ll. 77–80 and 85? Possibly they are bridled in cruel jest and then released, since they are not yet to be harnessed. When they are bridled at 5.1.147 they are immediately harnessed to Tamburlaine's chariot, and speak no more.

61 *Aldebaran*: a first-magnitude star in Taurus.

62 *threefold astracism*: constellation of three stars near Aldebaran, or perhaps threefold division of the cosmos into earth, planets, and stars(?).

63 *triple world*: consisting of Europe, Asia, and Africa.

65–6 *the funeral . . . son*: at 4.1.161, Tamburlaine gave order that the Turks' concubines bury his 'effeminate' son Calyphas.

70 *queens*: (with suggestion of *queans*, 'whores').

73 *serve all your turns*: be passed from soldier to soldier until every man's sexual desire is satisfied.

75 *Brawl . . . lechery*: Tamburlaine warns his soldiers against quarrelling boastfully over the women they are to enjoy.

81–2 *Live . . . heels*: Tamburlaine mocks Orcanes and the other defeated 'slaves' by suggesting that if they really wished to spare their 'guiltless dames' they should have lived continently and not marched to meet Tamburlaine in battle with 'troops of harlots' at their heels. The octavo reading, *Live content*, is hard to explain, unless conceivably Tamburlaine continues to address his soldiers as in ll. 75–6, bidding them be grateful and enjoy themselves but not to let the women follow them around too flagrantly. This could continue the idea that the soldiers are not to *brawl*—i.e. brag loudly—about their women (*OED*, v.¹ 2). It would seem odd for Tamburlaine to address his soldiers as 'slothful', but he does call them 'villains' in l. 84—a term not unlike 'slaves' in l. 81.

86 *'Twere but time indeed*: it is about time. (Said sardonically; Tamburlaine is scornfully amused at the notion of concubines' honour.)

91 *jest*: play sexually.

92 *soundly*: thoroughly, uninterruptedly; with suggestion of 'in a healthy manner'.

100 *controlleth crowns*: holds sway over monarchs.

104 *Sinus Arabicus*: the Red Sea.

108 *Jaertis*: see note at 4.1.107–8.

113 *Ilion's*: Troy's.

121 *Selinus*: the site of a temple to Jupiter in Sicily.

122 *Erycina's*: i.e. Venus', so named after a temple to her on Mount Eryx in Sicily.

125 *Saturn's royal son*: Jupiter or Zeus.

126 *Mounted*: mounted in.

127 *the path*: i.e. the Milky Way, as in l. 132.

5.1 S.D. *upon the walls*: in the upper gallery (a permanent feature, seemingly, of the stage for which Marlowe was writing), as at 3.3.14, representing here the walls of the besieged Babylon.

14 *of . . . conceit*: you would consider valuable.

15 *for*: despite.

17–20 *When . . . hell*: the bituminous lake turns all objects soaked in it into impregnable defences, resembling and surpassing the gates of hell.

33 *Will*: who will.

54 *I . . . throat*: I return the charge of 'traitor' down your throat.

61 *And . . . parley*: and that assault shall be delayed no longer for discussing terms.

62 S.D. *Alarm . . . Jerusalem*: Tamburlaine's forces ascend by scaling ladders to the upper gallery and thereby enter the 'city' of Babylon, exiting above into the tiring house. Tamburlaine's subsequent entry in his chariot on the main stage bespeaks his successful capture of the city.

63–5 *The stately . . . deep*: only the most remarkable hyperbole can imagine the pillars of Babylon, located between the Tigris and Euphrates rivers and over 100 miles upstream from the Persian Gulf, as visible from the ocean.

66 *carried thither*: blown all the way to Limnasphaltis' lake.

69 *Belus . . . Alexander*: Belus, legendary founder of Babylon; Ninus, the mythical founder of Nineveh, whose queen, Semiramis (see l. 73), was supposed to have built the walls of Babylon; and Alexander the Great, who conquered Babylon in 331 BC.

72 *with*: by.

75 *trod the measures*: danced in stately fashion.

77 *Saturnia*: Juno.

83 *used . . . of*: so greatly underestimated.

86 *Sirrah*: addressed to the Governor.

87–8 *the region . . . fire*: the upper atmosphere, below the fiery empyrean, in which, according to Aristotelian physics, ignited exhalations blazed as comets.

93 *quailed*: caused to quail; overcome.

97 *Cerberus*: the three-headed dog guarding Hades, captured by Hercules.

98 *black Jove*: Dis or Hades.

104 *the anger . . . Highest*: embodiment of God's anger or scourge of God.

123 *take*: take possession of.

126 S.D. *[Exit Governor]*: probably the Governor is led off and then is 'discovered' hanging on the walls at ll. 147 S.D. by means of a curtain drawn back, but it is also possible that he is strung up in sight of the audience.

131 *now*: now that.

147 S.D. *Re-enter Theridamas*: if Theridamas exits at l. 135, as seems likely, he could re-enter any time before l. 151, when he speaks. Alternatively, he could go to the stage door at l. 135 to see Trebizond and Soria on their way, guarded, but never actually exit.

157 *like Baghdad's governor*: as Baghdad's governor should hang. (Baghdad is seemingly equated here with Babylon.)

176 S.D. *a fire*: fires might seem dangerous in wooden playhouses, but the players did bring on lighted torches, set off cannon, and the like (and did manage to burn down the Globe this way in 1613). Perhaps a metal container is used to shield the stage.

193 *Or vengeance*: or why do you not send vengeance.

195 *abstracts*: epitome, i.e. the Koran.

213 *removed*: removed from.

5.2.9 *full from Babylon*: reinforced to full strength after the siege of Babylon. See l. 58.

58 *Or that*: before.

rejoined: reassembled.

5.3.8 *Cimmerian*: black. See Part I, 3.2.77, note.

19 *retain . . . holiness*: still deserve to be worshipped.

22 *Bear . . . burden*: do not join in the chorus.

31 *Sustain . . . inexcellence*: bear so vile a shame.

34 *they . . . out*: the devils think their allotted time of suffering is over.

36 *thy*: heaven's, Jove's.

37 *feel*: feel that.

38 *note*: mark, sign.

44 *a man*: a mere mortal.

53 *envy*: accented on the second syllable.

58 *charge*: level.

 his: i.e. Atlas'.

80 *govern*: to govern.

82 *hypostasis*: sediment.

84 *accidental*: abnormal.

86 *humidum and calor*: moisture and natural heat.

91 *critical*: astrologically unfavourable.

93 *alongst*: parallel to.

96 *organons*: bodily organs or fluids acting as instruments of the soul.

97 *argument of art*: medical diagnosis.

111 *endure*: harden, strengthen.

112 *only*: alone, all by itself.

116 *vanished*: dissipated, made to vanish.

131–5 *And . . . India*: Tamburlaine envisages a Suez Canal.

146–9 *Lies . . . Antipodes*: lies westward from the place where the Greenwich meridian line crosses the Tropic of Cancer (near the Canary Islands) all the way to the far East, where the sun, after setting here, begins the day again in the world inhabited by those who live on the opposite side of the globe. (Tamburlaine dreams of conquering the Western Hemisphere.)

151 *here*: i.e. in the Americas, the West Indies.

154–5 *And from . . . descried*: Tamburlaine points to Australasia, uncharted as yet but greatly wondered about.

164–5 *Your . . . flesh*: our grieving and humble selves derive their animating spirit from your soul, our bodies from your body.

168 *this subject*: the substance that is myself.

170 *his*: its.

177 *scourge*: chariot whip, mentioned at 4.3 S.D.

185-90 *With . . . dignity!*: how hardhearted would be my enjoyment of your gift to me of life and soul if, instead of dissolving into grief and mortification, I should gladden my heart at the prospect of such earthly dignity!

195-8 *How . . . sovereignty?*: how should I take such steps against the promptings of my heart, embracing a life of honour when I wish only to die, and pleading in vain with myself to accept an unwelcome sovereignty?

199 *thine honour*: your devotion to honour.

203 *steelèd stomachs*: obdurately proud spirits.

207 *damnèd*: doomed, wretched.

208-9 *And send . . . agony*: and may heaven transfer on to me the bodily suffering my father endures and thus reprieve him from death. (Alternatively, Amyras may simply ask that he be made to suffer along with his father, as befitting his grief.)

211 *my fatal chair*: the chair in which I am doomed to die; or, chariot.

225 *And when . . . sight*: Tamburlaine understands that his soul, freed of the limits of bodily sense, will be able to see Zenocrate's spirit.

231-3 *As that . . . fire*: on Phaethon's reckless guiding of the sun-chariot, so ominous in its implications, compare Part I, 4.2.49 and note.

232 *Phoebe*: the moon.

237 *Phyteus' beams*: the sun's (Apollo's or Pythius') beams.

238 *these . . . jades*: i.e. the conquered kings.

239 *take . . . hair*: proverbially, Occasion must be seized by the forelock.

240 *Hippolytus*: a young man who rejected the love of Phaedra and, as punishment, was dragged to death by his own horses.

251 *his*: its.

Doctor Faustus: A-Text

Prologue 1 *Trasimene*: battlefield in Italy where, in 217 BC, the Carthaginian general Hannibal defeated the Romans.

2 *mate*: side with.

4 *state*: stable rule and ceremony.

6 *daunt*: control. B1's *vaunt* is a persuasive reading.

9 *plaud*: applause.

13 *Wittenberg*: university famous as a centre of Protestant reform. The quarto reading, *Wertenberg*, probably suggests a confusion with Württemberg, though it has been argued the choice was intentional since Tübingen in Württemburg was known for its radical Protestant thought.

16 *The . . . graced*: having graced the university with his talents and presence; or, theology, that fruitful discipline graced by him and by the university.

18 *whose . . . disputes*: who take sweet delight in disputation.

21 *waxen wings*: the Chorus compares Faustus to Icarus, who flew too near the sun on the waxen wings devised by his father Daedalus and fell into the Aegean. A favourite legend of dangerous aspiration.

27 *his chiefest bliss*: i.e. his hope to be saved.

1.1 S.D. *in his study*: perhaps, in the Elizabethan theatre, Faustus is 'discovered' by means of a curtain withdrawn from a 'discovery space' backstage. If so, he presumably comes forward and plays most of the scene on the main stage.

2 *that . . . profess*: that which you claim as your area of expertise.

3 *be . . . show*: be a theologian in the world's eyes.

7 *'Bene . . . logices'*: Faustus translates this Latin (from Ramus, not Aristotle) in the next line.

12 *On kai me on*: being and not being, i.e. philosophical inquiry. (Greek.)

Galen: Greek writer on medicine in the second century AD, the standard classical authority.

13 *ubi . . . medicus*: where the philosopher leaves off, the physician begins.

16 *'Summum . . . sanitas'*: Faustus translates in the next line.

20 *Are . . . monuments*: i.e. are your prescriptions not the talk of Europe?

25 *being . . . again*: Faustus blasphemously dreams of performing miracles, like Christ's in raising Lazarus from the dead.

27 *Justinian*: Roman emperor at Constantinople, 527–65 AD, who reorganized Roman law in his *Institutes* (l. 32) and other writings.

28–9 *'Si . . . rei'*: if something is bequeathed as a legacy to two heirs, one shall receive the thing itself and the other its value in money.

31 *'Exhaereditare . . . nisi—'*: a father may not disinherit his son unless—.

33 *Church*: canon law relied extensively on Justinian. B1's *law* may be the correct reading.

34 *His study*: the study of Justinian.

37 *done*: said and done.

38 *Jerome's Bible*: the Vulgate or Latin translation, the canonical text for Christendom from the sixth century until the Reformation.

39–47 *'Stipendium' . . . die*: Faustus's quotations and paraphrases of the Vulgate Bible (Romans 6: 23 and 1 John 1: 8) wilfully omit divine promises of salvation to those who truly repent their sins.

51 *metaphysics*: occult lore.

58 *quiet poles*: motionless poles of the universe.

62 *But . . . this*: but the authority of anyone who excels in magic.

65 *try*: apply.

75 *That*: i.e. that 'damnèd book' of magic.

80 *conceit*: the very thought.

82 *Resolve me of*: clear up for me.

91 *Rhine . . . Wittenberg*: the Rhine borders Württemberg but is distant from Wittenberg, suggesting again a confusion of names.

92 *public schools*: universities.

94 *they*: the spirits who will serve Faustus (l. 81).

95 *Parma*: the Spanish governor-general who oppressed the Netherlands from 1579 to 1592 and was reviled in Protestant England.

97–9 *Yea . . . invent*: I will have my obedient servants devise even more ingenious instruments of violent warfare than the famous fireship used in Antwerp, 1585, by the Netherlanders against a bridge built by Parma.

106 *receive no object*: think of nothing else.

107 *But ruminates*: does nothing but ruminate.

115 *Gravelled*: floored, confounded.

116–18 *And . . . hell*: and caused the flowering youth of Wittenberg to swarm to hear me handle questions in debate, much as spirits of the underworld swarmed to hear the poet Musaeus (as they did also to hear Orpheus) when he visited there.

119 *Agrippa*: Cornelius Agrippa, 1485–1535, noted magician.

120 *shadows*: the shades or spirits of the dead whom Agrippa called up.

122 *canonize*: accented on the second syllable: can-ón-ize.

123 *Indian Moors*: American Indians.

124 *the subjects . . . element*: the spirits that inhere in and give bodily form to the four elements, earth, water, air, and fire.

127 *Like . . . staves*: like German cavalry with lances.

130 *Shadowing*: harbouring.

airy: heavenly.

131 *the Queen of Love*: Venus.

134 *old Philip's*: King Philip II of Spain's.

137 *object it not*: do not urge it as an objection.

141 *tongues*: learned languages.

well seen in minerals: skilful in alchemy.

144 *mystery*: secret art.

145 *Delphian oracle*: oracle of Apollo at Delphi.

156 *And . . . works*: and take along the works of Roger Bacon and Pietro d'Abano (or perhaps Albertus Magnus), thirteenth-century magicians.

166 *canvass every quiddity*: look into every particular.

1.2.2 *'sic probo'*: I prove it thus.

7 *that follows not*: i.e. it does not logically follow that if 'God in heaven knows', I do not know also. (Wagner parodies scholastic debate.)

10–11 *That . . . upon't*: more scholastic parody: it does not logically follow that you can demand an answer (since we have not established that I know the answer). A *licentiate* is the holder of an advanced degree short of the doctorate.

16 *Ask . . . thief*: ask anyone who knows me about my reputation for honesty.

19–20 *corpus . . . mobile*: a natural body and hence subject to change and motion. (Wagner's mock-learned point is that Faustus is, in Aristotle's terms, humanly capable of motion and hence likely to be anywhere.)

21 *But that*: were it not that.

23 *the place of execution*: (1) the dining room where food is being dispatched (2) the gallows. (Wagner jests that such rascals as these scholars appear to be are scarcely worthy to approach the place where Faustus eats, but Wagner will be indulgent for once and answer their question.)

25 *precisian*: one who is precise in religious observance, a Puritan.

32 *allied*: bound in friendship.

34 *Rector*: head of the university.

1.3.1–4 *Now . . . breath*: Faustus speaks of night as the shadow of the earth which, as the sun sets, reaches out in the 'welkin' or sky towards Orion and the other constellations.

11–12 *Figures . . . stars*: charts of the heavens showing every constituent element, and astrological symbols representing the zodiac and planets.

16–22 *Sint . . . Mephistopheles*: be propitious to me, gods of Acheron! Let the threefold spirit of Jehovah be strong! Hail to thee, spirits of fire, air, water, and earth! Lucifer, thou prince of the East, Beelzebub, thou monarch of fiery hell, and Demogorgon, we beseech you that Mephistopheles may appear and rise. Why do you delay? By Jehovah, Gehenna, and the holy water I now sprinkle, and by the sign of the cross I now make, and by our prayers, may Mephistopheles himself arise at our command! (*Acheron* is a river in Hades; *Gehenna* is the Jewish hell.)

34 *Quin . . . imagine!*: return, Mephistopheles, in the shape of a friar!

46 *That . . . 'per accidens'*: i.e. yes, I came because of your conjuration, but not because it gave you irresistible power over me.

49 *glorious*: (1) beautiful (2) vainglorious.

60 *confounds . . . Elysium*: denies any distinction between the Christian hell and the pagan Elysian Fields, thereby refuting the notion of punishment in the afterlife.

61 *His . . . philosophers*: may his (Faustus's) spirit dwell for eternity with those of Plato, Aristotle, etc.

101 *And . . . mind*: and then tell me what Lucifer says.

108–9 *I'll . . . Spain*: i.e. I will connect Africa to Spain at the Straits of Gibraltar.

114 *speculation*: profound study.

1.4.3 *pickedevants*: short, pointed beards.

4 *comings in*: income.

5 *goings out*: (1) expenses (2) being out at elbow.

else: if you do not believe me.

7 *out of service*: unemployed.

13–14 *Qui mihi discipulus*: you who are my pupil.

16 *beaten*: (1) embroidered (2) thrashed (so that the wearer will receive the blows).

stavesacre: flower seeds used to exterminate vermin. But Robin, no doubt deliberately, misunderstands and turns the insult back on Wagner, punning meanwhile on a *stave* or wooden stick that can administer an *ache*.

24 *bind*: apprentice.

25 *familiars*: attendant evil spirits. Robin plays with the word in l. 28.

31 *guilders*: Dutch coins, here spoken of as French. Robin gets this name wrong, too, and is patriotically wary of anything French.

34 *but . . . of*: were it not for the impressive-sounding name of.

35 *counters*: tokens used to count money, valueless in themselves.

48 *round slop*: wide baggy breeches.

49 *Kill devil*: a recklessly daring fellow.

53 *horns*: (1) devils' horns (2) cuckolds' horns.

54 *clefts*: (2) cloven hoofs (2) vulvas.

63 *plackets*: slits in petticoats.

69 *diametarily*: diametrically.

70–1 *quasi . . . insistere*: as if to follow in our (i.e. my) footsteps.

72 *fustian*: bombast.

2.1.23 *seigniory of Emden*: governorship of Emden (a prosperous port in Germany on the North Sea).

26 *Cast*: give birth to, or reckon, ponder.

29 *Veni . . . Mephistophile!*: translated in the previous line.

31 *he lives*: this B1 reading makes better sense than A1's *I live*.

42 *Solamen . . . doloris*: it is a comfort to the wretched to have had companions in misery.

43 *Have . . . others?*: do you suffer pain yourselves, you devils who torture others?

69 S.D. *chafer*: portable grate.

70 *set it on*: i.e. set your blood on the fire in a saucer.

74 *Consummatum est*: it is finished, consummated (Christ's last words on the cross; John 19: 30).

77 *Homo, fuge*: fly, O man (Timothy 6: 11).

88 *Then . . . souls*: then there are enough rewards to be worth a thousand souls.

105 *by these presents*: by this present document.

108–9 *inviolate*: having been fully carried out.

119 *these elements*: all beneath the moon.

122 *one self*: one and the same.

146 *in the devil's name*: this common profanity has ironically literal application, like 'the devil give thee good on't' at ll. 113–14.

150 *no*: this word, supplied from B1, seems necessary for the sense.

156 *Lucifer*: at the end of a list that includes the chaste Penelope, wife of Odysseus in the *Odyssey*, and the Queen of Sheba, whose wisdom impressed Solomon (1 Kings 9: 1), we might expect the name of a woman as the personification of beauty; but to Mephistopheles, being in hell, nothing could be more beautiful than Lucifer before his fall.

167 S.D. *(There turn to them)*: Mephistopheles turns the pages, here and at ll. 181 and 187, to the passages Faustus has asked for. These stage directions, in their original wording, represent the point of view of the author or stage manager giving direction to the actor.

175–7 *Here . . . thee*: when Mephistopheles pauses teasingly for a moment, Faustus expresses his sceptical view that this single volume can actually contain such a large volume of knowledge. Mephistopheles stills the doubt by turning the page with a flourish on 'Tut, I warrant thee.'

2.2 This comic scene occurs in the A-text after Faustus's visit to Rome in Act 3, where it awkwardly precedes another comic scene involving the same two comic characters (and a Vintner). It seems misplaced there. The B-text places it just before Act 3, evidently having mixed it up with a Chorus that appears in the present location but is intended for the beginning of Act 3. See Note on the Texts. Robin would appear to be the 'Clown' or rustic buffoon who took service with Wagner in 1.4, though here he and Rafe are horse-keepers in an inn.

2 *search some circles*: (1) find in the book some magic circles (2) find a sexual partner. (Sexual *double entendre* continues throughout the scene.)

6 *come away*: come along.

7–8 *rubbed . . . chafing*: Rafe hints at sexual play involving the 'mistress' or inn-keeper's wife. The sexual wordgame continues in *blown up*, *dismembered*, *forehead* (where cuckold's horns appear), *private study*, and *born to bear*.

18 *intolerable*: Robin probably means something like 'incomparable'.

24 *nothing*: naught, vile (but playing also on *nothing*, 'free', in l. 28).

27 *at midnight*: Robin chooses a time well suited for conjuring or for sexual adventure.

33 *in the devil's name*: the ironically literal application of this common profanity recalls Mephistopheles' use of the same phrase at 2.1.146.

2.3.15 *Be I*: (1) even if I am (2) even though I were.

22 *halters*: nooses.

steel: steel sword.

27 *Alexander's . . . death*: Paris, or Alexander (as he is usually called in the *Iliad*), deserted Oenone for Helen.

28 *he . . . Thebes*: Amphion built the walls of Thebes by playing on the harp with such 'ravishing sound' that the stones were drawn into their places.

35 *heavens*: i.e. spheres.

36–7 *Are . . . earth?*: are all celestial bodies part of one globe, like the earth at its centre?

38–9 *As . . . orb*: just as the four elements (earth, water, air, and fire) are hierarchically ordered, one above another, the heavenly spheres too are concentrically arranged, each one inside the next.

41 *Whose . . . pole*: the earth and the heavenly spheres move about the same axle.

terminine: boundary.

43 *erring stars*: planets, moving among the fixed stars.

44 *both 'situ et tempore'*: as measured both in space and time.

47 *the poles of the zodiac*: the axle of the planet's motion through the zodiac (which, because it differs from the earth's axle, appears to explain the planets' erratic motion).

50–4 *Who . . . days*: the planets revolve around the earth daily but also move through the fixed stars on different cycles.

55–6 *hath . . . 'intelligentia'?*: does every sphere have a particular angelic influence?

59 *the firmament*: the sphere of the fixed stars.

60 *the empyreal heaven*: the outermost sphere, sometimes regarded as the realm of God. (The quarto spelling, 'imperiall', suggests divine majesty.)

61–3 *why . . . less?*: why do the coming together in the sky of the moving heavenly bodies, their being opposite to one another, their relative positions, and their eclipsing one another not recur regularly on an annual basis?

64 *Per . . . totius*: because of their unequal motion with respect to the whole. Mephistopheles responds to Faustus's hard question—one that tested beyond its limit the Ptolemaic earth-centred hypothesis and led in the Renaissance to the new hypothesis about the sun-centred universe—with an answer that, as Faustus bitterly sees, tells him nothing he did not know before.

68 *Move*: (1) urge (2) anger.

73 *this*: i.e. what I just said, that you are damned, or, what you just said (when you are called to account for it).

78, 82 *can . . . Seek*: B1's *will* and *Help* give a subtly different emphasis with theological implications; *will* gives more volition to Faustus's choice.

92 *dame*: mother. 'The devil and his dam' is a proverbial phrase.

109 *Ovid's flea*: in a Latin poem wrongly attributed to Ovid, the poet envies a flea for its ability to go anywhere it wants—including, by implication, the most private parts of a woman.

122 *case*: pair.

124 *look to it*: watch out.

shall be: will turn out to be.

132 *Come . . . vengeance*: come down out of that chair, damn you. (Said to Faustus.)

135 *the devil a penny*: not a damned penny.

136 *bevers*: drinks or snacks.

136–7 *suffice nature*: satisfy the appetite.

138 *gammon of bacon*: ham.

140 *Martlemas-beef*: beef slaughtered at Martlemas or Martinmas (11 November) for winter.

142 *thou*: that thou.

152–3 *mutton*: a slang term for prostitutes.

153 *ell*: 45 inches.

stockfish: dried cod—slang for sexual impotence. Lechery prefers a little live action to a lot of failed performance.

3. **Chorus** 4 *mount himself*: ascend his chariot.

6 *yoky*: coupled by a yoke.

7 *prove cosmography*: i.e. explore the earth and see if maps are correct.

10 *And . . . feast*: and take part in the celebration of the Feast of St Peter (29 June).

3.1.1–18 *Having . . . top*: Faustus's trip takes him from Trier (on the Mosel River in western Germany) to Paris, then eastward again to the meeting of the Main and Rhine near Frankfurt and Mainz, then south to Italy.

6 *coasting*: exploring, or skirting.

9 *Campania*: today, the southern Italian province in which Naples is located.

11 *straight forth*: running in straight lines.

12 *Quarters . . . equivalents*: divides the town into four equal sectors.

13–15 *There . . . space*: Maro, or Virgil, was reputed to have carved a passageway through rock in one night by means of magical power. His tomb in Naples became a kind of shrine.

17 *of which*: of Venice. The temple is St Mark's Cathedral and the adjoining campanile.

23 *because*: so that.

24–5 *his holiness' privy chamber*: the pope's private apartment, where the latter part of this scene must be located. Prior to that, however, Mephistopheles' pointing out to Faustus the delights of Rome (ll. 29–43) suggests a vantage point from which they can enjoy a view of the city. The Elizabethan stage permits this flexibility of imaginative location.

33–4 *Just . . . parts*: these lines, supplied from B1, are missing from A1 but are needed to make sense of l. 35.

41 *As . . . year*: there are 365 cannon in the castle.

42 *pyramides*: obelisk. Accented on the second and last of four syllables.

45 *Styx, Acheron . . . Phlegethon*: three of the four rivers of the underworld.

51 *of*: in.

53 *summum bonum*: greatest good.

56 *charm*: put a spell upon. Theatrically, invisibility is here an understood convention achieved by words, gestures, and a garment that can be put on and removed.

61 *an you spare*: if you do not eat your fill.

66 S.D. *(Snatch it)*: as at 2.1.167, 171, and 177, the wording indicates the point of view of dramatist or stage manager directing the actor.

74 *a pardon*: an indulgence.

79 *Aware*: beware.

90 *Maledicat Dominus*: may the Lord curse him.

93 *took*: gave.

99 *Et omnes sancti*: and may all the saints (curse him).

3.2.1 *made*: i.e. made rich.

2 *Ecce signum*: behold the sign. (From the Mass.)

2–3 *Here's . . . horse-keepers*: i.e. not a bad bit of plunder for two simple stable-boys.

3 *hay*: i.e. ordinary fare.

4 S.D. *Vintner*: i.e. inn-keeper, whose main business is purveying drink.

6 *Drawer*: tapster, waiter. (An insulting title for Robin to use in addressing the inn-keeper.)

11 *etc.*: the actor is invited to improvise, or to treat *etc.* as insultingly suggestive.

12 *with your favour*: by your leave.

14 *somewhat*: something.

19 *'tis afore me*: i.e. it is not 'about' me, as you said, but right in front of me. Robin seemingly harasses the inn-keeper by showing him the goblet and tossing it to Rafe.

20 *scour*: whip.

25–7 *Sanctobulorum . . . Mephistopheles*: Robin speaks gibberish but manages (unintentionally, perhaps) to summon Mephistopheles by naming him. Summoning the devil is that easy.

27 S.D. *Enter . . . Mephistopheles*: the A-text here provides what seems to be a first shot at the rest of the scene, which the printer neglected to omit:

> *Enter Mephistopheles, sets squibs at their backs. They run about.*

> VINTNER *O nomine Domini!* What mean'st thou, Robin? Thou hast no goblet.

> RAFE *Peccatum peccatorum!* Here's thy goblet, good Vintner.

> ROBIN *Misericordia pro nobis!* What shall I do? Good devil, forgive me now and I'll never rob thy library more.

> *Enter to them Mephistopheles*

> MEPHISTOPHELES Vanish, villains! The one like an ape, another like a bear, the third an ass, for doing this enterprise.

4. Chorus 3 *stayed his course*: ceased his travels.

6 *gratulate his safety*: express joy at his safe return.

11 *As*: that.

14 *Carolus the Fifth*: Charles V of Spain and the Holy Roman Empire.

16–17 *What . . . performed*: whatever I leave untold of his magical demonstrations you will see for yourself.

4.1.10 *I'faith . . . conjurer*: said ironically.

15 *nothing answerable to*: not accordant in the least with.

16 *for that*: because.

22 *succeed*: follow as successors.

27 *spectacle*: object of admiration.

29 *reflecting*: shining.

30 *As*: to such an extent that.

motion: mention, suggestion.

48 *lively*: to the life.

56–7 *Diana . . . Actaeon*: picking up on the Knight's sarcastic allusion to Diana and the stag, Faustus compares the Knight's audacity to that of Actaeon, who was metamorphosed into a horned stag and torn apart by his own hounds for having dared to challenge Diana's ability in hunting (or, in some versions, for having intruded on her bath).

60 *meet with*: be even with.

71 *bachelor*: (1) knight (2) unmarried man.

71–2 *a wife . . . wear them*: horns were the conventional symbol of cuckoldry.

74 *concave*: hollow.

77 *There's . . . good*: i.e. haste makes waste.

95 *latest*: last.

96–7 *Therefore . . . Wittenberg*: without a scene break and probably without scenic effects in the Elizabethan theatre, Faustus and Mephistopheles signal, by means of their dialogue, their return journey to Wittenberg. When Faustus sleeps in his chair, we are to understand he is in his study.

100 S.D. *Horse-courser*: horse-dealer.

101–2 *Fustian*: bombast. (The Horse-courser's ignorant approximation of 'Faustus'.)

107 S.D. *[To Mephistopheles]*: Mephistopheles, now choosing to make himself visible in order to speed along the practical joke, is taken by the Horse-courser for Faustus's servant.

110–11 *great . . . child*: Mephistopheles mockingly pleads the neediness of one who has no family to support.

114 *at any hand*: on any account.

115 *drink of all waters*: i.e. be ready for anything. The proverbial phrase has ironic appropriateness to a practical joke about riding into the water.

119 *made man*: one whose fortune is made.

120 *leave*: i.e. sell.

120–2 *If . . . an eel*: i.e. if he's got spunk I'll make a fine living off him by lending him as a stud. ('Hey, ding' etc. is a bawdy refrain.)

125 *water*: urine, often used by doctors for medical diagnosis.

127 *fatal*: (1) allotted by Fate (2) ending in death.

129 *Confound*: dispel. (Said to himself.)

132–3 *Doctor Lopus*: Dr Lopez, Portuguese Jewish physician to Queen Elizabeth, was well known even before his notorious execution in 1594 for his purported role in a conspiracy against Queen Elizabeth.

133 *purgation*: purging by bleeding or evacuation was a regular (and vastly overused) medical treatment. Here the purging affects the pocket-book.

137 *known of*: aware of.

140 *bottle*: bundle.

143 *snipper-snapper*: i.e. uppity servant.

hey-pass: con artist, juggler.

149–50 *glass windows*: spectacles.

172 *Farewell, he*: i.e. good riddance.

178 *Vanholt*: Anhalt, a duchy in central Germany, not far from Wittenberg.

4.2.5 *great-bellied*: pregnant.

21–2 *the contrary circle*: i.e. the Far East, with its presumably warm climate. Faustus and Marlowe seem not to know about the reversal of the seasons in the southern hemisphere.

5.1.17 *For that*: because.

21 *No otherways for*: no otherwise in terms of.

23 *Dardania*: Troy.

24 S.D. *passeth over the stage*: enters by one door and exits by another.

33 *Happy and blest*: fortunate (but with ironic relevance to the issue of salvation).

43 *flagitious*: heinous.

68 *Revolt*: return to your allegiance.

74 *thy drift*: the direction you are going.

75 *crooked age*: old man.

83 *unto*: as.

91 *topless*: aspiring to the clouds.

Ilium: Troy.

99 *Menelaus*: Helen's husband.

101 *wound . . . heel*: Paris wounded Achilles in the heel—his one vulnerable spot, since his mother had held on there when she plunged her infant son in the River Styx to make him invulnerable.

105–6 *flaming . . . Semele*: when Semele, loved by Jupiter, prayed him (at the instigation of the jealous Juno) to visit her in his full splendour, Jupiter reluctantly did so. Semele was consumed by his lightning.

108 *Arethusa's . . . arms*: this nymph fled the god Alpheus and was trans- formed by Artemis or Diana into a fountain. The dramatist here speaks of her as one of Jupiter's amours.

azured: reflecting the blue of the sky in Arethusa's fountain.

5.2.15 *but not*: sooner than.

34–5 *God forbid! . . . done it*: to the scholars' conventional expression of pious shock, Faustus answers in a devastatingly literal sense.

45 *save*: this word, supplied by B1, is missing from A1 but seems necessary for the sense.

62 *Fair nature's eye*: O sun.

66 *O . . . equi!*: run slowly, slowly, you horses of the night! (Adapted from Ovid, *Amores*, I. xiii. 40.)

81–7 *You . . . heaven*: you planets of my horoscope, who determined that I was to be damned, suck me up like mist into yonder storm cloud, so that when it produces thunder and lightning it may violently spew forth my mangled body and free my soul to ascend to heaven.

99 *metempsychosis*: theory of the transmigration of souls, attributed to the sixth-century (BC) Greek philosopher, Pythagoras.

109 *quick*: alive.

Epilogue 9 *Terminat . . . opus*: the hour ends the day; the author ends his work.

Doctor Faustus: B-Text

(Where the A-text and B-text are similar, this commentary does not repeat information provided for the A-text.)

Prologue 6 *vaunt*: display proudly.

1.1.12 *Oeconomy*: probably a misreading of the A-text's '*Oncaymaeon*', i.e. '*on kai me on*', 'being and not being', but some editors see here a possible reference to Aristotle's term for domestic management.

62 *Here*: i.e. in this study of magic.

1.3 S.D. *[above]*: i.e. the theatre gallery above the main stage. Such a location for the four devils (probably including, Beelzebub, Demogorgon, and Mephistopheles) would allow them to observe Faustus without his being aware of their presence.

12 *erring*: this A1 reading seems entirely more convincing than B1's *evening*. (Also at 2.3.43.)

68 *fell*: the A1 reading; B1's *live* is probably a repetition from l. 67.

1.4.17 *lousy*: (1) infested with lice (2) contemptible.

31 *pressed*: (1) drafted (2) hired (3) ready.

2.1.19 *make them*: make those persons.

2.2 This scene is placed one scene later in the original B-text; in the original A-text it precedes the comic scene of Robin, Rafe, and the Vintner in Act 3, and features Robin and Rafe instead of, as here, Robin and Dick.

3 *as't passes*: as beats everything.

7 *'A'... gorgon'*: Robin tries to read, letter by letter, some spell that seems to contain the name of the devil Demogorgon. He begins, ' "A" by itself is "a", "t, h, e" spells "the", "o" by itself is "o" '.

11 *on't*: of it.

13 *with a vengeance*: with a curse on you. (An oath.)

14 *That's like*: i.e. fat chance.

14–15 *my master*: the inn-keeper.

15 *conjure*: i.e. constrain to do his bidding, or spirit you away (and playing on the idea of summoning the devil).

17 *horns*: cuckold's horns.

19 *my mistress*: the inn-keeper's wife, who, says Dick, has cuckolded her husband.

20–1 *there... talk*: Robin hints that if he and some others were free to speak, they could tell about the role they have played in the cuckolding. The talk about 'wading... deep' into 'matters' is sexually suggestive.

28–9 *sack... hold*: various strong wines and hippocras (a spiced wine drink), as much as the belly will hold.

2.3.37 *empyreal orb*: outermost sphere of the Ptolemaic universe, usually regarded as the dwelling place of God. See note on 'the empyreal heaven', 2.3.59–60, A-text.

40 *termine*: boundary.

59 *But... 'crystallinum'*: Faustus asks about two more possible spheres, the fiery and crystalline spheres, hypothesized in Renaissance modifications of Ptolemaic astronomy to account for the newly observed phenomenon of the precession of the equinoxes and an imaginary phenomenon called trepidation.

78 *will*: this word in the B-text places stress on Faustus's will to be saved, in place of the A-text's 'can', i.e. whether he is able to.

82 *Help*: the word here stresses a plea for divine assistance, in place of the A-text's 'Seek', with its emphasis on Christ's choosing whether to save Faustus's soul or not.

112 *wrought*: embroidered.

131–40 *these case*: this pair.

153 *On, piper!*: perhaps a piper led the Sins on and now leads them off, or perhaps one of them plays.

3. **Chorus 8** *The tropics . . . sky*: the tropics of Cancer and Capricorn and the polar zones which quarter the sky.

9 *the bright . . . moon*: the moon's 'circle' or orbit is the lowest of the eight moving spheres.

10 *Primum Mobile*: First Mover, the supposed outermost sphere that revolved around the earth in twenty-four hours, carrying within it the spheres of the planets and fixed stars. Equivalent in Mephistopheles' system to the 'empyreal orb' at 2.3.37 (B-text).

11–12 *with . . . pole*: on this circuitous course, within the limits defined by the axle of the universe itself (the spheres of which are, from the earth's point of view, concave in shape).

19 *his*: its.

3.1.15 *east*: A1's *rest* is tempting as a reading, but *east* is defensible as meaning eastern Italy.

16 *one of which*: i.e. Venice. (But probably an error for the A-text's 'midst of which'.)

36 *two*: the A-text's *four* accurately follows *The Damnable Life of Faustus*, the source for many details in this scene.

41 *As that*: that.

56 *victory*: i.e. victory over the German Emperor Charles in his attempt to name a rival pope, Bruno. See ll. 89 ff. below. This added episode in the B-text is loosely based on John Foxe's *Acts and Monuments*, widely known as *The Book of Martyrs* (1563).

62 *this bright frame*: (1) this splendid universe (2) this resplendent body of mine. Faustus hopes to be famous to the end of time, but the second meaning offers a more ironic comment on Faustus's rendezvous with damnation.

83 *antics*: foolish clowns.

triple crown: papal tiara with three crowns.

84 *beads*: prayer beads.

88 S.D. *[They stand aside]*: the B-text does not make clear if, in this added episode, Faustus is given the ability to be invisible as later at 3.2.15 ff.

some . . . pillars: the cardinals and archbishops are either preceded by clerics bearing crooks and pillars as signs of their exalted ecclesiastical rank, or bear those insignia themselves, while the clergy chant the processional.

93 *Peter*: Saint Peter, from whom apostolic succession descended. Both Pope Adrian and Bruno here claim to be truly entitled to the authority of the papacy.

98 *creep . . . wool*: i.e. approach noiselessly and without warning. Divine vengeance may have seemed asleep, says Pope Adrian, but now it strikes.

103 *consistory*: deliberative body consisting of the pope and his cardinals. (Accented on the first and third syllables.)

104 *decretal*: issued by papal decree.

105 *Trent*: site of the famous Council of Trent, held (1545–63) to reform the Catholic Church in the wake of the Reformation.

108 *election*: selection by vote of the College of Cardinals or (at l. 126) by imperial appointment.

119 *his holiness*: (1) his sanctity (2) his lofty title as 'his Holiness'.

134 *overpeers*: (1) looks down upon, as from a steeple (2) lords it over his peers.

136–7 *Pope Alexander . . . Frederick*: the emperor Frederick Barbarossa set up a rival pope, Victor IV, but was forced to submit by placing his neck under Pope Alexander III's foot. The pope, according to Foxe's *Acts and Monuments*, spoke the verses translated here in ll. 139–42. The present scene is a somewhat fanciful medley of history about Pope Alexander III (1159–81) and Pope Adrian IV (1154–9).

146–8 *Pope . . . lords*: the dramatist here invents history as precedent for the Empire's sway over the papacy, using familiar enough names; Sigismond was emperor in the early fifteenth century, Julius III pope in the mid-sixteenth.

152 *though we would*: even if we wanted to.

157 *Resign*: unseal.

160 *light*: alight (with a play of antithesis on 'heavy').

163 *served*: (1) obeyed in ecclesiastical office (2) played a trick on.

176 *Lollards*: i.e. schismatics, heretics (followers of John Wyclif, a fourteenth-century English radical reformer).

178 *if that*: if.

179 *Without . . . peers*: without being pushed into it by the emperor and his court.

193 *again*: in your return.

3.2.18 *are*: who are.

20 *forkèd*: i.e. snake-like.

21 *blue*: sulphurous.

tree: gallows(?).

55 *safe*: disposed of.

67 *Was*: that was.

3.3.1 *we were best look*: we had best see to it that.

2 *answer*: answer charges regarding.

3 *at . . . heels*: hard at heels.

23–4 *between . . . beyond*: Robin shows the cup as he jeeringly puns on the Vintner's accusation that between the two of them they have stolen his cup: no, it is not physically between us, it is out here in front of me.

27 *Ay . . . tell*: i.e. (mockingly) sure, right away.

4.1.1 *officers, gentlemen*: Martino may be addressing unseen officers offstage. Alternatively, some may enter briefly and be dispatched at l. 5.

5 *see the state in readiness*: see to it that the royal throne is made ready for Charles's entry. (See S.D. at l. 48.)

12 *Carolus*: Charles V.

19 *took . . . stoups*: drank deep with tankards-full. Perhaps this line is borrowed from *Hamlet* 1.4.8–10: 'The King doth wake tonight and takes his rouse', etc.

32 *the pope*: Bruno.

47 S.D. *Exeunt . . . throne*: the throne is presumably brought onstage at this point. Charles may be carried in on it.

58 *despite of chance*: in spite of what fortune can do.

71 *Blood*: by His (Christ's) blood.

88 *the devil's governor*: one who professes to be able to control the devil.

101 S.D. *Darius*: King of Persia, defeated by Alexander in 333 BC.

130 *calls*: who calls.

150–1 *'Sblood . . . torments*: possibly Benvolio is actually attacked by devils at his window, but he may simply mean here that he would not be strong enough to cope with such an attack were it to occur.

160 *Speak well of ye?*: this speech could be aside, but it may also be a defiant reply.

161 *of*: on.

o' this order: in this fashion.

162 *smooth . . . ruffs*: i.e. beardless academics, wearing the small ruffs of their profession.

4.2.12–13 *Here . . . infamy*: i.e. I am determined to kill Faustus, even if the price is my own life.

19 *this*: this time.

25 *Who*: whoever.

31 *in place*: here.

47 *Made*: that made.

71–2 *limited For*: allotted.

79 *horse*: mount.

83 *after*: after that.

89 *This traitor*: i.e. Benvolio.

94 S.D. *ambushed*: placed in ambush.

101 *these trees*: quite possibly some stage contrivance suggests that trees come between Faustus and the soldiers; Henslowe had trees among his properties. But perhaps they are to be imagined by the audience.

remove: move.

4.3.8–13 *Defend... again*: each knight is dismayed to see horns on his companions' brows and comes only slowly to the realization that he too is horned.

16 *spite of spite*: in spite of all we can do.

4.4.9 *stand*: haggle.

4.5.7 *on the score*: in debt.

11 *my score stands still*: (1) my credit is still good (2) my indebtedness is no bigger than it was.

12 *Ay... that*: i.e. your debt still stands, undoubtedly.

15 *Look... ho!*: the Hostess yells to her servants to attend guests in the other rooms of the inn.

18 *served*: played a trick on.

19 *on's*: of us.

26 *cursen*: Christian (with perhaps a pun).

27 *eat*: eaten.

29–30 *for... logs*: Robin has heard similar fabulous tales.

44 *went me*: went.

4.6.11 *are*: that are.

31 S.D. *bounce*: knock loudly.

45 *Commit*: commit to prison. (To which Dick insolently replies in the sense of 'fornicate'.)

55–63 *Nay... bottles*: the comic characters appear to be so drunk that they think themselves still in a tavern. Faustus has evidently wafted them here in their stupor to entertain the ducal court.

56–7 *and be hanged*: i.e. and the devil take you.

66 *gage*: engage, stake.

content: amuse.

74 *stand much upon that*: (1) put much stock in that (2) have a leg to stand on.

76 *flesh and blood*: i.e. memory.

85 *curtsy*: a low bow with one leg drawn back and bent—a gesture of courtesy, as the B-text's spelling, 'curtesie', suggests. The Carter is trying to put the presumably one-legged Faustus on the spot.

87 *'Tis . . . worth*: that is not much of a curtsy.

89 *Be . . . together?*: i.e. do you go to bed with two legs, or one?

90 *Colossus*: statue astride the harbour of Rhodes, with huge legs.

92 *make . . . you*: belittle you, have nothing to do with you (playing on *make* in l. 99).

101 S.D. *[He . . . legs]*: Faustus pulls up his long academic gown.

108 *carry it away*: carry the day.

109 *'hey-pass' and 'repass'*: mumbo-jumbo incantations.

5.1.40 *grow . . . nature*: does not become second nature with you.

47 *envy of*: enmity towards.

50 *Checking*: restraining.

5.2.6 *wait upon*: (1) lie in wait for (2) attend.

10 *demean*: conduct.

18 *come*: having come.

latest: (1) most recent (2) last.

59 *they*: i.e. the devils, who, in this B-text version, appear to be still visible to the audience as they witness this scene. Probably they gesture at this point.

86 *MEPHISTOPHELES*: if in fact the devils start this scene on the upper stage (see S.D. at 5.2), Mephistopheles presumably descends from above to the main stage by this point.

90 *Hath*: that has.

100 *Gave*: you gave.

104 S.D. *the throne descends*: a throne, with some theatrical representation of the saints in glory, is lowered by means of a winch from the 'heavens' over the stage.

110 *set*: sat.

114 S.D. *Hell is discovered*: probably a curtain is pulled back to reveal hell's torments, including a 'chair' or throne of hell that is vividly unlike its heavenly counterpart. Painted cloths, live actors, puppets, or other images may have been used to create the two contrasting spectacles of heaven and hell.

119 *quarters*: quartered bodies.

185 S.D. *Exeunt*: whether the devils carry off the remains of Faustus is unclear. In the chief source, the *Damnable Life*, Faustus's body is scattered all round the room. Possibly his body is carried off at the end of the present scene, and then in the next scene (not included in the A-text version) the scholars draw a curtain at l. 5 to behold some sort of spectacle of the carnage.

5.3.11 *self*: same.

15 *for*: since.

19 *heavy*: sad, solemn.

The Jew of Malta

Epistle Dedicatory Thomas Heywood wrote this dedication to his patron for the quarto edition of 1633, having contributed the prologues and epilogues for a revival in 1632.

3 *Alleyn*: Edward Alleyn, leading actor of the Admiral's men.

5 *Cock-pit*: a private theatre in Drury Lane.

17 *Tuissimus*: thine evermore.

The Prologue Spoken at Court 1 *Gracious and great*: i.e. the king and queen.

8 *a sound Machevill*: a Machiavel through and through. Heywood's spelling is retained here for scansion and rhyme.

The Prologue to the Stage 2 *best of poets*: Marlowe (Heywood's note).

4 *the best of actors*: Alleyn (Heywood's note).

5 *one*: i.e. Marlowe, author of the unfinished narrative poem *Hero and Leander* as well as of the plays named here.

7 *th' other wan*: i.e. Alleyn won.

10 *Proteus . . . Roscius*: the 'ancient one' of the sea who can change shapes at will, and the most famous Roman comic actor of his day (d. 62 BC).

11–13 *nor . . . day*: i.e. nor is this intended to derogate Richard Perkins, who now plays Barabas. (Heywood notes the name 'Perkins'.)

Prologue S.D. *Machiavel*: Marlowe introduces his play with a caricature of Niccolò Machiavelli (1469–1527), Italian author of *The Prince*, whose unconventional views about the pragmatics of statesmanship generated, in England especially, hysterical hatred of the supposed atheism and political cunning that Machiavel boasts of in this Prologue.

3 *the Guise*: Henry, duc de Guise, chiefly responsible for the mass killing of Huguenots (French Protestants) at the Massacre of St Bartholomew, 1572, was assassinated in 1588 on orders of the French king.

4 *this land*: England (even though the play is set in Malta).

6–8 *guard . . . words*: protect me against the slander of those to whom 'my name is odious', and let those same detractors know that I am mighty still and care nothing for their silly opinions. Alternatively, *let* in l. 7 may be imperative, with *them* referring to Machiavel's true followers.

11–13 *Yet . . . followers*: yet will those same detractors secretly follow my teaching to obtain the papacy and, when they then repudiate what I have taught them, will be murdered in turn by other disciples of my precepts.

16 *Birds . . . past*: Machiavel may be satirizing the pious notion that murder cannot be hid, as in the story of the flock of cranes that was instrumental in bringing the murderers of Ibycus to justice. Or he may mean that murder is an openly acknowledged fact of the natural competition for survival.

17 *such fooleries*: i.e. talk of murder and ambition as sins, or (in the next line) divine right of kings and hereditary inheritance.

19 *empery*: empire, rule. Julius Caesar was often regarded as a tyrant because he had seized power.

21 *the Draco's*: Draco codified in 621 BC a code of law for Athens that became proverbial for its severity; hence the word 'draconian'.

23 *letters*: erudition.

24 *Phalaris*: this tyrant of Sicily in the sixth century BC is said to have roasted his victims alive in a brazen bull, and eventually to have perished in it himself when he was overthrown. In Machiavel's view, Phalaris should have taken steps to suppress the rebellion against him instead of writing letters (l. 23)—the so-called *Letters of Phalaris* incorrectly attributed to him. The 'great ones' in l. 26 may be the aristocratic leaders who turned against him, or the phrase may represent the point of view of the bull's inventor, Perillus, whom Phalaris put to death in the bull.

26 *Of*: because of.

26–7 *O'th'poor . . . pitièd*: I would rather be envied (for my success) than pitied (as a victim) by ordinary folk. (The quarto reading of *wits*, 'wites', might also signify 'wights', people.)

29 *read*: give.

Britainy: Great Britain; England in particular.

1.1 S.D. *Enter . . . him*: perhaps in the Elizabethan theatre Barabas is 'discovered' in his *counting-house*, or room for doing accounts, by means of a curtain pulled back to reveal a recessed area backstage. Such a staging device would simplify the providing of *heaps of gold* in front of Barabas. In any case, the actor would soon move on to the main stage for better visibility and audibility. The name *Barabas* is derived from the account in Matthew 27: 15–26 of the criminal whom the Jews ask Pilate to release instead of Christ; in this play it is stressed on the first and third syllables.

1–3 *So . . . satisfied*: Barabas gloats that the capital he ventured has made handsome return, paying back the whole amount in return for only one third of the cost.

3 *summed and satisfied*: totalled up and paid off.

4 *Samnites*: a people of ancient Italy.

Uz: the biblical land of Job (Job 1: 1).

6 *silverlings*: shekels, silver coins (hence less valuable than gold).

13 *make a miracle of*: think it a miracle to behold.

21 *the eastern rocks*: the mountains of India, proverbially rich in precious minerals that can be gathered *Without control* (l. 22), without any restraints.

24 *Receive ... weight*: can gather them at no cost, and sell them by the bagful rather than weighing each individually.

29 *As ... rated*: that one such jewel, impartially appraised.

31 *in peril of calamity*: in a time of great crisis.

34–5 *frame ... trade*: conduct their commercial enterprises by methods quite distinct from those used by ordinary traders.

39 *halcyon's bill*: a weathervane made of a stuffed halcyon, a species of kingfisher, suspended in such a way that it will indicate in what corner or quarter the wind is blowing.

40 *how ... vanes?*: where is the weathervane pointing?

42 *bordering isles*: islands nearby, such as Cyprus and Crete.

43 *Are ... by*: have approached.

46 *gliding ... shore*: sailing along the shores of Crete.

52 *custom them*: pass them through the custom-house, pay the duty.

57 *as I*: as if I.

62 *The very custom barely*: the custom duties alone.

68 *So ... come*: well, at least some of my ships have arrived.

72 *Caire*: Cairo.

74 *main*: sea. (The Nile is a tributary to the Mediterranean.)

80 *they are wise*: i.e. a lot they know about it.

82 *And ... in*: and bid my agent bring me his bill of lading.

83 *at*: about.

88 *chance*: chances it that.

90 1 *Belike ... oils*. perhaps they came by way of Crete for a cargo of olive oil.

93 *conduct*: escort (needed for protection against pirates and Turks).

94 *wafted*: conveyed.

95 *within a league*: within three miles or so (of Malta).

96 *had ... chase*: were chasing the Turkish galleys.

97 *they ... Sicily*: the Spanish vessels were no doubt on their way to Sicily (in pursuit of the Turks).

101 *trolls*: flows abundantly.

104 *Abram's happiness*: God gave Canaan to Abraham and his descendants for ever (Genesis 15: 14–21, 17: 8).

109 *To . . . blasts*: to propel their cargo-laden vessels with fortune-bearing gusts.

114 *fruits*: compare Christ's 'Wherefore by their fruits ye shall know them' (Matthew 7: 20).

116 *profession*: professing of Christian faith. (Pronounced in four syllables here and elsewhere.)

117 *hapless*: unfortunate (playing on *Haply*, perchance). Those few Christians who live by their faith, says Barabas, suffer the consequence of poverty in a merciless world.

120 *I cannot tell*: I cannot say as to that.

122 *Kirriah Jairim*: a city's name (Joshua 15: 9 and 60, Judges 18: 12, etc.) is here given to a person.

127 *come not to be*: do not succeed in becoming.

136 *Agamemnon*: his willingness to sacrifice his daughter Iphigenia to appease Artemis, and thereby obtain a favourable wind for the sailing of the Greek fleet to Troy, motivated the revenge enacted by his wife Clytemnestra, and bodes ill in this play for Barabas's daughter Abigail.

138 *Tush . . . policy*: the Jews are evidently discussing whether the arrival of the Turks, and the ominous summons of the Jews to the senate-house (ll. 165–6), are devices of *policy* (i.e. cunning statecraft) or not.

146 *they*: the governors of Malta.

156 *What . . . league?*: why would those who are mutually bound by a treaty need to discuss terms of peace?

162 *With . . . attempted*: whom they have attempted to subdue.

169 *Provide him*: prepare himself.
     fashion: fashion's, form's.

170 *state*: welfare.

178 *contribute*: accented on the first and final syllables.

184 *make sure for one*: look out for number one.

187 *Ego . . . proximus*: no man is nearer friend to myself than I am. (Varied from Terence, *Andria*, IV. i. 12.)

1.2 The scene is imagined to begin in Malta's senate-house (1.1.165); but the Elizabethan stage allows flexibility of imagination, and at l. 306 we learn that we are now in the vicinity of Barabas's house. (*Ferneze* is stressed on the second of three syllables.)

S.D. *Governor*: Q uses the plural *Gouernors* here and elsewhere in the dialogue of this scene (ll. 10, 17, 27, 32, 129). Perhaps when Marlowe began writing the play he intended that a body of 'Governors' would rule Malta, but later decided upon a single governor, Ferneze, and did not make the necessary adjustments in the earlier scene.

2 *Knights of Malta*: Knights of St John of Jerusalem, headquartered on Malta after 1530.

11 *my father's*: i.e. the Grand Signor or Emperor (l. 39) of Turkey's.

13 *leave*: permission (to consult privately among ourselves).

15 *send*: send word.

20 *We*: i.e. we ask that we.

24 *their time*: what time they require.

45 *there's . . . so*: there is more to it than that.

50–1 *Alas . . . prince*: Barabas pretends to be obtuse, and to understand that the Jews are being asked to serve in a military capacity.

59 *strangers*: i.e. resident aliens, the Jews. Such people, argues the Second Knight in ll. 60–1, should pay taxes even though they are not citizens, since they are given leave to acquire wealth on Malta.

91 *Corpo di Dio*: by God's body! (An ironic oath in Barabas's mouth, since it refers to the crucified Christ.)

99 *one want*: that one individual should suffer privation. Compare Caiaphas' argument at Christ's trial 'that it is expedient for us, that one man should die for the people' (John 11: 50).

108 *your first curse*: i.e. the cry of the Jews as they demanded the crucifixion of Christ: 'His blood be on us, and on our children' (Matthew 27: 25).

117 *The man . . . live*: Barabas himself paraphrases scripture, pitting Old Testament ideals of righteous dealing (see Proverbs 10: 16, etc.) against New Testament and especially Pauline doctrines of original sin and the new covenant (Galatians 3: 13 ff., Romans 4: 13, etc.).

121 *profession*: i.e. being a covetous Jew. (Compare 1.1.116.)

126 *take . . . me*: again, Barabas paraphrases the Old Testament (Exodus 20: 15, 'Thou shalt not steal') in reply to what he views as sanctimonious Christian preaching on New Testament themes of rejecting worldly covetousness (as in the Sermon on the Mount).

136 *other*: other Jews.

137 *take . . . residue*: see to the proper disposal of all this confiscated property. (Ferneze does not plan to seize the entire wealth of all Jews; he does, on the other hand, need to sell the properties for money to pay the Turks, as he says at ll. 156–7.)

152 *distinguish of the wrong*: make false distinctions between the good you profess and the wrong you do.

153 *right*: justice.

154 *extreme*: harsh. Accented on first syllable here and at ll. 168 and 196.

159 *break our day*: fail to meet our deadline (with wordplay on *break . . . break*, miss . . . violate).

165 *Primus Motor*: First Mover—the Old Testament God who inflicted plagues on Egypt on Moses' behalf.

166 *upon my knees*: Barabas must kneel at about this point; perhaps he rises at ll. 169–70.

183 *Was written*: is set down (in Job 1: 3, which Barabas quotes almost exactly).

189 *last*: most lately.

192–6 *So ... eyes*: Job curses the day he was born in Job 3: 3, and proceeds in 3: 4–9 to wish for eternal night and clouds of darkness as Barabas does here, though Barabas also insists that his deprivation is more extreme.

193 *forlorn*: accented on the first syllable.

198 *vanity*: Barabas uses the term in its Old Testament sense of the futility and emptiness of human striving, as in Ecclesiastes 1: 2.

201 *patience*: Barabas plays bitterly on their urging him to be patient by using *patience* in its root sense of suffering (Latin *patior*, I suffer). This colloquy of Barabas and his fellow Jews is reminiscent of Job's talk with his comforters.

202 *pleased with want*: content with having little.

216 *for*: since.

220 *framed ... mould*: fashioned after a finer pattern.

222 *A reaching thought*: one who ambitiously plans ahead.

232 *urged thereto with*: incited thereto by.

240–1 *And ... turn*: and time, which cannot immediately serve our turn, will provide us an occasion in due course.

287 *Entreat 'em fair*: speak courteously to them.

290 *shall ... dissemble*: I will be dissembling, indeed, if I do that.

291–4 *As ... hypocrisy*: deliberate dissembling from start to finish is no worse than lapsing from honest dealing into deception. Swearing false vows (to be taken into the sisterhood) is better than a hypocrisy so inward that it shows no visible signs. (All nuns, in Barabas's eyes, become hypocritical dissemblers.)

302 *It ... seen*: it is necessary that I not be seen.

303 *seem*: pretend to be.

311 *waters*: water-source.

314 *you ... guide*: i.e. you friars who act as confessors to the fortunate virgins in your charge.

317 *hopeless ... hapless*: despairing ... wretched (with wordplay).

323 *want ... us*: Jewish faithlessness.

329 *moving spirit*: (1) soul moved to religious ecstasy (2) animated sensuality. Both friars' speeches are erotically suggestive. The Abbess and the

nuns may not hear all of this, or may simply miss the innuendo, but they may instead perfectly well understand what is being hinted at.

338 *As . . . worth*: Barabas plays on Abigail's word *profit*: (1) benefit spiritually (2) increase in wealth.

340 *What mak'st thou*: what are you doing.

343 *mortified herself*: killed what is worldly in her. (Barabas's repetition of the word is presumably caustic in tone.)

349 *back*: Barabas pretends to address her as though she were a fiend to be fended away.

355 *blind*: spiritually blind. (Barabas may find this Christian metaphor amusing in its physical sense.)

356 *reck . . . persuasions*: pay no heed to your arguments.

375 *in a dump*: down in the dumps.

380 *Cytherea's*: Venus'.

387 *countermined*: i.e. impregnable. A not uncommon error for *countermured*, fortified with walls inside the main fortifications; as also at 5.3.8.

391-2 *How . . . sir*: Lodowick's sugestion that he go along is met with a stiff reply: 'I am going, say what you will.' A rivalry is established.

393 *it . . . hard*: there will be trouble. (With erotic double meaning.)

2.1 S.D. *with a light*: the light is not for illumination in the theatre but to signify that it is dark. Barabas is imagined to be outside his house. Abigail's appearance *above*, l. 19 S.D., in the gallery above the main stage, signifies that she is upstairs in Barabas's house.

1-4 *Thus . . . wings*: the raven, as an omen of ill, was popularly supposed to announce by its croaking voice the coming of death and to hover over a house of sickness with its contagion (as in *Othello*, 4.1.21).

1 *tolls*: sounds the knell.

2 *passport*: permit to pass over from life to death.

4 *contagion*: night air was thought to be contagious.

12-14 *O Thou . . . offspring*: Barabas's prayer recalls the deliverance of the Jewish people when Jehovah led them with a fiery pillar out of Egypt and through the Red Sea (Exodus 13: 18-22).

24-5 *those . . . tales*: the legends about ghosts hovering near money that come now to Barabas's mind are typical 'old wives' tales', such as he might have been told by a nurse in his days of prosperity.

31-2 *Now . . . place*: i.e. would that my father were fortunate enough to be here now! (A dramatic irony, not only because Barabas is there, as yet unseen by her, but because he has just talked of his hovering spirit being continually there, drawn to the money.)

36 *Morpheus*: god of dreams.

37 *wake*: Q's *walke* may be a remembrance of l. 30, though possibly it is the word Marlowe intended; 'walke' is an obsolete form of 'wake'.

39 *Bueno . . . era*: my flock (i.e. wealth), good for everyone else, is no good to me.

41 *But stay . . . east*: the closeness of this line to Shakespeare's 'But soft, what light through yonder window breaks?' (*Romeo and Juliet*, 2.2.2) prompts one to wonder if Barabas, like Romeo, sees candlelight in the gallery above as though in a window of the house.

53 *practise thy enlargement*: work to obtain your freedom.

54 *O girl . . . bliss*: Barabas's blended passion for his gold and his daughter anticipates that of Shylock in *The Merchant of Venice*, 2.7.15-22 and 3.1.101-16.

59 S.D. *He . . . kiss*: conceivably Barabas reaches towards Abigail on tiptoe and nearly touches her outstretched fingertips, as in some productions of *Romeo and Juliet*, 2.2.

61 *for the raven*: in place of the raven (whom Barabas invoked in ll. 1-4 as suited to the night and his dark curses).

63 *these*: Barabas's moneybags, his 'nest eggs'.

64 *Hermoso . . . dineros*: beautiful pleasure of money. (Perhaps Barabas sings this line.)

2.2.1 *captain*: senior officer (here, vice-admiral).

11 *Turkish*: although Q reads *Spanish*, it is clearly the *Turkish* fleet that is intended.

12 *creeping*: with suggestion of timorous sluggishness.

14 *luffed*: came up into the wind in preparation for tacking. The technical sailing terms, *luffed* and *tacked*, apparently baffled the compositor of Q who set instead *left* and *tooke*.

31 *from whence you came*: when Suleiman II conquered Rhodes in 1522 and thereby displaced the Knights of Saint John, Charles V gave the Knights the island of Malta (in 1530).

32 *stated*: settled, installed in office.

47 *So . . . succeed*: you will be doing as the Christians on Rhodes did before you.

48 *their*: the Turks'.

2.3.2 *Fear . . . sale*: do not worry they will not be sold.

10 *Titus and Vespasian*: Jerusalem was besieged in 66-9 AD by Vespasian, and, after his becoming Roman emperor in 69, by his son Titus (later emperor, 79-81 AD). Jerusalem fell to Titus in 70. During this era the persecuted sect of Christians became increasingly visible.

16 *hand*: authority (to prosper again, as Ferneze proposed, though perhaps mockingly, at 1.2.103). Barabas also plays bitterly on the proverbial connection of *heart* and *hand*.

18 *the tribe of Levi*: the Levites in Judges 19 and elsewhere are anything but forgiving, but Marlowe may have had in mind Joshua 21: 13–27, telling how the Israelites gave to the Levites various cities serving as refuge for slayers. Alternatively, he simply nodded, or intended this line to mean, 'Being of the tribe of Levi, I am not the sort . . .'.

23 *Florence*: the city was known in the Renaissance as the home of Machiavelli and secret intrigue.

24 *Heave . . . dog*: the language anticipates Shakespeare's *The Merchant of Venice*, 1.3.109: 'Still have I borne it with a patient shrug.'

26 *stall*: bench in front of a shop, used during the day for displaying goods, but at night often used as a sleeping place for the homeless in Elizabethan London. Barabas wishes upon his Christian enemies a life of extreme poverty and vagrancy. See next note.

27 *be gathered for*: have a collection taken up for them.

29 *Even for charity*: (1) as my offering (2) to show my love for them.

31 *One . . . sake*: (said ironically).

33 *insinuate*: ingratiate myself (with Barabas).

39 *Ay . . . command*: Barabas mocks the self-confidence of the young lover.

41–2 *I would . . . wish you*: Barabas seemingly plays with the proverbial idea of 'like father, like son': If it is good to be your father's own son, it would be good also to have such a son of your own. Beneath the fawning, Barabas jeeringly suggests that this father and son are indeed alike, and that (as the Old Testament teaches) the sins of the father are visited on the son.

42–3 *a hog's . . . singed*: i.e. pink, hairless, and porcine. Orthodox Jews are forbidden to eat pork as unclean (Deuteronomy 14: 8).

47 *purge*: cleanse from spiritual (and physical) defilement.

48 *the promise*: God's promise. (See 1.1.104.)

51 *serve your turn*: (with sexual suggestion).

53 *I'll . . . wood*: Barabas's imagined sacrifice of his only child recalls the stories of Agamemnon and Iphigenia (see 1.1.136 and note) and of Abraham and Isaac (Genesis 22).

54 *poison of the city*: i.e. a poison readily available in Malta (or some Italian city, such as Florence or Ancona; see 3.4.70).

55 *white leprosy*: at one stage, leprosy forms shining white scales on the skin.

57–8 *foiled . . . foiled*: provided with a *foil* or metal background . . . defiled.

60–1 *pointed . . . Pointed*: tapering to a shapely point . . . appointed, intended.

63 *Cynthia's*: the moon's.

65 *an if . . . it*: if you take it, the diamond (Abigail).

67 *give't your honour*: (1) give the diamond to you (2) give you what is coming to you.

70 *it*: (1) the gift (2) revenge. The ironic double meaning is continued in ll. 71–7.

73 *in catechizing sort*: in the question-and-answer manner of religious instruction.

84 *reap some fruit*: (1) reap the reward of their holiness (2) become pregnant as a result of their *doing* (l. 84). In l. 86 Barabas pretends to correct these sexual implications as if he did not mean them, though 'fullness' can suggest pregnancy as well as completion.

86 *glance not at*: do not refer to with oblique satire. (Lodowick has heard the sexual innuendo.)

87 *burning*: (1) ardent (2) incendiary.

90 *I'll . . . nunnery*: I will have something to say to, or settle accounts with, that nunnery—implicitly responding to the nuns' propensity to 'increase and multiply' (as God bade all creatures do in Genesis 1: 22) with some equally commonplace saying from the Old Testament, such as 'in sorrow thou shalt bring forth children' or 'dust thou art, and unto dust shalt thou return' (Genesis 3: 16–19).

92 *there's . . . part*: quarrels about the price shall not come between us (with the more sinister suggestion that Lodowick will never leave alive).

102 *new . . . purse*: new way of stealing a purse.

104 *So that*: if only.

104–5 *So . . . gallows*: a thief of the profitable sort Barabas comically imagines would need special protection from the city government to save him from the gallows; without some such immunity, his talents would soon bring him to a bad end.

106 *sessions day*: day of trial.

107 *purged*: (1) cleared of guilt (2) made to atone (by hanging).

113 *philosopher's stone*: a reputed substance supposedly able to transmute metals into gold and prolong life. Barabas comically wonders if a slave with many *qualities* (l. 113) might not possess the secret of the 'stone'—something to be desired at any price, even that of being hit on the head with it.

115 *FIRST SLAVE*: Q attributes the remarks of this anonymous slave to Ithamore (*Itha.* or *Ith.*); also ll. 119, 122, and 126.

116 *shaver*: (1) one who shaves with a razor, as the slave says he can do (2) fellow, chap, swindler.

118 *youth . . . Lady Vanity*: in morality plays like *The Interlude of Youth*, the young protagonist usually found himself in the sinful embrace of an abstraction like Lady Vanity.

121 *Some . . . other*: 'to serve somebody's turn' has the connotations of doing that person in. Barabas puts a sly interpretation on the slave's offer to *serve* him.

125–7 *an't . . . chops*: if only for the sake of saving money on food. It would take more than fourteen pounds of beef a day to maintain your fat jowls.

131 *for my turn*: fit for me to use.

133–4 *mark . . . mark*: brand . . . notice, keep an eye on.

142 *stay*: stay and observe.

143–5 *He . . . governor*: these lines might conceivably be said aside, but Barabas has already plainly indicated at ll. 134–5 that Ithamore is to do his villainy, and Barabas proceeds at ll. 164 ff. to speak with complete frankness without any further testing of Ithamore's dependability.

155 *comment on the Maccabees*: to hoodwink Mathias's mother, Barabas pretends to have been offering to lend Mathias a learned commentary on the apocryphal Books of Maccabees, detailing the deliverance of Judea from Syrian persecution in 175–164 BC.

169 *that . . . thee*: something worth your remembering.

174 *nose*: Jews on the Elizabethan stage (of whom there were few) may have been fitted out with hooked beaks for noses. Barabas is 'bottle-nosed' or swollen-nosed at 3.3.10.

183 *Italian*: Italians.

195 *And . . . hospitals*: and furnished charitable institutions for the destitute and infirm with a supply of orphans.

196 *moon*: month (but alluding to the supposed influence of the moon on the insane).

197 *one hang*: i.e. caused one to hang.

198 *Pinning*: he, the suicide, pinning.

199 *with interest*: with threats of foreclosure for interest due.

221 *walk in*: the scene, set originally at the slave market, is now imagined to be at Barabas's house (perhaps adjacent to the market), represented visually by the façade of the Elizabethan tiring house. Abigail can exit with Lodowick at l. 242 as though going indoors.

224 *Ormuz*: a trading city at the mouth of the Persian Gulf.

229 *Philistine*: a Palestinian people on unfriendly terms with the Jews.

237 *made sure*: betrothed.

241 *it is . . . hand*: this letter is in my agent's handwriting, with his accounts.

243 *The account is made*: (1) my agent's accounts are here before me (2) the matter is settled, the die is cast.

249 *manna*: a food that descended like dew to feed the Israelites during their wanderings in the wilderness (Exodus 16: 13–15 and 35, Numbers 11: 6 ff., Joshua 5: 12).

266 *When . . . come*: to see if you have come.

268 *slipped me in*: slipped in past me.

273 *in . . . not*: into the house—but avoiding Lodowick. (See ll. 342–3.)

275 *As*: that.

284 *Of*: of losing.

288 *He*: Don Mathias.

291 *hold my mind*: conceal my thoughts and feelings.

294 *unfoiled*: (1) unprovided with a background to set it off (2) unsullied. Barabas and Lodowick allude to their conversation about the 'diamond' and its 'foil' at ll. 49–67. (Q's *unsoyl'd*, seemingly an error for 'unfoyl'd', limits the meaning to 'unsullied'.)

297 *golden cross*: gold coin bearing the representation of a cross.

298 *posies*: pious sentiments engraved.

302 *This offspring . . . Jebusite*: descendants of Cain, who murdered his brother Abel (Genesis 4), were considered accursed. Jebusites were a tribe of Canaanites, dispossessed of Jerusalem by David (2 Samuel 5). The term became an abusive nickname in England for Jesuits.

305 *Messias*: Messiah—not Jesus, whose divinity Barabas denies, but one yet to come.

306 *gentle maggot*: well-born worm. (An oxymoron; with wordplay also on *gentle/gentile*.)

312 *Faith . . . heretics*: that one not need keep oaths made to unbelievers (from which it follows, in Barabas's view, that he is free to deceive any non-Jew as a heretic).

317 *I cannot . . . bids*: probably Abigail speaks aside, though conceivably aloud in a coy way that Lodowick could complacently interpret as a sign of obedience.

318 *Nothing . . . me*: Abigail uses an evasion to avoid her promise: (1) I will love you till death do us part (2) I will die before I give up my true love, Mathias.

341 *Suffer . . . him*: evidently Barabas restrains Mathias for a moment to prolong the game and then whets him on at l. 352.

343 *accessory*: accented on the first and third syllables.

353 *Nay . . . herself*: i.e. if you do not believe me, just wait till your mother comes, when it will be too late.

355 *die with grief*: i.e. explode in grief and rage at the prospect of my marrying a Jewess.

356 *I . . . tears*: I could not even say goodbye to Mathias, I was weeping so.

374 *poisoned*: i.e. so that the smell of it will kill (like the nosegay in 4.4).

3.1 S.D. *Courtesan*: the establishment of a courtesan, Bellamira, much in evidence in Acts 3 and 4, recalls a familiar stage setting in Terence and Plautus' Roman comedies and in neoclassical adaptations.

1 *Since*: ever since. (The siege does not actually begin until after the negotiations break down at 3.5.19 ff., but Bellamira may refer more generally to the Turkish threat and its dampening effect on trade.)

2 *bare*: (1) sole, mere (2) naked.

8 *liberal*: (1) well educated (2) free with their money.

10 *from*: absent from.

20 *hooks*: climbing hooks, part of the professional thief's gear.

24–5 *Zounds . . . anon*: for Christ's sake (literally, 'by Christ's wounds'), watch out how you keep looking back at him furtively! You will give away our secret, before you know it.

27 *by her attire*: i.e. by the loose-bodied flowing gown worn by courtesans.

29 *the challenge*: the feigned challenge sent to Mathias as if from Lodowick.

3.2.1 *the place*: the place for a duel, as specified in Lodowick's supposed letter (see next note).

2 S.D. *reading*: Lodowick is reading a letter that Mathias wrote him in response to the feigned challenge carried by Ithamore to Mathias as if from Lodowick (2.3.375–80). Lodowick, not knowing of that feigned challenge, bridles (in l. 3) at the curt letter from Mathias, whom he supposes to be quarrelling with him over Abigail. Mathias, in l. 4, comes forward to acknowledge his writing the letter and to demand satisfaction. Q accidentally assigns l. 3 to Mathias (*Math.*) and l. 4 to Lodowick (*Lod.*).

8 WITHIN: i.e. offstage, as from the town, not from Barabas's house where he is perhaps assumed to be in his gallery *above* (l. 4 S.D.).

13–14 *O Lodowick . . . death*: Ferneze's point is that, though he holds Katherine responsible for Lodowick's death, he cannot avenge himself on a woman by challenging her to a duel. Katherine, in l. 15, sees herself as bound by no such chivalric convention.

23–4 *Lend . . . me*: Katherine's offer to commit suicide with Lodowick's sword is part atonement and part grief.

28 *their blood . . . heads*: the blood of our sons upon the heads of their murderers.

34 *reveal*: since Q provides no verb for this line, editors generally add *reveal* to fill the gap; *disclose* might also be possible.

35 *divide*: to divide.

3.3 Ithamore and Abigail appear to be at Barabas's house; the sense of scene is continuous.

3 *held in hand*: led on.

10 *bottle-nosed*: swollen-nosed. (See 2.3.174.)

to: as.

19 *imprimis*: in the first place. Ithamore chooses the word ineptly; he first carried the feigned challenge to Mathias and then Mathias's reply to Lodowick.

21 *In . . . days*: Ithamore sardonically inverts the usual ending: 'And they lived happily ever after.'

28 *Saint Jacques*: i.e. the Dominican order, often called Jacobins for their church of Saint-Jacques in Paris.

29 *them*: i.e. one of them.

32 *feeling*: (1) heartfelt (2) having to do with the sense of feel. The 'sport' he imagines is sexual.

34 *sirrah sauce*: you saucy rascal.

37 *pursuit*: aim. Accented on the first syllable.

39 *by my favour*: through love of me.

40 *Admit*: conceding that.

sire: Q accidentally prints *sinne*. See next note.

43 *sire*: the Q reading, *Pryor*, has been defended as referring to the title of 'Grand Prior' awarded historically to the commander of the priory of the Knights of Saint John or of Jerusalem (the Knights of Malta), hence appropriate to Ferneze, but the play shows no awareness of this history.

50 *Virgo, salve!*: Hail, Virgin! This version of the famous salutation *Ave, Maria* (from Luke 1: 28 but more familiarly from the Catholic 'Hail, Mary') would suggest blasphemous Mariolatry to Protestant audiences.

51 *When, duck you?*: what, are you curtsying and bobbing like a cleric? (Jacomo has presumably just genuflected.)

55 *for*: as.

57 *labour*: labour for.

73 *pardon me*: excuse my not answering that.

3.4.6 *Spurca*: base, low, dirty.

pretendeth: portends, means.

15 *second self*: although the Q reading, *second life*, could be defended, it seems more probable that the compositor's eye simply skipped up to the last word of the previous line.

37 *lest*: unless.

46–50 *Here . . . fire*: Barabas tantalizes a dazzled Ithamore with the promise, but not the reality, of power and advancement.

51 *I hold my head*: i.e. I would bet my life.

hold: wager.

76 *This . . . use*: on this night, the inhabitants make it a practice.

79 *Among the rest*: along with others who are carrying *alms* or charitable offerings to the convents.

92 *'tis . . . spared*: it will do us more good this way than if it is kept for our eating.

93 *by the eye*: as much as your eyes can desire.

98 *Of . . . died*: Alexander died at Babylon in 323 BC of a fever (or, according to one tradition, by poisoning), aggravated by heavy drinking at a banquet.

99–100 *And . . . poisonèd*: Pope Alexander VI was erroneously thought to have died accidentally in 1503 from a poisoned wine prepared for some other victim by his son, Cesare Borgia (1475–1507), hero of Machiavelli's *The Prince*.

101 *In few*: in short.

Hydra . . . bane: the monstrous water-snake of Lerna, near Argos, whose many heads grew back and multiplied when severed, faced Hercules in the second of his twelve labours. Its blood was poisonous.

102 *hebon*: ebony, the juice of which was considered poison; or perhaps related to *henbane*, a poison, or *ebenus*, yew.

Cocytus: a river in Hades.

103 *the Stygian pool*: the Styx, another river in Hades.

104 *the fiery kingdom*: hell.

112 *drench*: (1) poisonous draught (2) dose administered to animals.

112–13 *Flanders mares*: a famous breed of horses, here unflatteringly compared to the nuns as breeding mares.

113 *with a powder*: impetuously, violently, in haste (playing on the idea of the literal poisoned powder in the broth). Or it may mean, 'with the poison in it, bad luck to them'.

114 *And . . . boot*: i.e. and other diseases and inflictions, too. (Horse disease would be especially devastating to a stable full of breeding mares.)

117 *I'll pay . . . vengeance*: I'll give you what's coming to you, with my curse. (Barabas plays on *pay*, give money, and *pay*, settle scores.)

3.5.9 *passed*: duly given.

18 *refluence*: flowing back.

32 *profitably*: (1) in your own interests (2) in a good cause.

3.6.3–5 *The abbess . . . me*: the friars' particular concern for the Abbess and 'fair Maria' suggests an amorous connection. See also l. 41.

31 *work my peace*: bring about my peace of soul, eternal peace.

35 *degraded*: stripped of ecclesiastical orders.

49 *has . . . child*: wild stories of Jews crucifying children and the like were rife in medieval and Renaissance Europe.

4.1.1 *to*: compared to, equal to.

6 *swell*: become pregnant (as opposed to swelling from the effects of poison).

21 *Cazzo, diabole!*: a vulgar Italian oath of defiance or contempt. (Compare 4.3.12 and note.)

24 *God-a-mercy, nose!*: Ithamore has admired Barabas's hooked nose before at 2.3.174 and 3.3.10. Now, he jokingly thanks God for such a nose that can smell out rascals.

52 *Lie*: a plural verb following the plural idea of 'the burden of my sins'.

57 *A hundred . . . ta'en*: I have taken 100 per cent interest. (Usury was regarded as sinful in Christian Europe—though often hypocritically so, while tacitly allowing Jews to practise it.)

63 *And . . . serve*: Ithamore laughs privately at Barabas's absurd hyperbole (which is of course feigned) about whipping oneself penitently to death. Yes, says Ithamore sardonically, but penance will not do any good, so why bother?

66 *sollars*: granaries or lofts (solariums) used as store-rooms.

80–111 *O good . . . come*: Barabas plays with the friars by auctioning himself off to the highest bidder, agreeing first to go with Barnardine, then with Jacomo, who offers less strict rules about the wearing of shirts and going barefoot. When the friars quarrel openly, Barabas offers private reassurances to both, sending Barnardine off home with Ithamore and agreeing to receive Jacomo that night. (This reading depends on a slight reassignment of speeches. Normally in this play Jacomo is Friar '1' and Barnardine Friar '2', but at ll. 90 and 93 it seems more likely that the speech assignments should be reversed, though the speech is assigned to '2' in Q. Also, ll. 103–4 in Q are assigned to Ithamore or *Ith*.)

98 *thee, rogue*: Q's *thee goe* must be a mistake; otherwise Jacomo's response in l. 99 makes no sense.

107 *Jacobins*: Dominicans. See 3.3.28 and note.

110 *requite*: repay with charity (but with hidden meaning of 'revenge').

114 *the Turk*: i.e. Ithamore (a splendid choice for godfather).

118 *he that shrived her*: i.e. Barnardine, who heard Abigail's dying confession at 3.6.12–32.

122 *One*: i.e. Jacomo, who *turned* or converted Abigail at 3.3.53–76.

123 *The other*: Barnardine, who, having heard Abigail's confession, knows incriminating facts about Barabas.

137 *order*: ritual. The friars sleep in their robes as a matter of religious observance.

138 *if*: even if.

143 *shake his heels*: i.e. dangle from a rope's end.

143 S.D. *discovery space*: this scene, which began in some indeterminate place in Malta away from Barabas's house (since he sends Friar Barnardine home with Ithamore), is now, by theatrical sleight of hand, to be imagined within his house. A 'discovery space' backstage in the Elizabethan theatre is perhaps used to bring the sleeping Barnardine into view, though the action thereafter must move quickly on to the main stage.

148 *Yes . . . confess*: Ithamore wryly suggests that anyone who hears confessions deserves death and that in any case Barnardine knows too much.

149 *Blame . . . hanged*: Barabas elaborates on Ithamore's joke. The proverbial expression really means something like 'Tell the truth and take your punishment,' or, more simply, 'Go to hell'.

150–3 *Pull . . . amain*: Barabas and Ithamore strangle Barnardine by pulling on the rope belt from two sides, shouting 'Pull hard' at each other.

151 *have*: The Q reading, *saue*, which hardly makes sense in this context, seems to be an error for *have*, which accords nicely with Barabas's response in the following line.

154 *no print*: no rope markings on the neck.

157 S.D. *[He . . . body]*: we are now, through more theatrical fluidity, outside the house. Barabas and Ithamore probably conceal themselves in such a way as to be able to spy amusedly on Jacomo as he arrives and finds the body. The re-entry indicated in Q at l. 176 may mean simply that he and Ithamore come forward.

164 *proceed*: make progress, prosper.

170 *intercept*: meaning to intercept.

187 *his*: its.

188 *give in evidence*: testify.

194 *stayed*: were late in coming.

200 *a Turk . . . more*: Ithamore comically quotes an ethnic stereotype about Turks. Compare the proverbs 'To be worse than a Turk' and 'To turn Turk'.

203 *touch me not*: Jacomo's claim of clerical immunity to prosecution by the State ironically recalls the reply of another 'sacred person', the risen Christ, to Mary Magdalene at the sepulchre: '*Noli me tangere*', 'touch me not' (John 20: 17).

204 *touch*: censure, accuse. Barabas plays with Jacomo's *touch*, above.

4.2.12–13 *as . . . 'Is it even so?'*: as one might say, 'Is that how it is?'

13 *nonplus*: standstill, perplexity.

16 *freehold*: i.e. property, turf. Pilia-Borza hangs around the public gallows to pick pockets of spectators at executions, as his name (compare the Italian *tagliaborse*, cutpurse) suggests.

17 *conning his neck-verse*: memorizing the verse (usually Psalm 51) that an accused person could read in order to claim 'benefit of clergy' and thus save himself from execution. Pilia-Borza sizes Ithamore up as someone likely to need such protection.

17–18 *looking . . . execution*: witnessing the execution of Friar Jacomo.

18 *hempen*: (1) suited to a noose of hempen rope (2) homespun, made of hempen cloth.

18–19 *Hodie . . . mihi*: today your turn, tomorrow mine. Pilia-Borza reverses the usual proverb, 'Today is my day, tomorrow shall be thine', not being eager to hang first.

20 *exercise*: ceremony (of hanging)—with ironic suggestion of a devotional *exercise* better suited to a friar.

23 *tippet*: garment for shoulders and neck, i.e. noose (playing again on *hempen* as pertaining to cloth and to rope; see l. 18 above).

24 *cure*: spiritual charge, parish.

27 *muschatoes*: pair of moustaches.

28 *warming-pan*: long-handled pan able to contain hot coals to warm a bed, resembling in a way an absurdly fat-handled dagger.

30 *effect*: gist.

43 *stand or fall*: with bawdy double meaning.

46 *Now . . . way*: both 'Clean out of the way' and 'I am a foul way out' (as in *Twelfth Night*, 2.3.185) mean 'I have lost my way'. Ithamore plays with the paradox of *clean* and *foul*.

80 *in his kind*: as his kind deserves, as he treats others. Proverbially, to 'treat someone like a Jew' is to use harsh treatment.

83 *maids*: possibly maids actually appear in answer to Bellamira's summons, but more likely her promises of sybaritic pleasures are meant to string Ithamore along.

running: slight, quickly prepared and eaten 'on the run'.

88 *Content*: agreed.

90 *golden fleece*: the image of 'fleecing' or plundering ironically undercuts this poetic invocation of the story of the Argonauts' voyage.

91 *Where . . . hurled*: where meadows are carpeted with brightly coloured flowers.

94 *Adonis . . . queen*: the story of Venus' love for the young Adonis and of his untimely death (compare Shakespeare's *Venus and Adonis*) is again an ironic and ominous one for Ithamore to invoke.

97–8 *Thou . . . Love*: the language closely resembles Marlowe's 'The Passionate Shepherd to his love', published posthumously in *The Passionate Pilgrim* (1599) and *England's Helicon* (1600).

97 *Dis*: king of the underworld, not ordinarily 'above'. Ithamore means something like 'by almighty Dis'.

112–13 *Here's . . . not?*: Ithamore sardonically complains that Barabas's stinginess keeps him in rags.

114 *ten crowns*: this appears to be Pilia-Borza's tip, or a bribe to encourage co-operation, since we learn from ll. 100 ff. and at 4.3.18–23 that Pilia-Borza came away with all 300 crowns demanded at 4.2.75; what is more, he can expect a larger commission of one hundred crowns on his second such errand (see l. 119).

116 *ream*: 480 or 500 sheets; but with wordplay also in the next phrase on *kingdom*, i.e. *realm*. The two words were often spelled and pronounced alike.

129 *runs division of*: plays musical variations on.

4.3 S.D. *Enter . . . letter*: Barabas is still fuming over Ithamore's first letter.

5 *coupe de gorge*: cut the throat.

12 *catzerie*: roguery, whoring (from *catso* or *catzo*, Italian for 'penis').

13 *crossbiting*: swindling, outwitting one who has cheated you.

14 *husband*: i.e. pimp.

15 *And . . . crowns*: Barabas paraphrases the letter. He has evidently sent all 300 crowns, as ll. 18–23 indicate.

16 *he*: Ithamore.

19 *want'st . . . tale?*: are you lacking any of the total amount you earlier specified?

27 *what . . . for you*: i.e. the 100 crowns that Ithamore has demanded (4.2.129) for the bearer of the letter.

29 *make . . . away*: do away with this rascal.

34–5 *You . . . meaning*: i.e. do not pretend you do not know the way to climb up to the window of the room where I do accounts and keep my gold (as Pilia-Borza boasted of doing, at 3.1.19–20).

48 *as unknown*: whom I have not yet had the pleasure of meeting.

60 *demand*: this word, missing in Q, has been editorially added to make sense of the next line. Other possibilities include *and fetch*, *convey*, or *force from me*.

4.4.1 *pledge*: offer a toast to

drink it off: anyone to whom a toast was offered was supposed to drink to the bottom of his cup; see l. 7.

2 S.D. *whispers*: probably he proposes that they go to bed soon.

4 *Of*: on.

5 BELLAMIRA: Although this line is assigned to Pilia-Borza (*Pil.*) in Q, Bellamira is the more appropriate person to demand that Ithamore finish his glass.

5–6 *Nay . . . drop*: both Bellamira and Ithamore insist that the other drink up every drop as proof of affection.

10 *Rivo Castiliano*: pseudo-Spanish drinking slang, meaning something like 'Let the drink flow', that turns up in varying forms in *Twelfth Night*, 1.3.42, and *1 Henry IV*, 2.4.110.

A man's a man: proverbial.

11 *to*: let's drink to.

12 *you were best*: if you know what is good for you. Ithamore threateningly apostrophizes the absent Barabas.

20 *snickle, hand to! fast!*: put the noose around him, hold tight! snug!

22–3 *for me*: as far as I am concerned.

27 *Love . . . long*: a proverbial expression, perhaps a song title.

28 *incony*: dainty, sweet (with an obscene pun on woman's lap: in cunny).

37 *A vôtre commandement*: at your command, as you wish.

46 *fill*: pour full.

50 *So . . . gold*: Barabas plays on *finger*: (1) finger the lute (2) pilfer, pinch.

52 *run*: more punning: (1) run up and down the scales (2) escape with stolen goods.

66 *elder*: popular tradition held that Judas hanged himself from an elder tree (see, for example, *Love's Labour's Lost*, 5.2.606). Much was made also of the similarity of sounds in 'Judas' and 'Jew'.

68 *the Great Cham*: i.e. the Great Khan, the Tartar or Mongolian ruler whose wealth was described by Marco Polo and Mandeville.

69 *masty*: burly and fat, like a mastiff or a swine fattened on mast (acorns etc.). The association with swine is particularly offensive to a Jew; see 2.3.42–3 and note.

76 *rice*: i.e. the rice pudding used to poison the nuns. Ithamore's allusion to Friar Barnardine is couched in the same ominously suggestive way.

79 *The meaning . . . meaning*: speaking with an obscure profundity, Ithamore hints at more knowledge than he has let on to.

80 *charity*: Christian love(!).

5.1.18 *feared*: mistrusted.

S.D. *Enter . . . Ithamore*: theatrical foreshortening of time allows the officers to complete in a few seconds a search for and arrest of Barabas and Ithamore that would take hours.

20–1 *O, my belly*: the poison is beginning to work.

34 *him*: Barabas.

37–9 *law . . . law*: a fair trial . . . the full penalty of the law.

41 *As . . . souls*: may their souls be punished for what they have spoken.

46 *made*: that made.

55 *buried*: pronounced in three syllables.

56 *For*: as for.

57 S.D. *[Officers . . . aside]*: by staging convention, we understand that Barabas's body is thrown over the walls of the city, and that when Barabas, alone onstage perhaps at the front of the platform, arises at l. 60, he is now outside the walls where he can be found by the Turks.

59 *Well . . . drink*: Barabas offers praise and thanks to the sleeping potion he took to feign death (ll. 79–80).

64 *Take*: take back, recover.

80 *So . . . else*: thus, or in any case.

84 *against the sluice*: adjoining the opening where the sewers and streams empty out of the city. Q's reading of *Truce* for *sluice* is probably a typographic error.

89 *vault*: covered sewer drain.

90 *rise*: come up (out of the sewer).

94 *And if*: the Elizabethan 'And if' could here also mean 'an if', 'if'.

5.2.11 *them*: the captive Maltese warriors.

22 *entrance*: a first step.

35–7 *And . . . not*: Barabas speaks as a disciple of Machiavelli (*The Prince*, chapter 17). See also Gentillet's *Discourse against Machiavelli* (1576).

42 *snap*: feed by biting. The ass in this fable (not actually by Aesop but recognizable as a type) typifies the person who is easily distracted by immediate concerns and so loses sight of long-range objectives.

44 *Occasion's bald behind*: one must grab Occasion by the forelock (as the proverb puts it), seize the opportunity. (Occasion was portrayed iconographically as bald except for a forelock, to emphasize that Occasion gives you only one chance.)

47 S.D. *with a Guard*: under guard. (Perhaps something is missing from the text in which Barabas orders the guard to bring in the prisoner Ferneze.)

58 *no reason*: nothing to expect reasonably.

61 *good words*: speak calmly.

63 *for me*: as far as I am concerned.

64–6 *think . . . place?*: don't you think it would be a stupid stratagem for me to burn Malta down?

67–8 *sith . . . that*: since.

68 *got my goods*: acquired my wealth.

72 *as . . . distress*: as one whose friendly intentions are not recognized until one is in distress.

81 *outhouse . . . city*: building outside the city but belonging to it (in this instance a monastery).

94 *make*: gather, raise.

96 *cast it*: devise the strategy. (Luring one's enemies to a fatal banquet is described in Machiavelli's *The Prince*, chapter 8, as an example of power wickedly gained.)

106 *Ottoman*: ordinarily meaning 'Turkish' or 'Turk', but here used to signify 'Turkey'.

107 *about this coin*: get to work gathering this money.

121 *My . . . prevention*: being detected and forestalled by the enemy is most inimical to my stratagem.

123 *I know*: I alone know.

   lives: deaths.

5.3.8–11 *Strong . . . town*: strongly provided with a secondary defence by other small neighbouring islands, backed on the Calabrian side by Sicily (where Dionysius the Elder reigned as tyrant over Syracuse, 405–367 BC), and having on that same side two lofty turrets that overlook the town. (*Countermined* is seemingly an error for *countermured*, fortified with walls inside the main fortifications, as at 1.2.387. *Calabria* is in the heel of Italy.)

16 *Ottoman*: Turkey. (See 5.2.106.)

26 *for that*: as for that.

5.4.3 *culverin*: a cannon, to be fired by means of a *linstock* or notched stick holding the match (l. 4) as a signal for the Maltese Knights to 'sally forth' and 'issue out' from hiding against the Turks, and also for the trap to be sprung at Barabas's house (see 5.5.39–41).

4 *kindled thus*: the cannon is to be fired thus, by a linstock. (The actor demonstrates.)

7 *Or . . . servitude*: or, if all goes well, you will all be released from Turkish domination (and from Barabas as governor under the Turks).

5.5 S.D. *above*: Barabas is to be imagined in the gallery of his house. It is accessible by stairs (l. 58). Calymath and his bashaws enter on the ground floor or main stage at l. 50. So may a Messenger at l. 12. Whether Ferneze enters above or on the main stage is harder to say. He offers Barabas the money at l. 42, most easily done if both are above, and receives a knife at l. 36 which, however, could be thrown down to him. Barabas shows Ferneze 'this cable' at l. 34 (evidently near at hand) that the governor is to cut, and Ferneze does so at l. 62, thereby releasing a trapdoor in the gallery which must be devised in the actual gallery of the Elizabethan theatre.

3 *levelled to my mind*: directed toward my intent, as I would wish.

10 *so*: so long as.

25 *for*: as for.

41 *fire the house*: set off the explosives underneath the monastery.

49 *worldlings*: i.e. the audience.

56 *How . . . him*: Ferneze, in hiding, marvels at Barabas's hypocrisy toward the ruler he intends to kill.

61 *Sound . . . there*: evidently a knight, on a signal from Ferneze, relays to a trumpeter the order to sound a charge which will in turn signal the cannoneer in the tower (l. 39) to fire his warning shot, thereby commencing both the sallying forth of the knights and the exploding of the monastery.

S.D. *a cauldron discovered*: a 'discovery space' backstage and underneath the gallery is suddenly revealed by means of a curtain. Possibly the curtain opens with Barabas already in the cauldron, thus allowing his fall to be effected by his sudden disappearance from the acting space 'above' and a quick descent behind the scenes.

76 *you . . . now*: Barabas feels his strength going.

77 *thy latest fate*: the last that fate allows.

98 *all's one*: it makes no difference.

118 *come . . . world*: even if all the world should come.

Epilogue Spoken at Court 4 *Thus low dejected*: bowing thus humbly.

Epilogue to the Stage 1 *In . . . contend*: to contend in statue-making with the sculptor whose statue of Galatea came to life.

2 *Apelles*: the greatest painter of antiquity, fourth century BC.

Edward II

1.1 This scene, and several following, appear to take place at or near London and the court of King Edward II.

8 *Leander*: a youth who, according to legend, drowned attempting to swim across the Hellespont to reach his love, Hero—the subject of Marlowe's

Hero and Leander. Gaveston similarly has just crossed the English Channel from exile to reach Edward.

14 *die*: swoon.

22 *Tanti*: so much for that. (The actor gestures dismissively.)

first: sooner than that.

33 *against the Scot*: in Edward I's military expeditions against Scotland.

39–40 *the porcupine . . . plumes*: porcupines were thought to be able to shoot their quills.

54 *Italian masques*: courtly entertainments, thought to be imported from Italy, with performers in masks.

59 *antic hay*: grotesque country dance.

60 *Dian*: Diana, goddess of the moon and of chastity.

66 *Actaeon*: a hunter in mythology who, because he offended Artemis or Diana by coming upon her in her bathing, was transformed into a stag (or hart, l. 69) and torn apart by his own hounds (see Ovid, *Metamorphoses*, iii. 138–252).

81 *Mine uncle*: Mortimer Senior.

this earl: Warwick.

89 *Mort Dieu*: dead God, i.e. the crucified Christ. (A French oath.) Gaveston puns on the 'Mort' in 'Mortimer', as he did at l. 80.

94 *so stiff*: i.e. too stiff to kneel in obedience.

100 *obscure*: stressed on the first syllable.

107 *to the proof*: to good effect, irrefutably.

117 *Preach upon poles*: traitors' heads were impaled on battlements etc. as a public warning against treason.

119 *grant*: consent.

127–8 *All . . . friends*: said sarcastically; there is no love lost for Gaveston in Warwickshire or Lancashire.

143 *Hylas*: a favourite page of Hercules who was drawn down into the water by amorous water-nymphs and lost during the expedition of the Argonauts. Hercules looked for him in vain.

144 *exile*: stressed on the second syllable.

162 *envied*: stressed on the second syllable.

165 *Fear'st . . . person?*: are you afraid for your personal safety?

167 *seal*: the Great Seal, used on documents of the highest authority.

182 *reclaimed*: corrected, subdued.

185 *Saving your reverence*: (1) with due respect for your high clerical position (2) begging your pardon. (Said mockingly.)

186 *stole*: ecclesiastical vestment worn over the shoulders.

187 *in . . . anew*: this violence offered towards the bishop anticipates the use of 'channel water' from a ditch or sewer to shave Edward at 5.3.27.

197 *Fleet*: a London prison.

200 *True, true*: the bishop comments bitterly on the ironic multiple meaning of *Convey*, l. 199: (1) conduct (2) make away with, suggesting theft, *conveyance* or transfer of property, and sleight of hand.

1.2.19 *For vailing . . . bonnet*: in return for humble submission, signalled by doffing of the cap.

25 *take . . . slave*: express objection to this wretched fellow.

33 *my lord . . . grace*: his grace the archbishop of Canterbury.

35 *his*: the bishop of Coventry's.

42 *his peers*: the king's nobles.

47 *Unto the forest*: i.e. into seclusion.

53 *as who should say*: as if he were saying.

62 *lift*: steal (with sarcastic pun on *lift*, raise, in l. 61).

68 *but*: only.

69–71 *his . . . his*: the king's . . . Gaveston's.

75 *New Temple*: a building in Holborn belonging to the Knights Templars until 1313. Edward II gave it to Spencer Junior in 1324.

1.4.7 *declined*: turned aside; with sarcastic play on 'abased, lowered'.

13 *Quam male conveniunt!*: how badly do they suit! (Adapted from Ovid, *Metamorphoses*, ii. 846, where the spectacle of mighty Jove assuming the guise of a bull in order to seduce Europa elicits that wry observation that majesty and love do not go well together.)

16 *Phaethon*: son of the sun-god, who arrogantly aspired to drive his father's chariot and was destroyed.

19 *faced*: outfaced, bullied.

overpeered: (1) looked down upon (2) condescended to as if by a peer of the realm.

43 *patient*: pronounced in three syllables.

50 *Inde*: India (either east or west).

54 *Curse*: excommunicate (and thus cancel his subjects' obligations of duty to him).

57 *Curse me*: even if you curse me.

92 *common sort*: commoners.

97 *imperial grooms*: imperious and aspiring base fellows. (An oxymoron.)

100 *I'll . . . buildings*: I'll burn your ruined churches to the ground. Edward perhaps suggests both that the churches have been neglected by the clergy and that the churches will be *crazèd* or destroyed.

102 *Tiber's channel*: the River Tiber in Rome. *Channel* may also suggest 'gutter', as at 1.1.187 and 5.3.27.

140 *bear . . . way*: accompany you on the first stage of your journey.

172 *charming Circes . . . waves*: Circe used potent magical spells to turn Odysseus' companions into swine, and was able to walk over the waves (Homer, *Odyssey*, x, and Ovid, *Metamorphoses*, xiv). *Circes* means Circe.

174 *Hymen*: deity of marriage.

178–80 *frantic Juno . . . Ganymede*: Jupiter's (Jove's) jealous queen was resentful of Ganymede, Jupiter's cupbearer and amorous favourite; see Ovid's *Metamorphoses*, x. 155–61, and Marlowe's *Dido, Queen of Carthage*.

195 *Cry quittance*: get even, retaliate.

214 *Plead . . . resolved*: no matter who pleads for him, my mind is made up.

223 *torpedo*: electric ray, a fish known for its wiliness and benumbing effect.

248 *mark the respect*: consider the special set of circumstances.

276 *vail the top-flag*: lower his colours or topsail in a naval salute of respectful submission.

280 *borne it out*: maintained our position, argued the case; made it seem.

281 *up*: in arms.

282 *of*: on.

284 *brook*: tolerate it that.

285 *my lord of Cornwall*: Mortimer Junior sarcastically refers to Gaveston by the title given him by Edward at 1.1.155.

288 *'Tis . . . Gaveston*: even the king himself will not be able to shield Gaveston.

299 *in happy time*: by fortunate chance.

304 S.D. *mourning*: dressed in mourning.

305–18 *He's . . . Gaveston*: the king may speak to himself or to his attendants, but he brazenly allows the queen and nobles to hear his distress, as they indicate in ll. 311 and 319.

308 *revenue*: stressed on the middle syllable.

313 *Cyclops*: giants who worked in Vulcan's forge.

314 *up*: upside down.

316 *had . . . rose*: would that some pale and deathlike goddess of revenge had arisen.

319 *Diablo*: the devil.

328 *golden tongue*: Edward (perhaps hyperbolically) offers to have made for Isabel a rich jewel that would symbolize her eloquence.

331 *these*: i.e. Edward's arms.

357 *marshal*: dispose of, put in proper place (playing on *Lord Marshal*, a high officer of state).

369-70 *Clerk of the Crown ... Beaumont*: these could be two different persons, but the king's order appears to be a single command.

371 *Iris*: the rainbow, messenger for Juno as was Mercury for Jove.

378 *made him sure*: betrothed him.

379 *cousin*: i.e. niece.

381-3 *That ... love*: on that day, even though I know you are reluctant to honour Gaveston in this business, yet for the sake of myself, who intends to take the leading role as challenger in this tournament, let the entertainment be lavish; I will show my gratitude. (A challenger dares all comers to fight.)

391-7 *The mightiest ... Alcibiades*: Mortimer Senior cites several instances of male favourites of great men: *Hephaestion* of Alexander the Great; *Hylas* of Hercules (see note at 1.1.143); *Patroclus* of Achilles in Homer's *Iliad*; *Tully* or Marcus Tullius Cicero, a famous writer in the time of Octavius Caesar, the Emperor Augustus, though not in fact a personal favourite; and *Alcibiades*, an arrogant patrician friend of Socrates.

393 *Hercules*: although the early texts print *Hector* here, Marlowe clearly intended to cite the relationship of Hylas and Hercules; see note at 1.1.143.

407 *He ... back*: i.e. he dresses richly enough to consume the income (from rents etc.) of an ordinary lord. (*Revenue* is accented on the second syllable.)

408 *Midas-like*: as if made out of gold. Midas, legendary king of Phrygia, wished that all he touched might be made of gold, only to find that his food turned to gold also.

409 *outlandish cullions*: foreign rascals (literally, testicles).

411 *Proteus*: ancient god of the sea, capable of assuming different shapes to evade questioning.

416 *other*: others.

2.1 The scene is imagined to take place in the house of the earl of Gloucester, who has just died.

28 *My life for thine*: I bet my life against yours.

30 *read unto her*: tutored her.

32 *court it*: play the courtier.

33 *black coat*: the traditional dress of a scholar.
    band: neck-band, collar.

34 *faced before*: trimmed in front.

35 *smelling to a nosegay*: sniffing decorously from a bouquet.

38 *making low legs*: curtsying low.

44 *formal toys*: trifles done for form's sake.

53 *propterea quod*: because. (Formal Latin, evidently regarded as pedantic as opposed to *quandoquidem*, meaning 'since', in the next line.)

55 *to form a verb*: at engaging in elegant or effective rhetorical argument.

2.2 This and the following scenes are unhistorically imagined to take place at and near Tynemouth Castle (see l. 51); according to Holinshed, Edward went to meet Gaveston at Chester.

11 *device*: heraldic emblem with motto on a shield.

18 *a canker*: a plant disease or canker-worm, here suggesting in Mortimer Junior's view that Gaveston is a parasite attacking the royal tree of England that aristocrats occupy by right.

creeps me up: creeps up. (*Me* is an archaic dative.)

20 *Aeque tandem*: equally at length (suggesting a claim of social equality).

23 *Pliny*: author of a natural history, 77 AD. Renaissance writers made plentiful use of his lore and occasionally fanciful biology, sometimes using him as an authority for fabulous stories of their own invention (as in this instance).

28 *Undique mors est*: death is on all sides.

35 *my brother*: i.e. Gaveston, one who is to me a brother.

41–2 *And ... Britainy*: i.e. and the one you call a canker—Gaveston—will indeed have reason to say 'I am equally high' to the proudest peer of Britain.

45–6 *'Tis ... him*: not even the largest whale or most hideous winged bird with a woman's head will succeed in swallowing Gaveston.

53 *Danaë*: a king's daughter, confined to a tower, whom Jupiter craftily visited in a shower of gold.

62 *painted*: decorated with flowers.

73 *Return ... warrant*: return their defiance, and I will be your protection. (Gaveston proceeds to do so.)

74 *leaden*: spiritless, as opposed to *mounting*, l. 77.

80 *Treason*: drawing a weapon in the king's presence was a treasonable act.

81 *Here, here*: i.e. Gaveston is the traitor, not the barons.

86 *answer*: justify. But the king, in the next line, replies in the sense of 'atone for'.

88 *you both*: Mortimer Junior and Lancaster.

101 *Moved*: playing on *moved*, angry, in Warwick's speech, Mortimer hints at 'dislodged'.

102 *it is*: there is.

109 *defy*: (1) renounce allegiance to (2) challenge to combat.

122 *gather head*: muster forces.

129 S.D. *[Enter a guard]*: the guard may well consist of several men.

130 *Ay . . . well*: Mortimer Junior is sarcastic: isn't this fine, that the royal guard now denies us access to the king!

146 *the broad seal*: i.e. authority granted under the Great Seal. (See note at 1.1.167.)

148–52 *Your . . . these*: Lancaster and Mortimer Junior are affronted at being offered authority to collect taxes in the king's name for Mortimer Senior's ransom, as though they were beggars.

159 *The murmuring . . . hath*: and have stretched beyond limit of endurance the grumbling commoners' ability to pay.

163 *O'Neill*: the name of a famous Irish rebel clan in Edward II's reign and in the late sixteenth century.

164 *the English pale*: area around Dublin protected for the safety of English settlers.

166 *drave away*: drove off with.

167 *narrow seas*: English Channel.

171 *Valois*: the French king (though not a historically accurate name for Isabella's three royal brothers).

176 *Libels . . . thee*: pamphlets defaming you are distributed.

182 *But once*: Edward's one military adventure of any scope led to his disastrous defeat by the Scots at Bannockburn in 1314. He went to the battle with an army 'gorgeously apparelled', according to Holinshed.

186 *labels*: slips of parchment such as would affix a seal to a document.

195 *Wigmore shall fly*: Wigmore Castle, my property, shall be sold.

196 *purchase*: acquire (by military action).

221 *so I*: provided only that I can.

225 *him*: i.e. Mortimer Junior.

238 *let them go*: that is enough talk about them.

241 *arms*: coat of arms.

242 *gentry*: rank of gentleman (derived in Baldock's case from his having studied at Oxford rather than through a family coat of arms).

2.3.4 *adventure life*: risk death.

5 *of policy*: as a stratagem.

8 *cast*: reckon, fear.

doubt of: mistrust.

16–17 *Gaveston . . . king*: Lancaster's telling the lords here of something they already know and was not secret is probably the result of Marlowe's compressing his source, Holinshed's *Chronicles*.

22–3 *that . . . Mortimer*: a popular and erroneous etymology in the Renaissance derived 'Mortimer' from the Latin '*de Mortuo Mari*', 'from the Dead Sea', invoking the ideal of the Crusades.

2.4 S.D. *[Alarums]*: as in other battle sequences the action is virtually continuous from the previous scene.

40 *Forslow*: waste, lose or spoil by sloth.

42 *going several ways*: being sent against two enemy forces.

45 *begone*: i.e. hurry in pursuit of Gaveston before his reinforcements arrive.

47 *him*: Gaveston.

2.5 S.D. *Enter Gaveston, pursued*: presumably the barons catch up with Gaveston in the vicinity of Scarborough, having pursued him at first by water.

4 *unsurprised*: not taken unawares by military attack.

5 *malgrado*: in spite of. (Italian.)

15 *the Greekish strumpet*: Helen, the occasion of the Trojan War.

18 *King Edward*: although the Q1 reading, *Kind Edward*, might make sense in this context, the adjective is wholly uncharacteristic of Marlowe, and the line was corrected to *King Edward* in Q2.

27 *for*: because.

28 *so much honour*: sardonically said; Gaveston is not to be beheaded, like one of truly noble rank, but hanging is at least better than some more demeaning deaths.

36 *Entreateth . . . may*: asks you through me only that he may be allowed to.

42 *No . . . not*: i.e. no, there is no need to oblige the king or for Gaveston to get his hopes up.

46 *Will . . . hopes?*: cannot I hope that these negotiations will prolong my life a little?

54–5 *Not . . . earned*: Lancaster sarcastically suggests that returning the dead body will only prompt the king to give Gaveston a far more elaborate burial than the wretch deserves.

59 *When . . . tell?*: a sarcastic colloquialism meaning, roughly, 'Tell me another one'.

62 *seize*: repossess. 'Zease' and 'Seaze' in Q are sometimes interpreted as 'sees', and in the theatre the word is sounded ambiguously, but *seize* is both closer to the quarto reading and the more arresting metaphor.

64 *in keep*: in the matter of custody.

67 *for*: because.

70 *over-base*: the accusation of being a thief (l. 69) is excessive even among the base comparisons that have been inflicted upon Gaveston.

72 *companions . . . mates*: both words are contemptuously weighted with social disdain.

84 *'had-I-wist'*: if only I had known. (Warwick scorns the idea of regretting the seizing of Gaveston as a rash act and thereupon deciding to let him go.)

101 *to*: as.

102 *balk*: refuse.

103 *ARUNDEL*: here and in the S.D.s at l. 97, 3.2.88, and elsewhere in that scene, the early texts mistakenly refer to Arundel as Matrevis (*Mat.*). The confusion may indicate that one actor doubled the two parts.

104–5 *Your . . . prince*: i.e. your gracious offer is powerful enough to attract a prince. (The *adamant* or magnet is Pembroke's wife and hospitality.)

3.1.1 *thy friend*: i.e. Pembroke, Warwick's 'honourable friend' (l. 9). Gaveston and Pembroke's men, trying hopelessly to evade the ambush of Warwick's armed men, realize that Warwick has no intention of honouring his promise to Pembroke to allow Gaveston to visit Edward.

5 *Centre . . . bliss!*: O day (or king) that was to have been the centre of my bliss! (Gaveston then addresses Pembroke's men, imploring them to save him.) Alternatively, *centre* may mean centre of the earth, the lowest spot for falling.

13 *My friend*: Warwick sardonically refers to Pembroke with the term used by Gaveston in l. 1 and James in l. 9. The term could also apply condescendingly to James: 'my dear sir'.

watched it well: was vigilant, kept a night watch.

3.2 This and subsequent scenes appear in the theatre to follow continuously from what has recently happened near Scarborough, in Yorkshire. The battle in 3.3 occurred historically near Boroughbridge, in Yorkshire, after an interval of troubles in 1320–1.

12 *Edward Longshanks*: Edward I, renowned as a great warrior of large stature.

16 *Did you*: if you did.

19 *Be counterbuffed . . . nobility*: to be rebuffed by your nobles.

20 *on poles*: see 1.1.117.

22 *they*: i.e. their rebel followers or potential followers.

27 *We'll . . . tops*: we will strike with swords on their plumed helmets and cut off their heads.

29 *affection*: caprice, inclination.

36 *pikes*: soldiers bearing long iron-pointed staffs.

37 *Brown bills and targeteers*: soldiers bearing halberds or axe-spears that have been bronzed to prevent rust, and *targets* or shields.

42 *For . . . all*: for favours done to us all in that they were done to him.

44 *in lieu of*: in return for.

54 *in hand withal*: negotiating in this matter (to buy Lord Bruce's land).

57 *largess*: extra payment or treasure to be distributed to the soldiers.

63 *homage*: Edward had been summoned to do homage to the French king for his holding of Ponthieu and Guienne.

66 *Sib*: kinswoman, i.e. wife.

72 *bear you bravely*: comport yourself with dignity.

76–7 *heaven's . . . shoulder*: heaven on its axis, borne on Atlas' shoulder.

79 *towardness*: precociousness—sign of a short life to follow, as in *Richard III*'s young prince of the same name, Edward (3.1.94).

85 *go in peace*: a conventional blessing at departure, but here played off against *wars at home*.

87 *once*: once and for all.

88 *preparation*: pronounced in five syllables.

107 *to receive . . . him*: to take assurances from me that I would bring Gaveston back. (See ll. 98–100.) *Me* is probably an error for *my*.

121 *part*: role performed, deed.

125 *them*: the barons.

127 *starting-holes*: holes in which hunted animals take refuge. The enemy are to be 'fired' or smoked out of their hiding places like animals.

129 *moving orbs*: heavenly bodies moving in their orbits.

145 *merely of our love*: solely out of my love for you. (*Our* and *we* are the royal plural.)

149 *access*: accented on the second syllable.

150 S.D. *coat of arms*: a herald's coat or shield emblazoned with his lord's emblematic device.

160 *You . . . remedy*: you wish to find ease and remedy for this civil mayhem.

165 *Whose . . . dim*: the brightness of which is dimmed by such pernicious upstarts.

181 *lords*: Q's *lord* is possible, but probably the king addresses his lords including Arundel and Spencer (now earl).

3.3 S.D. *the noblemen . . . side*: these probably include Arundel and the bishop of Winchester.

6 *part*: side in the battle.

20 *in thy face*: Spencer Junior retorts to the accusation of being a traitor by throwing the word in Lancaster's face. (Q1 reads *on thy face*, probably making a simple unidiomatic error.)

34 *Alarum!*: sound the alarum!

35 *Saint George*: England's patron saint (beginning in Edward III's reign).

3.4 S.D. *with the barons*: Pembroke is missing from those who are captured and sentenced in this scene. The play treats him ambivalently; he might be supposed to have changed to the king's side after Warwick's treachery towards him in 3.1 (as was historically the case), but he enters with the rebels at 3.3.10 and rebukes Spencer Junior for his effrontery towards Lancaster. The role remains a loose end.

S.D. *Kent*: Kent's status is problematic. Last seen in 2.3 when he joined the rebel barons and promised to fight with them, Kent makes no appearance in the battle now ended, and we are not told whether he took active part. If he is led on captive at this point (an uncertain matter), the king does not keep him captive but orders him out of the royal presence (l. 12) without armed guard. As brother of the king, Kent would provide a special case.

4 *advance*: elevate (on poles). See 1.1.117 and 3.2.20.

9 *made him away*: did him in, killed him.

17 *watched*: see 3.1.13.

19 *overlook the rest*: i.e. be placed on a pole higher than the others.

23 *to live*: i.e. to live eternally.

25 *my lord of Winchester*: i.e. Spencer Senior, who was made earl of Wiltshire at 3.2.49.

36–9 *What . . . far*: possibly an aside, but possibly said in open defiance.

37 *Immure thy virtue*: close up in a walled prison your strength and power.

42–3 *Levune . . . land*: Levune, we are entrusting you with a mission upon which the security of England depends.

44 *with advice*: judiciously.

45 *that treasure* such wealth. Levune, himself French, is to bribe the French lords to deny aid to Queen Isabella.

48 *Danaë*: for her story, see note at 2.2.53.

53 *levelled at*: aimed at. The early texts mistakenly print *leuied at*.

54 *lay . . . together*: a grim jest: the rebel barons' putting their heads together will result in their being beheaded.

56 *clap so close*: deal so secretly.

59 *obdurate*: accented on the middle syllable.

4.1 Kent is to be imagined near the Tower of London, waiting for Mortimer Junior to escape. On Kent's being free even after the fighting against the king in Act 3, see note at 3.4 S.D., above.

3 *Nature*: i.e. natural attachment to a brother.

11 *Stand . . . device!*: be favourable, dark night, to Mortimer's plan of escape (by providing deep darkness)!

14 *potion*: sleeping potion.

4.2 The queen and Prince Edward have been at the court of France for some time.

5 *my uncle's*: i.e. Kent's, who appears to have good connections in France. See 4.1.6.

10 *jar too far*: are too out of tune.

Unkind: (1) lacking in feeling (2) unnatural towards a sister.

11 *Unhappy*: (1) wretched (2) unfortunate.

18 *stay time's advantage*: await favourable opportunity.

20 *shake off*: get rid of, leave behind.

24 *break a staff*: shatter a lance in jousting or fighting.

30 *Tanaïs*: the River Don, in Russia, regarded as at 'the utmost verge of Europe'.

40 *reserved . . . hap*: set apart by Fortune for a better fate.

43 *How . . . lives?*: why do you speak of advancing my cause, or my banner in battle, since my father lives? (The prince will have nothing to do with an offer of help from one whom he instinctively perceives as his father's rival, politically and sexually.)

an: if, if we grant that.

45 *I . . . worse*: we could do worse (than accept Mortimer Junior's offer).

55 *Would*: who would.

56 *appointed for*: equipped to encounter.

59 *deserved*: earned.

66 *to . . . base*: to challenge Edward to risk leaving his home base (alluding to the children's game of prisoner's base), i.e. to come out and fight. *Match* and *outrun* in ll. 67–8 continue the metaphor. *A base* punningly suggests *abase*, lower himself.

74 *brother*: i.e. brother-in-law.

76 *forward in arms*: ready and eager to fight.

77 *anchor-hold*: the hold that an anchor takes; hence, chief ground of trust and hope.

4.3 The scene is imagined to take place at Edward's court.

3 *And . . . uncontrolled*: and may Edward and his supporters triumph, free from the constraint their enemies would impose.

11 S.D. *the names . . . [executed]*: Holinshed gives the names: 'The Lord William Tuchet, the Lord William Fitzwilliam, the Lord Warren de Lisle', etc.

28 *premised*: put first, prefixed, taken for granted.

30 *France his*: France's.

51–2 *And . . . forth*: if the winds are truly *equal* or even-handed, they will balance their *injurious* or wrongful act of letting the traitors escape from England by bringing them back where they may be fought with.

4.4 The queen's party has just landed in England—according to Holinshed, near Harwich in Suffolk, though Marlowe does not mention this location and instead, by compression of his historical sources, gives the impression in the previous scene that Edward is hastening to Bristol in anticipation of her landing. The fighting in the next scene and following is clearly located by Marlowe near Bristol, where the encounter did historically take place.

3 *Belgia*: Hainault is located in Flanders, in modern-day Belgium.

4–5 *To cope . . . knit*: to encounter our own countrymen in fight—a sad turn of events, when opposing forces (of Englishmen) are interlocked in combat.

7–8 *Slaughter . . . gored*: seem, in killing Englishmen, to kill themselves and inflict wounds upon themselves.

29 *Edward . . . him*: i.e. if we stay here talking, Edward will not take us as a serious threat.

30 *I . . . more*: i.e. would that our talking were the greatest flattery Edward ever received, instead of the actual flattery that has ruined him.

4.5.3 *to Ireland*: according to Holinshed, Edward's reasons for going to Bristol were to raise support among the Welsh, where he was popular, and to be in a position to escape to Ireland if things went badly.

4.6.5 *of all unkind*: the most ungrateful and unnatural person of all.

16–17 *Bristol . . . false*: i.e. Bristol has gone over to the queen's party, deserting the son of Edward Longshanks (Edward I; see 3.2.12 and note).

17 *single for suspect*: suspiciously alone.

19 *Successful . . . kings*: the God who rules over rulers gives success in battle.

25 *Of*: out of.

26 *the Fates*: the three sisters who spin, draw off, and cut the thread of destiny.

28 *in this*: the queen refers with deliberate vagueness to the affairs of the nation after Edward's defeat and to the disposal of Edward himself.

40 *knows our mind*: i.e. understands and supports our wish that Edward's favourites be apprehended (as ll. 47 ff. indicate). The queen's exchange with Mortimer Junior, ll. 40–3, though cold-blooded in tone, is public enough at least for Sir John to join in at l. 44, unlike Mortimer's aside at ll. 38–9.

43 *A goodly chancellor*: said sardonically, presumably to Mortimer Junior. Sir John then agrees with her caustic evaluation of Edward's favourites.

45 *This . . . realm*: Kent's aside seems aimed not only at the favourites, whom the others are discussing, but at what Edward's follies have now led to: the conspiratorial intimacy of Mortimer Junior and the queen. Without the two commas (missing in Q), the line blames Edward directly.

45 S.D. *Rice ap Howell*: a Welshman sent into Wales to apprehend the king.

48 *this presence*: by this phrase, normally meaning 'the king's presence', the speaker hints at the momentum behind the transfer of authority to the young prince.

51 *Catiline*: a dissolute Roman patrician and conspirator in the 60s BC.

59 *Some . . . all*: this line is often regarded as an aside, since it does express a wish for Edward's death, but the speaker is an intemperate man not given to hiding his feelings.

60 *started thence*: forced from their lair.

63 *what . . . muse?*: what remains to be done? What are you thinking about?

70 *Your . . . head*: i.e. your pretty titles cannot save you now.

71 *prince*: king.

75 *Being of countenance*: having good credit or estimation.

4.7 According to Holinshed, Edward was apprehended by Rice ap Howell at the Abbey of Neath in Wales, after having unsuccessfully attempted to sail to Ireland or the Isle of Lunday (see ll. 33-6) and having landed instead in Glamorganshire. Queen Isabel meanwhile had moved from Bristol to Hereford. Marlowe does not mention Neath but clearly envisages a Welsh abbey. The religious disguise may be that of monks or penitents.

14 *what is he*: what person is there.

18 *nurseries of arts*: i.e. universities.

26 *sit secure*: rest free from care.

28-9 *Not . . . below*: even if no one alive knows where they are, Spenser *shrewdly* (sorely) fears that the *gloomy fellow* or Mower who saw them as they passed his *mead* or meadow will figure things out. The Mower in fact identifies them at l. 46.

35 *fall on shore*: run aground.

47 *I pray be short*: i.e. come along quickly (said to the king).

51 *he*: Edward (who is evidently has been sitting since l. 16, resting his head for a time on the Abbot's lap).

53-4 *Quem . . . iacentem*: he whom the approaching day saw so mighty and proud, the declining day now sees in flight from battle. (From Seneca, *Thyestes*, 613-14.)

55 *leave . . . passionate*: stop being so emotional.

56 *by no other names*: Leicester scornfully refuses to recognize the patrician titles Edward has given them.

58 *Stand not on*: never mind, do not attempt to take refuge in.

67 *in rescue of*: in return for the releasing of.

70 *earns*: grieves.

73 *so . . . heavens*: thus the angry heavens decree.

81 *Killingworth*: Kenilworth.

89 *hags*: infernal beings such as Furies or Harpies, or ghosts.

Charon: the ferryman who conveyed the dead across the Styx to Pluto's kingdom of Hades (l. 88).

90 *these, and these*: the monks and Edward's personal favourites.

91 *these*: Spencer and Baldock.

94 *that . . . shall be*: what must be shall be.

98 *Life . . . friends*: I must bid farewell to life itself when I say goodbye to my friends.

101 *fire . . . orb*: in earth-centred astronomy, one of the outermost spheres of the universe was thought to be an orbit of fire; or the image could refer to the sun. In either case, the apocalyptic images recall the Book of Revelation.

110–11 *To . . . fall*: we are born to die, and rise only to fall.

112–13 *the place appointed*: i.e. the place of execution (where such pious statements of farewell to life will be appropriate).

114 *your lordships*: said sardonically to Baldock and Spencer Junior (compare l. 56 and note).

115 *remember me*: i.e. reward the service I have done.

116 *What else?*: i.e. rest assured.

5.1 The location is clearly imagined to be Kenilworth Castle, called Killingworth (as in l. 2). The bishop of Winchester and Trussell are there '*for the crown*' in that they are a delegation charged with reporting back to Parliament and to Mortimer Junior and the queen on the outcome of these abdication proceedings. See ll. 38–9, 84–90.

10 *an herb*: the herb dittany, from Crete, which was fabled to have the power of expelling weapons from wounds.

14 *mounts . . . air*: i.e. rears aloft, as in royal heraldry showing the lion 'rampant'; with suggestion here of the soul mounting to heaven, as in ll. 19–22.

18 *mewed*: shut up as in a 'mew' or cage, as one might a hawk or falcon (a royal creature, like the lion). The image of flight continues in ll. 20–2.

20 *As*: that.

22 *plain me*: make my complaint.

27 *perfect*: mere.

35 *exchange*: change of fortune.

44 *a blaze . . . fire*: i.e. a crown that will burn its wearer's head, like that prepared by the deserted Medea for Jason's new wife Creusa.

45 *Tisiphon*: one of the Furies, who were often represented with snakes for hair.

47 *vine*: the emblematic vine on the English crown.

51 *weigh . . . brook*: consider with what difficulty I can endure.

52 *lose*: Q's *loose* may suggest 'let loose of', but is also a common spelling variant of 'lose'.

54 *That*: who.

63, 70 *wishèd*: (1) sought after by others (2) desired by me.

66 *watches . . . element*: i.e. stars and planets, that watch over us from the *element* or sky and mark the passage of time.

67 *at a stay*: motionless.

76 *fondly led*: i.e. foolishly misled by fantasies of power.

86 *be king*: these words, which do not appear in the early texts, are supplied by editors as a probable conclusion needed to fill out the metre of the line.

89 *seal*: attest to, ratify; be the ending of.

112 WINCHESTER *My lord*—: the early texts call for Berkeley (*Bartley*) to enter here and speak this line.

115 *protect*: act as Protector for.

128 *post*: Berkeley, though not a messenger in the ordinary sense, brings the news that Leicester is to turn the king over to Berkeley.

130 *to . . . breast*: i.e. as though the message itself were a dagger.

147 *as lieth in you*: as you can.

149 *Mine enemy*: i.e. Leicester, until now the king's gaoler.

5.2 The scene is at court.

5 *Be ruled by me*: follow my advice (with a suggestion of 'let me be in charge of everything').

9 *grip*: clutch, seize (Q's *gripe* is actually a separate word, but here with identical meaning; also at 5.3.57).

10 *imports*: it concerns.

11 *erect*: elevate to the throne, crown.

13–14 *For . . . writ*: for the advantage we now enjoy will gain more authority when the name of a king is signed below whatever we decree.

17 *so*: provided.

22 S.D. *and then . . . Winchester*: Winchester's entrance and exit are both unmarked in Q, but seemingly he enters in time to be present as the Messenger delivers correspondence from Kenilworth—either the sealed document containing news of the abdication which Winchester announces himself (ll. 27–8), or possibly a private correspondence from the king.

27 *Thanks, gentle Winchester*: perhaps the queen is acknowledging Winchester's efforts in bringing about the abdication of Edward, having gathered from his bringing in the crown that those efforts have succeeded.

30 *this letter*: i.e. the document of abdication signed and sealed by the king. The phrasing suggests, though not certainly, that this is the same letter brought by the Messenger.

31 *he*: the king. (See 5.1.144.)

33 *no more but so*: i.e. I have said enough; that's the sum of what I've heard.

34 *so*: as.

37 *Here . . . seal*: perhaps Mortimer Junior delivers the privy seal to Winchester to authorize something delicately confidential for which the bishop would need protection (a gesture that would motivate the bishop's exit at this point); but, since Mortimer Junior entrusts his secret mission instead to Matrevis and Gurney, he may here simply mean, speaking to the queen, that with the privy seal in his possession he has all the authority he needs to do whatever he wants.

39 *To . . . drift*: to foil the plot of the dull-brained earl of Kent.

40 *removed*: i.e. from Berkeley Castle. See ll. 59–62 below.

54 *him*: the king.

68 *this letter*: i.e. the letter written by Matrevis for Mortimer Junior to sign.

82 *enlarged*: released (with a hidden suggestion of 'released from life').

93 *him*: Edward II.

102 *That wast*: you that were.

111 *'sdain'st thou so*: are you so disdainful.

112 S.D. *[Seizing him]*: Mortimer Junior may do so playfully, as though he were a jolly uncle, like Richard III.

114 *strive not*: perhaps Kent tries to intervene, though the words can more simply suggest his dismay and anxiety about the way Prince Edward is being treated.

115 *nearer*: nearer in blood (to Prince Edward).

116 *my charge*: as Prince Edward's uncle and next of blood, Kent has a claim to be Protector instead of Mortimer Junior; see l. 89.

121 *thee*: apparently said apostrophizing the departed queen, though the exact points of her departure and of Mortimer Junior are uncertain.

5.3 The shaving with puddle water at ll. 36 ff., and l. 48, make clear that the scene is imagined to take place near Kenilworth Castle.

6 *the nightly bird*: the owl, shunned by smaller birds as ominous.

10 *unbowel*: open up and empty.

17 *air of life*: breath.

22 *rends . . . heart*: i.e. breaks my heart.
   closet: chamber.

26 S.D. *[Ditch water]*: in Stowe's *Annals*, a barber comes to Edward with a basin of water from a nearby ditch.

44 *remain*: dwell (in the afterworld).

46 *'Twixt . . . enmity*: Matrevis sardonically reassures the king that he need not worry whether the ghosts of his former favourites will be at enmity with his.

49–50 *How now . . . Kent*: in the darkness after their torches are extinguished, those guarding the king are vulnerable to a surprise intrusion and unable at first to see who is there. On the Elizabethan stage, with no artificial lighting, the putting out of the torches conveys total darkness, even though the spectators can see as well as before.

52 *Thrust in the king*: one staging possibility is to have some of the soldiers remove the king at this point, thus motivating Kent's insistent request in ll. 53 and 60 that he be allowed to speak with Edward. The king's exit is clearly marked in Q at l. 62, but such markings in this play are approximate; compare the end of 5.2.

5.4 A throne is presumably needed for this scene in honour of Edward III's coronation (ll. 72 ff.).

14 *That, being dead*: that when Edward is dead.

27 *use much*: am much accustomed. (Said ironically.)

31 *poison flowers*: i.e. in such a way that anyone smelling them will die.

32 *a lawn*: a thin strip of linen, here thrust suffocatingly down the throat in such a way as to conceal the means of death, as in all of Lightborn's Italianate methods of murder.

42 *At . . . horse*: post horses have been provided every ten miles to speed your journey.

43 *never . . . more*: i.e. do not come back here and arouse suspicions about me (but with darker hidden suggestion that Lightborn is to die).

51 *seal*: i.e. make decisions and put my official seal on them.

54 *Aristarchus*: famous scholar, librarian, grammarian, and teacher in the second century BC, noted for his severity of judgement.

57 *And . . . desire*: and beg me to accept the very thing I desire.

61 *onus quam gravissimum*: a very heavy responsibility.

63 *Suscepi . . . provinciam*: I have undertaken the responsibility for government (literally, of a province).

69 *Maior . . . nocere*: I am too mighty for Fortune to harm. (From Ovid, *Metamorphoses*, vi. 195.)

72 S.D. *Champion*: one who, in a formal coronation ceremony, offers to fight any who challenge the claim of the new king to his crown.

80 *here's to thee*: the king may follow a coronation ceremonial of drinking to the champion and then presenting him with the silver-gilt cup, or he may present a purse.

81 *Lord . . . charge*: unless the queen is asking Mortimer Junior to offer patronage to the champion, she is confirming Mortimer's role as Protector of the new-crowned king.

82 *with blades and bills*: guarded by soldiers bearing swords and halberds.

5.5 Edward's dungeon at Berkeley Castle may have been represented in the Elizabethan theatre by means of a trapdoor (since it is said to be a sewerage vault in the depths of the castle, ll. 2–4, 56–7) or a 'discovery' space rearstage. The bed could be thrust onstage at l. 38.

16 *for the nonce*: on purpose.

24 *Pereat iste*: let this person perish.

25 *What else?*: i.e. did the Lord Protector send any further instructions?

lake: channel, sewer, moat.

33 *A table and a featherbed*: according to Holinshed, Edward's murderers rushed into his chamber as he lay asleep and threw upon him 'heavy feather beds, or a table, as some write', to hold him down while he was murdered. Marlowe here specifies both, though whether the acting company used both is uncertain; Lightborn calls for a table only at ll. 110 and 112. A featherbed is a kind of mattress stuffed with feathers.

36 *Fear . . . that*: don't you worry about our doing our part.

38 S.D. *[Exeunt . . . Gurney]*: conceivably, Matrevis and Gurney retire without exiting completely; at l. 28, Lightborn bade them 'be not far off'.

41 *with all my heart*: i.e. I must say.

54 *Caucasus*: mountains between the Black and Caspian Seas, fabled for their ruggedness.

66 *dropped*: had dropped.

69 *ran at tilt*: jousted in a tournament.

104 *never*: never shall.

113 S.D. *[The King is murdered]*: according to Holinshed, some of the men held Edward down with a table or featherbed while a hot spit was thrust up into his body through the anus. Whether such a horrible method of murder was simulated by the Elizabethan acting company is not certain, but the act is easily simulated in the theatre, and this present scene does require that the table be thrust upon Edward to hold him down. Lightborn specializes in secretive forms of murder that leave the

body outwardly unharmed to make detection of the crime difficult (see 5.4.30–6), and here he expresses concern that the body not be bruised (ll. 112–13).

5.6 Matrevis reports to Mortimer Junior at court.

4 *I'll . . . father*: (1) I will offer you absolution as your spiritual confessor (2) I will make a ghost of you.

9 *Fly . . . savages*: i.e. flee beyond the reach of civilization, beyond the arm of the law.

11 *Jove's huge tree*: the oak.

24 FIRST LORD: although the early texts assign speeches to unspecified *Lords* throughout this scene, editors generally give ll. 24, 38, and 93 to a First Lord and ll. 77, 89, and 91 to a Second Lord.

45–6 *[aside]*: these asides need not be said by Mortimer and the queen to each other.

47 *'Tis my hand*: earlier, at 5.4.6, Mortimer Junior said in soliloquy that the letter was 'written by a friend of ours'.

51 *Why stays he here?*: i.e. why has he not been taken to his death?

52–4 *Bring . . . me*: Edward III sentences Mortimer Junior to be hanged, drawn, and quartered, the prescribed harsh punishment for high treason: that is, to be dragged through the streets to the place of execution on a *hurdle* or sled used for the purpose, to be hanged, to be divided bodily into quarters which might be hung up or variously distributed, and to have his head dishonoured. (*Drawing* might also involve being eviscerated while still alive.)

76 *I . . . unnatural*: Edward III's natural feelings prompt him to believe his mother's protestations, despite the evidence of her *unnatural* adultery and conspiracy to murder her husband.

92 S.D. *[attended]*: ll. 89 and 91 perhaps indicate that the Second Lord is to escort the queen.

94 *where it shall lie*: wherever it is at present. (Conceivably, the phrase could mean that Mortimer Junior's head is to be placed on Edward II's hearse.)

GLOSSARY

'a he.

abject *v.* abase, debase

abjection degradation

abroad out of doors

abuses ill-treatment

aby pay for

adamant lodestone, magnet

adjoin join

admire wonder at; regard with approval

admitted granted

adry thirsty

advance raise aloft

affect *v.* desire, seek to attain, indulge in

affections feelings

after afterwards

again *prep.* against; *adv.* back, still

against in anticipation of

a-good in good earnest, heartily

aim *v.* aim at

alarm, alarum call to arms; military assault

Alcoran Koran

allied connected by family or affinity

amain with all one's might; at full speed

amaze stun

amazed stunned

an, an if if

annoy molest, harm

anon immediately

appoint decide

approve find by experience

approved proved by experience, tested

arbitrament disposal, command

Argier Algiers

argosy large merchant ship; also, a fleet

argument subject

armado large ocean vessel

arms weapons, tools

art skill, discipline

artier artery

asafoetida gum resin of plants used in medicine and cooking

aspect countenance; astrological position

aspire mount up to, attain

asseized seized

astonièd stunned

at large in full, in detail

attend await

Aurora goddess of dawn

avail *n.* benefit

avouch confirm

awful awe-inspiring; filled with dread

aye ever, at all times

bait *v.* harass, torment

baleful deadly, wretched

ban *v.* curse

banco bank

band bond; ribbon

bandy exchange blows (as in tennis)

bane plague, curse

baneful pernicious

Barbarian Barbary

bark boat

bashaw, basso pasha, Turkish aristocrat and military leader

basilisk a fabulous reptile, able to kill by its looks; a cannon

basin plate

batten thrive by feeding

battle army

beard *v.* oppose defiantly

become suit

beguile cheat

behest command

beholding beholden

behoof benefit

behove be needful, befit

Belgia the Netherlands

belike perhaps, probably

benighted overtaken by darkness

beseem befit

beside besides, in addition to this

bespeak fair address courteously

betide happen to

betimes early, in timely fashion

bewray reveal; betray

bide face, encounter
bill halberd
blast *v.* blight, ruin
blubbered flushed and disfigured with
    tears
bolt fetter
bombard a large cannon
bondman slave
boot *n.*, *v.* avail, help
bootless unavailing
Boreas the north wind
brave *n.* taunt, insult; *v.* defy; *adj.*
    fine, splendid, presumptuous; *adv.*
    splendidly
bravely well
brawns muscles
brazen made of brass; hard or
    coloured like brass
breathe catch one's breath
breathless dead
breeching whipping
brent burned
breviated abbreviated
brigantine small pirate craft
brightsome bright-looking
broil quarrel
brokery the business of a broker
brook tolerate
brunt attack, onset
buckler *v.* shield, protect
but late only recently
buzz murmur
by'r Lady, by Lady by Our Lady
    (the Virgin Mary)
by this by this time
camp army
car chariot
carbonadoes meat scored across for
    grilling
careless unrestrained
carouse drink down
case pair
cassia a fragrant shrub
cast *v.* reckon
cast about scheme, devise
cates delicacies
celebrate observe ceremoniously
censure *n.* judgement
certify inform
champian level and open

chance happening, fortune
channel gutter
character stamp, distinctive mark
charge *n.* responsibility; *v.* command;
    entrust
charm *n.* spell; *v.* put a spell on
charmed protected by magic
charming *pple. adj.* using charms or
    magic spells
cheer *n.* mood, countenance
cherish encourage
chitterling sausage made with the
    intestines of pigs etc.
choler wrath
circumscriptible subject to limits of
    space
civil civilized, well-governed
clap *v.* pat
clean *adv.* entirely
clear *adv.* utterly
clift cliff
close secret, well-concealed; closed,
    lowered
closely secretly
closet private chamber
cloth of arras rich tapestry
clown stage character representing a
    rustic buffoon
coast *v.* sail along the shore
cockerel young cock or rooster
coil fuss, commotion
college deliberative body, often
    ecclesiastical
colour *n.* excuse, pretext; *pl.* military
    banner
commons commoners
compact of made up of, composed of
companion fellow
company *v.* accompany, keep
    company with
compass *n.* range; *v.* encompass, lay
    hold of; devise
competitor partner
complete perfect, consummate
complices accomplices, allies
conceit fanciful or witty notion;
    thought, understanding
conduct *n.* leadership
confess acknowledge
confines borders

confound defeat, destroy; throw into confusion

confusion destruction, perdition

congé ceremonial bow

consort *n.* musical group; spouse; *v.* attend

conster construe

consul chief magistrate

consummate fulfilled, perfect

contemn scorn, slight

contemner scorner

continent solid land; a containing space

contract, contracted betroth, betrothed

contributory tributary

control challenge, censure, hold sway over

convent convent or monastery

convertite convert

costermonger fruit seller

countenance sanction

counterfeit likeness

countervail match

county count

court it play the courtier

cousin kinsman or kinswoman; fellow member of the aristocracy

cozen cheat

cozening cheating

crazèd cracked, unsound

crest crested helmet

cross *v.* thwart

crown *n.* a gold coin

crownet coronet

culverin large cannon

cunning skill, erudition; deceit

curious intricately wrought

curstly malignantly, severely

curtle-axe cutlass

Cynthia the moon

dainty delightful, pleasant, choice, delicately wrought

dalliance delay

damp *n.* an exhalation, a noxious vapour or gas

dated limited to a fixed term

dead *v.* deaden

dear expensive

decay death, fall

degree rank

delicates delicacies. Compare 'cates'.

deny refuse

desert *adj.* uninhabited, desolate

desperate reckless(ly)

device plan; heraldic emblem

devoir duty

devote dedicate

diablo the devil

diet *v.* regulate as to diet

digest undergo digestion

digested endured, got over

Dis god of the underworld

discharge unload

dispatch be quick

distain stain

distained stained, dishonoured

distempered disordered, ailing

divers various

divine *v.* have premonition of

doom *n.* opinion, judgement; *v.* give sentence

dread, dreadful inspiring dread or awe

dress prepare

drift purpose

ducat a gold coin

earn yearn

earth-mettled base in temperament

ebon ebony-dark

ecstasy frenzied passion

egregious distinguished

elements i.e. earth, water, fire, and air

Elysium abode of the blessed after death

embassy, embassage ambassadorial message

empery dominion, rule, and the territory subject to it

empyreal heaven the highest heaven of light and fire

enchase *v.* adorn, set

enchased *adj.* set, adorned

engine instrument (of assault, sight, etc.)

engineer constructor of military engines

engirt encircled with

engraft implanted

enlarge set free

enroll wrap up, enfold

ensign military banner

entertain receive, welcome, maintain; employ
entertainment reception, welcome
enthrall enslave
entreat persuade; treat, deal with
entrench surround with trenches; place in a trench
ere before
Erebus the gloomy space between earth and Hades; hell
erst formerly, before now
essay *v.* try
estates states, positions
esteemed estimated
eternize immortalize
Euxine Sea Black Sea
exceeding very great; very
except unless
exclaim on or **against** accuse, denounce
exclaims *n.* exclamations
excruciate *v.* torment
excursion sortie, military foray
execution haste
exequy funeral ceremony
exigent extremity, emergency
expect await
expedition speed
exquisite excruciating
face *v.* turn up with another material; bully, confront
factious given to forming factions, quarrelsome
factor agent
fain gladly
faint *v.* lose heart, flag
faith by my faith
false *v.* falsify, violate, betray
fame rumour; reputation
family household
fancy *v.* fall in love with
fast *adj* secure
fatal ominous, prophetic, fated
Fatal Sisters the Three Fates, Clotho, Lachesis, Atropos
favour *n.* attractiveness, appearance, countenance; token of affection, such as a ribbon or glove; *v.* resemble; show favour to
fearful fear-inspiring; timorous

fell cruel, fierce
fence *v.* protect
field-piece light cannon
figure likeness, image
fire *v.* consume by fire
fit bout of illness, crisis
flat utter, final; **that's flat,** that's certain
flatly utterly
flatter court, try to please
fleering jeering
fleet, fleeting float, floating
Flora deity of flowers and vegetation
flourish trumpet fanfare announcing entrance of a distinguished person
flout mock
fly flee
foil *n.* overthrow; thin metal leaf placed behind a jewel to set off its lustre; *v.* trample underfoot, defeat, defile
fond foolish
forceless weak
forlorn abandoned; sad
for [one's] turn for one's purposes
forsooth truly (often ironical)
fortune *v.* turn out, come to pass
forward zealous
forwardness zeal
forwhy because
frame *n.* fashioning; *v.* fashion
framed made
framing fashioning
fraught *n.* freight, cargo; *v. pple.* freighted, laden
frayed frightened
friends kinsmen
frolic *adj.* sportive; *v.* make merry
front *v.* confront, oppose
Furies primeval beings that avenge human crimes
furious fierce, passionate, raging
furniture armour and accoutrements; furnishings
furtherer contriver
gage engage, stake
gallant fine young gentleman
gat got
gear business
generally without exception

gentle well-born; kind
gentles gentlefolk
ghostly spiritual
girdle belt used to carry purse or weapons
give the lie accuse someone of lying
glad *v.* gladden
glaive long-handled bladed weapon
glorious boastful
glozing flattering
God-a-mercy thanks (literally, 'God have mercy')
god of arms or **war** Mars
go to an exclamation of impatience or expostulation
grace *v.* be gracious to, show favour to; adorn, provide oneself
Graces Greek personifications of loveliness
gramercy many thanks (French, *Grand merci*)
gratify requite
grave *adj.* respected, influential, worthy; *v.* engrave
graven engraved
grief pain, suffering
gripe seize
groat a coin of small value (four pence in predecimal currency)
groom servant, base fellow
guise custom
habit demeanour
halberd long-handled spear and axe
hale draw, pull, drag
hap *n.* fortune; *v.* happen
haply, happily perchance; fortunately
happy fortunate, propitious
hardiness boldness, daring
harmless innocent; unharmed
hart male deer
haught, haughty courageous, lofty
haunted persistently followed, plagued
have at have a go at
have done with cease
havoc *v.* create havoc with or in
head behead
heading beheading
heartless spiritless
hearty heartfelt
helm helmet

hie hasten
high, high-minded arrogant
hippocras a spiced wine
his its; his
hogshead large cask
hold stronghold; grasp
home *adv.* all the way
homely plain, unrefined
horse cavalry
hospital asylum for the needy and aged, especially disabled soldiers
host army
hostry hostelry, inn
house dwelling; family
hoy a small vessel usually rigged as a sloop
hugy huge
humours the four vital bodily fluids, blood, bile, phlegm, and black bile
hurdle a frame or sledge used to drag criminals to their execution
husht hush
imbecility weakness of any sort
impale encircle adorningly
import signify
imprecation prayer
incense set on fire
incivil barbarous
incontinent immediately
indifferent, indifferently impartial, without bias
influence supposed streaming from the stars or heavens of an ethereal fluid acting on human destiny and character
injurious, injury insulting, insult
intercept anticipate, prevent
interdict cut off
intreated treated
invasion assault
invest establish in office
investion investiture
issue *n.* offspring; *v.* result, turn out, issue forth
it shall go hard there will be trouble, things will turn out worse than expected, unforeseen difficulties may arise to prevent (it)
iwis certainly
jack fellow

janizaries Turkish soldiers
jar *n.*, *v.* quarrel
jealous, jealousy apprehensive, suspicious; suspicion
jess leather strap fastened to a hawk's leg
jet *v.* strut
jetty jet-black
jig jocular ballad
joy *v.* enjoy, rejoice at
Juno wife and sister of Jupiter
kern footsoldier
kind favourable, natural, rightful, fitting
kindly readily, naturally
lade load
larded interspersed, garnished
larum alarum, call to arms, military assault
late *adv.* lately; *adj.* recent
latest last, most recent
lavish *adj.* unrestrained
lay song
league about three miles
leave *n.* permission; *v.* cease
leman sweetheart
let hinder
let it pass never mind
let me alone leave it to me
letters often meaning a letter (Latin *litterae*)
level aim
liberal generous, gentlemanly
licentious unrestrained by law or morality
lie reside
liege lord to whom feudal obedience is owed
lightsome light-giving, radiant
like *v.* please; *adv.* likely
list desire; listen
litter curtained couch carried on men's shoulders
lively life-giving, pertaining to life
loaden laden
loading cargo; bill of lading
lodestar pole-star, guiding star
'long, 'longing belong, belonging
long of on account of
loon boor, lout

lording lord
lour frown
luckless presaging evil, malignant
lusty vigorous; pleasant
magnanimity lofty courage
Mahomet Muhammad
maim *n.* serious bodily injury
main *n.* ocean, sea
mainly mightily
manage arms wield weapons
mandrake mandragora, a narcotic plant
marry *int.* indeed (originally, 'by Mary')
masque a court entertainment with dancing and acting in masks
Mass by the Mass (an oath)
massy solid, weighty
masters sirs
mate companion
mated daunted
mead meadow
mean *adj.* of low social station, lowly; *n.* means
meat food
meed merit
meet suitable, fit
mere pure
mess serving
meteors any atmospheric phenomena
mickle much
minion favourite
miscreant misbeliever
mistrust *v.* suspect
mortal deadly
motion proposal; impulse, emotion
move *v.* anger; persuade
muscadine, muscatel a strong, sweet wine
napkin handkerchief
needs of necessity
Nilus the River Nile
no more but so an ominously vague threat: enough said, just wait and see
nonplus *v.* a state of being nonplussed
nor . . . nor neither . . . nor
novice probationer
no whit not a bit
offer prepare, try, make as if
offering preparing
ope open

operation efficacy
order rule, custom
orient lustrous, precious, as generally of jewels from the East
orifex orifice, wound
orison prayer
ostler stableman, groom
out! an exclamation of indignation or reproach
outface impudently contradict
outrageous unrestrained
overthwart across
overwatched exhausted from lack of sleep
overweighing prepondering, overruling
pace traverse with steps
pale enclosure, district
paragon mate, consort
parcel an essential part of
park pale edge of the grounds surrounding a mansion
parle talk, hold a parley
parley *n.* conference under truce with the enemy; *v.* discuss terms
partake share in, be acquainted with
partial unfair, biased
parti-coloured variegated in colour
pash dash to pieces
pass *v.* care; pass sentence
passenger traveller
passing *adv.* surpassingly
passionate moved by strong emotion
pathetical earnest and full of pathos
peasant low fellow, rascal, boor
peevish silly
pelf money
pennon streamer
perforce of necessity
pericranion skull
period end, stop
petty lesser
Phoebus Apollo; the sun
physic medicine
pill *v.* plunder
pined tormented
pinioned shackled
pioner sapper, digger of mines and countermines
pitchy pitch-black
plage region

plainer complainant
plaint lament, complaint
plate silver coin
players actors
pleasant jocular
pleaseth may it please
pleasure *n.* will; *v.* please
pledge hostage
plight faith give formal promise to marry
plumed adorned with plumes
policy political sagacity or cunning
port gate
portagues Portuguese gold coins
portcullis grated metal gate
portend foreshadow; signify
portly stately
post *n.* messenger; *v.* hasten
posy bouquet; verse motto
pottage porridge
power army
pox *exclam.* i.e. a plague, the curse. (Pox is syphilis.)
practice doings; intrigue, treachery
practise devise means to bring about
precinct sphere of control
precise puritanical, strict in the observance of religious rule
prefer recommend, advance, promote
presence, the a place prepared for ceremonial attendance
present *adj.* immediate
presently immediately
present money ready money
prest ready, prompt, eager, keen
pretend put forward, set forth, intend
pretty amusing
prevail avail
prevent anticipate
principality sovereignty
privy *adj.* secret; privately aware, in on the secret
procure bring about; obtain
professèd proclaimed
promise *v.* assure
proper own, unique
prorex viceroy
prosecute pursue
protest swear, vow
prove test, experience; turn out

publish proclaim
puissant powerful
purple blood-coloured
purse *v.* put into one's purse
quaff drink deeply
quaint, quaintly skilful, elegant, handsome; skilfully, elegantly, handsomely
qualify mitigate
question dispute
quintessence the 'fifth essence' thought to be latent in all substances
quit *v.* requite; *adj.* acquitted
quittance requital
quotha says he, forsooth
Rabbi wise man
ragged with jagged outlines
rail *v.* utter abusive language
raise a siege lift or put an end to a blockade
rankle fester
rape abduction
rapine plunder, pillage
rare infrequent; excellent
rare-witted of excellent understanding
rate *v.* put a price on, evaluate
raze scrape, graze, destroy
read unto teach
readiness alacrity
reave deprive of
rebated blunted
record *n.*, *v.* witness; call to mind
recreant traitor, villain; one who breaks faith
recure cure
redeem free, restore to rightful authority
reduce restore, revoke
refined purified
reflex *v.* reflect, throw beams
refluence flowing back
regiment *n.* rule, control
remit abandon
remorse pity
remorseful compassionate
rend tear apart
renied apostate
repair *n.* arrival; *v.* betake oneself
repeal recall, as from banishment
require seek, ask

reserve *v.* keep intact
reserved set aside
resistless unresisting; irresistible
resolve dissolve, melt; satisfy, convince
rest remain
retire *n.* withdrawal from military engagement
retreat military signal to retire from the attack
revolted having deserted, rebel
rifle *v.* plunder
road harbour, roadstead; raid
room place
round *n.* dance
roundly bluntly, unceremoniously, briskly
rouse drive (a beast) from cover or lair
rout mob
royalize render famous, celebrate
rude barbarous, brutal
ruled advised
rumbelow a meaningless refrain
runagate vagabond, runaway
rusty rugged, rust-coloured
ruth pity, compassion
ruthful pitiful
ruthless lacking compassion
sable black
sack *n.* plundering; a Spanish wine; *v.* plunder
sadness earnest
salute greet
salve heal, remedy
satisfy pay the price
satyr lustful woodland deity, part human in shape but with goat's ears, tail, legs, and budding horns
sauce, sauced season, seasoned
savour *n.* stinking smell
scald contemptible
scamble up scrape together
scathe harm
scutcheon heraldic shield
search explore, probe
seat throne
sect sex; religious group
see throne, official position, especially that of the papacy
seed offspring
seld seldom

sennet trumpet signal accompanying a ceremonial entrance or exit

senseless lacking sensation

serve one's turn suffice (sometimes with sexual meaning)

service homage, obedience

servitor servant, follower

set *pple.* pitched

several different, various

severally separately

sexton church employee responsible for gravedigging, ringing bells, etc.

shadow shade, ghost

shag-rag rag-tag

shift *n.* expedient, device

shipwrack shipwrecked

shrewd mischievous, hurtful, irksome

shrive hear confession (**shrift**)

silly helpless, innocent, wretched, feeble

simple innocent; simple-minded

simplicity folly

sink cesspool

sirrah a term of address to an inferior or child

sith, sith that since

slave rascal, wretch

slightly easily, weakly

slip *v.* allow to slip by

smart *n.* suffering, pain

smooth insinuating, flattering

'snails by His (Christ's) nails (on the cross)

so *prep.* provided that

soft *exclam.* gently, take it easy

solemn ceremonial, holy

solemnize celebrate, do ceremonial honour to

something *adj.* somewhat

sometimes sometime, formerly, recently

sophister one skilled in sophistical arguments

sort *n.* kind, variety; multitude; *v.* turn out, assign, arrange

sovereign *adj.* efficacious

space space of time

speak (one) fair address (a person) courteously

sped done for

speed *v.* succeed

spend expend, employ

spial spy, scout

spoil *n.* booty; act of plundering; *v.* plunder

spurn strike, kick

stand stay

standard military ensign

start *v.* swerve, withdraw

state condition; rank; person of noble rank; common weal; throne

stay hinder, stop; wait for, await

still *adv.* perpetually, always, constantly

stilts crutches

stole ecclesiastical vestment worn over the shoulders

stomach *v.* resent

store supply of wealth

stout proud, haughty, brave, mighty

stoutly resolutely, arrogantly

straight *adv.* immediately

strait *adj.* strict

stratagem artifice, trick (often with specifically military sense)

strake struck

strange unsympathetic, cold, estranged

stranger foreigner

stripling youth

sturdy fierce, violent, disobedient

style title

subscribe sign one's name, give assent

substance possessions, wealth

success outcome, fortune

suddenly quickly

sue petition

suffer permit, tolerate

sufferance patience, respite

superficies surface

surcharged filled to the brim

sure secure

surprise *v.* attack without warning

survey *v.* look into, see

suspect suspicion

swain man of low degree, country bumpkin

sway wield, rule

swell be puffed up with arrogance

'swounds (see '**zounds**')

synod church assembly

table tablet

tall brave
target shield
tax *v.* censure
tell count out
temper *v.* mix; restore to proper 'temper' or health
temporal having to do with this world rather than the next
tender *v.* have a tender regard for
Terrene Sea or Ocean the Mediterranean
tester sixpence
thorough *prep.* through
thoroughout throughout
thrall slave
threat *v.* threaten
throughly thoroughly
'tice entice
tilt *n.* joust, tournament; *v.* engage in a joust
tilting jousting
timeless untimely; eternal
to boot in addition, into the bargain
tottered tattered
touching regarding
toward *adj.* promising, forward
Tower Tower of London
toy jest, trick, trifle
trade *v.* engage in trade, deal
traffic *n.* commerce; *v.* bargain, buy and sell
train *n.* retinue of attendants; course of action; trap; *v.* entice
treat of discourse of, discuss
trencher wooden plate; hence, place at table
tried refined
triumph *n.* tournament, triumphal procession; *v.* hold a triumphal procession
troth in truth
trow believe
trull strumpet
truncheon military baton
trustless treacherous, untrustworthy
tun barrel
turtle turtledove
tush an exclamation of contempt or disparagement
tyranny cruel act, outrage

unacquainted unexampled
unconfirmed unsettled
uncontrolled uncensured, free of domination
uncouth strange, unpleasant
unhappy unfortunate
unkind unnatural; lacking in kindness
unpointed unpunctuated
unvaluèd inestimable
ure use
urge compel
use *n.* custom; *v.* practise as a custom
vail lower flag or sail, or remove hat, in salute
value *v.* appraise
valurous valuable
vaunt *n.*, *v.* boast
villain ignobly born person; scoundrel
villainy indignity, insult
villeiness bondswoman
virtue force, commitment, valour, power
virtuous powerful
voided cleared
vouchsafe deign, confer, permit
wag chap, fellow
wait, wait on attend
want *v.* lack; are lacking; *n.* privation
wanton frisky, lascivious; of free, even libertine, imagination
warn notify
warning notification
warrant *n.* assurance, token; *v.* assure
wasteful destructive
wax *v.* grow, increase
wedge ingot
weed, weeds garments
ween think, suppose
weigh value
welkin sky, heaven
well said well done
Welsh hook curved-bladed pike
welter roll about, writhe
wend depart, turn, go
wheel an instrument of torture
whenas when
whereas where
wherefore why
whilom formerly
whit bit

wit judgement, good sense, cleverness; learned or clever person
withal with this, in addition
witty wise
wont, wonted *adj.* accustomed
wot know

wrack destruction
wreck *v.* destroy, avenge; *n.* shipwreck
wroth angered
you were best it would be best for you
zounds by his (Christ's) wounds (a strong oath)

OXFORD

MORE OXFORD PAPERBACKS

This book is just one of nearly 1000 Oxford Paperbacks currently in print. If you would like details of other Oxford Paperbacks, including titles in the World's Classics, Oxford References, Oxford Books, OPUS, Past Masters, Oxford Authors, and Oxford Shakespeare series, please write to:

UK and Europe: Oxford Paperbacks Publicity Manager, Arts and Reference Publicity Department, Oxford University Press, Walton Street, Oxford OX2 6DP.

Customers in UK and Europe will find Oxford Paperbacks available in all good bookshops. But in case of difficulty please send orders to the Cash-with-Order Department, Oxford University Press Distribution Services, Saxon Way West, Corby, Northants NN18 9ES. Tel: 01536 741519; Fax: 01536 746337. Please send a cheque for the total cost of the books, plus £1.75 postage and packing for orders under £20; £2.75 for orders over £20. Customers outside the UK should add 10% of the cost of the books for postage and packing.

USA: Oxford Paperbacks Marketing Manager, Oxford University Press. Inc., 198 Madison Avenue, New York, N.Y. 10016.

Canada: Trade Department, Oxford University Press, 70 Wynford Drive, Don Mills, Ontario M3C 1J9.

Australia: Trade Marketing Manager, Oxford University Press, G.P.O. Box 2784Y, Melbourne 3001, Victoria.

South Africa: Oxford University Press, P.O. Box 1141, Cape Town 8000.

WORLD'S CLASSICS SHAKESPEARE

'not simply a better text but a new conception of Shakespeare. This is a major achievement of twentieth-century scholarship.' Times Literary Supplement

Hamlet
Macbeth
The Merchant of Venice
As You Like It
Henry IV Part I
Henry V
Measure for Measure
The Tempest
Much Ado About Nothing
All's Well that Ends Well
Love's Labour's Lost
The Merry Wives of Windsor
The Taming of the Shrew
Titus Andronicus
Troilus & Cressida
The Two Noble Kinsmen
King John
Julius Caesar
Coriolanus
Anthony & Cleopatra
A Midsummer Night's Dream
Twelfth Night

WORLD'S CLASSICS
Late nineteenth- and early twentieth-century plays

J. M. BARRIE
PETER PAN AND OTHER PLAYS
Edited with an Introduction by Peter Hollindale

Contains *The Admirable Crichton*; *Peter Pan*; *When Wendy Grew Up*; *What Every Woman Knows*; *Mary Rose.*

ARTHUR WING PINERO
TRELAWNY OF THE 'WELLS' AND OTHER PLAYS
Edited with an Introduction by Jacky Bratton

Contains *The Magistrate*; *The Schoolmistress*; *The Second Mrs Tanqueray*; *Trelawny of the 'Wells'.*

J. M. SYNGE
THE PLAYBOY OF THE WESTERN WORLD AND OTHER PLAYS
Edited with an Introduction by Ann Saddlemyer

Contains *Riders to the Sea*; *The Shadow of the Glen*; *The Tinker's Wedding*; *The Well of the Saints*; *The Playboy of the Western World*; *Deirdre of the Sorrows.*

OSCAR WILDE
THE IMPORTANCE OF BEING EARNEST AND OTHER PLAYS
Edited with an Introduction by Peter Raby

Contains *Lady Windermere's Fan*; *Salome*; *A Woman of No Importance*; *An Ideal Husband*; *The Importance of Being Earnest.*

WORLD'S CLASSICS
Seventeenth-century texts

APHRA BEHN
OROONOKO AND OTHER WRITINGS
Edited with an Introduction by Paul Salzman

*The Fair Jilt, Memoirs of the Court of the King Bantam,
The History of the Nun, The Adventure of the Black Lady,*
and *The Unfortunate Bride* are complemented by a
generous selection of Behn's poetry, ranging from public
political verse to lyrics and witty conversation poems.

APHRA BEHN
THE ROVER AND OTHER PLAYS
Edited with an Introduction by Jane Spencer

Contains *The Rover*; *The Feigned Courtesans*; *The Lucky
Chance*; *The Emperor of the Moon.*

(Forthcoming November 1995)

JOHN BUNYAN
THE PILGRIM'S PROGRESS
Edited with an Introduction by N. H. Keeble

JOHN FORD
'TIS PITY SHE'S A WHORE
AND OTHER PLAYS
Edited with an Introduction by Marion Lomax

Contains *The Lover's Melancholy*; *The Broken Heart*;
'Tis Pity She's a Whore; *Perkin Warbeck.*